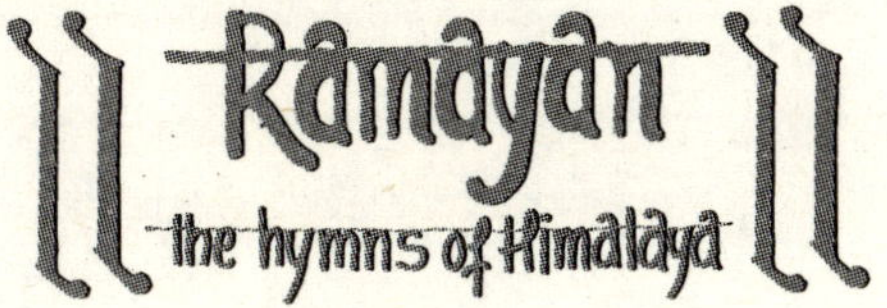
Ramayan
the hymns of Himalaya

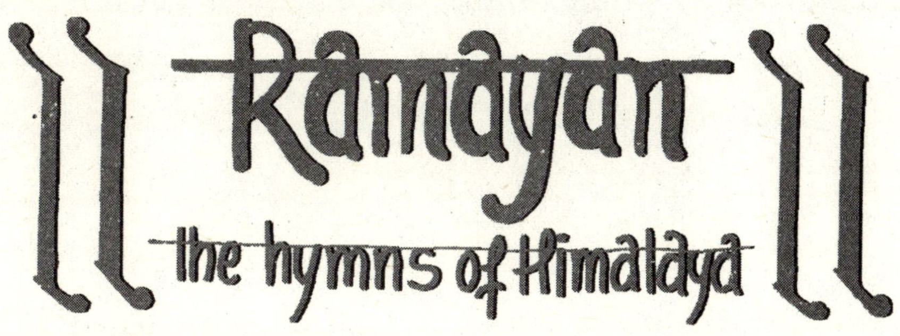

akhilesh gumashta

Published by
PRABHAT PRAKASHAN PVT. LTD.
4/19 Asaf Ali Road,
New Delhi-110 002 (INDIA)
e-mail: prabhatbooks@gmail.com

ISBN 978-81-7315-910-7
RAMAYAN : *The Hymns of Himalaya*

Edition
2025

Price
₹ 1500.00 (Rupees One Thousand Five Hundred only)

Printed at
R-Tech Offset Printers, Delhi

Dedicated to

Ramkrishna Paramhans,

who has

Given to the world

the Monk,

Swami Vivekanand

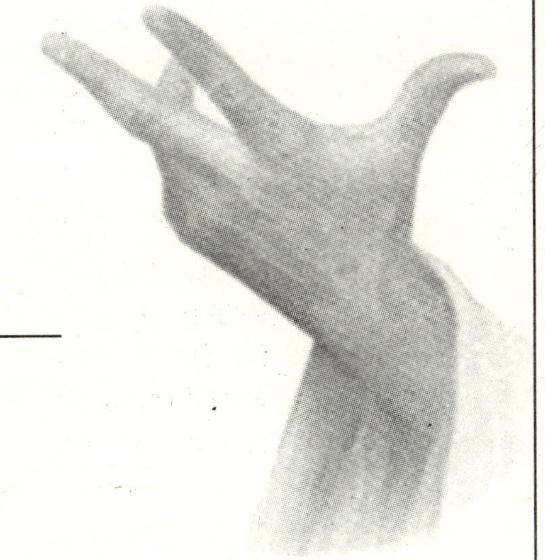

O Greatest bard of Ram, the Lord !
Thy rhyming songs and metres,
I do find in, waves of the Ganges,
In streams of Sarayu and Rewa, I do see,
How noble and simple thou singest.

O Tulsi ! the great laureate of Ram's court !
In the ocean, I see thy devotion fathomless,
and in pearls, the phrases of muses,
And to enlighten the world, thine paeans of Ram,
doth shine as, The Everest.

FOREWORD

Through the present work the author has done a signal service to both modern English literature as well as to the cause of spiritual awakening by presenting a versified version of the unique epic "Ramayana".

Dr. Gumashta's creative rendering "Ramayan — the hymns of Himalaya" is the latest literary work on the Ramayana. Casting a glance at both prose and poem, verbal translations, and original and imaginative rendering spread all over the world literature, both classical and modern, Ramayan has no equals. The tradition still continues unabated as we see in these latest poems.

Ramayan, universally accepted as the Adikavya or epic, has fascinated people of all countries and of all times. So far as countries of the Asian continent are concerned, Ramayan has not only captured their imagination but also influenced profoundly their creativity and produced everlasting contributions in all fields of life. The reason for this phenomenon is not far to seek. It is deeply ingrained in human nature. Man is potentially Divine. There is a dominant desire in every individual to manifest this spark of divinity. He seeks out ways and means to express the same. He yearns for perfection. Perfection can be achieved by emulating persons who are embodiments of such perfection. The quest for such icons is inherent in the heart of every man. It is this quest that makes Ramayan so attractive, and so fascinating, and draws people everywhere to the personality of Sri Ramachandra, who was the very personification of the highest ideal one can imagine. In fact, that is how the story begins. Valmiki, the first among poets, asked the all-knowing Narada about such an ideal person with no faults or foibles. Unhesitatingly Narada pointed out Sri Ramachandra as the "Maryada Purushothama". He epitomised the highest perfection that man is capable of achieving. That is how

Valmiki Ramayana came into being. And from that epic sprouted a number of Ramayans in various languages, realising and portraying Shri Ramachandra not as a perfect man, but as God incarnate.

It is human quest for an ideal personality as well as an ideal society that has made Ramayan unrivalled in its status among all the world literatures. It promises to be so for the future as well. Here again man yearns for an ideal situation where all sufferings are eliminated and perfect freedom and happiness prevail.

Ram's rule is characterised by such heavenly perfection. Ram Rajya is the replica of heaven on earth. The governing factor of this enviable state of affairs is the dominance of "Dharma". Dharma is spirituality in everyday life. Ram Rajya is actually "Dharma Rajya". Spirituality pervades every activity of even the common people. That is the understanding of Ram Rajya.

Dr. Gumashta in his work describes this ideal state of society in an exquisitely beautiful manner reminiscent of Sri Aurobindo's superb poetic style.

Spirituality filled the peopled air,
Blessedness filled citizens with colours of rapture.
It's spirituality, and not the rocks and bricks,
That makes the towers of national edifice.

Ramayan is not only the primal, the earliest poetic expression of mankind, it remains, forever, as the greatest poetic expression that mankind has ever known. World literature, as contemplated by Goethe for the first time, "demands that the author belonging to some other nation should be brought over to us, so that we can regard him as our own". For this cross-cultural exchange, there can be no one greater work in the East than Ramayan, to be brought over to the West. This exchange is "for providing an important channel for the flow of international influence" as Goethe says. There are already a few versions in English, but many more are needed, especially this poetic expression was needed more as the aspiration, taste and cultural ethos undergo change in every nation as time progresses. The author's attempt to build a bridge between two cultures is praiseworthy for this simple reason. This need is accentuated by the fact that the two cultures belong to two nations which are ethnically and geographically different. On account of this, Dr. Gumashta's is like the task of Bhagirath. This has proved successful in this English version, which leaves a pleasant surprise in regard to its truthfulness to the originals i.e. to Valmiki Ramayan, Ramacharitamanas and others, in so far as the message, character delineation and poetic beauty are concerned.

Presumably the author has depended on both these original sources and probably some others for rendering this free, creative and innovative work in verse.

The invocational beginning of this epic closely follows the sequence of Ramacharitamanas, but is considerably precise. The music, the emotional fervour of Bhakti, the introduction of Ram as the Avatar (Supreme Lord) and extolling him as belonging to a higher realm than that of Lord Siva, the unlimited strings of eulogy producing a magical spell of sheer emotional Bhakti, devotion etc. are common both to Ramacharitamanas and to Adhyatma Ramayan. This is recaptured in the English version, closely following Ramacharitamanas, but with utmost sense of propriety in condensing the loose and elaborate outpourings of the ancient, intended to create its magical spell of profound devotion to Lord. This precision is preferable as it suits English readers since the music and rhythm cannot be imbibed by them. The Anglo Saxon phrases and verse structure do not yield to music and rhythmic beat as we practice in India. Similarly, the entire story of Siva-Parvati wedding so lucidly and elaborately narrated by Goswamiji in an elevated style with alliterative sound effect yielding to rich music is almost omitted here. This may naturally result in diminution of poetic beauty and incessant flow of Bhakti, but is justifiable from the point of literary relevance as related to the reader's interest and to the main story of Ramayan. It goes to the credit of Dr. Gumashta that contemporary message is segregated and brought to our notice at appropriate context. It is also noteworthy that the ethos of a classic is carefully maintained by employing archaic expressions wherever necessary.

Regular meters with regular beats, charming natural flow of alternative adjectives and synonyms, an unfailing end rhyme are the characteristic features of Ramacharitamanas. It is at once a folk style astonishingly getting elevated to classical style, with no rigidity whatsoever. English style, on the other hand, can hardly escape from Anglo-Saxon rigidity and alterations which betrays their contrived effort. To overcome these unavoidable hurdles in the process of inter-lingual transmission, the author has carefully chosen the heroic couplet in its simpler form with end rhyme and has taken care to provide alternative effects. Certainly, there is no deviation from the original epic and all characters are truthfully drawn in spite of the total change of medium. His wonderful mastery of the English language and tone, familiarity with its archaism and above all his own poetic genius is evident in the almost natural flow of the expression. He has taken much care to:

i) Substitute the sound function of the source language with appropriate sound function of the target language (in poetry, as we know the metre, form and sound are integral to the theme or message)

ii) Employ elongated vowels wherever pauses are required

iii) Resort to regular alliterations, recurrence of consonants and pitch variations.

Before concluding my foreword to this graceful, poetic gift of Dr. Gumashta to the public at large, I would like to quote a few words written by Sri C. Rajagopalachari, scholar, politician and one of the foremost leaders of our freedom movement, in a similar context.

"Once again, I confess that in the evening of my busy life during a great and eventful period of Indian History, the writing of these two books wherein I have retold the Mahabharata and Ramayana, is, in my opinion, the best service I have rendered to my people. At any rate, they embody the best joy I have experienced; for in these two books I helped our great sages to speak to our dear men and women, elevating their minds through the sorrows borne by Kunti, Kausalya, Draupadi and Sita. The real need of the hour is a re-communion between us and the sages of our land, so that the future may be built on rock and not on sand. In presenting this English version to a wider circle of readers spread all over the world, I think I am presenting to them the people of Bhaarat just as they are, with all their virtues and their faults. Our classics really embody our national character in all its aspects and it is well the world sees us as we really are, apart from what we wish to become."

The Ramayan is immortal. There is no doubt that it will last forever, and continue to nourish the cultural and spiritual values of people in India and elsewhere, in ever-increasing measure and extent. It is correctly stated that "As long as the Himalayas continue to exist and Ganges continues to flow, the story of Ramayana also will continue to enrich humanity and its culture". Dr. Gumashta`s literary venture is, in effect, the outcome of this eternal urge of our great cultural heritage for self-renewal and self-propagation. I am sure the author's labour of love will be richly rewarded by the discerning readers and devouts in all parts of the world where English language is understood.

—P. Parameswaran
President, Vivekanand Kendra,
Kanyakumari, India

PREFACE

Enough!...!! Let's talk spirituality now. Enough we have talked of energy, nuclear power, weapons, weapons against weapons, ozone layer, strokes, drugs, life beyond and so on.

Now, let's talk spirituality, all above sects, faiths, paths and fragments of religions and its man-made cruelty. Divorced from God, we have endless hunger for lust and greed. May the hunger for Truth prevail, now.

Spirituality is the life-blood of India, the ancient land, where wisdom (the Gyaan) made its first home before it went into other parts of the globe. The great seers of ancient India saw so far ahead of their time that the world has to wait centuries yet to appreciate their wisdom.

Let's talk about the approach of those pure seers and seekers of this land of uplifted mankind. Let's explore into India and Indian valley of civilisation, by the rolling rivers, by the pinnacles of temples, by the chanting Ashrams, on the material planes as well; from sub-Himalayan terrains to the ghats of the three oceans, having geographical limits of the land frame.

Let's visualise into the vast treasure of India through the window of the epic, 'Ramayan', the very temple among books. From the time of the ancient bard Valmiki, the Ramayan has been told retold and retold in many ways, in many a languages of the world. The poetic excellence of Valmiki can be seen reflected in the later poets of different parts of India, who have chanted hymns of Ramayan in their own tongue e.g. Ezhuthachan (Malayalam), Kamban (Tamil), Shri Moll (Telugu) and many more, to come to Ramcharitmanas of Goswami Tulsidas, who had poured '*Bhakti*; (the devotion with surrender) to it's brimming level.

Every verse of Goswamiji proved itself and became 'mantra' in the minds of readers. Tulsi's Chaupais (Quadruplets) and Doha (Couplets) have already descended into the daily life of every Indian.

Some times, I think of the height of the will of our ancestors that had toiled to bring to us the great epic 'Ramayan' from the time when they had to make the paper of palm leaf (*Bhojpatra*) and also the ink before bringing it for readers. Having born in the age of computer-command, I even can not imagine their determination and ambition to make handwritten copies of literature for readers of the generations to come. We feel and must feel indebted to those forefathers and ancient poets. The people of this era respect the toilsome work done by our ancestors to bring such a literary treasure to us. Should we not be very keen to read and reread such a treasured text of world harmony and fraternity?

Ancient bards have made the epic ageless, beyond time, still they had realized that after a couple of years (may be centuries) any opus need be reviewed, lest the ageless flow of the epic may suffer stagnation.

I started making the work of Tulsidas as the prime guide but later studying Adhyatma Ramayan, Valmiki's Ramayan and the other Ramayans which have already stood the test of time, I have tried to make the present work more widely acceptable to the present-day readers and devotees. I sincerely hope the present work lives up to the expectations for which I have tried my best.

I'm neither the native nor the scholar of English, have only learnt a little bit from books of my medical studies, but I understand that the language of the heart may stand the test of devotion. This is a literary and not a scholarly work; scholarly work follows some norms while literary has its own style, nay, it goes out of style.

Many text-prose and sermons on Ramayan are available, but as verses have inherent power to penetrate through the soul and being more permeable into the mind, these verses should have more powerful impact of the missive of Ramayan. I agree with Ralph Griffith, an Indologist, who writes 'even far inferior poetic powers are, I think , much more Homeric than any literal prose'.

In my verses I have confessed that I'm not a poet, but the thief stealing the 'Bhaav' of the ancient poets, so much so that I have picked

the meters of the same vowel marks as have been used by Tulsidasji, i.e. Couplets (Dohas), Quadruplets (Choupais), Distich (Sortha), Stanzas (Chhandas). Seldom have I amplified, condensed or omitted as the situation permitted me to do.

To speak of the popularity of Ramayan, I may not be called a braggart if I firmly affirm that every one of the Indians living in the province of this part of the land is well versed with the story of Ramayan and they enjoy reading, and rereading this epic, again and again. Even every remote village of India has its own drama-team that enacts the stage show of Ramayan. Such worship is popularly named as 'Ramleela'. Characters of the play enjoy being participant characters of the epic. Sometimes I also 'think' how wonderful it would have been if I could have lived as a monk in the forest watching the wandering Ram or could have lived as a monkey in the army of the Warrior Ram. Such thoughts bring this epic closer to the reader and reciter.

Ramayan is the panoramic view on the canvas of India, showing spiritual sunshine over mystical quiet peaks with green trees of Deodars of moral richness, with mountains of patriotism, having cataracts of 'Bhakti' joining 'the Ganges of bliss.' Let this Ganga flow through the oceans to lands of different languages, as said here:

"Bhakti', the very treasure of my motherland,
I do share with the language of aliens."

In this fragmented world of the five elements, the spiritual philosophy and the realistic facts of the Indian way, may prove to cure the sick earth.

One of the most valuable assets inherited by children of this piece of land is ***cross culture respect***. The great threat for humanity is the active antagonism among the world's great philosophies of faith and religion. I think it's not those philosophies that stand antagonistic but it's the ego of the mere man which clashes. How can we live with each other until we have mutual respect and understanding? What's the need of the day? What mankind needs today is interfaith movement, the breaking of the ice with the warmth of understanding to bring

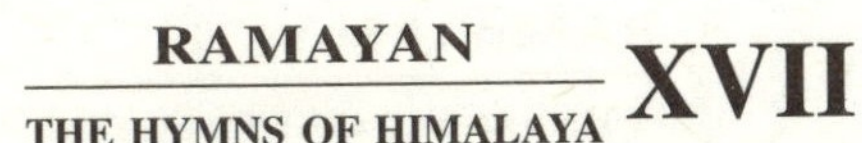

about the new age thought. May this opus, through its verses permeate into iron curtained egos of 'my and your faith'

It took me about seven years to complete this work. I see myself as a medium to bring words and thoughts together. I find that verses which inked my pages are guided by somebody else behind me.

Here, I most humbly accept that no wonder occurred during this work but while I look back into the registers and diaries and recite these verses, my jaw simply drops, 'It can't be me!'.

To confess this, I wish to dissolve my individual 'I-am-ness' because every word descends on the page with the grace of God. I pick the work here as Lord Ram says–

"Whose self is diffused to all with no 'I-sense',
My binding to him is more intense."

Hope, though the story is known to everybody, yet from the new readers to the intoxicated reciters of Ramayan, all will sure pore over these verses in bliss.

May the tender narrations of Ram fill our lives with innocence; May the pupil Ram bring into our minds, the real wisdom — the gnosis; May the bridegroom Ram bring to our thought the ecstasy; May Maa Siya reflect in today's womanhood as chastity; May the wanderer Ram fill all with altruism; May warrior Ram appear within everyone to fight ten-headed evils; May Ram Rajya be the goal of every soul, above caste, creed, race and faith; and May the echoes of 'The Hymns of Himalaya' with rich melody impact to modulate fragmented hearts, sects, lands and faiths into one good image of *Homo sapiens*, the Best creation of the Lord.

At the end of this work, when I look back I find how selfish I was, having drowned myself so much into my study-desk that my family had little space in my tubular vision. Today, I feel proud of God-sent blessings embodied as my wife Sadhana, and two children Varsha and Kartikey.

I would be failing if I do not mention the name of Sadhvi Gyaneshwari didi, who in spite of her busy and hectic life took lots of pains to bring the book and its text to the present form.

Line-sketches are depictions beautifully drawn by the well-known creative artist of Central India Mr. Vinay Amber to visualise Nirakaar (the Absolute) out of Saakaar (the Avatar) or vice versa. The picture sketches bring vision-thought exactly between Nirakaar and Saakaar.

With these wishes, I narrate the story in the words of Sage Yagyawalkya (as told to his pupil-saint, Bharadwaj)—

"O Child! Now I begin Ram's epic,
From the vast ocean few pearls I pick."

—Akhilesh Gumashta

05.11.2010
(Deepawali)

BLESSINGS

This is meticulously rendered literary piece. May it stand true to the test of time and public acclaim.

—Swami Satyamitranandji, Former Shankaracharya, Haridwar

I'm working in England for more than 30 years to introduce to the world the spirituality of India. Suddenly when I found the 'Ramayan' in its vesified form in English, that too with its high literary impact, I was overwhelmed with joy that the present work will serve the purpose of my Guruji, and thousands of his disciples working all over the world. I am not moved just because of its literary standard but I have met the ancient *Bhakti* and knowledge in it, which is the very soul of India. It seems to me natural that I should be moved because I read Ramayan everyday. May this epic prove to be so for ages to come, for generations to come.

—Swami Vishwa Bharti, Brahmrishi Mission, UK

Ramayan is the pride and joy of India. Present work will prove to be a milestone in the endeavour to make the great Epic reach to the world and I recommend to all English knowing devotees to make this great work as part of daily reading, just as the Hindi knowers read Shri Ramcharit Maanas.

—Swami Divyanand Teerth,
Member BOD Akhil Bhariya Sant Samiti, India

His verses are vital and full of life. The rich erudition and high scholarship abiding faith as well as *Sanatan* traditions is eloquently visible in every line of the work and has left me spell bound.

—Baba Kalyan Das, Amarkantak (M.P.)

The narrative of Ram needs its knowledge to depict the sap and essence of its muses. The present work is the outcome of devotion and determination. "Raṁ's *charit* is poem in itself, one becomes a poet, who ever narrates."

—Dr. Swami Shyamdasji, Vice President, Akhil Bharatiya Sant Samiti

Indian philosophy is an art of life (and not just the theory), now it comes in English. Author presents a precise illuminating narrtion to those who do not have knowledge of Indian languages. I wish to express my gratitude to the author who has kept the spirit of the Ramayan, as hymns of Himalaya as high as the Everest.

—Sudarshan Bhatia, President, National Council of Temples of UK, London

Today we live in an age of doubts of science engulfing the art of faith, but the challenge has been accepted by the author writing between the current materialism and perpetual flow of eternal divinity. I am very happy with this writing which keeps the very message of divinity live.

—Ron van der Post, Teacher, Indology and Yoga, Netherland

Marvelous is the work, marvelous is the concept, to bring to the world the spirituality. As the spirituality is the life blood of India and Ramayan, the epic is the soul; it is the right time that the life blood and soul together bring life to the dying mankind. The present verses of Ramayan will sure prove to be globally popular for centuries to come. May these verses stand the test of time to bring to the world the peace and harmony among all the faiths and sects followed by the men. Verses in the present work are reflection of the ancient glory of this piece of land and will prove to be so in time to come.

—Vishwamitraji, Shri Ram Sharanam Parivar, New Delhi

The present work is commendable. l send my compliments for the innovative and fresh views on Ramayan. l will try my utmost support of this great work in European countries.

—Swami Raghwanand, Suriname

CONTENTS

Chapter-3

Chapter-4

Chapter-5

Chapter-6

Chapter-7

॥AYODHYA KANDAM॥

Chapter-8

Chapter-9

Chapter-10

Chapter-11

Chapter-12

Chapter-13

Chapter-14

Chapter-15

Chapter-16

Chapter--17

Chapter-18

Chapter-19

॥ARANYA KANDAM॥

Chapter-20

Chapter-21

‖ KISHKINDHA KANDAM ‖

Chapter-22

‖ SUNDER KANDAM ‖

Chapter-23

‖ YUDDH KANDAM ‖

Chapter-24

Chapter-25

Chapter-26

Chapter-27

‖UTTAR KANDAM‖

Chapter-28

Chapter-29

Chapter-30

GLOSSARY

Avataar	Incarnation.
Ayodhya	Capital of Awadh, wordly meaning-A land of no war.
Bhakta	Devotee, votary.
Bhakti	Devotion with surrender.
Brahma	The Creator, One of the Trinity.
Brahman	High and pious class of society.
Chaitra	The month falling in April.
Dharma	The duty as laid down by religion and custom.
Guru	Preceptor, the Teacher.
Gyan	The Knowledge, Gnosis.
Hari	One of the name of Lord Vishnu, the sustainer among the trinity.
Indra	The chief of gods, godules (the celestial being).
Jaamvaan	Also Jamvant, leader of bear Army.
Kaama	The lust, the Desire.
Kailash	The mount Kailash, the very abode of Lord Shiva.
Karma	The Action.
Kashyap Aditi	The first couple (Kashyap, the celebrated sage).

Mahadev	Also Shiv, Shankar, The destroyer among Trinity.
Manmath	God of love and desires, the cupid.
Naarad	Celestial rishi with Lute (The divine celebrated sage).
Paaduka	Foot wear, Sabot.
Paataal	The nether region.
Parwati	Also Uma, Consort of Lord Shiva (who listens the epic).
Pushpak	Ariel car of Kuber stolen by Raavan later used by Ram to come back from Lanka to Ayodhya.
Raghu	An ancestor of Ram, King of Solar Race.
Raghuveer	Also Raghuvar, Raghvendra, other names of Ram.
Ram Rajya	The ideal governance.
Sarayu	River in Ayodhya joins Ganges.
Shloka	Strophes.
Siya	Siye, Janaki, Vaidehi, other names of Mother Seeta, the Divine Consort of Lord Ram.
Tapa	Austerity and penance.
Tilak	A mark put on the forehead.
Ved	Oldest scriptures in world library in the form of four books-Rigveda, Yajurved, Samved, Atharveda.
Vishnu	Naraayan, The Sustainer, one of the Trinity.
Yagna (Jagya)	Sacrifice, A religious ceremony accompanied by oblations in fire-altar.
Yama	God of death.

THE INVOCATORY STROPHES

THE INVOCATORY STROPHES

1

The syllables, very first who etched,
As mother script; on the palm foliage,
Engineered who the muse of verses
That first worshipped Genius is Ganesh.

2

The Devi, in all tongues of piety,
Who, in sentiment of all sacred texts,
Reflects as the Divinity,
That sentience is Saraswati.

3

In the province of the faith,
As, very Truth what is perceived,
Either is true or becomes true,
Its all glory of Lord Shiv.

4

He, who, discovered
Within bosom his own Master,
Nay, His Master he mastered;
Is Hanuman, the chief of Vaanars.

5

The pilgrim journey of Ramayan
On the palm-leaves, who opened
And etched on souls, the epic,
is the ancient bard, Valmiki.

6

In the cloudy heresy,
Whose, illuminating strophes
Dawned rich on twilight of folly
As sun of gnosis, is Tulsi,

7

In the range of Sahya and Malay
Its' Ezhuthachan's verses, that breathe
And Kamban's poesy wreathed
The Mahendra, Kaling and ghats of East.

8

With ancient of ancient poesy
Ved vyas etched leaves of palm tree
Thus evolved, with every sun
Uplifted Sub-human unto Human.

9

In deeps, steeps that creeped,
Are the unnamed lyrics,
Unclaimed folks on cymbals and reeds,
Turned this holyland further seraphic.

10

Who cherishes us, that creator Maa,
Who liveth in each biota, nay each iota
Who the friends' reverence, fiends' awe
Is non dual form, Ram-Siya.

11

Who is above all causes and Cause to the causes,
I worship 'Ram', in very verse of Ramayan who lodgeth.
In the frosty blur of illusion,
It bringeth solar road of devotion.

12

Whose conscious presence roots,
In the Geeta, the gnosis.
He ist Krishna thro' His flute
Puffs in Gopis all-bliss.

13

Sages from ages sung the sacred saga,
That embalmed pilgrim souls with Rama's aroma.
I do claim no penance, no worship
To cross, may the same epic be my ship.

14

I revere and I refer from holy text,
From ancient poets and quotes
May the alien tongue be further blessed,
With facts of Ram's anecdotes.

15

Story from the land, where, each canvas is a fane
And the soil is elixired with reverence,
From the Land, where heaven needs no season to come,
Where strangulates none of pealing anthems,*

16

The story is from the land of primeval seekers
Who, the astral issues from the ground measured,
The ethyreal touch in the Earth who discovered,
And Thro' mounts, sylvans, rivers, who revered nature.

---

* All the faiths are honoured

|| BAL KANDAM ||

1

God in you, alone can worship God

—Swami Vivekanand

"BACK ME UP! O LORD!!"

Distitch:

O Ganesh! Make task be coped
Thine Genius ist generous,
Thy first worship ist the hope
That taketh up the opus.

O holy wonder ! thou dost puff,
Into dumb, the voice
On path steep and tough,
Me, the crippled mayst be buoyed.

O Hari! Thy Swarthy hue,
Reflects in Ocean and Azure Dome,
Through this rich milieu,
Mayst Thou, make my bosom Thy home.

What Shiv is, just the thought of trust,
Which crushes the lust to dust,
Behind Shiv, his consort enshrines
That Uma is, the troth of mind.

Opus = work (composition) ; buoyed = encouraged/ cheered up; Troth = Surrender to faith.

Where trust and troth in mind dwell
Ramayan reveals as Shiv's gospel,
Troth in mind listens as Goddess Uma,
Thus within runs Ram's Saga.

To Guru, I make obeisance,
Who bringeth mercy of the Supreme.
On frosty chill of ignorance
Whose words shine as Sun beams.

MAY HELP EVERY ONE!

Revering Guru is revering his teachings
Bliss and blessings ever it brings.
Even dust of Guru's feet is soft salve,
It cleanseth eyes, maligned look it absolveth.

This salve once applied to mind's eye,
Gives insight, Thy holy epic to recite.
With such insight, mundane is transparent,
The unseen is seen thro' mines, mounts, mains.

Saints, their seance, Ashrams, abbeys,
Thro' whom governance of spirituality sways.
I pray them and their pious souls,
For they, the mankind, uphold.

Lord shapeth a man, and man un to-
Saints, himself reforms; that's due.
Saints know the way, hallow the way,
Saints go the way, and show the way.

Couplet: *Saints, The Teerth, as they are,*
Their sermon is holy Ganges.
Take in it holy dip,
For life's four largess'* 1

Agastya, Valmiki, Naarad had such dip,
Holy texts witnessed what they had achieved.
Wisdom, wealth, weal, fame and fortune,
By any mean, anybody gets, is saint's boon.

Saints give something more than wisdom,
The Séance, to Sansar, brings equilibrium.
They settled code to mankind's good,
Renouncing everything, by the Truth they stood.

Satsang, the séance brings wisdom at hand,
Freedom from folly is a great gain.
That too is not easy to access,
Sans Ram's excellence and His grace.

Thus wicked may be chanced to reform,
Even as, with elixir the metal transforms.
So I pray, as well, the wicked and villains,
Hostile who are with no cause, no sense.

Who are bloomy at ruins, gloomy at reigns
The Loss of others' are their gains.
Ill omened they are like a comet,
Like Kumbharan may they be sleep's intimate.

Dread not the troops of foe, draw near,
But nighing of one vile, who pose friend, fear!

---

*1.Truth (Dharma) 2. Glory (Arth) 3. Vitality (Kama) 4. Liberation (Moksha)
Séance=gathering of saints, satsang; Sansar=world, mundane.
Sans=without.

Couplet: *To trap in noose they,*
For the chance, lurk.
And never loose on prey
their evil work. 2

As duty I do greet viles as well,
But fear! their duty they may not fail.
With all longing heart any crow you treat,
But raven ceases not consuming meat.

Brahma*, hath created just a thought in human,
In to Sage or savage, the mind turns.
Sages and savages both I do revere,
The two give tho' pain, but modes differ.

Parting a Sage is a severe ache,
While arriving of savage is a set back.
Lord hath made good and evil,
Evil is praised to kill, while good for the good will.

Light, twilight, night, delight and plight,
Lord hath shaped some slight and some wight,
In sweets of grapes, the bitter juice,
And in mire, the lotus is His produce.

He maketh oasis among wasteland,
Through thirsty rocks He breaketh fountains.
In dark benthos, in brittle shell of Brine,
With own wonderous hands He maketh pearly shine.

Each day, He, for man, maketh way to bliss,
But Alas! Feeble race topples to abyss.

---

* the Creator.
Abyss =Lower world (pataal)

Couplet: *Whole of the creation is mixed*
With the good and the bad,
Man gets what he picks
Word of Ved or sword of mad. 3

The exact man finds his path exact,
He glows and grows with great éclat.
A confessed sin, depletes sin,
And virtues reveal then, hidden within.

Fumes lift up tho' form, the stain black,
But then spread as ink, on sacred text.
Further sublimed fumes, make the clouds,
Those shower on land, thus the life sprouts.

Thus even rubbish heap hath potential to heal,
Grace of Lord uplifts any evil.
For that innate potential, I pray,
The heaven, haven, heathen, human and even hay.

Nay, all species, measured eighty four lacs,
From mite, kite to treaders of height, Lord reck.
Ram's consciousness in every one dwells,
So I implore every bit, every cell.

Couplet: *The evil and good are conjoined,*
Before the both I bow
They are obverses of same coin,*
Evil goes with the good as shadow. 4

THE THRUST

The exploits of Ram I crave to etch,
My mind is shallow, His deeds are fathomless.

Reck=take care; Hay=grass; Wight=supernatural;
*two sides of coin.

My childish play on quicksand of shore,
Hath stubborn thrust but feeble lore.

The wit is whit, vast is aim,
With wealth of whey, the nectar I claim.
I dare, for the parents delight at child's lisps,
When he crawls on knees, the parents lift.

More so, every one likes his own opus,
May it be limerick, and a shallow verse.
Not a Laureate, the thief as I am,
I quote and recite from ancient names.

No waves of music no depth of strains,
But streams of Ram's glory it maintains.
Sure! I am ; with thrust it happens,
High goal may be achieved by a dunce.

Couplet: *With feeble luck, wish high,*
Yet I do confide,
Lofty will pore in lief,
Tho' a few may deride. 5

May it be an unlettered poesy,
Yet sure, its piety of a devotee.
In world of anarchy, it may not befit,
For those, this may be dull vapid.

It's substance keeps it ever above,
For it's impregnated with faith and love.
With no why? How? But with love for His feet,
Into such soul this epic reaches deep.

Dunce=fool.

My unnamed signature, knows 'His' name,
So beyond lyrics, excellence it claims.
My Lord Himself will goad my pen,
To fill mortal pages with immortal paeans.

Valmiki, Tulsi, Kamban, Ezhuthachan,
May please back me at every moment.

Sthnza: For pure bliss, blemish to abolish,
Tulsi lavishes pages with paeans.
Valmiki portrayed, Ram's sketch,
On palms he etched Ramayan.
Like pious Ganga, Kamban's verses
Traversed along the East coast.
Ezhuthachan picks, Ramar's scripts
With honour depicts the Malay's boast.*

Couplet: From Himalaya to Malay, the land,
In itself is an abbey.
Godward, where, souls wend,
May the world know that heritage. 6

MAY THIS PUNYA BHOOMI BLESS ALL!

The ancient land of gods and saints,
Where wisdom had early experiments.
Where wisdom made its first home,
And introspection pronounced echo of 'OM'.

Where every hamlet is a 'Teerth'.
And soil is trodden by great sages' feet.
Where Himalaya hymns the mystery of heaven,
Where spirituality is sung on material plane.

---

*Pride and joy of Malay.
Abbey=monastery; Paeans=verses of glory and praise; 'OM'=Sonic-manifestation of the Supreme.

Where first arose the man's doctrines-
That 'not the invasion, but introspection wins.'
The tidal waves of purity on the Earth,
Had deluged world with this spiritual worth.

From involution, where man first evolved,
Through inner quest, every query the seekers solved.
May this land bless me and bless all,
May the Spiritual Truth find no wall.

Couplet: *Towering edifice for man,*
On the bed rock of the Truth,
Was built by the saints,
For every soul to soothe. 7

This soil has been singing pure anthems,
With aplomb and calm as its theme.
Its message hath tinged every drop in veins,
May I bring on pages the same current.

To the dying race, of the Human, so called,
May the thin words break the fragmenting wall.
May the spiritual forces, all gather,
of the siblings of One Truth, One mother.

Most ancient land brings message modern,
Walks differ, tasks differ, yet goal is one.
The deluge of spirituality from time to time,
Hath, from this land, taught teachings of the Divine.

The Divine manifestation of the Immortal,
Descendth here as mortal's ideal.
And bringeth teachings of the Immortality,
And destined every soul to do great things.

Involution = entanglement
Aplomb=serenity, dispassion.

Couplet: *World has yet to learn,*
From the text of Ram's narrative,
Soul may create heaven
Once inner Shiv is perceived. 8

I pray motherland, with glory, full to the banks,
Where prudence is ever backed by experience.
Land, where texts had expedition from the truth to greater truth,
Thus, recorded and established the truth, Absolute.

On the Banyan of wisdom 'the Dharma is perched',
It's based on searches, researches' research.
Many visions, researches, here, have been accepted,
And were not hushed for corrupting fossilized texts*.

From subtlest atom to the galaxies,
The Age of ages, where mind's eye sees.
The almanac of the infinite hours,
And the Zero which this land discovered.

The spirituality and the materialism,
Where, were uplifted with equilibrium.
The sun, everything under it and beyond,
Seekers realized every science through Gyan.

Couplet: *May Saraswati descend*
Incite my conscience,
To Rich heritage of sentiments
Insight n sentience. 9

*Ram's memoir is ksheer Sagar***
And I have a little urn,
If, hope to lap it entire,
Through cat's eye I discern. 10

---

* old text usage changed with time;

** ocean of milk. Gyan=Gnosis, Real knowledge. Sentience=conciousness ; Almanac = calender of stars planets (panchang)

FORGIVE MY FOLLY

I have no muse's flame, I'm unknown to fame,
I know 'His' name, its my humble claim.
Ram's peaens I sing to my lore,
Can't fathom, with wavy froth of my mind, from shore.

Realizing His glory is infinitive,
My mind wavers to proceed with narrative.
All ineffabble is the sway of Ram,
Yet, I feeble must not leave chance to say of Ram.

The One, only one with no form or name,
He is ultimate bliss and the final aim.
To hallow my tongue, in mellow mood,
I sing sweet paeans, tho' my words are too crude.

Know not any text, little know of Veds,
My stubborn pencil, colours the page, yet.
Scriptures, Veds, texts are fathomless ocean,
And my Lord on other shore stay unseen.

Couplet:

Over Vast and deep Main,
Once a bridge is built
With no toil even an ant,
Can cross over it. 11

Solacing my soul in many such ways,
Sweet narrative of All time I portray.
Ancient and recent bards are my sires,
They may bless me, for what I aspired.

Before old muses ray and laureates of today,
As well I bow, to laureates of coming days.
I pray Kaliage, the uncivil era,
Where, this narrative is panacea.

Brahma, The Creator of the blessings and blemish,
Who created my dull mind and in it a high wish.
I bow to Him, His creation and His creating hands,
With one who made boon and with other the bane.

Who is my sire and the sire of my desire,
Who created Ganges, at the same, the mire.
My mind is crazed in this frame of garbage,
Me, the man of straw, walk on the path maze.

Couplet: *But the potential in garbage*
From Seasons and seasons of penance,
Becometh manure, an asset
Which is blossom's fragrance. 12

There is possibility even in the garbage,
So I am assured of His grace.
The mystery spelt by Shiv in 'Sabar Mantra',
Hath sharp majesty, tho' in muses are blunt.

May Shiv in me and in these verses dwell,
And create in the Epic the same spell.
May Lord Shiv initiate me inly,
May I be wise enough to see my folly.

Tho' Moon is stained but serene are its rays,
My mind is stained, may bring pure lays.
Even as chilly Himalaya hath warm cataracts,
May my cold limericks have warmth of faith.

May mind, thro' His grace be excelled,
Which is seasoned to make nothing but doggerels.
May, my slumbering pencil on the blank pages,
Dance enthralled with the epic's verses.

Inly = inwardly, lays=poems; Doggerels=worth-less verses

Couplet: *The serene rays, from holy planes,*
Impregnated with His paeans.
May brighten my conscience,
May very sense of hymns become séance. 13

MAY THE BLEST PLACES BLESS

I worship Awadh's people and pious milieu,
And revere worthiness of holy Sarayu.*
Who lived in Awadh and Ramrajya who witnessed,
All the peopled air is worthy of praise.

I adore every brick, every niche of Awadh,
Which still sing virtues of King Dashrath.
I bow to Awadh's people, where I sought,
The breathing love for Lord of my thought.

Janakpuri where alleys and abigails,
Witnessed ancient love of the Divine Couple.
Where Ram tore the shankar's old bow,
Before, that Janakpuri of Siya, I bow.

From the womb of the Earth, the holy wonder,
As Siya descends, the place I revere.
Where Janak surpassing the wealth of town,
Lived with inward glory, crowned.

Couplet: *Where Ram sojourned to tribes,*
To the holy Chitrakoot I bow,
Where fraternity gained new height
Where Bharat took Ram's sabot. 14

May the soil of Awadh initiate me on duty,
May fraternity in epic become my piety.

---

*Sarayu, the river of Awadh
Sabot=Wooden sandal

May the Sarayu river fill my pitcher,
From its pellucid stream, with the holy water.

Now, where Ram's visage filled every path-way,
And 'Bhakti' had woven the wedding bays.
May that Janakpuri fill in me the love,
May Ram pick me up as a flower in grove.

May me for once feel His divine touch,
May my empty colours in His lotus hand's blush.
May I be simple tribal of Chitrakoot,
And offer the Prince, handful of wild fruits.

May I be a shrub in Kamadgiri's parterre,
Be implanted in holy soil, by Siya be watered.
May I ask wind in such a way to blow,
So that me, that shrub ever bow to Siya-Ram's grotto.

Couplet: *May holy places bring,*
May bless me with boon.
That my Empty soul becomes a pilgrim,
me with 'Me' to commune. 15

THE COMPANION - CHAMPIONS/COMMONS

Couplet: *May vivid colours winsome,*
Of epic fill my dark bosom,
With crimson of Lakhan
With sanguine of Bharat, Shatrughan. 16

The chief among warriors, chief among devouts,
To Hanuman I bow, the soft heart in frame stout.

Bays=garland of victory; Grotto= beautiful Hut, Parterre=flowerbed.
Sanguine=hopeful(colour of blood relation.)

Every soul, who, to Ram goads,
Whose heart itself is His Lord's abode.

Jamwant, Vibhishan, Angad, Sugreev,
As dedicated warriors they are ever perceived.
The personified devotion I see in them,
For peace they warred to fulfil Ram's aim.

Birds, beasts, gods, godlings and men,
Whose souls have one and one very same flame.
I bow to lotus feet of all of them,
Who are daas of Ram for nothing in return.

I bow to saints, seekers, ascetics, hermits,
Walk, the whole mankind, on whose foot prints.
Every soldier who faught, still fight for the cause,
Or have fight within to bring Ram Rajya.

Couplet: *Those play-mates of care-free days,*
Whom He didth make win
'Be defeated' is His feat,
I bow to them to win blessings. 17

The doer of all blessings, dear of The King of kings,
Words of praise lack for Siya, Me think and think.
Her lotus feet I do implore,
May Her halo, lit in me serene lore.

Whose feet in itself are 'Teerth.'
Before Her feet as son I beseech.
Whose feet ever follow the Master's foot prints,
May in me be etched those moral imprints.

Those feet, those footprints winsome,
Hath guided men, 'll guide in time to come.
Glad tidings of truth on untrodden glades,
The winsome wanderers in the wood lead.

Glades=Forest path

Lakhan, at service of Siya Ram both,
A blinkless vigile, was his solemn oath.
Great Hanuman, the Great gallant I implore,
Whose glory, glorious Ram, Himself adoreth.

Couplet: *Full of light and might,*
Virtuous Hanuman I adore.
As wight, his deeds delight,
His simple devotion delights more. 18

HIS NAME IS ABOVE 'HIM'

Ram is essence, His name is raceme,
His name is greater, holdth higher esteem.
Ram-Name is in itself the compressed Ved,
Its abridement of all holy texts.

The sweet twin letters, ever fascinate,
The two orbs for devout, in sky of alphabets.
Letters, genial to all and simple to recall,
Are friendly in this very world; in next, pals.

Tho' these have no phonetic concordance,
But are joint as the Supreme and souls' alliance.
In embodied Bhakti 'Ram-name' as jewel shine,
Me fool! should niche the Name within, turn the clay into shrine.

Ram Name is Rampion, on it Bhakti's bee-hum,
and thus spirituality, in life's grove, blossom.
Fame cometh to him, who becomes a name,
Name goes far beyond the frame.

Wight=Supernatural being
Raceme=bunch of flowers

Couplet: *With chisel of His virtues,*
Shapeth out unshaped frame,
And mind carves statue,
And soul enshrineth 'the Name'. 19

Lacking name, the frame is alien,
Yet with Name, the Unseen cometh in presence.
The Name is interpreter of Formless Visage
Of the Supreme; to bring the Absolute to grasp.

'The named' is the same, the Nameless Absolute,
Yet it comforts mind with palpable statue.
Once named form is enshrined in bosom,
Mortal clay turns easily into sanctum.

So 'Ram-Name' is greater than 'Ram' Himself,
The statue of devotion in us it jewels.
So, devouts chant name, flooded to the banks,
With no toil, they quell, race of ignorance.

They roam in own world of bliss,
Independent of candle of gnosis.
Out of millions of texts, narratives and tidings,
Ram-name is Lord Shiv's finding.

Couplet: *His name is above Himself,*
Its final gain of all knowledge,
Shiv picked it from millions of tales
And imparted into sages. 20

Naarad, the divine sage became a Name,
Realizing and muttering the holy Name.
Prahlad became himself a sanctum,
Niching the Name within bosom.

Dhruv* fixed his mind on His very Name,
To astrayed sailors it guided to aim.
Hanuman, holding in heart the pious Name,
Keepth his hold over his Lord Ram.

Tulsi says he was a shrub cannabis.
The Name reformed him to holy Tulsi**, the sui generis.
Any age, any era under the blue,
The Name shielded the souls from the blues.

In this wheel age, the Name bringeth weal,
It bringeth success in life's ordeals.
Empty of piety and penance,
This empty Age on Very Name depends.

Couplet: *So, Keep on the doorsil tongue,*
Ram's Name as glowing jewel,
Urged Tulsi-for enlightening
Inside, the out as well. 21

Ascetics burnt midnight oil of Name,
And toiled to enlighten with the constant flame.
Many unnamed seekers of the mind's depth,
Found pearls of very Name as the ultimate.

Ram exerted Himself for army to cross,
Bridging the ocean from marge to marge.
But for devout the very Name is barge,
Should the wise ponder- 'what is less what's large'.

A constant change in manifestation may occur,
But very Name of Avatar never alters.
With manifestation the Eternal limits
Himself; yet the Name is infinite.

---

* A tale is wellknown that soul of Dhruv is sublimed to become pole star, lode-star, Dhruv

** Tulsi=Basil shrub, present in every house as holy shrub; Sui generis=peculiarity (of holiness.)

In this desert age, the Name is wish-tree,
Its only asset of empty handed Votary.
But the name becomes the Name,
Thro' the deeds of the manifested Supreme.

Couplet: *Formless Absolute is unseen,*
'the Name' as interpreter,
Reveals the very Supreme,
For easy access to Him. 22

THE POEMS OF PROEM

The Absolute, whom the seekers sought,
May Shiv bring that Avatar to my thought.
Lord Ram, the Supreme incarnate,
And his glad tidings are devout's assets.

Even who utters His name as a reflex,
Or rapt in Him, who utter, are blest.
Ram released, Ahalya, but a single,
Name doth free from millions of evils.

Ram Himself broke the Shiv's bow,
Name's glory shattered world's woe.
By all means, the Name, my err, will mend,
By Whose mercy, the Mercy never ends.

Whose beginning is unknowable, non menon,
Now narrative of that Supreme, I begin.
Prosperous, penniless, classy or son of clay,
Dull or lighted, bright or cloudy ray,

A Slight poet, or a laureate of height,
All sing paeans of Lord to own insight.
While I portray and ink pages,
I impregnate faith in these lays.

'Bhakti', the very treasure of my Motherland,
I share with the language of aliens
It's narrative of faith and theTruth,
In manifested form of the Absolute.

Couplet: *In kaliage, false, fallacy*
Frauds and fouls grow
Virtues of Ram for these
Are the fierce inferno. 23

Lord incarnateth in many forms,
Millions and millions are paeans of Ram.
In novel words, in novel tongue,
Noble deeds in novel ways sages have sung.

It was Tuesday, of Lunar Chaitra, ninth,
In Awadhpuri dawned Lord's exploits.
Veds, Valmiki, warbled His virtues,
Tulsi inked verses of banks of Sarayu.

Sarayu- flow is pious, its glory is deep,
Waves seem dipt in swarthy form, with ripples of 'Ram' on lips.
Verses, strophes, and couplets, stanza,
Are chants of the Ganga and the Hymns of Himalaya.

From ancient days on solar road,
Where ever the men went, the virtues trod.
May the honest efforts and my sincere opus,
Fulfil, 'for the men', its very purpose.

Couplet: *Not fond of Ram with no fund of faith,*
And who never found the reverence,
They may not get the muses
Nor will perceive its nuance. 24

May it, in the wise, stream as Ganges of devotion,
With depth of dispassion, waves of reason.
Frolicsome Leela of the Divinity,
May fill in this mature world the infant's purity.

Here, the natural bond of sibling's deeds,
In the fragmented world, is the time's need.
May Siya's wedding with Prince Ram,
Fill every canvas with rich panorama.

In the joy of crowning of Ram, as regent,
The turn in story, may bring 'strong spirit' in men.
Crabby counsel of kooney to Kaikeyi,
May warn and save men from selfish 'I'.

'The renunciation is the great gain,
The path of duty, is the joy not pain'—
The story brings this message,
'The path of thorns, are winning alleys.'

Couplet: *'The natural paths of natural heart,*
bringest Lord to the sill,
Through Kewat, hamlets and path plebs,
This, the holy story reveals. 25

Bharat cometh as if for fraternity's cause,
And on which was built the Ram-Raaj.
The determination is ever bound to win,
This message the warrior Ram brings.

The narrative is confluence of the three,
The devotion, determination and the divinity.
Determination is Ganges, Yamuna's devotion,
With Saraswati, the unseen divinity, have made confluence.

On its bank dwelt Bharadwaj, the hermit,
For Ram, in heart who hath a flame lit.

Thus Bharadwaj in Triveni of the narrative
Taketh dips in séance, with other ascetics.

The place that depicts Bharadwaj's wisdom,
Is the confluence of Prayag, the sancto-sanctum.
In winter solstice when sun enters capricorn,
Every year to be witness of that morn,

In holy Prayag would gather seers and saints,
And would share their thoughts in the séance.
With fervour in Triveni they would dip at wee of day,
And in Ram's narrative they would dip all the day.

Couplet: *Rituals, spiritual and real,*
The Divine and elements,
Of mundane and of riddance,
All would share experience. 26

While orb of sky, the Sun changeth path of rays*,
With solemn dip all would discuss of solar race.
Once, after plunge during solstice,
Returned to their abbeys all ascetics.

Yagyawalka, the most prudent sage,
Was detained by Bharadwaj at his hermitage.
Asked-" O pious ! my mind hath a doubt,
And thou havest mastered all about.

"lacking light of Guru, one can't get,
The serene rays of holy palm foliage.
"Is Ram the same Supreme element,
Who hath come mansized for men's riddance?

" Is same Ram wanders in alleys and glades,
Are the same Ram's tidings praised by Veds?

Sancto-sanctum=holiest of the holy.
*during winter solstice.

Couplet: *"Who stays in Shiv's heart,*
Is that same prince or else?
Thou must havest realized,
O wise! Tell me in detail." 27

VERSES OF SHIV'S CONVERSATION

Yagyawalka knew all about Bharadwaj,—
'For the coming men's race he had asked.'
Yagyawalka began Ram's narrative,
Bharadwaj and his pupils all sat attentive.

'O Child ! I begin now Ram's epic,
From vast ocean few pearls I pick.
What was told to Uma by Lord Shiv,
To my lore, I begin the same narrative.

Shiv said "O Devi! I had heard in days of old,
Narrate it, what Ram Himself had told.'
The Supreme's descent was for world's woe,
And to eradicate the Earth of humanity's foe.

Some say He descended for Kashyap-Aditi's love,
Some say He came for devouts like sage-crow.*
Bharadwaj! I value the cause all above,
For devout's worships, He came for Sabari's sloe.

Couplet: *When rose up falsehood,*
In the anarchic mayhem,
To establish the Truth,
The Unseen as the Apparent came. 28

For seers, seekers, friars and saints,
For long petrified Ahalya's riddance.

---

*Kakbhushundi (a divine sage in the form of crow)
Sloe=jungle plum (ber)

For every whispering vesper Lord descends,
For page's reverence and sage's penance.

The Creator Brahma creates thro' penance,
The penance maketh Vishnu, the Supreme providence.
With powers of penance Shiv ruinates,
With same power Shesh holds earth's weight.

Penance maketh the Supreme to manifest,
And the mankind nay the Earth as a whole to bless.
"Thus seated in pavilion of Kailash,
Shiv began the story O Bhardwaj!"

So calmly sat Shiv, the Slayer of Kama,*
As the serenity itself hast taken a form.
Hour was right, time was just meet,
Bhawani wished to know more of Ram's feat.

Wifely love bringeth increasing respect,
Shiv asked Her to sit very next.
"exoteric concealed is revealed by saints,
To soothe a man smitten with pangs.

"My eager soul implores Thou and ask,
To grace me with narrative of Raghu's Lord.
"If Thou are pleased with me,
O my Lord! And knowest me true to Thee,

"Then tell to me and detail His paeans,
And disperse my clouds of nescience.
"The realized and enlightened sages,
They define Him as the ancient of ages.

"Is this same as, son of Awadh Naresh,
Or else, unseen, unborn, formless?

Kailash=the mount kailash; *The winner of lust and passion;

Couplet: *How come unborn Lord cometh as Prince,*
With the earthly wail and toil,
I see plain acts, but hear divine facts,
doubts around my conscious coil. 29

"Lord ! my folly shouldst not tease Thou,
Disperse all clouds, wipe out my doubts.
"First tell me what caused the Supreme,
True formless Lord appearth in form.

"Relate to me the story of Ram's advent,
And divine deeds of divine child then.
"Tell me glad tidings of the wedding,
What happens then which, sad plight brings.

"then detail about the Chitrakoot,
Reverently which is reference of brotherhood.
"Then reveal to me His deeds in dense,
How didth He kill Raavan and demons.

"O Ultimate seer! Tell me ultimate truth,
For souls what should be the godward route?
"Tell! of path of gnosis, subtlest knowledge,
And vast devotions with distinct alleys.

"Thou are greatest Guru, holy texts say so,
Lest how canst, the story, feeble race know?

Couplet: *"Wonderful wonders of the Holy wonder,*
Tell me O Lord ! next,
How did He move to Elysium,
Blessed His abode to His subjects. 30

Charming words of Uma's natural heart,
Her serene faith, gladdened Her Lord.
Holy wonders of Ram all gathered within Shiv,
And thrill welledth over the eyes of Shiv.

The Supreme Deo, Mahadev, Mahakaal,
By thousands of names Shiv is called, recalled.
Only Siya-Ram knew the truth of transcendent Self,
that very truth then Shiv began to detail.

Revering Ram, full to the banks, Shiv,
Poured nectarian heart, voicing narrative.
"O Uma! So great, so blest I see,
None else is benefactor of world like thee.

Those beating hearts with no genial faith,
Art just breathing machines as good as dead.
Skilled tongue that sing no Ram's praise,
Like that of a frog is unlettered flesh.

Couplet: *Lost in bliss, Shiv went in trance,*
Hush and silence stretched.
Then regaining began the story,
Poured His heart in sketch— 31

"Uma ! I see in thee, the mercy of Ram,
Tho' natural hearts may show simple qualm.
Ram's truth is too vast and too subtle,
Nuance of His paeans are noble.

To misery, mistrust, and mistakes,
The mind binds not, with this very knowledge.
'Ts glory of future, today and glory of past,
Doctrine of the discourse may help at large.

Its an axe to boughing, growing sin-tree.
With heart and soul Uma ! listen to Me.
Veds enchant the advent of Ram,
His deeds virtues, His feat, His charm.

Who bringeth all blithe, who ist bane of blight,
May His light grace, which graced Dashrath with exploits.

Under dark canopy of folly and qualm,
On threshold of troth, dawns Truth of Ram.

Couplet: *"It's unwise to say 'one is wise'.*
Its folly to say one's ignorant.
Man's wisdom the Lord decideth,
All puppets in Supreme hand. 32

Sightless, lightmen, dolt, humblest,
Having mirror of heart blurred with blue dust,
Toiled at earthly thirst, soiled with lust,
Never met Holy Shine, they, the mortal rust.

Averse to Holy verses, they can't sense,
The fragrance of Veds, their endowing gains,
Their surfing mind, never dipt in Supreme,
Ever they aver a folly thing.

To, lushy of wine of fleshy world,
None shouldst give ear to their absurd.
Ram is Sun on threshold of true bliss,
How can linger there any cloud of fuss.

Man tilt for cheers under clouds of fears,
And toilt in vain for goals of Earth.
Suffused in all soul, He, the serenest Light,
Is the earliest ray, the true halo of delight.

All matter, all soul havest within,
Subtlest, serenest ray of the Supreme.
His paeans have no beginning and no end,
Veds chant *mantras* to their ken.

With His hands unseen. he workth every thing,
Supreme, the Earless, tho hearth every sigh and din.

Lushy=drunk; Troth=faith; Ken=knowledge.

He is pure bliss with no rise or fall,
He is substratum of changing Maya, the tall.

Couplet: *He is formless so is His grace;*
Yet the conscious in us,
Once dipt in Him lost flesh,
Perceives His divine touch. 33

Who is envisaged within sages,
Enshrined within saints,
Who is extolled in holy pages,
Same ist Ram of Awadh, All-friend. 34

Shiv says—

Ram name I impart in dying mortal coils,
In Kashi's soil, that freeth all from toils.
Very same is my Lord at the same, Master of matter-man,
Who masterth all threads of His puppets.

"Uma ! He the Sovereign Spirit,
He meetth in all, omnipresent as He ist".
Words of Shiv occupied Her seat of thought,
And faded finally the blurs of fog.

And deep within Her seeded faith in Ram's feet,
Now unbelief in Ram became Belief beyond belief.
"Clouds of any doubts that vapoured in feverish sun,
O Lord ! are now wiped by healing breeze of sermons.

"Thy kindred spirit havest lit me,
The sacred visage, my mind can foresee.
"My askance faded, now to mine asking,
Be pleased and reveal Ram to me.

"Lord is Supreme truth, in all nests, all breaths,
Though the conscious in all, yet of all separate.

"The Supreme, Absolute is tho' ever nigh,
Appeared as Human tell me Lord! why?

Shiv rejoiced hearing a natural heart,
With a natural beat craving story of His Lord.

Couplet: *"I tell blest words that echoed,*
In Himalayas' valleys
And reached to Malay's coast,
From Ayodhya's alleys. 35

□

Let each man see and take of God what ever suits him

—Ram Krishna Paramhansa.

SAINT YAGYAWALKA'S SERMON IN SÉANCE

"Who ist cause of all causes, His holy Advent,
Hast very many causes and many relevance.
"*Bharadwaj ! Ram is beyond mind's reach,
His sway is above the limits of speech.

"Whenever virtue is won over by vice,
Demonic deeds multiply and rise.
"When the outrage ravages the Benigns,
To the troubled mankind when law of nature is blind.

"Then, appearth unfailing the Supreme Mercy,
In various forms to wipe misery.

"But Lord cometh not just for demonry,
His coming ist more for virtues and votary.
In one round of creation, thus the Supreme on the earth.
Holy deeds He performed in His holy birth.

In one round Kashyap Aditi were parents,
The blest couple came as Dashrath-Kaushalya next.
"Many causes of 'His coming' the verses reveal,
Truly Lord Cometh, on Own will.

*Yagyavalka said to Bharadwaj.

Couplet: *"O Sage ! Ram's Glory I say*
Let more reverence in you stay,
Let minds not swell astray,
His nectarian story I portray. 1

"The Supreme wonderment hath varied advents,
With wonderous charms of His attainments.
In every cycle of creation of this clay,
Cometh Lord, enacts in lot of divine ways.

"Hallowed fountains of muses' mountain,
Were warbled by Valmiki in Ram's advent.
Hari is infinite so art Hari's feat,
Varied ways about Whom, saints pick and depict.

"No lays, no ways, no sage can reach,
To the finite of His endless feat.

THE FIRST COUPLE WAS BLESSED WITH DARSHAN

First parents of men, Manu and Satrupa,
The first couple evolved by nature's law.
Later sons of Manu were named 'Man'
Thus Creator's thought came to existence.

With height of faith and depth of penance,
Prayers of first couple reached to the Lord's conscience.
A vision, a visage, came in sight the form,
Appeared before them the Wight form—

Couplet: *The celestial splendour in celeste colour,*
A sapphirine swarthy form,
Whose sapphire shone the azure,
And dazzled all the world's pomp. 2

Wight form=super human form.

Couple's thirsty eyes kept lids ope,
Accomplished, was their long waited hope.
Heavenly bliss blunts worldly sense,
Both fell at feet of the visage in reverence.

"O devout couple! I shall accomplish,
I ope before thou my hands rich."
"Thy holy sight O Lord ! is greatest asset,
We are fulfilled, its all Thy grace.

"Yet a keen longing linger within me,
Its sternest for me but sport for Thee.
"My wish is high, humble is my reach,
It's easy for Thou but I have a hitch.

"Thou art soul of all souls and so of mine,
Grant me as Thou knowest my mind.

Couplet: *"The Bliss tempts for bliss further more,*
So a wish grows in my core.
O Gracious Supreme Lord!
A son like Thou, I implore. 3

For Lord, the true prayers are ever concern prime,
And the merciful Lord said "so it be".
"But where shall I get one alike Me,
Your son, so I, Myself shall be.

Then Satrupa was asked by the Lord,
Her words welled out of Her natural heart.
"The light, the height, the delight, bliss,
Lord! What's attained by true devotees,

"Very same bliss, same love, same faith,
Grant us same light, same life and same fate."

Truth ever echoes more intense—
In the heavens gets the high deference.

Most reverently then Manu spake-
"I have one more request to make.
"Let me have love for Thou, as a father to a son.,
So intense, that I may be called insane.

Lord said "O heavenly souls on this earth,
O father! I shall be thy son in Awadh.
"O father! meanwhile go to Paradise,
Till the right sun calls me from Awadh's sky.

"I fulfil Myself, when I fulfil thou,
I shall come mansized, its' My vow,
"Men's fruition is My fulfilment"
Saying so the Lord evanesced.

"Both enshrined within, that wight visage,
For rest of the life they lived in some hermitage.
The Age picked their holy souls from holy cage,
They sojourned to divine plain, next.

Couplet:

Shiv told to Uma-this text
is a solemn stream,
and there are many more causes,
Of advent of the Supreme. 4

The primitive souls saw many colours,
Some were real blest, some were accursed.
Great Magician masterth the fate,
Every Soul in His hand is marionette.

The friends' claiming law, or fiends' taming awe,
Are all His Maya's extravaganza,

Evanesced=dissolved.

He made treaters and traitors too,
The blush of blossom and blues under the Blue.

Made rocky mounts and rosy dews,
With His colourless brush made prismatic hues.
Made He devils, who devour the peace,
And made devotees who adore every species.

Made hate and heart with the same hand,
Honey in bittercomb, a boon and bane.
The world, with skilled words, His bards do flood,
At the same, He, with sword, spills the blood.

Couplet: *The colours in the destined frame*
All its greens and blues.
Are in creases of the hand
All gleams, all glooms. 5

With message, on purpose, he made hand's crease,
'He ist at hand to change the fate with ease'.
On the hands on duty, and on worshiping hands,
Doomed creases melt, and doomed fate mends.

With chisel of troth and axe of truth,
Lord appreciated, the man, own fate who hews.
A transparent soul hath taintless fate,
It purifies others as the chaste Ganges.

Man of consequence walks on narrow strip,
With no balance of reverence, he is bound to slip.
Only concern, in to and fro sojourn,
Is not the glory but the virtues earned.

Whoever incurs, the Nature adverse,
The curse follows him to its' worst.

Hew=carve.

The curse, turns man unto demon,
Truly, it proved in the frame of 'Raavan'.

Couplet: *Since providence hath puffed*
*life into nuclei**
Virtue and Vice tugged
The right and the wrong vied. 6

THE RAVENER RAAVAN**

Curse has twenty arms to raven virtues,
In Raavan's case it became true.
Ten times shrewd head, twenty times prowess,
Thus curse multiplied in Raavan's case.

Even as a sin follows the sin,
Curse gathers more curse as kins.
Raavan became the king of Lanka,
Ahimardan, Kumbhakaran were his fra'.

lesser to say, the better; but with some scope
providence made Vibhishan his brother with hope.
At all odds, Vibhishan was a different soul,
Of different soil devoted to Ram.

Kings' sons, his kins, even underlings,
Were havoc to the Earth and earthlings.
My words awe-struck, my verses tremble,
To tell of those ruthless wretches' rebels.

---

* subtlest form of life,

** Raavan is said to have Twenty arms and ten heads making him a monster; Fra'=brothers. Rebels=revolt against law of Nature.

Couplet: *Tho' scions of line of a saint**
Of Pellucid Pulastya race.
The curse blown in them a Satan,
All behaved a Sin Incarnate. 7

Three brothers performed tough penance,
not for the rise but for the low gains.
They asked the boon from the Creator, Himself,
Beyond the heaven, their reign to swell.

They wished not to die at any hand,
But forgot to mention monkey and man.
Kumbhakaran's palate had diabolic repast,
Guided by Sharda**, long sleep he asked.

With all odd faces and all odd frames,
Race of base was skilled in phantasm.
Phantasm and pomp never charmed Vibhishan,
He asked for, in Ram, his true devotion.

The Trikuta, three peaks stood out of the Blue,
And Lanka seemed Creator's own work too.
On the face of nature, the grace of architect,
Both worked together to make land great.

Bricked with gold, it blushed heaven,
Its splendour faded all show of paradise.

Couplet: *The guarding Ocean all around,*
Protected Lanka like a moat,
Heaven descended in town,
With paves of jewels and walls of gold. 8

Thus the chief of mischief, Raavan,
From the Earth to heavens, he ravened.

---

* Raavan belonged to the race of Saint Pulatsya.

** Goddess of wisdom.

He assigned to his friends and fiends,
The ravishing life, and lavish living.

One day, in a play he ran to Kuber,
And carried away Pushpak, his aero car.
Own power to test, mankind to harass,
In odd funny mood, he lifted the Kailash.

His awe, his army, his allies, affluence,
Fame, feral fun, family with no fence,
All grew with every new dawn,
Even as the greed grows with the gain.

For six months in sleep, Kumbhakaran would bury,
His wakening would make the world worry.
His brawn, his arms and his might,
Were strong, staunch stalwart in fight.

Eldest son Meghanaad was family's proud,
An archer, a warrior, a champ stout.

Couplet: *More champs, Kumukh, Akampan,*
With the jaws of steel,
Dhumket, Atikaaya, many unnamed,
Wer' breathing mounts of ill-will. 9

Raavan's haughty look viewed his naughty throng,
He assessed his assembly and his pomp.
In the pomp of power sprouted proud,
The ruthless spake in wrath aloud—

"Listen ! sons, all demons and kins !!
I'm to heaven and heaven to me is hostile.
"They live on essence of Bhog of altarage,
And alms of Yagna by humble human race.

Feral=brutal.
Altarage=sacrifice of holy eatables in altar. (FootNote)

"Prayers of men, deify celestials,
So go ! ruin ! man's piety, yagna and rituals."
Saying so he rose, shook the earth itself,
He scoffed heaven, challenging gods to battle.

The demon King, more over with lust of fight,
None dared him, all went in hides.
He snatched away, mirth of hearts and hearths,
Adepts, men, heaven he wilfully accursed.

The wind, water, wealth and welkin,
The time, death, planets were at his will.
The awe whispered in every breath of life,
The Earth suffocated in Demon's strife.

Frail mortals and immortals failed,
All bowed their will to Raavan's fad.

Couplet: *His mighty paw gripped universe,*
With his mightier awe,
His thoughtless thoughts accursed,
The Earth with draconian law. 10

Couplet: *Top of brutality claimed top beauty,*
And the excelled dames,
His lust crossed morality,
He wedded many of the women. 11

Demonic outrages faded holy pages,
All was adverse to morals-ethics of the text.
They preyed on pious, pure, poor plebs too,
Things of thick terror thumped through and through.

Welkin=sky.
Draconian = rigorous; Fad=craze, whim.

Pure piety was perished by satanic crew,
Dharm vanished in blue sceptic milieu.
Flaw knew no law, filth knew no faith,
They subdued *Dharm* and ruined holy veds.

Stanza:

The faith faded, fraud pervaded,
Flawful law only stayed.
The bust of lust, Raavan made the Earth,
The worst of it's state.

The hell fell upon men and heaven,
Anarchy ruled the reign,
Feeble innocents, pious and saints
Were subdued by brutal hands.

Distitch:

All sins, embodied as Satans,
Won over the innocence,
Words dumb on face of demons,
Whose lust was just violence. 12

THE LADEN EARTH PLEADS

Viles, knaves who craved others' wealth,
Thirsty blood tides in their minds swelt.
No piety, no prayer, no pity for parents,
They exacted sweat of exalted saints.

The innocent-breath struggled to survive,
Even sylvans, penates, Veds homed in hides.
With rare life, the bare sylvan,
Looked at withered rivers and seasons.

Tho' rich environ wrote the green bequest
But very next, the greed of demons axed.

Lord shiv Said to Uma--

O Bhawani ! Who act in this way,
Those creatures are demons of today.
The flood of innocent blood, on the façade
Of the feared Earth, made herself scared—

Anarchy turned men unto beasts
The world looked then to the East.
Here, the spirit of Earth brooded in herself,
'My lap hath turned into the hell.'

'I am not rocked by hills, rills, rocks,
But Laden with ills by wretches and rogues.'
Perverted deeds distorted the Earth's lot,
Yet for fear of Raavan, she uttered not.

Laden with the debris taking form of heifer,
Went she to hidings of gods, seers, friars.
The Earth, the heifer, her laden soul,
Could not be helped, could not be consoled.

Stanza: *The gods, godlings and pious beings from hides*
Headed to Brahma,
With the Earth in tears, as poor heifer,
Looked deserted struck with awe.
Seeing white and blues,*
Of hues of His own creation,
Unamused Creator then mused
'Let our sigh may raise to the Lord of lords.

Debris=decays of life and Dharma; Heifer=the cow.
*White (fear) blues (gloom)

Brahma consoled the earth—

Distitch: *"O Earth! Not be edgy,*
Let ease may come to thou,
The Eternal shalt hear thy elegy,
Thy eclipse shalt ebb now. 13

Troubled gods sat in a counsel,
"Where we may find Lord, where should we appeal?"
Some said Lord liveth in high paradise,
Some said not this, its mare nectaris.

Shiv said- "A seeker strives best to his love,
In return always manifests holy touch.
"I too happened to be in the concourse,
And put to them my discourse"-

"Hari dwellth alike in all bits, all breaths
And ist revealed on beats of faith.
"Any trace, any place, any face, any part,
Tell me! Where the Lord Hari is not ?

"He is soul of all souls, He revealth by fervour
Even as by friction manifests the fire."
Brahma agreed 'well said! well said!!'
With all, my words found favour.

Couplet: *Thrill ran through the veins*
Of Brahma and eyes brimmed.
With lofty heart, lifted hands,
He began to hymn— 14

THE PRAYER-HEARD

The hymn: *I do belaud O Lord of lords!*
O all bliss to supplicants!!
O mercy hand ! O slayer of fiends!!
O benevolent to the innocents !!

O Master ! O mystery!! O wonderous wonder!!
*O kind to mankind and cow**
Thou naturally doth show, the grace on low,
O Glory ! All glory be to Thou . A

O Providence! Thy nuclear presence
Ist divine radiance in all beats,
O Unseen divine!, Thy holy touch
In Thy holy feat doth meet.
In all souls Thou meetst,
And all souls meetst in Thou,
Holy soul and saints ever chant-
O Glory! All glory be to Thou. B

Thy crimson of dawn, the green of great lawn
The blue of the Blue and the azure hue,
All these colours died, and blues dyed us,
More over no liturgy our elegy knew.
O Delight of sages! Dark night Thou razest,
Our artless heart, our deeds and vow
With folded hands, ever chant -
O Glory! All glory be to Thou. C

O Ancient visage! Beyond thoughts of sages
And holy pages, even Sharda goddess,
Let Thou bestow, on poor and low
Let Thou be moved to pity with grace.
O Eesh! O bliss! Churn our fuss
That bringeth glory, all glory be to Thou. D

Couplet: *Soft sigh of love and pain,*
Ever doth echo intense,
All awe of men and heaven, to drain
Grave revelation came — 15

---

*Cow represents innocents.
Liturgy=worship, Rituals

"Fear not! O heaven! O Earth! O saints !!
For your sake my coming ist at hand."
"I shall come in shining Solar race,
My divinity in human form, will manifest.

"Kashyap-Aditi strived for Me,
It's time their penance be fulfilled
"Pious souls art glowing as Kaushalya-Dashrath,
In human frame art the Rulers of Awadh.

"Me, the Supreme shall come in their palace,
As four brothers, the best of Raghu's race.
"What Naarad had told, I shall uphold
I shall descend with full Light and Force.

"Pale face of Earth and her laden heart,
I'll relieve burdens, courage! O gods!"
–The Heavenly voice poured bliss in heaven,
Soothed all worshipers forthwith returned.

Brahma, then buoyed up burdened bereaved
Earth; and was reassured, was of fear, rid.

Couplet: *Brahma said "ye art ever*
Monkeys in Lord's hand,
Go! Be born as monkeys, its proper,
To serve Him during His advent. 16

THE INCARNATION

And reassured they all went,
Knowing coming of Lord was at hand.
Behest of Brahma was a boon for gods,
They took no time to carry out command.

In the form of monkeys they came on earth,
A terrific might, a fright in fight and robust.
Rocks, paws, jaws, boughs wert their arms,
But they unrocky, calm, waited coming of Ram.

During this truce, the trappean troops,
Swarmed wide in world, on mounts, in woods.

Shiv narrated to Uma—

'This divine discourse I have portrayed,
I pick up now which I left half way.

Lay to north of Ganges kingdom of Kosala,
With Ayodhya the winsome town as capital.
Built on the banks of the Sarayu,
Where solar dynasty ever ruled.

This kingdom none, had dared to challenge,
For its impermeable array's strength.
Groves orchards added to its charm,
Only bees had right to disturb town's Calm.

True to it's name, Ayodhya defied all foes,
No spill of blood, it's soil did know.
Comfortable was the commerce in every corner.
Comfortable were the people and peopled air.

The King of Ayodhya, in this happy state,
Was Dashrath, as mentioned by Veds.
A human by soul with godward move,
Accessible to all, he, the champ of virtues.

Couplet: *Kaushalya wast king's blest part,*
And so wert other queens.
For King, queens had wifely faith,
And great longing to the Supreme. 17

Awadh was a very vast reign,
Only few could claim to cross end to end.
Some happy dawn, king's kudos poured,
'He had no son', a sore in his core.

Good reign ever revereth goodliest virtue,
The King, so, hastened to Vashistha, His Guru.
He shared with him, own bliss and blues
And wast, many ways solaced by Guru—

"Take heart! thy lot shineth, I find.
Thy pride four sons wilt care mankind."
Vashishtha referred name of a seer,
In the state of Anga, who lived.

King Dashrath himself went to bring Rishya Sringa,
Thus, Yagna was performed under his guidance.
Yagna continued for full cycle of seasons,
For the Supreme to bless a peering Son.

The Seer offered oblations, poured his heart,
With blest 'paayasam urn' reified, the fire into god.

Fire-God said—

"whatever envisaged by Vashistha, the sage,
For thou! O king !the object is now blessed.
"O king! Take this urn the divine offering,
And divide among queens as thou dost think.

Couplet: *The fire reified in form ,*
Guided them and dissolved ,
And flood of bliss and it's warmth
Brimmed out of the King's soul. 18

King prompt, sent for his beloved consorts,
Swiftly Kaushalya and others turned up.
Half of kheer he gave to Kaushalya, the eldest,
To Kaikeyi, the king gave the rest.

Both the queens made their share's halves,
And Sumitra accepted both the parts.
Now queens proceeded on the family way,
All big with child, all great with gay.

Since Lord found his way into the womb,
All milieu wast pregnant with new bliss boom.
The splendour of queens fell on palace,
With a shine of beauty, virtue and grace.

Sometime was, thus happily spent
till moment of advent of Hari came at hand.

Couplet: *He, who ist luck itself in all signs,*
And astral bliss of planets,
Zodiacs stars lined up fine,
When the Lord didth incarnate. 19

Bright day of crown Chaitra in new year,
In Abhijit asterism, to New Born, so dear.
High time, high noon, no scorching no chill.
Coming of Lord was nigh and the coming of the thrill.

Nature spake in blooms, smilt in mount gems,
Nature hummed in pellucid rivers and rills.
Nature whispered in fragrant soft breeze,
Holy earth pleased, heaven gave up ill at ease.

When Brahma kent, Ram's advent at hand,
In aero-cars came the crowd of heaven.
On the vault of earth, flocks of the heaven,
Gods, songsters warbled Lord's paeans.

With seraphic crowd in the tabernacle,
Sky strummed, gods drummed in revel.
Echoed drums' roll, gods', sages' carols,
They tendered services, extolled manifold.

Couplet: *Celestials crowded sky*
Implored and returned back,
Thus, Lord Himself came for sighs
Of the Earth to solace. 20

Stanza: *Descended a marvel, an Advent for humble*
To grace Kaushalya taking nascent form,
Pleased all mothers, eased all seers
As He revealed His ancient charm.
Light of His eyes, wast delight of all eyes,
And fright for the plight of the Earth ,
Having celestial glow, Celeste hue of the Blue,
With divine emblems in His sporting arms. A

"O Lord of lords! How can I belaud !"
Prayed divine mother joining palms,
"nae tone, nae tome, can intone,
Thy paeans, O Oeon ! In neo form."
"O Virtue incarnate! O bliss ultimate!
Holy pages, and sages ever do say—
'To gladden my laden heart,
Thou descendst now in my arms! B

"Veds adored that in every pore of Thine,
Galores of galaxies room,

Tabernacle = decorated canopy (colourful sky)

Even man of lore marvels, that "Thou, The Marvel
Had dwelt in my womb."
The revelation was graced by chubby face,
Many acts he wouldth perform,
Revealed to mother, prior birth of her,
To seed in her motherly warmth. C

Not at stake, now mother spake—
To give up that Supreme form,
"Be a child, as child ist mother's need
And childish deeds, art a mother heart's warmth."
Hearing her words, the Lord of world,
The Ancient became infant and began to cry,
Tulsi doth say, who warble this lay,
Whirl not in carnal bay, and attain Shri Ram. D

Couplet: *To benefit heaven and human*
For sake of saints, innocents,
Beyond tents and wonts of mundane,
At His Will, He shapeth n descendth 21

A youthful joy heard infant's cry,
With gust all queens rusht by.
Hushed working hands, rushed worshipping hands
Revelry flooded with hustles of content.

Reached to the king tidings of son's birth,
Tidal gush drowned the rapt Dashrath.
Thrill and love welled from his core,
He sought to rise, flooded to the shore—

Whose very Name bringeth bliss, and grace,
The same Lord cameth at my palace.
Melody of bliss strummed heart of the king,
Asked for drumming, thrumming, strumming of strings.

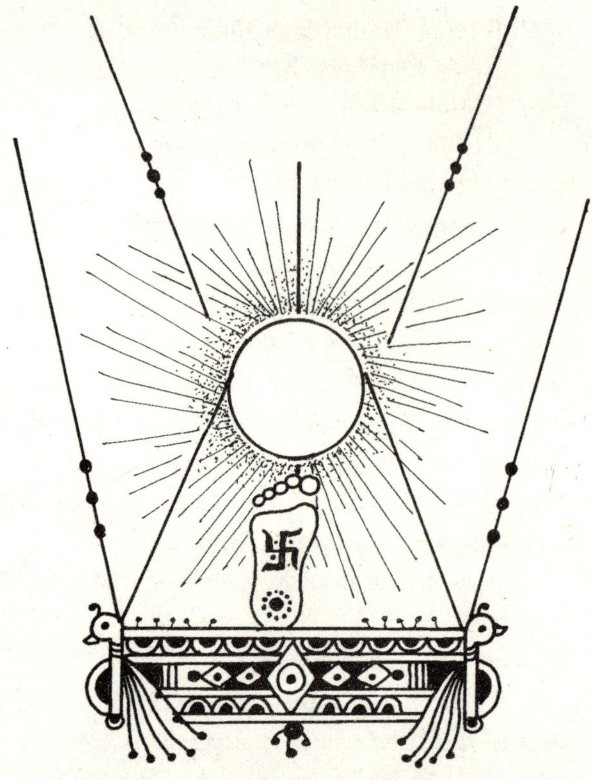

Guru Vashishtha, then, was also summoned,
Who called at, with convoy of Brahmans.
All gazed welling halo, hovering over cradle,
At the beauty of child, the Beauty herself failed.

Couplet: *All Rites, rituals of the gifted hour,*
and the customs king performed.
To Brahmans, His ope heart conferred,
Gems, raiments, ornaments. 22

THE CELEBRATIONS

Decked town with florals, frills, festoons and flags
To figure splendour of festivity, words dost lag.
In the grandeur of town and, colours of citizen,
Richness was further added by floral rains from heaven.

With festal breast and in casual dress,
Glad Bevies rushed with pompless grace.
With auspicious articles in auric plates and Urns,
The glad hearts, moved in palace, Carolled they, much concerned.

Waved worshipping lamps, raised worshipping hands,
See! the Divine child to rid from ills, wished plain hands
All skills, muses, the poetic excellence,
All bloomed with Lord's solemn paeans.

This golden hour faded all riches to gratis
Who received, retained not the gold, but the lavish bliss.
Colours filled the peopled air of the town,
Lanes mantled with musk, sandal, saffron,

Couplet: *Every lane in colours, every man in cheers*
Joy mantled the peopled air,
For, the Wonder Himself appeared,
Every door peered palaces' cheers. 23

Big with child, two queens meanwhile,
Sumitra gave birth to twins, Kaikeyi to one child.
The latest pride, as the king enjoyed.
Having not one, not two but four bonny boys.

The go, glow, and the golden hour,
Nae bards can word, nae gods can utter.
The splendour of town fell on the night,
It came abashed as threshold twilight.

Taken a back at the sight of the Sun,
The night stayed as very eve at horizon.
Incense fogged up as dusky horizon,
Wafted Gulal looked even as eve's crimson.

Bevy=company of women.

Like twinkling stars, gleamed gems on walls,
Kalash crowned the palace as moon in night fall.
Chanting of Veds in palace resembled,
As the time befitted for the bird's warble.

Gala and fun raised high to the Sun,
Dazzled Sun, also moved with the Earth's spin.

Couplet: *The wide day tarried for a month,*
That no one could ken,
Sun moved dazzled by spendour of fun,
How could the dusk come ? *24*

This strange none could grasp
At last Sun returned to the stable-self,
Celestials and pious souls to their abodes returned,
With content of witnessing the great Advent.

Shiv said to Uma—

"And here I tell my covert fact,
For I know, thine steadfast faith,
Me and Sage Kak taking in the human cage,
We, both, were there no one could guess."

"The gale of gala aired on the bliss loaded roads,
And Thrill filled we two, all lost, roamed.
Our adventure of rapture he alone can ken,
Blest grace of Shri Ram who hath gained.

Blest King hadth blest, at this blest moment,
Every desire, whatever way it came.
Elephants, mounts, ornaments, raiments,
Gladly he granted gold, gifts, garbs, gems, lands.

Dusk = Night
Sage Kak=Kakbhushundi, (Crow sage); Mount=Horse.

Couplet: *All were appeased and eased hearts,*
Invoked their blessings,
Upon Tulsi's Lord, the Lord of lords—
'May long live all sons of the Kings'. 25

INFALLIBLE INFANCY

Some days thus passed in such fashion
Some suns rolled unnoticed, moons some.
Knowing time had come for naming children
King sent for Vashishtha, the Sage Enlightened one.

Paying homage to the Sage, the King spake—
"Name the kids, that thy mind arrived at"

Vashishtha, the royal priest told —

"The One only, but with names more and more,
Yes ! I will declare names to my light and lore.

"Infinite ocean of joy, the infant as He is,
Who bringeth all bliss with His bit of fizz.*
"This eldest little one, hath for His name 'Ram'
Who graceth to cosmos the warmth, charm and calm.

The chubby cherub who cherisheth cheerth,
Who supportth Dharm, will be called Bharat.
And that face of faith and the fate of foe,
Veds named as 'Shatrughan' the enemy's awe.

Couplet: *Noble thoughts, that ripple in heart*
Of embodied virtue,
Mainstay of world, beloved of the Lord,
Named 'laxman', by the Guru. 26

---

*little froth of the Ocean of joy

From Ocean of vision Guru pearled out 'names',
"King! Four sons art four Veds themselves.
Ram is holy pages' gem and sages' gold
for devouts all in all, He ist Shiv's soul".

Vashistha, the regal Guru further said—

"That Infinity longed to do deeds of infant,
For Laxman, Ram's feet are ever fane.
"Bharat and Shatrughan hath increasing love.
Their reverence 'll gain new height with every sun up."

One swarthy worthy, one fair pair,
'Let they be saved from evils'- mothers prayed ever.
Fine virtues of four divines didst shine,
Yet, Ram was par excellence, the Bliss Brine.

In sky of His heart shone moon of the grace
And blest moon-rays welled through smiling face.
On lap, now on nape, now on cradle,
Calling 'Darling! Soul of my soul' mother fondled.

Four sons as they were parent's jewels,
Won by pranks, gestures and prattles.
Revealing just sprouting pearls in gums,
Enriched more grace on adorned rich gems.

Couplet: *Unborn, ageless Ancient,*
above any play of clay;
For love, for devotion, as infant
Came under Kaushalya's sway. 27

The celestial face and celeste visage,
At the swarthy mien, the Beauty herself amazed.
On His ruddy feet glistening nails resembled;
As pearls set on red lotus petals.

Fane =temple

Adorned long arms, those ever carest,
A tiger-claw-wreath hangth around neck.
Gems, diamonds hangst as necklace,
Elegance is raised by footmark on the chest.*

Conchshell tellth the beauty of his neck,
The beauty charmed chin-deep by chin and face,
Two rows of pearls, veiled by lips of rose
R'markable nose and holy Tilak on brows.

Chubby cheeks and the cheery ears
And His lisping words art to sweeten the air.
Thro' His untrimmed locks brimmed more grace,
Holy mother dresst curls in several ways.

Garbed in amber, ameable to Tulsi, Valmiki,
B'fore Whom world kneelth, He crawlth on knees
Nae poem, nae poesy, nae paeans can pen,
One, who hath insight can only rightly ken.

Couplet: *The Creator who ist above mundane*
Above fleshy, carnal coils,
Sported like innocent child,
For the divine love of parents 28

Shiv said to Uma—

"Uma ! People of Ayodhya were delighted, thus,
By the Supreme Parent, Ram with His infant touch.
Pure whispers go up and echo more intense,
In return Ram graceth; it's certain.

Averse to Ram however one may toil
In vain; and is never freed from mortal coil.

---

* Bhragu, son of Brahma once kicked Lord Vishnu on the chest, since then Lord Vishnu has ever borne on his bosom the print of sage's foot as a mark of honour.

Maya, the delusive pomp which dazzles all world
Even that trembles before the Lord.

Sway of Maya danceth to the play of Lord's brow,
Where else should we go? Where else should we bow??
Not art but the heart, that ever wrought,
For, Ram, ever bless, devoted deeds and thought.

Thus Ageless Lord as a child sported,
And all the peopled air of Awadh was spirited.
Motherly touch now rocked him in cradle,
Now tenderly handled, dandled and fondled.

Couplet: *In whispering hour she cradled,*
In warbling hour fondled,
So rapt Kaushalya dipt in love,
More than heaven, of her child. 29

To her daily joy, once happened,
She washed, arrayed, put to sleep her Son.
Herself she had bathed, the order of every day,
Before patron deity of family to pray.

She offered worships, offered relishes,
Returned back again to the queen's kitchenette.
Mother came back to the place of worship,
She found her Son relishing bhog-dish.

Troubled at this, she rushed to cradle,
Found Son in cradle, that raised a puzzle.
Coming again she saw her Son in temple,
Saw again in cradle, now she trembled

Now in cradle, and now in temple,
'Is 't my rapt temper or something real?'
Her pale face mirrored her inner puzzle
And the Infant Lord smilt soft gentle.

Couplet: *Mother saw the form, to the fore*
Nae Infant but the Infinite,
She didth see in His each wee pore,
many creations , universes, spirits. 30

Her vision saw the Terror, the Wonder, the Heavens
Many suns, moons, gods, woods, mounts, oceans.
Mien of the moment, modes of all means
Time's pace, Nature's face, she traced more unseen.

All delusive riches of mundane, she saw,
Pomp of 'Maya' stood befo' Him in awe.
She saw souls threaded to the mundane webs,
and also liberating face of Godliness.

Thrill ran through her veins, chilled her lips,
She dropped at Lord's feet and drooped her lids.
Her mind was palsied by wondrous ecstasy,
Kenning this, Lord reassumed infancy.

Churnt at thought, she worshipped not
She learnt, not the son in her lap but the Lord.
Lord solaced many ways her stirred thought,
This is your son, O mother! Rest you reveal not.

Couplet: *More and more Kaushalya implored,*
A prayer of great devotee-
"Let Thy Maya casts no more,
It's spell upon me" 31

Nonage acts in caress arms,
Delighted devotees with budding charms,
The infants' joy was a daily bliss,
As the infants grew up, the joy increased.

For 'the Father of Creation' as 'the son of man',
Ceremony of tonsure, the Guru performed,
Innocent pastimes of the four princes',
Became life of lives of queens and kins.

Above science of conscience, who in above grasp
Glad blessings on Dashrath! In his house, the Lord plays.
He would not turn to dine on king's asking,
Loth to leave playmate, rapt in play.

When motherly call would reach Him,
The little strides would run away toddling.
Whom Veds termed limitless, and is above Shiv's thought,
It's the lot of the mother, she ran and caught.

With His body all over besmirched with earth,
Took in his arms, mirthful Dashrath.

Couplet: *Even while sat he, the fickle child,*
As He got chance to flee,
His mouth daubed with curd rice ,
He would run with scream of glee. *32*

□

No man can really see God except through human manifestations

—Swami Vivekanand.

BRINGING UP OF THE BRILLIANTS

Deity of poesy, the Veds, even Shiv,
Havest sung His sports loving and naïve.
In His sports, whose mind findth no heaven,
They livest in vain, with no divine gain.

Parent's toys grew, at the same grew the joy,
Guru invested with sacred thread, the four boys.
Reached learning age, they went to Guru's place.
Soon, the Master of the world, mastered all knowledge.

What a great fun, What a surprise,
Vashistha schoolth Him, who is Lord All-wise.
Sharp in Learning, simple in reverence,
The four sober princes, are skilled in regal games.

Armed with tiny arches in their arms
Their beauty and visage are for world to charm.
Beauty of four princes, as they pass by
The unstirred common eyes, with picturesque-look, imbibe.

Couplet: *In Awadh, the gracious Ram is,*
Soul of the common souls,
Larger than any largess
Dearer than their own soul. 1

Ram wouldth, perdiem, call brothers and playmates
For venery in dense, and sports of chase.
As the Holy wonder grew, grew more content,
A fuller meaning king's life attained.

Repast was the part of play with his friends,
He, the parent of all-sways, ever obeyed his parents.
He, the Bliss incarnate contrived the means
For joy of town, happiness of common men.

Listened to Veds, imbibed with rapt attention,
Imported to brothers what the truth it contained.
Rising with first blush at the Eastern edge,
To the parents and Guru, Ram ever paid first homage.

With permission, busied self, in affairs of state,
King's heart was more content with such noble acts.

Couplet: *Who is named 'Nameless' perceived Frameless,*
And timed Ancient of the days,
For aevotees, that Soul of all souls
Performed marvels many ways. 2

SAGES' ADORATION / SAVAGES' ADO

So ist His wonder, so it's text,
Hear ! Me attentive what happened next.
Vishwamitra, the enlightened hermit,
In woods at sacred spot he lived.

Perdiem=daily

Worshipping hands of the sober souls
Ever trembled awe-struck of satanic lour.
Seeing sacred yagya, worships and rites
Sages felt sore about, demons' running riot.

And Vishwamitra was struck with pang—
It's none but Hari could lay them low.
Having understood that Hari already had come,
To relieve the Earth heavily laden.

'My holy-Will chanceth me, seeing His feet.
To bring two brothers, I shall entreat.
'He ist Virtue incarnate, Wisdom embodied,
That, very sight of Hari, my eyes shall feast.

Couplet: *Unhushed high hopes rushed in heart,*
His hurried steps rushed too,
Soon reached he, to the royal court,
For duty of a sage, due. 3

The holy steps at the royal door
Welcomed by king with Brahmins of his court.
The Peer of realm bowed at the seer of realism,
On His own throne the King seated him.

Hands of might havest more reverence,
King felt more blessed and more content.
The courteous heart, that dwelt in king,
All welled to welcome and win him.

" It's certain day of glory for us,
Thou havest blest the court with steps so pious."
When asked for the rest after long journey,
He answered "No need its no first priority",

Lour = Frown

King asked is there any thing I can do?,
Sage said "yes! A favour, here, I ask you."
Mean while the four sons came, they bowed befo' sage,
The Sage lost flesh in the flash of visage.

The visaged sight was the sage's delight,
As partridge is enamoured by full moon light.
"O seer !", the king adored full to the shore,
"Thy such grace, never crowned me before.

"What's holy purpose what's thy behest?
Before thy words melt, I shall act"

Vishvamitra said—

"Monsters molest our meek Monastry,
To militate against them, I ask monarchy

"The storming ravaging savages to ebb,
I will feel saved, Ram-Lakhan if I have"
"Why Ram? My Ram! Soft Ram !! Child Ram !!
Me, Dashrath is, here to save Dharma from harm"

Couplet: *"Your lofty heart have vain passion*
Entrust your sons to me,
High esteem you will earn,
And they 'll earn more glory" said he. 4

As thunderbolt, this demand fell,
King's heart heaved and face turned pale—
" Brood ! O Brahmin ! Make a guess,
I'm blest with sons at the declining age.

"Ask me for heifers, treasures, land,
Gladly I'll give with liberal ope hand.
"For soul, breath is most precious thing,
Even that I'll part on thy asking.

Partridge = Chakora bird

"All sons to me are above my life,
Ram is soul of my soul, I can't survive.
"Heavy demons are hideous hadean,
Here pretty princes are yet too young."

The tides of love that surged, to the shore,
The core of Vishwamitra immersed, enamoured.
Vashishtha, then cleared Dashrath's doubts.
Then in sun of wisdom, all clouds wiped out—

"There must be Divine purpose working thro' seer,
It's a privilege for Prince Raghuveer.
"Seed's growth at parent tree is stunted,
Till in the free care its transplanted.

Diffidently King asked to send Lakhan too,
Vishwamitra agreed to reck the two.
"I'll look after both its my concern,
Tho' looking after me is Their mission.

Mannerly the King called near, two sons,
Preached them and squeezed them to bosom.
His heart, his soul King gave to the sage—
"Like father let thy hand be crowned on them".

Couplet: *King committed them to the sage,*
And poured on them blessings,
Ram called at mothers for homage
Stepped out for cause of All–beings. 5

Ram, the Ultimate Cause to every cause,
Moved as lion, mankind to save
Versus hovering savage over hermitages
For showering on the saints, His grace. 6

Eyes-O-Charms, Long arms, buxom bosom,
Celestial handsome, celeste hue winsome.

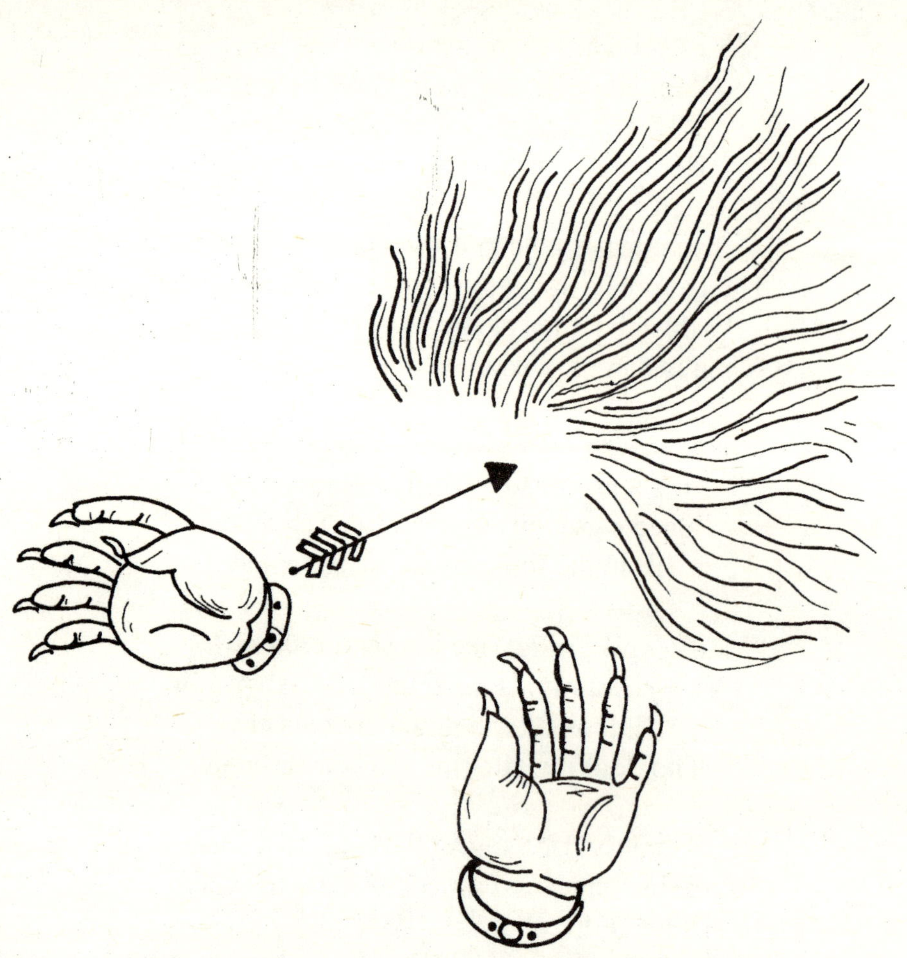

A quiver on back, yellow rob on waist,
One hand with pretty bow, one with thirsty shaft.

One visage dark gem, one with fair hue,
The worships treasured, for Vishwamitra, the great value.
As they accompanied, Vishwamitra then kent,
'Me concern, His own Parents, Ram left.'

The pure, the sure steps on their ways,
Were witnessed by Taraka's* demonic rage.
Fighting Rakshasas, as was a new sport for them,
And were excited for the adventurous game.

---

* A demoness. (Rakshasee)

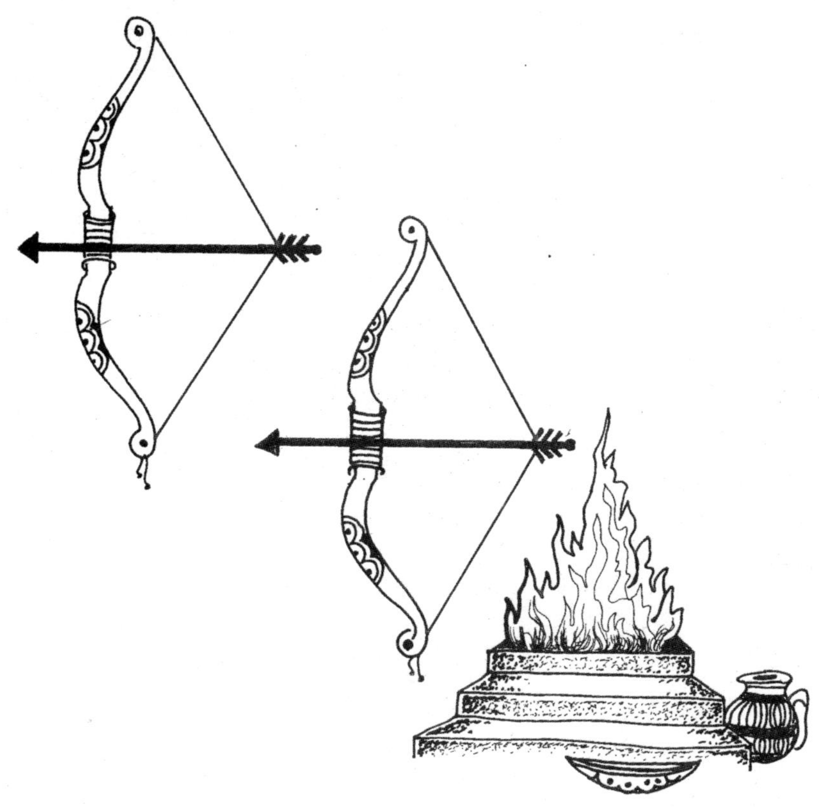

Grave hearts, brave arms needed just one shaft,
Killing Knave, Lord gave her, His own state.
Seer felt along the heart, 'Lord is All-wise',
Still imparted to Him, a sacred advice.

The formula to win thirst and hunger,
To have nitid valour and rigid vigour.

Couplet: *Making over to Lord Ram,*
The divine weapons and divine arms,
To Ashram, the sage took Lord Ram,
A real welcome, with cordial warmth. 7

Morn broke on the guard of Ram, the Saviour,
Begun worships, yagna in fearless air.
To save holy oblations, sacred fire, sacred hearth,
In wary mood, guarded the Saviour of earth.

Praying whispers are ever din for dingy demonry,
To hush prayers, Marich rushed with troops in fury.
Ram struck headless shaft on Marich,
Miles and miles beyond sea, he reached.

Next His flaming arrow fired demon 'Subahu'
And there Laxman wiped out demon troops.
He crushed demons, thus blessed Brahmins,
The heaven and human offered praises to Him.

The saving hands of Lord further graced sages,
Lord Ram Stayed with them for some days.
They talked of old legends, and new trends,
Everything, even though, Lord doth comprehend.

"There is a great deal yet ahead of you,
For the present let us proceed to Mithila.
"You may enjoy Ram ! this diversion,
Where King Janak is performing Dhanush Yagna."

AHALYA'S RELEASE

On the way, A grotto gathered the gaze of Lord,
But the hush was stretched lifelessly odd.
Seeing odd stone with a stern face,
Abou' it, Lord inquired of the sage.

Couplet: *"Accursed stone, she is Gautam's wife,*
With stunned gaze and stern face,
Dust of Thy feet, may blow in her a life,
She is craving for Thy grace. 8

Stanza: *It was Holy feat, with touch of Lord's feet*
Shaped out Ahalya, the Penance embodied,
She did stand with folded hands,
Seeing before her the Lord, the All-bliss.

A grotto= Nice hermitage.

Fulfilled she, and thrilled she
Her ills did flee, love muted her words,
Nae words, nae sighs, only rills from eyes,
Were prayers, only prayers that teared. A

She realized grace, and the gracious visage
That had emerged before, to the fore,
"Glory of Raghurai ! only one canth eye,
And canth realize, who hath ope mind's door''
"Thou shrivest world, I'm soul shrivelled
And Thou art delight of devouts-
"O Saviour ! Thou dispellest dismay,
I do pray, save me! save me !! Thou." B

" It was the boon and not the ruin,
Nor curse of my consort sage,*
No bane but benefit, I do feast, with eyes these,
My Ish, the One who liberateth.
Nae taint, nae talent a wish doth dwellth
In my natural heart,
Like pollens for bee, my heart to Thee
Let whirl around Thy feet O Lord !" C

---

*Gautam who accursed his consort Ahalya.

"To those feet, that issued Ganges
And Shiv borne that in His Locks,
And Brahma adored, those holy feet,
To the fore, blessed grace on my Lot".
Thus, her stony bane, brought her boon
And wrought for her great gain,
With warmth, she extolled Ram
Went to consort's Dham, flooded full to the banks. *D*

Couplet: *If knows such Ram, who,*
lifts not the praying hand
are the poor fool,
befooled roam in mundane. 9

GANGA'S STORY

Ram and Lakhan accompanied the sage,
And reached at banks of Holy Ganges,
From heaven the descent of Holy Ganges
The legend was told to Them by the sage—

"Mother Earth has been here since beginning,
And will stay until Time swallows everything.
"It's pious Ganga flows thro' Himalaya,
Picking essence of rare herbs on its way.

"She courseth thro' many a kingdoms
The Holy, every piece of its ground becomes.
"Her descend involves your ancestors,
Before she could earth, she had to be mastered.

"Bhagirath knew fate of his accursed ancestors,
So he took pains, bring Ganga to Earth.
"He devoted his life entire,
To the mission of Moksha to his sires.

"For salvation of his sires he sought,
From high Heaven the Ganga might be brought.
"His intense penance continued for chiliads,
Brahma and then Shiv now conceded.

"But then Bhagirath had to try for another Chiliad,
Ganga appeared as little girl and said—
'No doubt, till my stream on the earth roll,
The earth would remain no better than sheol.

"I'm pleased on promise of Lord Shiv,
Yet if Ganga descends, Earth may not bear shove.
"Go to Shiv, pray to Him once again,
The mission of your life to attain."

The mission, the determination was worth,
Shiv again appeared before Bhagirath.

Couplet: *Shiv said-"O Bhagirath!*
I'll help in summum bonum,
For, Ganga's every drop is worth,
The Earth to make sanctum." 10

"I willst see, none wastes a single drop,
And thrust of descend to vanish in my locks.
Thus, Ganga whose origin was in Creator's heaven,
Started her roaring deluge in descent.

Shiv appeared just when deluge was about to hit,
Eyes fixed, arms akimbo and planted firm feet.
Vanished in Shiv's lock, became a tame end,
Bhagirath mulled "nothing comes in the end."

Conceded=agreed, Sheol=place of spirits and devil,
Chiliads=thousands of years.
Summum bonum(£)=highest welfare; shove=thrust, drive ; sanctum=holy place.

"Shiv realized, Ganga was totally enveloped,
So He let her trickle out drop by drop.
"Pleased Bhagirath with reverent look,
At the banks of the Ganga then stood.

"Paid his first prayer to pellucid stream,
Laved ashes of ancestors to fulfil his dream.
"Bhagirath's name thus became a byword,
For his determination and tireless efforts.

Bhagirath gave shine to all the mankind,
Ganga's every drop in itself is a shrine.

Couplet: *" O Ram ! in strenuous efforts*
Resides power to prevail.
Firm determination works,
What this old tale tells. 11

"Firmness brings fortune; its absence,
O Child ! leads to nothingness.
"One who dares the despairs,
prevailing power with fortune, shares.

"Every drop on Ganga as the story narrates,
To Bhagirath the mankind incures debts.
"Ram ! see none of her drop is wasted,
Today, tomorrow even in kaliage.

Ram was happy getting holy task,
'What next?' Ram most reverently then asked.
At the banks of this heavenly flowing gift,
With sages Lord took a holy dip.

On the quick-sand following holy foot prints,
Obediently were listening to the sage's hints.
There is a great deal yet ahead,
Turning face, sage would perfect Him at every step.

Couplet: *"O Ram ! be a Ram,*
Of my perfect vision,
May this prince be transformed
In to true Paragon." 12

TO THE MIRTHFUL MITHILA

A hallow company and mellow heart
Makest easy and short, the path.
Lord Ram and Lakhan with Vishwamitra, the sage,
Crossed holy Ganges on a raft.

And so, quick reached they at Janak's capital,
To add to His delight, town's splendour fell.
Nectarian streams, wells, falls, brooks, rills,
Nature pencilled marges with mounts and hills.

Men jewelled further, the nature's rich drawing,
Preserving cooing birds and bees droning.
On winsome blossom, aired threesome breeze
Nature, at own beauty, blushed on lotus' and lilies.

All the virtues and the perfect learnings,
Sprang in right sceptre of the king.
To childless Janak Seeta was earth's gift,
Whom, the royal parents lovingly cherished.

As the daily joy came the Divine Cherub,
As a treasured child they brought Her up.
Today, Her wedding Yagna turned festive
every alley, every door and every niche.

For the Earth's daughter, the Nature too,
Spreaded vernal colours in festive mood.

Couplet: *Green mat was spreaded,*
As lea, leaves, laden orchards,
Fruits, blooms in green studded,
Became charms of herds and warmth of birds. 13

Nae muse can sing, nae words can bring,
All sights, all things were eye catching.
Flooded markets, it's stately face,
Was moneyed with riches, adorned with grace.

Honest commerce graceth growth to the Haat,
Thus, glow of Bazaar seemed heaven's art.
Ope hands of nature, fine hands of men,
Made lae, leaves, lanes, all pleasant.

From bricks and hearths welled bouncing bliss,
Lively predella breathed, on walls, the master-piece.
In blest environ, peopled air was blest,
With broad mind, fine hands and soul chaste.

Hearths looked heavenly, houses with stately grace,
Man-made paradise was King's palace.
Rampart fortified palace's beauty but failed,
It's glory fell on walls, welled over as well.

Couplet: *Stood towering milky palaces,*
With gold waving tapestries on face.
For Seeta's palace, words tremble to express
My muses crawl a little space. 14

Doors decked with gems looked doors of heaven,
With festive environ ever ope to commons.
'The beauty and art delightst with the might'—
King had tough army, chariots, elephants, knites.

Predella=painting on wall.
Tapestry=curtains.

Had cleve' and brave his helping hand,
With honest bond of obedience.
Town looked fevered with royal event,
And crowd of guests camped in lae, lawns, banks.

Princes from Magadh, to Matsya and Malay,
From Mahendra to Mewad, Sahya to Himalaya,
Sindh, Gandhar, Kashi, Salve, Laat, Pandya, chol,
Utkal to Konkad, of fifty six states enrolled.

Rammed on Rajpath, they crowded the road,
They crowed, rowed, bowed, elbowed as they trod.
On Rath, Chariots, Palanquins and knites,
To reach to arena, princes vied.

Here, the green spread under laden boughs,
For stay, Kaushik, chose a Mango grove.
Blest sage naturally liked blest place,
Which was further blest by Ram's grace.

Lo! The fortune of this orchard,
Where all holiness all divinity gathered.
The schedule, the crowd, in which king was engaged,
Could not camouflage the arrival of the sage.

Couplet: *Tidings of Kaushik reached to King,*
And rose tides of joy,
Rushed he to welcome with his kins,
And with royal convoy. 15

Model host before the modest guest,
King bowed befo' sage and was blest.
King greeted pious gathering, praised own fortune,
As the reverence chanceth more luck and more heaven.

Kaushik= another name of sage Vishwamitra, Camouflage=keep hiding, veil.

The sage from his heart, more than courtesy,
Asked King's welfare and offered him a seat.
That very time, the two brothers appeared,
Who had gone to see the orchard.

One dark, one fair tender lads handsome,
Through their eyes, alighted in their bosoms.
All got up from place, caught in visage,
Sage asked both brothers to sit next.

The gazing thrill chiefly drew,
To a worthy fair and a swarthy hue.
Revered Janak lost in elated reverie,
Befo' the revealed visage, revelled he.

Couplet: *Rills of thrill ran,*
Along the veins of Janak,
In tides to the banks,
All lost he spake— 16

"The visage to the fore, the pretty incarnate,
Who are they and whose assets?"
"Whether absolute realm hast come in dual forms,
Whom even Veds canst not fathom."

"My detached passionless mind as I knew,
Why intensely currents to these boys, two?
"Me think, self possessed, is possessed by them,
What drew me? and what's true?

"My sight is adhered since I saw them,
My steadfast mind strayed from the Supreme."
The sage admired, "you have spoken well,
What you said is ever true, what you saw is real.

Reverie=dipt in thought, Revered=honourable, worshipable.

"From edge to edge, where exists life,
Hath thriving love for Them with inner drive.
"Two sons of Dashrath, the Raghu-race gem,
For my cause King has sent Them."

The sage, Vishwamitra further said—

Couplet: *"The charm-embodied in noble forms,*
As brothers Lakhan n Ram,
Their valour, virtue, worth and warmth,
Won demons, saved me from harm". 17

"Ram killed Taraka, and keeled Marich,
Redeemed Ahalya by touch of feet.
"To this Event, Now he hath turned,
To see Shiv's bow and to enjoy diversion.

"To join His father He'll go to Awadh,
In need, He'll serve my purpose.

Janak said—

"My merits have earned thy holy steps,
To touch thy feet sage ! is an asset.

"One boy worthy swarthy, one fair bright,
Both brothers art delight of itself, the Delight.
"Loving spirit that binds, the two boys,
It's lifetime bliss and daily joy.

"What binds them is natural affinity,
O Sage ! Even as the soul and the Divinity."
King's thrilling gaze feasted visage more,
And flooded heart stormed the shore—

Praised own fortune, fortitude of the sage,
King, then, escorted him to a nice palace.

Fortitude=Moral strength/ patience.

King lodged the sage, the guest of pride,
In the palace prime, conditioned for all time.

After further homage, taking leave of sage,
Courteous king returned back to palace.

Couplet: *With hallow escort, with mellow heart,*
Both dined and rested a while,
Slow and slow sun strolt,
A quarter day remaint still. 18

In younger's heart* pure yearnings dwelt,
So Lakhan craved to see the capital.
But some deference and some diffidence,
In his heart ; that maintained silence.

Passing in tides from Ram one can't hide,
And so He kent Lakhan's mind.
Seeing sib's love, a love of the pious,
To the sage Ram's shy words voiced—

"Lord ! Lakhan intends, in town, to go,
His modesty asked not for thine awe.
"If I have thy permission I'll take
Him round the town and, quick come back.

Words touched the soul of the sage Vishwamitra,
"No wonder, Ram! If you value all merits.
"You are the help hand to the virtue's Helm,
Son ! you bringst bliss, to the devotee, out of love for them.

Couplet: *"O sons ! see town's splendour*
And your splendour, let town gaze,
Go ! bless eyes of peopled air,
Reveal to all your charming visage." 19

---

*Lakhan

THE WANDERING WONDER

Passer by who beheld, held off steps,
Enamoured some, shadowed behind the two chaps.
Graced with bow-arrow, clad in yellow,
The fond-path gazed, as they did go.

Loving pair with a contrast hue,
They drew the souls of peopled avenue.
Dighted with sandal paste, bright apparel on waist,
Neck with floral wreath and a sparking crest.

Face of lion with grace of blossom,
A soft heart dwelt in buxom bosom.
Thick lids, thin lips and cheeks dimpled,
Swift walk left behind halo of sparkles.

Dazzling eyelashes and the eyeful gaze,
Between embowed brows, show of Tilak graced.

Couplet: *The face fenced by curly locks,*
With careless elegance.
Graced as should be, from toe to the lot,
All eyeful and pleasant. 20

Like tides, the tidings waved in air,
That two divine princes had appeared.
People rushed as paupers for eyeful riches,
Leaving their errand, at hand business.

Citizen gathered all along surprised,
Thro' worthy, thirsty eyes, the visage they imbibed.

Paupers=beggars,
Fond path= enamoured people on street.

With charmed peeps, maiden peeks rolled and stayed.
On the passing by two pretty visages.

Thus dazzling visage became talk of town,
In the ethereal beauty all town drowned.
"This beauty is true, that is all it's limit,
O friend ! above trinities and beyond infinite.

"Among mortals, immortals and celestials,
None stands none equals to this form eternal.
"A vision, a dream or a charming sway,
O friend! Tell ! unstirred can any one stay?"

"Like wondrous lay*, like thunderous ray,
Penetrate in bosom, who are they?"
One elder voice came in gentle tone,
"Abigail! I tell, as I have been told.

"They art cygnets, king Dashrath's sons,
This tender visage but, had ravaged demons."
"One, in swarthy form, eyes having Lotus charm,
Demonry who hath harmed, known by the name 'Ram'.

"Wielding bow and arrow in His arms,
He's son of Kaushalya, known by the name 'Ram'.
"Who walkth close, as shadow in fair frame,
Younger to Ram 'Lakhan' is his name.

Couplet: *"Ram redeemed Ahalya,*
Ravaged savage', saved abbeys,
Sage brought them to Mithila,
On their ways." 21

Charmed by Ram, some lass spake—
"For beauty of Princess He is perfect match.

---

*Wondrous lay (such beauty is only read in peoms); Peek=stealthy seeing (peep)

"If the King doth but see Him now,
He'll go for this match and abandon his vow*."

One sighed, "King hath come to know Him.
Welcomed Him, yet not left his whim".
"O Friend! For king the vow is prime.
Folly masters over great chances sometimes."

"If providence is good as it is said,
Then Seeta with Ram sure 'll wed.
"had the providence been a lovèless soul,
He would not have made such matching moulds.

"My soul says yes but mind argues,
King's vow is tough, for the tender beau,"
Twin tender teens, with alluring mien,
Passed thro' roads along such whispers and din,

Couplet: *"It's this event that takes place,*
Bestowed on us such grace,
(Or else) Again to see him for feeble race,
Only rich merits can bless." 22

"It's Healing thought it's appealing thought,
But Shanker's bow to lift is hard.
And this swarthy lad hath a tender form"
—some-one expressed her qualm, her storm.

Some spake "all is at stake
Everything my dear! is out of place."
One consoling voice came "some people say
His form is small, but, wields vast sway.

Mien = aspect, visage

* King Janak had a vow that who ever upholds the Shiv's heavy bow and strings it, will only wed princess Sita.

"Celestial power of His Lotus Feet dust,
Redeemed Ahalya, - His gracious touch."
"Bow down ! doubts, He'll bend bow as toy,
Toy not with mind, me ye rely.

"The Creator who carved Jaanki at His leisure,
He preordained swarthy match, worthy, to be Her."
This consoling plea was all souls' glee,
Together all prayed, 'so it be'.

Couplet: *Thus, where ever they passed by,*
Spreaded colours of joy,
blithe faced dames and bright eyed,
Rained blooming buds on blooming boys. 23

The eager steps then moved eastward,
Where arena for wedding-yagna was made.
A huge cope canopied under earth's canopy,
A richly adorned altar was a beauty.

Encircling gold seats for royal suitors,
Were fixed all around the stately altar.
Closely behind that for common eyes
Circular tiers of seats were raised high.

The feebles, the royals, the commons, the riches
For eyeful event all had privilege.
Glowing grandeur of gallaries in gyrates,
Were made still high, raised still great.

Overwrought beyond all thoughts and vision,
Gallaries wert made for galaxies of women.
Thrilled youth showed arena to these elite guests,
From garth to hearth with elated interest.

Cope=canopy.
Garth = lands ; Hearth = Altar(in yagna shala.)

Couplet: *Dazzled youth imbibed visage,*
filled their thirsty-soul,
They gazed and they grazed,
Thrilled along veins to the core. 24

Flooding affection as was seen by Ram,
He attended all of them with due warmth.
'See ! this hew, this hue!! And see this view!!',
Youth drew attention, Ram looked with love due.

All delighting artistry Ram shared,
With his younger brother with caress care.
Who tracketh in all breaths, who waketh all souls,
Who decketh all scapes, who maketh all spells,

He, the Supreme won by simple love and faith,
Man-made arena, He glanced amazed.
Rushed to Guru, two brothers thence,
Getting-late, uneased by awful reverence.

Whose power overawes the Terror itself,
He esteemth glory of love and faith.
Against will of the youth, he bade them adieu,
See ! the duty is reverence, reverence is duty.

Couplet: *It's mingled awe of deference,*
With that of love n devotion.
Submissive both, bowed in diffidence,
Sat by Guru with permission. 25

Delighted Guru, saw twilight, the time of vesper,
Gave words; all followed, performed prayers.
As night strolt from on high to nigh,
Guru told tales till night laden his eyes.

Grazed =touched lightly.
From on high=from sky, vespers=evening prayers.

Both brothers sat by, bedded down Vishwamitra,
Four reverent hands cared, the reverenced feet.
The Lord, whose feet art hallowed path's hightest gain,
And art aims of all means, of the men,

The same Divinity, the same Almighty,
Conquered as it wert by love of devotee.
When the sage asked him again-n-again,
Lord Ram went to sleep only then.

A brotherly bond is chain of reverence,
Lakhan caressed Ram's feet embraced to bosom.
Ram asked more and more Lakhan only then kipped,
Enshrining in his bosom, Ram's feet.

Couplet: *Laxman woke up befor' night closed,*
When still was the threshold,
And the wee watch did behold,
That befor' Guru Lord Ram awoke. 26

Aft' routine of dawn, and rituals of morn,
Both stood bowed to Guru, with high concern.
As the Sun drew, and picked up pace,
To pick up florets, both took leave of sage.

To the charming royal garden, their sight drew,
Robed in beauty of many vernal hues.
Nonage foliage, floriage and lea,
Overhanging creepers and engaging trees,

Wattles bowed with riches, boughs were Laden,
Nature put to shame, even pomps of heaven.
Sweet notes wandering in bush, trees, sky,
Lo! Peacocks are dancing on that warbling birds' voice.

Heart of this scape, have a serene lake,
Dighted with flights of bright steps.

Wattles=twigs, small branches.

See ! on lake, water-birds floating making coo,
Heed ! on floating lotuses, floating bee-loud too.

Couplet: *Blessed garden, that gladdens Ram,*
Must have been more blessed,
Which charms, the charm of all charms,
Must have been most charming place. 27

THE DIVINE MEETING

Ram, the Supreme Gardener looked for gardeners,
With consent, with content began picking up flowers.
Blessed was the place, blessed was the occasion,
Seeta was sent by mother for Girija's orison.

Escorted with Her wise abigails,
Environ filled with their sweet warbles.
Sacred to Girija, there stood a fane.
At the lake; its beauty was beyond any pen.

Taking holy dip with all her friends,
Glad heart Seeta went to Girija's fane.
With daily devotions and orisons of ceremony,
She begged of Goddess a match worthy.

One of abigails strayed and parted,
Her eager heart wished looking at parterre.
Glance of two brothers chanced to her strayed vision,
Mesmerized she, to Seeta returned.

Couplet: *All eyes were upon meek face,*
Yet her shining eyes spake.
"where you gaze, and where engaged?,"
They asked, but not guessed yet. 28

Fane=temple; Orison=worship of supplication.

Reply came—

"In garden I witnessed two princes,
Both of tender age and charming visage
"To say of their charms my words numb,
For my speech is blind and eyes are dumb."

A wave of joy aired among friends,
But the longing stormed Seeta, full to the banks.
Some said "they must be the two princes,
Who arrived day before with the sage."

"That envisaged beauty from the two princes welled,
Captivated the town by casting the spell.
"Warmth of their charm filled peopled air,
We must see them, for worthy they are,"

Friend's advice was voice that did meet
The heart of Seeta to the yearning beat.
Eager steps of Seeta that followed Her friend's,
An innocent walk to Her love Ancient.

Couplet: *What Naarad divined, that standth nigh,*
In pang of yen and angst mingled.
With amazing gaze all round She eyed,
Like a fawn startled. 29

Melody of bangles and mellow of jingles,
In carol of bells as Manmatha hailed.
Ram said "Lakhan ! what bells is no bell,
Its truly Manmatha bellowing for battle."

Again Ram looked whence sound came,
His gaze stayed at coming comley countenance.
True beauty of Seeta was true bliss to Lord,
True bliss forgets words and forgets the thoughts.

Angst=fear, auxielt ; yen=longing; Manmatha=cupid, the god of love/ the deity of beauty;

Creator's skill had come embodied,
The holy expertise, the world at large, to feel.
Divine hands carved Her with feather touch,
Said within Himself, Ram charmed and touched.

"As if in fane of beauty, a flame is lit,
With glow beyond bards' words and Laureate's wit."

Couplet: *Thus a visage flame lit an image,*
In Ram's mirror-breast,
It's sheen reflected on Ram's face,
Simply to Lakhan He spake— 30

"O brother! she is none other, than
For whom this ceremony is arranged.
"In Goddess Gauri's fane, with Her friends,
Came She for orisons of the occasion.

"My unstraying heart is clear transparent,
How this beauty seemth etched on that.'
"It's natural trait of sober Raghu's race,
On courser course they have never astrayed.

"No wild pleasures, no lewd anchors,
Can move Me, the pure, I am sure."
"Who are grave in life, brave on battle front,
Who never crave for coarser want,

"Who are kind heart for deprived hands,
On the land such breed, is a rare trend."

Touched=impressed.
Etched=(Engraved as on glass)
Orisons of occasion=special worship of Gauri done by bride.

Couplet: *Deep He was enamoured,*
While He talked to Lakhan,
Imbibed the nectar to the fore,
Like a bee on the blossom. 31

The unseen thread, that chains the two;
Made Seeta eager, those princes to view.
Where ever keen sight of Seeta moved,
Everywhere sheen dight spring bloomed.

Her friend, then, pointed out to Her,
Through the creeping greens, peeping, two wonders.
One fair, other swarthy worthy for Her,
Her joy, valued as if, found lost treasure.

Stirred within and body motionless,
Seeing Ram, emotions stormed on the face.
Deeply moved She, unmoved Her gaze,
Her moved soul and mind forgot the flesh.

Receiving Ram through doors of eyelids,
And niched in Her heart, wisely closed exits.
Friends saw Seeta dipt in emotional gush,
Wordless abashed they, spreaded hush.

At the same appeared from arbors,
Two comely princes came to the fore.
Two gallant heroes wert the perfection of show,
As blooming Lotuses a blue, a yellow.

Petals and buds were playing in Locks,
Fore head is decked with feather of peacock.

Dews of toils and coils of locks,
And a 'Tilak' dights between arched brow.

Peeping=becoming visible.
Arbors=bower of trees; Carpet=Greens of garden.

At vernal smile, the spring of garden blushed,
Lo! cute chin, cheeks nose and face cut.

Supreme craftman casted a perfect mould,
As comely as He could, He carved both.
"the Flowers, one who carries in left hand,
That swarthy prince is most charming, O! friend."

Couplet: *The brawn, the grace, the beauty in One,*
Those blest eyes of abigails,
Dazzled they saw solar scions,
In glad souls faded flesh. 32

Recovering herself, one clever friend,
Said to Seeta grasping her hand—
"O Seeta! see heavenly princes first,
Meditate on Gauri afterwards."

Seeta opened slowly lids abashed,
And saw two lions of Raghu's race.
Lids heavied of shyness, toe to the head She eyed,
But Her father's vow, heavied Her psyche.

Her gaze stayed, totally swayed,
Alarmed friends said, " let's go getting late."
" O Seeta! next Sun shall bring again,
A chance for this Blest divine vision.

Time of gold runth faster; lingers not,
'Getting late' this awed Seeta's thought.
Enshrined Ram within, with a shine of fire,
Tho, was conscious of reverent trust of Her sire.

Couplet: *Pretending to see birds, deer and bough,*
Her gaze turned to Ram's visage,
Lit deep fire, not the spark shallow,
Ageless Love more and more waxed. 33

'Unyielding is bow of Shiv, unyielding is vow of sire'—
Drooped She moved niching swarthy form within Her.
Ram gazed going princess, the pompless grace,
The Breathing Glory He saw face to face.

The divine-love that flashed the image,
On the plain heart of Ram, was etched.
Too full of thoughts, and sublimed hands,
Her reverent steps moved to Bhawani's fane.

"Jai! O All Glory!! O All Grace!!
Mother of Kartikey! O Mother of Ganesh !!
Thou appearedst in crowning heights of Earth,
Thou breathedst life in all, even the inert.

"Before beginning begins, after all end ends,
O! Ancient !! Thy presence standth.
Thou carvest, carest, crushest cosmos,
Thou controlst all puppets, and dost puppet cosmos"

Seeta further worshipped—

Couplet: *"O! Mother!! thy vestal deeds and vesting heart,*
And the pellucid soul,
Ever Thy supremest moral,
And Thy virtues standst foremost." 34

"Thy ope hand ever bringest,
Fulfilment upon devotion and faith.
"Be it godly, saintly or a plain worship,
Thy motherly hand crownth, O beloved of Shiv!

"A flame lit in Me Thou knowest well,
Thou art the glow, in every one, dwell.

Crowning heights of Eartn=Mountains; Vestal=Pure/clear; Vesting=Bestowing.

"Thou needst nae word nae worship,"
—with this, Seeta clasped idol's feet.
Before lively faith, enlivened statue,
Wreath's flowers smilt, Bhawani's idol too.

The Wreath dropped, even as cometh divine grace,
The smiling face, to Seeta spake-
"Near Me if any call is drew,
I can't contain Myself in statue.

The suitor who, reflectth within You,
Indeed be Yours, my words are ever true."

Stanza: *"That Swarthy hue, that worthy beau,*
Who lit in You-an actual flame,
That ancient flame, that Omniscient,
Indeed ! 'll be yours; its mutual flame."

Abigails adored Gauri more and more,
Seeta was enamoured further more—
Blessing words of Gauri poured,
And fulfilled all full to the shore.

Distitch: *The grace that fulfilled,*
It's thrill ran along Seeta's Veins,
My poesy babble a little,
To say of Her content. 35

With rose in bosom and aroma in soul,
Ram stepped back to Guru, with Lakhan.
Before Guru, Kaushik Ram oped His heart,
That guileless heart knew no mask.

Ram picked flowers for orison,
and the chance blossomed His own bosom.
princes two, were gladly blest by Guru—
'let your desire may come all true.'

After mellow meals, with hallow gospels,
Whole joyous long day, seemed curtailed.
The Sun seemed fast and the dusk whispered,
The self-disciplined disciples performed vespers.

The Lord descendth performth common feats,
To guide mankind for Godward deeds.
Night served bright moon in the dish of sky,
Faded; all twinkling beauty that fell in Ram's eyes.

Couplet: *Vivid moon garbed vivid,*
Lookth timid in the day.
hungth eclipsed before Seeta's face ,
Could the petty moon stay ? *36*

□

Vivid = bright

We, all are projections of one Absolute Energy.

—Brahmrishi Vishwatma Bawra

THE LINGERED NIGHT

"Face of moon eclipseth, waxeth and waneth,
It's rays pinkth pining lass and pilest up pang.
"Moon causes buds sere, and causes birds fear,
O ! moon, the fair ! but a pool of error !!

With countenance of Seeta, if some doth compare,
The blame, he would incure for it's improper,
Finding moon a pretext, befo' Seeta's face,
To Guru He returned, while the swart spreaded.

Here, tho' Ram was sleepy, reverence was awake,
Before He retired, He bowed at sage.
There, Siya felt unease, in night's stretch,
Agitated by bangles, bells, bays, even own breath.

Even rustling of silk and tapestries
Agitated Her, with drift of the breeze.
Her maids had never seen Her in such mood,
Became concerned tho' at first amused.

They found Her prattling to Her own–
'He was here, He was there, and forever gone'.

Sere =withered dry; Pink=pierces; Pining lass=lovesick ;Swart=darkness.

She smiled within Self with crease of pangs,
On the arched brows appeared pearls of strains.
The question went on drumming in Her mind,
Who was He that quelled this heart of Mine.

The night spent itself with little sleep,
Only hope that dawned was Girija's worship.
Before the east knocked Ram was awake,
To the younger Lakhan then Ram spake—

"Lo! Lakhan lo! twilight lo ! the delight to lotus,
Motley fun of east, lo! Heavenly treasure."
The golden ball hopped-up the threshold,
And the words within himself Lakhan couldn't hold—

Couplet: *"The sun came, lo! Sere lily,*
Lo ! thinned stars.
Just as Thou dawned in city,
The feared are all prince-stars !" 1

"For the crowd which gathered how can it dare ?
Bow of Shiv is for them, a night-mare.
"Not the feeble stars, but the nimble Sun, Thou!,
Canst only fulfil the Janak's vow.

"The dusk downs, earth smiles at day break,
Thy devouts wilt smile, as the dusk of bow breaks.
"Lo ! the play of first ray at the far threshold,
Dusk downed before casual dawn, behold!

"This sun in its shine, revealth a stand,
That at shine of the Sun, stars can't stand.
Glimpse of Thy might, all world to show,
Wise vow he hath set, that is breaking of bow."

Chains of brotherhood, thus fastened between two,
With regards, and love and care ever new.

Nimble=bright.

After daily routine and daily rituals,
Both worshipping brothers bowed to the sage Vishwamitra.

Satanand, Royal Guru was summoned, meanwhile,
And sent at once to the sage Vishwamitra.
Satanand conveyed the humble proposal,
And his words gladdened the sage Vishwamitra.

Couplet: *Adoring Satanand's feet*
Ram sat by the sage,
Vishvamitra gladly agreed,
To Janak's humble message. 2

RAM WAYS TO BAYS

"How bride decides on? let us see,
Whom the providence pickth as Her would-be?"
"One who chanceth to get sage's blessing hands,
Wilt be proud groom"- thus said Laxman.

Apt words of reverence touched all saints,
They blessed both princes with ope hands.
Both brothers, with this holy company,
Proceeded to visit the arena of event.

Brothers reached arena, this tidings aired,
And there, the peopled-rush gushed, gathered.
Stopped hands at work, stopped chats and chants,
All age gathered where ever the Two went.

The crowd flooded in, swelled in and swelled in,
From town to arena peopled river welled in.
And the rill of thrill welled out of Janak's face.
People all disciplined sat on due place.

Bays=wedding wreath (garland of victory)

Couplet: *Flooded glut of viewers*
On the royal request,
Ebbed all around all eagers,
To their cadres they sat. 3

Twin beauty princes, holding all sways, stepped in,
Thus further splendorous rays stepped in.
Their divine steps like vernal spread,
Blossomed every bosom, while they stepped in.

The two moons shone ahead, in fading galaxies,
Viewers' souls pleased, suitors' hopes ceased.
It was perception and not just the view,
Some saw the foe, rest saw the breathing statue.

"Lo! the warrior!', 'nay! He, the terror!'
Lo ! the Almighty, nay He, the tender!
"Lo! Handsome, winsome','nay! awesome!"
Wicked kings thus eyed the terrible form.

Commons in Him saw the Faith incarnate,
Demons in Him eyed the breathing death.
In delight, common gaze, on Him was fixed,
In fright, crooked gaze had heavy lids.

Couplet: *Among bevies in galaries,*
Waves of praising-whispers hummed,
Seeing Ram, the suitors benumbed
Despaired they kept mum. 4

The wise, saw in Ram a Godhead ahead,
A might of Almighty, and a sight of the Great.
King saw a very kin befo' his sight,
While Yogis saw embodiment of the formless light.

Yearning mind's eyes beheld in Him, loving child,
Learned mind's eyes beheld in Him, the Father.

Looked to the ground, Seeta in the bridal grace,
But magnet-eyes* wer' drawn up at the Magnate.

Discovered She, content, in Her the ancient flame,
She could see now the very unseen chain.
People's thirsty eyes imbibed all charms,
All gazes unstirred wer' absorbed in Ram.

King Janak saw, two brothers and the Great sage,
He clasped Sage's feet with all homage.
Every one found Ram, as if was looking at him,
No wonder! Lord ever lookth everyone, the even.

Couplet: *For the best of the guests,*
Seats specially made,
On high tier above the rest,
King seated the sage and two princes. 5

All gathered princes, blushed at Lord's sight,
Like, the stars fade, at very first light.
They felt panic they couldn't vie—
"No way we stand befo' this guy."

"Even if Shiv's bow for Him proves sturdy,
Seeta'll choose Him for the wreath of victory."
Some didn't vie, for fear of being guyed,
Turned back, casting to the winds all pride.

But some who wer' blinded with pride,
Said "For Ram, Seeta is a far cry."
"Even if death cometh, we will vie,
And win this battle for the bride."

The terror, some showed, some bowed, some crowed,
But pious, wise and loyalists glowed.

---

*charming eyes; Magnate=chief. (Crow=boast, show off (self praise.)

They smilt at such ego and pomp,
What did they intuit, they did prompt—

Couplet: *"Dashrath's son? Who can vie?*
Ram'll guy their airing pride,
False cry of pomp'll die,
This swarthy is only worthy for the bride." 6

"They fools need no vaunt in vain,
Befor' His glory where do they stand?
Befor' their dreaming becomes their nightmare,
'Seeta ist Creator mother,' make them this clear.

"Ram is mare nectaris, rest all is mirage,
Rest all is mere the mass of pottage.
"My view, my say is only true way,
Holy ancient light shineth in new ray."

—Thus, wisdom, prevailed, unveiled all faith,
Ram's virtues among good princes prevailed.
Whenever true prayers and faith is raised,
Heaven dropth spring and rainth grace.

When mirth touched zenith, zeal gained height,
Janak sent for abigails to escort the bride.
Seeta's beauty defies any language,
How can the Creator-mother, She, appear on my page.

All earthly similies for seraphic visage,
All my muses babble at this stage.
Miles to miles me and my mind's eye, in vain, saw,
For lovely and lively simile of Siya.

Divinity of beauty, divinity of Riches,
Deity of the wisdom and deity of the faith,

Guy=mock (laugh at); Crow=t

Put together their glory on their face',
Can't analogue Seeta, in goodness and godliness.

Couplet: *The Heaven was dazed by splendour,*
Of Her paradise face.
'cause heaven gets its colours,
From Her heavenly riches. 7

"Lo! Here! comely Seeta comes,
Hear ! abigails are singing nuptials.
"Lo! Heavenly dress and the human countenance,
A youthful frame, motherly innocence."

Her splendour is falling on ornaments adorned,
The shine that shone is Her own.
Her steps in arena are steps in all hearts,
In circles, galaries and beyond ramparts.

The celestial crowd in sky gathered,
Heaven seemed lesser heaven before the Earth.
In her Lotus-hands wedding bays sparkled,
She floated rapid eye on all princes herd.

While Siya's avid look was locked on Ram,
All royal flock was stuck on Her charm.
Like, on ancient treasure, Her eager eyes fell,
And imbibed the visage, to the fill.

Couplet: *Lost in the lost treasure,*
But Her modesty was aware,
And she withdrew Her stare,
And drew Ram's mien within Her. 8

Nuptials=wedding songs, avid=anxious, keen.

The Spectators lost in charming splendours of Ram,
And stare was locked in Siya's splendorous charms.
All thought–"should it happen somehow,
Should destiny favour over Janak's vow";

"Its folly on the part of king now,
After finding good match, he is stuck on his vow.
"Janak should edge way through his pledge,
Destiny's wed-lock made a perfect match.

"Oft logic of mind is an ache for the soul,
It's folly to take on, now highminded role.
"Worthy Seeta is made for this swarthy match,"
This common feeling every common possessed.

Then, Janak called his royal heralds,
To make public what he had resolved.
To proclaim king's vow, the royal heralds,
Moved on their errand with jovial hearts—

Couplet: *"Heed! All suitors' ! King- prince !",*
Heralds softly avouched.
"With all resolve we announce,
The king janak's vow . 9

"Suitors' might will be assayed on Shiv's bow,
Its massive, its heavy every one knows.
"Demons like Raavan who are heavy for the soil,
They saw massive bow and quietly recoiled."

"Who ever breaks Shiv's bow, or bends it,
Shall be wedded with Jaanaki with no touch of hitch."
Heeding this some high-headed, headed to the bow,
Filled with folly, blinded by ego.

All princes prided on their pomp and show,
Bowing to their deity, they rushed to the bow.

Some had ego, some to have a go.*
Exerted all strength at Shiv's bow.

Some did crow, some did trow,
'they are mightiest'-but refused by the Bow.
But those princes, their limit who did know,
They narrowed and didn't go to the bow.

Couplet: *In folly, annoyed some turned,*
Trowed like a toy, the bow.
But failed and coyed they returned,
Foiled and toyed by the bow.

"So huge, a Single glance could not comprehend,
Is this a bow or the Meru, the mountain.
"Even if some one lifts and strings it,
What target is there, the shot to receive."

Together, then, tried thousands hands,
But baffled, the bow toyed their all attempts.
Massive bow of Shiv stirred not,
As the virtue stays before stray thoughts.

Thick-head princes trowed, 'the bow is none,'
Their pomp-pride pruned, like what a prude earns.
Their strength flagged, their own flags drowned,
Before bow they bowed their fame, name, renown.

Bleached faced kings, clinched their fists,
With a set back sat back amidst
Their own company, amidst known assemblage,
Here Janak vexed impatiently spake—

"Hearing my vow, with all their show,
Kings came from diverse parts of the globe.

Crow=self praise, boast; *Go=Attempt; Narrowed=confined; Trow=believe.
Prude=Hypocrite, pretender

"From plains, hades depth and from heaven heights,
In human forms came, all heroes of fights.

Couplet: *"A Winsome win of bride,*
A handsome gain of fame,
For such a triumphant prize,
Me think, none is made by providence. 11

"Stringing breaking bow, wrongly I trowed,
Alas ! none stirred a little of the bow.
"Leave here your ego, your go, and go!
Me think of valour on earth, No ! No !!"

"No glory, No glee, no gala now here stay,
For Seeta's fate chanceth no family way."
"Heavier than bow, with heavy low lids,
With all longings failed, long faces here sit.

"Giving up vow is giving up virtue,
She remains unwed, this I view.
"Valour is vapoured from the earth, had I known,
I would not have sowed the fun of my own."

"I question myself, in linking Her bride groom,
With this mighty, and divine heirloom."
Faded faces of commons and dewy eyes saw,
The wrath of Janak, and the wreath of Seeta.

Aloud words of Janak whispered a jolt,
And hammered Lakhan's heart as a thunder bolt.

Couplet: *Kept mum for Ram's reverence,*
With hearth in heart, fuming face.
Yet, at last Lakhan broke silence,
Revering Ram's feet he spake— 12

"Such light words before the Light of Raghu's race,
Though Janak told none dared, none spake.
"Janak was conscious of presence of Ram,
A Being of Great presence is Ram.

"It's no ego, it's front against affront,
Raghu's race is my pride inherent.
"O ! revered Ram ! on Thy words,
Nay bow, nay arena, I can lift universe.

"Words pierced like arrow, into my marrow,
Thy splendour can break mounts, this is just old bow.
"I can finish the story of the old tough bow,
I can lighten Janak's burden, who slighted us though.

"My Lord ! let me have Thy say,
Thou see ! what wonders I do play."
"Belittling words of Janak have heavied hearts,
Let those be thrilled by Thy glory magnate.

Couplet:

"If I fail to break the bow,
If I crow in vain,
I'll swear off quiver arrow,
Never to handle again." 13

Like thunderbolt fell Lakhan's words,
That scared kings of Earth and itself the Earth.
Further bleached suitors on thunder of Lakhan,
Further pleased Siya; Janak turned crimson.

Ram was glad as well the holy assemblage,
On poise of Lakhan and his pledge.
Word for word Lakhan follows Ram,
Elder gestured and Lakhan sat by Ram.

Affront=insult ; Belittle=Undervalue ; Being of great presence=attraction, man of self possession; Magnate=great.

Vishwamitra perceived, the time was meet,
In most endearing and soft pitch
Said, "Up Ram! Up Ram!! Break, bow of Shiv,
My child ! from anguish; Janak you relieve."

He bowed to the behest of the sage,
To the bow He trod with His natural grace.
He moved with no throes or no ego,
Yet, by the bow, He stood like a leo.

Couplet: *Like the first-sun Ram reached,*
Like the orb hops up the East,
All saintly lotus hearts pleased,
In common eyes appeared birds-bees. 14

Dark hopes of rival suitors ceased,
All faded, as befor' sun, the stars serried.
All sham-Kings ashamed like owl befo' Sun,
The silly kings dulled like lily in the morn.

Sages' and peoples' craze looked winged,
Their wings of joy to the heights reached.
Ram revered sages feet with love and homage.
And wished for holy blessings of holy assemblage,

"Lo ! the feat of Lord, lo! the feet of Lord,
With natural modesty, He steppedth forth"
His divine grace into eyes of citizens
And through eyes thrill ran all over their veins,

"If all my merits are of any value."
They whispered "if my vespers are true,
"Let all my true Sadhna, all my faith stand,
O Ganesh ! for Ram as a helping hand,"

Couplet: *The heart which mothered bride,*
With love and care and pangs,
That heart filled to the eyes
Sighed Sunayana, could not contain— 15

THE TURBULENCE WITHIN

"My friends, dear ones and royal kins,
Are they mere viewer and let this odd happen.
"Two princes are yet tender boys,
Don't make them coy, bow is not a toy.

Queen, the mother of bride spake further—

"At the bow fop kings failed and flopped.
Raavan and others flocked but touched not.
"Grey–sense has taken leave of the king,
Can a cygnet ever lift the mount with the wings.

"Wonder! For the bow, people put to test young prince,
Easy prey of innocence, brutal way of providence."
"O Queen ! only your motherly eyes witnessed,
Belittle not the glory, splendour hast no age."

" See! The victory arch, small Sun doth march
Among mobs of planets, tiny orb, winth all dark."
Further, Augastya, the saint drained vast ocean,"
Some wise friend of queen, thus convinced.

Couplet: *"Not hollow din, but hallow chants,*
Sway over Trinity Lord,
As the mighty and most mammoth elephant,
Is swayed over by tiny goad. 16

"Belittle not the little one, belittle your qualm,
Me think, bow 'll be broken by Ram."

Thus assuring words were balm for queen's qualm,
Now her anxious bosom, was filled with warmth.

Casting eyeful at Ram, bride Seeta then,
Each deity, each holy power She prayed in turn.
Turbulent moments lit in Her, the ancient flame,
Her idolized eyes turned into imploring anthem.

Her eager murmurs communed with Uma and Shiv—
"My firm faith should lessen bow's weight.
"O ! Ganesh ! it's for this day I did plead,
O Bestower ! rain grace in my sore need.

"Let bow be stirred for my unstirred faith,
My strong will should lessen it to trifle for weight."

Couplet: *—A dreamy glance, in a waking trance,*
On the Person of Ram stayed
For what She saught and what She thought,
Calling courage Seeta prayed. 17

In brimming dew in Her eyes, reflected Ram's glow,
Recalling vow and bow, dews shone in woe.
"Alas! My father, what hath he sought?
He wronged all good and thought not.

"Not in awe, the counsellors should see unseemly things,
But the reverence should more relevance bring.
"It's a fib or gibe-"this hard bow is presage,
And 'll favour that slender cage, that tender age.

"My gloom brims seeing father's adamant mien,
Could a plume trim ever an adamantine."
"Here stands stone-faced assembly,
O ! Shiv's bow! Only hope lieth in thee.

Trifle=next to nothing; Adamantine=Hard diamond; Presage=Omen.
Plume=feather,

"Impart ! thy weight on this grave assembly,
Lighten thyself at Ram's lightening glory."
Her heavy heart shared Her woe,
And each hung moment was heavy like heavy bow.

Couplet: *Her restless floating glance,*
Now gazed Lord, the very Heaven,
Now at floor, at bow now danced,
With Her lids Laden. 18

Within Her Lotus lips, speech was caged like a bee,
And aired not for afraid of night of modesty.
Speech cornered as miser's gold lies,
And dews wert confined to the corners ofHer eyes.

Her anguish swelt, but before it did melt,
She pluckt Her heart and tried to abate.
"My faith my heart my thought and true soul,
The truth is 'the true might' that I do hold."

"True in Love is true in Luck and due for all blessings,
Here heaven hypes up as helping thing."
Unwavering flame that lits two souls into One,
Is the holy spark that cherish the pure bosom.

At the Lord Ram, Seeta casting Her sight,
Resolved to be His, even at the cost of own life.
All swayed by love, Seeta prayed,
Ram kent Her mood grey* and scant the bow like a prey.

Couplet: *Lakhan perceived, the Raghu's chief,*
Casted a glance at bow,
In high spirits he did speak,
Pressing the Earth under toes— 19

---

*grey(in doubt and gloom); Abate=Ease; Hype up=help.

BREAKING OF SHIV'S BOW

"Heed! Hold on! Behold ! O Earth !!
Read Ram! Be ready ! I make you alert.
"Cardinal guards! Awake!, the earth may not shake,
Bow of Shiv, Ram seeks to break."

To the stern bow Ram then turned,
Stunned citizens bade all virtues they earned.
'May the bow turn light' on-lookers yearned,
For the merits whatever their deeds had earned.

Some dolt, some doubts burdened the bow,
But doting and devotion lightened the bow.
Its perverse of suitors that laden the bow,
But holy blessings lightened the bow.

Vain ego of kings and their pomp-show,
Vow of Janak and queen's woe,
All further added to the bow, though,
Lessened by Lakhan's go.

In bevy some said 'if He fails we will die,
As soul 'll leave soon, the frame of unwed bride.'

Couplet: *A hush in crowd, Ram Scant,*
A still like predella,
A mute pang, then He kent,
With in stirred Seeta. 20

Her hung time stretched like an age,
Ram saw, the awe sketched on Her face.
Time crawls on the road of the throes,
On the lea of glee, it hops and goes.

Dolt=foolishness ;Doting=excessive fondness ; Stunned=shocked.

What's gain if it rains on sere crop
An opportunity lost bringeth all bathos.
Ram saw tempest in Her modest eyes,
And Her heart Ram treasured within, as prize.

With auric heart and adamant's go,
Ram bowed to Guru and then to the bow.
Nimble He gripped bow, simply He held,
Archaic arch touched the roof, people beheld.

In swift flash Ram held, strung, drew it tight,
Mixed up bow's glare-Ram's flare, fixed all eyes.
All saw one dazzle and then two halves of the bow,
Ram broke it, echoed bow's aweful roar.

Stanza: *Uproar of bow, soared high,*
shoved planets off their row,
Though suitors crowed,
but saints did know
Ram ist one and the only prow.

All heavens, demons, commons
wer' awed by the odd din,
When they did know,
'Ram had broken bow'
they belauded loudly Lord's win.

Couplet: *None saw it happen,*
He was so quick and swift.
Roar of cracking bow deafened,
The bow, could not stand Ram's grip. 21

Ram didst throw down two pieces of the bow,
Thus eased among commons, tumult of throes.
Roar of joy soared up and up to heaven,
And blossom of blessings dropt in return.

Sere=withered; Prow= worth, gallant.

In the shouts of paeans of Ram's win,
Breaking din of the bow, drowned in.
Dumb gyres* wondered, yelled in joy; "Lo!
Ram broke Shiv's bow, that very massive bow!"

Muses of bards and music of minstrels,
Medleyed in lays; aired amusing revels.
Peopled air was intoxicated with ballads,
Town itself turned to the auspicious ode.

On parted lips of queen, the unheard-strains,
Yet, can be read on her face in seeming silence.
Janak poured whispering lay in his throat,
In the dinned air he dropt some sober note.

Couplet: *Flatly laureates could crawl,*
Swift feat of the Lord to depict.
Tho, within spectators it scrawled,
And wrote a lasting script. 22

At breaking of bow peerage suitors peeved,
Just as breaking of the day, dims lamps of the eve.
To Her antique love Seeta's heart winged,
First time She felt 'bliss is aching thing.'

With praise to its fill Lakhan eyed,
Though, Ram's feat for him is a daily pride.
Royal priest, Satanand then gave words,
And Seeta softly advanced Ram-wards.

Couplet: *Moved She like a cygnet,*
Shy steps and serene gait.
Though she possessed grace, yet,
Her pace spake, She was possessed. 23

---

*Gyres (Spectators sitting in circles)
Peerage=Aristocrate, Peeve=upset.

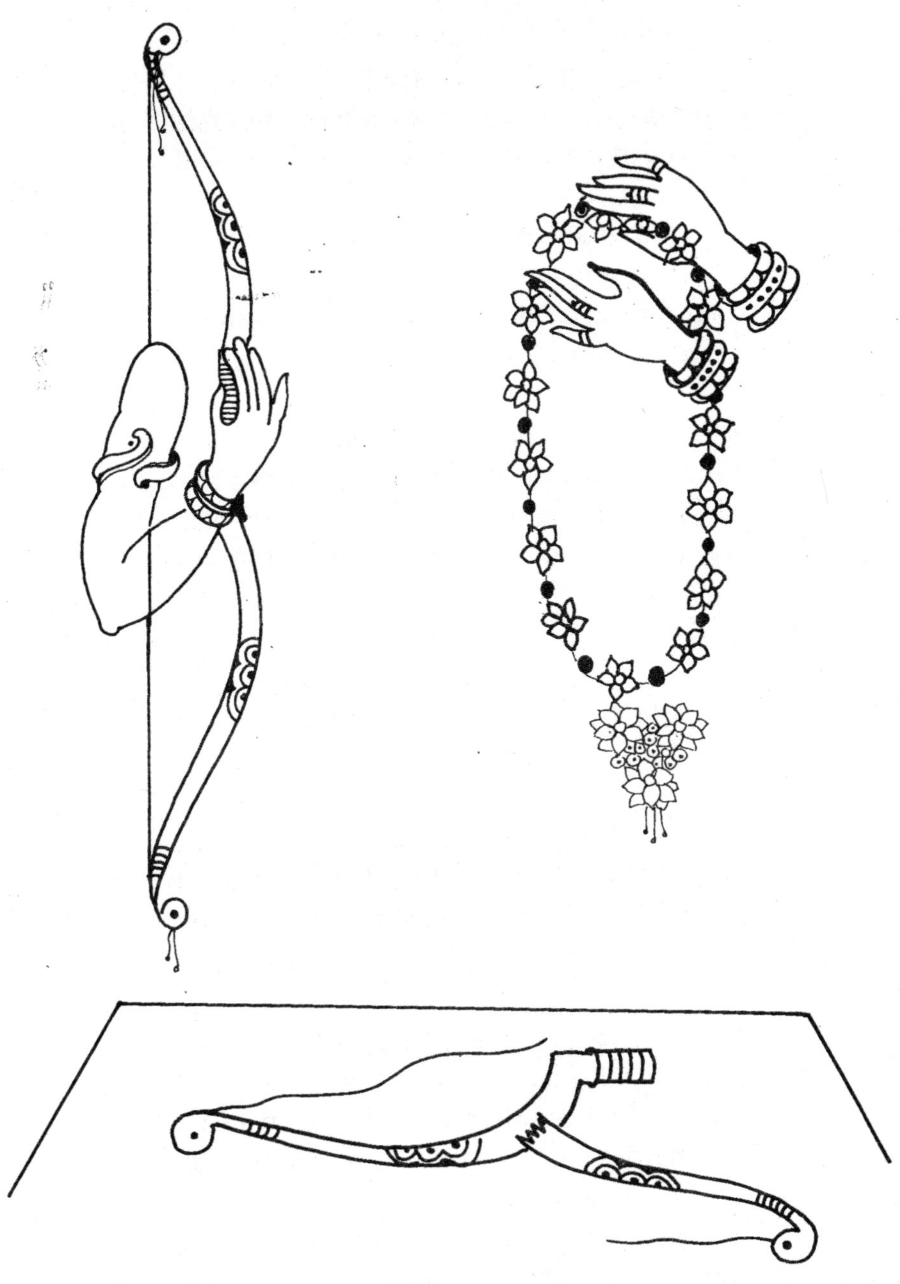

Startled and thrilled abigails didst escort,
As Seeta passed by, Her beauty surpassed.
In Her vernal hands the wedding wreath that bloomed,
Was to wreathe worthy beau, that swarthy groom.

Her blush added more crimson to Her hue,
And, Her arrays, Her gaze, Her bays wooed.
To the draw of Ram, She drew near Him thrilled,
Even as drew on canvas, She remaint still.

Her apt abigails ardently said—
Invest the groom with wedding bays.
As She raised wreath with hands sublimed,
Her arms froze and warmth overwhelmed.

'Beauties dazzle each other'- is a perfect match,
Ram didst propend little, to reach hands stretched.
With bashful nerve and brash fervour within,
Siya invested Ram with the wreath of wedding.

Couplet: *The Bays blossoms on Ram's bosom,*
Seen, a deep blossom in His eyes.
A glee blossom rained from on high,
But fop kings looked flopped and dried. 24

Music purled very nigh, warbled from on high,
Heaven alighted on the Earth, Earth delighted to sky.
Gladdened hearts revered from inner core,
Laden hearts turned fevered further more.

Music, lyrics and panegyrics,
And rollicks in milieu aired thick.
Heaven looked lesser, Earth looked paradise,
Wondrous Festivity itself looked surprised.

Among Vedic chants, world warbled lays
Of winning palm of Siya, and of winning the bays.
Ope hands' offerings, ope hearts' blessings,
Were invoked on the Divine couple by common beings.

Brash=bold/self confident; Draw of Ram= Attraction of Ram,
Bays= wreath of victory.(wreath of the wedding)

Abigails urged "Seeta ! touch yo'r Lord's feet"
But in bashful awe She was freezed.

Couplet: *Feet didst wonders for Ahalya,*
This was Her awe.
Ram kent transcendent love,
And innocent lore of Siya. 25

□

You are not the body, but the mind and thought.

—Brahmrishi Vishwatma Bawra

THE CHAOS

Some fop, flopped names, cropped their shame,
Their heart burn smelt in their claim.

" So what if Ram broke merely the bow,
While we live with more fire in the marrow."
Crass cranium rose from seat one by one,
Undoing their morals, armours they donned.

"Seize Seeta, and teach the two princes,
Should Janak have for us little bias."
Righteous kings reached on their gross words—
"The shame itself should abash on such crass conduct."

"All your go, your ego, and pomp-show,
Shattered with the shattering of the bow.
"Your shameless chaos had charred your face,
Your vaunting vault is daubed with ash.

Couplet: *"Hush ! the scorching tongue,*
Hush up! Ye all ego,
Before your words reach to Lakhan,
Ye know Ram and to Ram ye bow." 1

Vaunt=Brag, crow.

"As a hare should covet the lion's share,
As a gnat should gauge the whole mere.
As a glow-bug should beg for sun's glare,
As a knave should crave a divine favour.

"As a thorn should thrive for a vernal throne,
For cygnets' crown as a crow should drone.
As a fraud should feud for ceaseless peace,
As a wanton should want a heaven's cheese."

"Same way, the passion fayed, and faded your thoughts,
Your folly further flops you unto all odd."
Drums dumbed, frolic dimmed to this din,
Here Seeta feared and moved to the queen.

They sighed " the Destiny's hue, is least understood,
On vernal Canvas, brushed a gloomy blues.'
Sheer din there, here Ram's reverence,
For fear of the Dearest, Lakhan kept contained.

Couplet: *Hushed lips in reverence;*
But more fevered brows,
Lakhan's look was fiery silence,
As on berserk elephants, the Leo. 2

THE RAGE OF SAGE PARASHURAM

Vain yells swelled high and high,
And curse fell on them, from the common eyes.
And the tidings of bow reached far and wide,
Sage Parashuram heard that and arrived.

Crowing coward Kings cowered down,
And fear whispered hush in the town.

Fayed=befitted, socketted.

He, the revered sage with severe rage,
A terrible face and noble cage,

Matted locks, knotted looks, knitted brows,
An awesome aura and austerous halo,
High born, High brow, Highly strung,
With quivering quiver, vexing axe-all thirsty weapons,

Serenely garbed but armed severe,
Frame of Seer, with wearing of a tough warrior,

Couplet: *Harsh face, serene dress,*
Looked embodiment of rage.
Parashuram came like tempest,
None knew what happens next. 3

All flocks of gathered blokes wer' shocked,
All lips locked, only hush knocked.
Swallowed by fear nor they crowed nor rowed,
Not just to his holiness but to his awe they bowed.

Now, the host royal couple rushed to the sage,
Called on Seeta, to pay homage.
Royal modesty ever getth noble blessings,
And Parashuram blest the bride, the queen and the king.

Next, Parashuram and Kaushik*, the two sages,
Met like two streams of holy Ganges.
Kaushik placed Ram-Lakhan at holy feet,
With the feelings of honey seer's gape kept fixed.

His gaze couldn't gauge the godly glow,
That engraved glee in his grey-marrow.

Highly strung=short ignitibility.
*another name for Vishwamitra; Blokes=men, boys; Gape=Amazing Gaze.

Couplet: *Tho' Parashuram knew things;*
With his wrath garnering,
He asked Janak, the king,
About the gathering. 4

A thin voice of Janak faced grim face,
Reverently he revealed the straight fact.
He turned round, espied the shattered bow,
Like gathering storm, he gathered brows.

His fiery words then chilled every soul-
"Tell O Janak! fool ! who has broken the bow.
Now show to me, that odd accursed,
Lest your realm and the crest meet the dust."

The awe palsied the tongue of the King,
Odds and wicked were glad within.
All colourful rave bleached in fear,
Smeared in dark mood of raving seer.

'T fell upon the Queen mother as a thunderbolt,
"Alas ! fate has undone the accomplished goal."
Here Seeta learnt of the rage of the sage,
Her moment stretched like an age.

Couplet: *Ram learnt the airing nerve,*
Kent Seeta at stake,
Ram saw sinking verve,
So stoically he spake— 5

"Who hath broken the bow O thy holiness!
Must be some one of thy pages."
"Tell me! What ist thy behest?"
Nursing the ire then said, the sage–

Rave=Celebration; Raving=Raging, Lost one's temper.
Page=Servant, attendant; At stake=in difficulty; Verve=enthusiasm.

"A page is not to master but to obey,
He paged the way to affray."
"Heed! Ram! Whoever has broken Shiv's bow,
Indeed, ist mine greatest foe.

"Let the odd bloke stand out of flock,
Lest all high gathering shall be knocked off."
Spearing smile of Lakhan, then, jeered,
Who sneered at Parashuram, the seer—

"I have toyed with my infant hands,
have broken many bows, you never grew so tense.
Why should you be sick of this bow?"
Parashuram uproared nursing the row—

Couplet: *"Itself toyed by death,*
Your voice is strayed,
Prince! would you ever match,
Famed Shiv's bow, with your arch-play." 6

Said Lakhan with a grin,
"all Bows are alike, all arch and string,
"what's wrong in breaking of a worn-out bow,
It was heir loom, it was just a show."

"O Sage! Don't rage Ram took it for a new,
At His very touch, it broke in two."
Words offered in the hearth new fire, it waxed,
Said "don't you know temper of my axe?"

"Your tender age should see temper of this edge,
O Clot! take me not a mere mild sage.
"With the fire of the truth and fervour of celibate,
I'm sworn-enemy of Kshatriya-race.

Paged=summoned, called for; Affray=war.
Celibate=chaste/ monk

"Once vexed, I axed the whole of Kshatriya-race,
I hewed all hues of royal flags.
"My axe many times ruined the reigns of the Kings,
And crowned it all times upon commons."

Couplet: *"O block bloke! bring not,*
To your parents gloom.
My thirsty axe has knocked off,
Even tiny, whose world was womb." 7

Seeing him in a flat spin, Lakhan with wide grin,
Said, "hallow spleen making hollow din."
"To mount up awe, his axe he flaunts,
As if he would blow out, in a breath the mount.

"Your blaming index* should have blessing nerve,
We would wither not, like lander mimosa herb.
I bend to, My lord! Your sacred ego,
My lordly words are for axe, bow, arrow, tho;

"Now that I have known thou art heir of Bhragu,
I'll pick up thou, ebbing my pique.
"It's family trend, we never show strength,
Never challenge cow, devotees and saints.

"Thy words are enough like a thunderbolt,
Axe and bow-arrow, in vain, thou dost hold."

Lakhan added—

Couplet: *"For my words, Pardon me,*
I bow before thee,
My row is for weapons, I see"
But then sage uproared in fury— 8

Hew=Chop down, slay with axe.
Flaunt=show off; Pick up= hear, get to know; In a flat spin=frenzied/ in a panic/ wild.
*Index finger which was pointing

"O Kaushik! This halfwit, is making sick shout—
And will fell on his race as a weeping cloud,
"For solar race, he is a moth,
With nerveless verve he is all mouth."

"His scorching words'll be chill of his breath,
No blame, if high-head comes in jaws of the death.
"On the mere of dare, tides of his proud,
Enough foaming bubbles should ebb now."

"Forbid him, save him from my gruel,
My glory, grudge, gruel, O Kaushik! you tell,"
Said Lakhan, "O Sage! who else can praise,
Where your honour! you brag blowing own trumpet?"

"Your vivid voice with volatile virtue,
Void this fire of volcano, that's blazing in you.
"You are champ, the name, pure and broad,
Pouring of abuses, all echo odd."

Couplet: *"It's not words but the verve,*
That worked in holy cause,
At foe, not ego but the Go serves,
And not the self applaud. 9

"O Sage! The death seems to be your pet,
You carry on calling it, for my sake!"
Lakhan poured, oblations in volcanic hearth,
And through sage's veins ran lava of wrath—

"He is prey of my rage, prey of carnage,
Slayed not till now, for his caress age.
"Spearing tongue'll not be spared,
His haunted words have vaunted dare."

Gruel= extreme punishment

Said Kaushik "O Sage! heed, such deeds, with smile
It's not his sin, it's prattle of a child."
"With holy touch with unbias blessings,
And with sober grace, O Sage! forgive him."

"His fate hath a shield of your hand,
Lest my axe is keen on his stern offence."

Couplet: *Vishvamitra thought with grin,*
He weighs Lakhan, easy prey,
Dark folly is ever green,
Folly brags, drags mind stray. 10

Thus, More vexed Parashuram aimed his axe,
Flocks taken aback 'Alack! Alack!!
As fiery as simple fire Lakhan said—
"Saved, what from me, is you being sage.

"You must have thwarted no sword but the sward,
Your strayed vow, must have never faced the hard."
No one agreed to such a fracas,
Ram as well asked Lakhan to stop.

Couplet: *Oblations of jeer, Lakhan poured,*
In the hearth of the wrath.
Serene sprinkles Ram implored,
The cool tongue, and the warm heart— 11

"My lord! have mercy !, on him be mild,
Wreak not thy wrath on babbles of child."
"Child's chirpy chats are cheer for parents,
Had he known thee, could he ever affront."

"At child's jeers, the sires, the seers ever cheer,
Such pranks, preachers and parents rear.

Wreak = punish out of revenge; Sward=grass; Thwart=To defeat.

"Me, the benign bairn is thy page,
O High minded ! O High brow ! Sage !!

Hearing warm heart, seer cooled down a bit,
But again Lakhan smilt and uttered in Lips.
Seeing his jeer, Seer again turned sick,
Said - "Ram! your brother is gross wicked.

"This proudy fair hue hath cloudy dark shade,
Real poison saps from his deceiving face.
"His nerve seems to be more perverse
His verve, is not after you, will bring him curse".

Couplet: *Lakhan said "O holy sage!*
The rage is the cause of sins,
Such craze brings all mess,
And all sourings. 12

"The wrath ever follows the folly course,
And ever ends at the point of remorse.
"O! chief sage! Put away thy rage,
Be good upon me, I am thy page.

Lakhan added—

"Heal thyself, wrath will not mend,
For the broken bow, let's call master hand."
In fear of further fracas Janak said-
"Pray hush!, Me Pray !! maintain the grace."

A common fear hovered in air,
That Chevy of child is a vain chatter.
But the glow of Lakhan's go, and brave bravado,
Burnt sage with rage into ashy ego.

Chevy=Shouts
Bairn=child;

Posing himself poised, Parashuram obliged–
“He is your fra, sic I spare sick child.
“This fair skin bams tho’ he is all blot,
As if bane is brimming out of the gold pot.

Couplet: *At his wry smile, Ram hushed Lakhan,*
Viewing miff in milieu,
All stern strife's to end,
Lakhan turned up to his Guru. 13

Decent palate maketh a difference,
Ram spoke with wining reverence–
“thy presence is holy, thy blessings are pure,
The acts of child, thy wisdom’ll ignore.

“Saint is innocent, so is a child,
Frank feats of the two are flawless mild.
More so, he hath not done any misdeed,
Who wronged thee, my lord! It’s Me.

“What fulfils, deal to Me, as thy page,
Be it a favour, or frawn or even death.
If thy rage flags, will be my soul’s ease,
Sage ! tell means by which, thou mayst be appeased.

Said sage “how can my rage die,
While your brother still pulls a face wry.
“My vexed axe hath a gory thirst,
That will be quenched only by Lakhan’s blood.

Couplet: *“The iron fight in my axe,*
Is fright for royal crests.
But irony of my axe,
Perplex me today. 14

Wry=mock up; Bam=deceive; Bane=Poison; Sic=so
Iron=strong; Irony=Sarcasm

"Which, won all palms that palmy axe,
In my palsied hand, is held lax.
"That bold axe has today gone blunt,
The fate against me is turned.

Mercy in my heart now strain my mind,"
Hearing this, Lakhan mocked, smilt—
"O kind ! mercy dropth from thy statue.
Thy words are less a word and more a honey dew".

"While the mercy scorches me,
May Lord help when thou art angry."
"Lo! Janak this low bloke is such a block-head,
Beholds he not, the hovering death".

"Can't brook this wicked, enough is laid on thick,
Let he be out of my look, he maketh me sick."
Lakhan murmured "on your eyes let thick lids overlie,
Not just me but world 'll be away from sight,"

Couplet: *"You raised my rage O wretch! "*
As the hearth blazes, the sage spake—
"Ram! You teach me now to patch,
Your foul deed and my heartache." 15

"You pose poised, while he poisons,
You pray, he plays; you confess he cons.
"Do not join the palm but win the palm,
Give battle to me or give up name 'Ram'.

"No trick 'll have the edge for you two,
Befo' this vexed edge which looks at you."
Sic sickly sage gaged calling him a foe,
While Ram smilt within and bowed.

Brook=tolerate; Palmy=glorious
Edge=upper hand/advantage; Edge=edge of axe ; Cons=tricks ; Palm=triumph,Victim

He thought "modesty hath a mute appease,
Yet sometimes it too begetth evils."
"No one braves the raving slips,
As the crescent moon hath no eclipse".

Ram prayed sage to cease the spleen,
" I bow before axe, thy rage to win.
"Thy vexed axe, here my flexed head,
Reverence of thy page toils to ebb thy rage".

Ram said—

Couplet: *"What bindth thou and Me,*
Ist thy mercy and My homage,
Any duel how can there be,
Between master and his page." 16

"Lakhan's shallow look could not fathom,
The hallow in thee but the garbs and arms.
To the bow of the warrior; a warrior never bows,
Thy martial mien triggered all rows."

"Not to the hearth of rage but to heart of the sage,
Lakhan would not disparage but pay homage.
"Would not have erred had he known thee,
He is green for the sin, and not wronged thee.

"To lapse is child, to grace is saint,
We, green for the world, need thy pious-rains.
"Before saintly pearl, can ever dust stand,
Even my petty name shrinketh befor' name Parashuram."

"We art a dew, thou art a helm,
Thou art pearl true, and we, the sand."

---

raving slips=crazed error
Disparage=insult; Green=innocent.

"In every view I'm lesser to the chief of Bhragu,
Befo' thee I am ever subdued."

Couplet: *Nor Eulogy nor apology,*
Worked on the fixed mind,
Sick thoughts zeroed on him thickly,
In Ram all tricks he did find. 17

Whispers of worship wrought not,
On fevered head, brows were more taught.
A berserk mind is more hectic,
All, he finds, sick, all pricks and tricks.

"I find both princes are running wild,
To win their will, they use all wile.
"Their scorching tongue had parched more my thirst,
Their perverse verve 'll be their own curse."

"Me think ! They think of me an innocent saint,
Their taints and taunts are not to exempt.
"My heart is hearth, my wrath is fire.
My glory needth prince's gory offers."

"Ram ! you broke the bow so you blow about big."
Ram said, "thou slamst more, at my slim slip."
"the archaic arch, and the bow was warn out,
My mere touch broke it, vain matter to be proud."

Couplet: *Ram said, "Truth needth no trick,*
And so is My truth.
My truth or thine is matter of strife,
Till the truth is one Absolute." 18

"The truth is ever one, may be in shell,
If one seeth not, it needth be unveiled."

Wile=craftyness, trick; Gory offers=offer of blood.
Blow about=proudly utter; Slip=error; Slam=attack/ criticize.

"My sturdy sinew, my sturdy view,
Hath very true reverence for thou."

"The sceptical prism distorts truism,
Mind's eye, if possessed, intuits pessimism.
"We, the scions of the warrior Raghu's race,
In war, are ever bellicose to meet even Death.

"since he who fearth thy race, is rid of all fears,
Such is the glory of thy pious race."
Grave words knocked the sage's raving core,
And opened eyes of minds' stern doors.

"O Ram ! Same Ram ! and not a sham,
Take ! draw ! this divine bow to withdraw my qualm."
The sage offered, the bow moved into Ram's hand
Of its own accord, what a strange!

Couplet: *The ravings melted in to rave,*
And ran along the nerves.
The rage froze into homage,
The thrill welled over in words— 19

Parashuram, the sage said—

"O! Glory dawned in Raghu's race,
O! Ram to save men from savage.
O! Strange Craft Man of the greens,
O! Fire for forests of the fiends.

"O Ram! O glory!! All glory be to Thee,
Thy flaring flag wilt flag all demonry."
"O! Heaven for devotee! O havoc for demons!!
Here O blessing hand!, there O lashing hand. !!

Ravings = wild talks; Rave =celebrations.

“O light of high lore! O delight of common core!!
O might of the pure! O fright of ill scores!!
“O Lord of lords ! my loud mouth booed,
But Thy parental pardon still wooed.”

The sage rued in worships, in worships sage wooed,
Sic, praising both brothers, he withdrew to woods.
Mutiny muted, galling suitors’ princes fled-sad,
And the gale of gala turned the whole milieu mad.

Couplet: *Heaven hovered to the fore,*
Over Earth, the greater paradise.
And showered flowers more and more,
And gods joined, the common rejoice. 20

THE GALE OF GALA

‘She louds’ drowned in heaven’s drums,
Seraphic songsters poured pealing anthems.
Far and wide spreaded vernal paints,
With lays of winning bays and saintly chants.

Like pauper Janak gathered, the treasure, he gained,
His heart and soul wast full of gems.
Heart of Seeta wast drowned in to despair,
Now, tides within Her, nitid eyes shared.

Above flesh were nerved, ever Janak’s mind and soul,
But his verve swelt much beyond control.
When initial excitement moderated,
King Janak approached Vishwamitra again.

To Vishwramitra he made obeisance –
“Its thy blest grace and holy presence

Mutiny=revolt; Booed=made sound of disapproval; Rue=regret; Scores= swarms
Nitid = shiny

"That Ram hath been able to break the bow,
That two brothers could conserve my vow"

"Now tell O holy sir ! what behoves me?"
"With broken bow, bays won, wedding is done O King!,

Couplet: *"still, what holy pages say,*
Follow your family trend,
Take up usage of the grey,
Follow royal preceptor's stand." 21

"Go ! invite Dashrath, send honeyed message,
To Awadh, some envoy, fast be dispatched."
To send invitation at once went the King,
Called court-poets, epistle-writers for the glad tidings.

Poets would write an epic on the event,
But then need of time, was, message be fast sent.
In the ristling silk embossed words rolled,
In brief epistle, they poured the soul.

The lucky emissaries holding epistle,
Moved fast on the mount, with left hand on bridle.
To pour more colour to the zeal of the town,
Every door of Mithila was decked to appeal of the town.

To deck doors, corridors, bazaars and lanes,
To deck groves gardens dense' and planes,
To deck forts, fronts, fountains and fanes,
Citizens poured their souls intense.

The King asked his helps to raise canopy,
A welkin under welkin for wedding panoply.
Skilled hands, thrilled hearts of the artisans,
Worked Gold pillars look-like plaintains.

Panoply=splendour

Couplet: *See ! aurum stems add decorum,*
Emerald fruits leaves leaven,
Further painted red by ruby blossom,
See ! the craving of men, carves heaven. 22

Bamboo sticks are tricked to bamboozle,
Whether its of emerald or wood real.
The heart capers as the gold creepers creep,
And to see carved emerald as betel leaves.

Tidily tied the nitid pearls,
In strings of gold and knots of emeralds.
The Gems have taken shine of Ram's eyes,
Worked ruby have taken more crimson from the bride.

A heaven is erected under the sky,
Riches spread richly, a posh panoply.
Wisely devised they, Lo! birds and bees,
Hark! sweet hums with whirls of breeze.

Lo! Deities, on pillars sculped and fixed,
No soul have they, but still speak.
The earth is clad in the nuptial fit,
Lo! Itself earth looks a bride's kin.

Couplet: *The timber shows, golden summer, hewed,*
Wroght mangoes to fill the core,
Emerald fruits, on silk, re sewed,
With blossoms of gold loading to the floor. 23

Decking wreaths, swathes, whorls and vignettes,
As if the cupid should spread a trap net.
Festoons florals flags and frills,
In the fill of festival, are fevering more thrill.

Leaven=enliven.
Bamboozle=confuse.
Swathes=line of grass/corns; Whorls=ring of leaves (Toran);

Gold tapestries ristling with silk curtains,
Gold urns are making earning of blessed omens.
Studded with gems, shine the lamps,
The confusing, whether glitter is of gems or the flames.

Where Laxmi, the Supreme comes with all radiance,
My muses dazzle at Her bridal presence.
The Perfect beauty that masters all beauty,
See! that Ram, the bridegroom!! under groomed tepee.

Couplet: *Where Goddess of riches is bride,*
Lord of lords is bridegroom.
Town's brilliance to describe,
My poesy is too pigmy. 24

No that, No this is king's palace,
Every door fascinates by its royal grace.
Plain lanes have the splendour of paradise,
With heaven; every roof-every pave vies.

THE ENVOY OF JOY

Spirited soul speedth up steps,
Happy envoys reached the holy place.
Overwhelmed they saw most of Ayodhya,
Then, gaze fixed on royal boast of Ayodhya.

Entranced they sent in words at entrance,
Hearing, King Dashrath called them to his presence.
With all due esteem, they delivered the epistle,
King rose in joy, in person received.

Like His own Ram, he took letter as own life,
Words filled his marrow upto his eyes,

Tepee=Canvas, shade, canopy.

Words of the message he read aloud,
In tides of tidings were dipt, the court and the crowd.

At the same time Bharat happened to reach there–
"What new in daily bliss is added O father?"

Bharat asked–

Couplet: *"Should this letter flow in me life,*
Should its words blow in me breath.
Its words 'll, revive,
If news of my brothers, it hath." 25

In the frame of a father, the King was lost,
"O friends ! O messengers !! close ! come !" King asked.
"Have your own eyes feasted on them?
Should their beauty still in your mind hang.

"Since the sage took them; with the authentic news,
Aching stretched time, only today is soothed.
"do you know them? Seen them? O messengers !
Tell ! if you know them, their welfare.

"Doth ever the best needth inquest,
Ram standth ever above the rest.
Whose splendour awes the sun's face,
And the moon never faces upto whose grace."

"How did we know - ist thy doubt,
Me ask, O Lord ! how be They in a shroud?
"It's like a lampoon, to lamp in sun's search,
Glory of meek sun needth just a marge touch."

"In vain, there gathered pomps of champs, princes,
None could stir Shiv's bow for Seeta's bays.

Inquest=enquiry; Lampoon=mock, jock.

"Shiv's bow stirred not, massive vow stirred not,
Show of reigns went in vain, failed their strayed thoughts."

"Men, demons, even Bana and Raavan,
Who lifted mounts were counted short.
"Few frustrated, few feared and few flop fops,
Their painted pouts seemed, predella, hung lost.

Couplet: *"A Single stood among the flock,*
To relieve the common pang,
Ram broke the bow as lotus stalk,
Would be broken by elephant. 26

"High-brow sage, Parashuram heard of the bow,
With brows on the tenters, came he in row.
"But then, sage bowed to Ram, the divine prow,
Fulfilled sage went; fled all fop foes.

"Lakhan's lightening look hath loyal spirit,
A lordly lore of lion's fit.
"Warmth of verve that streamth in his nerve,
Hath a soft control of his elder brother."

"He is hiss of snake for the wicked,
He is bliss of seraph for the devoted.
"Our mind's eyes keep, fresh, their visage,
Rest all look pale to our eyes' catch."

Lavish love that flooded their paeans,
Thrilled court lavished messengers with gems.
Dashrath heaped presents, on messengers, and the blessings,
"Go !Tell them, in Ayodhya we heard sound of bow snapping."

Fops=vain showy persons, Pouts=face of displeasure

Couplet: *Reverence that dealt in king,*
Welled out before Vashishtha.
King shared heart with him,
And shared letter's gist, 27

Said pleased Guru hearing the news-
"the bliss ever courses to the virtues,
Though never be desired by the Ocean,
Still to the brine brooks and brooks run."

"All riches of mind, all riches of the hand,
Unasked these tend to the pious man."
"Treading all along footprints of virtue,
The Heaven pours upon Kaushalya and you."

"The pious path is tough that you tread,
'll be untrodden in the time ahead.
"Your crown deeds, crowned blessings upon you,
With four worthy sons, the four mines of virtues."

"Ram, valiant sapient; Ram mute innocent,
Ram, kin of commons, Ram ist face of a friend.
"Let, the Kins and friends from this reign and foreign,
Fast! Prepare for Baarat* for lifetime gain."

Couplet: *Reverence that dwelt in king,*
Bowed head at Guru's mandate.
With behest of envoys' lodging,
Post haste he rushed to palace. 28

The epistle king shared with gynaeceum,
And read aloud as if puffing life in them.
Rills of thrill rushed along veins of queens,
Soon the town was filled with flood of tidings.

* wedding processing

This flood painted the town red,
Glad tides in populated air stayed.
Queens rejoiced like pea-hen at rumbling skies,
Their bursting emotions rained the eyes.

Mothers took the epistle to the bosom,
The message of sons seemed like sons had come.
King recounted brave deeds told by envoy,
Many times, as if taking dip in the Ocean of joy.

Ideal is royal joy, which pervadeth common life,
And far and wide this festivity was rife.

Couplet: *Heaven bestowed upon reign,*
With its lavish hands,
Queens with ope hearts ope hands,
Gifted with same lavishness. 29

A beggar in the reign was an amazing thing,
Few vagabonds were brought before the queen.
Queen felt indebted to who so-ever received,
The gifts; queens' feelings to accomplish.

Prone or supine hands* had the same spirit,
What was donor's go, receiver had same grit.
The peopled air with this glad tidings,
Filled every lane, thrilled every dwelling.

The charms of Ayodhya looked ever new,
People groomed it more, for Ram, the groom.
The soul of every soul in this single crowd,
Had one Ayodhya within that decked Ayodhya without.

With flags, festoons, fragrance, florals, frills,
Feelings figured out Ayodhya, which was within.

Rife=widespread, prevailed.
*giving and receiving hands; Grit=Nerve, feeling.

Tapestries, tabernacles tented in many patterns.
Vases, canvasses, glasses, glosses and gold urns.

Couplet: *The face of every door,*
Had décor of bridal grace.
Bricks, becks, brinks, brooks bore,
Groomed beauty of the palace. 30

See ! Rows of damsels like rainbow assemble,
Their lightening show hail, as on roads they amble.
On the roads they rock like rainy rills,
Their beauty is breaking the brinks of thrill.

Their hymns are honeyed hummings of bees,
Their whispers, their warbles are whistling breeze.
As if all the spring is drained on lanes,
All paradise paints 'r paralyzing brains.

My million-words shrink befo' King's palace,
See ! it's décor, See ! its pompless grace.
On hanging silks gold tapestries ristle,
To vie the sky, erects the tabernacle.

In Milieu of melody and mellow lays,
Chants of hymns, thrills of trills are medleyed.
One Ayodhya within and one Ayodhya without,
Couldn't contain excess joy, and it welled all about.

Couplet: *Splendour of King's palace,*
Dazzled poet in me.
To say of Ram's birth place,
My opaque muses flee. 31

☐

Bricks=houses, becks=brooks(mountain streams), brinks=banks.
Amble=Move with joy (slowly.)

The feeling of The Divine is awakened, when I see a great crowd of people.

—Ram Krishna Paramhans

THE WEDDING PROCESSION PROCEEDS

The content king, called Bharat next
To prepare mounts, elephants, and chariots.
"My glad feelings fitting no delay,
My gaze stay, where my Ram stayth.

"Let the proper announcement be widely made,
That every man, woman, child, in Mithila, is invited."
To witness Supreme's deeds riders speeded to stables,
Soon stout steeds stood stately saddled.

Their equine toes had avian go,
Mastered swiftness had a majestic show.
Rare breeds glaring hides and brave knights,
They outstripped winds in, light-footed strides.

Bharat mounted all youth, all were high
Jaunty to vie, they wished to hie.
All handsome, winsome all richly adorned,
With bow arrow in hands, quiver fastened at the side.

Steeds=horses/ mounts, Fitting=agree with.
Jaunty=sportive; Hie=hurry, run, rush; High=cheerful, overexcited

Couplet: *Blithesome blessed builds beaux,*
All brilliant brave brains,
With each knight were two,
Footmen clever at brands. 1

The fight in knights had might of chivalry,
Zeal sallied forth them, halted at outskirts of city.
Their steeds they put through varied speeds,
Filling leisures* with pleasures of martial deeds.

Chariots and cavalry were chasing charms,
In cared caress of revelry's arms.
Face, dress, pace spake of enthusiasm,
All minds w're crazed into tabors and drums.

The rapture, open hands, they would earn,
Array of treasure, out-did rays of sun.
Horse' hooves; wheels' moves synchronized with beats,
To charm even sages, was the lavish exhibit.

In the saddle carefree, they as in the cradle,
Champs mounted chariots fearfree of hurdles.
In Baarat's move, nor hearts nor horse' were bridled,
Winged hoofs would just kiss rill, runnel, pebbles.

Couplet: *Crowded the blessed men,*
Nigh wheels and hoofs,
Crowded up blessed omen,
All themselves to prove. 2

Cavalcade, chariots and processionists,
Elegant elephants with canopied seats,
All gathering arrayed at out limits,
To loot lavish rains of heaven's gratis.

---

* Leisure time.
Revelry=celebration; Cavalcade=Procession on horse.

In milieu of purlieu aired jubilee,
Under glad lee, on the lae, all drowned in glee.
High brows, high borns, in high spirits,
Were offered palaquins, sedans to sit.

With mellow hearts, all Pandits, priests sat,
They looked embodied Mantras of Veds.
Joined all muses' bards, all music wizards,
Famed figures and champs of fanfaronade.

The Grey, looked more green in their gay,
Peopled air drowned in hums, drums, hymns, lays.

Couplet: *Thrill spilt over to outlimits,*
Welled and swelt infinite.
All spirits vivid, and eyes avid,
Wished the Two Heroes to meet. 3

The Air soloed one carol medleyed,
With chants-chantey, hums hymns, lilts-lays.
Neighing of the mounts, nigh creaking wheels,
The din of drums would drown thunder peals.

Palace's door had such peopled flood,
That stone thrown there, would turn to dust.
Bevies marged nigh, in terrace, on tops,
On flocked din, Sweet folks they dropped.

Their joyous strains touched and passed by,
As a far flute blowth, under rumbling sky.
Now, two chariots yoked, for the King by Sumantra,
With steeds that would outrun even horses of Sun.

Of the two, the one splendour on wheel,
Was equipped with royal paraphernals.

Lee=air; Lae=ground of grass; Purlieu=Out skirts; Avid=keen, Vivid=strong, Peals=Loud/great sounds.

Other chariot was more than a royal meet,
King's first reverence offered it to Vashishtha.

Couplet: *Causing Guru to get in,*
Moved to other chariot, the king.
His fond steps like winged thing,
Recalling Divine grace, stepped in. 4

The King looked like heaven's mellow face,
And Guru like heaven's hallow grace.
King did rites to the usage and to holy text,
And then ensured for each one's ease.

To Guru bowed he head, but to Ram, the mind rushed,
King sallied forth Baarat as the conch-shell was puffed.
Blooming bosom on the lap of earth,
Full many blossoms from heaven it bringeth.

Drums, hums, hymns, trumpets, neighing, all muddled,
All overwhelmed hearts welled and the air revelled.
Trills to tolls, from rings to roars,
From ding to din, to yell from bell's clamours,

All added honey, to sweet air, more,
On the beats in and out, all danced enamoured.

Couplet: *Delights made steps to pirouette,*
On beats of melodic core,
Knights made steeds' curvet,
On beats of drums and tabors. 5

Arrayed procession was on its move,
Glad omens gathered themselves to prove.

Muddled=Confused
Curvet=frolic of horse; To Pirouette=To dance.

Blue Jay in gay on left, cow appeared on right,
Everyone saw in field auspicious mongoose.

A blessed woman appeared with filled urn,
Then a cow suckled her calf in front.
Air brought with it a vernal wind,
And on wild wattles warbled the winged.

A fox turned around again and again,
Deer herd came on right in wild land.
Wide roads narrowed, narrowed, narrowed,
Then, along whispering untrodden leaves they trod.

Feathered friends of the Blue, under green avenue,
Like a predella with their colours painted woods.
On the people's face whatever took place,
Procession noted it as the omen of grace.

Couplet: *Mother-nature craddleth men,*
With strings of omens,
To fulfil own strength,
blessed omens occurred at blessed moment. 6

At hand Dashrath hath all blessed omens,
Who hath the Supreme as his own son.
The secluded passes in the way, impressed
With trailing trespasses, the foliage's bridal dress.

Soft they marched under dense bowers' arches,
On it's roof, sun showed some peeping torches.
Then on skirting glades they lingered not,
For untired minds were staying on Lord.

On rides, on strides they vied each other,
Nature caressed them as they cared nature.

Wattles=small branches of tree, Jay=bird; 'Neelkanth'(magpie bird.)

Learning that the 'Awadh was already on way',
Janak had rivers bridged and raised stays.

The forward party had already reached,
With a continuous line of movement between two cities.
Lo ! some of youth vied to perch on the trees,
Some were managing the stampede.

Some strong arms were employed,
To help declining genuflexed strides.
In bustle and huddle, sleeping babes startled
In mother's lap, by mother's tap again were lulled.

In feigned quarrels, the fairlady who was till now mild,
Put into husband's arms, her difficult child.
The couple who had had some quarrel, walked in hush,
But was side by side to avoid missing in rush.

One such husband smilt within himself,
"May not speak, my support she will need at river's edge.

Couplet: *Camels went bearing loads,*
Having their parched throats,
Sighting far for ponds,
Picking juicy leaves while they trod. 7

Brahmins ever who practiced austerities,
Secluded they walked away from bevies.
Some hopped to save the life of passing ants,
Not to incur even trivial violence.

In trumpets and drums people moved dumb,
Communicated through gestures, or kept mum.
Bulls of carts snapped off of yoke suddenly,
Ran helter-skelter, adding to melee.

Suddenly came in Discipline, the running riot,
When they saw Bharat Shatrughan's chariot.
King Dashrath with Kinglet neighbours,
Journeyed all along with hundreds of followers.

After journeying a distance of two yojans,
King and all in shadow of Mount Shail sojourned.
Next Sun saw camp moved along quicksand,
There, begun coming in, into Mithila contingents,

Getting lavish lodgings with cozy fits,
With riches to comforts, dishes to own meets,
In mellow milieu they reached purlieu of the town,
In view of great event all were drowned.

Couplet: *Far drums and distant dins,*
With hazy stirs at horizon,
Janak learnt, Baarat was approaching,
And sent troops to welcome. 8

Rushed hearts, rushed souls, rushed ope hands,
On rides, strides, chariots, elephants.
Cherries, berries, fruits, nuts, beans,
Relishes, delices, dishes dry and green,

Every offering had a fervent touch,
To greet was like greed, only too much was enough.
Flavour of feelings flavoured the fervour more,
Aroma of ardour enriched the air more.

Offered jars, plates, trays, all lavished,
With wreaths, rings, riches, robes and rubies.
Seeing welling over hearts and welcoming hands,
In the reach and beyond*, rich rapture reigned.

---

*Near and far;

Dried out all toiled-pearls on the lot,
In view of witnessing the winning wed-lock.

Couplet:

Storms of warmth that hit,
The two oceans of bliss.
Spirited waves to meet, to greet,
Rushed transgressed their limits. 9

Glad tides crossed and hit the limits,
The Heaven hailed with colours and music.
By just witnessing the Heaven on the Earth,
Paradise bestowth, more blissful showers.

The welcome team with great esteem,
Befo' King Dashrath placed all offerings.
Accepting gifts on this gifted hour,
King passed them among all with concerned care.

Guests were absorbed in houses, camps, palaces,
And in homely comfort, in the cozy cottages.
A soft spread of the huge carpet,
Was host's feelings spreaded under Baarat's steps.

The divine bride* who bridleth every existence,
Manifested Her glory to a large extent.
Transference of Her will personified as godlings,
She consigned those siddhis** to wait upon guests and King.

Couplet:

Godlings godules hastened,
On the divine behest,
More and more heaven opened,
With lush comfort, upon guests. 10

The Baarat camped there in cozy ease,
With all comforts at easy reach.

---

* Seeta, Herself; Toiled pearls on the lot=Sweat on forehead.
** Siddhis=Miraculous powers personified.

A plush marquee and posh mates,
Silken spreads and velvet carpets,

Every cell was a heaven compressed,
None knew runic hand, but Janak all praised.
Sita's splendour only Ram could discern,
Pleased to realize Her caring concern.

Lap of father is earth's paradise,
The two princes were overjoyed hearing father had arrived
Eager to meet father yet the princes modest,
And to meet him, they looked for Guru's behest.

The modest faces, gratified Guru,
Thrill brimmed through eyes, he embraced the two,
They all hastened to king Dashrath's place,
Thirsty souls winged their steps.

Couplet: *Before king as if, hath opened paradise,*
He moved seeing the sage with prince'
His hands full with skies,
had footing in ocean of bliss. 11

Reverence broke all royal stretch,
As the flood of soul breaketh ego's hedge.
The king rushed and fell at feet of the sage,
Kaushik* pressed him to bosom and blessed.

Intense reverence of two brothers for the King,
Fulfilled the purpose of all his being.
King pressed his two sons to the bosom,
and the scorch of separation was balmed.

As the withering leaf getth honeyed drop,
As the thick sky bestowth upon drought,
As the dying gasps get ambrosia,
Like-wise the two as of his own soul, Dashrath saw.

* another name of Vishwamitra

He saw, then the two were meeting Vashishtha,
Both laid themselves at the sage's feet.
Like the two brooklets, met Bharat, Shatrughan,
Rushed and dissolved in the mirthful ocean.

Couplet: *Kins, friends and citizens,*
The courts, pets, minions,
Ram greeted everyone
With concern, convention. 12

THE WEDDING

Just the sight of Ram was delight for guests,
And the zing touched the zenith of the zest.
The king stood and the four sons next,
As validating virtue ist vividly vouchsafed.

Heaven on Earth and earth on the seventh heaven,
Hovering between two, was the golden occasion.
The dew which impregnated the souls,
It honeyed the air with, hums, revels, drums' rolls.

The sky danced, like the damsels do,
And filled further mellow hue to all milieu.
Preceptor*, the pious, and plebeians,
Mentors, ministers, minstrels, minions,

With joy all, received the guests,
With rich thoughts returned back, rapt.
Baarat reached there a day earlier,
All prayed let the hour stay longer.

*Satanand (the royal preceptor of Mithila)

Couplet: *The Mithila talked all wides-*
" The Beatific beau is true,
Beauteous bride is pride.
And two kings are frames of virtue. 13

"Merits and worth of Janak hath come true,
The Divinity breatheth as daughter in Siya's statue.
"Ever moral ist merited by the Gain due,
Ram is personified Dashrath's virtue.

"Being born in blessed soil of Janakpore,
The grace hath crowned upon us too.
"Who could else be highly blessed as we?
Who have eyed Siya-Ram's visaged beauty."

"Further witnessing wedding of Ram, there by,
Shall reap rich for these* and minds' eyes.
Damsels, abigails softly cooed—
"O friend ! providence hath ordained us boon.

"This wedding further addeth to our delight,
For, oft this visage will be visitant to our eyes."

Couplet: *Janak's love will reck,*
'll send for the princess,
Ram to take Her back,
Will chance us with His visage. 14

"Our eyes 'll ever stay on the path,
Which goes and cometh from the Awadh"
Hosts and guests were stringed with warmth,
Of hospitable openness of hearts.

Nae glitz, nae greed that ties the two,
Nae metal but the mettle of honey in you.

---

*these eyes; Metal=gold, Mettle=Nature, temperament.

"The sprouting kinship that we view,
Their frequenting 'll bring town's joy anew.

Some told – "one more pair came to my sight,
With Baarat similar twins came as elixir of eyes,
"Bharat's visage is the Ram's image,
Same hue, frame true and the soul exact."

"like swarthy pair, Shatrughan and Lakhan named,
One fair pair from toe to crest is the self same.
Mortal grey matter of the mortal clay,
Can't say up to such divine portrait.

Stanza:

Tulsi says- "No page no sage,
Spake of such a visage.
No poem, No proem, no prose composed
No muses, no music phrased."
"The noble twins, with marvel sheens;
Only They stand in Their compeer,
We forlay, all four They, may be
Married in town, to add cheer."

Couplet:

In whisper of heaven's fill,
Thus, thrilled damsels cooed,-
"May Lord Shiv fulfil
Merits of two kings and their virtues." 15

In many ways they prayed providence,
And rill of thrill inundated their veins.
Royal suitors who were little sick,
One by one joined the colours and frolic.

Enlivened with praise and grace and lore,
Each returned enamoured, extolling the four.
Whole day witnessed the frolic and fun,
The Sun marched fast and fast, along the arched run.

Sun's glaze then inclined to the early autumn's grace,
At the same, winged time brought the wedding day.
Reading planets, stars and astral effect,
Noting auspicious hour and the date,

Brahma Himself sent epistle, a surprising pride,
For, the time was same that Janak's astrologers derived.
People heard of this and observed—
'Our astrologers are so many creators as it were.'

Couplet: *From Hoof's dust, the dusk spreadth,*
When cows eagerly home back,
Most sacred is hour befo' sunset,
Brahmans apprised the King at that. 16

King's urn of merits with sweet kernel,
Of blessed hour now overwelled.
King asked ' O priest! What's causing delay?'
Satanand was already on the way.

Conched, drummed the Celestials, filled more paradise,
Din of men vied with tabors and pipes,
Chants of holy verses and music of gay,
And nuptial lays with melody medleyed.

Meanwhile envoys proceeded to invite
The Baarat, for the blessed hour was nigh.
Splendour of King Dashrath they beheld,
Heaven looked a lesser heaven befo' that.

Informed they, 'the blessed hour hath come'
King's beats in the bosom, kept up with drums.
With permission of Vashishtha, King sallied forth,
All moved like brook of bliss hath broken the shore.

Couplet: *Lavish hands of providence,*
Poured luck, light, lore upon King,
Immortals believed own ens,
Is very little befor' him.* 17

Celestials extolled Dashrath, the Blessed,
For their own being, they believed fruitless.
Best thing in life are not the things,
But life of merits as of the King.

Elyseal spread on the Earth, tempted
Gods, godlings and goddesses.
Winged upon thrill, they stationed themselves,
In the sky, to look at the wedding festivals.

Raptured gods dazzled at Janak's realm,
Own heaven appeared lesser to them.
Heavenly cope with heavenly craft,
Greater heaven on Earth made the heaven-beings, rapt.

Peopled air hadth the essence of lore,
The deiform charm, and the warmth, they adored.
Finding fabulous, fair, fulfilled folks,
'Whose handiwork is this?'- The Creator Himself was shocked.

Couplet: *"Be not lost in wonder"*
—Shiv advised gods, godlings,—
"Let us calmly ponder
On the Wondrous Wonder's wedding." 18

Shiv revealed—

"Whose very Name is all charm, very Flame in all forms,
Who is the very spirit of your deiform,
"They are the same, ancient Siya-Ram,
Little while ago, were together; came together again."

*Dashrath; Ens=Existence/ entity.

Gods, then rapt in words of Shiv,
Beheld that Dashrath had just arrived.
The assemblage of sages and the holy folks,
Accompanied the King, as in town he walked.

The four princes moved in, together with Dashrath,
As four* gains of treasure of his worth.

One worthy swarthy, one fair pair,
—All citizens imbibed through thirsty stare.
From swarthy spread of Lord Ram's hue,
The sky treasured it's worthy blue.

Clad in clouds adorned with lightening,
It's clout of Lord's countenance on the welkin.
Dressed in splendour of nuptial occasion,
Graced with ornaments that adorned His person.

His countenance delighted as full moon of autumn,
For my dazzled accounts my muses kept mum.
Ram mounted** with transcendental grace,
My depiction, drag to sketch, is like a Jade.

By the sides three brothers paying heed,
Rode curveting their restive steeds.
Other youth of Awadh, too displayed speed,
With bridle free glee, on their steeds.

Fleet of steed, which Ram bestrode,
Seemed as if the Cupid himself, was giving a prod.

---

* four types of Moksha (liberation). 1. Salokya –residing with the Supreme. 2. Sarupya-attaining the form similar to the Supreme. 3. Samipya-living in approximity with the Supreme. 4. Sayujya-Complete absorption.
Clout=influence, power.

** Traditional wedding procession in which bridegroom goes on the mount(horse.)
Jade=worn out horse.

Stanza: *Speed of steed that Ram rode,*
Was charmed by Cupid's prod; it seemed,
Or else steed, was himself the Cupid,
To meet the Rider's esteem.
Bejeweled saddlled with beaded pearls,
All eyes beheld, lost puzzled,
Braided bridle, bells tinkled
Mortals as well immortals were dazzled.

Couplet: *On the mount Ram rode,*
The mount rode on joy,
And danced in His control,
As do cosmos as His toy. 19

Which Ram bestrode, beauty of that mount,
Even the Wisdom herself, could n't account.
Shri Ram's true beauty Lord Shiv imbibed,
Treasured value of His own eyes, He, then recognized.

Vishnu saw Ownself mirrored in Ram,
Was enamoured by the visage charm.
And Brahma with own vast sight fulfilled His delight,
Felt sorry He, for limits of His eyes.

The sight hath limits but not the vision,
And mind's eye beholdth boundless heaven.
A beauty perceived is a beauty but more faith,
Kartikey* imbibed six folds of that.

Tho' one thousand eyes of Indra are less,
Yet one blessed mind's eye canth see His vastness.
Thus, heavenly-beings overjoyed fulfilled,
Imbibed, imbibed cloyed not their fill.

---

*Kartikey-the warrior god is six faced.

Stanza: *Joyed and thrilled, cloyed not to the fill,*
Were enamoured in courts of king,
Drums tabors, on beats of rapture,
Floated in air, glad-shoutings.
While festive din reached welkin
Heaven showered flowers on Raghu's prince.
With auspicious things, thrilled within,
To welcome stood queen with her kins.*

Couplet: *With a flame in heart, lamps in hand,*
Women moved to welcome bride-groom,
In feminine pace, festive dress and,
on face with a grace of bloom. 20

With eyes of gazelle and dazzling faces,
In makes of dresses and in make ups of tresses,
In pompless grace and in egoless show,
Along lanes loving lasses stood in a row.

When the wedding warbles wooing women cooed,
Sweet lays honeyed whole milieu.
Shining bracelets, chiming anklets,
Their charming gait, further charms added.

Goddesses of wisdom, wealth and vigour,
All wise virtuous and naturally pure,
Assuming disguise, joined royal women,
Could not keep themselves from gynaeceum.

Their divinity brought more festal fire,
All muses and music, all arts and lyre.
Further bloom was added in royal bevy,
Tho' None could recognize them as the Devi.

---

*Queen=Sunayana(Seeta's mother.)

Stanza: *"Where ever minds bloom; who should know whom,*
't was over the moon to welcome bridegroom,
All gynaeceum moved, in mellow mood
Stood befo' the bridegroom.
Joy fountained, along the veins,
And ran through their Lotus eyes-
"Siya's Beau is a beauty true"
Their eyes bedewed spake of the delight.

Couplet: *Paradise that dwelt in,*
Soul of Sunayana,
Bliss brine that swelt in,
Even Saraswati herself canst not draw.* 21

Bliss brine that swelt within,
Brimmed in bedewed eyes of queen.
Welcomed she, with waving lights to the family usage,
Performed she, rites to the holy text.

Flutes, lutes and hymns and hums,
Trumpets, tabors, cymbols and drums,
Chants, verses paeans as well,
In the studded din further more swelt.

And the heaven, that dwelt in every soul,
Welled up end to end uncontrolled.
Town carpeted hearts, to receive Baarat,
And carpets, mates gates all along the path.

As Dashrath trod with his rich spread,
To the wedding canopy, Shri Ram proceeded.
Ram entered canopy, was escorted to the seat,
Heavens poured more roars, earth's din to meet.

---

*Goddess of wisdom.

Stanza: *Ram sat on seat, decked to divine fit,*
Vented holy chants jolly events to meet,
In wave of delight ladies waved lights,
All did sight Ram's blithe feat.
Great gods, goddesses witnessed scene,
Disguised in earthly thing;
As they gazed on the visage,—
Felt privileged to fulfil their being.

Couplet: *Peals on lips and pearls in hand,*
Ladies scattered offerings over Ram,
Panoply was filled with poets' paeans,
Dancing warmth too added more charm. 22

The two Monarchs*, the two submerged,
Rushed, embraced and immersed into each other.
Nor usage, nor rites, nor protocol,
Heart workth only on heart's call.

Marvel spectacle of two monarch's meet,
Was divine wordless, proved poesy's defeat.
All muses were washed by flood of sentiments,
Panorama failed puns, paeans, poetic prudence.

At panoply of the wedding, the heaven entranced,
To the tie of Oneness and to two kings' alliance.
Since any past such panoramic paradise,
The heaven had never eyed.

All witnessed, the eyeful scene,
Janak Himself conducted Dashrath, the new kin.
Carpets unrolled under his steps;
With great honour Dashrath was brought in.

Vented=revealed, expressed; Panoply=display, show.
*Janak and Dashrath.

Stanza: *Panoramic pavilion, a phenomenon,*
With all plenties in its prime,
Its panoply vied sky
For all eyes 't was prized surprise.
As the thrilled kings entered in,
The zeal touched its' zenith,
With zest Janak, seated the guests,
Dashrath, Vashishtha, and Kaushik.

Couplet: *Janak revered Vamdeo,*
And other hallow guests.
Elegant seats he gave,
In return, and was blest. 23

Janak once again bowed to Dashrath with great honour,
Taking him as Shiv and none other.
"My riches, my race and my rank,
Being connected with thou, hadst been enhanced.

His joined palms for the other guests,
Had the same warmth and same respect.
What beguiled each of Awadh's party,
Was nae gifts, grants, glare but King's gentility-

'Ts not the riches, but rich tongue,
Which lavisheth bindings of relations.
Celestials felt pride taking human form,
To eye bride Siya and bridegroom Ram.

Janak honoured them, though they wer' disguised,
Assigned good seats, though were not recognized.
Heaven or human all rapt in raves,
Were dipt n lost their ownselves.

Stanza: *The beatitude, embodied stood, as bridegroom,*
Whom they gazed.
Their rapt hearts, in raves lost, everyone forgot,
his own self.
The One All-wise, Ram recognized,
the disguised gods, as human,
Ram revered them in his own reverie,
And they revered Ram deep within.

Couplet: *Such sheen heaven had never seen,*
As was on countenance of Ram,
All drank in, in and in,
Sated not, imbibing the charm. *24*

At the same, Vashishtha in full spirit,
Sent for Satanand, Bride's family priest.
Mutual reverence with no ego,
Maketh go of souls more hallow.

Said Vashishtha—

"Should thy kindness O Sage ! now be swift,
And 'll bring Seeta now quick."
He gladly left taking it as behest,
Queen received message with more zest.

Nuptial trills filled the gyaneceum,
Trains of thrill ran along veins of women.
Principal deities, the consorts of Trinity,
Came disguised, veiling identity.

Unaware queen but, paid great entreaty—
Canst ever hide, rays of divinity?
Abigails adorning Seeta about her making gyre,
Conveyed her to pavilion, with notes of lyre.

Reverie=in vision.

Stanza: *Principal deities, warbled ditties*
Other ladies accompanied them,
The beauty of bride looked pride of the Beauty,
Abigails in whirls dazzled the vision.
Jingles of bangles, tinkle of ankle-bells,
Were musical in nuptials.
All kept tune with lovely warbles
Of lovely damsels' ensemble.

Couplet: *In the centre of bevy*
Siya shone forth great,
The essence of native beauty,
graced much all ahead. 25

To Her wealth of grace, my dearth of wit,
To Her riches of charm I'm pauper to depict.
How a mind of clay with pencil of charcoal,
How can it portray, the glow of gold?

As with golden play, the East bringeth the day,
As the silvery orb* in its full display,
As the brush of petals colourth the spring,
As the holy rill rollth in the marble cliffs,

She entered pavilion, all glad eyes saw,—
"She ! the bride ! the pride princess Siya !!"
Ram looked at Her, as desires fulfilled,
Dashrath and brothers, all were with thrill.

Gods revered Her and Her feat,—
'The Ancient Two, hadth, plotted their earthly meet.'
In patronage of sages, they did family usage,
The rites, customs, rituals as in holy pages.

Ensemble=assemblage, Bevy=flocks/ company of ladies.
*Moon

Stanza: *Sages observed family usage,*
Paid homage to Gauri Ganesh,
First worshipped Ganesh accepted homage,
Greatly gratified he blest.
Demigods, gods, godules, godlings
As traditions earned worships,
To the fore appeared enamoured,
Their visible forms bestowed blessings. A

Bride performed rites, as Guru did guide,
Then sages assigned Her pride throne,
Ram-Siya's finding of mutual binding,
The two Ancients could ken alone,
Mutual string, the unseen thing
Which clingth the Two into One,
The ancient flame, between Them,
None kent, remaint beyond bard's span. B

Couplet: *The Fire-deity reified in figure,*
Accepted sacred alterage,
As the priest came the Sun, Himself,
For rites as per Vedic text. 26

"Lo! the queen-consort of Janak, Sunayana,
Looks like a Devi, being mother of Seeta"
The Creator had exhausted in fashioning her.
All world's virtues, wits, vision put together,

A real ethereal, with goodness of the earth,
With winsome wisdom and all winning worth.
Sages sent for queen as the time did meet,
Thus, the zeal zoomed high to zingy zenith.

The royal parents* with bliss on real high,
With pearls of joy, pearled their eyes.

---

*Janak and Sunayana

Came forthwith the two, to bid welcome,
Brought with own hands auspicious urns,

And gold vases filled with the holy Ganges,
And full many jewels in auric trays.
Their inner reverence with raves running riot,
Welcomed Ram with love, the customary rite.

Stanza:

With raves running riot within,
The queen and king performed rites.
With feel of charm, loving feet of Ram,
Laved they as welcome rite.
More than tradition, thrilled with emotion,
In passion, they touched Ram's feet.
Two mellow frames touched hallow feet,
And marrows were filled with Ram's feat.

Shine of these feet, enshrined by Shiv,
With rich regard in His bosom's niche,
Stunned stone, the accursed woman,*
Was turned to life by these feet.

These heavenly feet, the human benefit,
Whose nectar issueth Holy Ganges,**
The lovely Ganges is lively goddess,
Ist the holiest on the mundane clay.

Boon for Janak, fortune for queen,
Bride-groom ist the King of kings.
They laved the feet, its Lord's feat,
Its all mirth for the Earth indeed.

---

* Ahalya;

** The holy Ganges is issued from feet of Vishnu,

They joined palms of Siya and Ram *
And priests recited sacred psalms.
Thus, nuptials of divine couple was performed
And Ram accepted bride's palm.

Janak lost his flesh, in swarthy flash
Of blooming bridegroom's visage,
Sages recited holy pages, while
Priest performed usage of the race.

Offerings offered to the holy altar
In holy fire as a due rite,
Ancient flames with neo names
For wedlock their garbs were tied

'Ts a message to world, They pledged and whirled
Around the blest wedding fire—
" 'Ts tie of vow, its fast to last,
Witnessed by the pious wedding altar.

Couplet: *Among high huzzas and humming of hymns,*
Wedding couples were tied.
Flutes, lutes, drums making din wide,
Flowers showered from the high. 27

Couple's circumambulations about altar place,
Is firm, staunch and the holiest.
Both circumambulated the fire of pledge,
All feasted their admiring gaze on pleasing pace.

Which bindth, that tie hath a clear message,
Tho' thin fine its fast on family ways.
About fire as they whirled, their visage flickered
The images; pillar-jewels itselves treasured.

---

*The ceremony known as panigrahan
Huzza =noise of glory

Some images revealed, some went out of gaze,
Numerous forms of images the jewels of pillars displayed.
Enamoured spectators saw in jewels they wore,
The reflections of image of the visage, to the fore.

Ram applied Sindur* to Siya's forehead,
As if the Charm itself painted all wides red.

As if blooming lotus with pollen lookth more graced,
Bride's bashful blaze of beauty looked great.
The sight of newly wed, was seat of all bliss,
The two sat on bright seat on behest of Vashishtha.

Stanza: *Boasts of all charms, both Siya and Ram,*
Sat on the bright seat,
Blest blithe touched the beatific height,
Thrilled Dashrath eyed this divine treat.
Dashrath beheld, the divine couple
His joy doubled in high spirit
Wedding of Siya-Ram had been performed,
And the charms stretched to zenith. *A*

Any wise on Earth, can't voice of mirth
Of paradise that spreaded wide,
On march of rich hues, my parched muse,
Trail a little, but fail to write.
'T was Vashishtha and his priest's behests
Janak sent for princess', the rests,
Came Mandavi, Shrutikeerti, Urmila
All bridally clad. *B*

Carved of virtue, the divine statue
The one, among the rests, eldest,
Janak content gave Mandavi's hand
To Bharat, all goodness embodiment.

---

*Vermillion mark

Urmila the bride, in her shy stride
Then moved into pavilion,
Janak was privileged, as he placed
Her hand in marriage to Lakhan. C

A pretty frame, Shrutikeerti named
King gave her hand to Shatrughan,
Thus four brides four bridegrooms
To the fore stood as prized vision.
All perfect match' a predella sketched,
Did catch every-every gaze,
To the fore panorama, of Ram and Ramaa
And four paired Splendours amazed. D

Couplet: *Dashrath's mirth touched zenith,*
Seeing four sons with brides,
As tho' bright merits had brought to king,
Four goals of life realized. 28

All princes were wedded to the same usage',
As were performed in Siya-Ram's case.
With lavish hands Janak and others,
Showered and dowered ope hand's richness.

Garbs, grains, gold, gifts and gems,
Countless cows, mounts, maids and men,
Arrays, apparels, aurums, antiques,
Ultimate articles and art's unique,

Elephants, servants, chariots, what not,
His ope host hands were so, to speak his heart.
Dashrath accepted all to his pilgrim soul,
But kept none with him; handed on to all.

Couplet: *To see the Divine in guests,*
Was Janak's praxis,
Then for, in Dashrath's case,
His feelings touched the Zenith. 29
□

Praxis=Habit.

7

Once a man has faith and fortitude he achieves all.

—Sri Sai Baba

REVELRY, RAILLERY AND RETURN

Stanza:

Janak paid homage, to great sages
And praised them with great reverence.
Filled with cheer, thrilled in tears
Glad Janak bade praises to saints.
Then the sages returned to abbeys
With sketched minds and etched hearts,
Niched their bosoms with Siya-Ram,
'The divine couple their own Lord.' *A*

Not the gold but soul, not the show but love
That only moveth and moveth the saints,
Saints were enchanted by heart felt words
of Janak with his sublimed hands.
Again, he polite with love and delight,
Did submit before King Dashrath—
" thy Kindred ist my prayers-fulfilled
(Lest) Me thy serf, is of what worth. *B*

"How my worship is wreathed with thy kinship,
The best gain on the Earth,

Kindred=Kinship; Serf=slave.

Me and mine haves, now are thine slaves
Pray accept all, O ! King of Awadh!"
Reverence, that dwelt in Dashrath
Swelt and welt out,
His flooded soul adored Janak
And poured on him the honey. C

Mere drop of honey in Kinship
Is the divine brine, the mare nectaris,
'Ts warmth vapourth up and up
Then, the Heaven rains more and more bliss.
In enthralled pause, all moved to lodge,
'n' with Guru's consent, bride's friends'
Then conducted the pairs for worships of
Family deity to the family fane. D

Couplet: *Again and again Seeta gazed,*
Out of modesty did shrink ,
With shy eyes imbibed the Ram's visage
Athirst of love wished more drinks. 1

Charming eyes of Siya had a charmed gaze,
And fixed athirst on Ram's visage.
Her lids dropped down loaded with modesty,
Her sight stayed at Ram's Lotus feet.

Dyed with red lac His Lotus feet,
Ever which drew sages' minds like bees.
These holy feet in Her bosom She niched,
And image etched thro' modest lids slit.

With a mellow appeal, Ram's apparel yellow,
Outshown the Sun's play of it's wee-halo.
On the swarthy hue, with silk's aurulent glow,
Gleaming grace of bridegroom was further hallowed.

Lac=red auspicious colour painted on feet/Mahavar

Yellow hallowed thread*, further boosted charm,
Hanging across broad chest of Ram.
A yellow scarf with fringes of pearls,
As the dresses graced, so the tresses curls.

Her glance moved quick on His face,
Brows, nose charmed, charmed forehead visaged.

Stanza: *Lavishly adorned limbs ravished all,*
In the gleam of crown drowned all sights.
Pretty celestials, city damsels
They prayed all well of the groom and bride.
Damsels prayed, they warbled lays,
And revelled in festal carols,
The Paeans, bards chanted; heaven vividly painted,
Viewing to the fore, the four couples. *A*
Adorned great, damsels richly clad,
Glad they, lead the twains,
For piety, to tutelary deity,
Thus, to the family fane.
Abigails, damsels let their hearts,
Run riot, when they performed rites,
All rituals of new couples,
Performed by bridegrooms and brides. *B*

In the wrist-jewels, Jaanaki beheld,
With dazed eyes Ram's image.
For fright of losing the sight of charm,
She moved nor arms nor Her gaze.
Thus, mirth on the earth that surpassed all words,
Only Siya's friends alone discerned,
In the vae of glee, abigails' bevy
And all the gynaeceum plunged. *C*

---

*Sacred thread
Tutelary=Guardian; The vae of glee=depth of rapture

They did escort, with consorts, the brides
To the lodging Janvaas
Where ever they passed, every single, and in mass
Blessed four couples with huzzas.
Here peopled air in the vital fervour,
Poured their souls on pairs
There real ethereal, celestials
On four couples showered flowers. *D*

A lavish banquet then richly was arranged,
Rich variety and ranges fragrant.
Beauty of carpet told of heart of host,
On which Dashrath and sons sallied forth.

Warmth of Janak's soul, vapoured up clouds,
And rains of love washed Dashrath's feet.
No pomp no show but reverence and go,
'T was not the two kings, but the kins' true meet.

And every eye revered, the reverence of the host,
Unending flood of love immersed all coasts.
For all the guests in the banquet,
Janak's honour offered the apt place.

Here, skilled cooks served eats of choice,
There, damsels warbled sweets of voice.

Couplet: *Cooks served eats of choice,*
Polite, in light mood.
They served all in a trice,
The curry-n-boiled rice, light food. *2*

First morsels was offered to the Divine,
All guests then commenced to dine.

Janvaas= the lodging of the Baaraat (wedding guests)

With Eats, sweets dishes of four category,
They revelled to hear lays of raillery*.

The repartee in lays of raillery,
Medleyed ambrosia in confectionary.
Experts served four foods and six flavours,
With warmth of love mixed with fervour.

Some common, uncommon, some real surprise.
With verve they served some preserved and dry.
At dinner ladies in melodious strains,
Railed at men and women mentioning by name.

At an apt moment even raillery,
Is agreeable and becomes revelry.
Felt amused King Dashrath and Baarat party,
To hear railing folks of the repartee.

Couplet: *Janak's Lavish hands and loving heart,*
Offered lavishly what not,
Dashrath, retired with Baarat,
Thus, feast ended yet, fiesta not. 3

Revelry and fun every sun saw,
Red of the threshold blushed seeing colours of Mithila.
The crossing passage of the Suns,
From dawn to dusk was a swift run.

Dashrath would wake up in wee cloaks,
Minstrel would warble paeans-folks.
Beholding Sons and brides, very souls of his soul,
His bliss welled over the lip-threshold—

Rills of his thrill streamed and rippled,
"O Chief of Sages ! I am fulfilled.

---

*Songs of good humour (Gaari) as a custom in wedding banquet.
Repartee=quick witty words; revelry= celebrations.

I have realized all my purpose,
'Tis all thy grace O Generous!!"

"Heaven have poured upon me lavish,
With ope hands prized me this bliss."

Couplet:

Vashishtha sent for sages then,
Came Vamdeo, Valmiki,
From abbeys given to penance,
Came Named Jabaali, Kaushik. 4

Dashrath prostrated on the ground,
At holy feet with honour profound.
He sent for lacs of cows; next,
All tamed and pretty; for abbeys.

No gold, no riches art as holy,
And as cherished as the cow is.
King bestowed cows upon the pious ones,
"the fruit of my being now, I have attained."

Crown King was crowned with blessings,
Drowned he in the ocean of bliss, within.
Then his altruism poured upon plebeians,
With chariots, mounts, gold, garbs and gems.

The wedding of Lord of lords, its colour, splendour,
Can not be worded in Man-sized words.

Couplet:

Reverence that dwelt in King,
His crown shone its pure touch,
He bowed at feet of Kaushik,
"Its thy grace that prized us." 5

Warmth and ways of the host King,
Dashrath extolled affection, his doings.

Every dawn, now Dashrath asked to return,
Each morn, Janak would lovingly detain him.

In rich stream of affection and attentions,
Every heart drank life, every soul plunged.
Greater fiesta, frolic for the coming days,
Million ways of festivity, the city witnessed.

The mirth gainsays with Dashrath, wishing to go,
Warm hospitality detained, saying no.
Sic, none liked to go but the call of onus,
One should live upto, be honoured by us.

Out of love it's hard even though,
Guru advised-"now you must let Dashrath go."

Couplet: *Janak messaged gynaeceum,*
Awadh-King longs to depart,
It was soul-stirring,
And peopled air came to halt. 6

Along gardens, ghats, grottos and glades,
Tidings of departure anxiously spreaded.
All revelling feet, retreated crippled,
At the dusk, even as, the lotus-bed shrivels.

All eyes iced, all faces dried,
All hearts melted, all souls cried.
Vernant dawn faded in the hue of dew,
In the eyes of town, in every wide view.

Here, solaced some grey advice,
"Days of festivity can't be a daily prize."
There, Janak dowered, showered his heart,
Looking at gifts, prizes even Kuber surprized.

Gainsay=disagree; Onus=responsibility.
Vernant=spring.

Chariot, carts, mounts and troops, carriers,
Cows, oxen, elephants, and heifers,
Gold, apparels, gems, jewels on the back of mules,
Large largess' lavish dishes food-fruits.

Couplet: *Tho, It's mettle and not the metal*
Which floodth heart to the shore,
The Guests at the fare well
Bade adieu to host's door. 7

The door, which witnessed fancy fiesta,
Where Lord of lords stood for Seeta,
'Ts prized surprise, it's door of paradise,
Where Mother-Creator cometh with Her exploits.

Having got all equipages well set,
To Awadh, everything Janak dispatched.
As the queen heard of the time to part,
Her world turned to desert, a fish her heart.

Now, on lap, now in arms she blest,
"Seeta ! May you be ever the beloved of your Lord."

"Be soul of all souls, serve the parents,
Do the bidding of yo'r Lord, 'tis my daily compliment."
Parting soul palsied queen's bosom,
"Why did Creator ever create a woman?"

Couplet: *At the same the Best of Raghu-race,*
Ram with his brothers
To take leave, reached palace,
With innate, modest pace. 8

Lonely eyes of town, crowded
By the Ram's way to imbibe the grace.
"They intend to leave"-said one,
"Let us fill thirst, and drink this winsome.

"What virtues we have earned from providence,
For we witnessed this Divine radiance.
"May the vitreous views, with rich view be etched,
May the virtuous statues be in the heart niched.

"Behold ! this riches to the fill of eyes,
Hold ! asset 'neath lids for life after life.
"May the guest of our eyes, be guest of mind's eye,
And be prized vision for aeons of lives.

Queen moved, at sight of Ram, in bliss,
Immersed she, as if in mare nectaris.
With nerves of verve she blest bridegroom,
Offered caressing care, the whole gynaeceum.

while spake Ram like pouring honey-dew,
Amiability and affection filled the milieu—
"King-father intendth to leave now,
And has sent us to take leave of thou."

"Mother! Thine affection shalt grant us permission,
Thine love will see us ever as own children."
In Tumult of parting soul of her soul,
Queen embraced brides, most humbly she told—

Stanza:

Queen's meek voice and bleak eyes,
Told words of her soul, even before her lips,
Committed Siya to Her Lord and
Submitted she in humble lisp—
" What passes within, may O Ram ! Ken-
Your betrothed Siya is our breath,
She is your maid, She is made for You,
May She be ever Your beloved."

Vitreous view=view by mortal orb of eye.

Mother sunayana said at farewell—

Couplet:

" I give my child to You,
And my soul in Her dwells,
Can I still bid adieu,
When me, is empty of my-self." 9

Her sight, in tears blurred, her voice in ache slurred,
As if lost helpless in slough of the love slush.
Purport of the purest meek words,
Is like pellucid stream with an iceburg.

Wordless aches are heard wide and more,
If whispers sigh from depth of the core.
Thus, Ram kent the nerve of mother,
His reverence bowed at this parting hour.

Infancy of new ties, had grown up kindred,
The bindings heavied four pairs' departure.
Imprinting within, the departing Ram's visage,
With rapt gaze, queen called brides and embraced.

With bridegrooms parting of daughters,
'T was even as cow may be, parted from heifer.

Couplet:

Regals, plebs, abigails
Huts, haats, castles,
All filled with sorrow to the level,
That the town seemed pathos' capital. 10

Parrots and pets wailed in sorrow,
"O Siya! O Princess! O! Where She goes ?"
Innocent wings fluttered in the blues,
As to the parting calf, the pet cows mooed.

Slough= (used for) helplessness, slush; Mooed=cry by cow.

When such was the fit of beasts and birds,
No words befits the spirit of human breast.
Then came King Janak with emotion's deluge,
His brimming eyes told of inner blues.

Famed Janak*, who tamed all bliss and blues,
The parting, moved rampart of wisdom with sickly dews.
Embanked wall of wisdom toppled down,
Rills rushed as he clasped daughter to bosom.

'On peak of pleasure its helm of pangs,
A father partth his soul with own hands.'
In a trice, realized this wailing meets not,
Healing back, he ordered palaquins to be brought.

Couplet: *"All rapt King, kins and queens,*
Yet perceived the moment blest,
Helped brides to ride palaquins,
*Prayed for first worshiped Siddhi Ganesh**.* *11*

A child is ever child for parents,
Janak primed in brides 'the duties of a woman.'
Bestowed upon daughters many friendly maids,
Who had been their trusted, favourites, pets.

Single, slender bride, heavied of saying adieu,
To town's deserted faces with cataract of tear dews.
All stills, and seeming stills, stirred as She moved,
Appeared all good omens, themselves to prove.

The priests, pious, plebs and himself the King,
Followed parting souls to convoy palaquins.
The rings, strings, pipes, flutes, lutes,
Struggled to fill hush of odd mutes.

---

* Janak is known for his stoical nature

** Recalling name of Siddhi Ganesh, who is first worshipped deity to accomplish.
Convoy=Escort

Partying slackened in the parting air,
Saying, bliss and blues are clasping hands'-pair.
Betimes, revering Durga, invoking Ganesh,
With Baarat, Dashrath set on his journey back.

Couplet: *Fulfilled heaven made floral rains,*
Filled Baarat with drive.
Divine nymphs sang paeans
And all set forth with life. 12

Reverent heart of Dashrath called mendicants,
Bestowed gems, jewels, garbs, horses, elephants.
Sublimed heart of Dashrath bowed to Janak,
Begged again and again to return back.

But out of affection, he would not turn back,
Getting down of Chariot Dashrath begged—
In flooded heart of Janak immersed the guest King,
Got down of His ride, kept strides standing.

In the heart of nectar, the Ocean of love,
From both the sides, mutual high-tides billowed.
From the deep of bosom, from benthos of hearts,
Janak pearled out words of no pomp no art.

His stirring soul one could trace on face,
With eddy of emotions, four princes he embraced.
All able, amiable, amicable, all apt,
Ace of artless acts, adepts, affectionate.

Like a gale whispers far wide from helm,
Or as prayer swings between joy and pang.
Like a breeze of love or a hymn in the fane,
Janak spake then, full to the banks—

Betimes=At proper times.
Billowed=rose big waves; Benthos=Bed of ocean

"O Ram ! who roamth in Heart of Shiv,
And in minds of seers as a seeking flame.
"Seizing upon whom, all meum ceases,
Edging all gloom, here, as bridegroom pleases.

"Who is spark that blazes the mundane pomp,
Who is in hermits' hearts-the one flame, Ram."

Couplet: *"Whose very name saveth a recluse,*
From flash, flesh, fisk, lust–flux,
Whose name unbindth world nooze,
Here, is cause of my binding nexus." 13

"You have exalted me, and my feeble race,
This kinship in no words can be praised.
"Far above the best, my fortune is blest,
Now a Name, I am, my esteem is raised."

"O Ram ! You'll ramble in my rapt thought,
Upon astral wings sublimeth my lot.
"I am bold to confess on Your face,
Tho' I lack virtues, deeds and riches,

"but entire of my soul, I have,
My strength hath only the current of love."
"O Ram ! I beseech let me be blest,
Should never my current to You be faded."

Ram valueth as pearls, ever words from depth,
Ram honoured in honeyed words, Janak to Sate.
Approached to Bharat, then humbly the King,
Embraced him, poured more blessings on him.

Flush=shine of pomp; fisk=treasure(maya); meum=ego; seizing=grasping (mediating); flux=flow.

Couplet: *As he reached young ones,*
All embarkments broke,
He embraced two in flux of emotions,
His blessing words choked. 14

Moved by Janak's words; As the four moved,
Paid respects anew, and bade him adieu.
Janak clasped feet of Kaushik, next,
" O pious ! O poise !, this blest nexus is thy grace."

" My words are bold on my soul's conviction,
Thine hallow presence proved to me, a halo of renown.
The flag of glory on such renown's peak,
To attain has many cliffs and steeps."

"Thy gracious sight blessed this glorious height,
And hath brought this within my reach."
"Unknown, Unknowable, O Gracious sage!
Cometh to my door, it's thy sagacious grace."

Bowed head again and again the mellow King,
The sage poured upon him, the hallowed blessings.
Thus, started bridegroom's convoy,
Thrums of drums dipped in the din of joy.

Couplet: *Sating gaze of passing by hamlets,*
And halting on ways,
Appeasing on path's abbeys,
Returned Baarat on some sacred day. 15

Melody of pipes, tabors, drums and conches,
Trumpets of elephants and neighing of horses,
The clashes of cymbals, timbals, timbrels,
Chanting of hymns and chyming of bells,

Poise = dignity/elegance
Timbal=Nagada, drum ; Timbrel=Mradangam

In mellow hearts, the billow of moods,
Attuned end to end with flutes and lutes.
Roads, crossroads, markets and gates,
And whole of city was painted red*.

Alleys and ways showed the glad-craze,
Florals frills flags decked, their festal grace.
Trade of haats coined up new commerce,
'T was no coinage but currency of cheers.

Spreaded Carpets, mates, arches, canopies,
With pomp of pennons and planted showy trees.
Reverence of citizens for their own nation,
Reflectth in the story of the celebrations.

Couplet: *They adorned doors with vases and urns,*
Stood with hearts in hand,
What pearls of life they earned,
Envied even lives of heavens. 16

Every common brick had a regal touch,
Every avenue viewed even as Rajpath.
Nature, as well, sketched with it's divine brush,
Every milieu showed the vernant colours.

Within every bosom dwelt one Ayodhya,
With it's drive, they decked exterior Ayodhya.
As the crown adornth more charm to the face,
As the auspicious Kalash crownth the fane,

As the Everest is the crest of the sacred spread,
In Ayodhya shone King's palace ahead.
Grace of ingress of the royal palace,
As ever, was wide-ope for common plebs.

---

*city celebrated; Pennons=Triangular flags
Raj-path=Royal street; Ingress=entrance

The peopled horde; could ramparts hold?
To win a look at Ram, all sallied forth.
Mothers faded their flesh, in surpassing bliss,
Their pilgrim souls were dipt in depth of zenith.

Couplet: *Worshipping, first worshiped Ganesh,*
Glad mothers conferred gifts,
Upon the needy and godly plebs,
Who treasured it as life's gist. *17*

Bliss in soul dissolveth flesh and mind,
Behind halo of bliss, all dazzleth blind.
The motherhood bliss knocked the summit,
Their limbs locked, to walk refused feet.

Their recovered souls, primed their eyes,
For loving sight of Ram with bride.
Mothers prepared, then for reception of sons,
While Sumitra rushed with wares of good omens.

Grass, curd, betel-leaves, paddy and basil blossoms,
Mother brought for son, who is Lord of all omens.
Glad melodies floated and keen gaze roved,
Every trice lingered, waiting for beloved.

Essence filled the milieu, and urns filled with the Sarayu,
Thrill ran along veins, brimmed as eye dews.
Mothers got ready for waving of lights,
In the waves of delight, they sang melody.

Couplet: *The Emotions, mothers throbbing with,*
Rushed, their sons to greet,
The mothering warmth melted in lids,
Tho' queenhood tried to hid it. *18*

Sublimed fumes of the perfumes, incense,
Hovering as tho' laden clouds of rain.

Lovely jewelled festoons on the door arches,
Looked like in a row iris arcades.

Delighted dames came and quickly went out,
Like fitful lightening in the clouds.
The Beats of drums, timbrels, tampours,
Resembled the high crash of thunders.

Noisy presence of godules, plebs, flocks,
Was like warbling wrens and gambolling peacocks.
Kenning timeliness of the blest hour,
Vashishtha, the preceptor gave words.

Then King Dashrath and the pride of Raghu's race,
Stepped in Awadh, recalling Shiv Uma Ganesh.

Couplet: *See! Divine dames dancing on drums,*
Omens proving their goodness.
Dazzled heaven drizzling blossoms,
As the comely Baarat comes back. 19

See! Laureates are pouring their heart in muses,
Dancers are pouring soul in steps of nautches.
Bards are draining their marrow in strains
Of glory of Ram; His triumphant Paeans.

Here hymning of Veds, here chiming of bells,
Town is painted red with brush of revels.
In the heart of Awadh, one heaven dwellth,
And in heart of heaven, one Awadh swellth.

The Heaven, as ever beholdth men's revels,
And showerth more and more heaven on the Earth.
Every gem of moments, citizens picked,
Prized, pearled and preserved in inner niche.

Gambol=Dance; iris arcades=rainbows.
Nautches= Indian dance.

Happy town then greeted Rath of the King,
Princes' chariots and brides' palaquins.
Glad women of town could not contain,
Their stealthy peep eyed through slit of curtains.

Thus, to the door of Kaushalya, the queen,
Arrived Son Ram, Long unseen.
Her wondered gaze was won by Wonder visage,
And she failed to perform family usage.

Recovered she, waved lights in delight,
Then all queens'sights were caught on brides.
Petals, jewels, pearls and what not,
They scattered about new weds as family rite.

Mother's bosom is Ocean, but to this bliss,
Pouring in and in, seemed a bowl, little.
The charm of Ram and beauty of Siya, the bride,
Amazing visage, the dazed eyes imbibed.

Passing thro' gates, walks, arches and doors,
The waiting corridors and greeting floors,
While couples entered hall, their halo did fall
On the walls and hallowed whole environ.

On the comely thrones mothers seated them with love,
Their holy feet they lovingly laved.
For ownself delight and Vedic rites,
They worshipped blest couples and waved lights.

For a mother, a child is child, ever a tot,
In her nerve, her lot, her verve, and her thought.
Queens felt, as ambrosia dropth on the gasp,
Or as true as nirvana realized in her lap,

As sight cometh to blind, eloquence to dumb,
As the flame enkindleth moribund.

Moribund=dying;

Mother worshipped Penates, Paters, manes,
to the heaven echoed Te deum.
Long dynasty of race of Raghu,
A name of prowess, power, vows and virtues,

At this happy moment mothers worshipped all them,
Begged blessings for sons, with sublimed hands.
"Blessed be this race, blessed be this palace,
O Manes! O Gods! O Godly men! Confer thy unseen grace.

Grace tho' unseen, 'ts palpable,
In the ocean of bliss, as the treasured pearls.
Here, King sent for the guests of nuptials,
Conferred articles, jewels apparels.

They all treasured moments as priceless prize,
As the good moments art carried life after life.
King's content heart welled thro' fistless hands,
And conferred gifts to mendicants, attendants.

Couplet: *With filled hands, fulfilled bosom,*
Joy loaded, they blest king.
With Vashishtha, and Brahmans then,
Full to the banks king stepped in. 20

By the family usage, by the holy pages,
The rites, King performed as the Guru said.

Reverence is paragon in royal crown,
That shineth in race as the renown.
Holy guests were flooded with devotion of hosts,
Manners, morals, merits touched, their cores.

To Kaushik he paid, homage in many ways,
"O Sage ! as I am, no one is so blessed."

Te Deum=Thanks giving hymn.
Fistless hand=Open hand, liberally

Bowed crown couple, bowed the newly weds,
To Vashishtha, the preceptor, the wise of lineage.

Meek eyes spake the wordless homage,
Doth ever heart and soul need a language?
King placed reign, all sons before his Guru,
However he accepted only customary due.

Penny pervadeth not into prosperous penance,
Over blessings of Guru no glitter standth.
Empowered by worships hardships in woods,
They are never swayed by the clay, who way into truth.

His blessings, Guru crowned upon the King,
'Ts crown of the crowns, most pious thing.
Thus, the lord of state, with loving lavish hands,
Granted largesses, livery, lands and alms.

Couplet: *Melics of melodic frolic,*
Diffused heaven in milieu,
Poetics, limericks, worships, music,
Confused the celestial crew. 21

AYODHYA-THE GREATER PARADISE

Awadh, a greater heaven confused gods,
Should they, mellow stay, linger or now should depart.
At length fulfilled and thrilled they,
Swayed by Ram's glory, gods proceeded.

Then the King visited the inner ring,
Beheld princes brides with bosom over-brimmed.
He gladly gathered boys in his arms,
Embraced them as tho, gathering the world.

In acme of joy his sinew benumbed,
In deluge of delight his voice swamped.
In the rill of thrill, in the spate of gay,
Stayed not humble tongue, my stave strayed.

The king then related how the wedding had happened,
That honeyed more heaven in gynaeceum.
King worded Janak's worth and the wreathed welcome,
His winning will, wealth and wide wisdom.

Couplet: *As the sun glided down slow;*
On the train of events to go,
Gladsome moments with a go,
Rose up on the eve of show. 22

Melics of frolic in melodic ways,
Men women of town sung nuptial lays.
The delights ignored, passing stars' drill,
Then drowsy touch knocked joyous vigil.

Ope lids strained with nightly drowse,
Keeping Ram's visage, all proceeded to own house.
For the brilliant beat, for this boast of life,
For the beauty, for bliss, for blooming blithe,

For the crown moments, for the crayoned events,
No words stand for such merriments.
Wifely love bringeth increasing respect,
King summoned then queens, and seated next.

The King asked, as ever, in gentle tone—
"Brides are yet child, came to strange home,

Delicate damsels, innocents as they are,
Like the lids care eyes, ye caress and take care."

Deluge=Flood, spate; stave=poetic lines.

Couplet: *"See ! the boys are tired,*
Go and put them to bed,
So said King, then retired,
Enshrining within Ram's visage. 23

King's request taking as the behest,
For the tired boys the mothers turned sleepless.
Mothers made ready couches themselves,
The auric bed bejewelled with pearls.

Whose Name is the fruit of all efforts,
Whose Name is the root of all comforts,
Mothers efforted for comfort of charming chaps,
Prepared couches as soft as mother's lap.

Asked wonder gaze, asked mother's love,
"How did you kill Tadaka with dainty little gloves?
Did those worthy arms* that dared the savage,
Or these swarthy arms that cared the sages.

Mother continued—

"Ye, two** scourged scores of savage,
Lord kept ye from evils by great sage's grace.
"Even while ye both, saved every alterage,
Must be that through some sacred knowledge.

"This sacred lore is secret of success,
That saved my motherhood, and the demons ye ravaged.
" Its god's will, sage's wit and your grit,
That torched in ye, hard staunch spirit.

"But then how? Mere soft touch of dust of your feet,
Blew life in stony wife of the hermit."

---

* weapons given by Vishwamitra.
** Ram and Lakshman; Scourged=punished, whipped.

"Your hard feat, slew savages, ravaged awe,
Your soft feet, blew life, salvaged Ahalya.

You won lei of Jaanki in princes assembly,
Braking Shiv's bow, making Janak's vow, under the lee.

Couplet: *" O Child ! you act Suprahuman,*
Must be only grace of sage,
Our longing life, now gains fruition,
Long-waited seeing your face. 24

"Pray ! Creator may reck upon us,
Days without you may be reckoned a minus."
Ram gratified mothers in polite and sweet,
Then His mind He cradled on Shiv's feet.

His nerves were lulled by thoughts of Guru,
Then He laid his lids, swayed by sleep.
Ruddy lotus gleamed in bit of shut eyes,
As crimson petal is half closed at even-tide.

Every door, corridor kept rejoicing vigil,
Women railed at each other in glad lilts.
From hearths to sills, drowned in revels every house,
Every niche of town, rich in raves not drowsed.

Motherly arm enfolded, lulled and cradled,
As if treasuring the brides, as lost child.
As the pets and birds made the wee-knock,
Before the East crimsoned, Lord Ram awoke.

Couplet: *Melics, melodies filled milieu*
As the daily joy begun its routine,
With brothers He bathed in Sarayu,
And performed His matins. 25

Under the lee=Defending from wind blow.

As they returned to their sire,
He embraced the four, as fulfilled desires.
The king sat down and the four sat next,
Court accounted their eyes highly blest.

Then, came Kaushik and Vashishtha, the Guru
The King, four sons prostrated before the two.
On the seats holier than the highest seat,
The two were seated, King laved their feet.

While echoed prayers, sermons and precepts,
Unhurdled rush gathered, tho' in hushed steps.
Vashishtha belauded Vishwamitra's virtues,
Vamdeo vouched Vashishtha's view as true.

From birds' whisper to the bard's vasper,
From toddler to grey, boosted increasing rapture.
The very Earth looked real ethereal,
The Nature dandled vernal dance on beats of man's revels.

Couplet: *The daily joy that dwelt in hearts*
Of palace, pious and plebs,
That swelt beyond ramparts
And Earth was dipt in its waves. 26

Sage Kaushik every morn intended to leave,
Was detained by Ram's loving entreaties.
Bidding the Sage adieu, speech failed King's tongue,
"Thine drudge, judge in me, family and sons.

"My haves art all thine, let thine grace bless us,
Thy benisons art our lives' purpose."
The sage then departed from the palace,
For quite a distance Ram escorted.

On his way to abbey, praising to himself,
The glory, glow, goodness of Raghu's race,

He went gladly to the lonely dense,
Fixing mind on Ram, as holy-rememberence.

Vashishtha,Vamdeo voiced virtues once more,
And narrated Kaushik's pious anecdotes.
In the haats, on the ghaats, in the lanes and fanes,
The class or the mass talked of Ram's paeans.

From the day Ram came home duly married,
All merriments took their abode in Awadh.
Glory of Siya-Ram is live's very grit,
To say of festive spirit, ever fumble my wit.

Of the Unknowable, I, on purpose narrate,
For it pourth grace, purgeth race of poets.

Stanza: *Lord pourth grace, and purgeth poets*
On purpose, I compose, it's my greed,
Unknowable, unknown as He is, still
I do repeat His feat. *A*
Me unhallowed, drifting in shallows
Can't fathom Ram's ocean,
Dipt bard can only cross who
Get on to bark of Ram's paeans. *B*

Couplet: *Who find radical in these lays,*
To preserve spiritual radical
Beloved of the Lord they,
Ever win the Laurels. 27

□

Radical=main principle ; Radical=rootlets.

AYODHYA KANDAM

Nothing is good or bad in this world, it depends, how you use it.

—Brahmrishi Vishwatma Bawra

STROPHES

As the embodied stoicism,
Even glades of exile, gladdenth Him,
Who is Lord in nonmenon form,
I belaud Him, as phenomenon Ram. 1

Shiv in Ram, and Ram in Shiv, I salute,
He is ancient and Absolute.
Whose celestial reflection is azure,*
Which is spread of Ram's celeste hue.
Ever who is at the helm
on brine of mundane's storm,
May, in me enshrine that Nameless,
As the attributed Ram. 2

AWADH'S FROLIC/NAARAD'S PANIC

My wooden head and purblind eyes,
Revolve around Ancient bard's insight.
They 'll awake my soul, that loll,
Vyas, Tulsi, Valmiki, Kamban, Shri Moll.

*sky ; Celeste hue=blue; Loll=lie in lazy attitude.

May antique texts become my instinct,
Thus, I colour native pages in alien ink.
Those bards are the Guru, the verses are sermons,
To guide and goad me, as vade mecum.

Holy dust of Guru's feet, good as precept indeed,
Pray! Guide me sing, Ram's holy feat.
From the day, Ram came home duly married,
Daily merriments rose up to new peaks.

On the moral peaks, helms of merits,
Poured showers of joy and peopled clay enriched;
With rills of riches, affluence and heaven,
Flowed amain down into, city's pious ocean.

On sinuous moral hills, rolls of virtuous rills,
Nourished life in lives, prospered vernal fills.
People like pearls bedecked, the bed of this ocean,
Deep, pretty, pacific dwellers, prized, hyaline.

Mellow majesty rejoiced rapt in merriments,
All maids, menials, with family and friends,
On hills of hilarity, the coppice of charm,
Dawned upon more colours, in aurora of Ram.

Couplet: *Each hearth hadth one fire,*
Each heart a common desire,
Ram, as the regent be declared,
By Dashrath, the sire. 1

On the wheels of cheer, the chariot of the Suns,
Winged bridleless chasing more of heavens.
Sic, some days lapsed on lap of paradise,
Palace, pious, plebs all filled with rejoice.

Vade mecum=Manual book (guiding text)
Dawn upon=to be visible; Hyaline=transparent; Amain=with force.

King, the virtue incarnate, a fair name,
In courts, with transports would hear Ram's paeans.
Every coronet, crownet and wide reigns,
Would Solicit Awadhs' favour in great reverence.

As on King flown felicity, fortuity
None can be blest so now and in time to be.
What ever might be said, lingerth short
Of him, who hath for his son Ram, the root of bliss.

Thus, the festivity and Ayodhya's frolic,
Became the Heaven's and its beings' panic.
One day, Naarad, the divine sage,
To the presence of Ram, from own skies descended.

Couplet: *The sudden arrival of Naarad,*
Was not amazing for the Prince,
Along with Siya, His consort,
Prince Ram bowed before him. 2

"O holy one! Must be some merits of ours,
Havest brought thy pious steps here.
"Pious company moulds the clay-earth,
And bringeth, to a worldly life, a worth.

"Hath it just happened or some purpose,
What hath brought thy grace here, O pious!
To this, Naarad most humbly said—
"Ram! Talk me not like a mortal clay.

"like a pigmy mortal Thou, the Supreme
Ask me, while Thou knowest every thing.
" By mere Thy presence Thy Maya createth,
Pinnacles, pictures, planes, peaks, planets.

"Thou art flame, and Siya is its warmth,
She ist luminosity, Thou art Sun O Ram!

"Thou art 'White', Veds call Thou Sattvik,
Yet from it, Thy Maya, in all colours, is picked.

Couplet: *"Thou art beyond time,*
Thy maya is time wheel,
The 'changing Maya' mimes,
Thy unchanging strength to reveal. 3

"Complex body constituted to the I-sense,
Grossly is composed of five great elements.
"Beyond these five energies and five senses
Make 'Jiva'*, through Thy Maaya, 'the causal adjuct.'

And Thou art the very Self in all 'Jiva*',
As Pure consciousness, Thou dost live.
"All super impositions of 'Maya' dissolve,
When Thou, the substratum, art perceived.

"from gross unto subtle unto causal adjunct,
The knowledge in stages, is experienced.
" Sic, who are devoted to Thee,
Towards 'Salvation' they move quick.

"Let nor Thy Maya superimpose
On me, traversing the conscious course.
"O Ram ! deign to save me; 'am Thy devotee,
But frolic in here, is heaven's panic.

Couplet: *"Thy advent, is Thy own will,*
For the cause of the Virtues,
Is to efface all the evils,
Is to place all the values. 4

"but Thy father wish to see Thou, as Raja of Awadh,
But then that will restrict Thy purpose."

Mime=Show in gesture.
*vitality of the life.

Ram declared–

"I shall carry out Naarad ! What I have pledged.
There is nothing, beyond My knowledge.

"I shall be destroying whole tribe of Rakshas',
That is my very and foremost purpose.
"Very morrow-sun will see my exile,
Wild spoil sports of Raavan, I'll spoil.

"Making semblance of Sita the occasion–,
I shall destroy with kith and kins, Raavan."
Fulfilled Naarad returned to his divine plain,
Here, Ayodhya was unaware of the undercurrent.

Here, in mirror glass once, blest King in blase'
Seen through his crown, coming curls of grey locks.
Busy hands are unaware to watch,
That the wheel of the time, runs fast.

Fingers pointed out, tremors murmured,
"O King ! wilted season of the decline knocks.

Couplet: *The ruthless brush of the age,*
With mastered hushed pace
Daubing mortal cage; messaged
"King make Ram your regent." 5

Peeping through the crown, the silver streaks,
And creased cheeks did appeal, did speak.
His eyes, seeing under shadows deep,
Shone in wake of making Ram, the regent.

Greying is a gaytime for the saintly man,
Who endorseth the order's change.

Blase=uncarefully, casually.

About Shri Ram, the king having a think,
The fulfilled mind, shared with Guru, the thrill.

"O sage! Ram hath proved His prowess,
His apt, act, art say 'He is the ace'.
"Thy grace hath shaped Him in a lovely form,
Ram is soul of all souls, Ram is everyone's charm.

I gained what not to this earthborn heart,
But still my longing hath a fevered thought."

Couplet: *" That will sure be done,*
By thy grace my lord!"
To the Guru, Dashrath opened
His devoted heart. 6

"O King ! in pious soul the plough of good deeds,
Fruits with ripeness all sowed wish seeds."
"Any desire, even before you entertain,
O King Dashrath ! is ever half-done."

"Your name Dashrath itself, is wish-tree,
Its lavish grants pourst name and glory."

Dashrath requested—

"Let me and people, eye this before my death,
All may be set on, but for thy behest."

O Guru ! lingering may have to repent later,"
"O King ! it maketh one repent when Ram is averse."
" Ram treadth on the heels for real love,
That very Lord is your son, O king! a joy!!"

Couplet: *"for good cause wait not far,*
Crown Him by morrow forenoon,
When the auspicious Pushya star
Is in combination of the moon". 7

Prayers seemed fulfilled, and Dashrath,
Paced to palace on pinions of mirth.
At the same He summoned minions, ministers,
And placed before them, the auspicious offers.

"If it meetth all favour with ye,
Then install Ram's sway, with no linger, no delay."
Very same seed of dream all they had,
Showered King's words, on their hearts' bed,

Budding beatitude shooted up in shouts-glad,
"thy glory may live long, O King!" They prayed.
"May thy grace and blessings, rain on reign,
May millions of seasons see thou, O Sovereign!"

"This's a glad plan for the reign and foreign,
This pious proposal may promptly be commenced."
Wise counselor's support encouraged King,
In sprouting bliss, he swiftly primed.

"let everything, every little detail be ready,
Let the feast and zest spread unlimitedly."

Couplet: *"For crowning of the crown-son of Raghus,*
Speed up ! Everyone speed!!
On behest of Vashishtha, Guru,
Carry out all requisites." 8

The pious Guru worded a honeyed behest,
Holy water from all places, get holy Ganges.
Get Roots, nuts, fruits, flowers, foliages,
Suede mats, herbs, grass, garbs, many more sacreds,

Chattels, apparels, articles, jewelleries,
All goods of good omens, chowries, draperies."
Fetched they things as per the holy text,
For the coronation of king as laid in Veds.

"With empyreal decks, what ye have inside,
Go ! Now, to Ayodhya add more paradise."
"with garlands, fountains, plaintains it be decked,
With avid celebrations, paint the town red."

In Every shore, every core from floor to welkin,
Let drowsy revels have new vigil waking."
" Wee matins, glee of vespers and yea ! the vigil.
With worships, chants, rites, all milieu be filled."

Couplet: *Fastoons, frills, florals, flags,*
Elephants, mounts chariots,
To prepare all, asked by the sage,
All rushed to their own work. 9

The behest, was accomplished by every one,
So haste as if before-hand done.
King's breath worshipped the Supreme,
Prayed Ram's welfare in the days to come.

To the gynaeceum reached glad-tidings,
Of further adding in her son's esteem.
Kaushalya who treasured the Creator into womb,
That Son is Creator of all fortunes, all dooms.

Kaushalya who mothered the child as her first worship,
Her child's very Name, for God, ever came in her lips.
Who cradled Him as the soul of her soul,
In the child-doll who saw her God's idol.

Mother, became the puppet to childish demands,
And to command of the unseen bonds.
Never was alone in mind, ever who thought thrice,
Once for herself, and twice for her child.

Who impregnated fullness to child's empty words,
And mother and toddler became each other's world.
Since then a long way, mother's daily joy saw,
At this hour, each event rolled in eyes of Kaushalya.

Mellow news puffed through sills, hills, rills
And filled peopled air with zenith of zeal.
On the trains of bliss, in chains of festivals,
Jovial town re-echoed strains of revels.

With melics of men, frolicked good omens,
Amain on Awadh poured more heavens.
The divine couple, Shri Ram and Siya;
Who art, themselves blest omen in Person,

Felt upon them, omens proving themselves,
And kent "Omens hint of Bharat's return."

"Omen is true that clues of his return,
All my love ist embodied as Bharat in Person."

Couplet: *At the same queens were enthralled,*
On gush of tidings' stream,
As the ocean-tides swell
With flux of Lunar gleam. 10

Those who broke here news first,
Were richly rewarded with ope treasures.
With reverence in heart and not ravenous wills,
They wished see Ram's feat; and accepted worldly gilts.

Ravenous=greedy.

Messengers earned, the blessings of queens,
Queens prepared festal urns, to let all auspicious omens in.
With coloured meals Sumitra limned the floor,
All queens mirthfull hymned the choirs.

The blest current of Kaushalya's bosom,
Flown through openhanded grants and alms.
A son is soul of the soul of mother,
She is ever be consumed with his welfare.

Gods, nagas, godlings, godules, deities,
Kaushalya prayed ensuring Ram's good-n-gaiety.
Fresh fair faces, fawn-eyed beauties,
Graced more the affair with festal ditties.

Couplet: *Once more every core,*
Every door, corridor.
Leaving chores, they, enamoured
Rushed to the Awadh's festal course. 11

To prime opportune advice, then Vashishtha,
Was sent by Dashrath to his fond-passion, the Ram.
Ram rushedst to welcome Vashishtha,
Bowed at his feet, the laven devotion of Ram.

The Grace of Guru is a boundless gain,
His feet was laved by lavish emotions of Ram.
Siya Ram clasped holy feet with lotus palms,
Eager to be mastered, spake, the Master workman Ram—

"Thy visit, the bliss ocean, panacea of ills yet,
The better would have called Me, thy slave man, Ram.
"Its a pleasant ache that thy feet toiled to us,
Tho' laid aside customs, would have summoned, Ram.

Limned=painted.

"Thy affection hath graced our souls, our sills,
Thy pious practices moulded Me, unto this lucky Ram.
" Its my privilege if 'm bid, O holy sage!
Serving Master is all welfare of this lackey Ram."

Couplet: *Hearing words, in love steeped,*
Sage did commend Ram,
"You should say so; it's but meet,
O ! Raghu's ornament, Ram." 12

Nectarian words of Ram further honeyed,
The heart of Vashishtha, and his speech-
"O Affectionate ! O Virtue incarnate !!
With regal onus You'll be invested."

"Its day of austere, rituals worships,
So that divinity bringeth to it a great finish.
"What masterth the fate its Ram ! Your feat,
The Austerity yet, ist the customary meet."

Sic, went back Guru, here Ram drowned broody,
Was caught in puzzle, in a brown study—
' Our birth, hearth, mirth were all one,
Our plays of chase, craze, pledge were one.

'Under one roof we had bringing, preachings, weddings,
Bias custom now voice for the one aine."
—May this fraternal flow in these verses; Flood out
The filth of crooked faults of the devouts.

Couplet: *Then, Lakhan steeped in love*
Stepped as if on wings
Of gaiety, gleesome, go;
And Ram's fond words greeted him. 13

Aine(F)=eldest son.

From earth to ceilings, from hearth to sills,
From vales to hills, from wells to rills,
All walks, all wheels, all talks, all trills,
All wides, all sides were full to the fills,

With increasing revels and swelling thrills,
With upgoing peals and echoing squeals.
Bharat's return was soul's will,
'would he come to cherish his eye's fill?'

Doors, corridors, shores, moors and ports,
Roads, crossroads, haats, forts, courts, resorts,
From peopled milieus to the far purlieus,
Sole text, which filled the talk of the hordes,

Was-" Pray ! divine make the swift, in crawl of the Sun,
To bring in town and in us a new crimson."
"When will greeting knock of golden morrow come,
To offer Seeta Ram the august throne of aurum.

For last few days Dashrath was scared
Of night mares and heard screeches from no where.
He was seized with anxiety and doubts,
He was told his mars and Jupiter were aspecting same house.

Which means death or near death catastrophe,
His worry to end, the event needed an urgency.
He wished the golden morrow to dawn,
His all ill-stars, to superimpose upon.

Couplet: *All prayed for golden morrow,*
Tho' Sick gods, the so-called high,
Brewed trouble in their shrewd marrow,
On rejoice of Awadh, they sighed. 14

In sun of delight wicked gods saw murky night,
As the thief is scared of milky moon light.

Sic, sick of tricks, rushed the wicked they,
Before Goddess of wisdom, Shardaa, they prayed—

"O mother! ignite something malignant,
Should our grave calamity end."
"Let more the divinity of Ram's feat
Spread; and our purpose may not defeat."

"Just not for Awadh's sun and moon,
Coming of Ram is for all suffering commune.
" O ! mother design things for our cause,
So that Ram resignth, retireth in exile."

"Attacheth with thou not the least blame,
For unstirred of throes or throne, is the stoical Ram."

Couplet: *Sic, shardaa came and possessed,*
The remote-witted sick Kooney,*
She, the bale of bale, Kaikayi's maid,
Shardaa perverted her, a Loony. 15

THE VICIOUS ADVICE

In the Kooney's pass came colours of views,
Melics, melodies, merry-making moves.
Her asking 'for what is this new?'
'Ram's anointing painted her blue.

In her eyes fumed few evil-dews,
To drain Awadh's joy thro' overnight deluge.
A pulled pale face, in pernicious pace,
Loony Kooney approached Kaikeyi's palace.

Kooney bowed at Kaikeyi's those very feet,
To get simile 'the lotus' performed austerities.

---

*Kooney was also named Manthara; Loony=crazy; bale=parcel ; bale=woe

Like a lull before storm, to teach mischief,
Embodied venom stood in hushed speech.

Smilingly Kaikeyi asked her to know,
'What brews within your fevcrėd brow?'
Her hushed hiss heaved only deep sighs,
And beads* bade bale in her crocodile eyes.

" Is it Lakhan who taught you some lessons?"
Her muted hiss only spake a serpent.

Couplet: *With in queens' bosom,*
Stirred obsessed storm.
Asked she well of Ram
And King, Lakhan, Bharat, Shatrughan. 16

The cry of Kooney carried canard,
In honeyed shield a septic tirade—
" I'm poor servant, how can be puissant?
What makes me cheeky?" thus said the peccant.

"thou askst but for Ram who else,
Is happy whom king investing all regals."
"Today Kaushalya is the providence's pick,
Huffs me, puffed up high head of that uppish."

"Why not thyself go and see the egoist?
Her vapouring vanity maketh me sick."
"Thine Love for Ram Alas ! is from heart,
While Kaushalya's to Bharat is mind's art.

"Thine son is abroad and thou keep abreast none,
Heedless of cunning king but for this silky cushion.

Puissant=powerful; Peccant=Sinful, producer of disease; Canard=false, fabricated news or report; Tirade=censure.

* Tears; Deluge=flood.

Keep abreast=know, be aquainted; Huffs=tease; Puffed up=arrogant; Uppish=egoistic.

"While Siya Ram will succeed to throne,
Think of loving Bharat on bare floor alone.

The Queen smelt rot in honeyed kernel,
In her words like bells, a call of bale.
Queen's choler roared " Enough ! hush !! now,
Knave ! you braved to sow a row in house."

Couplet: *" See ! in Lame a mislead,*
In hump backed a crooked.
In half- blind a sightless,
More so if 'ts a hand-maid." 17

Keeping poise but then, queen smiled "O girl !'
You are a lackey, my shade, an Abigail."
" I keep poise, never try poison O you !
Ram is regent, my dream cometh true."

"You have brought all honey all heaven to me,
Tides in full to banks, this glad tidings.
"When the beau-Jour comes to threshold,
And brings new joy, I can't hold."

"The eldest should be lord, is D' accord in race,
Younger ones his page, it's blessed usage."
"Ram is soul of my soul, my son, my bairn,
His innate reverence to me hath great fond.

"When will oriental sloth knock the dawn,
And bring to The crown of Raghu-race, the crown."
Asked from Jealous Kooney the zealous queen—
"While town is painted red, why you feel green?"

Beau Jour=Great day.
Feel green=Be jealous.

Couplet: *"Capital is keen O Kooney !,*
While city is crayoned crimson,
Why should you croon cloudy?
On crowning of Ram, my son." 18

"In Bharat's name, tell me ! don't hide,
Kinky cry is strange in kingly rejoice."
Even as the crop was kissed by chill of cloud,
spake Kooney all ill in sweet beats of clout—

"My palsied tongue is now fulfilled,
Thy hammering hampered it into chill."
"Truth may be billous, truth may be bitter,
My chore defeats if I just flatter."

"My tunnel vision is ever behind
queen ! whether thou dost berate or be kind.
"tho' mind approves all wrongs, all unctuous,
Gib, glid is no bitter, so I choose a hush,

" Or speak palatable it's my vow from now,
'll contain self even if, it harmth thou."
"Whoever rules over me-maid, I lose nothing,
Forgive me for I why broached the thing."

So swift Kooney spitted words pungent,
As if bitterness of words, the tongue refused to contain.

Couplet: *Sick words poured upon sic,*
Had headlong volley,
Stirred queen became fate's pick
Through Loony Kooney's hooey. 19

Croon=hum.
Berate=Scold, criticize; Unctuous=flattering; Clout=influence.
Kinky=Strange off beat
Volley=a heavy attack; Hooey=nonsense talk.

Alas ! how the apathy, can whirl,
Can twist the fate and turn one's world.
Queen's faith mistaking for a friend in foe,
As the jungle tally-ho beguiles the doe.

Decree of destiny changeth mind's depth,
Craft of Maid proved to be trap of the fate.
Canards of Kooney crafted a mesh,
And queen's mesmerized mind was caged in that.

The queen questioned Kooney for nostrum,
Then lull of storm opened her mum—
" Me, a cheap-lip and a frame of mischief,
But thou hath mistaken me and my missive.

'ts true thy current ever flows to Siya-Ram,
And they repay it with little-some warmth.
"But Boast of majesty maketh modesty sick."
—thus the pervert worded in the way oblique.

Couplet: *"Thy eyes of love and innocence,*
Art blind for coming days,
Keenness of cunning king stays,
Only till thy youth swayth. 20

"Thy pellucid eyes pickst no guile,
In tricks of King and Kaushalya's ill- will.
"Jealous Ram's mother and devious king,
Biased both sent Bharat out of scene.

"Tho' King's fondness for thou ist just skin deep,
Yet green-eyed Kaushalya ever envied.

"Befo' thy nod acceptth the cheek's sag,
And through thy face plays ploy of passing age.

Missive=message, report; Nostrum=Secret cure.
Tally ho=sounds of hunter; Ploy=trick, dodge; Green-eyed=jealous

"Before this silk* ist wrinkled with creases,
Should the plot be wrought before thy sway ceaseth.

"Thy puissance ist naturally co-wife's awe,
Thy clout is cloud hovering on Kaushalya.
"Ram becometh King, it's fair, I too welcome,
But qualms daze me for thy days to come.

Couplet: *With canard of the cruels,*
Kooney venomed the queen,
Put her off the scent, unfailed
That her sour might prevail. 21

Alas ! as the fate, would have that
Tho' Kooney faked, queen took as the fact.
The closed mind is an empty vase,
It's folly fills it with fishy filth, fast.

Through the clouds of doubts, the queen's mind blurred,
That the trap of words, would raze her world.
Queen's folly was convinced by cajoling chat,
Kooney held the threads of now, a puppet.

"Under thy tutelage" Kooney further held forth—
"that I am thy page, blame me not for my faith,"
"If I invent words and lie a flam,
.Let nemesis fall upon me for the same.

"Should Ram be crowned, the very next aurora,
'll bring for thou the murks of awe."
"in varied moments of emptied puissance,
You may be jilted or treated as maid servant."

---

*Skin.
Put off the scent=deceive by false indications
Fishy=doubts.
Nemesis=ill fate; Flam=trick; Jilted=abandoned.

Couplet: *Kooney convinced Kaikyi,*
Colouring crafty canards,
The crooked cooked cunning plot
Quoting fibs of the past. 22

"For thou, Kaushalya is a rival-cowife,
The time is nigh, she'll tyrannize."
Kooney further wrought and poisoned—
"and My Bharat, your son; 'll rot in the prison."

Worked up queen was stirred stunned,
Her mind stormed and voice mummed.
Through her limbs shriveling shock ran,
She struggled to keep herself contained.

Taken a back, the humpback* ceased further to puff,
Lest for the feeble heart, it was quite enough.
Some honeyed words on the heep of bitter,
Koony poured upon the queen to comfort.

Mistaking a heron for a swan,
Confused queen, to kooney's crafty words drawn.
Adulterated flam addled the queen,
A scorching flame that burst all within-

Couplet: *"My life ist a naïve,*
Deeds have no blot.
What a pain fate gave,
For no flaw on my part." 23

"Simply I can't pickout friends or foes,
Nor flam nor blame my heart knows."
"My casual mind was confined to ramparts,
Ever to Ram, did current my heart.

Addled=confused; *Nicknamed Kooney had humpback, a Kyphotic(Manthara)

"The fate headlong pourth-sufferings on me,
In only you, O Kooney ! an aid I see.
"My say, my sway if I barter in life,
To serve a co-wife, better not to survive."

"or else I would fain go to my father's,
In this palace on my grief who bothers.
"My heart hath lotus my thoughts a rose,
Ecce ! in palace I'll rot as grass ross.

Availed the humpback of these humble words-
"it meets not if thou speakest such,"
"Lo! thy fortune ist more and more bright,
Don't give up; make right, the wrongs thro' fight."

Kaikeyi said—

Couplet:

" Your cardial bidding,
I shall follow O Kooney!
I can forsake anything,
You are my only crony." 24

"Worry not ! the mischief whoever tricks,
Shall eventually reap it's fruits of pricks.
"thy puissance shalt lead Bharat to reign,
He shall be the King, this much is certain."

"For thine obliged King, upon a plan, I hit,
At my humble bidding, do act upon it."
"thy éclat shalt ebb this eclipse,"
Sic poisoned Kooney in words honey-mixed.

"Tell Koony ! Cure ! Cure !! of my dire distress,
Sure ! my son, Lord, the sire I can forsake."

Ecce != look, lo ! ; Ross=Debris.
Crony=intimate friend; Éclat=impact.

Wily way winning over wit of Kaikeyi,
She told as if whettling the knife of trickery.

The knife of cheat with it's cold edge,
Stabth back of race, severeth to soul-depth.
"The King won Shambar in some early battles,
And promised thou two boons, for being his help."

"Added the hand-maid " it's just right now,
Ask for two boons that king promised thou."

"Ask him, two promises be fulfilled,
One realm for Bharat, two for Ram the exile.

Couplet:

"But ask that not till,
He hath sworn by Ram,
Lest he may not fulfil,
I have my qualm. 25

□

·Whettling=sharpen.

Dare to seek the Truth even through hell.

—Sri Udiya Baba

TWO PROMISES REVIVED

One sick design, sic, Kooney hatched,
Further stuffed into queen, that wretch.
"Confine thyself to the sulking room*,
Discreetly manage for couple of boons."

A viper in visage of the good,
Queen extolled over and over, the shrewd-
"if my genuine morrow cometh to be true,
As apple of my eyes I shall cherish you."

Lavishing bright words on that personified murks,
Queen retired to darks in the sulks.
The Lady of house as a puppet of mistrust,
Bringeth to the house a certain curse.

In the perverted soil, prickly seeds of deceit,
Bloom all the blues, for its fruits, the defeat.
While enjoying the sway, betrayed by loser lore,
In the murks in the sulks, she laid on the floor.

* in a palace a separate place for sulks.

Couplet: *With the festive charms and warmth,*
Crowded the denizens;
To and fro they swarmed,
At the lively barbican. 1

Childhood cheer Ram shared with whom,
Those, companions, thronged and met with new bloom.
Ram talked with them in same intimate accent,
Ram recalled every single of His friends.

They returned talking together very high,
'Busy yet Ram is, same easy spry.'
'In him I see still a playmate,
Some said,' He ist whole world's intimate.'

"With whom we played, fate hath chanced us,
In His child's play; He creatth the whole cosmos.
"Pray ! in this and next births to come,
May His playmate, even maid we become.

'May He be ever Master and we His puppet.'
The same desire every single had.
But for onc Kaikcyi's heart with the flame of flam,
Was set ablaze in wily will's name.

Came the tired sun, in the west solar-line,
Even as, to bath the sweated sun sunk in Sarayu it's shine.

Couplet: *It was the happy evetide,*
Perhaps last in king's life,
His winged steps did guide,
Him to palace of Kaikeyi. 2

On the soft wings of affection, the King,
Seemed, on harsh blaze, as if, was hovering.

Barbican=gate house of palace; Spry=Cheerful, intimate; Flam=trick.

All his colours faded to pale and murk,
As he heard of the queen in the sulks.

King's winged stride froze and shrivelled,
A chill ran through as he crossed the sill.
Oft mightiest hath some weakness,
Here King had sickly silky trap.

Oft Bills, bolts, brands who have endured,
With flowers of Cupid, were found injured.
Thus, his timid steps approached the sulking room,
Was taken a back seeing the Embodied gloom.

Was lying on the floor attired in coarse,
As if foreseeing impending mishap on door;
Drawing himself nigh to the beloved queen,
Asked King the reason of her spleen—

Stanza: *"All in festive din, meets not this scene,*
Vent out cause of your spleen.
I have never chanced, such angry glance
Untimely frawns, O my queen!"
Kaikeyi threw flash, as live as a snake,
Knitting her brows enraged.
Worded Tulsi, under sway of destiny
King took the lethal as lithe plays.

Couplet: *To the queen's firy askance,*
And wrath that meet not,
The King asked of her misfeasance,
"O beloved ! tell me the cause. 3

"Beloved who dared to hurt you,
Who had the liking for the death noose."
"Ask me for any bare head be crowned,
Ask me for any crowned be dethroned down."

Bills=Axes; Lithe=flexible, pliant; Misfeasance=wrong doing; Brands=swords.

"My brand is no blunt, my hilt is hell,
For a crowned or common, who ever has libelled.
Your knit of brows is a noose-trap,
Even for immortals, where stands a pleb?"

"My entire self bows under your ire,
My sons, my soul, my power, my desire.
"My unfeigned words have sincere warmth,
No canard, all candid I say by Ram."

"Your cheery countenance ever cherished me,
Angry mute meets not, it's unseemingly.
"I may not agree of what you speak,
Yet to the death,'ll defend your right to say it.

Couplet: *Kenning candid vows,*
Weighing oath of the King,
With cunning-smirk queen rose,
As the murk of that evening. 4

She rose as if huntress was laying the noose,
Roses on her face had thorny ruse.
Unaware of the murk in her smirk; the king
in winning accent, poured all honey—

"What have you desired, has come to pass,
This news has won whole Awadh's applause.
Morrow Sun will fulfil your marrow's desire,
I make Ram, the regent, (so) put on festive attire."

Winsome words of king touched wilsome marrow
Of queen, it cracked it was hard tho'.
Her knitted forehead looked fierce odd,
In her fiery eyes drew, poisonous ruddy cords.

Candid=honest; Libel=insult.
Ruse=trick; Smirk=hidden smile.

Fluttered sickly outspread of her hair,
Still her smile shared not her inner affair.
The smirky face brought a murky eve,
But the imposter grace further did deceive—

Couplet: *"Ever you ask me to 'ask'*
But your words evanesce,
On Dear's face I see mask,
For your two promises. 5

"You promised me dear ! a couple of boons,
But my getting them is still a question."
Dashrath smilt kenning it a petty mean,
He opened his hands and heart before the queen.

"You are overfond of feigned annoyance,
This keeps wifely love verdant."
"It's daily joy in the consort's meet
But the union after feigned anger is more sweet.

"Oblivious as I am, that I did forget,
Means not from my words I retract."
"Pray ! O beloved !! blame me not,
For, no fault lies on my part."

"I say-ask four boons nay just two,
My lips know no lapsus but are ever true.
"It has ever been a rule with Raghu's race,
At the cost of even death to hold promises.

"Truth is worship, and route of virtue;
Is said by Veds and declared by Manu,
"Moreover it chanced I have sworn by Ram,
Who is Best of Raghus and embodied virtue.

Evanesce=Dissolve.
Verdant=fresh

Couplet: *Finding him bound to his words,*
Sic, a sick smile she stretched,
Head-long on King she poured
All Awadh's smiles to snatch— 6

"O beloved ! I pray to vouchsafe,
As the regent of Awadh installation of Bharat.
"For your promises dear ! I have no qualm,
Second boon I ask with folded palms—

"Detached as ascetic, for just fourteen years
In woods as hermit, the exile of Ram."
—How does a moment ruins the worlds,
Alas ! how does one spell, spell fate's words?

How is mortal canvas daubed by brush of fate,
Could be read on the king's bleached face.
Struck by lightening as stands a palm tree,
As the cloudy fear had frosted springing seed,

The king stood stunned mind, and hammered soul,
Soft words of queen fell like thunderbolt.
Her sweet words soured Dashrath's core,
The salty flood broke the eye's grieved shore.

Couplet: *Her flam and fury, was helm,*
Clouded Awadh's sky,
A woman's clout had aimed,
At vernal twigs, a frost-dry. 7

Thus, in feigned friendly words, King saw,
A hovering fiendish curse over Ayodhya.
As a homeless pauper, the King in palace,
Stood palsied as the prey of fate.

Seeing King in bad plight queen further sulked,
"Do you see me through the mirror of commerce?

"Is Bharat your son? Or a hay or whey,
I find your mind in thick of fray."

"If my words as spear pierced through,
You may turn down promises as untrue.
"If it's lapsus I 'll never mind,
But it bringeth infamy if you decline.

"Loud in self boasting of being steadfast,
I would ask for the grain, you might have thought."
Sic, she belched all foul, what she learnt,
As though applying salt to the burn.

Couplet: *A warrior of virtues,*
Was stabbed on back,
Beating own head he sighed out,
'she has put me at stake.' 8

The queen stood as the fury's own sword,
World's most awe-some is the curse of consort.
Fury's sword with hilt of malign mind,
The edge of rage the humpback* did grind.

"The dreadful, rigid sword that pierced through,
Will drain my life, it seems true?'
Steeling his heart and gathering his soul,
In polite mask, the King, then told—

" O my good lady ! your words meet not,
Ties of love, faith will you cast off."
"My stand with no bias seeth, the two,
I vouch my view hath no skew."

"At the first knock of east,'ll send a dispatch,
For Bharat, Shatrughan, 'll soon come back.

Skew=slope(favour for somebody); *Humpback-kooney

"And sure 'll bestow the kingdom on Bharat,
Reckoning planets and auspicious date.

Couplet: *Ram-Bharat 'r two breaths, one soul*
Have no eye for worldly pomp,
For this 'apple' no grapple,
It was me, for the eldest Ram. 9

"It's usage of Race what maketh you sick,
None tricked only, in my mind it clicked.
"To me, Ram, or Bharat it maketh no difference,
A few days hence, Bharat will be regent."

"To ignore you, I never did mean,
But for surprise gift what you cherished within.
"Me and your Awadh shall make no difference
But for second boon is a piercing pang.

"Is it just quip or a whip of queen consort,
If, is gage or a grudge I'm gallow's bird.
"Ram ever loved you and Ram, you too,
Cool ! tell of His guilt, is this His due.

" I fathomed the depth, Him you ever blessed,
Alas ! was it just on surface."
To mother, who cradled, cared cherished child Ram,
That kindred Ram goeth crude, it's a qualm."

Couplet: *"Cease ! sally and sulk,*
What chilled me to bone,
So that my eyes regale,
On sight of Bharat on throne." 10

Grapple=combat, close fight.
Quip=joke, jest, gag; Sally=witty remarks; Regale=feast.

Dashrath said further—

"A winged without wings can live
Rather fish without water may out-live."
"Ram is soul of all my soul,
Ram is vital flame, lest this mould is too old."

"A Ramless* breath is a lifeless toil,
A sapless machine in my mortal coil.
"My life without Ram is deserted rampike,
All lustre of the ramparts is, then worth soil."

True words, like fuel blazed up fire,
Her heart seemed a hearth consumed with ire—
"Your cajoling words now shall not sway,
Here, no wile works, no ploys play."

"Ram is a prize, you too are wise,
Now for Kaushalya's device, she gets a reprise.
"It's straight now grant my request
Let ignominy fall on you lest."

Couplet: *"If Ram is not exiled;*
This morn will bring
Death to me, while
Ill-famy to you king ! 11

"Ram should doff royal for garbs of hermit,
Go must in dense as an ascetic."
—then this wicked women saying so,
Stood up, seemed an erupting volcano.

Oped mountain of passion through portal of awe,
And her swollen anger seemed the terrible lava.
As happens, creeping hot flood has no governance,
Uprooted King's life and of Sarayu's banks.

---

*Ramless depicts godlessness (more specifically without Ram).
Reprise=retaliation; Rampike=stump of a tree; Ploy=trick.

'ts no jest', King kent 'I'm put to test',
'In disguise of consort, the death hovers very next.'
Mind's hang up, sunk heart and funk face,
Lips trembled, tongue rattled, then the King spake—

"Pray ! do not play axe on solar race,
My parting from Ram is my death itself."
"A short folly adds up life long-pangs,
Retain Ram or carry unending repents."

Couplet: *All mellow melody, in this murk,*
Faded in King's Bosom,
Queen's malady smirked,
n' King screamed 'Ram! Hey Ram!!' 12

King dropped on ground, his limbs drooped,
his hands froze, on brows shone chilly dews.
Parched tongue, bleached face, speech failed lips,
A fish squirms on stormy sand, as if.

But the urn of poison spilt once more,
As if, scorching a non healing sore
"King ! then why you bragged 'ask ! queen ask !!
Your malicious mind has mellifluous mask."

"You are tight-hand yet known a generous,
Only I behold your twin faces."
Lacking scathing attacks you remained the Hero,
Now keep your ego, or your words you forgo."

"Pray do not linger a dilemma within,
Reck ! the pledge or reckon ! the passion."
"Well said ' the life, wife, sons and land,
Are like straw for a trueman."

Malady=sickness; Smirked=grinned, leered
Mellifluous=sweet(honeyed); Scathing=criticizing.
Reck=take care; Reckon=consider.

Couplet: *On her hiss king ex'claimed,*
" hush not ! say what you will,
You are not be blamed,
Possessed by my doom-devil." 13

"Possessed ; you muse on, your words a sermon,
You thought not, it was all poison."
"This reign, Bharat, I know, 'll never covet,
He'll not agree to this decree of fate."

"The tide hath turned adverse to me
No blame, you came as my embodied sin.
"Ram ist the flame of all fraternities,
Ram ist the name of all majesties.

"The cloudy murk of sky shall drift,
The Ram's reigh, again,'ll soon be a gift.
"to today's men and mankind to come,
Ram and Ram's reign will be a paragon."

"A blot on you and on my lot,
None length of suns-stars can wash.
"now, till this cage, of mine toils for breath's job,
Hush! hush!! unto you repent and sob.

Couplet: *'Bring no ruins' King urged her,*
In vain argued and fell
But the wile did not utter,
As tho' busy in evil spells. 14

In vain he argued, he failed and fell,
On acme of emotions, his nerves turned motionless.
Stopped wrangles, as his heart was wrung,
His senses drained, further parched the tongue.

Like a glum bird's pinions were clipped,
King fell in fate's grip, stricken with grief.

Wrung=peirced; wrangles=row, quarrels.

On acme of pain, in stupor fits,
Only sigh 'hey Ram!' repeated his lips.

"To tell all this to Ram should go none,
"Go, Stray!; Rise not O God-sun!!,
"Thou shouldst fade O Sun ! at plight of the town,
Pray ! night may linger, day may not dawn."

The King soft delicate, queen hard ruthless,
Lo ! two extremes, puppets in play of the fate.
Sleepless King wailed, while Awadh yet revelled,
Till East broke with strange appeal in ruddy apparels.

Couplet: *Melics, melodics filled,*
The milieu of King's door,
Bards extolled, the birds trilled
Crowd wished Ram to the fore. 15

To the melodies, dins and the rush,
The King's door had all odd hush—
"The Sun hath come up and King yet,
Hath not woken up, we never ever met."

Crowd of plebs and the pious asked Sumantra,
To go into Mahal to get the behest.
A mortal hush had it's wide-spread.
Gynaeceum wore dismay, froze feared steps.

As if whirls of storms of calamity,
Were having unebbing waves on sorrow's sea,
The milieu of melee and not mellow,
Looked a monster, all Awadh's joy to swallow.

Sumantra forcely pierced himself deep more,
His limbs numbed finding the King on the floor.

Sumantra uttered not, his throat choked,
But then in smirky voice, the silence, queen broke—

Couplet: *"King was through out winkless,*
His secret is his secret,
His Vigil creeped on anxious wake,
Only 'hey Ram!' he repeated. 16

Kaikeyi said to Sumantra—

"Hope ! he wisheth to see his son,
Call on Ram and bring him soon."
Wished to blink at queen but for King's blank face,
Minister left judging 'the queen designed some mess.'

On his last legs, he failed to move,
And forced himself out, and tried to recoup.
His roaming thoughts struck him headlong,
'Can Ram set right what's going wrong?'

As he rushes out and in hush he goes
The Joy calms, follows him qualms of crowded brows.
Reassuring crowd, Sumantra rushed to Ram
Who received him with reverent warmth.

With few stealing and few looking in the face,
Sumantra conveyed him the royal behest.
In an odd haste Ram followed Sumantra,
All about anxious citizens, awefully stunned.

Couplet: *The tress, dress and crest,*
All in great mess,
Ram saw sire all wretched,
Like aged elephant sees a lioness. 17

Blink at=ignore.
On last legs=exhausted

Parched lips bleached face and barren eyes,
Scorched frame lying like a rampike.
Then, Ram saw next to His father,
Kaikeyi with brows on the tenters.

As if embodied death, on the abacus,
On the head of Dashrath counting his last gasps.
Soft princely life of Ram within ramparts,
Was ever stranger yet to such odds.

Ram brooded—

"Down-visaged what gnaws father's heart,
May I be lucky nostrum for His blues' dart?"

Kaikeyi then burst out—

"The sole cause, Ram ! is his lust in You,
But he promised me, my choice boons two."

"Simply, I asked two promises to fulfil,
My begging, however, struck him with chill."
"This dilemma has laden his lips,
On your score can't shade off the hitch."

Couplet: *"Here plighted words, there for son the lust,*
Puts him on dilemma,
Haste ! you obey his behest
Rid him from such awe." 18

Sic, Kaikeyi was too sickly bold,
All sore she poured, all pungent she told.
As if tongue was a bow with words for the darts,
And bowman's trick was piercing King's heart.

All ill was her skill of bowmanship,
The King quivered beholding the quiver of lips.
Conveyed all to Ram, she, the Poison incarnate,
As if prophesying the words of doomed fate.

Then the All-wise Ram, the Statue of innocence,
Was in stoical bliss, as is in joy or pains.
His vernal heart bloomed within,
His nectarian tongue spake all honey—

"O! beloved mother! it's all My bliss
My proud luck has blest Me all this.
"Who obeyth parents, that son alone is blest,
Who gratifieth them, with worshipping faith."

Couplet: *"Hallowed forest is blest,*
To me in every view,
On top it's father's behest,
And thou approvest too." 19

THE STOICAL RAM

"With ope hands fortune to the fore stands,
My Bharat, my soul will be regent.
It's worth while to go to exile,
Lest both sides I shall be deprived.

" 'ts all rare to find such bliss,
Must I avail favour before the time slips.
"Should I barter away divine tree for a cactus
Not just thine its My boon with every plus.

"But the aching puzzle, thick upon me came,
Is King grieved with strange pang.
"For a trivial matter My father is so grieved,
O mother ! it's more than I can believe.

"Looks sick, a grave and a brave as he was,
I must have erred and trespassed.
"His hush is the witness of my lapse,
Speak out to Me My father's distress."

Couplet: *How can shallow foam fathom,*
The pellucid oceans,
Blurred eyes of wicked flam,
Perceived not pearls of Ram's innocence. 20

Then, kenning Ram, His in and His out,
She spake out spreading her clout.
With easy yes of Ram, with her pomp of love,
The hypocrite mind began to gloze—

"By you I swear and by Bharat too,
For King's grief none else I knew."
"O Brother of brotherhood ! O son of heritage !!
"You are true to parents-You truly said."

"May You not slacken a virtuous son's duty,
May not fall on staunch King, the infamy.
"May his words stand high and his virtue,
That have fetched him a son like You."

Her odious lips had polite accent,
Like a sacred fane in accursed land.
To her cunning words Ram was winningly engaged,
As all kinds of brooks are hallowed in Ganges.

Couplet: *With regain from stupor,*
Dashrath turned his side,
Humbly submitted minister—
'Ram hadth arrived' 21

Gloze=flatter; Odious=loathsome.

Little hushed hint of Ram's presence,
He felt all along his stuporous sense.
Like a key of hope, for the cage of slumbers,
He unlocked eyes as word 'Ram' touched ears.

Sumantra comforted his Sovereign to sit,
King to the fore saw Ram falling at his feet.

He took Ram to embrace close and close,
Even as good treasure was being snatched perforce.
Thro' his hushed eyes gushed rills of tears,
That told sad-tidings of his very state, untoward.

Tears told of his silent missive to Shiv,
That prayed for his hugest pang to relieve—
" O Shiv! ever blissful!! Thy celestial grace,
Can veer the tortuous trains of fate."

Couplet: *"Since, Thou promptest every breath,*
Thy clout mayst inspire Ram
To flout my words and stay back
At her frail flam and my filial flame." 22

"Thou Shiv! canst see my filial flame,
And canst judge her frail flam.
"Let all wide infamy and shame,
May come to my lot and my name.

"To perdition I would fain be damned
Rather than have Ram lost to my panoram.*

Sic, his mute prayers had all stiff lips,
Tho' his mind trembled like aspen leaf.

Frail flam=unchaste trick ; Filial flame= parental love; Veer=sudden change in direction.
*go out of sight; Perdition=depth of hell

Ram judged his simple, filial love,
And guessed mother's feelings may further echo.
Suited to time, it did behove,
Ram spake words rich in love—

"My immodesty to speak is breach,
Pray ! forgive me father ! for a childish deed.
For a trivial matter thou art so grieved,
Now, mother hath told me, I am relieved."

Couplet: *"Sire ! anguish meets not*
Having this festal cause,
Command me with glad heart,"
Worded Ram with applause. 23

"Celestial blessings happen upon, the one,
Whose sire is content by the doings of the son.
"Who is committed to parents like his own breath,
He is worth four rewards* of the earth."

"Blessings of thy command that crowned upon Me,
Is the blest behest, is the best thing.
"Let Me now go to bid the mother adieu,
I shall be soon back after obeying you."

Thus Ram departth, thus King's real soul goes,
Leaving frame of breaths with puffs of woes.

THE AWE-STRUCK AWADH

On the Awadh's Blue**, King's muted helms of blues,
Stormed peopled air, as spreaded the news.
As the touch of sting poisons all limbs,
As through slight slit, the whole bark sinks,

---

behove=befit.

* Religious merits, material riches, worldy gratification, final beatitude.

** sky of Ayodhya.

The odd silence of stunned revels,
Filled awe in milieu of the Capital.

Couplet: *Paeans, melics sounded bathos,*
And Awadh's festive crop,
Was swarmed by locust of pathos,
Some sickly screamed, some stood shocked. 24

All sick and shocked screams asked,
"How the fate hath designed all odd?
Vexed victimized people voiced against the vixen,
Rebels rebellowed and reviled the queen—

"She seeks to perceive after gouging out eyes,
Venoming veracity she wishes ambrosial life.
'ts like in vernal grove, the jungle fire,
Hath scorched the nectarian hue entire."

"Having set fire to a newly thatched house,
What brews within King's wretched spouse."
"Heat of the tidings is as chill as death,
Sitting on bough itself, the tree she axed."

"As real mother she pretended herself,
But the foster reality hath come to face."
" 'ts easy, a man may catch his shadow,
'but for the ways of woman to know."

"Poseur's soft pats lulled Ram in cradle,
Same fickle mind exiles Him unto jungle.

Veracity=truthfulness; Vixen=unpleasant woman (Kaikeyi)
Poseur=poser, not genuine

Couplet: *"What not is faded by fate*
What can't bury in ocean
Alas ! who can't be a puppet,
To power of the feeble woman. 25

"What's not be consumed by the fire
Of woman's thin brow on tenter of ire.
"A mundane's play is not a fair game,
Alas ! what cometh and what we dreamt."

"For us fate bricked a castle in air
The mirage of mirth was a mirk of night-mare."
—the raising hell had all helpless hue
Of sighs of laden plebian view.

"Words to wicked woman" some said,
"May be turned down, it's no breach of promises."
"Ram was her daily bliss, her daily worship,
Hope me ! she may forgo her last wish."

In past cure state, some hope they possessed,
That proved to be their lives buttress.
"Mastered by weakness, king hath lost wisdom,
And realized not what calamity cometh."

But the saner didn't blame king's verdict,
For he upholdth all firmness of ethics.
'Bharat connived? 'some whisperedth in qualm,
Negation screamed for love between Bharat and Ram.

Couplet: *Moon may shade no silver but flame,*
Nectar may poison,
Bharat can't even dream a flam
Prejudiced to Ram. 26

To connive=to plot, scheme; Negation=denial.

Turmoil of fury had self-restraint-hush,
For honour of words of revered Dashrath.
In palsied crowd some blamed the Creator,
Who in poisonous urn had offered nectar.

From fitful fury vapoured up weaping cloud,
In flood of melancholy, drowned the town.
Peopled air was filled with sad squall,
Along the nerves chill ran with tragic hail.

Rushed to Kaikeyi her kins and friends,
Found not the same queen but all strange.
They reminded her of current of her soul,
That her flooded heart ever told,

Of the ambrosial warmth that along her veins,
For Ram's good, Ram's loving care, ever ran.
"Mind ! you connive the Ram's exile; why?
Tho' feminine, yet you had no jealous to co-wives.

Couplet: *'Will Lakhan choose home over Ram?*
'Will doom part Siya-Ram?
' Will Bharat pick throne over Ram?
'Will King outlast without Ram? 27

"Will Awadh ever now see the vernal spread?
'll reveling brush ever paint Awadh red?
"Will time reward same Awadh anew?
But can King survive this moment, can you too?

"The silly mind and sickly askew,
Will bring shame and obloquy to you.
"Agreed ! Bharat be crowned, but then,
'What's need for Ram's exile in the dense?

"Ram is above lust of power and pomp,
Not covetous of dazzle of glittering charms.

Obloquy=infamy

"Suggest ! Ram may leave to live with Vashishtha,
As your second wish ask the King this'

"Does a son like Ram is worth exile,
And need to pass life in wild.
"Its lone chance to avert the impending grief,
Heal all sores, up ! up !! be quick.

Stanza: *"Discern Queen ! devise means*
Not be demeaned and save the race,
"Dissuade Ram, discourage Ram, persuade Him,
Not to go to forest,
"Ram ist part, of this ramparts
And Ram is warmth of Bharat's heart
"Let Bharat sway, but Let Ram stay,
For Awadh's sabled night Ram is sunny day.

Distitch: *Salutary suggestion did stab*
Through and through the queen,
Tutored as was by humpback,
Overheard it as hollow din. 28

To the wise advice she made up pose,
As hungry tigress looks herds of does.
The mute volcano through sullen mask,
Only thro' her ired askance she asked.

All caring caution came again and again,
But on stern glebe they toiled in vain.
"Twin edged tongue of queen sabred us,
Betrayal of doom have sabled all colours.

The Haats stunned, lamented every brick,
While milieu sighed, the Sarayu flown sick.

Salutary=beneficial
Sable=to put on black; To sabre=strike by sword.

"Ramless breath is just puffing fit,
Ramless life's like lifeless rampike.

Anguish of separation struck all with awe,
Meanwhile, Ram called on His mother, Kaushalya.
A carefree, cheerful look he wore,
With the bliss overwhelming full to the shore.

Couplet:

The bliss is broad,
With no bias, no anguish.
As is stoic Ram, thought,
Well freed from chains of Kingship. 29

☐

10

One glance, one touch is enough.

—Ram Krishna Paramhans.

THE BRAVE MOTHER

The Perfect one was embodied stoicism,
Lest King would have detained him.
Firm Ram went to mother in no ceremonial robes,
And the doom of palace followed behind Him in sobs.

Ram revered mother touched feet; while,
With fond breast mother embraced child.

With overwhelmed joy took she, son to bosom,
Unaware of the brewing flam against her son.
Seeing soul of her soul, the life of her life,
Her joy rolled over brims of her eyes.

Every mother is 'a blessed paradise' in herself,
In her depth, in her height meetth selfless self.
The holy love asked in her hallow terms—
"When the glad auspicious hour Awadh 'll earn?

"When my virtues and piety 'll help,
to touch me- life, the blessing alps?
"When'll yearning impatience of the town,
Fill with newborn bliss while you are crowned.

Couplet: *"O Son ! my soul ! my Ram !,*
Tell me I beseech You,
When the reward 'll come,
Of our piety, virtues. 1

"O Son ! it's by now over delayed,
Quick ! bathe, be ready for anointing usage.
"Take some sweets, see Your father after that,
I alert it's already getting late.

Even regal couch or motherly touch,
The charms of mirth or the warmth of hearth,
Even, Mother's cradling lap-n-nestling arms,
Unstirred to duty, lured not Ram.

The sacrifice is the godly humanity,
It puts by, strife between greed and duty.
Accepting as a boon, the mandate of fate,
To mother Kaushalya, Ram, thus, spake—

"Ope hands love of my sire,
Hath bestowed upon me jungle's empire.
"He favoured for cause and chances in forests,
Cheerfully grant leave and not be obsessed.

Couplet: *"For years just four and ten,*
Having obeyed father's behest
At thy feet'll be back again,
Poise ! poise !! not be upset." 2

Son's words tho' all gentle and tender,
Pierced mother's heart, her soul shattered.
Taken a back on Ram's taking emphasis,
World whirled around her, her zeal languished.

'in monsoons some shrubs may wilt'- well said,
Green bowers have no season, no reason to collapse.

Her leafy heart withered in vernal summit,
Face chilled in fevered heat and freezy fit.

Thro' eyes melted her frigid core,
Dismayed as if doe had heard a roar.
Containing herself, with wavering lips,
In words she dragged the heartfelt nips.

"You are his daily bliss, is it worth while,
for the King to command you to exile?
"I ask, my Ram ! for what offence,
King putth You in such a penance?

Couplet: *A weighed and wet reply came,*
*From the ushering person**
He told reason and flam,
And mother was struck dumb. 3

She read shri Ram's tacit eyes,
She felt stifled in hands of plight.
Caught in the strife of the dilemma,
She stood petrified as the statue of awe.

Nor could detain Ram, nor yet say 'Go'.
Will of the fate had decreed woe.
'Creator deceiveth, and the fate his puppet,
'the Grape of joy burst and soured the palate.

"May not be created bad blood
Among brothers; May be retained the moral code.
"but how a mother can ever accept."
—thro' stoned eyes flown stunned mind's cataract.

Languish=droop; Summit=peak
Nips=bites, hurts
*Sumantra's son was accompanying Ram.

Librating dilemma of mother and that of moral,
The guileless she spake gathering the mettle—
"Well ! my child ! that you hold is the course, most blest,
" Of all, father's command is most sacred.

Couplet: *"He promised realm, gives exile's whip,*
It moves me a bit not,
Ramless life is balmless nip
For Awadh, Bharat and my lord. 4

"For the palace, pals, plebs, posh and the pious
Your absence is an ordeal rigorous.
"Any case, if it be just father's; then go not,
'but heed ! mother is ranked on the top.

" more, if mother* have asked to proceed to jungle,
Then, the woods will equal Awadh in centuple,
" With sylvan penates for your parents,
And parrots birds, beasts for your friends.

"tho' grey epoch of life, for jungle doth meet,
So your green age, maketh me little sick.
"You go to woodlands how much 'ts blest,
Alas ! Ayodhya is now luckless, deserted.

"Your exodus, even it's very thought,
Deserts Awadh; it wrongs lives to odds.
"if I ask you to take me with You,
That 'll put you in dilemma anew.

Couplet: *"May not my love's manacles*
Be noose to slacken You,
Up ! my child ! up !! with morale,
May Your firmness be true. 5

Librating=weighing; Mettle=courage.
*Kaikeyi
Exodus=departure; Centuple=equal to hundred times; Ordeal=put to test.

"May! penates, paters and the Earth itself,
Escort you ever at every step.
"May the nature spread it's green silk,
May hills be home, let be deserted this sill.

' 'Ts untrodden path that you tread upon,
Ram! be for coming men a virtuous dawn.
"May your steps lit, the stray goers,
May it be at cost of darks at Awadh's door.

"May the arched leaves bless the strides of a lone,
But will let parched city live with piercing thorns.
"Go Ram! Go ! may jungles cradle You,
Go Ram! Go ! may sylvan-gales lull You.

"May the pebbles kiss Your supple feet,
Let the Awadh's plebs miss Your marvel feats."
Voice of mother could hold no strength,
Wailed she calling herself, most fortunate woman.

Mother's wailing beads, paled her phiz,
Ram pressed her to bosom and tried to ease.

Couplet:

Tides of tidings aired
As a jolt to Seeta,
She rushed to Kaushalya and revered,
And sat in tight lipped awe. 6

Mother beheld in Her a benign statue,
In the fate's fane being plundered by doom's crew.
Seeing grace of her Beauty's quintessence,
Seeing fineness of Her innate elegance,

—For the time first, the mother was distressed,
Seeing pleasing charms of Siya's seraphic face.

Phiz=face; beads=tear drops; Penates=deities.

Wifely devotion of Siya's soul,
With trains of thoughts sat in Her dazed mould.

Siya brooded—

'My Lord ist stoic, tacit lips His 'Yes'.
Who goeth with Him, knowth only His hush.
'To accompany Him, how can I merit,
Whether body goes as well or only my spirit.'

As Her toe nails scratched ground, in thought of Her own,
Even anklet bells belied not; made a moan.
Agony of Her soul thro' Her eyes melted
Her mute tears dropped nigh moaning anklets.

Couplet:

The mother saw pearls of pang
In eyes of in-law princess,
She broke the odd silence,
To Ram she thus spake— 7

"O my child Ram ! she is all beloved,
She is genteel, gentle and delicate.
"Her feet knew the silk, since days of play,
The go, glow, gaiety she saw in both houses.

"Her grace, face, race, goodness is a gem,
She is all a stranger yet to the pain.
"As very apple of my eyes I treated Her,
She is my life, nay, my life is hers.'

"At Her every step I carpeted my lids,
And was cared by all Kindred spirits.
"I have fostered with love this seraphic creeper,
Woe is me ! fate averses in blossoming hour.

Belie=contradict.

"The current of my heart is so possessive,
That I never asked Her to stir a lamp's wick.
"mere touch of grass pinks whose sole,
'Wish to follow you in woods, thinking, sinks my soul.

Couplet:

" 'ts not just wild breeze
Nor just crags cliffs steeps
'ts hosts of brutes, fiends beasts
That make me all sick. 8

"Siya, who is all a heaven's creeper,
To live in heinous groves it ill-behoves Her.
The Creator hath carved some different moulds,
For dwelling in woods, lasses of Kirates and kols.

"With born hearts of rock and unrocky limbs,
Fearless they roam in twilight dims.
"Or else an ascetic's wife who choose wood's life,
Who renounce mundane for hard-crude life.

"In woods how 'll Siya's days pass?
Who petrifies seeing apes on the canvas.
"One, who sported in pellucid lake, that cygnet,
It behoveth not if foam, moss she gets.

"Judging this, what ever is your emphasis,
To my beloved Siya I'll bid.
"She is too good to lose and a great solace,
if She stays at home, our life stays."

Couplet:

Honeyed speech of Kaushalya
Imbued in mother's love-n-grace
Ram imbibed as ambrosia
For, at hand far- days. 9

Pink=pierce like sword.

SIYA AND LAKHAN JOIN

Ram comforted the appaled mother in words of aplomb,
Tender words for the tender heart to balm.
His modesty saw His mother's presence tho',
What forced Him to speak to Seeta, was an odd scenario.

'O Princess ! I depict strange woods demerits,
'What's fit, what not, what's family benefit.
'My Comfort, Thy ease and family's need,
'If Thou stayst back, it really meetth.

"While Thou shalt be obeying my words,
Thou'll be chanced rendering services to mother.
"Rendering onus to parents is great reverence,
And is worship of Lord, most sacrosanct.

" Let Thou be mother's same daily bliss,
Lest pangs may add to her panics.
" A mother's pangs only a woman can ken,
Her sore may be balmed by Thine presence.

Couplet:

"Take behest as My request,
All virtues it bringeth,
Any obduracy Lest,
May plot with it straits. 10

"For mother's sake, I leave you here,
It's my mind-ful heart's advice, sincere.
"Me-go, my soul stayth within ramparts
With parents, and Thee, with fras, plebs and pals.

"My suns will steal times in swift rush,
I'll be back soon redeeming father's words.

Appaled=shocked ; aplomb=poise
Sacrosanct=holy.
Obduracy=stubbornness; Straits=difficult position.

"Hardships of homeless, travails of travels,
Hard heaps, high hikes, heats, hails and hassles,

"Copeless camps, chasms, cliffs, caves crudes,
worms, wasps, wicked wilds will welcome Thou in woods.
"Gritty bed of stones, thirsty ways of thorns,
for Thine bare feet, those wait all along.

"Even wild winds shiver in yells, hauls, barks, roars,
In hush of gloom, soaring bowers snore.
"While reptiles, wilds, bugs and gnats,
for Thou, rills brooks are innate inapt,

Ram further added—

Couplet: *"The Earth, for Thy couch,*
Bulb roots for food.
Sylvan barks, for Thou,
Will be robes in woods. 11

"There, only the discipline of the seasons work,
Free commerce hath paucity or a bulk.
"No hierarchy works but the nature-hex holds,
With anarchic clout and it's lout control.

"In lawless Sylvan dwell devils, cannibals,
Who master stygian air of jungles.
"Hoards may end but hardships have no end,
Woods life is penance with un-asked pangs.

"No man but Satan, no friend but fiends,
In various forms imposters deceive.
"Wild beaks, jaws, claws, horrifiy the air,
At very thought of woods even the boldest shudder.

Travails=pangs.
Hierarchy=celestial governance ; Hex=witch; Stygian=hellish ; Hoards= resources

"Noiseless poise there, is a Satanic ambush,
Foretells of gory revels in hush or seeming hush.
"So; O Cuckoo of mango ! O Cygnet of milky lake!!,
Shouldst Thou stay back; not for hardships Thou art made.

Couplet: *"Medic's, Mentor's Master's*
View of mates, intimates
One who does not revere,
Surely has to regret." 12

Seeta heard Her beloved's winning views,
Mist of milieu, but, filled Her eyes with dews.
'Her pious beloved would leave Her behind'—
This very thought pierced through Her every sinew.

His soothing advice proved scorching to Her,
Her wifely devotion could make no answer.
Containing Self by perforce, the Holy damsel,
Her damp eyes she dammed, to mother's feet fell—

"O reverent maa ! forgive ! My great impudence,
Lord of My life tendered Me advice to My best.
"None the less, I have mulled and realized,—
'Away from the Beloved is; the worst compromise.

"No gold, no glitter no pomp can daze,
Concord with Lord is, life-Cord of a page.
"Can wifely devotion ever compromise,
With parting of the soul, for comforts of life—

Then, Siya told to Ram—

Couplet: *" O Benign ! Blossom of my bosom !,*
O Becoming! O Bliss !
Lacking Thou even Elysium,
'll be nasty as abyss. 13

Impudence=shamelessness.

"Mother, father, mentor, sister, fras,
All kinships, friends and parents in laws,
"All ties of blood and all ties of kindred,
Are pangs to a woman bereft of her Lord.

"Charms of castle-chattels are chains of chagrins,
for bereft woman, her breath is grim.
"Luxuries are loathsome, ornaments a load,
a lavish home is like hellish abode.

"Even fondling breeze is a jerky jolt,
moon rays pierce through as thunderbolt.
"Me-life ! Me-Lord ! Me-soul ! parting Thou,
This mould of clay, Say ! surviveth how?

"Even vernal groves 'll look herds of cacti,
if the nectar of Thy mien, Me not imbibe.
"In woods, whatever falls, 'll be crest prize,
Thy presence makest 'every odd, a paradise.'

Couplet: *"There, winged will be mates,*
Sylvan green's regal grove
Zoic-life my pal-pets,
In company of my Beloved. 14

"Meadows will be my mellow and leas my glee,
Under blest crowning hands of sylvan deities.
"The sylvan penates like parents,
Will, sure take care at every tramp.

"High bowers with arched corridors,
Will carpet all along a litter, vernant floor.
"pebbles and dust for this daughter of the Earth,
'll back up my every effort.

Chattels=movable property ; chagrins=worries.
Tramp=sound of foot steps.

" My fortune boon, with some pricks stubborn,
'll chance me Thy care, in plucking out thorn.
"Gazing upon Thy lotus feet,
I shall be cheerful like a bee.

"I'll see in tribes, the innocence of crude lands,
Who fathered mankind with ancestral hands.
"Thou depictst woods-a home of awe and woe,
Yet is lesser to the parting sorrow.

Couplet:

"Humbly I refrain O Kind !,
Bearing this in mind—
Fate's design I decline,
Pray ! leave me not behind. 15

" Pray ! leave Me not, O Soul of My soul !
Lest; brood ! what befallth to this mould.
"Long before Thou shallst come back from exile,
This frame of clay will puff it's last sigh.

"Toils of luxury can't toy with Me,
Me see no hurts in Thy buoying company.
"Thy ambrosial lotus feet art the life,
Just on their nectar, Me, the bee survives.

"At times, stretched path may fill Thy calves,
Labored pearls may shine on Thy lot.
"The eager path blest by Thy feet,
May cling all over it's dusty fleet,

"During pauses of passes and halts under trees,
I shall fan Thou and lave Thy feet.
"Doth it behove that Thou toil in penance,
And me Thy page loll in opulence.

Toils of luxury=chains of luxury; Opulence=richness

Couplet: *"My wretched Self has hard-heart,*
And beats stopt not.
Still survives, the words harsh—
'Of separation, from My Lord," 16

Sic, saying sick Siya could not bear
'The pangs of a bereaved' even in words.
Wilting mould looked as if the soul had left,
Ram realized Her ache of being bereft.

Ram spake to Siya, not to brood,
To make no moan and join Him to woods.
'Hush up grief, sob is inapt,
'Poise ! prepare for the journey, fast!

Ram fell at mother's feet to bid adieu,
On mother's cheeks rolled anew, warm dews.
Her hand's touch and parched tongue blest—
"come back soon O Children! relieve people's distress.

"Shall the tides of fate ever turn in favour,
and my eyes witness arrival of charming pair.
"O Time ! pass in a wink and stay O Breath !
Till my winkless petrified eyes, see the two, back.

Couplet: *"When again it 'll chance,*
That I clasp You to bosom.
When again 'll I glance,
The daily joy of my son." 17

"When the curfewed air of the tempest,
Will turn to peopled glad-gale in this palace?
"When 'll again my eyes imbibe my child's mien,
'When 'll I summon you calling 'Son ! my darling.

"My life is lifeless rampike without my son,
When again 'll I have Ram as vernal blossom."

Her words choked yet thoughts fatigued not,
Ram consoled many ways, the consumed heart.

To bid farewell Seeta bowed to mother,
"I go leaving thou while I should have served.
'Unfavourable heaven hath fallen on Me,
And I am slacking my duties towards thee."

Tears of a mother fadest any ink of any bard,
Sic, I can't pencil pain of Kaushalya's heart.
Gathered she blest-"Siya ! your wifehood,
Like holy Ganges flow, may that continue."

Couplet: *Looked as if the noose of fate,*
Is parting cow and heifer,
Going Seeta touched mother's feet
And hugged, bowed, hugged, bowed and revered. 18

When, the tidings reached to Laxman,
His doleful rush moved in confusion.
Ocean of emotion pearled through wet blink,
He fell at Ram's feet, with hasp of arms he clinged.

In hush of reverence, with humble gaze,
Yet his tender sore through mute face spake—
An anxious silence waited elder's behest,
Whether forsaketh or to forest He taketh.

Ram kent on Lakhan's face the vent of turmoil,
As if already had decided to go with; in exile.
Fraternal warmth, temperth kin-threads to steel,
Needth no cramped peal but a mute appeal.

Ruby threads in eyes, melting heart on cheeks,
Ram read Lakhan, spake soft, as He is—

Consumed=obsessed.

"No conclusion should cloud your mind Lakhan!
What cometh in end is ever happy one.'

Couplet:

"Mother, father, mentor, Master,
Who obeyth with reverence
He upholdth his birth,
Lest life goes in vain." 19

"Such pious stride is a deifying step,
Lest, in mundane, dwarf's life is ever strayed.
"Bear this in mind and serve parents,
Balm and heal, their sores of My absence.

" 'ts for the grief of King and for his age,
'ts worth, if a son like you stays.
"Besides, Bharat-Shatrughan, the two of us,
are not at home to take up the onus.

"Unescorted father, and unmastered Awadh,
if, be ignored by us, is not worth.
"To subjects, see!, bringeth sufferings whose reign,
He is rated for earnings all stygian."

Warmth of Ram's word for Lakhan had,
Pangs as fevered as the chill of the death.
In misty dismay Lakhan lost his flesh,
Wilted he, as if frost had kissed lotuses.

Couplet:

Over powered by love,
Lakhan clasped Ram's feet,
'Thou the Master and me, the slave,
Mayst take me or quit. 20

"tho' Thou havest advised what doth meet.
My faint mind, but, can't take it.
"Thy advice is for Self-possessed and noble,
Who are fit to be taught Ved's gospels.

"Me, ever was sheltered, as a mere little one,
Was nurtured in Thy pampering affection.
"Thou art my world, I know no else,
Nor parents, nor patrons, nor preceptor nor pals.

"Thou art father's fostering, a motherly touch,
A fraternal fervour, a friend's fidus.
"All affluence Thou art, all afflatus,
Thou art my Lord, I know this much.

"The piety, propriety are the teaching for the one,
Who aims at glory, riches or the heaven—
"But in Thy feet who findth his home,
Should ever he be forgone to stay forlorn?

Couplet: *"My life's every while,*
For Thou ist made,
How come Thou goest in exile,
Discarding own conscious shade?" 21

Fraternal words full of fondness,
Pierced thro' unto the soul's depth.
"Go ! take leave of mother, soon come back,
Come on ! the sovereign of Sylvan waits."

A favouring command was Lakhan's delight,
As if every wrong hath proved for him just right.

Persistent devotion prevailed, and on pinion of thrill,
He approached Sumitra, the mother queen.
The Reverent son, Lakhan before her, bowed head,
While his mind yet with Siya Ram stayed.

Mother's keenness kent the hidden melancholy,
When asked; Lakhan related the whole story.

Fidus (*L*) =Faith ; Afflatus=Knowledge.

Every word hammered over awed mother,
As a doe is woe-begone at fire around her.

He feared mother's love, might frustrate his plan,
'Things would take a turn wrong.'
With timid pause, fumbling he asked to go,
Brooded he 'she bids me or says no.'

Couplet: *Recalling genial Siya-Ram,*
And King's genuine fervour,
'Yet mean queen tricked the flam',
—brooding this Sumitra was stirred. 22

Soon Sumantra setting back storms in mind,
Perceiving it was no grieving time.
She mulled over milieu of melee,
"May her modesty be mute with no mutiny."

Possessing as she, in her gentle tone,
Spake soft " heed O my son!
"You discover in Siya, the mother,discern the father, in Ram,
Let your faith make, you ever dear to Ram.

"Splendour of this town, before the woods fails,
That alone is 'blest-Awadh' where Ram dwellth.
"In this place, without Ram; let me make you clear,
You have no business to stay here.

"The father, family, fraternity and friends,
Through their affinity to Ram; judge them.

Couplet: *"Your fortune and mine too,*
Have rewarded to serve Siya Ram,
Your blest mind is solemnly drew
To the holy feet of Siya Ram. 23

Melee=dispute

"A mother just only is said, blest,
Whose son solemnly is, to Ram, devoted.
"For the bairn, hostile to Ram, the womb is blamed,
Lest she had better remained barren.

" 'Ts only due to your chance worth while,
That Ram is moving to the exile.
"Greatest reward of all virtues, merits, deeds,
Is instinct of devotion to the fraternity.

"With no morbid feelings but the pellucid stream,
serve Siya Ram with great esteem.
"Sylvan greens 'll, for you, be regal carpets,
On the paths which 'pedestrian Ram' ll tread.

"The Riches of nature fade pomp of man's hand,
Further more with Ram 'ts all benevolent.
"You exist just for comfort of Ram,
See Him ! gravely gorges may not harm.

Stanza: *"Yes ! O my son, thus you discern,*
To you this is my gospel,
"Watch ! gales intense, watch gallaries in dense,
Be vigilant of grazes, gravels.
"See ! none may harm, your Siya-Ram,
They may not recall us, in their daily bliss."
Thus blessed she and gave him leave-
"may faith in you ever cherish."

Couplet: *Having bowed before mother,*
Niching in heart the behest,
With his anxious chill more fevered,
Laxman departed in haste. 24

Bairn=child.

THE LEAVE TAKING

Where Ram was, Lakhan went straight,
On glad wings, finding the company of beloved.
Bowed to the feet of Ram and Seeta,
Accompanied them to the King's palace.

Excepting Lakhan, whole town was emanciated,
Wailed all grieved hearts and sad faces—
"Well nigh the fulfilling shore of mellow,
The barks of our fortune havest shattered in shallow,"

They beat their heads and wrung their hands,
Like the Clipt bird, helplessly laments.
Peopled air seemed storm of wail,
With sleet of sighs and weeping hail.

Minister woke the king out of his stupor,
Who struggled with lids and saw to the fore;
Stood Ram Siya with Lakhan in reverence,
Highly strung dilemma of father turned intense.

Couplet: *King eyed with helpless hope*
And hopelessness of the dilemma,
His weak arms enveloped
Ram Lakhan and Siya. 25

His words drowned in flood of emotions,
Overwhelmed he pressed them to his bosom.
Sick grip held arm of Ram but slipt,
Gaze of King asked Ram to sit.

During parting of the dearest of dears,
Tongue shrunk yet moments hung as long as years.

Sleet=frozen hail ; Hail=storm.

Ram touched father's feet, the reverence of adieu,
And begged blessings for the time to ensue—

" I beg thy blessings and behest with delight,
The hour of blithe, why thou dost take as blight?
'From path of duty, one if strays,
Earns ignomy and incurs disgrace.'

Still under spell of love, the King asked—
"My boy ! of you sages say 'Ram is Lord?'
" Its verdict of man and words of Ved,
The fate judgeth the doer and fixeth good or bad."

Couplet: *"But here, the sin one sows,*
The Benign reaps fruits,
This puzzle none knows,
When the fate blights and when bestoweth." 26

King filled his words with all honest means,
To detain Ram, but all in vain.
He discovered in Ram, an opinionated Will,
The virtuous drive until fulfilled;

The strong minded, fore-sighted as He is,
Will not stay back for ease or cheese.
Then seeing Seeta, fatherly soul fevered,
Recollecting himself, the King admonished Her;

With hardships and uneven life of woods,
For what She was not made; why pick up She should.
But then home's cheese, wood's tease could not mould,
Only Ram's foot prints Seeta treasured in Her soul,

The King, Kins and preceptor's wife,
Everyone else too warned with miseries of Jungle life—
"None hath exiled you to the forests,
Take words of elders as the behest."

Couplet: *Tho' advice was to allay*
Thick came like noose
Upon Seeta; like moon rays,
Makest restless, the goose. 27

Seeta's modest mum had no words,
But then, Kaikeyi's flare went berserk.
She brought xanthic robes as was her flam,
Shameless she spake, in sham soft tone-

"Lust of the King for you, is his life,
but his virtues, his words need to survive.
"He is too soft to shake off this lust,
He may fall into disrepute lest.

"He will forfeit his virtues for the next world,
than ask you to proceed to the woods.
"What is now desired, what pleases you,
O Ram! O Best of Raghu's!; you do."

Kaikeyi's advice for Ram, was rejoice,
But pierced like thunderbolt, the King, through and through.
While fainting bout consumed the King's wake,
As a hermit at once Ram, costumed self.

Couplet: *Reverently bade adieu,*
To the parents and He left,
Having equipped for jungles due,
He left every one bereft. 28

□

Allay=soothe, relieve.

11

Every idea that strengthens you, must be taken up and every thought that weakens you, must be rejected.

—Swami Vivekanand

HERE JOY/ HERE JOLT

Ram, Siya, Lakhan in reclusive apparels,
Out of regal doors they appeared.
Meanwhile Siya asked Mandavi, shrutikeerti, the Sisters,
For care of Her heifer, Her doe, Her birds.

At the pious doors of grotto of Vashishtha,
The Lord, stood as a suppliant hermit.
Crown hand of Guru ist the crest shield,
Is the unseen care, under the lee.

Guru crowned his hand over the three,
Ram captivated all hearts by His courtesy.
Moaning friends, maids and groaning civic,
Ram entrusted them to the Guru's aegis.

The Lord lauded Guru, spake with folded hands—
"Me Lord ! be to them, their own parents."
Then to bereft faces, Ram turned for farewell,
Gazes welled seeing him in hermit's apparels.

Aegis=care, protection; Under the lee=Protected from storm.

Couplet: *"Parting is parlous for all,"*
softly Ram voiced—
"He alone is my best pal,
Who brings back King's blithe". 1

"See! ye all! O attentive citizens!"
With aches none of my mothers is smitten."
To the perilous plebs and panicked town,
He bade advices to the grieved throng.

Uma-Mahesh, Ganesh, He invoked,
Bowing to Guru, Ram set forth,
What to say of livings, every brick and stone
Of the town seemed as if making a moan.

Whole Awadh drowned, as He sallied,
In the deeps of oceans of melancholy.
And above, sallow face of low welkin,
Clouded and wailed over town, melpomene.

The King woke, when his stupor broke,
With new spell of woes, he was walloped,
'Ram hath left but my soul lingers,
and now to what this body of clay adheres?"

Recovering a bit the King muttered—,
"O Sumantra ! follow Him with your chariot."

Couplet: *"Siya's world was within ramparts,*
Lavish care, my sons, too had,
Pick them up on chariot,
Show round jungle, then bring them back." 2

Parlous=perilous, troublesome.
Melpomene=tragedy muse; Sallow face=sickly look.
Walloped=Stroked, whipped.

"The twins are true, firm and stoical,
And may decline to your proposal,
"Then you do entreat with folded palms,
to send back Seeta, ask my Ram.

"Avail yourself of the opportune time,
When seeing jungle Seeta getth alarmed.
"Tell to Her my behest, my advice, my request,
To return back home, not to go to forests.

"Now here in Awadh, now there with parents,
Can stay where ever you feel content.'
"O Sumantra ! try ! by all possible means,
She cometh home, try to convince.

"It 'll be the succor of my breath,
Lest, this episode 'll end in my death."
With acme of aches he fell into swoon,
Muttering,'O! bring them to me! bring back soon!

Couplet: *Sumantra bowed head to behest,*
Got ready a swift chariot,
To the Three, rushed he in haste,
To the city's outskirts. 3

In the flood of peopled purlieus of town,
Sumantra viewed the moaning crowd all around.
Sumantra submitted to Ram King's message,
And to mount them on chariot he persuaded.

Ram, Siya, Lakhan mounted the chariot,
In the mind, they bowed to own land of Awadh.
Wheels rolled on aching breast of motherland,
And Ram's sacred journey, thus began.

Purlieus=outskirts.

Madding crowd saw Ram had already left,
Followed they, bare feet, barren heart and bereft.
The Lord used many ways, them to dissuade,
They turned back home, but again came back.

Towering town, richly spread looked doomed,
Every lone looked alone in the crowd of gloom.
None shared their own world of night mare,
In the din, every sigh had its own flare.

Couplet: *Their hearths seemed to them death,*
Men, women looked like manes,
In riches peeped wealth of shades,
Ayodhya looked barren land. 4

It's not the orbs but mind's eye views,
So in groves, greens, people saw deserted blues.
Even gentle breeze scorched, gardens looked parched,
On curfewed Rajpath, melancholy's troops marched.

Equine, bovine, taurine, inmates,
Oscine, passerine and cornine pets,
All dumb pets petrified, stood by the paths,
Seemed penciled predella on the canvas.

The divinity painted the Awadh evergreen,
But Kaikeyi, the queen axed that, it seemed.
In the peopled air, the poison, she puffed,
Without Ram-Siya, the Awadh turned tough.

Heavenly homes, all haves they forwent,
'For us, without Ram luxuries 'r not meant.'

Dissuade=Discourage from.
Equine=Horse; Bovine=Cow; Taurine=Ox; Cornine=Crow; Passerine=Sparrow; Oscine=Song bird

Sic, in their minds resolved all they—,
"Where Ram taketh abode, we 'll stay."

Couplet: *Leaving in their homes,*
The aged grey and nonage green,
All populace accompanied Ram,
Ayodhya ran along Ram's wheel. 5

THE FIRST SOJOURN

Happy, Full to the banks of his heart,
At the banks of Tamasa, Ram made first halt.
Ram saw His people overwhelmed with love,
His compassion was filled with woe.

'bivouac with Ram is equally blessed.
And is equally holy as Awadh, itself.'
Nor glebes, nor blebs for the plebs mattered,
Assured of itself the Ram 's succor.

Their dews of toils* under the bare feet,
Those touched Ram and ached Him in deep.
Ram told of their duties in honeyed words,
Duties to the Hearts, hearths and to the Mother Earth.

But amiable Self of Ram was at an odd,
For this love of people to bid adieu.
In the nocturn cradle worn people fell asleep,
And the two watches of the tranquil slipped.

Then Ram addressed minister with hushed lips
'Drive ! Chariot making tracks mixed.

Bivouac=temporary company; * blebs

Couplet: *There was no other way,*
Tho' was heavy to leave.
For, it was time's mandate,
For the object to fulfil. 6

The three, mounted the chariot, recalling Lord Shiv,
The minister, right then, did drive.
Tracks of wheels he muddled and blurred,
Mysterious Lord's mystic purpose to serve.

All they woke up at the wee dawn,
They cried and yelled " Lord Ram hath gone."
"Ram! O Ram! where are Thou?
Benumbed we were, lost everything now.

"My heavy lids have laden my life,
My Ram is lost I can't survive.
"Without Raghuveer, O ! Woe is me,
A curse will, on my life be.

"Less to say of our miseries, the better,
O fate ! prize death for this life, the better".
Their empty steps dragged back in remorse,
They survived the shock for the glimpse of hope.

Couplet: *'That long exile 'll end,*
Ram 'll be back again,'
They for ensuring Ram's return,
Began sacred observance. 7

AT THE GANGES

At the holy banks of pellucid Ganges,
By the name of Shringverpur' a township dwelt.
Reached Sumantra with Seeta and the two,
Glad hearts they beheld the celestial flow.

Delighted Ram alighted from the wheels,
And fell prostrate with esteemed zeal.
Ganges motherly touch driveth all sorrow,
Ganges blest then, now, and 'll bless morrow.

Ganges ist celestial gift to mankind,
Today on its sands, Ram's footprint signed.
Thro' the Lord's gaze, the waves of the Ganges,
Filled His hearts full to the banks.

They plunged in Ganges, to the fill they drank,
The water, the nectar; their fatigue to drain.
Whose, very name relieveth the toil of worldly freight,
Felt fatigued; for He followth the world's ways.

Couplet: *Ram, the formless Almighty*
Descendth from paradise,
To show path of immortality,
The Immortal came man-sized. 8

Tidings of princes got deep among tribes,
Guh, the tribal king rushed in joyous surprise.
He gladly called near and dear ones,
With eats, fruits roots he ran to welcome.

His endless thirst fixed his distant gaze,
And imbibed, through eyes, the ocean of visage.
Doth sincere soul need ever decorousness,
Or commerce of pomp or boasting business?

Thus, won by the heart of the host,the genuine.
Ram accosted Nishaad as His friend.
"Sight of thy feet ist sign of welfare,
Thy care dispelth all despair.

"Tho' Thou seest a pal, I'm Thy page,
By Thine feet, let my door be blessed.

'Guh ! your true heart I kent, realized,
But My father hath commanded Me otherwise.'

Couplet: *"For just four years and ten,*
Me life shall be of hermit,
In the Sylvan dense; hence
It meetth not to go in hamlets." 9

Words as thunderbolt pierced thro' and thro'.
Stood as rampike, looked at Ram, Guh.
Puzzling words heard Guh and the rest,
Their toes plunged into sands in distress.

Their crude folly could not ken,
The exile of Ram by wisdom of Good reign.
'Can they be mother-father or parent of perils
Who have sent such children to exiles.

A voice wronged them that King had done right,
There by chance had blessed our sight.
Then the chief of tribes, chose for the three,
For resting place a rose-wood tree.

Ram declared it as a beautiful place,
Villagers returned back paying their homage.
As, from on high, blanketed the twilight
Ram retired for prayers of eventide.

Couplet: *Meanwhile Guh carpeted bed,*
*Of the leaves and Kush**
Brought in cups of foliage,
The tubers, fruits and roots. 10

Having partaken with Siya, Sumantra and Lakhan,
To sleep Raghuveer layed down.

---

*Kush(a type of grass)

Lakshman then kneaded Ram's feet,
Till he perceived Lord hath fallen asleep.

Then he rose and to sleep he asked Sumantra,
With bow and arrow he sat on alert.
On a vigil of his own-mandate,
Worked by duty, a warrior sat.

Guh called on his trusted watchmen,
Carefully at various points he stationed them.
Guh saw King of kings lying on grass,
His heart aches over his eyes' brim crossed.

He poured befo' Lakhan, the deluge of his dolor,
His palsied anguish with Lakhan he shared.
"King's palace, where all ye dwelt,
Hath it's splendour where heaven fail—

Couplet: *"Where boggy couches cradled,*
And fragrant breeze drowsed ye,
"Where cozy tapestries lulled,
And the Trills rose ye— 11

"Where splendour of Ram falls on jewels inwrought,
And of jewels falls on the ramparts.
"Where, on richly bed rustles the silk,
Where lactescent sheet whispers its crisp.

"Apparels', jewels', pearls', petals' lush,
maketh pride of cupid and Rati, to blush.
"Through oriels moon peeped in leisure-winks,
Of Siya-Ram into such cozy attics.

"Very same Siya-Ram lie on pallets,
My laden heart is fevered to behold that.
"King, kins, queens, and pals and maids,
All cherished whom like own breath,

Pallets=Sheet of grass; Oriels=big windows ; Leisure-winks=sleep.

"Alas ! today sleepth on ground, spent,
Nay, Seeta, the princess of puissance, affluence.
In Her both houses was lavished endless,
Pastime of fate puts Her on pallets.

Couplet: *"for Siya-Ram, the new-couple,*
It meets not for Kaikeyi,
To put them on her crooked spell,
And Awadh in misery." 12

"The wicked woman hath become an axe,
And fell on the Banyan of solar race.
"Woe is me ! whole world is a woe,
They lie in bareland, O Lakhan ! Lo !."

But then Lakhan treated of doubts of Guh,
Spake sweet wit, all honey imbued
"No trap, trapes, trapan, No trick, No treason,
The Mundane is a trade of own action.

"The life is fragrant garland of bliss,
Wreathed by aching thorns to make it.
"Rapture or the tortune are captures of fate,
And are all illusions of worldly freight.

"Man's nescience dazzles the mortal coil,
At the glittering affair of pomps of soil.
"The hearth, home, haves, the heaven, the hell,
These hoax the Human through folly's veil.

Couplet: *"In fancy or in nightmare,*
A beggar turns to Lord,
Or King reduces to pauper,
So, must waking eyes look to world." 13

Hoax=play practical joke on; Treason=Treachery; Trapes=Idle suit (Kaikeyi); Trapan=design, share

"In the business of breath, think in wide sense,
The earthly commerce hath no loss or gain.
"Reasoning thus do not blame anyone,
it's night of delusion, so grieve not in vain.

"It's mere folly to be clever for mundane,
Which is delusive race of greed for gain.
"Only to mystic yogi's this mystery is known,
In dreams of slumber, they are awaken alone.

"Aloof from the clay, the potteries and puppets,
For the highest truth, these yogis quest.
"Dazzles of pomps, lest, is mist of delusion,
None the truth it bringeth, but blurth the vision.

"When virtues bring 'dawn of wisdom' in man,
From his long slumber he, then, sees blessed eaon.
"Then votary's devotion to the Ram's feet,
With thoughts, words, deeds, is achieved."

Couplet: *"Ram, the immortal behaves,*
As mortals by own will.
To right the wrongs of knaves,
He came to right all ills." 14

"Let this anthelion enlighten your core,
Let infatuation may cloud in you no more.
"With divinity of Ram, may your soul be hallowed,
Know! Ram as infinite, that much you need to know."

With paeans of Ram; Lakhan dispersed Guh's mist,
While he was yet recounting, unveiled the East.
Before the Sanguine orb, the Sun had hopped up,
The very hope of Sanguine world; Lord Ram woke up.

They had already doffed regal dresses,
But still had crowns of princely tresses.

Sanguine world=confident world; sanguine orb=Red orb(sun)
Anthelion=luminous light about.

With the tree-sap; the two matted their locks*,
While Sumantra stood completely sapped and shocked.

What the king had charged him, he then spake—
'to escort ye on chariot, to the banks of Ganges.
"All scruples and doubts setting at rest,
Do bring Ram, Lakhan Siya back.'

Couplet:

His melancholy fit,
Had burst into tears,
He fell at Ram's feet
And further he beseeched— 15

"Mercy! me Lord! O Merciful!! Mercy!
Awadh may not feel desertion, you see."
Sumantra kneeled, Ram lifted him and admonished,—
"O Elder! thou havest experimented the Truth."

"For the virtue, Sibi, Dadhich, Harishchandra suffered,
Hardships of Truth have aching pleasure.
"Through many trials, many more in the past,
Had upheld virtue, till their last.

"Secret and Sacred pages said
Above all virtues standth the Truthfulness.
"With no efforts no penance, My chance gains,
The easy road to virtue, with no pains.

"Hard paths of Truth, the blistered steps trod,
And made easy for Me this untrodden road.
"If I forsake Truth, for the sake of comfort,
'll bring infamy and purport wilt not be served.

---

*Ascetics with some tree-sap keep tresses matted.
Desertion=Act of deserting.

Couplet: *"Convey my words to father,*
Conveying obeisance to him—
'Dear sire ! pray ! do not bother,
And be not troubled for Me.' 16

"Now we see possibility in thy puisance,
That thy prudence shalt care my parents.
"that thou 'll care my father is not dipt
In the miserable scorch of the grief."

All immersed full to soul in the depth of colloquy,
The circling crowd and the tribal chief, Guh.
A poignant whisper from Lakhan then came,
But Ram asked him to hush, instant.

Embarrassed Ram, adjourned Sumantra, then
'to repeat not, to father the remarks of Lakhan.
In defeatism minister, then reproduced King's message.
For Seeta, at least, to return back.

"For King's survival and revival of Subjects,
Let She back home, both homes* eagerly wait.
"King's entreaty was all love and ache,
Siya 'll be panacea if returnth back."

"Language of eyes those conveyed King's grief,
With my mortal lips I can't brief."
Then, the merciful Ram in countless ways,
Admonished Siya the Awadh's distress.

"Siya ! be panacea for pangs of palace,
The parents, preceptors, plebs, pals, populace.
"Must you return for Awadh's essence,
Must you return for Sarayu's existence."

Prudence=clever management ; Colloquy=conversation.
*Palaces in Ayodhya and Janakpuri

Seeta replied to Sumantra—

"Heed ! O Wise Elder ! can ever a shadow,
Be torn away from its substance.
"Without Sun, Sunlight hath no subsistence,
Nor moon be uncoupled from it's radiance."

Couplet: *"My hush revereth in thou, a father*
But my pang speak out
Lords' lotus feet's nectar, the elixir,
I can't survive without." 17

"A rich brought up, with it's splendour,
My childhood witnessed all lavish care.
"and in earnest care of My in-laws,
Attribute of My own sire I saw."

"But, my heavenly abode to me is desert,
And hearth is a pyre, without consort.
"Daily crimson of the eastern horizon,
Wilt poison My bleached life with more affliction.

"Every vernal bloom will bring to Me new gloom,
Only thorns of doom in Me 'll mushroom.
"The celestial pomps added in worldly fete,
At My Lord's lotus feet, all do negate.

"All sickly-prickly passes have heavenly comfort,
In the fortunate company of My Consort.
"As the Sylvan syke is vital pellucid,
Through impassable rocks fearlessly proceed,

Syke=brook, rivulet.

Couplet: *"Likewise My Sylvan life,*
With tribes, beasts and birds,
Wilt bring Me a natural blithe
In company of My consort." 18

"Make request for Me at parent's feet,
Not to be' pensive for Me, the least.
"My Master, I have ever nigh Me,
And his Younger brother on vigilant duty.

"My toilfree strides 'll cheerfully cross,
The peaks, pricks, rills, hills, rocks hillocks.
"Nature hath carpeted lae, for my strides blister-free,
And for melting toil-dews, it'll fan soft lee."

Soft jingling of Seeta's lips,
Deep to the soul of Sumantra pricked.
In the fainting fit, failed his wit,
Ram tried to ebb minister's stormy fix.

Sumantra set on his efforts to go with,
But then, Ram replied very persuasive.
Ram's behest either could not be breached,
And then fate had dictated it's cruelties.

Bowed to the three, then he turned back,
Heavy of soul with burdensome steps.

Couplet: *As he drew bridle, wheels to drag,*
Horses jaded and neighed.
It was dumb animal's language,
Turning gaze to Ram they conveyed. 19

Lae=green lawns, lee=the wind

THE ARTLESS HELMSMAN

When even beasts felt so sombre,
Of father, mothers, priests least to say, the better.
Ram compelled and sent Sumantra back,
Forth with they reached holy banks of Ganges.

Ram called the helmsman, yet he cometh not,
Though he kent who standth, is 'at the helm of world.'
This artless boor, denied his boat to moor,
For, the wonderful wonders of wonderous feet, he knew.

"My heart rocks for my means of panary
By this canoe-boat I maintain family.
"Dust of Thine lotus feet have some nostrum,
'ts said if transformed a rock to woman.

"My boat is further soft so it's easier task,
Thy touch will puff soul in my boat to a lass.
"at a loss, my boat goes as hermit's spouse,
At a loss I'll be, for up keep of my house.

"Commerce of my folly, knowth none other trade,
So command me Lord ! Thy feet to lave.

Stanza:

No fare of ferry I do seek,
And my affair is only one,
I can't afford and let Thou board
Until I fulfil my sine qua none.
I do swear, by Thy O Sire !
I can dare even Lakhan's shaft,
But until I have, Thy feet laved,—
'll not ferry Thou cross the waves.

At a loss=puzzled; panary=earnings ; boor=rude fellow; Nostrum=secret remedy.
Sine qua none(*L*)= prerequisite (i.e. to wash His feet.)

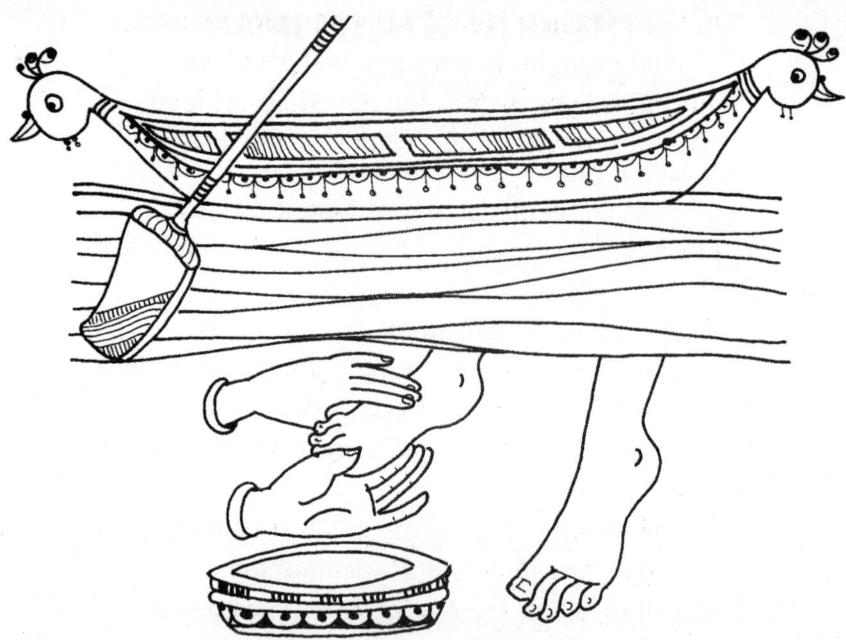

Distitch:

At lout utterance and blunt,
But from his fond breast,
Lord smilt gazed aslaunt,
At Siya's and Lakhan's face. 20

With a tender smile blest then Lord,
"Do ! what prevents your loss,
"Be quick ! bring Ganges and lave My feet,
The time runs out; promptly take us across."

Whose name, in mundane it-self is bark,
For the mortal coil, to cross the bar,
The Divinity who is at the helm of cosmos,
For whose three strides the universe was short,

Very same Ram, maketh a mansized request,
To the helmsman, to cross the Ganges.
The celestial stream was bemused by Ram's voice,
Looking to the sire-Nails of Ram*, she rejoiced.

---

*Holy Ganges hath originated from the toe nail of the Supreme Vishnu.

On Ram's behest Kewat rushed to pious waves,
And brought, in a trough, water to lave.
From his eyes over flown the eddies of love,
Medleyed with water; Ram's feet he laved.

Blessedness of this man even Saints cannot vie,
Which the holy Sand viewed, even heaven envied.
Joy of Ganges, full to banks, on his boat splashed,
While the welkin witnessed, scene of innocent faith.

Couplet: *Having laved feet, took holy sips,*
With family and kiths,
First crossing the souls of his stirps,
Took the Lord across, in bliss. 21

The silky-milky spread, was creased by oars,
The waving of boat, waved glad tides in core.
As if Ganga Herself took the boat in her hands,
They crossed the stream to the other bank.

Getting down Siya Ram stood on banks,
With Guh and Lakhan, on carpet of quick sand.
While fell prostrated before Lord, the helmsman,
For empty to pay coins, Ram felt diffident.

Jaanki keenly kent Her beloved's regret,
Gladly She took out Her signet.
The gracious Lord offered 'take your toll.'
Clasped feet of Ram, the distressed soul.

"On what else wage, my will should wait?
While all wants, wails, woes now have wilted.
"For wages from ages I made toils,
Only this dawn earned for me the earnest toll.

Kewat=helmsman, boatman; Stirps=forefather

"Thy ope hands graced upon me, a pleb,
With handsome gains, me, the par-venu is blest.
"What ever Thou, while returning back,
Bestowst on me, I'll gladly accept.

Couplet: *The three travellers tried utmost,*
Took nought he, the thrilled
True Bhakti then Lord bestowed
And let him go fulfilled. 22

Then the Lord of Raghus bathed in Ganges,
And worshipped Lord Shiv making a clay image.
Folded hands Siya worshipped celestial river,
To accomplish Her simple desire

"Wish to worship at Thy banks, maa !
In safety My return with Husband and His fra."
From the depth of stream response came back,
Steeped in the nectar of love and grace—

"Whatever divine I do find O Seeta !
And the shine world do hath, is all Thine O Seeta !
"Thou, the mater, puffst Soul in dummy raw,
Thine divinity deifieth the man of straw.

"Thou deignedst me, for a prayer to me,
'ts no humble prayer, it's a favour to me.
"Yet O reverenced ! bless Thou, I must,
Just in view to prove my words."

Couplet: *"With Lord, His fra ; Thy self,*
From my depth I bless
In safety shall return back,
With divineness wide-spread. 23

Par-venu=the poorman who suddenly becomes rich.
Mater=divine mother; Deign=think fit.

GUH, THE ESCORT WITH FOOT TRAVELLERS

Seeta rejoiced and felt composed,
To find the Ganges favourably disposed.
When Ram bade Guh, the farewell,
Guh's throat dried and wet eyes welled.

Parched words hesitantly from scorched heart,
Of Guh came out all with no art—
"Thou callst me a kin, a friend,
Let me observe my duty at my end.

"O Lord ! I'm Thy slave, a bond page,
May I usher Thou to woods as cortege.
"Among the bowers in the manless dense,
I wish to fashion grotto with own hands."

When Ram kent depth of his love,
Lord took him with, for bliss of Guh.
Then, Guh summoned all his kinsmen,
And sent them back with kind assurance.

Couplet: *At the brink of holy spread,*
On sloppy bed of ticklish sand,
To the Ganges adieu They bade,
Bowed They with reverence. *24*

□

12

If I am in dark, let me light a lamp.

—*Brahmrishi Vishwatma Bawra*

IN ASHRAM OF BHARADWAJ

With thoughts immersed in Ganesh and Mahesh,
They all disappeared into Sylvan bushes.
Ram with Siya Lakhan and His friend,
Halted under a bower, while bowing leaves fanned.

Comfort is there in cozy mind,
Ram slept in cradle of all odd-nite.
The next dawn, begun their southernly strides,
Till they reached Sacred Prayag at the twilight.

In the setting crimson shone flags of fanes,
At the holy triune confluence.
In confluence, the trine influence of streams,
Vie with each other, men's sins to cleanse.

The triteless trust on this sacred place,
Had turned tristesse into triumphs since ages.
Among rests, this place hath its exquisite throne,
And the immortal Banyan, as umbrella, denoteth.

Trine=threefold; Triune=three in one situation.
Tristesse=sadness; Triteless=not decaying.

Couplet: *'ts hallow milieu creates mellow,*
In the pilgrim throngs.
On the chants of saints, waves rebellow
And dance-far all along. 1

For some mo inky flow* hath discrete go,
As if vieing with milky flow for own ego.
But then worthy swarthy Yamuna dissolveth herself,
Into pious poised flow of pellucid Ganges.

Thus is claimed 'on the both holy banks',
Are sitting pilgrim souls dipt in endless penance.
Some visible forms, some unseen frames,
Are sitting all along leaving no sand.

Ram was delighted reaching Prayag, the Holiest,
And the Prayag was delighted receiving the Supreme Guest.
The green glory scattered along the two flanks,
Ram witnessed in bliss, full to the banks.

Ram retold the glory of divine spot,
Thus splendour of Prayag was further raised aloft.
Befo' Vesper could scatter it's dark,
Ram performed worships and reached doors of Bharadwaj.

Couplet: *At Bharadwaj's feet Ram fell,*
He clasped Ram to bosom,
The bliss what high sage felt,
Was of Oneness with Brahma. 2

The visible form of The Ancient of days,
Cometh as palpable bliss to the abbeys.
Sure ! merits of chains of lives of the sage,
Had fructified and today was blessed.

Rebellow=resound.
*Dark flow of Yamuna river.

The sage offered loving homage to the Supreme Guest,
And offered fruits, tubers, shoot, orchard-fresh.
The prolific life of sage was, thus teemed,
He offered fruits to Lord, it's all frolic of Supreme.

In the lavish welcome ; with much relish,
Siya Ram Lakhan, Guh parlook every dish.
Refreshed Ram forgot long journeyed Calves,
Then Bharadwaj addressed in accent of love

"My penance, prayers and pious practices,
My patriotic piety to this pilgrim place,
"Have fully been rewarded this eve,
O Ram ! Thy sight in person I perceive.

Distitch: *"I had meditated on Divine,*
for ages and ages.
The very divinity I find,
O Ram ! in Thou, that exact." 3

Bharadwaj extolled–

"Thy perfect goodness appeared before me,
Thou must have accepted me as Thy devotee.
"In the mirky mire of mundane,
All arts, arms, arks are in vain.

"When man hath in Thou, unfeigned faith,
True ecstasy of soul he, then getth."
Shri Ram abashed on words of sage,
He then extolled the High sage in many ways.

" O Sage ! one getth true esteem, true raise,
Reverently, whom, Thou O pious! praise."

Art=trick ; Arms=power ; Ark=treasure.

Thus, the current of true souls had courteous exchange,
And the deluge of transport they gained.

The tidings aired from brinks to the bricks,
Flocked in plebs, saints, hermits, friars, ascetics.
The crowded eyes feasted on visage,
To all then Ram paid His homage.

Couplet: *Nightly-repose Ram had,*
In the Bhardwaj's hermitage,
At dawn in Prayag He bathed,
Revering Sage, the travellers proceeded. 4

Ram asked lovingly the High sage,
What road should they follow next?
"O Ram ! all roads, from Thee commence,
And in Thou all the roads end.

"Thou makest the path for the astrayed,
None the road is remote for Thine tread."
Yet, the sage called his pupils to escort,
Dozens eagerly vied their rush to go with the Lord.

With love they claimed 'I know the path',
But then Bharadwaj chose four of them to escort.
Reverently Ram bade the sage adieu,
And travellers proceeded on unknown move.

Deliberately the escort took them through Populous Purlieu,
Common eyes to chance on, The Blest view.
Common gazes were stuck until nimbus on path,
Went far and far and was lost.

With dazzled eyes and puzzled heart,
Grieved they returned sending hearts after strangers.

Brinks to the bricks=from river to town.
Purlieu=outskirts of town.

Couplet: *With great courtesy sent Ram,*
The fulfilled pupils back,
Gathering beatific moments in bosom,
Returned they, on winged steps. 5

Ram went below, bathed in Yamuna's worth-flow,
Which was as swarthy as His own glow.
Hearing that divine strangers were passing by,
Riverains ran unmindful of their toils.

The strange passers, they all beheld,
Feasting on visages, felicitated own self.
In the dauntless minds grew unlettered puzzle,
'Who? Are they real or ethereal ?'

Hearts seized with longing, and gazes were dazed,
Modesty could not ask, naivety could not guess.
Years grizzled whom, with ripeness of reasoning hints,
They recognized Ram with grey wit's dint.

Précis of pastime of princes pained plebs,
Mob moaned, "Regal couple had not done well."
The same mo, an ascetic with spiritual glow*,
Whose mystic ways, neither the plebs nor poets know,

Seemed, in pious shrine like a statue of faith,
Came with long waited sight with longing eyes wet.

Couplet: *The longing conscious recognized*
His own adored incarnate,
Brooks in bosom brimmed in eyes,
The sublime soul, fell prostrate. 6

---

* This mystic ascetic episode is the thrilling creation of Tulsidaas. May it be Tulsidaas himself or else but the reader may place himself in this episode to immerse self in the depth of Bhakti.

Dint=power ; Grizzled=grey haired; Riverain = inhabitants at the bank of river.

Ram upraised, locked him in embracing arms,
In warmth of grace melted, all chills of qualms.
As if the soul was blest by the elixir touch,
The gold, shone on his face, was splendorous.

Some said 'the Lord favourth the fervour of man,
Lo ! the Embodied compassion meetth embodied devotion.
Next the ascetic clasped the feet of Lakhan,
Overpowered with Love he took him to bosom.

Again he gathered dust from lotus feet of Mother,
And placed on his head this richest treasure.
Siya blest the child knowing to be Her own,
His mystic soul only Siya-Ram had known.

In his turn Guh fell at the feet of mystic Saint,
Who took him to bosom knowing him Ram's friend.
With the beauty of Ram, he filled his eye's bowl !
And poured this nectar into his hungry soul.

Couplet: *Ram, then several ways,*
Admonished Guh, the soul mate,
Bowing to his Master's behest,
Guh went his way back. 7

THE DAZZLED HAMLETS

They made to Yamuna, a renewed stoop,
Non-stop with Siya further proceeded the two.
Through Laes, under trees, on untrodden gneiss,
Trod a Determined, a Delicate and a Devotee.

With conquered conscious, in any crude course,
The cogent drive, even the odds can't coerce.
The passerby stood stagnated, amazed
Their nomadic move was chance, as if a pilgrim place.

Gneiss=stones ; Cogent=powerful; Coerce=stop

Confused by royal visage and regal marks,
While barefoot they, were in common garbs.
Nor clue hath wrought, nor dints of hints,
Failed their wits, failed all inklings.

They asked "we find all signs of high born,
Astral calculation fail at your guise, a vagabond.
"We doubt troubles are afoot, under your feet,
Thorny peaks, thirsty pricks, thickets and cliffs.

"On uneven passes your unskilled strides,
We enjoin to escort ye in the wilds."

Couplet: *Thus, the passerbys offered*
Overmastered by Love
Concerned they asked to Usher,
the strangers, on strange rove. 8

Lo ! Lord dost rejoice on their humanly concern,
However Ram gently askth them to return.
Hamlets that lay by the Lord's alleys,
Are envied by the Paradise itself.

Gods godules are quoted as saying today,
Lord's endless blessings crownth the plebs.
Wayside dwellers toiled on honest earthly fret,
Daily duties today, help them be upraised.

Their hands at work, their honest earthly deeds,
The Fruits of penance, piety, have achieved.
Denizen of Elysium praised 'it seemth, thus,
Here, for poor hearts, poor hearths Ram desertth Awadh.

Much blest are they, the men of clay,
At the doors of hay, on foot Ram wayed,

Enjoin=advise strongly; Afoot=around; Underfeet=in the way; Rove=wandering.

That day the peasants, the very saints of soil,
Were freed from to and fro business of mortal coil.

Couplet: *The umbrella of cloud's drift,*
And the green silk made the path,
The clime primed all with vernal sheet,
Glad nature opened it's rich ark. 9

Looked like welcoming arms, the green boughs,
The leaves oblated their lives on Ram's road.
As the travellers entered high Bamboo Sylvans,
Creaking welcome was bade by the litter cushion.

The birds warbled, brooklets recited,
On beats of nature, danced rills, cataracts.
At every step the three travellers felt,
The stretched soft palm of the Earth itself.

Bellowing beasts, lowing doe, cooing dove,
Ram beheldth all His own toys with love.

They moved in umbrella of corridors of green,
And in peopled alleys under sunny welkin.
Nameless people, the frame of earthly duties,
With shapeless wishes and unlettered piety,

Their colossal trust with their ample heart,
Goodly generosity got godly generous reward.
Blest inhabitants, those befell nigh Ram's passes,
Rushed to imbibe the nectar of the visage.

Couplet: *Sipped they the Elixir to the brim,*
Through their stunned view,
Dipped they in the brine of bliss,
As a pauper becomes par venu. 10

Clime=climate ; Ark=treasure box.
Litter=Dry leaves making floor of forest.

Thus, the bounty clouds blest the rains of blessings,
Thus flooded their souls full to the brinks,
And the gluts of desire were all vanished,
B'cause of the ope gate of grace that lavished.

Seeing cool lap of way-side Banyan,
They prayed Bhagwan to rest there till dawn.
Some brought urn full of soft water,
The voice of patois, conveyed all nectar.

Ram took request as behest of a child,
Under banyan shades rested for a while.

The dew of toil shone on divine faces,
The wrinkled dresses and crinkled tresses.
People, on visaged strangers, fixed the gaze,
All souls captivated by beauty peerless.

Couplet: *The crest of matted locks,*
And garbs of the hermit,
Crowd's strange gazes were locked
With imprint on their spirit. 11

Appearance of prince, apparels of hermits,
With Arms of warrior, charms of manifolds of cupids.
Strangers were curiosity among plebians,
And the strange mien of strange aliens.

Matted locks making crown over head,
Quiver on waist and bow by the broad chest.
The pearls of sweat shone as ornaments,
For etheric grace, poet's earthly pen wanes.

All stood there, with unstirred gaze,
Like a painted canvas, all men, all lasses.

Patois=crude language of village.

Each statue in love-thirst looked amazed,
As if by the flash of glow, a doe is dazed.

The women folk drew near, encircled Siya,
Shrank to ask in modesty and some awe.
Village damsels in the extreme of love,
They would ask Her but diffident to do so.

Couplet: *But then they threw themselves at feet,*
Of Siya, all modest
"Though civility doth not meet,
We ask about Thou yet.' 12

"One swarthy one fair both of tender age,
Princely glow shone both faces visaged.
"Autumnal full moon and aurum of Earth,
And emerald must borrow from Them, the worth.

"Our incivility, Thou please ! mayst pardon,
For our unformed utterance, we, the unlettered women.
"To any beauty, who bestowth Own grace,
How stand They to Thou? Tell us!"

Blooms of roses blossomed on Siya's face,
With Her smile She looked at Them abashed.
She looked at Them and to the Earth again,
With double delicacy, Her face crimsoned.

With fawn-eyes gesture whispered, Siya,
'Named, Lakhan fair frame is my brother-in-law.
With hem of garbs veiling faces glow,
Side long aslant spake through eye brows–

Hem=corner of cloth.

Couplet: *With a quick side-glance,*
With half veiled half revealed eyes
With angled slant,
Spake She in comely voice. 13

Not Her murmur but Her mum did nod,
that 'there, He ist My Lord.'
The bliss, women gathered was more than any gift,
Over anything which can be achieved.

With utmost devotion they all bowed,
To modest Divinity, the Ashish, they bestowed—
"Heaven's good grace may bless Thy goodness,
May Thy virtues spread boundless.

"O good lady ! may Thy wedding chain
Like of Uma-Shiv, have endless gain.
"Prithee ! shouldst Thy return by the same route,
May we be blest with divine vision again."

New kindred Strangers were soothed by patois,
But then kenning Ram's mind, Lakhan voiced,
And gently asked 'the way they should take',
All villagers felt sad and depressed.

Couplet: *Ebbing high tides of pain,*
Their palsied hands took courage,
Some sublimed hands showed ways
Some sublimed hands prayed. 14

As the people out of love followed, the three,
Ram sent them back with soothing plea.
Though returned back, their hearts Ram took with,
A moment's bliss brought the lifelong miss—

Nod=indicate ; Ashish=blessings.

"The providence is unmastered perverse,
Its heartless autocracy never remorse.
"it disfigureth the moon, in roses putth thorns,
In the vasts of oceans it pourth the salt.

"tho' crude, our daily joy, knew no pains,
Why providence lavished upon us and took back again.
"if the providence who hath exiled the princes,
Then for whom had He created luxuries and riches?

"if They repose on ground of grass, hay, dirts,
Why doth providencc take trouble of making comforts.
"if fate assigns them caves, huts, hovels,
In vain had He thought of Chattels and Castles.

Couplet: *"if these handsome, delicates,*
Attired in hermit's dresses
Barefoot they treaded,
Wearing matted tresses,

"then the glitter of gold devised by God,
And swish of silk, is all fanfaronade.
"if They live on bulbs, roots and flavourless tastes,
Why the Creator caterth, elixirs, lavishes.

"Bright, They seemst not begot by God,
Wight, They came of Their own accord.
"Anecdotes, holy quotes, notes never had taught,
These wights, self wrought, on this path are odd.

"Creator's failed toils, tried to make their match,
But then, princes in envy to the woods, dispatched.
Other said "our folly masters our sense,
Yet we do account ourselves highly blest,

Chattels=movable property.
Odd=strange; Wight=Supranatural; Fanfaronade=vain glory, pomp.

"Their virtues and merits for them brought a deal,
Who see or 'll see or have seen these Three."
Their lout words, in longing patois,
Were as loud as lauding Ved's voice.

Couplet: *Fond spirits, filled with tears,*
Fond remarks thus they made–
'How such benign 'll traverse
Such an untrodden track?' 16

A flame of love overmastered villagers,
Breasts scorched, eyes melted for strangers.
Unstirred all gazed upon tender lotus feet,
All stirred within, with their fevered feel.

Scorching flame in their breast sighed a chill,
"With the touch of soft soles, both, our hearts and the Earth shrink.
"The ruddy are the soles and muddy the soil,
Should God make Rajpath if fated Them exile.

"A boon of our asking, if the Heaven bids,
We 'll secure these Three, within our lids.
"Their toilsome march scorch our lavished souls,
As well who saw them not, those famished souls.

Famished souls wished to accomplish their lives any how,
Asked 'how far must have they gone by now?'
Crazed they, dashed the ways and thus, gazed,
The blest, then returned in bliss, amazed.

Couplet: *Couldn't see, ailing, trailing, failing frames,*
Wrung hands in repentence.
Thus, people were smitten with love flame,
Where ever Shri Ram went. 17

Famished souls=starved, hungry(who had not seen them)

Ponderously the Creator, Brahma hadth placed,
And Ram passed by those pious populace.
As the inkling of the exile some got,
They blamed royal couple for their cruel part.

But then, some wise mind thought otherwise,
'the mercy King vouchsafed the reward to our eyes.
"Blest are parents and citizens as well,
That hamlet is heaven from which they hail.

"Blest are bowers, bushes, brinks, brooks,
Every brick, every bank which Ram passed through.
"Every life, every leaf, every lee, every lae,
Is blest which is looked at by the three lovingly.

Couplet: *The news ; through the jungle routes*
Flashed before Ram reached to,
As to how the Divine moved,
Through the mazes of the woods. 18

Beholding hamlets, huts, hills, hillocks,
On common paths trod they bringing heaven to the flocks.
Proceeded Ram leading in the front,
While in the rear followed Lakshman.

Their weighed steps moved modest and swift,
Both conspicuous in robes of ascetics.
As between mortal coils and the immortal Supreme,
Dazzleth the rich Maya, thus Siya was seen.

Anew, beating my brain I muse simile,
Between twin lotuses afloats white lilly.
Caring foot prints of Ram on the dust,
In spaces Siya planted Her feet on Earth.

And the Earth, herself cradled on her pious breast,
The coupled foot prints' long spread.

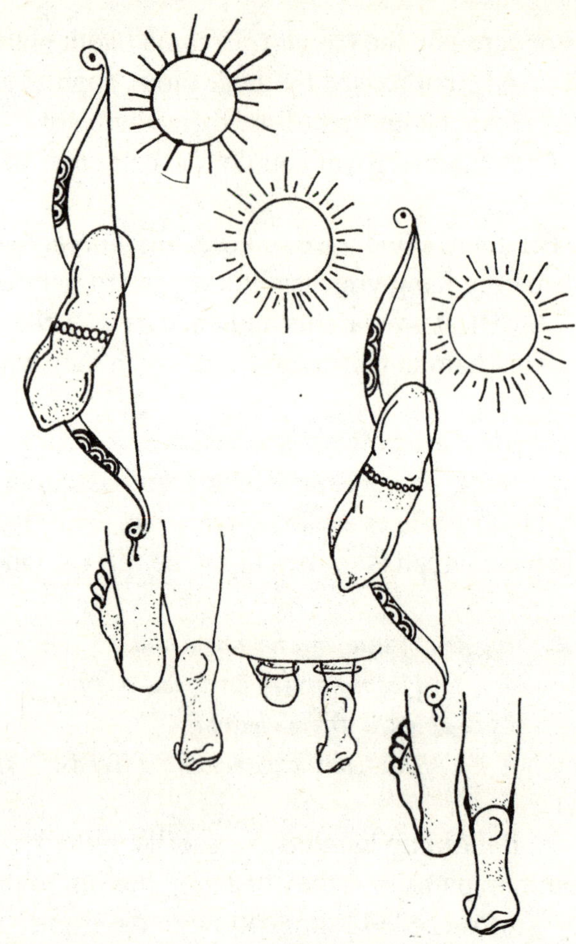

In the rear Lakhan traversed cautious to avoid,
The coupled foot prints, keeping on his right.

Couplet: *The firmness of footprints,*
So concreted on alleys,
On this pious land did imprint,
For all ages, the spiritual ways. 19

Foot prints of Truth, on the untrodden soil,
Ever get fossilized* in hearts of mankind to guide.
Visage treasure that moved on alleys lone,
Mellow antiques sung**, i trail to intone.

* Fossilized (used for permanently imprinted); **Verses of Ancient poets.

Through the droves of trees and drones of bees,
Lo ! through mind's eyes, beauty march of the three.
Even today, whose mind drags for a while with them,
Will blissfully cross the journey of mundane.

Seeing sanguine play of the orb in the west,
Seeing Siya's sanguine soles exhausted—
Ram stayed overnight under tree Banyan,
And proceeded further in the next wee dawn.

Couplet:

Ram's beauty birds, beasts beheld,
To the brim filled revelery
Bewildered they enthralled
Forgot innate rivelery. 20

IN THE ASHRAM OF VALMIKI

Rivulets hopped through the pebbles with gurgles,
And vernal hue crayoned the canvas of jungle.
On lone alleys through hills, cliffs, steeps,
After long wandering, a wonder grotto they reached.

Bees plundered honey from scattered blossom,
Blind drunk they, in joy making sweet hum.
Attuned to hymns, birds warbled their lays,
Ram rejoiced to behold comely, welcoming hermitage.

In the Ashram dwelt, the sage Valmiki,
Who penciled his piety into pious poesy*.
He poured into populace what his Person picked,
Pure strophes of epic he perceived and inked.

Hearing coming of Ram, the sage came forth,
Before holy bard, fell prostrated the princes, both.

Grotto=Beautiful hut.
*The Ramayan.

Blest was the bard, nay birds bees as well,
Who eyed with mortal orbz, the Immortal's arrival.

Couplet: *The muses of Valmiki home in on whom,*
That roaming Ram was his guest
Whole cosmos is whose room,
Sojournth in hut of the sage. 21

The blest sage offered fresh fruits, roots,
The accomplishing Lord lavishly partook.
Gathered within him, the sage, the ocean of bliss,
Could put a drop of it in his strophes*.

Reverence of Ram, voiced "O ! pious of Sages !
Tho' thou canst perceive all three watches.
"must be known to thou My exile to woods,
That had chanced Me great gain great boon.

"Obeying My sire, gratifying My mother,
And crowning of Bharat, My dearest of dears,
"Moreover I'm chanced to see thou,
I gather gains further, being bestowed.

"Beholding thy feet is My deeds rewarded,
O crown sage of sages ! guide me further ways,
"May not My hovel in the dense disturb,
The hermitages, habitats, lives, hives and herbs.

Innate, innocent Ram's request,
Further enlightened Sage, he then thus spake

Stanza: *O Ram ! Thy acts wait upon tenets of Veds,*
O Ultimate cause of the cause!
And Siya the deity, with Her divinity
Chances, charges and chars cosmos.

---

*Strophes of Ramayan.
Hovel=hut of leaves and twigs; Tenets=principles.

And Lakhan, Thy fra, the demon's awe,
He is path, the dogma of life.
The virtue, who maintains in the mundane,
And truly supports the truth in flaws of the life.

Couplet: *"Thou ! the infinite comest man sized,*
For the cause of gods, godly men,
With unknown, unknowable pastime,
Even beyond Ved's depiction. 22

"Thou dost dwell in every nucleus,
Thy fingers puppetst mundane's minus-plus.
"Even trinity dance on Thy divine tune,
Thyself is revealed by will of Thy alone.

"The blessed alone, can know Thou, whom Thou makest known,
Once he knows, becometh one with Thy unknowable own.
"Thou the cause of all causes, the Aim of all aims,
Thou art every mould's soul, and every soul's name.

"Devoid of any change, O Ancient of time,
O Infinite ! shaped into limits for the sake of mankind.
"Thou, the Master Lord, yet speakest as worldly monarch,
Who realize Thou, crosseth bar without bark.

"Thou the unseen, assumedst a palpable frame,
Thou the bliss incarnate, treadst road of pain.
"While the mortals in folly are blind at Thy deeds,
The same pastimes enlighten, the Wise discreet.

Couplet: *"For the place to thatch hovel,*
Thou askst O Omnipresent !
Where Thou dwellst not ; tell !
Then alone I can show place pertinent. 23

Bark=ship

"Every niche, nook, nidus, every nucleus,
Have nothing of its own but all Thy nimbus."
like the gurgling river of sweet poesy,
Like the chiming bells with chants of piety,

Sage's words, dropped into Ram, the honey dipt,
And blush blossomed on face, hearing panegyric.
Then, the hush conveyed verve through mutual smile,
And wordless warmth wayed new fervour for a while.

A new gush of thrill flooded out the hush,
Where mayst Ram dwell, the sage made request
"Who listen thy lavish feat like lovely rills,
They replenish, with no surfeit, inner mare nectaris.

"In the bosoms impregnated with patience and faith,
In those living fanes, enshrine Thyself.
"and in hand of peasants, the very saints of soil, who till,
Dwell! in such pious hands of no pompous will.

Whose lips ever sing Thy epic,
Their heart, as home Thou mayst pick.

"Ever who eye at Thou, with mind's eyes imbibed,
O Ram ! in their hearts, Thou shouldst abide.
"Ever who offer eats before taking it,
And never feel surfeited listening to Thy feats.

"Every garb, gem, grain, gains who dedicate,
And then take as blessings of Thy grace.
"In the depth of the Blue and in the heights of the Blue,
Ever who perceive Thine visaged hue,

Nimbus=Halo; Panegyric=Eulogy, Praises
Depth of the Blue=depth of the sea ; Height of the Blue=sky.
Surfeit=satiation; Replenish=fill up and refill.

"Whose verve perceives Ram, in Ocean's silky crease,
Whose nerve feels Ram's touch in kissing breeze.
"and who meet Ram in every bit, every beat,
In core of such hosts enshrine Thy seat.

"Thou shouldst dwell in warriors' courage,
In farmers' tiltage, in friars' hermitage.
"Whose reverence know no gain of bargain,
But with pigmy prayers and plain penance,

Couplet: *"All those worships and walks,*
Are winsome ways to Thy feet,
Thou shouldst live in their hearts,
And bless them refuge in Thy feet. 24

"With no lust, no lapse in the limpid hearts,
With blameless Bhakti, free from fraud,
"It is in their hearts that Thou shouldst dwell,
In whose hearts, over passion, the reason prevails.

"With bricks of benign belief, and guileless glue,
With purlin* of purity, builds heart, who,
With swept dust of lust on floor of flawless faith,
Thou shouldst room, under selfless roof of that bosom-fane.

"Who are resigned to Thou, with heart and soul,
Not in blind race of world; slow they move to true goal.
"Other's women, wealth nay the treasure trove,
Whose steadfast steps, to the greed; never drove.

"Never the cheap commerce could cheat whose chasteness,
Whose plain folly knows no sums business.
"Whose straight virtues tread on true yet tortuous road,
Let those hearts be Thy blessed abode.

---

*Purlin(here used for roof); limpid=pure, transparent
Treasure trove=hope of unexpected riches.

Couplet: *"To, whom Thou art at once,*
Perceived in the mind's eye,
"a pal, preceptor, parent
In those pilgrim hearts Thou reside. 25

"Thy parental hand ist crown of all crowns,
Thine pally hug ist bond of no bounds.
"All pompous craze who sets aside,
For one only one kinship of Thine,

"Who perceiveth in Thou, the master, mother, mentor, mate,
At once all such kins' faith who hath,
"What's shallow in other's ignoring that,
What's hallow in them, who selectth,

"Who behold the heaven, hell, this world and the next,
All filled with Thou, composed of none else,
"Who is laden with knowledge, bows more and more,
Learning of sums adds reverence in whose core,

"Whose head, heart, hands are set to Thee,
Thou shouldst setup Thy abode, within his being.
"Whose mind's eye in waking or drowse doth sink,
In clearer vision of Thy pastime, unwinked,

Couplet: *"Whose spontaneous devotion,*
Knows no gain, no bargain
That heart asks for none,
Should be Thy very mansion. 26

"If I, as Valmiki recall my past,
My deeds were curse, the mankind to harass.
"I was driven on the evil course of sins,
Not to slacken in my duty, towards my kins.

"I do confess I was Brahmin mere by birth,
I had brood of children by low born perts.

"Having deadly weapons, I was a curse,
One dawn, seven saints, thro' my noose traversed,

Moved by greed, I desired to rob,
I forced my own way, the pious souls to stop.
They asked I bragged-'its not my greed,
But to feed my house to fulfil the need.'

They asked me to go to my kiths and kins,
To ask them 'whether they wish to share your sins?'
"Coming home was return of my real sight,
All wished to share earnings, not the sins-they replied.

"Words drove me to mood of severe repentance,
I confessed every thing before those saints—

Couplet: *"Save me from abaddon,*
I am destined to
They replied "up ! up! ! your confession
Will certainly bring fruit." 27

"You are degenerated Brahman, fated for hell,
Tho' difficult but we extend our help.
"O Lord! they initiated me into Thy name,
I enshrined into mind the very same."

"They guided me to repeat and repeat
Thy name, till they returned to see me.
"Initiated was my concentration slow and slow,
Brought Thy name from tongue unto mind unto soul.

"From gross to subtlest microcosm,
My consciousness witnessed Thy very causal form.

"Lost of I-am-ness to countless ages,
I sat unstirred, on me ant-hill raised.

"It happened seven saints returned and perceived
My meek penance, in ant-hill, the Valmik*.

"They broke the fossilized ant-hill dome,
As if born again, I came out of the womb.
"By a different name, Valmiki, this twice born cage;
With every breath convey a sacred message.

Couplet: *"My life thus, conveys,*
The potential of upliftment
Every soul is sacred,
May sublime from Satan to Saint." *28*

□

*Ant-hill raised by termites is called 'Valmik' in Sanskrit language.

13

Ethics is unity, it's basis is love.

—Ram Krishna Paramhansa

THE CHITRAKOOT

Voice of Valmiki was like chants of Ved,
Not for Ram alone, but for coming men to tread.
Melodic muses of the bard-sage poured,
Honeyed mellow as Ramayan into Ram's core.

Ram bowed Himself under Sage's soft commands,
Which guided Ram for the present wants.
"Ram canth not be confined to ramparts,
No forts, no comforts, Ram is nature's own cord.

"Bless Chitrakoot let that be Thy host,
On the holy hillock take up Thy abode.
"Within all Sylvan hush, and in green's lush,
In the wild slug, sloth and wild rush.

"In the charms and warmth of nature's lap,
On the banks of Mandakini, the very stream of Ganges.
"Let Thy feet bless more, make it more sacred,
Which is graced by Atri, Ansuiya and many sages.

"Wend ! Thy way thither and reward the penance,
And longing of sages and long waiting patience."

Thus proceeded Ram, taking leave of Valmiki,
Yet He ever dwellth in strophes of His epic.

They walked further south on spread of broiled gravels,
But those turned to soothes of scattered petals.
In parched tender climbers smilt out twigs,
With verdant cloths, bare peaks got wigged.

"Lo ! Siye !! that monkey's apish play,
Shins up-springs down making in rill splash.
"Unstirred lizards feign as if meditate,
But on hypocritic move for bite on its prey.

"Like lizards, the imposters in Kaliage will feign,
Then, the holy texts should sure guide the men."
Thus, commenting on the passing by scenes,
The three divine guests, entered Vindhya-range.

Couplet:

Wide known Kudos of Chitrakoot,
Chanted by the sage-bard,
The Two with Siya came in holy woods,
In the pious stream they bathed. 1

Shri Ram asked Lakhan seeing good descent,
To thatch the hut near the banks.

Lakhan said–

"Hark ! O Lord lark's welcoming warbles,
Lo ! dancing brooks join holy flow with gurgles.

"Watch ! vernal mosaic on green carpet,
As if heaven cometh forth befo' Thou, the divine guest.
"Some mounts encaved in lofty bosom, for the saints,
The rocky homes for their unrocky penance.

Lakhan selected a site, to prove true,
A spot for grotto, as per Vastu.

The holy site, with delight Ram hath approved,
Came in forms of the tribemen, gods and godules.

Came Heaven's architects with artists' flock,
Put up huts clad in green, over Kamad-hillock.
To serve, there came celestials in Bheel's guise,
Made huts, one little fine, other larger in size.

Couplet: *The twin thatches of straw,*
Looked splendorous lofty fanes,
Where lived Ram Lakhan and Siya,
Like vagrant, the Supreme reign. 2

The Sylvan incense of Samphire,
Intoxicated the glad milieu entire.
'Mid rocky trembles, rolling waves warbled,
As the holy stream gurgled, the sand tickled pebbles.

'Mid the slumbering copses, the slug life,
'Mid vernal groves the hum in hives,
'Mid awe of jaws, paws and claws,
'Mid wild run of unbridled laws,

Ram kent in nature's arms of hailing boughs,
The wreath of welcome in landscape's show.
The hallow throngs* in the mellow moods,
Streamed in the blest woods of Chitrakoot.

Ram made obeisance to them all,
They poured blessings tho' they knew who is Who?

Couplet: *Ram reassured with reverence,*
They dispersed freed from woes,
And began performing penance,
Prayers, yagna vigil and yog. 3

Thatches=Huts; vagrant=vagabond
Samphire=wild plant with aromatic leaves; *Crowd of saints.

Like jungle fire the spread of news,
From Chitrakoot reached to wides of purlieus.
The tidings penetrated deep into tribes,
In joy they flocked from dense, caves and hides.

Their penury knew no penance but labour,
Men's simple deeds had brought Lord to their doors.
With fruits, roots filled in bowls of leaves; they rushed,
With their fruits fulfilled in soul's heave, they rushed.

Their dauntless toils of mute prayers,
Hath chanced them to gather great treasures.
Their plain anthem knew no commerce,
Not the flattering din the Lord seeth but meek whispers.

Though wild they, so-called, are naturally civil,
Tribal's unlettered deeds knew no ill.
Steeped in love, peeped they thro' foliage,
Like a pictured canvas with unstirred gaze.

The hitch vanished soon, came they out of greens,
Soon, this unknown seemed to them their next of kin.

Couplet: *They greeted and spake,*
Dauntless tho' strange—
"Thy grace blessed this place,
Thy feet took pains. 4

"Blessed is our tribe, nay trails and tracks,
The trees, its twigs, green turf is blest.
"Thou must havest not choosen this, for ownself,
But to right our wrongs, woes and wails.

"Our fortune hath chanced Thou, to the fore,
Fulfilled we, now feel secured.
"We Plebs, Pagans nay the plants, plains, peaks,
Are blest where Thou havest planted Thy feet.

"O Ram! receive, a rave from rills, ripples, rocks,
A hail from hovels, huts, hills and hillocks.
"On Thy visage; our felicitous eyes feast,
We the base, are blest nay all birds, all beasts.

"Jungle's sunless roof, floor of dreary crawls,
Even ghostly trees shiver with roars, hawls,
"Thy grace shalt turn those wilds to pal, pets,
And we, thy pages are already at Thy behest.

Couplet: *"Thy hut on the holy holt,*
For us, ist blest shrine,
Thy dwelling is heaven's own abode,
For us, ist divine. 5

"The Kamadgiri, the holy holt,
ls hallowed more being Thy host."
Seers trail, Veds fail whom to describe,
Same Ram's parental heed, listenth to wild-tribes.

Ts Love alone that attractth Ram, most,
Let the curious seekers may take this note.
Ram, then, poured all honey in His words,
Gratified, blest foresters then, dispersed.

No worships, no hardships, no text, no chants,
They knew no, piety, pomp, no penance.
Their unstyled, unlettered natural truth,
Hath chanced them this treasure of many lives' fruit.

Thus, the great grotto and the greatest guests,
Gladdened godly souls and gratified the place.
Ever since Ram came and here in dwelt,
Whole jungle swelt, in vernal robes revelled.

A rave=welcome.
Holt=hillock surrounded by forest.

Couplet: *The parrots, cuckoos and jays,*
Lavished, the milieu more,
Oscine honeyed, in sweet lays,
Ravished every core. 6

Big cats, cattles, boars, bears, doe, deer,
Free from enmity sported together.
When the soul getth from nature a vernal kiss,
The cruelity drownth in the ocean of bliss.

More over, its Lord Ram's gracious touch,
All animals abandoned their animus.
Very soul of all souls, Ram, the Lord,
Abhorth Knave's art, adoreth naïve heart.

Nature's law eased befo' Ram, the Creator of discipline,
And Ram's keen grace looked at all them, as kins.
Blossom-clad-land showed its revels,
The holy hut, on holy holt looked as glowing temple.

The Sylvan deity opened its arks,
And painted spring tides on whole the canvas.
Through the woods pellucid Mandakini rolled,
Whom, holy Ganga, Yamuna, Rewa, Godawari extolled.

Couplet: *Man-sized forester Ram,*
To bless plebs, beasts and birds,
Descendth for Saintly swarms,
For mirth of the Earth and every hearth. 7

The merits, merriments of this jungle life,
Belittled all glitter of celestial life.
Among, pricks of pebbles and pinks of thorns,
Among crass courses and coarse environs,

Oscine=song birds.
Animus=Enmity

They all, got rid of pangs of their lives,
Who, eyed Ram and whom Ram eyed.
Glad was the deity of mount Vindhya's line,
Hosting Ram, whose own holt became a shrine.

Ramulous and even axed rampikes,
All blossomed by the glance of Ram's eyes.
Men, leaves, trees rejoiced Lord's touch,
Enlivened all by His ambrosial feet's dust.

Hugging of creepers tickled the glad trees,
Hymning of seers mingled with humming of bees.

Couplet: *Laxman, waited upon,*
Ram, in thoughts, words, deeds,
Such depth of the devotion,
None else thought, none else did. 8

Siya-Ram's feet were Lakhan's world,
Who never recalled anything else.
Siya valued none, those regal luxuries,
Before the daily delight of Ram's company.

Wifely devotion of selfless faith,
Was witnessed, in love with increasing oneness.
The current of Her soul ever streamed,
To Her beloved Lord of Ancient of days.

For Seeta; in company of Her Lord,
Millions of joy of Awadh, this woodland brought.
While the ducks, dove, doe became Her abigails,
And roots, bulbs, sloe Her lavish dishes,

Lovely litter of leaves, with Her beloved,
Much over lonely glitter of silk, She weighed.

Ramulous=Branched.

No odd seemed any odd to Siya,
For, the company of Her spouse was ambrosia.

The strange environ brought homely care,
In Ram's caring love and puntillious manner.
For Siya as well for brother Lakhan in woods,
Ram would say and do for their good.

Old legends and tales Ram would narrate,
Would unveil as well the truth of Veds.

But in vernal colours which supervened,
Was the thought of Awadh to turn pain green.
In the chill He would recall warmth of mother's lap,
Sun's scorching would remind shelter of father's love.

Seeing pellucid Mandakini, the very Ganges,
Ram would recall His own soul, the Bharat's face.
'What is Awadh now, but citizen's grief',
With this grim thought, Ram's eyes would brim.

Couplet:

Melancholy would paint on face,
Of Ram a different crease.
Noticing His distress,
Siya-Lakhan would try to ease. 9

In His turn to divert from sadder Siya and Lakhan,
Ram would narrate some sacred anecdotes, sermons,

And the very name of Laxman, the signature of reverence,
Through vigils, duties proved itself.
Thus some cheer, some tears, some joy, some woe,
Filled milieu of this heavenly grotto.

And Thus, here Ram sojourned to the woods,
Now Lo ! there Sumantra waited with petrified looks.

Punctilious manner=every minute care.

SUMANTRA RETURNS

As he saw Nishaad returning alone,
Gone into his heart the current woe begone.
"O Ram, Siya Ram! Lakhan !!" cried the forlorn,
And looking to the south, mounts neighed and mourned.

Couplet: *While in pool of own tears,*
The minister dropped on ground,
As birds whose wings were shorn,
Mourned the restless mounts. 10

Overt sobs of Sumantra and covert sobs of the meeks*.
Moistened core of returning Nishaad, deep.
Nishaad then consoled the minister, and asked,
"tho' lightens the sob, but it delays the job.

"While the king is sick and Awadh at stake,
"thy job, thy duty is on test.
"Compose thyself the hour meetth not,
"give the soothing touch to Awadh and it's lord."

By force Nishaad seated him in chariot,
Drove not he, driven by the fate, running riot.
His mind got numbed, hands getting fatigued,
The Horses would not move, were getting fidgety.

They would topple down as if untammed in harness,
Neighing bewildered like rabid horses.

Couplet: *The grief benumbed Sumantra,*
And the grief untamed the Meeks,
Then the four charioteers of his troop
Were sent by sad Guh. 11

Overt=obvious ; Covert=hidden; *horses.
Fidgety=restless ; Run riot=raise hell, go wild.

The language of bridle, in hands skilled,
Followed then by hooves and the wheels.
Bereft of Ram, tortured by remorse,
Lamented Sumantra, the prey of throes—

"the woe is me ! with this business of my breath,
Bereft of Ram why not it ceases?
"Alas ! soul missed a win, and stays in vain,
Even now heart breaks not into twain.

"Still sticks to the flesh" his soul he accursed,
His grief was too deep for the words.
Like a ruined Sumantra rued his lot,
Like a prey of fate laid in chariot.

Pricking memories those hang by the treasured delight,
Bringst more of tears day and night.

Couplet: *Agony benumbs when,*
The ache touches acme,
It blunts and declines the pain,
When grief touches climax. 12

His withered look uttered thro' his meekly sobs,
And thro' his blunt orbs-that all treasure was robbed.
In tears dissolved all his wisdom and will,
Sat he, dissociated from chariot and bridle.

In the slumber of stunned brain,
His feeble flesh sat, with soul completely drained.
Scorches of his heart parched the lips,
And dried his eyes, within wet eyelashes clips.

Eye's slits had life for hope of Ram's glimpse,
Unawake of ways, winds, wheels, whisk, whips.
He thought of the odd Awadh sans Prince Ram,
The wheel of his grieved thought had no cam.

Cam=protecting part of wheel in motion.

"Now the soulless Awadh's skeleton I 'll view,
With ruined bricks, sick road, spooky look.

Sumantra thought—

Couplet: *"Wide stares will run for Ram,*
Along the chariot's course,
But will not ask me in remorse,
Their mute 'll prick me more." 13

"Then I shall stuff them with my heart's load,
And pour the tidings like a thunderbolt.
And the questioning eyes of the citizens,
Will follow me long to sever my bosom.

A spark of hope ever which stays,
In queen's eyes; seeing me, 'll fade.
"I'll recoil at the rush of Ram's mother,
Like an eager cow for her own heifer.

"Mother's empty eyes 'll question,
'what good in woods, 'll happen to her sons.
"King, queens, town nay birds and pets,
Them I can't face, I can't solace.

"My brash rush unto Ayodhya,
Will prove to be a thunderbolt of awe.
The moment king sees me returning alone,
His soul 'll discard body as a piece of Straw.

Couplet: *My hard heart cracks not,*
This flesh, my soul, doth cherish
This frame is in my lot,
Fit for agony of abyss. 14

Spooky=ghostly
Brash=bold (not attractive); Abyss=hell

On wheels of grief whipped by anguish,
The banks of river Tamas then he reached.
The escorts then humbly bade adieu,
To Sumantra, the melancholy's statue.

The feet of Sumantra, was baded with guilt,
As if a cow or his own Guru, he had killed.
He passed day under trees in purlieus,
In fit of dumps, glum, gloom and blues.

The weary wheels, withered hooves, worried ride,
Entered Ayodhya in the dusk of eve tide.
His slug feet, hung frame, slunk into palace,
Leaving the chariot at the gate.

Some who recognized gathered near chariot,
Found restless horses fatigued and tired.
Who heard the news thronged those citizens,
All dipt in waves of melancholy's ocean.

Couplet: *With news of minister's arrival,*
A chill ran along veins
Their souls melted as hail,
Even hope of the hope was drained. *15*

Sumantra saw mute arches, in hush of corridors,
Heard whispers of tapestries through ghostly doors.
The moan of gynaeceam that very moment,
Raised as queens heard of coming of Sumantra.

Scorching of queens flared afresh,
Asked their brimmed eyes, grieved faces asked,
But his stunned mind and his palsied tongue,
Replied His hung face, only palms he wrung.

Slunk=moved in abashed; Slug=sluggish.

His eyes turned blind and ears deaf,
Asked about the King his perplexed self.
Some maid guided muddled ministers, to the King,
Who found no King but feeble breathing thing.

Bleached face, parched lips and scorched breath,
Heaved a sigh muttering 'Ram' in every next.
Tangled hair, and the toppled crest,
He quizzed through his squeezed eyes raised

Couplet: *Gathering his failing warmth,*
Gathering his flaccid arms,
Gathering his fidgeting qualms,
Asked the King—'Where is my Ram?' 16

DASHRATH'S DEMISE

Bewildered King lifted prostrating Sumantra,
Asked 'where is Ram, Siya and Lakhan?'
His limbs and bosom were all chilled,
The warmth he had, was rolling on cheeks.

"Where are Ram Lakhan Siya? asked he anew,
Tell me ! welfare tell me !! all true.
"Light of my soul did you bring back?
While the light chariot speaks some else.

"Did you usher them to woods and left there?"
Sumantra's blank face replied ; replied his tears.
"I intended to install but exiled my sons,
Declining age rewarded in my name a great sin.

Recalling Ram's virtues, vision, vigour, visage,
His soul melted to brim out of the cage.
"I had to part such son" the King cried,
"my soul didn't depart what a sinner I am?"

Couplet: *"Before pupils petrify in wait,*
And soul recoils bereft,
Friend ! take me to the place,
Where Ram, Lakhan, Siya do stay. 17

"How this mortal coil without soul of my soul,
'll carry on affair of breath for this mould?
"On this mould constricting close rope of anguish,
Soon 'll strangulate hope, my soul to squeeze.

" The parting from Ram itself means*,
Departing of soul from its means.**
" O Friend ! contrive some quick mean,
My beloved sons where by, you may bring.

Recovering himself then Sumantra replied—
"Thy majesty is brave nay learned and wise.
"Fate's paw maketh its pleasure drapes,
Unfolds pain, then, as feeble man's traps.

"Time-span's wheel spins on fate's fulcrum,
Bringeth bane-boon, blues-bliss, blight or blossom.
"The twist of fate brought this tempest of life,
But for thyself, the stoic, gloom-bloom are alike.

Couplet: *"O Sapient ! thou art stoic,*
Take up the courage now,
Be not sad and sick,
Give up sorrowing somehow. 18

"First halt was made at Tamasa's side,
And at holy banks of Ganges the next night.
"They took dips and sips of holy water,
Remained without food Siya and two brothers.

Pupils=part of eye responsible for sight.
*meaning, ** body, frame, medium.

"then simple devotion of Nishaad is worth
To be mentioned; and his warmth.
"the two coiled their matted curls like crest of sages,
Then, Ram called for a boat to cross the Ganges.

"My bidding dews, the sacred flow did accept,
And Ram in sweet accent, addressed.
And conveyed his obeisance to thou,
And asked me to convey His humble message

"O Father ! worry not on my account,
Thy blessing hand over head is ever crowned.
"Thy rites merits and deeds 'll wrought
For us, the journey and sojourn in woods, a comfort.

Stanza: *"Thy behest is my crest and strength*
in the forest,
All sorts of comforts I shall have
As greatest asset is thy grace.
My quest in woods and rest in woods
'll have happy halt and jovial jaunt.
Console thy soul and mothers' as well,
I'll be back having obeyed command."

Distitch: *He told Ram's message, for,*
Mothers to cease sorrow,
And for Guru to exhort
The King ; his woe to forgo. 19

Sumantra repeated what was conveyed by the prince,
His message to father, brothers, mothers and kins.
"The King, queen, kins and citizens
Convey to them my submission

'He alone is my bosom friend
Who ever ensures the King's content.'

'When Bharat comes and as regent he assumes,
Tell him to be cautious on the road of virtues.
'The fine foot prints of Bharat shall define,
The path of rectitude for the mankind.

"Bharat is embodied duty and devotion,
And forlorn Awadh, is his own.
"Tell him 'not the name Ram or Bharat',
It's wisdom, virtue and work that works.

"Ram hushed Lakhan for his harsh words,
Asked me 'not to mention his juvenile jabbers.'

Couplet: *Sending reverence and greetings,*
Siya could say zilch,
Only flood in eyes brimmed,
Her words on cheeks chilled. 20

"On the command of Ram, at the same,
They boarded a boat Kewat began play of helm.
"As the boat floated across; my soul sank,
And heavied soles petrified into sand.

Nettled by the sting of the fate,
Returned my palsied limbs and frame helpless.
Sumantra's choked throat stopped to speak,
'He took Ram to woods', -this was his grief.

Charioteer's story fell like a thunderbolt,
Own melancholy, the King could not hold.
Bereaved of Ram in deep anguish,
He writhed like, on sands the fish.

Wails of queen touched heights of echo,
In the fate's hands danced embodied sorrow.

Zilch=Nothing ; Juvenile=childish ; Jabbers=disapproving talks.
Nettled=agitated, annoyed.

The endurance itself could no longer tarry,
This grief, itself the Grief could not carry.

Couplet: *Out-crying in gynaeceum,*
Filled Awadh with chaos,
And tidings so glum,
Treaded into Awadh on toes. 21

All the hopes of the King died,
Only flickers of lips showed some palsied sighs.
Flame of soul seemed in eyes to be extinguished,
Sluggish breath knocked the throat to quit.

In voice-hush flourished more, his anguish,
That toiled for the soul from mould to split.
With sluggish pulse and sere of his sense,
Kaushalya kent the sun of race was abou' to set.

Gathering courage she said in stoical term,
" O lord ! thou art at the helm
"Of bark of boarded sad Ayodhya,
And the separation from Ram is ocean of awe.

"Thy patience O lord ! wilt be drive,
Lest how drowning family will survive.
"to see Ram Lakhan and Siya, we are sure,
Courage ! My lord! take up what I assure."

Couplet: *The nectarian words of hope,*
Worked a bit on king,
Laden lids he toiled to ope,
Like water works on fish writhing. 22

Healing own sorrow, the King got up and sat,
'Tell ! Where is Ram, where is his grace?
'Where is Lakhan, where Ram is?
'Come ! Vaidehi ! my child, me, to appease,

Monarch moaned all endless stretch of night,
Every mo brought missive of massive blight.
Reminded of blind hermit's curse that mo,
To Kaushalya he narrated that anecdote

"Bereft of Son the hermit accursed,
And now upon me, same plight occurs.
"Better dead I should be without Ram,
None else can charm, none else can balm.

"Ram is soul of my soul, now this mould is carcass,
Fie ! fie !! on, my soul which denies to shed off.
"Siya-Ram ! O Lakhan !! now I cross,
Ram is my calm, Ram is my cause.

Couplet: *For 'Ram' cried lips and King's eyes,*
'Ram ! O Ram ! Alas !!
'Ram-Ram' yet again he sighed
Again gasped 'Ram' in his last. 23

Dashrath reaped boon of his pious life,
And his death had rewarded him great prize.
As long as he lived 'Ram' he gazed,
And bereft from 'Ram' became excuse for his death.

The holy flame shed off the mould,
Thus, his glory, whole cosmos extolled.
Wails of queens welled over the palace walls,
Every hearth hushed every heart howled.

Queens fell on floor their keens touched sky,
Lamented every view, every milieu sighed.
Every heart wailed far, far and nigh,
Flood of anguish welled over every eye.

Howl=doleful cry.

Pals, plebs, pages abused Kaikeyi,
Who had robbed world of its eyes.
The sore eye of the east brought grief to the town,
In clouds of melancholy, wailing Awadh was drowned.

Couplet: *With the spread of tidings and sun,*
Holy hermits gathered from wides,
Vashishtha solaced all with sermons,
And his wise advice. 24

THE BENIGN BHARAT RETURNS

Then an oil filled boat Vashishtha caused,
And placed in it Dashrath's corpse.
To call Bharat quick, he then summoned envoy,
And warned not to reveal the news in the way.

"Approaching Bharat tell the two,
Thou both art quick called by the Guru."
On behest, in haste in winged speed,
Rushed they, put to shame the excellent steeds.

Ever since in Awadh, things went wrong,
Before Bharat occurred many ill-omens.
Dreadly mares filled his nights,
And his days came with ill thoughts and frights.

There are ever some unknown chains,
Those bind men with shackles of clairvoyance.
Bharat would perform tough prayers,
And rites to rout any rough hour.

Couplet: *Thus while Bharat was ill at ease,*
Along with words of Guru,
The anxious couriers reached,
Eagerly received, the two. 25

Bharat oped palmleaf enveloped with Loam,
Was eager to read the words from home.
The epistle summoned in hurry, the two,
Immediately started in worry, the two.

Urging the horses not on hooves but on wings,
The two crossed spans, steeps and streams.
Every moment hung heavy in their thought,
Every hurdle was humbled by anxious heart.

The two rued, would that they could fly,
Thro' out they brooded and the town drew nigh.
All ill omens welcomed them in town,
In the hovering murk Awadh was drowned.

No usual melody but, melancholy filled milieu,
Wails, yells, yowls, had chilled the two.
The bloom in its gloom and the Blue in blues,
Awadh looked ghostly in its ugly hues.

Colours of men's heart, the nature-mother follows,
Gloomy looked greens, gills, gardens and grove.
Like lifeless ghosts seemed citizens,
They moved lost, and totally drained.

Couplet: *Their countenance to Bharat,*
Mute obeisance to Bharat,
Was all strange to Bharat,
Brought more pangs to Bharat. 26

His mind was possessed by fear unknown,
Obsessed Bharat, Shatrughan asked none.
The pompless Haat had lost it's riches,
He was scared by sad doors and niches.

Gill=brook, rivulets ; Rue=regret.

In this air of sorrow, the narrow queen,
Rushed with broad smile to the prince.
With lamps she welcomed the Would be King,
From very door she brought them in.

To Bharat's surprise in the Awadh's odd,
Kaikeyi's joyous face looked more odd.
Kenning awe-struck son and his melancholy,
She asked about her mother's family.

Bharat's empty eyes and hollow voice,
Asked about father, mothers brothers in reply
"Tell! where are father mothers and Siya?
Where are Ram-Lakhan my beloved fra?"

Couplet:
Drawing back her smile,
Bringing tears of crocodile,
The words more than turmoil,
Said the sinful wife— 27

"I have accomplished for you son! a great plot,
Poor Kooney was great help among all odds.
"Only fate has marred a little in the way,
To the paradise the King has passed away."

As soon as Bharat heard of father's demise,
As if words hammered head and heart was sliced.
His soulless body fell on floor,
His lamentation went high more and more.

Broken into tears he accursed himself–
'Woe is me ! I was absent at his last breath.'
Kaikeyi tried to console the soul of her womb,
But that further scratched Bharat's wound.

The wicked conspiracy what she devised,
She oped befo' son in bragging voice.

Glad heart she vaunted her haunted plot,
She thought of reigns but the ruins she wrought.

Couplet: *Hearing of Ram's exile,*
Forgot he King's demise.
Accursed self for he realized,
As the cause of all spoils. 28

Puzzled mother for the distressed son,
Tried to solace, more to aggrevate burn.
How anything could balm that ulcer,
Which was shaped by his own mother.

"It meets not, the King be mourned,
With merits and lavishes, His life was adorned.
"Rich harvest of the vast renown,
Ever had blessed his deeds, his crown.

"As the true reward and will of your sire,
As heir accept this entire empire.
"Son ! sorrow be ceased, follow fate's decree,
In you, the King, not just me but populace see.

Doab heart of Bharat dipt in between dismay and dole,
And his scorches were touched again by live coal.
"No morn of reign, but thou broughtst ruin and mourn,
Why didst not thou kill me while I was born.

Couplet: *"Claiming Ram-Lakhan for brothers,*
Blessed with father such a great,
But mother ! I have thou for mother,
Woe is me ! befo' the fate." 29

"When thou germinated this malign seed,
How hard was thy heart that remained single piece.

Vaunt=brag, crow.
Doab=raised land between two rivers.

"Asking boon where thy conscience fled?
Nor thy mouth festered, nor thy tongue fell.

"Thou didst deceive the trust, King's faith,
Fate had robbed King's sense to design his death.
"How could naïve, pious king discern,
The expertise of the knave, the expert pert.

"Ram is dearest to all ; but to my woe,
Yet that Ram appeared in thy mind as foe.
"Tell me the truth ! who thou art,
An alien machine with no soul, no heart?

"Not should; reign but may I be arraigned
Of Ram's exile, King's death and all ruins.
"thy drabbled deeds that designed speck,
Away ! away !! daub thy face in black.

Couplet: *"nay ! my sin runs in my vein,*
Being born of poisonous womb,
I slight thou in vain
Being averse to Ram is my doom." 30

Mother Kaikeyi's words scorched Shatrughan,
But no remorse could reverse, the wrongs done.
That very moment the hunch-back maid,
Came in made up face, lavishly clad.

The fire of furor filled youngest fra,
He kicked her at hump she screamed in awe.
Kooney's hump was smashed and she spewed,
Blurred sight, slurred voice, in spurts and bruise.

"To Kaikeyi, me, the Kooney has keen committment,
For that I get this ill-recompense."

Arraign=accuse ; speck=spot, defect.

On words of Kooney, Shatrughan in his rage,
Seized her by hair and began to drag.

The pert Kooney designed all as expert,
But the trust of brothers she could not hurt.
By soft-soul Bharat then she was rescued,
To mother Kaushalya then both moved.

Couplet: *'Who she is?' They thought,*
Wasted frame withered with woe,
In heavy look and shabby robes,
Sat figurine of sorrow. 31

Kaushalya's empty eyes and empty core,
Kent coming Bharat at her door.
With filial fills she rushed to her fils,
Like a cow to heifer, she ran to the sill.

Rushed she up to meet him at the door,
In reeling faints she rotted on the floor.
Her lids drooped she dropped in swoon,
To see her plight, Bharat was deeply moved.

In regard, in regret he fell in her feet,
"Tell ! father, Siya-Ram, Lakhan where can I meet?
"In this world why Kaikeyi was born?
And if born why 'didn't she remain a barren.

"Who else is in world so wretched as I?
I caused father's death and Ram's exile.
"I lead to all troubles woe be to me,
Mother! pardon me not! peccavi.

Filial=relating to son ; Peccavi(*L*)=I have sinned; Fils=son

Couplet: *With healing words of son,*
Kaushalya was revived,
She filled him into bosom,
Grief rolled through her eyes. 32

Mother, the naive creation took him to bosom,
As though Ram Himself had come.
Then, the Shatrughan was clasped by her naïve arms,
Medleyed with grief's chills and love's warmth.

Every one who saw, said ' she should be so,
For Ram's holy mother that she is, with holy core'.
In the lap of mother Bharat found his world,
And calm in balm of the soothing words

"Compose yourself O my wise child !
Should time not be mourned while hour turns wild.
"The fate walks on the time's course,
It's unalterable move, so shed off remorse.

"In the hands of providence, the puppets we,
Dance, Son ! blame no one for the destiny.
"Such a trying jolt of the fate I could sustain,
He maketh me survive, what is his gain?

Couplet: *"All his father's behest,*
Stoical Ram obeyed,
did submit crest for hermit's dress,
For the Truth went on crude ways. 33

"With cheer within and without,
With no dilemma, no dole, no doubt,
"Solacing all souls of Awadh,
Picked up He the untrodden, over the Raj-path.

"As an adherent devotee, and Ram's shadow,
How could Siya stay back, and She followed.

"Laxman heard, sprang up and accompanied the two,
Ram tried to detain him but he joined them to woods.

"Sic, Ram left, leaving Awadh bereft and sick,
While ramshackle king died, and me live like rampike.
All ruins these very eyes witnessed,
Yet this wretched soul drags on the business of the breath.

"The King knew well how to live, how to die,
Bereft of Ram who refused to survive.
"I, the mother of Ram claim to love my son,
Yet survived His exile, my heart of adamant.

Couplet: *Bharat saw in mother,*
Wailing statue of love,
And the King's palace appeared,
Very shrine of sorrow. 34

And lamentation of two brothers echoed,
Whole gynaeceum looked melancholy's abode.
Kaushalya clasped them to her bosom,
Comforted them with tender words of wisdom.

The tears shared, is the torn hearts shared,
Brothers and mothers consoled each other.
Recalling of joyous time with the King,
Brought to all of them more aching sting.

Insisted him his innocent instinct,
With folded palms he imparted his modest thought.
Bharat fought back the tears-roll,
Overwhelmed he then, to all told–

"A Sin attaching to the parricide,
Or sin of slaying cow, woman or child,

Ramshackle=crazy; Parricide=murder of father, mother.

"blames of bloodshed, all blemish all blots,
Let all be mine, had I concurred this plot.

Couplet: *"For men who worship manes, spirits,*
Resigning Ram and Shiv,
May fate reward me same nemesis,
If I ever agreed this trick. 35

"If mother ! all this has my approval,
Let me share fate of those who sell morals.
"Who revile the Veds and are hostile to world,
Who weigh wealth over the worth of words,

"Who are fiends in the mould of the men,
Whose filthy feat put mankind ashamed,
"On other's wealth who cast green eyes,
On other's female, who are blue eyed flies,

"Put together all these major sins,
Let all be hung upon me.
"Nay! All sins of the world be mine,
If I ever knew this crooked design.

"The imposters, traitors in thoughts and deed,
Whose blue thirst has lecherous greed.
"May Lord Shiv allot me ferule of fate,
If any concord with this plot I ever had."

Couplet: *"O ! incarnate of brotherhood !,"*
To Bharat, mother spake—
"O brother of faith ! O son of Truth,
Do not be at stake." 36

□

Ferule=cane of punishment; Green=jealous; Blue eyed flies=sensuous.

14

Seek the science of the maker and not that of the made.

—Swami Vivekanand.

BHARAT, THE NAME OF FRATERNITY

"You! Bharat ! a name till ages infinity,
Your affinity will be mark of fraternity.
"For the mutual love between you and Ram,
Can anyone on earth have qualm?

"Ram is your soul, Ram is your life,
And you are Ram's soul, likewise.
"Sky may fall on floor, Snow may emit fire,
Moon may diffuse poison and not the elixir,

"but in no case, will you for a while,
O Bharat! to Ram can turn hostile.
"Those who look at Bharat with askance,
They err in here with major offence."

Motherly warmth melted through her eyes,
She clasped Bharat, and lamented all night.
With the dawn sages and court gathered,
Vashishtha solaced, in words to meet the hour

Couplet: *"Brave the hour ! dear Son !"*
Said, Vashishtha the sage—
"What passed can't be undone,"
And Bharat rose gathering courage. 1

Vashishtha escorted him to the sleeping sire,
In endless sleep, waiting for bier.
Bharat caused holy bath, as per Vedic trend,
And caused pure bier with own hands.

'T was hardest mo for the queens,
Came they all for King's last glimpse.
With herbs aroma, aloes, sandal woods,
A pile was raised at banks of Sarayu.

In the holy cage stayed long the pilgrims soul,
A shrine, itself, was Dashrath's mould.
The priests put the corpse on the pyre,
And asked Bharat to do obsequies for his sire.

But, then Vashishtha said "You are abandoned,
By the King, Himself for last services as son."
"He was in difficult set of mind O dear Bharat!
Such move was issue of mood of a bereft."

Stunned was Bharat, sad steps stopped short,
Fell he as was severed of his vital part.
"Me, Alas from the funeral rites who is abandoned,
How, for father's throne, am a privileged son.?"

While the pyre of his sire was still cold,
By the side stood Bharat with ashes of own soul.
Bharat asked Shatrughan to do funeral rites,
More sad who, then, the pyre set to ignite.

Thus was performed Dashrath's obsequies,
All the ruined steps, then dragged back in blues.

Couplet: *Aching words of Kamban,*
Along foot prints of melancholy,
Of Bharat and Shatrughan
Dragged Laden muses in his poesy. 2

All rites for next ten days,
As guided by the Guru,
Performed as per holy texts,
the two brothers gone through. 3

Garments, garnets, garbitures, grains,
Gee, goats, grots, gold, gems,
Gifted Bharat with ope hands,
Among the pious and the plebs. 4

Bharat, the fils with none fills of guile,
Performed rites for departing King to fulfil.
The glory, nor the gain is slain, but body dies,
His deeds, and paeans, in peoples' heart sighed.

Then calculating an auspicious date, Vashishtha,
Came summoned all the court and elite.
Brooding pack sat in the chamber of court,
Two brothers Bharat-Shatrughan were also sent for.

Vashishtha seated Bharat to his very next,
And quoted references from holy text.
Sage repeated with exploitation of the Cunning,
And worthy exploits of love of the King.

As Vashishtha spake of Ram's virtues,
Along his body a thrill ran through.
Then he extolled the affection of Siya and Lakhan,
In his overwhelmed eyes melted grieved emotions.

Gee=horse; grots=beautiful grotto, houses.

Couplet: *Sad Sage then spake—*
"Bharat ! formidable is fate.
Loss-gain, name-shame, life n death,
're all providences' puppets." 5

"Thus discern Bharat ! whom should we blame,
Fret not ! for the freak fate's game.
"Ponder ! my son ! how King Dashrath lived,
And his glorious death should not be grieved.

"behind thumb-sized thing*, the mortal coil is nothing,
That soul ever liveth with it's virtuous workings.
"None needs be piqued, none needs be pitied,
Change should not be grieved, as challenge, be greeted.

"Unlearned of Veds who brags own prudence,
Needs be pitied for his nescience.
"Unlearned of hymns, who chant by rote,
Pitiable are parrots, crammed up Veds who quote.

"Pitiable the King, who careth not his subjects,
Pitiable the subjects, own nation who betray.
"Pitiable, the pal who stabs in back,
Pitiable the pupil who disobeys.

Couplet: *Pitiable, the woman who betray,*
Her own spouse,
The seer who in world go astray,
And the worldly who spurn own house. 6

"Pitiable, the fraud friar and his false penance,
The fils, fra, friend with no faith in concerns.
"Pitiable are those who harm others,
For own charms, those self centred.

Rote=cramming; * (The soul is thumb-sized) from Shvetashvatar Upanishad (ch-3/13)
Spurn=neglect; fils=son; fra=brother.

"Pitiable the apostle, who appals other's faith,
Who abhors other's faith and appeals hatred.
"Pitiable the monk who go astray narrow,
Who create an ado for sake of own ego.

"the man dazed by anarchy of mundane,
Pitiable the human frame, who is not a humane.
"to grieve for the king, is not worth,
Whose splendour illumineth all spheres.

"In the past and now and in time to be,
'Ts a mark lead by your father's monarchy.
"From infant world to the mature heaven,
His paeans filled all, with pealing anthem.

Couplet:

"Tell me dear child !
Who begot such pious sons,
My words deplete to glorify,
Reach nor depth nor height. 7

"Nor the self nor the soul but mould dies,
Change is nature, mourn not, but realize.
"Obey King's command and repay his due,
He has bestowed the Kingship on you.

"For His own words who embraced the death,
To redeem those words follow his behest.
"The King, weighed over anything, his words,
Dear Son ! therefore redeem, his words.

"Sons like Ram, Parashuram have set lessons,
In obedience of father are legends.
"thus, the King's command you reverently obey,
This meetth the hour in every way.

---

apostle=missionary.

Couplet: *"Over father's dictum,*
Whose, wit dictates not,
And, reverence keeps the reasoning mum,
Is beloved of the Lord. 8

"Cherish subjects, redeem King's behest,
It copes with ethics of Vedic text.
"Earn merits, heal sores of populace,
Then, King's soul 'll sure derive solace.

"Crown is his, whom father bestows,
So come ! rule kingdom, feel no remorse.
"Right all wrongs, accept the throne,
Awadh 'll owe you, heal it's throes.

"It fitly fulfils need in crisis,
'Ts your duty to draw the Awadh from nemesis.
"When Ram-Siya 'll hear, they 'll please,
Our anguish 'll cease seeing you the liege.

"Who have witnessed the divine oneness between,
Ram and You, and found it to be supreme,
"They say rule Awadh enshrining Ram in bosom,
When He returnth home, may hand over the Kingdom.

Couplet: *"You need must obey Guru,"*
All submitted with joined hands,
"With coming home of Lord of Raghu,
Do ! what you think fit then." 9

Kaushalya added "O Bharat! Listen!,
For us, and all Awadh it's statuary lesson.
"Guru's command is ever conductive,
Care of Awadh is your concern; you conceive!

Liege=King, lord.

"While King is gone, and Awadh woe begone,
It meets not you stay forlorn.
"While Ram did depart to the forest,
In and out of ramparts you are the one buttress.

"In this obscure occurrence onerous,
Your ownself is only option for this onus.

"During nemesis of fate, the crisis on state,
It meets to accept the call of royal crest.

"Obey with reverence Guru's behest,
Vanish blues of Awadh, cherish the subjects."
Most reverently Bharat heard the Guru,
Patiently Bharat heard mother's nectarian view.

Stanza:

Guru's behest and court's request
And mother's account for the crest,
Though words imbued in nectar
But grew Bharat's blues to the climax.
His remorse, through eyes coursed
Welled over in silence,
Who were present, lost existence,
That event Tulsi could not pen.

Couplet:

Bharat, the embodied altruism,
To assuage the assembly,
Picking up the pluck firm,
Made a pellucid plea— 10

"Voice of preceptor is said to be Lord's voice,
Whole assembly has endorsed good advice.
"To her best thought the mother has injoined me,
Every asking intends to anoint me.

Onerous=burdensome
To injoin=to order

"Words of Guru, parents, Master and friends,
Certainly I ever took to obey with reverence.
"One fails his duty incurs loads of sins,
If he weighs such advice by a pause to think.

"Though ye advised all conducive to me,
But along my nerves runs something pensive in me.
"I realize it's all good, but still
In my grieved veins crawls the chill.

"Arguing into thy sincere goodness,
Forgive me, reckon not, fault of my craze.
"Heed me ! heal me ! a perplexed soul,
And advice me which my grief can hold.

Couplet: *"Father 's dead, Siya-Ram are exiled,*
Where as, ye offer me the Sway,
While melancholy smiles,
And teases me, as the prey. 11

"My good lies under Ram's shadow,
On in his glow, me find mellow.
"My love is bond-slave of Siya-Ram,
But the tricky fate framed for me this wrong.

"My perverse mother robed me of this privilege,
She had snatched the master from his poor page.
"I have pondered my good lies in none the other way,
Without Ram Awadh is a noose, a cage.

"Like a wreathed and jewelled body without cloths,
All glitters of Awadh without Ram look odd.
"Like luxuries, lavishes for the benumbed,
Like melodies, rhythms are of little use to dumbs.

"Without dispassion as the search of 'Brahm',
Like wise without Ram is this Kingdom.
"Grant me leave, let me go to my soul,
Ram is my life, Lest this is just mould."

Couplet: *"It's folly of infatuation*
That asks me, the wretch to reign,
I'm hostile to Ram, the Kaikeyi's son,
Perverted, lost to the shame. 12

"A virtuous man, not me, the earthling,
Should be allowed be crowned as the king.
"If by perforce you install me, the perfidious,
The Earth 'll shrink; into under-earth will it sink.

"As the urn of gold holds toxin,
My body is all embodiment of sin.
"I'm the cause of Siya-Ram's exile,
I'm the cause of my father's demise.

"My adamant breast braves country's cries,
With lost shame gazes into people's sad eyes.
"My thirst for luxury, hunger for lavishes,
My passion for reign, longing for riches,

And some more lusts dwell within me,
To prove and proclaim 'Alas! peccavi!'

Couplet: *Begotten of Kaiykeyi, me peccant,*
A son of the hard core,
Harder I'm like adamant,
As iron is harder than its ore. 13

Peccavi (*L*)=I have sinned; Peccant=sinner; Perfidious=treacherous.

Bharat continued to say—

“Being born of such a hard womb,
My wretched life is highly doomed.
“Where I have survived even this tempest,
Stone in me shall have much to see yet.

“Words are short for the Kaikeyi’s praise,
The three beloved who exiled and husband who dispatched.
“Fostering craze for her cradle, she clinged to widowhood,
She ruined hearts, hearths for her son’s good.

“On this evil course of impious infamy,
Trod bold steps of my mother and me.
“Kaikeyi gave throes to all, to me the throne,
Born of her womb she thought, of me hers alone.

“She had offered imperial robes for me,
And spreaded perilous barbs for the three.
“Providence himself has fulfilled everything,
‘and ye now as well help my way to be King?’

Couplet: *“It’s incurable sore,*
Nor cure I see nor nostrum,
No balm can soothe my core,
’m sinner of high treason. *14*

“For me all ills the providence, ordained,
But why he bestowed Dashrath as father, in vain.
“Me keep gimcracks of being Kaikeyi’s son,
Deep pricks, dirty tricks, deceiving decorum.

“Being Dashrath’s son I gained praise,
Called ‘brother of Ram’ which meets no match.
“I became now, name, being Kaikeyi’s son,
And claim all happened, is fitly done.

“I’m hostile to Ram-it’s certain,
Who else exiled him? - it’s very plain.

Gimcrack=worthless show.

"While Ram's exiled it's Awadh's bane,
While countrymen 're lashed, I'm lavished with reign.

"The Bane of Awadh, ye say, is my good gain,
It's my pitiable misfortune to be blamed.
"Your fearing folly that does compromise,
Ye have me, the crippled option and no other choice.

Couplet: *"Among changes, unchanged is mother's love,*
In guileless mother of Ram,
Unchanged her voice with same lull,
'n-her lap with same warmth. *15*

"Her distress intended my distress to lull,
Her affection words out, its her natural impulse.
"as if all adversities of fate, today, plea,
Even Guru's mind is set to anoint me.

"My Guru, whose wisdom ever enlightened us,
And torched our paths of ethical onus.
"But for Siya-Ram, I'm butt for every mind,
But then Guru's views find me benign.

"These showers of words should flood my heart,
But then, such water bringeth mud in the last.
"I shrink not to think if world calls me a vile,
My anguish is one, Siya-Ram's exile.

"What makes sick, what pricks through me thorn,
Is it for Ram's banishment, I was born?
"Lakhan reaped reward of his being,
On Ram he fixed mind, discarding everything.

Butt=target, (victim of joke)

Couplet: *"With laden head I bow,*
Heavy heart I lay ope,
My woe shall not go,
Without Ram, I can't cope." 16

"What throbs in me, who else than Ram
Can behold that sore, and can balm.
"Bereaved of Ram, can but be relieved by Ram,
Deceived soul, a sieve can but be healed by Ram.

"For my sore, only cure, is Ram,
I must, at first dawn, rush to meet my Ram.
"though I'm vile, cause of exile of Ram,
May, my wrongs be undone, be condoned by Ram.

Me, the mean, in my mangy mien,
'll sure be met by meek, modest mannerism of Ram.
Who's never woe of even a foe, that Ram,
'll forgive me, mere child, hostile though, to Ram.

"I cann't part Ram, let me depart to Ram,
The cord of my life is with, one accord to Ram.
"Bless me ! so that may I achieve my mission.
Hearing my begging Ram mayst return."

Bharat concluded—

Couplet: *"Born of wicked womb,*
My design is all-known
Still my nerve never numbs,
That He'll accept me as own." 17

Ope heart of Bharat spake, the honeyed lips,
All glad gathering in its nectar was dipt.
For sting of being bereaved of Ram,
Bharat's ambrosial words came as nostrum.

Mangy=hateful, odious; Condon=Pardon.

On the shocked citizens and on havoc of city,
Like a vernal wind came words of fraternity.
Mothers, mentors, ministers, minions,
All were moved by Bharat's opinion.

Couplet: *"We shall sure make it happen,*
What you brood,
To bring back Ram,
Let's proceed to woods." 18

All praised— "Your love to Ram hath no but
It's like Bharat and only Bharat.
"It's folly nay, it's great a sin,
Who sees no Ram in you, and not you in Him.

"Blinded of bluff what Kaikeyi brewed,
Will blunder, if some one blaims you.
"Like a dew on grass, like lotus on morass,
Your pellucid thoughts are above worldly dross.

"In ocean of melancholy and dark,
For us, the drowning souls, Bharat became a bark."
An Awadh of past, enlivened on their face,
In the flood of thrill all lost their flesh.

That eve brought on Awadh full moon of hope,
Cheered people returned back home.
'Blessed is Bharat' was talk of the town,
Not the crown, his soul is his own crown.'

The deeds, thoughts, words are crown of saints,
Thus, pure soul rule the souls of men.
It's now nay, in the time to be,
Bharat 'll be monarch of fraternity.

This town is no Awadh but Awadh is in woods,
This hour is reward of Bharat's brotherhood.

Parson=preacher; Morass=slough, soil

With the earnest wish, none would stay behind,
The journey, thrilled everyone wished to join.

Couplet: *Perish ! that penny, pleasure, pomp,*
Person, parson and pals,
Who keeps eyes from Ram,
Parting Ram making own rampart. 19

The dawn of hope had already hopped,
But eager citizens waited eastern knock.
Carts, cars, carriages, chariots,
Curious wheels waited the command of Bharat.

One thought that pervaded Bharat's mind,
The Kudos, Kingdom, Keeps and Kind,
Protecting this splendour and treasure spread,
Should be prime concern of mine.

It's all His treasure, I'm a trustee,
Safe keeping it, is my moral duty.
As a caretaking servant, not a usufruct,
Must I abide to this trust.

Peopled air is loyal in honest politics,
From their duty, none in Awadh never flinched.
Picking pickets, troops and entrusted them duties,
Ever who picked the charge as pure piety.

Couplet: *To Kaushalya, rushed then Bharat,*
Brooding abou' mother queens,
Thinking of their comforts,
He got equipped palaquins. 20

Vigil eyes of town witnessed starry drift,
Till morn star made eastern lamp lift.

Usufruct=one who has the right to use.

The threshold torched the whole canvas,
To rouse the zeal from shades of past.

Bharat asked some of his quick men,
For the installation of Ram to arrange.
" It's longer lingered, sage will invest
Beloved Shri Ram, even in the forest.

Glad ministers, kins minions moved,
And arranged an escort of the soldier's troops.
Agnihotra, the holy fire to be carried by Vashishtha,
Brought by Arundhati* as the prerequisite.

Holy steps of Chief Sage in this holy mission,
Mounted the chariot to lead the legion.
With the incandescence of penance,
Followed in various vehicles, the saints.

Then peopled flow joined on their means,
And all queens journeyed in palaquins.

Couplet: *Then, moved firmfeet of faith,*
In the last of the caravan,
The personified firmness,
Bharat and Shatrughan. 21

The throng lost the nerve, for thorns in feet,
For, Ram was balm for their heart's pricks.
Dews on forehead and aching pearls on soles,
Could not ebb the verve of the souls.

Realizing that Siya Ram wer' in woods,
The two brothers began journey on foot.
Moved in careless rush, barefoot princes,
Recalling Siya-Ram in every step.

---

*Sage Vashishth's wife.
Incandescence=shine.

The life without Ram, is acme of their aches,
Pricks, pierces nay, they forgot their flesh.
People dismounted and moved, when they saw the two,
Everyone of caravan thus, began journey on foot.

Got down the palanquin Kaushalya spake to Bharat,
"Children! mount you both on the chariot.
"All are drained heart and untrained sinew,
'll walk all the way, in reverence for you.

Both obeyed mother, their Raths they mounted,
At Tamas, next at Gomti they halted.

Couplet: *Leaving Lavishes, luxuries,*
They progressed on their ways,
They fasted for the three,*
Took journey as pilgrimage. 22

To the Sands of Sai, they then drew,
Next morn they reached Shringverpur's purlieu.
Nishaad heard news about troops and crews,
Felt concerned within and he did brood.

And some shapeless chaos took shape in his heart,
"What the evil in Bharat's mind do pass?"
"Doth the brotherhood ever need the troops,
Must have brought the army never to stoop.

"His blind greed must have designed wild,
With thought to kill Ram-Lakhan during exile.
"But the craft of Bharat knew no 'state-craft',
He stepped to taints, now he steps to his last.

"If all diabolic forces stand against Ram,
'll fail, as Ram hath truth as his arms.

---

*three-Ram, Siya and Lakhan

"That legion like a serpant crawls to the woods,
Like a charmer we'll crush its hood.

Couplet:

Pondering thus Nishaad,
Anxious of nighing speeds,
Alerted his squad,
Hearing neighing steeds— 23

"Be alert, set boats and siege ghats,
Sink loathsome those, loaded with pert crafts.
"Equip with arms against that flam,
Ye lived for Ram, now die for Ram.

"Bharat, I'll face, its open combat,
Soul may cross my flesh, he will not cross Ganges.
"Dying at sacred shore, for Ram's chore,
In the hands of Ram's brother, my death needs what more.

"For the cause of Ram, my life was blest,
For this lackey, the luck lavished such a death.
"With triumphant death the life is life,
It's just to and fro freight otherwise.

"If I win it's His, if I die it's no loss,
My life and the death too 'll serve the cause.
"All prayers, piety and penance,
In paucity of patriotism, all are in vain.

Couplet:

Not the least alarmed,
Thus Nishaad did prompt,
Demanded armours and arms,
Fixing his mind on Ram. 24

"Equip body for combat and mind to face death,
O Bretheren! make haste, do not hesitate.
"Let no one shrink hearing my behest,
All noded in yes, responded in zest.

Saluting him, the kins and champs left,
Bracing self, backed up Nishaad they, the brave breasts.
They fastened Arms, donned armours next,
Vexation waxed, they straightened axe.

On body fixed arms, in mind fixed Ram,
The chance to serve Ram, have charged champs with charms.
In batches, in bunches, the brave brigade,
Went upto their chief, glad greetings they bade.

Finding virile, agile the dare devils,
For vigil in battle, new zeal he kindled

Couplet: *"Great cause hath chanced upon*
A great death for us,
Life has it's many occasions
Let death give it a purpose. 25

"Spare not your life O brethren!"
Replied, uproared "O brave! have patience!"
"their fighting mounts and mounted crews,
Will amount soon to the ghastly dews.

"No size of fleet in fight that wins,
Its size of fight in fleet that wins.
"Our flame against flam hath triumphant warmth,
'Ts none ours, Master's might and majesty of Ram.

Seeing fire of fevered feud within them,
Nishaad exclaimed, "beat the martial drum."
Easy is very first beat of martial drum,
But has gory echo even after it mums.

But then, a hollow voice through grey-beard,
Slurred out his aged experience in words
"let's go and find what bringeth Bharat?"
Nishaad agreed; the feud need not be abrupt

Virile=manly, Strong; Agile=fit; Ghastly dews=blood shed; Flam=falsehood.

" it's nitwit act, hasty to rash,
The wise 'll read Bharat before clash."

Couplet:

"Ye brave ! let me first go,
And scan Bharat's brain,
If he is a fra or foe,
Let me ascertain. 26

"If he cometh with armada, armours, arms,
With own arms to hand over to Ram,
Or if haughty hatred in him do hatch,
Befo' me hidden heart can't be camouflaged."

Thus he proceeded to Bharat equipping himself,
With roots, fruits, eats sweets lavish dishes.
As he Kent Vashishtha, the Guru of the Lord,
He fell prostrate, his flesh he forgot.

The sage knew him to be Ram's soul-mate,
And introduced him to Bharat as Ram's intimate.
About Nishaad as soon as Bharat knew,
He alighted from Rath while wheels were still on move.

Alighted from the Rath, delighted he rushed,
His emotions filled his eyes with a gush.
And Ram's reflection in Bharat Nishaad found,
He greeted Bharat placing head on ground.

Couplet:

Nishaad would fall prostrate,
On that pious ground,
Bharat lifted and to bosom he pressed,
And met as if Lakhan was found. 27

Bharat felt warmth of a fra, of a friend,
Hand in hand both sunk in agony's sand.

On the high the witnessing sky,
Extolled the union with jubilant cry.

On the sandy banks new steady Kinship shaped,
Between prestige prince and the poor pleb.
Who surrenderth to the Lord, with selfless love,
Life entertains him all the saints, above.

For pure patricians or poor plebians,
Supreme vision hath a level glance.
One, who utters 'Ram' even while yawning, is blest,
By Ram Himself, this man* was embraced.

The ancient bard, Valmiki was a dacoit,
Till 'Ram' name honeyed his soul and defied.
Every brook betook into Ganges,
ts each drop is elixired with holiness.

Couplet: *The worthless, wilds, viles, worst,*
With little of their wit—
With little of their thirst—
For Ram ; they achieve(Him). 28

What Nishaad had achieved was all saints above,
For him, all witnessed increasing Bharat's love.
No wonder, for ages Nishaad will be a name,
Why not so it be? whom, Ram called a friend.

On the sands of Ganges, the ocean of bliss,
Swelt all along the two parties.
Seeing celeste reflections of Ram in Bharat,
Nay, his calm, care, canny, chivalric conduct,

Nishaad was dazed with unfatigued gaze,
His unwinked eyes imbibed the grace.

Patrician=high born; *Nishaad; Canny=gentle.

And to Bharat's anguish, being bereft of Ram,
The Nishaad, Guh's* union worked as a balm.

More and more charmed and with added warmth,
Submitted he honeyed words joining palms
"I have beheld Ram's lotus feet,
Further I'm blessed when thou didst meet.

Couplet: *"I'm crude, cad, catty yet,*
Ram granted His mercy,
None, I am for such grace,
Which the Lord crowned upon me. 29

"A cheat, chav, cheap, coward, crude cad,
An oarless, loreless torpid**
"Ever since Shri Ram took for his own,
I have become more, a gem, the world known."

Winsome words of wisdom were winning,
His words for Ram, rambled emotions in twins.
And next Shatrughan embraced Nishaad, as own kin,
Then, as a finding he took Nishaad, to the lost soul queens.

Nishaad greeted, queens treated, as own son,
Their motherly ope heart they could not contain
"May you live for ages and your name too,
Our blessings deluge is huge, but lips know few.

People praised Guh, the Nishaad for earning Divine hug,
That Embracing of Ram was embracing of goodluck.
As he heard these words it reminded Guh,
Of lavish warmth of Ram's close hug.

---

*Guh (name of Nishaad).
Cad=low; Catty=mean.
**Punning of the word(Oarless torpid=a boat without oar; Lore less torpid=dull minded)

Couplet: *On Nishaad's behest,*
Dispersed hosts of servants
To lodge all the special guests,
In haste, in zest they made camps. 30

Town's milieu and men earned Nature's rich gain,
Each frame was filled with lowing heifers, towering fanes.
Bharat felt revived with rejoice of the town,
He regained his soul which was long drowned.

Shringverpur, on one shore of Ganges,
Enamoured Bharat in his all gazes.
Bharat's brotherly hand on the shoulder of Guh,
Revealed bonds of affinity, as they moved.

Troubled Bharat, humble Bharat stepped with Guh,
And followed convoy of wheels, heels, hooves.
Then Bharat with kins, troops, retinue,
Imbued own soul with the 'Ganges' holy view.

Bharat's imbued soul, imbibed holy sips,
And immersed into waves for holy dip.
All reverence in Bharat, begged the Ancient flow,
Of all his conscious, to flow for Siya-Ram's love.

Couplet: *Long tired sinews and souls,*
Since Ram had left them,
At holy banks, citizens, prayed and extolled
For exiled Ram to return. 31

Camp was enlivened by the Ganges' holy run,
On behest of Guru, Bharat asked all to sojourn.
People took up their scattered lodging,
Caring Bharat asked about everyone, in person.

Taking leave of citizens, Bharat and his fra,
Both went up to mother Kaushalya.
All embodiment of reverence, then, the Bharat,
Politely looked for all mothers' comfort.

Then he entrusted Shatrughan, in their attention,
And summoned Nishaad, and moved hand in hand.
"to sooth my scorching show me that,
The spot, were Siya Ram and Lakhan stayed.

Bharat's scorched heart, parched tongue and eyes wet,
Poured a piercing chill through Nishaad's breast.
Sad Nishaad with his Laden heart,
Took Bharat swiftly to that spot,

Couplet: *Where under Asoka tree*,*
The Lord of Raghu rested,
Lost Bharat did kneel,
Before that shrine, the most sacred. 32

His lost soul, lost eyes found, some
Lost foot prints of his beloved Ram.
Reverently he put on his lot its dust,
Ocean of love which swelt, that have no words.

Bharat eyed some shines of gold spangles,
His reverence brimmed taking them as Siya Herself.
Recess of his lids filled with remorsed dews,
Then, he spake to Nishaad, all honey imbued

"the fallen bort, spangles from anklets and bangles,
Bereaved of Siya, look like Awadh's people.
"Helpless, sapless, without Siya-Ram,
Bleached faces have lost their charms.

"Siya whose father is monarch of affluence,
At the same, mastered ascetism as aplomb.

Bort = particles of diamond * Jonesia asoka (Sinsupa); Aplomb=dispassionate.

"and Ram whose majesty bringeth glory to cosmos,
That Ram Himself, is whose Lord,

Couplet: *"Hay-litter as I gaze,*
Used by virtuous Siya,
Adamant within me, not breaks,
Alas ! even at such awe. 33

"Worth-fondling prince, the little Lakhan,
Beloved of King, queens, Kins, Kingdom,
" 'Ts he, comely Lakhan had gone into woods,
Now and time to be, will be sign of brotherhood.

"A delicate mould, a dedicated soul,
A devoted mind and heart of gold,
"He bearth all hardships in woods,
Never been, who was exposed to wind or cold.

"Ram is friend of all, even praised by foes,
To Ram, every beat of Ayodhya owes.
"Shardaa * herself hath no word to speak,
To merits of Ram Lakhan, her tongue is weak.

Couplet: *"Ram, who is mine of mirth,*
And the mount of bliss,
Sleeps on grass, on earth,
It's fate's fitful fix. 34

"Ram had heard nor sobs nor sighs,
Father tended him like sapling of the life.
"Nay, mothers cherished him day and night,
Even as eyelids care the eyes.

---

*goddess of speech(Shardaa).
Fix=plight, tricky situation.

"Same Ram, bare foot wandered through woods,
Leaving lavish life, living on crudes.
"Accursed is Kaikeyi, who turned hostile,
The jewel of her life, Ram, she exiled.

"Me, occasioned troubles, me a blot to my race,
Twice accursed is my wretched own self.
"Me, the foe of fraternity; fie! fie!"
—Sic, sighs of remorse melted Bharat's eyes.

Nishaad solaced the soul in pain,
"why should Bharat ! you lament in vain?
"with the adverse fate rests the blame,
Mutual chain of love between Ram and you, I ken.

Stanza: *"Actual reverence hath mutual chains,*
That I kent between you and Ram,
It's fate's fitful fix, that deceived,
And bereaved you of Ram.
Nemesis bewitched, won the wit
Of mother Kaikeyi, by its trick,
You revere Ram ever, He rememberth you ever,
It's soul shared, so be not sick."

Distitch: *"Be not ill at ease !*
He recallth every humble call,
In every breast He is niched,
He is All-wise, pal. 35

"Courage ! this thought of Ram you do keep,
Take rest ! you Prince ! please go to sleep."
To the sores of Bharat words proved to be balm,
He stepped to lodgings, with the thoughts paced to Ram.

With spread of news, paced people to that place,
They saw the spot in swelling distress.

In brooding eyes, the view fell as thunderbolt,
And through their fatigued lids, the melancholy rolled.

For the stoical Ram, awe-struck they
Saw, instead of silky glitter, the litter of hay.
They blamed Kaikeyi and reproached cruel fate,
But, Bharat's Bhakti, they all praised.

Among some stunned mum, some did taunt,
Love of King for Ram was empty vaunt.
They skipped the kip, all kept vigil,
Passage across river began at wee-dawn.

Guru was put on a swift skiff,
And all mothers on one newly-built.

Couplet: *All crossed in short span,*
His mothers, Bharat adored,
To the Guru he bowed then,
And now started the whole host. 36

Bharat made Guh to usher the Van,
Started palaquins of mothers, then.
To escort palaquins, Shatrughan he summoned,
The Guru then proceeded with hosts of Brahmans.

To the celestial flow he made obeisance,
Himself set forth invoking Siya Ram Lakhan.
Bare feet Bharat on briars, barbs marched, on the bosky ways,
While led by the bridle moved harnessed bays.

Again and again pages, plebs did plead,
'Sire ! be pleased ! to mount thy steed.
"which Ram trod on foot ; its no wrong
Nay, it behoveth me I go headlong.

Kip=sleep; Skiff=boat.
The Van=front part of the troops; Harnessed bays=equipped horses.

"Let me not slacken my duty to the Lord,
For the duty of servant is ever hard."
Seeing Bharat's sick state and meek attitude,
All melted within with scorching lassitude.

Couplet: *In noon convoy reached,*
The pure purlieu of Prayag.
"O Siya Ram !" Bharat screeched,
"I have come to such a 'pass'. 37

Bharat's soul was blessed with blebs; the sole too,
Now, on bare lotus feet shone blister-dews.
Whole convoy was grieved to hear the news,
'Bharat continues all the march on foot.'

Taking care of everyone of accompaniment,
Bharat came to the banks of holy confluence.
Holy touch, holy dip in the sacred waves,
Healed body, healed mind and soul as well.

Sands of bank cushioned with its tickling drift,
Like healing kiss to the blistered feet.
Through eyes Bharat imbibed and quenched deep in,
The meeting of one swarthy, one pellucid stream.

"O Ganga ! O invincible waves of blessings,
Thou cleansest the souls of their sins.
"O mother ! I beg of thou alms,
Fill me, to the fill, with Ram.

Couplet: *"Willing no worldly weal nor wealth,*
Nor nirvana nor calm,
Only boon I ask nought else,
In my each lap, love to Ram. 38

Lassitude=weariness

" Let abuses and curses may fall upon me,
Let me be declared world's enemy.
"Growing up of my devotion, is my concern,
More and more, for Siya Ram, with every sun.

"May kins scold, may welkin pour coal
Upon me, the heaven may discharge thunderbolt.
"Even may Ram forget me and my love,
It's a gain if my faith grows above and above.

"The Master and the mastered, the world can't take back,
Ram within me, they can not ransack.
Tides within Bharat, touched the tides without,
From waves came sweet whispers, some aloud

" O Bharat ! thou art real pious soul,
Thine Love to Ram is unknowable, untold.
"the bout of doubt, in vain thou dost brood,
Thou and Ram havest mutual chain of brotherhood.

Couplet: *Thrilled Bharat heard Ganges,*
The rejoice shone Bharat,
And was appreciated
by Paradise, people and Prayag. 39

☐

15

Only those who want nothing, are masters of nature.

—Ram Krishna Paramhans

BHARAT IN PRAYAG

The people of Prayag, the pious pilgrim,
Praised Bharat as pride prince of pure realm.
As a fine benign, him they perceived,
Became he the talk of town, that eve.

Bharat's passes became avenue of applause,
Swiftly he wayed to the abbey of Bharadwaj.
The sight of the sage elixired Bharat with life,
But like lifeless came he, fell prostrate.

Running up, lifting, clasped him Bharadwaj,
As if embracing him fulfilled life's cause.
Guilt ridden, repent laden, as if Bharat would hide,
Sat the prince abashed, bent low contrite.

Conscience-stricken he sat mum,
Non plussed mind of Bharat found no word's sum.
Seeing abashed Bharat, the sage abated
"O Son ! all are puppets of some unseen thread.

Contrite=Abashed.

Couplet: *"Bharat ! be not ill at ease,*
For your mother's deeds,
Just faultless Kaikeyi
Was possessed by goddess of speech." 1

"Tho' nobody would approve what I moot,
But all have lauded your brotherhood.
"O Bharat ! singing your paeans and praises,
Holy sages, holy pages will earn accolades.

"Your sire was a goer of virtuous path,
For him world's tongue is filled with lauds.
"The will of King was to anoint you,
For the King, it was blessed point of view.

"But like thunderbolt fell exile of Ram,
That brought to hapless King, the hail storm.

"and the nitwit queen turned to the puppet of fate,
And now she repents of her own act.
"On you, who lays the blame, least,
His wicked folly need be preached.

"No blame falls down even if you accept reign,
Gratified Ram'll take it as His gain.

Couplet: *"Now your act excelled indeed,*
Bharat ! your stand is sound.
The devotion to Ram's feet,
Is the crown of all crowns. 2

"What's treasured in you that Ram is your wealth,
May that cherished vital thing be your breath.

Accolades=praises
To moot=to debate, propose.

“ ’Ts not to be wondered at, in your case,
Who is Dashrath’s son and Ram’s beloved.

“that night the three* till early wee,
Most fondly talked of you with me.
“In every step of Ram, Lakhan and Siya,
I noticed, for Bharat a nostalgia.

“Shri Ram cherisheth great love for you,
Nay, he cherisheth whole family of the devouts.
“While Ram is embodied Mercy itself,
You are it’s soul, the Love incarnate.

“ ’Ts one only soul that lies in two breaths,
You are shaped Devotion, He ist embodied Grace.
“Sameness of hue is not just skin deep,
The fathomless mutual love I have noticed.

Couplet: *“While you call it a slur,*
To us all ’ts a precept,
The world you have elixired,
With your nectarian faith. 3

“The welkin of devotion is canopied over us,
Crows not your devotion, glows like moon in hush.
“Unlike bragging meteors that ever melt,
You the spotless new moon shall never set.

“Nay, it will never wane and ever’ll wax,
It’ll torch the paths of generation next.
“Seers, seekers by seeing this new moon,
Like water lilies their souls will bloom.

“Your feet struggled not on path of love,
And calves ached not, on your moral move.

---

*Ram , Lakhan and Siya.

"In the blind folly of murky mundane,
You have torched a discrete path for the men.

"Your acts are elixir for Lord's devotees,
On earth even, you have made this path of ease.
Your truthness reflects your paters per se,
King Bhagirath's, Dashrath's virtuous way.

Couplet: *Dashrath, whose threads of love,*
Made the Lord to descend,
His heart and soul drove,
The Infinite's embodiment. 4

"Bhagirath's ethereal task on the real earth,
Flown down celestial Ganges for us.
"Such is your forefather's majesty,
Which made ethical path for posterity.

"You carry upright the very lit torch,
Of your pious race, on the moral march.
"The Elixir devotion that your bosom hold,
It's touch will make mankind of gold.

"You carry great onus as sung in Ved's opus,'
Your fuss at heart is of no purpose.
"My life has been fulfilled, while
I saw Lakhan , Ram Siya with my own eyes.

"Now, your sight is reward of that reward,
It's my gain nay it's gain of Prayag."
Healing words of sage thrilled the gathered throng,
And healed scorches of Bharat that sored him long.

Per se=by itself.

Couplet: *Rills of thrill ran,*
Along the veins of Bharat,
Molten eyes drained
All his searing hurts. 5

In the flood of emotions, words got choked,
Gathering himself Bharat, then spoke
"In the pious place among sages' throng,
All truthful should be my tongue.

"the pomp of sophism, here works not,
A cant can't cook, here it's plot.
"Even if I trick to cook a lie,
I will fail to word, before ye, All-wise!"

"And more, Raghuvar hath His access,
And can look every nook of heart's recess.
"Truth ! Nor mother's hellish thing is a sorry plight,
For me, nor father's heavenly passing, a blight,

"Truel not the least I fear for fated spoils,
Nor grieved a little for Awadh's turmoils,
"What pains me is dressing as hermits,
Ram, Lakhan, Siya roam in wilds bare feet.

Distitch: *"They kip on kush*
Keep self on bare roots,
Clad in crudes
Lonesome wander in woods. 6

"This agony is burning me deep,
Hath consumed my palate and my sleep.
"There is no remedy for the bereaved,
My sore is scratched with this toxic prick.

Molten=melted.
Cant=verbosity

"The warmth of my mother's lap had scorched me,
And fevered world is feeling like chill of agony.
"The infamous contrivance, what she employed,
Fell upon me and my world is destroyed.

"She spelt disaster, consumed vernal land,
Leaving withered lives, frosted end to end.
"The blues, blains of my bosom and the burns,
Wilt cease only when Ram returnth.

"Healing touch of Ram is only panacea,
With intense sore I stand in awe."
Gratified sage said, "Child ! Grieve not much,
All woes will disappear with Ram's touch."

Couplet: *The sage solaced sick soul,*
Asked him to stay—
"divert from the dole,
And be beloved guest of abbey." 7

Bharat in hard puzzle was perplexed,
In the difficult time, was asked to relax.
though confused was mind, consumed was soul,
Yet reverent words he had to hold.

Steeped in esteem he replied the sage,
"My Lord ! at thy command is thy page."
"monarchy-monastery if have mutual reverence,
It bringeth moral policy of governance.

"Ye Pupil ! entertain Bharat with fruits, roots, bulbs,
Care ! pious', priests, peers, pedestrians and plebs."
For the distinguished guest Bharadwaj thought,
'the divine powers' must be brought.

Blains=bleb; Peer=Aristocrat.

The atomic super-natural power of 'Anima',
Appeared embodied bidding "at thy service me lord !"

Bhardwaj ordered to power of 'Anima'—

Couplet: *"O power of tiny nucleus !*
I mastered you through penance
Entertain them, serve my purpose,
For they are drained and pained." 8

What hidden energy the particles conserved,
Embodied themselves became ready to serve.
All bowed down to the sage's order,
Deeming themselves highly favoured.

'Anima' the deity bowed at Bharadwaj's feet
"Let's serve the party, what's meet."
They raised tabernacles in stately way,
Equipped with luxuries and lavishes.

The ethyreal glory of this real camp,
Put, on high, the Immortals to shame.
The genius of such wondrous statecraft,
Is inner science that conceiveth state of art.

Provisions, pomps and pages at hands,
Were provided which ever can't be dreamt.
They assigned to the guests the heavenly abode,
The comfort of a fort with mellowness of meadows.

Couplet: *By dint of the penance,*
The Sage raised stately canopy.
Lavished with opulence,
Made far from Awadh, Awadh's copy. 9

By dint of=by power of.

Bharat was swayed by majesty of the Sage,
Cosmos looked petty before his sway.
The riches lavished camp's every nook,
The Sage spreaded canvas of a paradise look.

Through windows peeped in twilight of the eve,
And the breeze whispered into tapestries.
Canvas of vast Ganges viewed through windows,
And orchestrated melody of the twin flows.

As the ruddy roundel set in the west,
It's crimson adorned Ganges sandy crest.
In the bosky bushes, vernal breeze whistled,
And puffed in abodes making silks' rustle.

Essentials, especials, elixirs and eats,
Luxuries lavishes were all at easy reach.
Like caress of lap was the care of the couch,
But the enlivened eyes refused to drowse.

Couplet: *Keeping an opaque eye,*
On the glitter of opulence,
Bharat camped their in night,
Till blush in east commenced. 10

As the trill of birds called them for matins,
The party reverently took a Holy dip in.
The Bharadwaj's blessings, Bharat reverently received,
For, the up Sun was bidding him to proceed.

Healed cramps, healed blebs with touch of repose,
Bharat proceeded on journey taking whole host.
Expert guides joined Bharat on the route,
And his mind was set on the Chitrakoot.

Ruddy roundel=circle,(the setting red sun).

While Ram was enshrined deep in his marrow,
Hand in hand was Ram's friend* along the go.
With no shades, no sandals, the bare foot,
Stepped the determined devotee, on the rare route.

Every prick stabbed Bharat for the Three,
Who crossed the same in forlorn journey.
Bharat's speed drew up seeing the trees,
Guh told there rested for a while, the Three.

Couplet: *Nature-mother saw the love,*
And carpeted vernal bed,
Clouds afforded umbrella above,
For the devotee, ever cometh the nature's aid. 11

The birds, beasts, beeves, bees, beetles,
Even boughs, bushes, bowers, bosks, brambles,
Were blessed with boast of beatitude,
Who viewed Ram, or whom Ram's passing eyes viewed.

Now, Bharat's sight brought for them great gain,
They got rid of mirk and mire of mundane.
For Bharat, it was not a great thing,
Whom Ram ever cherished within.

Even they who utter Ram once in this world,
They are bark to take across bar, the others.

The tortuous passes which Ram rambled,
On that for the follower Bharat, the Nature helped.
Nature is good to the good while vile for the vile,
Worth winth the wreath, worst cometh to the wile.

Closer and closer Bharat neared to Ram,
Feared Indra brooded of the plot's spoilt.

---

*Nishaad, Guh.
Beeves=cattles; Boast=treasure; Bark=ship.

Couplet: *"The ocean of love Bharat cometh,*
With love Ram is ever won,
Let's find some strategem,
Lest our plan is undone." 12

INDRA'S PLOT DECLINED

"Ram's scrupulous nature that threatens me,
For help he asked divine Guru, Brahaspati.
In the words of Indra Brahaspati could find,
'Who seeth only 'Self', is better a blind.'

"Ram is craft Master and to His devotee,
who crafts artifice, it goes a miss.
"Past is not to be repeated for we thought,
It had tacit approval of Ram, the Lord.

"now, resorting to some treacherous means,
In return a sure disaster it'll bring.
"A hostile to Ram, Ram will skip,
One who hurts His devotee, he, sure gets His whip.

"Alike Bharat ; beloved of Ram, none can meet,
World mutters Ram's name, while his name Ram repeatth.

Couplet: *"Harbour no harm to devout,*
For it bringeth swarms of woes,
Let, here, no infamy sprout,
And in the next, trains of sorrow." 13

"O Indra ! O King of gods godules !
To Ram, just the Justness is most valued.
"And the service to devout is service to Ram,
It gratifies both so plan no harm.

"Although, Almighty watcheth with balanced eyes,
His look hath equal grace with no bias.
"Like a swarthy cloud that leaves no roof,
Showerth grace on the goers of false or truth.

"Yet, deeds of man only, rules the fate,
One reaps what he sows, it's tit for tat.
"Anarchy ruleth never, but the True belief,
Lord seemth to pass on devouts, His relief.

"No pomp but the pith*, no ego but the go,
He dwellth in benign, not the maligned show.
"Perverse to the truth, getth bonus of curse,
So trick no pricks for, true path who traverse.

Couplet: *"Devotees of Ram are gems,*
Are unbias for the mankind,
Bharat is highest among them,
Trick no malign to the Benign. 14

"Ram hath come for the cause of men,
For sick, weak, meek and for innocents.
"Devotion and love of Bharat is the height,
It's more a surrender and sacrifice.

"It's truth not the trick that pleaseth the Lord,
It's folly to be wise, in His cause.
"Blame not Bharat, blame your own interest,
That drives your mind and soul restless."

The heavenly word's of the celestial Guru,
Solaced Indra, gods and godules.
Now, solaced souls extolled Bharat,
For his fraternity, firmness, fidelity, faith.

---

*pith (for actuality)

Bharat's every breath was a bereft sigh,
Even rocks would melt, adamant would cry.
Halting at Yamuna, seeing its swarthy hues,
In Bharat's eyes brimmed the gloomy dews.

Couplet: *All were dipt in grief,*
Seeing swarthy hue of the flow,*
B'cause fate kept them bereaved
Of same swarthy hue of the Beloved. 15

THE SWIFT JOURNEY OF QUEST

All were dipped in the ocean of grief,
But, then hope of Ram's glimpse became bark of relief.
Enshrining swarthy Ram in their hearts,
On the banks of swarthy waves they made halts.

From the ghats all around, in the night's course,
For the holy cause came variety of boats.
So crowded, the boats as if making a bridge,
At the eastern break, all crossed in one trip.

To the Yamuna paying ablutions and regards,
Proceeded they, taking Nishaad as beloved escort.
Holy company first, then the royal crew,
people of Awadh, in the last the two.**

The quest of Ram was inner tempest,
So Swift moved toes as if equines' gait.
Their anxious rush had only little rest,
Reverently they bowed at places of Ram's stay.

---

* Dark flow of river Yamuna.

** Bharat and Shatrughan.

Couplet: *Reached to villages, the news and the din,*
Rushed they resigning routine,
And beholding the royal twins,
Got they gifts of their own beings. 16

Peasant's folly in saintly innocence,
Asked 'whether same twins hadst come again.'
They seem same prow, with same glow in visage,
Same amiable glow, same go in gait,

"look like Ram-Lakhan in every view,
But instead of Siya, accompanied by the crew.
"The twins have enlivened us a new,
With the same visage view and the contrast hue.

"but the twins who had gone, had divine smiles,
Here heavied with dews, are the empty eyes.
"Clad dresses, sad faces provide the clue,
Same bliss they bring to us, but are the different two.

One, who knew told 'Bharat goes to the wilds.'
To bring back Ram from his exile'
Reverence swelt in them, Bharat seemed their own,
In him they saw, a fra, a friend long known.

Couplet: *For the cause of brotherhood,*
Bharat renounced the sways,
To persuade he goes to woods,
None equalth Bharat today. 17

Faith, firmness, fraternity of Bharat,
Villagers viewed his virtues, vows and worth.
Let Bharat be the guide in mirks of mundane,
A legend who leads to a laudable lesson.

Talking of Bharat's ways, walking on Bharat's way,
Devout's will dispel their darks and dismays.

The bosom of Bharat is all mare nectaris,
'ts all ambrosia for men's species.

An affectionate heart in Bharat dwelt,
Though for brother of Ram, wonder not for that.
Tho' Bharat is pious yet for his forlorn state,
Some blamed Kaikeyi, while some blamed fate.

"While Awadh is accursed and wronged the worst,
But our wretched village is best favoured."
Thus, Strangers became delight of villagers,
A sight of life, like divine tree in desert.

Couplet: *Sight of Bharat was,*
Blessing showers on the village',
Their doors. the fortune had knocked
To the fore came itself pilgrimage. 18

Chance crowned upon the commons, the blessed marvel,
As if Prayag hath come in reach of simhals.*
Hearing whispers of his praises and his virtues,
Bharat further added to the pace of his move.

Crossing firaries, flows and fields, forests—
Crossing untrodden paths, some pedestrian passes,
Crossed planes, lanes, lands, fanes and the dense,
In penance, he, who was stranger yet to pains,

Moved he aimed at one and only need,
The sole devotion to the Siya-Ram's feet.
From peasants, saints, students of abbeys, convents,
He eagerly asked about Siya Ram and Lakhan.

The Little of tidings of Ram's comfort,
Tided over Bharat as life's support.

---

* dwellers of SriLanka.

Bharat looked eagerly every stranger,
For ambrosial words of Ram's welfare.

Couplet: *As the tired mounts of Sun,*
Crimsoned the crest of the west,
Party halted near some hamlet,
Started again at wee of the next. 19

The clear clairvoyance perceived by every one,
As if to prove themselves occurred good omens.
Omens suggested felicitous promise,
That woes and sorrows will soon vanish.

Thirsty Bharat and all rejoiced at very thought,
Soon they would imbibe the sight of their Lord.
With the souls elixired with wine of love,
After long odd days they had rave.

Ram's very thought became balm to melancholy,
Each one was engaged in his own fancy.
Their limbs danced, mastered as puppet of the soul,
All sinew were charged with emotive control.

Sametime, to Bharat Nishaad pointed out,
Through the bowers the glimpse of Kamadgiri mount
"That's hill by the rills of Mandakini,
There dwell, Siya Ram Lakhan, the Divine Three."

Couplet: *Beholding the holly hillock,*
Some fell prostrate in zest,
Searching Ram, eyes were locked
Zeroed on far quest. 20

The flood of joy that filled all the ways,
Engulfed poet's words to further portray.

Clairvoyance=intuitions.

What went in the heart of Bharat that time,
Those whispers of bosom can't be outlined.

The party was elixired with the wine of love,
Thrilled they all had a sluggish go.
Overwhelmed hearts benumbed their sinew,
Pace slowed and slowed as the bliss grew and grew.

Just a yojan they crossed till sunset,
Halted, waited for the twilight of the next.
The intuition, is unseen chain of mutual esteem,
It descended that very night in Siya's dream.

Bereaved Bharat, down Awadh, gloomy faces of mothers,
Filled Ram with glum, as Her dream She shared.
Who getth rid of sadness, He Himself was sad,
'Lakhan ! this bodes no good, something ist bad.'

Stanza: *Fretted for kins, upset for queens,*
After wee-routines, performed matins,
With Lakhan worshipped Lord Shiv,
He had brooded the time was grim.
Sat down the Lord, gazing to the north,
Seen dusty clouds to raise misty doubt,
Amazed he gazed, heath heaved,
Till came wood reeve to tell about.

Couplet: *The News, brimmed the eyes with bliss,*
Rolled on cheeks a beaded view,
As a blow of autumnal breeze,
Hath pearled lotus with dews. 21

Heath=forest land ; Wood reeve=foresters (guards).

LAKHAN'S ANGUISH

Very next mo vanished his joy and bliss,
'what reason brought Bharat' was His anguish.
Tidings and tidings were pouring in,
Some said 'comes with him forces with four limbs.'

'Manful military, mounts, monks, minions,
Martials, ministers, masses and myriads of men.
Between firmness to father's command and love to His fra,
The Master was muddled by this dilemma,

Fixing on Bharat's reverence, love and spirit,
Valued wisdom could not work out not even vague verdict.
He, himself consoled that Bharat was submissive,
At the same, Lakhan saw Ram's ill at ease

Lakhan said " I may pertly, but say unasked,
Blame no pertinence for the opportune cause."
"Thou the Master omniscient, O All wise ! Ram !
Me, Thy servent tell of my little mind's qualm."

Couplet: *"Thy pellucid mind's eye see*
Ever guileless the brotherhood,
Like Thyself know all to be,
And perceive not the mind's crude. 22

"In the glitter of pomp man's folly prevails,
In dazed eyes, ever the avarice swells.
"World heard melodies of Bharat's heart,
All the current of his soul seemed set to the Lord."

"But now his wisdom and righteousness,
Yet attaining 'Thy sways' may be swayed.
"Double the vision in my eyes dwells,
Mind seeth in him faith, while outward crosses else.

Avarice=greed.

"For, his eyes altering, may have altered all,
May have wrongly his rights, guided him to fault.
"Fallible faults may falter the faith,
Finding Thou in forlorn forest, cometh the foul face.

"Their folly playing foul, with forces they forayed,
Thus fixed feud, the fight for the secured sways.

Lakhan concluded—

Couplet: *"His mind ist ruined by reign,*
Swayed over by pomp the sway,
All his fraternity is drained,
Evil hath driven him astray. 23

"Sovereignity severeth the thread among kins,
Crown hath drowned many, in mirk of sins.
"Bharat read first lesson of the politic belief,
One should leave even, not single hostile seed.

"Sic, he cometh, the sick mind, with brewing poison,
'Thou art forlorn', he, but is mistaken.
"His grave esurience will be staved by Ram,
He who braves Ram, can only be saved by Ram."

With brows on tenters, and bows in hand,
His bellicose mind burst words of challenge.
Touching Ram's feet again Lakhan spoke
"By Bharat not a little I am provoked."

"My restrained fire, now trampet ballad-drums,
While Thyself art with me, shouldst I keep mum?"
"Pray ! do not take offence ! to conclusion I jump,
The facts I reveal as Thy factodum.

Fallible=erring; Falter=shake.
Esurience=greed; Stave=crushed; Factodum=confident servant; Bellicose=heading to war.

Couplet: *"Hush meets not a warrior,*
Further I'm Thy known page,
Thy support is my valour,
So I'm never at stake." 24

As he rose and with joined palms asked the leave,
It seemed as if heroic muses cometh embodied.
Binding his tress, fixing on waist quiver,
He strung his bow, with brows on tenters.

"me, the page of Ram with pelters of bows,
'll force Bharat to surrender and, to bow.
"Braving Ram, contempt of Ram, is misdeed,
Indeed in field it's fruit, they will reap.

"The hostiles, in the field, art sure disarmed
By the Doers for Ram, the goers for Ram
"Ram is with me, truth is my weapon,
Before its fought, the battle is won.

"To my past fire, I shall give today vent,
Even as a lion tears the herds of elephants.
"Even if Lord Shiv cometh to his aid,
I swear by Ram, he'll be defeated.

Couplet: *In the anger, wisdom was dipt,*
Took he the solemn oath,
Furious face, flaming lips,
Brought not the truth to his troth. 25

□

Troth=belief.

16

If you want to be spiritual, you must renounce.

—Swami Vivekanand

RAM PRAISES BROTHERHOOD

Dismayed Sylvan-deity fled, and godlings ran,
An oracle filled air with Lakhan's paeans—
"glory of thy bow, thy might O prow !
None can tell nay None even knows !"

"But think ! think ! before any feud, any grudge,
Words, weapons, go only one way, so think ! judge !!
"Acts not well thought of, ever go in vain,
So reck ! impulse lead but to repent.

"Such words of gold are penned on old holy leaves,
So the furor of fire, thou extinguish ! please !"
Shyness crimsoned the countenance of Lakhan,
But then Siya Ram eased him with comforting mentions.

Ram said to Lakhan—

"What you have said that sounds proper,
The swill that swells, worst is the wine of power.
"But for Bharat I tell, now and in time to be,
Creation may never create so good as he is.

Furor=passion

Couplet: *"Bharat is far above great,*
Would never be ruined by reign,
He is fraternity incarnate,
Unaltered by any gain. 1

"In mare nectaris of love, Bharat pulls a good oar,
Can that ocean of milk be ever split by drops of soar.
"A Gnat may blow great Meru in a puff,
The tolerant Earth may turn tough,

"But drinks of pomp can not intoxicate
Bharat ; who is elixired with love and faith.
"Bharat is benign, Bharat is divine,
Bharat is mine, a pious brine, pristine.

"In the mire of mundane and in it's mirk,
Virtues of Bharat, as swan, pick pearls.
"In the fumes of fib fraternity fades not,
Fidelity falls not in the fancy of fraud.

"Bharat is as dear to Me as you,"
Thus Lord of Raghu extolled Bharat's virtues.
World extollth Ram, Ram extolledst Bharat,
His troth, trait, truth his depth, his faith.

Bharat's birth is the boast of the Earth,
Lest the cause of virtue who would have served.

Couplet: *Hearing speech of Shri Ram,*
Drawn by merits the gods, demigods,
Nay all Sylvan to heaven were charmed,
Seeing lofty stance of the Lord. 2

Pristine=original; Pulls a good oar=a skilled sail.

BHARAT MEETS RAM

Here, Bharat bathed in pious Mandakini with hosts,
And then left all of them, at the river shore.
Taking permission of his mothers, preceptors, ministers,
He proceeded where Siya and Ram were there.

Taking Nishaad and Shatrughan, he, in timid steps,
With ill surmise moved the meek modest.
"God forbid ! Siya-Ram Lakhan may be annoyed,
They may leave place, me the wicked to avoid.

"Whether he abandonth this Knave, me think,
Hope ! he may allow me in his bosom to shrink.
"Whether He shunneth me in His rage,
Or welcometh me as His own page,

"Whether His healing touch balmth my wound,
My brotherhood whether 'll be pruned or ruined."
Doubts dragged his steps as he went nigh and nigh,
One stride was keen, one stride was shy.

Though, diffidence of mother's act, pulled him back,
And his own deference pushed his steps.
Glimpse of hope was Ram's disposition,
"God forbid Him see my vile, but the devotion."

"Me, a guile thing, in my shameless go,
find the only refuge in His sabot.

Couplet: *"thinking of mother's vice,*
no ill to me 'll be too much,"
He Felt shy in surmise
'May he forgive me with old hug.' 3

Sabot=wooden sandal (Paduka); Surmise=doubt

Divined Nishaad— 'thy sober wish,
Of delight will be accomplished,
But clad in saber, the bliss,
May turn in sorrow at finish." 4

Thus, discussing all pros and cons,
Near to the grotto they were drawn.
Bharat's thirsty eyes at the holy hillock gazed,
While his soul was winged, swift gait seemed dragged.

On the pinions of hope charged with assurance,
He moved as if flying, as he saw the hilly range.
In the vernal greeting of the greens of Chitrakoot,
The bereaved Bharat forgot his blues.

The laden bowers lightened his burdened bosom,
The virgin forest seemed revelling in his welcome.
Bharat wondered not at rejoices of jungle life,
As where Shri Ram dwellth, by itself is paradise.

In the blithe of buzz of bees in woods,
Recalled Bharat, Ram's lullaby in the childhood.
The breeze murmured Ram, brooks whispered Ram,
Cataracts muttered Ram, cascades uttered Ram.

Couplet: *A greater paradise was Chitrakoot,*
A vision or the waking dream,
Kamadgiri, like a shrine stood,
*In back drop of the holy stream.** 5

The holiest heaven with habitated hermitages,
Breeze unveiled vernal wrap, welcomed nodding thickets.
Folks of bushes rocked on the gale glad,
Soles forgot blebs treading on floral shed.

---

*Mandakini river.

The whirring bees and the warbling birds,
Orchestrated for frolicking beast herds.
In the crooks of brooks and spills' rills' flow,
Shallow pebbles creased some milky furrows.

The Earthern fragrance perfumed the milieu,
Grassy meadows sprinkled on toes the dew.
With the wind it drizzled from nodding avenue,
To freshen rued Bharat's countenance a new.

Gladdened avians made glad concert,
Laden boughs bowed in the path of Bharat.
The spread of spring went on a binge,
To balm all qualms and Bharat's sufferings.

Couplet: *Through bowers was seen Ram's hill,*
As to the fore Ram had stood,
Beholding it Bharat was thrilled
As if had reaped life's fruit. 6

Meanwhile Nishaad ran up a mound,
Lifting arms exclaimed 'Lo! that mount.'
"Lo! those huge figs and noble plums,
There dwellest Siya Ram Lakhan, the ibidem.

"Enriched by the fig, mango, Tamaal and plum,
Stands seemly, shapely, stately Banyan.
" it's silky foliage that makes verdure canopy,
With stitched on it the fruits ruddy.

"Under that unbroken shades, in its gremio,
With hay clay, leaves Ram had made a grotto."

Ram maketh the cosmos for own Joy,
Same way He hath erected that hut as own toy.

Go on a binge=make merry.
Ibidem(*L*)=in the same place; In gremio=on bosom.

Wavy pebbles fixed by Lakhan at the sill,
Seeta planted by the sides, holy shrubs of basils.

Couplet: *An altar raised by Herself,*
As seat for sermons, anecdotes,
Where crowds of hermit would tell,
Of veds, legends and the old. 7

Seeing medleyed bunch of trees of grove,
Through Bharat's eyes brimmed heart of love.
Two brothers were benumbed by emotion, reverence,
While soul winged far, dragged only their frame.

Even goddess of speech could not reach,
The statue of love that in two hearts was niched.
They found foot print on their pass,
To the bliss, as a pauper had stumbled on Paaras.

Rills rolled on cheeks dropped on prints' dust,
Tears mingled in dust, revealed mutual thirst.
Stirred by the scene, Nishaad was astrayed,
But then Sylvan deity carpeted floral ways.

Ascetics nay, alps, animals, avians,
Began to praise Bharat's true affection.
Only Bharat could make soulful, an inert,
Even could make lost soul, the life, with no exerts.

Couplet: *Bharat's deep heart was churned,*
By the Mathini of bereavement*
And nectar of love was earned,
For the mankind and heaven. 8

Paaras=elixir stone that converts base metal to gold.
*Churning stick

The nighing three, in the bushes shroud,
'Cometh who'? Lakhan could not make out.
Through the nodding shrubs, but Bharat could see,
The simple hermitage with its stately beauty.

Lakhan was standing with alert presence,
Hermit's robes girted loin, quiver tied on waist.
As the Lakhan moved a little; the divine glimpse,
Of his beloved Ram, filled him with bliss.

In the hermit's dress and matted tress,
Among blest assemblage sat He, in swarthy grace.
With hallow crowd, in mellow mood,
On the raised altar he saw Siya too.

The divine couple, doubled Bharat's thrill,
His limbs palsied at this divine sill.
Worthy smile, swarthy face, that time fulfilled
Bharat; healed sore-soul of diffident ills.

Couplet: *In the whirls of wise commune,*
Sat winsome Siya and Ram,
Looked like in circles of wisdom,
Dwellth with its bliss, the Truth. 9

Bharat imbibed the scene and absorbed in it,
And forgot his chilled ill, and fevered fit.
Mirth on its zenith is above pleasure-pangs,
Benumbed the new-comer, lost the frame and the sense.

And soon Bharat's conscious found his Master to the fore,
Flat he prostrated and fell on the floor.
'Save me Lord! Save me! Thy slave!
Lakhan Kent,'he is filled hearts,and empty haves.'

Lakhan, but at Ram's service, to meet Bharat though,
Was in the dilemma of the two beloved's love.

Same while, Lakhan told Ram in great reverence—
"Here about cometh Bharat and making obeisance."

The news as nectar poured, Ram started up lost,
There fell robes, here quiver, bow, arrow dropt.

Couplet: *To Bharat, thus, Ram paced,*
Lifted him in persuasive rush,
This meeting who ever witnessed,
Lost he flesh and all conscious. 10

The mutual fond of twins, and their fraternal feat,
And their meetings no words can meet.
In the flood of affection, its pellucid flow,
Dissolved the two looked One, the Embodied love.

Wet eyes of two souls had the same thirsty go,
Lost reason, wisdom, lost mind and ego.
Royal silk rustled meeting hermit's robes,
Jewelled wreath met rosary beeds and sobbed.

On Ram's bosom laurelled loops of lei,
Were laved by craved love of Bharat's eyes.
'Rama gatherth Bharat, this panorama,
And the pouring of affection's ambrosia,

Stunned wordless everyone, who ever did behold
All gazed the meeting, all filled to the soul.
Then, the godlings found some hurdle in the plot,
But when Guru* solaced them, they gave shouts of applause.

Couplet: *After fondly embracing Shatrughan,*
Ram met Nishaad, as friend,
At the same Bharat hugged Lakhan,
On the flood of love, rained the Heaven. 11

Likewise Lakhan eagerly met the youngest,
And clasped Nishaad to his bosom next.
Then they greeted the hosts of hermits,
Swift, placed their heads to Siya's Lotus feet.

In the rapture of love they made obeisance,
Overwhelmed to Her again and again they bent.
Most affectionately Siya, the doer of cosmos,
Blest them with Mother's touch, overwhelmed She was.

Laurelled=wreathed with leaves; *Brahaspati, Celestial preceptor.

When they found Siya propitious in every way,
Their anxiety vanished, gone their dismay.
In overflowing heart words had no room,
Comfortable hush ever sufficeth in the love bloom.

All lips did freeze and words did cease,
As the fraternity hath no words, no queries.
A hush from hearts filled the earth, the welkin.
But then Nishaad gathered words to say something.

Couplet: *"Lord ! whole Awadh was bereaved,*
The queens, kins, plebians,
Accompanying with Vashishtha,
All along, all have come." 12

THE THREE MEET ALL VISITORS

When amiable Ram, heard of Guru,
He proceeded at once in swift move.
Left Shatrughan by Siya's side,
His reverence for Guru put Him on winged stride.

Seeing Guru, Ram Lakhan prostrated themselves,
: The reverence dwelt in them, profoundly swelt.
from here,Vashishtha ran and clasped Them to bosom,
Even as after fourteen long years They had come.

Guru saw prostrated Nishaad prone on the earth,
He embraced, seemed as though gathering the love, scattered
This blest moment Nishaad treasured,
In the earth born bosom, as ethereal gain.

Nay, in chains of lives of penalty and pains,
Came as final beatitude, this rare moment.

The people of Awadh looked embodied Anguish,
For their restless soul, their sentimental wish.
For pangs of pious, posh, plebs, peasants,
Ram Lakhan relieved all, in an instant.

Among Ram's wondrous wonders, it's no a wonder,
Simultaneously Sun fills all, with it's splendour.
Then, the three grieved statues*, bereaved images,
Like, the frost bitten creepers looked empty faces.

In vain, mothers tried to hide inner blues,
With bloom on lips, in eyes gloomy dews.
But then brooding abou' mother, Ram realized,
The fate had thundered over them left into rampike.

Grieved Ram, retrieved, arrived to Kaikeyi first,
Reverently he bowed and soothed her hurts
'this mo, none but fate be blamed,
As Providence driveth the Time's helm.

Couplet: *Ram met all His mothers then,*
And balmed their sore,
'the providence is the helmsman,
Blame none, therefore.' 13

Then, the preceptor's wife and priests' ladies,
The two greeted them like Ganges and Gauri.
Ram and Lakhan then bowed at feet of Sumitra,
In her, the statue of melancholy they saw.

Both fell, now at feet of Kaushalya,
Even as humble thirsty would get ample ambrosia.
Mother's arms enveloped, bathed them in tears,
As the meek cow getth long lost heifer.

---

*Three queen mothers.

The warmth of joy with the chill of grief,
This divine meeting, no words can meet.
Mother's lap for son, is any reign above,
Endless is the sway of warmth of her love.

Recalling blest mo in hour of blight,
Bringeth more dolour and none the delight.
The day came well nigh done,
On command of Guru, encamped citizens.

Couplet: *Along with Lakhan and Bharat,*
Queens kins and the priests,
Lord proceeded to the holy hut,
Ushering His Guru first. 14

Siya came, threw Herself at Vashishtha's feet,
Implored by Her, the blessings She received.
Seeta greeted one and each of pious hosts,
To them, most reverently She bowed.

Scanned through the crowd, when the tender princess,
Looking at mother-queens She turned dismayed.
She closed Her eyes at the sight of havoc,
Her throat choked, lost She was shocked.

Shrunk She screamed engulfed by grief
'Alas ! providence had done big mishchief'.
Seeing tender girl on trials of the woods,
Mothers were sore distressed too—

"We must bear what's imposed on us,
To endure fate's curse is our onus."
Siya embraced mothers, filled with woe,
Seemed the Earth would tremble to bear pathos.

Couplet: *Siya let the rivulets of great love,*
through Her eyes, gush,
At their feet She Herself, did throw,
And was soothed by blessing touch. 15

And the melancholy swayed the whole milieu,
And one by one all dipt in the deluge of the blues.
Then wise Guru bade them and all sat down,
'ts fret of the fate, fear not its frown.

In the crowd every one was forlorn,
With his separate weeping world of moan.
Guru gave them lessons and sermons,
And then announced King's passing to the heaven.

Ram is stoical and firmest of firm, though
But the mo of moan filled Him with woe.
News fell as thunderbolt, through and through it pierced,
'His love for Me had caused his quietus.'

Lakhan, Siya, queens nay all assembly lamented,
As though King had died that very day.
That day the Lord fasted, even abstained from water,
Persuaded but none else took a sip either.

Couplet: *In the sorrow's hush none spoke,*
The night had sleepless tread,
And as eastern rim broke
Reverent Ram did what the Guru bade. 16

THE URBAN GUESTS-THE SYLVAN HOSTS

Ram observed father's obsequies as per olds*,
And performed rituals as the priests told.

---

*Old texts

In the little mortal eyes-'the Lord hadst performed,'
But the rites in itselves were hallowed by Ram.

Two suns saw ghostly woods in odd hush,
Then Ram approached to Guru and spake thus
"O My Lord ! it's my woe,
People live here on bulbs roots and sloe.

"Blight of both brothers bothers Me,
As well when ministers, mothers I see.
"Their distressed moments for Me pass like an age,
What worries Me, 'if more they stay.'

"Thou art here and the king ist in heaven,
To reck forlorn town, ye all may return.
My gross presumption, pray ! thou willst ignore,
Now, O Gurudev! do what's proper to thy lore?

Couplet: *"For thy words Ram I'm not amazed,*
O bulwark of virtues !
Let grieved souls derive solace,
Seeing Thou for a day or two." 17

On Ram's words feared assembly trembled,
As in brine, the storm had tossed bark on sail.
Words of Guru seemed as down dropt the breeze,
But still on faces reflected ill at ease.

People would bath thrice in Mandakini, the very stream of Ganges,
And ever would feast their eyes on Ram's visage.
Their matins, vespers, and their vigils,
Their prayers, entreaties had only one will—

"Should Ram return! should Ram return!!
Should qualm shun ! should our virtues earn!!"

They flocked at His abode, gazed with Eyes locked,
Their feet circumambulated the hallowed hillock*.

Founts, mounts, flaunts of flamboyant,
And breezes, boughs, birds, bees soothed their pangs.
The Creator painted forest with his vernal brush,
Sylvan-welcome had lively lavish lush.

Couplet: *Verdure carpeted the lae,*
Winged warbles filled the ways.
Contrast beasts roamed free,
Bees hummed, birds hymned lays. 18

Lotuses bloomed, and water fowl cooed,
Flown some quiet, some coquettish brooks.
Sylvan dwellers and remote races,
Eagerly welcomed their strange guests.

Making bowls of barks and cones of leaves,
Brimming with fruits, roots, bulbs and peas,
Sweet words of earthly touch, accented lout,
Offered they full hands, fruits-sprouts.

For their strange foods they would mention the tastes,
Seeing interest of guests, brought more lavishes.
People gladly offered a liberal price,
With humble submissions the foresters denied

"Ye are dwellers of Awadh, the virtuous soul,
Wild crude are we, Bhil, Kiraat and Kol.
"It's Ram's grace that had chanced us in forest,
Ye, the godly people are our guests."

Flaunts=boast; flamboyant=floral decoration; *'Kamadgiri hillock'

Couplet: *"Take aegle-bel* shake off scruple,*
We cater our love,
Our pigmy hands are ope liberal,
Accept roots, bulbs, grains, sloe. 19

"Forest taketh ye as welcome guests,
But we uncivil can't serve ye the best.
"None we can reach to recipe of your interest,
Roots bulbs we barter in friendly business.

"Our daily commerce is a crude bargain,
Preferth handful loss for the bosom's gain.
"Accept our token of goodwill in woods,
Else, our service is that, we don't steal your goods.

"We dwell with wild beasts, and we are no less,
We are coarse, cruel crooked creatures.
"Our daily toil is spent in sinful pursuit,
Our confined life is unrefined, crude.

"Since, worthless, we, gazed swarthy visage,
Our folly, flaws all are now fled."
Citizens thought of true faith of tribes
"Befo' such an innocence, its folly to be wise.

Stanza: *"It's prize of unstained life that blessed*
The plane tribes,
The divine visage, enshrined Himself,
In the Dense, becoming man-sized.

Prudence fails before such reverence,
Here prevails, none else but the faith,
Citizens souls extolled Ram's grace, as well
The lot of the remote race.

---

*Aegle marmelos=(wood-apple)

Distitch: *They wandered in wondered mood,*
Finding Ram In Chitrakoot,
Found pilgrimage in wondrous woods
Where dwelth Ram,That's their Awadh. 20

Rush of the time was the wink of the eye,
Thus passed citizens days and nights.
With equal attention Seeta waited on mothers,
Queens took these days as great treasures.

If one inclines to the declining ages,
Such service stands on worship's acme.
Keen hands of Siya ever served the queens,
Did win over them, Her reverence within.

Perceiving Siya and two brothers naive act,
The bitter queen, birtterly repented.
Guilt- ridden she would hide her into earth,
As well she sought help from the god of death.

Nor the earth afforded shelter nor did god grant death,
Those, hostile to Ram, find no shade.
Now, the question which stirred every thought,
'O Heaven ! will Ram return back or not?'

Couplet: *As the fish is worried and writhed,*
Sunk in the quick-shore,
Anorexic days and insomnic nights,
Filled Bharat's core. 21

□

17

All the heaven, that ever existed is now and here.

—Swami Vivekanand

ANGUISH IN ASSEMBLEY

"Disguised, as my mother, the fate's mischief,
Hath ruined the ripening crops of paddies.
"Me think, reached not, the way how?
Shri Ram accepth the Ayodhya's crown.

"I can hit upon no plan at this point,
Only Guru is hope for Ram to anoint.
"Ram 'll return on Guru's behest,
But then, Guru 'll first see Ram's interest.

"Biddings of mother may again force Ram,
But, will mother insist? – it's a qualm.
"As for myself, only vassal and nothing,
At the top, the providence is against me.

"More over due reverence bounds my limit,
If I ask; for me it's not meet."
—His anxious night was spent awake,
In the next vague morn he got to the sage.

Couplet: *Bharat bowed at preceptor's feet,*
With permission sat nigh,
Soon assembled executives, elite,
Making gathering a size. 1

Then, the Sage, in words, most appropriate,
To the gathered council thus spake
"heed ! the councellors and wise Bharat you !
Ram, Himself is the path and Himself goer too.

"the strophes of Veds are shone in His deeds
He ist trophy of blessings to the world indeed.
"His firm foot prints on the untrodden path,
For the Would be men, will be virtuous torch.

"A definite purpose carries His advent,
For Ved, Virtues, Values; He doth descent.
"Obedient to preceptor and parents,
Morals of holy pages He maintainth.

"The etheric, earthy, eerie, or else,
All affluence is mastered by His spells.
"Ye of clay, nay all rays and all the ways,
Are swayed over by His simple brow's play.

Couplet: *"Undecided the mind is caught,*
In the mesh of dilemma.
Only Ram'll find the path,
To rectify our awe." 2

"Coronation of Ram 'll bring sublimest joy,
Think ! some device may be employed.
"Ram, as He is, Vast virtue's epitome,
What way may prevail to bring Him home?

Eerie=wondrous, magical.

A spiritual thought with a salutary surcharge,
With regard, sages's words, every one heard.
While Ram is the question, the answer is Ram,
There, dumb founded people sat with joined palms.

In the brooding hush, milieu, a silence did hold,
Bharat bowed his head and thus told
"O Revered Guru ! the ancient reign of solar race,
Had increasing greatness, thou art witness.

"Every scion was a greater icon,
Further sublimed solar race's splendorous eoan.
"The birth, fruits, feats, defeats are destined,
Yet thou changest determined fate, what thou dost determine.

Couplet: *"Now, Thy asking at this crisis,*
While fate is defeated at thy feet,
Misfortune, to me, sticks,
My little mind hath little reach." *3*

Revered words filled and flooded Guru,
"What you have said is no doubt true.
"My wisdom, My vim is all Ram's grace,
Who is hostile to Ram, never can see success.

Vashishtha advised—

"Most hesitant I tell, what did I conclude,
Bartering exile ye, two* retire to woods.
"Ignore loss, when everything seems periled,
Empty hands should course a halfway deal."

While the Guru resolved the best of their choice,
The two withered faces, bloomed with rejoice.

Scion=heir; Eoan=dawn.
*Bharat and Shatrughan.

Happy, as the King's corpse was puffed with soul again,
Happy, as Ram had accepted Awadh's reign.

In the balance of bosom, people weighed the loss,
In this bargain, they bargained for a gain vast.
"I conceive no greater bliss" Bharat said,
"I will stay all life in the forest."

Couplet: *"Obeying Guru is my concern",*
—Hearing thus Káushalya wailed,
"No barter knows mother's bosom,
My glee and grief paralleled." 4

"Redeem thy words, if what thou sayst is true.
Me Mother am at same loss, if this is approved."
Bharat's heart rolled through eyes and lips worded,
All assembly was benumbed, lost flesh.

At the brink of brine of bosom of Bharat,
Helpless sage's wit stood without a raft.
Sought many a device to cross this brine,
But the boat, bark, brig; Bharat could not find.

Can ever in a shell, be contained a brine,
Thus the glory of Bharat can not be defined.
The sage was pleased with Bharat in his heart of hearts,
So, with whole assembly, he came to the Lord.

Reverently Ram welcomed, offered a raised seat,
Every one sat down all about receiving permission of Vashishtha.

Vashishtha said in assembly—

"O Unknowable Ram ! Thou knowst every thing,
O Virtue incarnate Ram ! Listen to me

Bargain for=anticipated.
Brig=a type of ship.

Couplet: *"Thou dwellest in every core,*
Thus, know our intent,
Tell us Ram ! therefore,
What serves Kins, queens, citizens." 5

In the elegant way Ram did speak
"Pious thou art panacea of all the panic.
"Carrying out thy behests, and acclaiming those,
'll be shower of blessings, every one knows.

"Any order from thou is our bliss,
Each will devote himself to thy service."
Further said the sage "What you said is true,
But Bharat's love hath robbed all, me too.

"Soft control of emotions hath muted my wit,
To the devotion of Bharat I'm sympathetic.
"My judgement hath lost it's lofty spirit,
Thus no conclusioin I do meet.

"Me think ! the love for Bharat what dwells in you,
For Bharat, will ever do every good.

Couplet: *"Listen ! Bharat's humble submission,*
Then think and again think,
Then with vedic, ethics, civic concern,
Come to the verdict." 6

For Bharat, the Guru's caring bosom,
For Ram, became a matter gladsome.
Bharat is virtuous-it's world known,
Ram, knowing him, the most beloved own,

Spake, soft as chiming worship-bells,
Hormonized with Guru's behest, in enthralling spells—
"There hath been no such, and in time to be,
Brother as Bharat, only rare world will see.

"More-over whom the preceptor hath blessed,
He is favoured both from earthly and ethereal ways.
"He is younger so my words of praise,
Recoil to proceed on his face.

"For Sure ! it will be conductive to the best,
To do what so ever dear Bharat suggests."

Couplet:

The Sage to Bharat now said,—
"Shake off all scruples
What for O Child! wait,
Let your heart unfurl." 7

He read Ram's mind and heard sage's favour,
He felt, on him, a warmth of shelter.
Glad he was, blest by the preceptor and Master,
At the same felt onus on his shoulders.

Bharat realized that he was on helm at tempest,
His tongue froze, Lips stiffened therefore, in unrest.
Thrill ran all along his sinews,
Gushed through his eyes the helpless dews.

In fevered warm heart, his words chilled,
The statue of love stood in assembly stilt.
But then collecting himself, he whispered a bit,
"the sage hath resolved already, I have nothing to submit."

"My Master is Kind to even a hostile,
His brows, at me even in child's play never coiled.
"Since cradle left me never, nor did He damp my spirit,
He would have me win a game, even tho' I had lost it."

Couplet: *"My meekness mummed my lips,*
Due to reticent reverence,
Tho' my mind's eye in Him dipt,
My thirsty eyes never quenched. 8

"Still craving the ambrosia of His sight,
Have not been sated to this day, my eyes.
"But the coveted fate could not tolerate,
In disguise of my vile mother it created a cleft.

"Even it behoveth me not to say such,
With the vaunting self, will I be pious.
"Nope ! to say mother victim, me, the son virtuous,
Itself is a mouthy mouth malicious.

"Can an empty vault produce a pearl,
None be blamed but me, my luck is dull.
"I pose of my faith, but my flaw unfurls,
My words may not stay in ye, like silky burl.

"I have scorched my mother in vain by taunts,
My plea, I'm sinless, is my sin that vaunts.
"I have Siya Ram as Masters, thy holiness as Guru,
So, my hope presumeth we will get through.

Couplet: *"In pious presence, at pious place,*
Have I craving for Ram or I crow?
I speak in my good faith,
The sage, Siya Ram dost know. 9

"The world is witness of the two extremes,
King's quietus for his love, and queen's ill quirk.
"Nay, the queens, Kins but the people at large,
With the deepest agony all are scorched.

Burl=a small knot at corner of cloth.
Quirk=trick.

"Weeping cloud I am, fell on Awadh as doom,
That clouded every soul with its gloom.
"Being root of all pains, it pains me more,
Realizing this, all sufferings I endure.

"Sorrow's crown of all sorrow is–'I 'm root of sorrow,'
The beloved Ram left to the woods, yet I survived this blow.
"Left Siya Ram, Lakhan as hermits, bare foot,
Still my hardest heart to break, refused.

"More, my block head, blurred eyes saw Nishaad's love,
To live with my shameless soul where should I go?
"At whose sight snakes, scorps forget to sting,
Woe is me ! the root cause of His sufferings.

Couplet: *"On whom-else, the wrath of the fate,*
Should fall as woes,
Than, Me, whose mother looked at
Ram, Lakhan, Siya as her foes." 10

Hushed his lips, in the modesty words sunk,
And the Laden heart was full of load on muted tongue.
Words were impregnated with prudence, patience, pang,
And whole assembly was plunged in pain.

Grieved long faces with inner utterless chaos,
Pale sickly countenances looked lost-glows.
The enlightened All wise sage then solaced,
Then the words to meet, Shri Ram thus spake—

"No feud within you, should frustrate you,
Fate puffth soul in clay, maketh tough rolls too.
"Souls are destined puppets of the providence,
So, no ! it's no fault in your part, it's alien hand.

"I see in past, today, and in the time to be,
Men of virtues before you, look pygmies.
"With level glance, not through lens of mother's deeds,
Tho' mute but your faith, yet one can read.

Couplet: *"Your name itself O Bharat !*
'll be bright elixir to cleanse,
In the mundane's murky freight,
Man of his evils and sins. *11*

"My words are ever true, the witness is Lord Shiv,
The earth is being sustained by you and like you.
"Hatred and the Love too, can not be disguised,
The face, can't conceal heart even if one tries.

"Even birds-beasts can pick out among hunters-hermits,
What to say of man who hath virtue and wit.
"Full-well of your soul, Bharat ! I know no doubt.
But My worked up mind doth not work out.

"The King abandoned me and kept his vow,
Nay, he gave up life to keep vow of the love.
"I am perplexed, his words to violate,
My scruple on your account is still great.

"Your request is added on Guru's behest,
For my dilemma better is to say less.
"Keeping vows of words, keeping vow of love,
What you suggest, should I keep above.

Couplet: *"With cheery heart shake off scruples,*
Bharat ! come on tell the choice,
This very day I wilt fulfil,"
—heeding Ram assembly rejoiced. *12*

Scruples=Hesitations.

In heaven perplexed gods, uneased the Lord
Here, Bharat felt a load on his heart.
After much deliberations, to conclusion he came,
That his welfare consisted in obeying Ram

"He hath kept my vow, forgoing His own,
His love and soul for me, He hath thus shown.'
Bharat read endless grace in Ram's silence,
Spake then Bharat in sweet accent–

"Should I be mouthy or bring some of my mouth piece,
O Knower of all hearts ! Thou knowst the cheese*.
"Now that Master's glad and Guru is pleased,
All torments, the creation of my folly, hath ceased.

"I was blurred, blocked by mirky obscession,
Till the ripe east broke; its no fault of the Sun.
"Deviation of mother, and device of destiny,
Designed the disaster of dishing me.

"Doom conspired gloom ; then like Sun didst come Thou,
To rescue me by redeeming Thy vow.
"O Ancient ! Thy feats art well known in Veds
O Saviour ! Thou protectst, it's an ope secret.

"If the whole cosmos turns bellicose,
Thou art the saviour and thou art the hope.
"It's told by eagers, seekers, adepts and wise,
Thy unbias hand is itself paradise.

Couplet: *"O Working hand of all hands !*
Thy shelter's panacea,
Very here any one can obtain,
All the relief from awe. 13

*Correct thing.
Dishing=deceiving; Bellicose=aggressive.

"In care of my Master and my Guru,
My unrest hath gone, and my chaos too.
"Now, O Compassionate! do take steps,
For me, devotee's sake, be not perplexed.

"A menial is mean who lookth own gain,
And placeth his master on embarrassing stand.
"Chance to serve should fulfil a servant's need,
Renouncing all personal comfort and greed.

"Everyone 'll be gainer, if Thou returnst back,
And obeying Thou, will be gain in millions of ways.
"Thou, Thy very grace wilt chance us, to be obedient,
Further it'll bring earthly and ethereal gain.

"nay on such souls 'll pour blessings of merits,
That 'll further add bonne foi, in turn all benefits.
"If it so pleasest Thou, heed to my request,
here, coronation is arranged, accept the Awadh's crest.

Couplet: *"Instead, send me into exile,*
Let subjects feel secured now,
Or ask Lakhan to go back; while
Let me be in forest with Thou." 14

"Or else we three may remain in the forest,
Thyself with Siya mayst return back.
"Which may favour us, do that some how,
O Lord ! which may as well pleaseth Thou.

"Laden with great onus the weakhead, I
Have nor nous nor knowledge, nor insight.
"Even tho' my entire is mire of faults,
Out of His affection He extollth.

Bonne foi(F)=good faith; Nous = Wisdom, Sagacity.

"I 'm guilty of such situation awkward,
Which hath put my Lord in odd weird.
"My submission I tell in all good faith,
This is only way, ensures happiness.

Couplet: *"Thy command hath healing touch,*
Lord ist balsum, Lord ist nostrum,
Thy behest ist blessing for us,
To end the disparity, doldrums. 15

" We 'll carry out command with reverence,
All ills and imbroglio 'll end."
Bharat's guileless openness of the heart,
Received praises from sages, nay heaven did exalt.

Ascetics, foresters were greatly amused,
While the people of Awadh got confused.
The uncertain hush Shri Ram did not break,
Mummed milieu muddled the whole assemblage.

Janak's messengers arrived that very moment,
Promptly Sage Vashishtha, sent for them.
They bowed to assemblage and looked up,
Through grieved gaze at Ram with breath half puffed.

Vashishtha enquired welfare of Janak,
Replied " thy asking itself is man's good luck.'
"O Seer ! O Sire ! thy love O pious !
Thy brooding care is blessing for us.

Couplet: *"Oh ! Our welfare other wise,*
If thou askst O wise sage!
Passed away with Dashrath's demise,
Mithila also is masterless. 16

Weird=fate; Imbroglio=Confusion.
Balsum=pain reliver (herbal fragrant.)

"Thunderbolt fell on Mithila hearing King's demise,
Our words can't reflect the country's sighs.
"Statue of stoicism, the Janak was so-called,
Poised image of King Janak, all looked false.

"It hurt him to hear; came from home, the hurl,
He was nonplussed by stunning puzzle.
"News of Bharat's crowning and Ram's exile,
Tossed his agile mind and wisdom felt fragile.

"What ought to be done ? all failed to brood,
Even long deliberations could not conclude.
"One step crossed the sill, one step stayed back,
King Janak's vague mind was at stake.

"In this unfixed hour of dilemma,
He despatched four spies to Ayodhya.
"To ascertain Bharat's news and Bharat's views,
Secretly to confirm truth of Bharat's virtues.

Couplet: *"Thus secret mission went,*
Bharat's ways having ascertained,
Bharat left for woods, the moment,
To the Mithila spies returned. 17

"Bharat's doings and Bharat's going to Chitrakoot,
The Spies gave account as best as they could.
"More reverence poured on sad hearts, on report,
Of the King, queen, Kins and the court.

"Tho' hard, he collected himself from grief,
And summoned guards, warriors, equerries.
"Posting them in town, right then he proceeded,
On this holy journey with his regal squad.

Hurl=tumult ; fragile=sickly, ill.

"His swift rush, had no time to wait,
Did'nt halt on the way, as was already late.
"This very morn they bathed in holy Ganges,
From Prayag, in advance we were dispatched."

They bowed their heads, saying so,
From sad faces reflected glimpse of new hope.
The great sage dismissed at once messengers,
Sending with them escort of foresters.

Couplet: *Response to the news varied,*
While Ram felt unease,
Diseased immortals felt sick,
But the assembly was all pleased. *18*

Lesser said of Kaikeyi's mind, the better,
With whip of remorse she was battered.
With the arrival of Janak, people felt assured,
They rejoiced getting chance of staying more.

Thus, further zeal was added to their daily joy,
In orisons to deities, their days, they employed
"From O Sylvan ! our orisons in the heaven,
May be heard and be fulfilled our devotions.

"O Ganesh ! Gauri !! Shiv, O Supreme workman !"
They worshipped favourites, tutelars, their manes.
"With Shri Ram our King and Sita our queen,
May Ayodhya be repeopled with its old sheen.

"It's splendour, as before, may daze the heaven,
May bliss fill us, ill-fate be undone.
May Shri Ram instat Bharat as crown prince,
Let everyone reap reward of his being.

Couplet: *From matins to vespers,*
Citizens were overwhelmed,
All asked in their prayers,
All prayed for Ram's realm. 19

JANAK'S ARRIVAL

Hearing this, wise, yogis and adepts,
Weighed their ways, lower to the Bhakti of plebs.
Wisdom is the torch that enlightenth the ways,
Love is sunny faith that never getth strayed.

Thus, the pious, posh, plebs and peasants,
All squeezed their souls to see Ram, the regent.
Chitrakoot, by then looked like Ayodhya—
Between bliss and fuss; the daily Sun saw.

With the compassionate sight of Ram and His healing touch,
Where Ram was, that was their Awadh.
Ram's very one look and a feel of tap,
All treasured that mo, in their memories' lap

"Since Young age Ram kept the faith above,
As well recognizedth the depth of love.
"As we are lucky, only a few are known,
Whom Ram recognizeth as His own."

Couplet: *They all were dipt in love,*
The milieu was cheery,
At arrival of Janak that mo,
rushed Ram and all in hurry. 20

Whole assembly proceeded led by Ram,
to receive King Janak with ope arms.
There, in Janak's view holy hillock was caught,
Made he obeisance dismounting from chariot.

His thirsty eyes searched for the visage,
Yet, too far was the eager sight to catch.
As his nighing steps came close and close,
It seemed 'the holy hillock farther goes.'

But exhausting feet while nighing the goal,
Felt no toil of calves with the untired soul.
While the mind was fixed on Ram and Siya,
Faded all the fleshy hard algia.

Elixired with love, with intoxicated core,
Moved further more to find Ayodhya to the fore.
Both parties adored sages and exchanged greetings,
And Ram and youngers, then greeted the King.

Couplet: *Lo ! Janak's party's river of pathos,*
Ram ist conducting it's stream,
Lo ! to His own Grotto,
Like sacred ocean of quietism. 21

Sad vessels are joining this stream of pathos,
Banks of wisdom are drowned in its flow.
Lo ! the sighs and wails are swelling waves,
Uprooting the craggy trees of courage.

Melancholy represents its flow that is swelt,
With fallacy and folly its eddies and swirls.
With the boats of learning, on helm of patience,
Learned are the boatsmen, standing at the banks.

But they know not the depth of flow of sorrow,
Tho' they oar but are unable to row.
Foresters are unknown passers, tho' stirred,
Are standing by the turbulent stream in a fix.

Algia(*L*)=pain.
Quietism=serenity, peace.

When the stream of sorrow joined the quiet ocean,
It, too surged up as it were with emotions.
Grieved all recalling the Dashrath's ways,
All plunged in ocean of woes and wept.

Stanza: *With wails swelt squall, in oceans of grave trial*
Prevailed the pang,
Citizens, sapients, saints did lament
They claimt the plaint of fate's hand.
Ascetics even mystics winced to witness
Janak's woe,
Tulsi at sea, could see all drowned,
None crossed the river of love.

Distitch: *Overwhelmed current of the souls,*
Here and there in many ways,
The great sage tried to console—
'be solaced ! keep courage !!' 22

Janak, who himself is the Sun of wisdom,
Could the mirk of worldly folly approach him.
Night of metempscychosis who eradicates,
Whose speech rids to and fro earthly freight,

That very Janak was plunged in grief,
Shows; his affection for Siya-Ram had triumphed.
Veds say framed souls have three types of flame,
The sensual, the seeker's, the sapient's.

But, he alone is the highly esteemed form,
Whose heart is honeyed by love for Ram.
Wisdom with no love for Ram, is imperfect,
Like a vessel without oarman is astrayed.

In the sighs, sobs, wails thus passed the day,
Many ways Vashishtha, admonished King Videh.

At sea=perplexed ; Squall=storm ; Plaint=grievance.

Stretched, sad time in the silence but no peace,
Sick hours ailed them anorexic.

Couplet:

In grief from the aged to the littles,
Even birds pets cattles,
Took nor a sip nor a nibble,
Ill, all sat on Ram's sill. 23

All bathed with retinue at the hour wee,
Then, wasted sad they, sat under Banyan tree.
The pious souls, from Awadh, who hailed,
Those who came from Mithila, as well,

Nay, the preceptor of Awadh and the priest of Janak,
Who had explored the ways to the blessed luck.
They toiled and toiled to collect themselves,
Were, solaced with references of Legends and tales.

With the topics of ethics, logics and civics,
The quotes from vedic chants they picked.
none took a drop nor a bit of morsel,
Once again all at Ram's sill assembled.

Couplet:

Blessed are they, who feel blessed—
That, 'they are of some help',
Their chances never lapse,
Such a chance, foresters availed. 24

Empty hands of penury, offered penniers of loads,
With roots, blossoms, leaves, fruits mellow.
By the grace of Ram, the range of hills,
Along rills, nature's fill had great yield.

The grace of Ram, in every frame spake,
Through the hue, the view, a new landscape.
Laden boughs offered picks of no exerts,
Birds bees made a melodic concerts.

The vernal robes adorned the forest,
The sweet breeze further burdened bowers' weight.
As if for healing touch, the nature came nigh,
As if for Janak, the land had turned to paradise.

Ram blessed the Nature with His healing touch,
That treatth man's spirit wandering on crutch.
All won by the Nature, encamped scattered,
Meanwhile eats like nectar were offered.

Couplet: *The Baskets full of Sylvan eats,*
First offering to Ram, preceptor and priest,
Having offered worships,
Citizens partook the holy feast. 25

Peopled air wandered on sylvan wye,
In this way swift, four days rolled by.
Getting eyeful of visage of Lord,
All felt gratified in their heart.

In both the camps this feeling prevailed,
'to return without Siya Ram is of no avail.'
'Living with Siya Ram in odd exile,
Is wiser, over dwelling in cozy paradise.

'That homesick is an accursed sick,
Leaving hallowed company who prefers shallow bricks.
'Privileged of Ram's nearness and dearness,
Can only be had by His own grace.

'Roaming about Chitrakoot, in mellow moods,
Living on bulbs roots, in hallowed woods,
'In a flash, will pass our nights and days,
Thus glad time 'll clock years four and decade.

Couplet: *Gathering in small crowds*
Thus wished they but for providence,
They had their own doubts,
As fate had deceived them once. 26

THE QUEEN'S MEETING

Their spontaneous current of soul ever flown
To Ram ; and indulging fancy of their own.
Thus affectionate air filled the milieu,
Meantime, to Awadh's queens, Sunayana* sent her retinue.

Having learnt Awadh's queens were at leisure,
Ladies of Janak's gynaeceum proceeded there.
With due courtesy Kaushalya received,
And offered the seat as hour would permit.

With such mutual affection the both sides met,
As would have made even the adamant melt.
Helpless they hushed their inner turmoil,
In the wordless sorrow, only their eyes voiced.

Along their veins ran the chill of woes,
Froze they scratched ground with nails of toes.
It seemed as if pathos had taken breathing shapes,
In the distressing hush, Sunayana spake—

Couplet: *"Befo' folly of awesome fate,*
None is safe of it's wrath,
Who chiselled with an axe,
To break up milky froth." 27

Queen Kaushalya replied—

"We look for the nectar, but the fate stings,
It spells it's doom on bloom of springs."

---

*Seeta's queen mother.

Hearing this, Queen Sunayana, dolefully observed,
'the ways of providence are most perverse.'

"He createth, careth and crusheth like a clay,
His designs are as absurd as childish play."
Replied Kaushalya "'ts none a trespass,
Bliss or fuss, gain or drain are designed by our past."

"Inexorable ways of destiny are exclusively known
To the Supreme, who dispenses all fruits, alone.
"to create, to care and to curtail,
Only the command of the Master Creator prevails.

"Such is fate's design immutable and wide,
So wailing out of infatuation is not wise.
"we mourn the contrast between King's company and his loss,
As our interests have suffered by his demise.

Couplet: *"Lakhan Ram Siya may stay,*
In exile I 'm not much bothered,"
Said Kaushalya dismayed,
" I'm nervous for Bharat." 28

"My sons, their consorts, by the god's grace,
Are as pellucid and pure as Ganges.
"Nor the words stand, nor the simile,
For Bharat's loftiness and modesty.

"The fraternity, feelings and firm faith,
What dwellth in him can't be expressed.
"Can't extol that soul which dwellth in him,
Can oyster ever ladle out the ocean.

"The King ever and ever had told me so,
—Bharat, as glory of house, I should know.

"Gold may need stone to prove it's shine,
But the heart of gold stands the test of time.

"Expert jeweller espies the gem through lens,
Man is valued through innate dispositions.
"It meets not me to speak this now,
But the grief and love, knows no when and how?

Couplet: *" O queen!" Kaushalya uttered,—*
Should I say no more,
Thou being Janak's consort
Who is embodiment of lore, 29

"Yet at proper mo, thou mayst speak,
To king as if it's your own plea.
"that from exile Lakhan may be detained,
Instead with Ram, Bharat may be sent.

"For the King this bid may stay,
And may find favour even if he weighs.
"At home, if inseparable soul of Bharat
Stays; may lead to something untoward."

Pathetic sentiments filled in, whoever heard,
The feat of a great mother and beat of her heart.
The purest current of her vast bosom,
Overpowered even apathetic ascetic's wisdom.

To see this all the ladies of gynaeceum,
Nay, all muses of bards struck dumb.
Consumed lamps told 'sleepless night goes'
Recovering herself, then, Sumitra interposed—

Couplet: *"tho' our sad hours crawl,*
O reverent queen ! recover thou !
May us reck the starry stroll,
Be quick ! please return now." 30

"Now only refuge is The Supreme Saviour,
King Janak hath come to us as succour."
Hearing to what Sumitra interposed,
Most courteously Kaushalya rose.

Hearing the mother, Creator's wondrous existence,
Janak's queen bowed to Kaushalya replied in reverence
"Thy revered soul is quite becoming of thou,
Thou being Ram's mother and King Dashrath's spouse.

"Greatmen ever honour even lowest of the low,
Mounts bear grass on top, fire crowned with smoke.
"Mithila's King* is thy menial in Awadh's need,
Thy indebted maid in thought words and deed.

"Worthy to serve thou, on Earth I find none,
Can a lamp ever brag to help the Sun.
"After serving His cause of heaven and men,
Endless will be, in Awadh, Ram's reign.

Couplet: *"Such are holy predictions,*
Of Yagyavalkya, the great saint,"
Said Sunayana with precision,
"His holy words never go in vain." 31

SEETA IN JANAK'S CAMP

Meanwhile to Her kinfolks Seeta reached and greeted,
In each case in the manner as was apt.
They saw their princess in robes of ascetics,
Pathetic pricks filled them with panic.

And there, for his camp Janak too left,
Finding Seeta here, to his bosom he clasped.

*Janak.

Finding soul of his soul and life of his life,
Welled up an ocean of love from his eyes.

A richest riches, a daughter, is asset,
With this wealth yet father, seemed poorest.
The father who had treasure of a child as his gem,
Before fate's design stood as beggared man.

His petrified face and palsied limbs quivered,
To his drowning mind, the thought of Ram was succour.
Not really as benumbed of craze, the passion,
What he bore for Siya Ram it was triumph of that affection.

Couplet: *And Siya was deeply moved,*
Could curb not the melancholy,
Awed by the awkward mo,
Racked She, recovered reckoning duty. 32

Siya in hermitess' robes when King Janak beheld,
Tho' grieved but was gratified as well
"You have brought more sanctity to both the houses,
You are a pious name, thus the world says.

"Your splendorous glory hath outshone
Ganges ; it hath penetrated cosmos and beyond.
"Unto the Ocean, the Ganges is extolled,
Endless is éclat of your pilgrim soul."

Tho' father's remarks were not just father's but true,
Lotuses bloomed on Her face with bashful hue.
The child shrunk in the blessing arms of the sire,
Parental warmth fulfilled Her soul entire.

What a father ever hath, bestowed that crown of blessings,
Seeta took it as most precious thing.

Racked=distressed.

Her modest disposition uneased Her and asked-how?
She could stay with parents with that vow?

Couplet: *Perceiving Her fair vow,*
Again, they took Her to heart,
Then politely they allowed
Their soul, their child to go back. 33

Seeta met Her mother, as she returned, now,
Mother ran to daughter as to lost-heifer, the cow.
Some tears of pangs, some tears of pride,
Welled over the bosom, through mother's gratified eyes.

Mother detained not her daughter, as daughter's duty
Towards her house, was the priority.
Now, Availing Herself of the time opportune,
Abou' Bharat, vividly told the wise queen.

As Janak heard of Bharat's Bosom, the ocean of love,
Moved he, his stable mind roved.

Lids wiped weeping eyes gathering dews of pains,
His emotions eulogized in ecstatic eloquence
"Be attentive O beloved queen! Hark!
In the mire of mundane Bharat sets pious mark.

"The world, the wisdom, values and virtues,
Are the various walks, where I have my views.
"But fo' Bharat's piousness, fo' his pilgrim soul,
My words are short, I fail to extol.

"All the boast of my wisdom is not much,
Even shadow of his splendour my mind can't touch.
"The current of his morals and essence of his deeds,
Purifies every soul with its flow, pellucid.

Couplet: *"His virtues surpass Ganges' flow,*
Bharat alone to be
The like of Bharat ; you know
All my heart is in lauding key." 34

"Lavish love of Bharat that won the laurels,
Lay-figures of language of laureates can't lay.
"Of Bharat, all poets baffle who attempt,
Even as the fish can't glide on the quick sand.

"Unknown, unknowable is Bharat's depth,
Tho' Ram alone knows it, He too can't relate."
Kenning queens' keenness, King further voiced
"Lakhan returns, Bharat goes, that will be wise."

"The mutual current of love between the two,
Its unseen, unknowable, none knew.
"Even tho' Ram seemth standing at stoical height,
Depth of love wells over Bharat's every sight.

"His eyes art fanes where enshrineth Ram's feet,
Above his ownself, his all wits, his spirit.

Couplet: *"Can never Bharat flout,*
The behest of Shri Ram,
In vain, is any doubt,
With Bharat stays no qualm." 35
□

Lauding key=appreciating spirit.

18

The thoughts are the main driver of your life.

—Brahmrishi Vishwatma Bawra

THE DIALOUGES IN DILEMMA

The real fraternity and its ethereal way,
Royal couple recounted, unsated.
Saying so, thrilled Janak's words choked,
Like a mo passed night, till wee hour knocked.

At the day break both the camping folk,
With the new sun and new hope, all awoke.
In the mechanized morn, they took holy dips,
Offered to Sylvan, heaven their daily worships.

Raghvendra in the morn, then called on Guru,
After tacit permission He opened His views —
"Holy Sir ! Bharat, citizens mothers too,
Are being vexed by sojourn in the woods.

"King of Mithila and his followers for many days past,
Stay with hardships for no fault on their part.
"Thus Me Lord ! all liest in thy hands,
Do please ! what meetth in this circumstance."

Couplet: *Feeling it a breach of grace*
Ram was much embarrassed,
But the joy filled the sage,
Thrilled he thus expressed.— 1

"In Thou Ram ! reverence and the core that dwell,
Maketh, the presence of Thy absence, a hell.
"Thou art life-blood in life, the flame in soul,
The thrill in the joy, and the aim of all goals.

"Cozy home without Ram is a barren sill,
Who prefereth, sure, his fate is ill.
"Worships, wisdom wits are valued waste,
With quiddity every quest will be quashed.

" A grieved is so grieved, only without Ram,
And who ever is happy is through, no doubt Ram.
"Thou dwellest in all, so Thou dost know,
Every glow of mellow, every sallow of sorrow.

"Think! think!! Ram Thy behest wilt stay,
May, please now, return to Thy hermitage."
Making obeisance Ram took the leave,
At the same King Janak called on Vashishtha.

Couplet: *Said Guru " O wise monarch !*
You uphold the virtuous cause,
See ! none getth scorched,
Find way in this impasse." 2

Words of Guru filled and thrilled Janak,
In the inconclusive impasse he was stuck.
In vain, every wise-talk was,
All lost way in dilemmatic impasse.

Quiddity=heresy ; Sallow=sick face.

Helpless Janak sobbed as if robbed by fate,
Hapless Janak whispered at stake
"We came here it was no just good,
We shall ourselves now send Ram to the other woods.

"Our wit is won over by our whim,
And bragging our wisdom, we shall return in triumph."
Holy assembly was overwhelmed by words,
Taking leave, then, King proceeded to Bharat.

The reverence that dwelt, welled in welcoming Janak,
In King's grief surpassed seeing Bharat, awe-struck.
"You know the disposition of Lord of Raghus,
And I know Bharat ! your dispassion too.

"Ram is devoted to duty,
You're dutiful to devotion,
In this mute of mutual courtesy,
I may take to Him your notion." 3

Janak's words filled Bharat's bosom and eyes,
Said, with great restraint imposing in his voice
"in thou, a sire, a Guru I see,
Tho' my own parents were not so liberal to me.

"In this great galaxy having Kaushik and Vashishtha,
Grave gathering is present in our amidst,
"if I babble before such a brilliant mass,
My brazen bragging 'll be an act, brash.

"Yet my hush will still surpass,
The unbashed bounds of my black heart.
"Know me a luckless lackey, mere a child,
O Master ! bid me as thy own page, a docile.

"My lip-wisdom, even so hath impudence,
O Pater ! pray ! forgive me for my adverse providence.

"Holy texts recognize the duty of servant,
Is indeed ever a hard challenge.

Couplet: *"Hatred is blind ever,*
Love too hath no mind's eyes,
Me, a subject to my Master,
Work out my work, O wise !" 4

Firm yet humble, strong yet soft
Words of Bharat, from Janak got applause.
With billow of emotions and flow of a wise,
Carrying vast meaning, tho' too concise;

At hand, yet the speech was beyond a catch,
Strange words of Bharat were even, as a mirror image.
Then Bharat, with Janak and holy assemblage,
Proceeded to Shri Ram, to His holy hermitage.

Brooding they moved even as crawling on the pass,
Their steps were heavied by indecisive impasse.
Anxious citizens after getting this news,
Some faces looked composed, tho' some were confused.

Seeing devotion of Bharat, disposition of the flock,
The Ate* attacked immortals, warned defeat of their cause.
'Bharat 's faith incarnate, Ram 's statue of bliss,
Unnerved gods beheld the two, thro' eyes selfish.

Couplet: *"Lo ! Bharat 's faith incarnate,"*
Indra said in his gloom—
"plot means as Ram's considerate
Lest we are all doomed." 5

The insecured immortals as wer' ill-famed for plot,
Reached again to Shaarda with prayers and applause.

Indra=chief of immortals(in heaven) ; *Ate(R)=goddess of mischief

Hailed goddess of wisdom and prayed for help,
For the heaven, as they wished, may not turn to hell

"Thy deluding spell mayst serve purpose,
If Bharat's core changeth, it's cure to secure us,"
Shaarda heard this and could understand,
Selfishness of immortals had robbed their sense.

"What? Bharat's reason how can I control,
While, even Trinity can't alter his soul.
"What ? can the moonlight ever steal away Sun,
Can ever a mollusc molest the ocean.

"Bharat's heart is, where Siya Ram art enshrined,
Can darkness ever enter, where the Sun shines."
Then Shaarda left immortals helpless,
Sick of selfcentric ego they turned much perplexed.

Couplet: *Among the Awadh's subjects,*
Puzzled immortals, the selfish,
Weaving deceptive nets,
Imposed unease, ennui, emptiness. 6

They imposed Ate's art on earthly aptness,
But, on Bharat their art could not act.
After all their tricks, were perplexed,
For, in Bharat's hand was their failure-success.

Very first to approach Ram, were Janak and Guru,
Raghuvar with reverence received the two.
Then the Preceptor of Ram commenced the dialogue,
As to meet, the clock and the gathered flock.

He oped the converse its crux, its view,
Among Janak Bharat and ownself too.

Ennui=mental fatigue.

Repeated he the charming speech of Bharat,
And also, the dilemma that occured

"At this stand, I propose the way,
What ever Thou dost order Ram! All should obey.
"In Thy presence and also of King of Maithili,
If I utter, 'll be quite unseemly.

Couplet: *"I swear by O Ram ! Thou,*
Thine word wilt be final."
All shrunk hearing Guru's vow,
All looked at Bharat, stifled. 7

Assembly seemed confused on issue,
With a look at Bharat and a look at Guru.
A great self-restraint, Bharat exercised,
And the real impasse he realized.

From every face dropt the awe,
No choice, had his voice in this enigma.
Bharat bowing his head, joined his palms,
Spake to blessed swarm and his beloved Ram

"My puerile wit hath piercing say,
For my unbecoming act, forgive me today."
He invoked then goddess of wisdom for help,
Who, with her glory, in pilgrim souls already dwellth.

Firmfaith, fraternity fired in him fillip,
And his mind then oped on his modest lips.
His piety, purity and prudence,
Bespake in word of patience and pains.

Stifled=silenced; Fillip=stimulus.
Enigma=problem; Puerile=Juvenile / childish.

Couplet: *Bharat eyed thro' mind's eyes,*
The assembly was fainted with love,
Invoking Siya Ram he voiced,
In words just those behoved— 8

"Lord ! Thou art pater, pal, preceptor,
The Master who masterth my all inner.
"Thou art at helm of every one's go,
Every ens is energized with Thy ego.

"Nay, Thou art Power, Paragon, Patron,
Thou art hope, help and healing path to heaven.
"Thou art at helm of my sinful mind,
Tho' me a disloyal, still Thou art kind.

"Voluble voice of no value, I brought,
My folly is mute, also set at naught.
"The mundane, that I see, is filled with evens-odds,
But have seen none, disobey Ram, even in thoughts.

"My insolence, the Lord approveth as my innocence,
And He took my presumptions as my affection.

Couplet: *"Me, a Loud brash is lauded,*
Lord's grace hath blessed me,
My failings have been rewarded,
Not the loss of face but the Glory. 9

"O Wonderful wonder ! Thy wondrous ways,
Are worded in world and chanted in Veds.
"The fraud, fake, fiendish and fabricated face,
Thou acceptst even such ever who cometh with faith.

"The glutton, guilty and godless,
Merely once bowed, surely are blessed.

---

ens=body.
At naught=at nothing; insolence=boldness

"Thou dost sum virtues, ever dost shrug sins,
Thou dost reck, ranked us as next of kins.

"Since my infancy, eyes ever perceived,
With recking company of my Master I lived.
"from the Age of toys, joys, boys to the Age to come,
Without Him no memory, no fancy I assume.

"I do say,— with sublimed my arms both,
Ram's my Lord, declare on oath.
"Warbling parrot or wandering puppets,
Their skill limits, where His Master sets.

Couplet: *"Out of odds reforming the devout;*
Thou makest him Thy own,
Taking care about,
Thou maintain his renown" 10

"In insolence of my verve, little innocence of my nerve,
For Thy behest, I am defiant to serve.
"Even me, such brash, is blest by the Lord,
And hath taken my boldness in good record.

"In spite of my folly failings and faults,
Continued grace ist bestowed by the Lord.
"Like a swarthy cloud, Thy worthy grace,
Lavished upon me, pour of blessings unbias.

"While I have wronged him, do I deserve this; Alas !
For my Lord, I am the cause of such impasse.
"Lesser is my devotion, His disposition is great,
Lesser is my passion, for the Most Compassionate.

"I have presumed too much, vaguely,
Being immodest befo' Lord and assembly.

Shrug=ignore.
Defiant=disobedient.

"Now my Patron, my Lord, seeing me concern,
With His compassion will surely pardon.

Couplet:

"My hush is harsh; n my words too
Befo' the beloved Master,
For me, what's now due?
Be pleased, give me order. 11

"For, Thou hast ever accomplished my object,
Be pleased ! command me what's to be done next.
"Swearing by dust of Thine lotus feet,
It's truth*, pilgrim souls havest perceived.

"One wish in my conscious is ever cherished,
Whether 'am in waking fancy or dreaming sleep,
" forgetting my existence that dost exist,
With guileless love to serve Thy feet.

"Greatest joy of a page is to obey noble Master,
Let this servant of Thou obtain this favour."
His lids sunk in the laden unease,
Grief choked his throat further he couldn't speak.

Bharat clasped Lord's feet in such lonely impasse,
From that only refuge, his wordless eyes asked.
Such was the warmth of emotions, that mounts would melt,
At the same, Ram took Bharat and seated him next.

Stanza:

Racked devout, it's no doubt,
is recked by the Omniscient,
when any impasse, in life cross,
it's certain, Ram very nigh stands.
Sombre Bharat touched sober Janak,
And the solemn assemblage,
Every one saw, love for fra,
Was shaped into Bharat's cage.

---

*of dust; Racked=distressed ; Reck=take care.

Couplet: *Peerless ethereal love,*
Seeing on the real Earth,
The Hallow gathering turned sallow,
And in woe, was withered. 12

Vile indra is known a worst specimen,
He loves other's loss and his own gain.
Citizens were dipt in Ram's love,
For them, a net of ennui, Indra wove.

Then, with deluding spell, he bewitched them all,
Their indecisive mind thus wobbled.
Now they conceived a liking for forest,
They would love their home, the very next.

Even as the river rushes to the brine,
But at the mouth is tossed back as if denies.
Between devotion and distraction the wavering of mind,
Was such that no solace they could find.

Their ill at ease, they tried to veil,
Even they didn't disclose among themselves.
The All-wise Ram kent their ailment,
He smilt at wavering in twin-shored sentiments.

Couplet: *The King, Kins, queens as well,*
The sentients and saints, senate.
Were touched of this spell,
Rest fell spell-rapt. 13

Ram saw people wavering between, love
For Him and the net what Indra wove.
Seekers, sages, saints and senate,
All lost their flesh seeing Bharat's faith.

Spell-rapt=Hypnotized

In meek modesty none spake,
Sat all in hush as if on canvas a sketch.
Their timid eyes gazed in hope
At Lord and uttered not as if taught before.

A modest hush on Bharat's face,
Had grief in a 'still', the delight to trace.
His faith and feelings, figured in his eyes a dream,
That reflected in his eyes a melancholy theme.

In depth of devotion, in decorum of modesty,
All assemblage was dipt in deluging Bhakti-sea.
All bards put together, all muses as well,
Can't portray in words, the sentiments those swelt.

Couplet: *On the welkin of devotee's heart,*
Renown of Bharat is moon,
With brilliance without spot,
Showereth on Tulsi it's boon. 14

Path of nobility which Bharat did tread,
Can't be easily grasped, even by Veds.
For the ethereal love of Bharat for Siya Ram's feet,
'Pardon me! if I portray with my nit wit.'

A sanction to mention of Bharat, for me is boon,
But the babbling infant, only little can croon.
None the little, Bharat had touch of ownself,
For his soul, in soul of His soul* ever dwelt.

None is so vile who is inspired not,
With love for Ram, in Bharat's very thought,
Seeing plight that was suspending over the milieu,
And knowing Bharat's truth and his virtues,

---

*Ram

Self possessed, prudent, Ram, prosprietious,
Poured nectar in His saluting words
"Dear Bharat! all the virtues you uphold,
Are well versed in secular lore, that holy verses* told.

Couplet: *"Adept in love, indeed*
You're your compeer,
Perfect in thoughts and deed,
You are dearest of the dears. 15

"Tho' it's nor time, nor the place,
For, should my words recount Your praise.
"You know how the glory of truth is raised,
By revered forefathers of the solar race.

"This gravity of occasion, hath put us on test,
Values are ever valued a crest of the crest.
"The feelings n the duty are two shores of the lore,
The dilemmatic surf puts in our oar.

"O Goer of right path!, O Doer of right deeds!
I'm confident you know, the hour's need.
"Snatching father from us, the fate had deceived,
It's a catastrophe, if sun sets ere the eve.

"Our fatherless course, now have only refuge,
In the Guru's blessings, and his guiding views.
"Our own, our Kins', our subjects' interest,
Are conserved by Guru and his precepts.

Couplet: *"Me, Ram, our reason, religion, race,*
Our renown, riches and reign,
'll be protected by Guru's grace,
And so, all will be well in the end. 16

---

*Veds
Puts in our oar=interferes us.

"One is at home or in woods roams,
Will be recked by Guru's goodwill alone.
"Obedience to the Parents and to the preceptor,
Is the prop of all piety, penance and prayers.

"You do obey Guru, help Me do so,
It's all success, this discipline ever doth bestow.
"It bringeth riches, renown and release,
For disciples, this discipline discoverth the ease.

"Dear Bharat ! up !! for subject with no lack of belief,
All are awe-steeped in their sack of grief
"Read ! empty faces share my woe, from a senile to a child,
But your lot will be hardest for the term of My exile.

"Parting Me for somewhile tho' is hard for you,
But with your hardships, people's hard days 'll get through.
"For your tender heart, my hard words are jolt,
But it's Just on my part, for time is so out of joint.

Couplet: *Beholding Bharat's bosom*
The Bharat's bona fides,
Ballads of bards blossomed
In lauding Bharat's bonne foi. 17

"Love's only form in which Love is loved and assayed,
'Ts alone fraternity that helps in hard days."
Hearing words of Ram, the assembly was stirred,
With nectar of love, the voice was elixired.

Bharat saw in his Lord, the love Personified,
From His words, great consolation he derived.
Now that his Master was benevolent to him,
His fix turned away, his bliss sublimed.

Bonne foi (*F*)=good faith ; Bona fides (*L*)=good heart.

Along creases of his face, now ran cheer,
His mind's fog cleared, gone his hearts fears.
He bowed again and again for this gain,
And spake joined hands making obeisance.

"Thy words comest as reward of my total existence,
I have derived the joy of going with Thou in the dense.
"Now whatever be Thy behest, I do obey,
But for my stretched days, grant me some mainstay.

Couplet:

"In obedience observing orders,
Of the revered Guru,
I have brought the holy waters,
Thy coronation to do." 18

"I 'll do the same, what ever be Thy behest,
It's ever crest of all our joy's crest.
"While my gloom is gone, blooms one great urge,
But due to diffidence I didn't divulge.

With permission, in honeyed words Bharat continued
" I would go and see the sacred Chitrakoot.
"the beasts, birds, brooks, banks, bowers, boughs,
Grace of ground of grasses, green get up of the groves.

"falling glad cataracts, calling clad caves, crags,
Lonely lanes, lively lands, lofty landscapes.
"I would witness reign of nature adorned with Thy foot prints,
Vivific view, velvet walk, in vernal ink.

"Go ! Bharat ! explore the pious woods,
The Sage Atri's land, and do as He bidth you.
"See ! the teils, rills, hills, lae, lee and trees,"
Heeding this reverently Bharat, bowed to sage Atri.

Teil= lime tree; Divulge=reveal, show ; Vivific=reviving.

Couplet: *The discourse that coursed between two,*
Bharat and the Lord of Raghu,
The fraternity, Immortals viewed,
On the Earth that heavenly virtue. 19

"Praised be Bharat! glory be to Raghurai!!"
Thus filled the milieu with immortals' voice.
The priest Vashishtha, King Janak holy company as well,
Hearing two brothers all were enthralled.

The thrill melted in all eyes and sighs
For the virtues of fraternity touched it's height.
People felt the earthly words were short,
For the divine brotherhood to exalt.

That bindth mutually, is unseen, tho,
Of all visible things the most visible is the love.
All witnessed how the Master serveth devotee,
How a devotee masterth the Master, all did see.

This discourse coursed all along veins of both camps,
And poured on the hearts the drops of pleasure mixed with pains.
Kaushalya realizing, the glee and grief alike,
Solaced souls of queens, kins in stoical voice.

Couplet: *Then Atri, the sage asked Bharat—*
"For Ram's anointing what you brought,
That sacred water may be kept,
*In winsome well nigh the holy hillock.** 20

"The water you brought from sacred places,
Will turn this well, more sacred.
"Honeyed brotherhood as well medleyed in it,
Will sweeten the well's eau benite."

---

*Kamadgiri hill.
Eau benite(F)=holy water.

With filled urns, on sage's behest,
Bharat reached at the fathomless well's edge.
Thro' the arms of arbours the well was little seen,
Sage said "The time made this holy place lonely concealed."

With the flood of emotions in his core,
Bharat heard far deep splash of holy water as he poured.
Seemed, even as the thirst of the well was quenched,
And divinity of the well, nay, of Chitrakoot was enhanced.

Well's fathomless depth became height of brotherhood,
And since then, it's named as 'Bharat koop.'

Couplet: *Lauding glory of the well,*
All returned to Ram's grotto,
Atri said 'since Ram dwelt
Swelt Chitrakoot's kudos.' 21

□

19

The Bhakta loves the Lord because He is lovable.

—Swami Vivekanand

A SAINT, IN THE REGENT

Narrating the legends the night was fast spent,
Even as stars leaped and rushed to the west.
Next east lit up the expectant day,
Sun of hope illumined the holy forest.

As the first rays torched thro' the bowers' avenue,
Taking permission proceeded into forest, the two.
The forest had already witnessed the Regent,
How that Bharat was transformed into saint.

As they moved barefoot on untrodden walks,
Path smoothened itself, hid into self, the rocks.
Hallow woods in its own mellow moods,
Stood with bowed boughs, with ope arms of shoots.

Rove in groves, roars of rills filled Bharat's marrow,
Sorrow waned seeing rows of hills, and vista's brow.
Clouds afforded shades, trees offered laden largess',
Beasts filled their gazes, birds trilled the lays.

Rove=wandering; Vista=scene through trees.

Couplet: *With every yawning, who uttered Ram,*
Nature offered him aegis,
In every breath who muttered Ram,
Nature blest that Bharat, the bliss. 1

The divine canvas was filled with viridian brush,
Nature spreaded all about the vernal blush.
Keeping Ram within, Bharat rambled through Chitrakoot,
Viewing wondrous wonders he wandered through woods.

Birds, beasts, breeze and buzzing of bees,
The bliss brimmed Bharat's bosom seeing laes.
Nature's carefree glory spreaded more bliss,
Bharat valued this treasure, over man's stately bricks.

Near and far oft in the way were seen,
Lone unknown hermits keen in discipline.
Abbeys altars sanctified the forest,
Even as they knew the coming of the divine guests.

Like meditating mystics looked the mute trees,
Some stretched boughs looked like performing yogis.
Seeing a saint within Bharat, Sylvan deity-blest.
On the third watch of the day roaming team returned back.

Couplet: *Bharat visited all spots sacred,*
In five days of his quest,
Tho' Chitrakoot is said,
'its' holy in every step.' 2

Trip was hallowed more in mellow Atri's auspices,
And made the worthy Bharat's days.
An auspicious dawn came the next morrow,
But Ram was hesitant to say them to go.

Aegis=protection
Ramble=roam.
Mellow=gentle; Auspices=direction.

Whole assembly met once again,
But His modesty mummed him in diffidence.
All looked at Bharat; the saints, subjects, senate,
Because, Ram seemed very considerate.

Finding Lord very together, Bharat rose,
With restrain on himself to the ground he bowed
His deference and diffidence medleyed,
In words of wisdom, Bharat then spake—

"Thou my Lord ! granted me all my wishes,
I find every one suffers for my sake.
"Lord! grant me leave, for my bulky days,
I'll stay in Ayodhya, till Thou art back.

Couplet: *"My laden soul finds no mean,*
For time to come bereft of Thou,
O Merciful ! admonish me,
How 'll I live now. 3

SABOT, THE SUCCOURER

"Awadh's people art blest, ever who love Thou,
Their this sojourn hath further hallowed them now.
"None of them felt the pain, for they had realized,
Their Master, their Lord is ever close by.

" 'Ts better to be battered for Thy sake,
Than getting even supreme state, masterless.
"O Saviour! Thou will reck in this and next,
And next to next chains of to and fro business.

"Not in ourselves but in Thy Lordship we see,
That ever fills zeal in the devotee.

Sabots=wooden shoes, (Khadau, Paduka).

"O Lord! correct the faults of my nerve,
This is Thy page, command ! me with no reserve."
Impregnated with love, Bharat's words,
Everyone applauded who ever heard.

Couplet:
All-wise Ram heard Bharat,
The speech guileless meek,
Then, Lord spake apt,
The place and time to meet— 4

"For everyone of us ever who brood,
Whether we be at home or roam in woods,
"The Revered King Janak and our Guru,
They are our repute, reward and rescue.

"More, we got good chance to obey father,
That chanced us, repute and reward further.
"more so, its voice of Ved, its a guide to mundane,
As well, father's glory My way 'll maintain.

"With no little reluctance who obey
Parents, priests, pious; they never go stray.
"They are blest whose firm decision cometh first,
And where action follows afterwards.

"Pondering this put away your awe,
Go and rule over the reign of Ayodhya.
"From Kins to denizens from welkin to horizon,
Reign not just the soil but win soul of everyone.

Couplet:
"Like the hedge row protects,
Reign sways and saves us,
King is parent, a child the subject,
With this view take up! the onus." 5

"The beauty of the King's duty is this much,
He reckth the subject with parental touch."

Thus Shri Ram comforted the younger in many ways,
But without some prop, Bharat found no rest.

Ram kent this, dearest Kin's keenness,
Finally he further extended his grace.
Own sabots Ram gave to Bharat, then farewell He bade,
Reverently Bharat took and placed on his head.

The Sabots were not just two wooden sandals,
But had glory of the name 'Ram', the two syllables.
Sabots were prop, to dare struggles, scandals,
In the mirk of mundane were two candles.

The Sabots were path, the goal as well, the foot prints,
To sanctify the soul with its imprints.
In the welkin of devotee, the blessing sabots
Are the Moon and the Sun, the Almighty's orbs.

Couplet: *Bharat felt repaired,*
A prop, his breaths got,
Like the divine couple, the divine pair,
He took on head the paired sabot. 6

Making obeisance Bharat begged leave to depart,
And Lord again claspedst him to heart.
Then again, immortal godules spelt trick,
Turned wits of people weary and homesick.

Trick proved to be boon to sustain their lives,
To be in Awadh, while Ram was in exile.
Lest, the soulless frames, how long would have breatht,
Had their bosom not frozen, bereft?

Thus people departed, with laden steps tho',
By Ram's grace resolved their imbroglio.

Imbroglio=trouble, confusion.

Ram locked His Bharat in close embrace,
And Bharat gathered warmth for coming lonely days.

This warmth melted their souls thro' eyes,
Dews blurred every sight, sigh filled every voice.
In the greens of Chitrakoot, with deserted look,
In the hope of Ram's return, all they moved.

Couplet: *The infinite hope begets,*
The infinite repose and ease,
With tease of being bereft,
Moved they to Awadh palsied. 7

Beholding the parting of Ram and Bharat,
Even stoic Janak was woe-struck.
Dipt in deep ocean of fraternal love,
None could reach or fathom the core's cove.

Bharat looked as if a soulless machine,
Lost flesh, stunned face, lost all sheen.
At this point, whose muses baffle not, that bard,
If versifies this parting, is real hard.

Even elegance of eloquence shrunk in itself,
To depict such delicacy, wits of all muses fail.
The lamenting canvas filled whole milieu,
It was severing of one soul into two.

Claspedth He again Bharat and solaced,
Then, Shatrughan He gladly embraced.
Bowing to both camps, esteeming holy crowd,
Bharat's crawling steps to Awadh set about.

Cove=depth/recess.

Couplet: *To hallow company, Both bowed,*
Both bowed to the Sylvan,
Once more their core overflowed,
Finding to the fore, Lakhan. 8

With same fervour with Lakhan, the two met,
But, joys of four together, were now, toyed by the fate.
Both touched Siya's feet with great devotions,
She pouredth benisons as on Her own sons.

Here, Ram Lakhan bowed to Janak with great gratitude,
For, he strived all the way to reach the woods —
"Thy compassion for us hath moved us,
Thou didst take this task as thy own onus.

"We have imposed a strain and taxed thou,
Be thy blessings our prop, mayst please ! return now."
Hearing this the King plucked to the bosom, the two,
And departed back, all struck with the blues.

To the saints and sages Ram bade farewell,
With the great esteem what within Him dwelt.
Ram-Lakhan then took blessings of mother-in-law,
Then bade adieu to the people of Ayodhya.

Couplet: *Then, the two met sages great,*
Kaushik, Vamdev, Jabali,
and sent back saints and senate
With due concern and courtesy. 9

Then Ram took leave of pious, priests and plebs,
Then He reached to Kaikeyi and embraced.
He spake to remove her grief and guilt,
And saw her off in palanquin equipped.

Meanwhile Siya saw off the maternal kins,
Bade adieu to mother, ushered her to palanquin.

That mo had such delicacy of nerve,
Mute are Kamban's verses, without any verve.

Receiving parental benisons from both camps,
Siya lost in love, was filled with pains.
Then Ram sent for elegant palanquins,
To mount He helpedth His mother queens.

For a son, mother's lap is all his existence,
But it's just not for, the son is meant.
Niching in core the three, Awadh's people advanced,
Mute caravan proceeded, as if going in a trance.

Couplet: *Adoring the feet of Guru,*
The Siya Ram and Lakhan,
With some bliss, some blues,
Bade adieu and returned. 10

Through jumbled jungle of Chitrakoot,
All left, but one Nishaad kept standing, mute.
"O Guh ! meeting you with fraternal drive,
We were four but now are five."

Ram sent him off, bereaved he did go,
In chaos of the core, he whispered 'Ciao!'
Bowing again n again, the Sylvan populace,
With medleyed gloom-bloom all returned back.

The melancholy dimmed more the shades of Banyan tree,
Where grieved of parting dears, sat the Three.
In the noble disposition of Bharat Lord wast dipt,
To Siya and Lakhan He revealed this.

Ram extolled Bharat with own blest lips,
And his love, faith in thought words and deeds.
The Sylvan was sad every milieu looked perturbed,
Yet godules were glad, their purpose was served.

Ciao(*It*)=Goodbye

Hush of gloom filled flocks, rocks, hillocks,
Baffled beasts, birds, forgot toils of sylvan clocks.

Couplet: *It seemed even as the Heaven,*
Hath landed in the dense,
Where dwelt Siya Ram Lakhan,
That grotto, in itself was a fane. 11

Here, dwelt in huts Siya-Ram and Lakhan,
Huts looked as the shrine of Bhakti, wisdom, dispassion.
And there, in grief the whole caravan was lost,
On account of their parting with the Lord.

Dipt in grief, rapt in virtues of Ram,
In odd hush they moved, with loads of Storms.
They wended their way to Yamuna and crossed,
With no sips, no eats thus that day passed.

In the sacred lap of Ganges, they had their halt,
Further northing the weary caravan crawled.
Ferrying Sai river, bathed at Gomti shore,
And reached Ayodhya on the eve fourth.

King Janak stayed there for a couple of days,
And looked into the affairs of the state.
Entrusting reigns to Vashishtha, Bharat and senate,
Then rapt in Ram, to his state he left.

Couplet: *Nestling in Ayodhya then,*
Leaving luxuries lust, leisures,
People lived in discipline and penance,
'Only one desire' they treasured. 12

With stonned gaze and stunned face,
Waiting Ram's return they begun counting days.

Fane=temple, shrine.

Sentinels, soldiers, servants, senates,
Their respective duties Bharat set.

He then sent for his kinsmen and citizens–
The pious, posh, poised, peasants, plebians.
A saint in Bharat, consoled one and all,
A regent in Bharat ensconced one and all.

He entrusted Shatrughan in service of mothers,
Then he called on and prayed his preceptor
"O revered ! charge me with any service,
I shall not slacken a bit of it.

"A life of discipline and a life of penance,
I should now live with thy accordance.
"Bharat ! What you do" the sage spake,
"is the pious deed and piety's stake."

Couplet: *Getting Guru's advice and benison,*
In hallowed hour, with mellow heart,
Bharat installed on the throne,
Holy Sabots of the Lord. 13

To Ram's mother and to the Preceptor he bowed,
Then taking advice he enthroned the Sabots.
Bharat, the upholder of all virtues,
Reached 'Nandigram' in the capital's purlieu.

Clad himself like Ram, in the hermit's robes,
Wearing a tuft on the head, the matted locks.
Lo ! low spirited Bharat with his callow travails,
Maketh with sallow foliage, a hallowed hovel.

He then beginth rigid vows of hermits,
Austerities and sacred pieties.

Ensconced=settled
Hovel=hut of leaves ; callow travails=inexperienced labour, unskilled toil.

In the thought words deeds he professedly,
Discardth leisures, lust and luxuries.

The Ayodhya was a surprise of paradise,
With its nitid riches was known all wide.
Yet in that opulence, indifferent Bharat dwelt,
As a bee sucks not champacc's scented floret.*

Couplet: *The soul of real gold ever jilt,*
For Truth, the gilded mundane,
And the glitter never fill,
The gifted eyes with pomp of opulence. 14

Before mettle of Bharat and his merits,
Maya of metal faded in defeat.
In the fire of penance and discipline,
His frame thinned, yet face charmed with sheen.

His frame became altarage, and gained more charm.
For his mind was altar with inner flame, for Ram.
Now cleared all sad-clouds from mind's welkin,
In self straints, observances, disciplines.

On the welkin of mind, the faith was Lode star,
In yearning eyes full moon of 'Ram's return' looked no far.
The fixed faith like Bharat in the bosom is a boon,
In the galaxy of thoughts it glitters as full moon.

Bharat's views, virtues, veneration and verve,
Even Wisdom, herself hath no word for the verse.
For the divine soul's deeds I do babble confused,
My words need eternal blessings for the muse.

Jilt=discard; *Champacca=Michelia champacca bear fragrant yellow flowers, the bee, it is alleged never sucks it.
Lode star=fixed pole star.

Couplet: *In daily vigils, matins vespers,*
The Sabots of Ram he revered,
And them, he ever reffered,
In clearing state affairs.

With rotes of Ram his tongue he enriched,
Visage of Siya Ram in his heart he niched.
While Siya, Ram Lakhan in woods, roamed,
Through penance, Bharat perceived even tho' at home.

Viewing both the sides, everyone did say,
'Bharat is praise worthy in every way.'
The peak of piety, penance and his pledge,
Put to shame the pious ways of even abbeys.

Acts of Bharat and it's anecdote,
Are delight in itself and to enlighten with its quotes.
In the mirk and mire of the mundane,
'Ts blessing lotus blossom, and beatific fountain.

Fidelity, fraternity, faith and just the faith,
Is the sacred secret of Bharat's greatness.
This epic is a bliss of the devotees,
It relieves from burden of to and fro journeys.

Stanza: *Bharat as a lead, for it was a need,*
What he did, was a hallowed deed,
Had he not born, who would have performed
Such feat, which was so meet.
A page in him, a sage in him,
Has razed our sacrilege,
His go dispelled our ego, his glow propelled*
Us to Ram's visage.

Sacrilege=impiety; * go=spirit, determination ; meet=proper.

Couplet: *As finding of the mankind,*
Cometh Bharat and Bharat's anecdote,
The fraternity who defined,
Defying the Ram's Sabot. 16

□

ARANYA KANDAM

20

Its through the many that we reach the One.

—Sri Sai Baba

STROPHES

1

Shiv, The Dharma in Himself,
For high tides of joy, The full moon.
Who is dawn to ope the Lotus mind,
For dooms of mundane, a boon.

The untrodden forlorn glades,
Feet of the Wandering Ram did tread,
'For the cause'-He descended,
The Feat of the warrior, Ram thus bade.

2

Ram's hue Swarthy, like worthy clouds,
And clad in yellow.
Quiver in waist, matted locks as crest,
In hand bow and arrow,

Large eyes gleam like lotus and
From whose body the bliss glows.
He doth go on narrows, Siya-Lakhan follow,
To such charming Ram, I bow.

LESSON TO JAYANT

Distitch: *With Rays of Ram, stay far away,*
Only learned seekers are lighted,
Mundane drives the rest, astray,
Blind at Dharma are benighted. 1

Troth of town, and the Truth of Bharat,
I have worded to my limits,
Now i heed n read, pious deeds of Ram,
His feats in forests will now fetch new charm.

From the treasures of blossom all about the grot,
Ram culled some flowers, some wreaths He wrought.
Shaping bracelets, bands, belts, bandeau, bays,
Fondly bedecked Siya, and on crystal rock they sat.

*Indra's son, a fop, did realize,
In folly, wished to weigh Lord, seemed to him man-sized.
Even as low lore ant would fathom the ocean,
He disguised self as crow for his wicked reason.

He bit Seeta on foot and waited not a bit,
And the foul creature flew away in speed.
Ram came to know when wound did bleed,
To His bow then Ram fitted shaft of a reed.

Couplet: *Ram's ever gracious,*
And is ever so, for the meek,
But fool came as vicious,
Even with Him played a trick. 2

Winged with a spell shaft of reed sped,
And the disguised crow more far to far fled.

Grot=grotto, beautiful hut.

Consumed by terror he assumed his form,
Approached his father* in alarm.

But Indra refused refuge to the Ram's foe,
His ego drained, found no place to go.
Dismayed he fled from stern to stern,
Yet from home to heaven he could find no haven.

With frailed wings fled further fretted,
Prince of heaven, found no haven even in the hell.
Thro' different planes, planets of galaxies,
But he, ill at ease was no where appeased.

Weary were his wings, stricken with awe,
He traversed to Lord Shiv and to Lord Brahma.
For the hostile to Ram even heaven is hell,
The nectar is a venom, and petal is a nail.

The Clouds on clouds hung upon his head,
Every bloom in this gloom, was doomed to fade.
A friend turns to foe and weal to wails,
Thus, the anarchy that dwell in atheists, ever fail.

The tender heart Naarad; as are the saints,
Was moved with pity, seeing Jayant.
His face with savours of boast was gone,
Sage sent him to Ram," O Saviour !" he did moan.

" O gracious Ram! mercy! mercy!
As a crow my crowing ego assayed Thee.
"For hostile to Ram, Ram ist only refuge,
Be my armour, arms of Ram only could."

---

*Indra, chief of the heaven; Haven=refuge.
Savour=smell ; Armour=shield cover.

Couplet: *Prince of heaven had ego,*
That drained in his piteous plea,
With grace Lord let him go,
Thus, Ram quelt the qualm's sequelae. 3

AT ATRI'S ASHRAM

This anecdote is quoted to Uma by Shiv,
Before proceeding further Lord's mansized narrative.
Roaming in hallowed woods of Chitrakoot,
Many exploits were performed by Lord of Raghus.

Then, Shri Ram thought, it would be wrong,
Everyone knew His stay and people would throng.
Brooding this left the place, then the Three,
And reached the Ashram of Atri.

Seeing divine visages on his sill,
Atri ran, and ran along his veins, a thrill.
As the two brothers with reverence did bow,
The Sage embraced them, laved them with tears of love.

Dazed he, gazed at Ram's visage,
Then escorted them into his hermitage.
He offered roots, fruits, and relishes,
The sage poured his soul in paying his homage.

Distitch: *The visage was in Atri's bosom seat,*
And he found now, Him to the fore.
That visage his eyes did feast,
And in apt words he adored— 4

The Hymns–

"I do worship Thee,
who doth cherish devotees.

Thy feelable form I do beseech,
Thou ever art within true thought's reach.

"Thou holdst the hue swarthy,
reflectth in the welkin and the sea.
Thy might O Almighty!
Mitigateth mundane's misery.

"Thy humane helping hands,
Art at helm of the human.
Thy humane helping hands,
Handth every human's errands.

"Thy visaged eyes winsome,
In vigil eyest every bosom.
Human-sized Thou dost come,
To humanize each and every one.

" 'Ts swarthy of Thy hue,
That colourth every milieu.
O Ancient ! yet ever new,
Thou art ageless, known to very few.

"Of Thou, what a man can mention,
As an ant wish to fathom the ocean.
Seekers strived and found seldom,
And derived that Thou art nonmenon.

"O wondrous wonder of all wonders !
Warmth of all fervour ! charm of raptures !
With ope arms, making arms as armour,
Save me from savage O saviour !

Handth=supports, helps.
Nonmenon=unknowable.

" O blithe of the benigns and blight of the brutes,
Thy divinity is expression of all fruits.
The goal, Thou art, as well the route,
The goal itself goadth the go to the Truth.

"The callow hands and sallow hearts,
Art hallowed by Thou O Lord !
Amidst devouts and O Lord of lords !
There is an unseen cordial cord.

"In every bit, beat, nit, niche, every nidus,
Thou art the nucleus of nucleus.
Thou puffest a heaven on earth's canvas,
Thou stuffest in spring a vernal blush.

"Thou dwellest in the minutes that swellest to universe,
To bless earthlings Thou comest on the Earth.
Thou art the Tamer of every atom,
O Master! Thou masterst every bosom.

"Thou, the warmth of all charms,
Glory ! glory ! ! be to Thou O Supreme!"

One who ist enlivened by this lively hymn,
Ever findth Thou enshrined within.
Glory ! glory ! ! be to Thou O Supreme !

Couplet: *His heart brimmed thro' lips,*
Then further spake the sage—
"May my spirit be ever dipt
In Thy virtues and visage." 5

With goodly esteem Siya, the modest,
There, Atri's godly wife, She met.
Overwhelmed Anusuiya in great delight,
Embraced Seeta and seated Her nigh.

With ornaments Anusuiya blessed Her,
In heavenly robes she arrayed Her.
Wifely virtues by which a women is valued,
Making Her an occasion, thus Anusuiya viewed.

"All Kins, sheens, means, gleams, their shine,
Before consort, but have confines.
"A husband however bestowth endless bliss,
Vile is a woman who believeth not this.

"Whatever falls on a lady's lot,
Shoud husband be her lord, above the Lord.

"Wholesome wifely service to husband,
Is women's sacred vow and penance.
"Most Pious is the dame, convinced in her heart of hearts,
She can't even dream of man other than her lord.

"The lewd viewed woman is valued worst,
Who deceives her lord for her blue bosom thirst.
"She, the most depraved, for her moment's miss,
Suffers ages and ages of nemesis.

"Every dame hath divinity but for her deeds,
Deify a deity, in her by degrees.
"celestial deity reflects in earth born woman,
If her eternal beauty she ever retains.

Couplet: *"Siya ! Thy very name itself,*
Is the truth's and trust's strength,
'I said for the earthly damsels,
n for mundane's good I spake". 6

"Thou art Bhakti incarnate O child Siya !
Staunch mould of mind, Jacta est alea!!"

Depraved=corrupt, debased; Jacta est alea (*L*)=the die is cast.

—Hearing this motherly discourse,
Reverently at feet of Anusuiya she bowed.

Then Ram said "O revered ! thy grace,
May never cease even if I leave this forest."
Learned sage lovingly replied Lord's words
"Thou art the same Ram, Supremest gain of the world.

"Thou art the same Ram, the friend of the meek,
The fire of seekers, the favour of the weak.
"Thou the same True soul, we, Thy soulules,
Thou art Master workman, and we, Thy tools.

"Fructiferous trees bow to the child's catch,
Same way cometh to me Thy fruitful grace.
"Thou art real ethereal, unequalled,
Why Thou best not to me so amiable?

"O Allwise ! in every heart Thou dost dwell,
How can I bid Thou, a farewell !"
Thrill choked sage's throat, he invoked no words,
Rills flooded thirsty eyes, lids wiped the gaze-blurred.

Stanza: *Rivulets of thrill filled eyes of the sage,*
He rivetted gaze on Lord's visage.
He thought what's that piety which brought,
For him the Lord, and His unending grace.
Unknown, unknowable, Ram roamed,
His visage rummaged hearts of sages,
So Bhakt doth praise in his own lays,
Holy ways of Ram in the dusks and days.

Rivetted=fastened together.

Couplet: *Kaliage in itself a havoc,*
And in mundane's mire and mirage,
Ram's totality is Bhakt's torch,
In this mirk of anarchic age. 7

THE SOUTHWARD - MOVE

The Atri-Anusuiya's hermitage,
Even for the Heaven, became a pilgrimage.
Then the wondrous wanderers, the Three,
Reverently bade adieu to Atri.

Foremost walked Ram, Lakhan followed after,
Most appealing they appeared in hermit's attires.
Siya, shone between the two, such a way walked,
Amidst Eternal and Earthlings, as the Maya rocks.

All along the passage, Sylvan spreaded heaven,
Caves, crags, clefts recognized their Creator's hands.
In the Kingdom of nature, shone the mount-crest,
With breeze combing trees, grassy laes, valleys and alleys.

Where ever Lord thro' woods made his shift,
Was comforted by Umbrella of cloud's drift.
On their untrodden ways, demon Viraadh they found,
As soon as he appeared he was laid down.

On their way as the trio wended,
Visited they Sharabhanga, the resigned sage.
Resigned world and resigned flesh as well,
Yearning highest earning, in this sublimed soul dwelt.

Couplet: *Elixir of Lord's countenance,*
Poured nectar into his fixed glance,
Reverently his two eyes drank,
A reward of ages of penance. 8

With esteem Sharbhanga did speak
"Within Shiv and Shivaites Thou art niched"
"With the tidings, that Ram roamth in forest,
My heart was stolen, my mind was rummaged.

"Lost flesh, the ways, day and night did I see,
My tubular gaze waited none else, but Thee.
"Walking to me, Thou havest blest the reward,
This humble page of Thine tho' deserveth not.

"didst Thou no favour, I mull now,
Thou havest only redeemed Thy vow.
"Now, I offer my gains of chains of births,
This bliss hath fulfilled my coming on the Earth.

"My sated soul would wing from this cage,
In my earthly life I see Thou, would see Thou in the next.
Sharbhanga, the yogi achieved final bliss
To sacrifice his frame he made a pyre.

Couplet: *"Let Thy embodied form sway,*
The conscious of my soul,
May Thy divine shine stay,
Enshrined within, I pray." 9

Saying so, to set apart the quinary's frame,
Sat on pyre, with Yogic vital frictions, set it to flames.
Ripe penance is above frame, with sublimed mellow soul,
Like a gourd it cuts off reaching hallowed goal.

No liberation, no absorption in person of Hari,
But wished the devotion, which was blest already.
Seekers, sages who saw such sublimed state,
On this goal, gladly, their goal they set.

Rummaged=robbed.
Quinary=of five elements.

Swarmed up charmed saints extolled and praised
"O mountain of glee!! O fountain of grace!!
"glory be to Thou! Thy feats, Thy acts,"
thus in silence of woods echoed Ram's éclat.

The Three went to hermitages, hideaways, havens,
Passing further into woods, hosts of sages followed them.
Ram paused witnessing huge osseous heap,
Of sages ravaged by savages' deeds.

With brows on tenters, eyes brimmed with tears,
With uplifted arms, Ram firmly declared—

Couplet: *"Enough is enough now,*
To rid the Earth of Demons,
Me, Ram take the vow,
For the cause I have come." 10

VISITS TO SCATTERED ABBEYS

On the ways, the abbeys, hermits He gladdened,
Visiting their hermitages one by one.
Then, Sutikshana by name Agastya's learned disciple,
Doped in devotion, dipt in discipline.

Ram was enshrined in furrows of his brain,
In line of his thoughts, in deeds of his hands.
From lines of his thought*, to the lines of his hands**.
Lo ! the Lord rushed in love, to give meaning to his penance.

On long awaited tidings of Lord's approach,
Thrilled Sutikshna rushed out on toes.
Any rush seemed him slug, the thrill pearled lids,
He was indulged in his own fancies

---

* His thought process;
** His luck.

"May Ram draw to this man of straws,
May He come to the fore, ignoring my flaws.
"No deserving wisdom, no unswerving faith,
And me, earned no weight in my earthly freight.

"Nor I claim any steadfast devotion in His feet,
Nor with the enlightening fire I am lit.
"On my part my worth hath all lacunae,
But then one ray of hope that delightth devotee–

"The Merciful holdth the devotee who depends,
Exclusive on Him, in the mirk of Mundane.
"With this inspiration my mind is doped,
This blest day wilt sure fulfil my hope."

O Uma* ! no riches, no rituals no rites work,
Worth is the man, his own who, surrenderth.
No genus, no genius but with the genuine love,
Lord holdth such devout, no doubt all above.

In flood of love wise sage was immersed,
Robbed eyes set keen, orbs danced in search.
His verve benumbed all his sense,
Nor his steps nor nerve could make out lanes.

Lost flesh, he knew not, who he was,
Knew little of the pass and the compass**.
He would go on, one pass and would turn back,
Then would resume his move on different track.

Lord watched him, hiding behind a tree,
Doped in love, dipt in bliss, such strange devotee.
The elixir of divinity when within sage poured,
Impregnated with thrill he sat on the road.

---

*Shiv continued to narrate the story of Ram to Uma.
Genus=sect, caste; **compass=directions.

Then, gladly Shri Ram, drew nigh and nigh,
The sage would not wake, many ways tho' Ram tried.
In his visionary ecstasy he was so lost,
That he felt not, the feelable Lord.

Then, Ram withdrew His splendour of visage,
As the bosom was emptied, the sage turned restless.
With his ope eyes, enlivened he saw same form,
Tho' as lifeless log he fell before Ram.

Filling him in long arms, Ram took him to bosom,
Felt, his soul as if passed through many passes of heaven.
To the fore stood shri Ram, Lakhan and Siya,
Fixed gaze of sage looked as if drew in predella.

Rush of his soul ended, hush of gained goal prevailed,
Slush of doubts ended, gush in the devout swelt.

Couplet: *Then, summoning within his courage,*
Feet again, 'gain he clasped,
Conducted Lord to his hermitage,
Many ways offered Him homage. 11

Said the sage " O Lord! O divine Guest listen!
How am I to chant Thy paeans.
"for Thy vast glory my wit is none,
As the flash of glow-worm before the Sun.

"Clad in hermit's robes, glad in matted lock's crest,
With bow arrow in hands, quiver fastened to the waist—
"This visaged glow endth mirks of mundane,
It's fire consumeth delusion and warmth the saints.

"Thou art the Sun that torchst road of the saints,
And the Sun that scorchest herds of satans.

Predella=wall painting(behind an altar)

"Thou art havoc to fiends and friar's bliss,
And art a hawk, whose game is metempsychosis.

"O Lord of Siya! O Lord of devotees!!
O Lord of Maya! O Lord of divinity!!
"A rapture Thou art that enamourth devouts,
Thou, the divine Vulture, devourth serpents of doubts.

"Thy name ist the bark for the mundane oceans,
Thy name ist the torch for dark of seven sins.
"Thy arms art the armours of the sages,
And Thy arms art fierce to savages.

"Thy hands art the Saviour of heaven's virtues,
Thy hands art the slayer of demon's crews.
"To help Sanaatan and to zap Satan,
Worked Ownself unto man, O Master workman!

"Mansized Thou art, the compressed divinity
Of Absolute, that Infinity cometh embodied.
"Wise-world defined Thou as with the Form or without,
Thou art the witness of hearts of devout."

Listening the words of sage, reading his soul,
Embracing him to bosom, Lord Ram then told
"I'm so pleased with you O Sutikshna !
For the great deal of virtues you have earned.

"I assay lofty hearts not the Lordly words,
I see the plain worships not pompous verse.

"My hands are ope to grant you the boon,
May ask Me what ever you choose."

The real gain of devout, that he knows not,
The business of bargain with the Lord.

Yet it's childish right to ask his Sire,
'To be parent's beloved', is his first desire.

The sage replied, "I know not
O Lord ! what's real and what's false."
"What pleaseth Thou, that would please me,
Thy delight, in itself, ist a blessing."

"May riches of wisdom, devotion, virtue,
All spiritual goodness, bestow upon you."
Thus benisons were poured upon sage by the Lord,
Then, asked Sutikshna what cherished in his heart—

"Thou havest lavishly blest me as sire,
Now accomplish my cherished desire

Couplet: *"From desires, may I be freed,*
My bosom be the shrine,
Of visaged statue of the Three,
Siya and Lakhan too, by Thine." 12

Gladly Shri Ram said "so be it"
Further to Augasthya he started His visit.
Said Sutikshna 'ts longtime since now,
I have seen my Guru, so will go with Thou.'

"to my Guru's hermitage if I escort,
I'm putting no obligation my Lord !"
Lakhan smiled hearing this,
"Company of Ram, a Wise 'll never miss."

On the course, discoursing the course of faith,
They arrived soon at Agasthya's hermitage.
Forthwith before Guru, the pupil-sage,
Prostrated himself and thus addressed

"O revered ! whose Name thou ever dost mutter,
Same Lord of lords have come to thy door."
The high sage, with high spirits hied,
And sight of Hari, filled his eyes.

The two brothers revered sage's pious feet,
Sage clasped them to bosom, yet was already Ram's seat.
Came, who was ever seated in his mind's niche,
Came, whose Name, sage's soul, ever enriched.

So thrilled was he while he said
"As I am today, there is none so blest."
Assembled in a rush the sage's swarms,
All eyes feasted on ambrosia of charms of Ram.

Couplet: *Midst assembly of Sages*
Sat visaged Ram,
All gazed the nectarian spread,
As by moon, the Patridge is charmed. 13

Then, said Ram to Augasthya with reverence,
The very cause of His awaited descent
"O Wise sage ! nothing is concealed in thy wit,
Thy far-sight is beyond time's limit."

"Thy benisons, opinions would help Me long,
To zap who wrong the hermit's throng.
Asking of the Almighty with deference,
Above Might of the Lord, sublimest the piety, the penance.

The Sage smilt hearing Ram's remark,
'with what resolve have O Lord ! asked?
"The ocean of Thy energy that's Thy Maya,
I know 'dwelth in every nucleus of the iota.'

"Thy Maya ist like a huge Banyan tree,
With fronds, fruits, foliage, the millions of galaxies.

"We, the rotary souls that dwell and rot
A Single fruit, and of the divine tree know not.

"The Time, itself hath palate for that fruit,
Even that Time ever trembleth in Thy fright.
"Thou, the paramount Lord, of all planets, paradise,
Mansized now havest asked of my advice.

"O Unknowable ! Thou art the endless brine,
On dugout, this devout can't fathom, can't define.
"nor Gyan, nor Bhakti, yet it's intense in my mind,
That my heart be the Trio visages' shrine.'

"Cataract of love that pourth on my heart,
May I be dipt in it's bliss O Lord !
"Some have explored and adored, finding Thou as Absolute,
I feel enamoured of the form with Attribute.

"Thou havest ever exalted Thy devotee,
That is why Thou simply askest me.
"Beauty of Dandak woods, as if wait,
For Thou; with Panchwati, a tree's pentad."

"Sanctify that spot and Dandak forest too,
Bless sage's of the place, taking abode in that woods."
Ram took sage's permission with great courtesy,
And soon drew near to the Panchwati.

Ram noticed on the way, Great Eagle, Jatayu,
Was friend of Dashrath in his battle field's crew.
Ram developed friendship, for the bird had
Even in that form, wisdom's ripeness.

"I shal lead,and, Thou mayst follow,
O Ram ! all along my wing's shadow."

Dugout=small boat; brine=ocean.

Couplet: *Ram reached Godawari's bank,*
Was charmed by nature's canvas,
He then thatched with own hands,
Hut of leaves twigs and grass. 14

IN PANCHWATI

Since Ram accepted Dandak as home,
The Sylvan entranced, sages unafraid roamed.
Nature painted richly the whole milieu,
More lovely day by day, the beauty grew.

Birds, beasts, bees, looked full of thrill,
Hills, rills decked self finding the Lord on doorsill.
From ripples of rivage* to the far rival heights,
The bosom of virgin nature was filled with delight.

*Godawari's bank.

Hummed bees, in the soft breeze tides,
Entranced bowers nodded in saintly quiet.
Verdant mat was embroided with vernal thread,
Lord approved the glory of nature's spread.

Thus tenderling guests as tenant of nature,
Lived in 'Dandak-Van' for stretch of ten years.
In such daily bliss, Laxman asked once upon,
"O Lord tell of Thy show which goeth on and on."

"Discourse to me course of Maya and it's pomp,
The wisdom, devotion, illusion, it's pros and cons.

Couplet: *"What's true ? what's dream?*
Tell of the hand at the helm,
What links the soul with Supreme,
Which masterth puppets of mundane? 15

"O Almighty ! tell of Thy Maya, it's might,
Tell of dreams of illusion in folly's night.
"I explain O Lakhan ! in nut shell the fact,
Heed ! with absorbed soul and intellect.

"I, Me, My, You, Your's this feeling,
Is the illusion which sways over All- beings.
"What's in reach of mind and of sense of sinew,
Is the Maya's mortal empire with many hues.

"In this empire, the gnosis-nescience go parallel,
With the pride of knowledge, the ignorance swells.
"Equipoise wisdom with no I am ness,
Ever that is bestowed by heavenly grace.

"With gnosis, the spiritual wisdom; the pride
Should not come ; Lest it's folly to be wise.

Verdant=green; Gnosis-nescience=knowledge-ignorance.

Dispossessed is the man, who thinks of himself,–
"as man of the straw, with Lord at the helm."

Couplet: *"All the Maya who masterth,*
Is the Master of cosmos, the Shiv,
The real souls ever perceive
The Supreme Truth; and rest all as the passive. 16

"Such wisdom cometh thro' virtuous practices,
And the Yoga guideth wisdom to the innerquest.
"Veds Sayst 'the Gyan is bestower of the Release,'
What melts Me is 'Bhakti', the delight of devotees.

" Free from folly is the fortitude and faith,
Requiring no prop, it stands by itself.
"nay, the faith is stake of wisdom of seekers,
It is root of bliss acquired through saints' favour.

"The Path of Bhakti, the devotion hath the easy go,
A walk of no pomp, thro' hearts of no ego.
"Should a man, first, from sleep of toxins of mundane,
Wake up hearing the tocsins of reverence.

"Next, on path of duty should he step,
And engage self as recited in holy texts.
"Let the weeds of passion be weeded from soul,
Then the seed of devotion will find it's soil.

"Then in warmth of virtues, in hallowed environ,
Germinates, grows up! up !! the seed of devotion.
"Me, the gardener, friend of man and fiend's awe,
Care as parent, preceptor, pal and fra.

"All the current of devout ever run to Me,
His mind is all heart, all vice free.

Gyan=gnosis; knowledge of truth.
Toxin=poison; Tocsin=Alarm bell; Weeded=root out.

Who hath no lout tongue, loud words nor doubts,
Ever I back him on call of such devout.

Couplet: *"Entire who surrenderth,*
With no petty niche but bosom broad,
Whose vespers know no barter,
That heart ist My abode." 17

From Ram thus Lakhan with keen heeds,
Heard of devotion, dispassion and human duties,
The science of wisdom, the arts of devotions,
How they go and reach the same one aim.

And thus, thro' high bowers many Suns witnessed,
And saw Ram's daily feat in the dense.
Thus Panchwati became the condensed Paradise,
On the banks of Godawari, the Dandak's pride.

Ram would say "see! that deer how looks into Your eyes,
Siye! You of same species, that deer decides."
"The tendrils tend to Your tender frame,
Seeing one of their own, the creepers, at You, aim.

"You planted Tulsi shrubs see! those hail,
In You, those shrubs find their own Abigail."
Siya replied "in cloud-veils those mounts abashed,
Stand O Lord ! dazed by Thy visage."

Couplet: *Thus, ten summers, ten winters*
With length of ten springs,
Witnessed many of such hours,
On the palms Valmiki had inked. 18

Tend=incline.

SURPANAKHA'S EPISODE

On one such day Surpanakha from demon race,
Saw the divine beau, the Ram while wandering in forest.
She peeped into the tree's pentad,
In her blue-eyed looks, the thirst raised.

Stormy lust flooded her swampy core,
Assuming charming form she dallied at the door.
Fevered with passion of the lust of Liaison,
Pert she, approached Ram, in demonry's fashion.

In wonderment Ram looked at,
She worded with smile of coquette.
In the rush of lust she spake straight
"Till now my youth I have wasted.

"Now that I have found You in this woods,
It's my finding to fulfil my womanhood.
"No err in Your person, same says to me mirror,
With great care the Creator made me and You. the pair.

"In the world tho' ; have ransacked,
Found none, so I remained unwed.
"tho' it meets not for a woman of breeding,
But, I dare, driven by the Cupid in me.

"My mind is at rest a bit, finding now You,
Viewing, winning winsomeness, for wedding I woo."
Casting glance at Seeta Lord said in short
"My younger is the suitor and I am not."

With new gush of lust, she rushed to Lakhan,
Who knew the imposter's race of demons.
Lakhan looked at the elder and replied soft
" O perfect lady ! I am slave of my Lord."

"for a slave, hath no will of his own,
No comforts are mine, so me you condone."
"Servant's cheer cherishes no wish for the cheese,
Aspires no voice, no choice, no ease.

" 'Ts beyond the realm of reason, for who begs,
That poor beggar if expects privilege.
"Should beauty be secured, coupled with power,
'Ts worthy of Him, He ist All-Power."

Blue-dumb she heeded not Lakhan's sarcasm,
Consumed with lust, rushed to Ram shading shame.
Even to a bluff, Ram could not be so rough,
He sent her to Lakhan ; tho' enough was enough.

Lakhan clad his ire in irony and said
"to such brash wanton, a shameless will wed."
There upon fretting, foaming to Shri Ram,
Knitting brows she revealed her demonic form.

A gesture to His younger, Ram made,
When He saw that Seeta was dismayed.

Couplet: *In litheness Lakhan quick,*
Struck off her ears and nose,
Thus punishing the minx,
As if challenged the mankind's foes. 19

Mean demoness wore a repellent mien,
As if from mountain red ochre springs.
Went to Khar-Dushan and did lament,
'fie ! fie !! O brothers upon your strength.'

High strung she sighed before the two,
Shamelessly told of her choiced beau.

Minx=pert lady, a flirt.

The Giants took it as a challange of pigmy,
Quick Khar and Dushan gathered demon's army.

Army of demons to the target rushed,
With horrific weapons and hostile thrust.
Like swarms of Locusts, they flooded the Sylvan,
In the Sky robusts drifted like winged mountain.

Headed by Surpanakha with inauspicious face,
Many more ill-omens had occurred to demon race.
In vanity of prowess, careless of the foe,
Doomed as they all were, to the death they did go.

They bullied, roared against two foe manikins,
Giants hovered in air making terrible din.
Stranged they, in rage some savages said
'how dare the men, our easy prey.'

Sun had dimmed in the sublimed dust,
High headed army hied, headed by robusts.
Said one " Capture the brothers and lay down them,
Forage the cottage, carry off the dame."

Ram asked Lakhan to take Siya in some mount's dugout,
Himself foralaid, the foray which was about.
Ram saw belial force of bellicose foe,
He Smilt as He strung His formidable bow.

RAM, UP IN ARMS

Stanza: *Ram beheld, the belial force of*
Bellicose foes coming before,
coiling tuft of tress, bearing tough face
He strung to brows the cowing bow.

Foralaid=waited for ; Foray=attack.
Cowing=formidable, awesome; Belial=devil; Bellicose=hostile.

fitting quiver on waist, knitting brows like crest,
Clasping divine arms, with His long arms,
He gazed in rage, the savage to ravage,
As if lion looks at beasts' swarms.

Couplet: *"Seize him ! seize him!!" they screeched*
Rushing came the champions
Like the sabled clouds in east,
Gather upon the infant Sun." 20

But, foraying fighters forgot the fight,
Even as their glance took Lord's first sight.
Mesmerised they stood as painted prows,
On the canvas with palsied arrows.

Charmed by charms of Ram, the champs said
'whoever may be this' prince is boast of man's race.
'We have daubed the earth with earthlings' gore,
With such a beauty, never been enamoured.

"Brethren ! He disfigured our sister, yet,
Khar Dushan murmured,'He deserves not the death."
Twin demons sent message " O Manikin !
Submit woman at once you keep in hiding."

"We spare You and Your brother too"
the heralds reached to Ram with demon's view.
Ram smilt "We are warriors by birth,
The wretches like you are the game, We search."

"Nor mammoth might, nor mammon means,
Canst come in the way of Truth's triumph.
"We are none dismayed by the foe's might,
'Ts truth in the combat that's on our side.'

"Brag not O Savage ! I will ravage,
For sages, your race ; tho', am in man's cage.
"If ye parley out of peril and pensive awe,
Go home, I kill not on back of bella.

" 'Ts debility in battle to play wily trick,
To show grace to foe is the face of the weak."
Herald's returned forth, with Ram's message,
Fired in the twin demons, the inferno of rage.

Stanza: *Screeched fiends 'seize Him ! seize Him,'*
In grim mien, in sabled array,
They stormed Ram, brandished arms,
Hovered daggers, sabres in battle array.
Here Hari looked at, as if fiends were gnats,*
Lord gave next, His bow a twang,
Demon's array, deafened-dismayed,
Had left in them no sense.

Couplet: *Dismayed they taken a back,*
Kenning the pluck of foe,
Some stampeded, some reacted stalemate,
Some moved with palsied go. 21

In a bit of the mo,
Ram tore hurled weapons into pieces,
In a fit of the woe,
Array fell to pieces. 22

Ballad: Then drew Lord string of His bow,
And let fly His own arrows.
Like snakes, hissing shafts did go,
Sped forth towards the foes.

Bella (*L*)=War
Sabled array=dark cloth ; Stormed=scolded; *the Lord Ram's another name.
Fell to piece=become agitated; Stalemate=stand still.

Piqued Ram picked from His quiver,
Arrows pelted on fiends to quiver.
Fierce arrows stormed the force,
Fell to pieces the swarms of foes.

Enmeshed shafts made a snare,
Dashed fiends fled scared.
The Trio* warned gust of escape,
'the fleeing fleet would be zapped.'

Resolved to die, returned demons,
If destined, better it be with wight hands.
Decided they made frontal array,
But they knew it was felo de se.

Facing such a Might, lost to fate, they knew,
Demons hurled weapons with no fight in move.
But proclaiming prowess in vain-ego,
The bizarre array was made by the Trio.

Lord discharged multifaced mutilating arrows,
Frightened fiends began be mowed.
Fountains of gore, gushed from the sores,
Dropt heads, daubed red, trunks were floored.

Pierced by the shafts they yelled in pain,
And fell lifeless like the mountains.
Pierced pieced fleshes had fierce facade,
In the canvas of the copse, piled up corpses.

Heaved they fell to pieces, stood up in deceit,
Then fell in pieces, severed to sieves.
Heads limbs hovered, trunks hared to and fro,
Wrangled in cruel way jackals, kites, crows.

Wights=supernatural ; Felo de se=suicide ; Trio*=Khar, Dushan,Trisira.(Demon chiefs.)
Hared=ran

Stanza: *Jackals wrangled in evil way*
Crows warbled eerie lays,
Flood of blood painted sabled wings,
Beaks, snouts feasted on the flesh.
Ram's rage to ravage the savage,
And to raze the sacrilege,
In the form of arrows, Ram's pledge
Forayed over the demon arrays. *A*

Nearly dead, in severe ways,
Stood they, ran astrayed
Cried 'forage ! sieze ! raze ! !'
They grinned making din in grim ways.

In claw's catch, in the beak's snatch
With piece of flesh vultures fled,
That weird sketch, was beyond match
Bards' words canst not portray. *B*

While a number of champs were zapped
And Lord laid low them in this bellum,
In front, to confront Strange Man,
*Came affronted Trisira, Khar-Dushan *.*

With verve a new in their Sinew,
On Ram threw, fiends crew, the weapons,
Spears, daggers, sabres they hurled,
With ardour all at once. *C*

In a flicker of mo, Lord warded off show,
And flag of fanfaronade,
Planted sharp shafts, through the champ's breasts,
Fell they into gory sward.

---

*three leaders of demon race; Eerie=strange (feary)
Fanfaronade=vain glory.

Yet they would not die, played many ploys,
Rose again, dashed and clashed in fray,
Animus spirit-high, they would vie,
And then Lord wrought His illusive play. D

Under Lord's spell, amazed dazed they,
In each-other gazed, the visaged Ram,
Ram's spell wrought, among self they fought,
In gory bath, perished scamp's swarm. E

Couplet: *Demonry vied, cried, sighed*
And in end at quitting gasp,
Called 'Ram ! Ram ! !' ; there by,
Attained beatific state. 23

Floral rains from sky,
Told of relief from the brutes,
Of the Earth as well of paradise,
And victory of the Truth. 24

For the mankind to relieve of demon's awe,
As manikin, the Lord fought the bella.

Before Might of the Lord, fiends were pigmy puppets,
Yet for Bhakt, His own Grace, incarneth.
Thus begun the end of demonry, as was pledged,
Lakhan brought, then Seeta to the hermitage.

Lakhan fell at feet, raising him Ram embraced,
And on delicate swarthy form Siya fixed Her gaze.
Thus the exploits of Ram under quinary trees shades,
Became daily delight of the pages, the sages.

Perceiving ruining of demon's reign,
At once to Raavan, Surpanakha ran.

Scamp=devil

In daily pompous routine of Lanka,
She entered bleeding like volcano's lava.

Awe-struck demon's weapons dropt from hands,
'Who could do this?' none could understand.
Wrestlers forgot the fights in rings,
Damsels dropt, from the heights of swings.

Droopt jaws in awe, all gazed her with sighs,
'with such a dare, who could survive?'

Couplet: *She stormed into the court,*
As the demonry's ill omen,
Her gore daubed the floor,
Stood embodied challenge before Raavan. 25

The ire within her instigated Raavan,
And ignited a fire that scorched his bosom
"Careless, O brother ! thou art in dance and dine,
Dipped in wealth and doped in wine.

"No heed thou takest that the raider assailed,
Who is now at thy very doorsill.
"A reign without control is bound to ruin,
A gain without concern turns to loss soon.

"The learning without wisdom is in vain,
Kingdom and Kudos, through slumber drains.
"Such maxims I heard so I harp on abou',
Lest it's silly to be sapient before thou.

Couplet: *"The master, the man, the minion,*
A foe, fire, fault and fate.
To these never turn blind, the vision,
The sickness, the sin, the snake." 26

Bella=war

Her lamentation raised,
In the Raavan's assize,—
"Should I be lessened to this state,
Even tho' thou art alive?" 27

Paying court to the words of weeping demoness,
The courtiers rose in great distress.
Lifting her up, solaced the grieved soul,
Knitting his brows, then Raavan told–

"Who dared, detail me O dear !,
To strike off your pretty nose and ears."
"Two princes of Awadh came for venery,
I estimate they'll rid earth of the demonry.

"They are boast of mankind, a lion in men I see,
Under His protection hermits roam free.
"Their charm is warm, young and delicate,
Yet They art terrible as chill of death.

"Our giants are dwarfs, before the size
Of fight, which within Them abide.
"With killing spirit, the skilled archers,
In combat two brothers had no compeer.

The elder winsome hath with Him, a young belle,
Millions of Rati's beauty before Her fail.

Couplet: *"From that belle lotuses begged,*
'Her mercy for petals,'
Looking to Her waistless waist,
The creepers seemed dazzled." 28

"About that damsel ever swarm deer herds,
Own eyes those found in Hers.

Assize=court ; Paying court=paying attention.

"In eyes shone oceans, but in mouth smile pearls,
With man She lives, tho' She is angel-girl.

"She is boast of beauty, carved by kisses of blossom,
She is sure Creator's one and only creation.
"Me fool ! why say of Her from tresses to the toe,
While you yourself may go and bring her by tomorrow.

"For Her beauty, I see Raavan you, as Her beau,
So, from Her man I wished on to snatch Her for you.
"But, His younger made a mock of me and chaffed,
Knowing I was thy sister, my ears nose he chopped off.

"In revenge to Ram, Khar Dushan, Trisira ran,
They and their army in a trice were slain."
Sorry plight of demon's might in the carnage,
Filled Raavan with the scorching rage.

Couplet: *His wounded sister he solaced,*
Own prowess he crowed,
But retired to his palace,
Feared he dozed, stirred he rose. 29

□

To Chaff=to joke.

21

The monk is greater than the prince.

—Swami Vivekanand

SATAN DISGUISES AS SAINT

The glitter of gold, and creases of silk,
Pricked overnight, his eyes wink.

Raavan brooded—

"Among deo-demons, winged, finned, other else,
None can dare me and even my elves.

"Dear Khar-Dushan were peers of my prowess,
Who else? Had it not been the Lord Himself?
"If therefore, He cometh to gladden, Laden Earth,
Resolutely to fight with Him is worth.

"Against my prowess, my proud, persistence and my person,
If Lord Himself descendth, I have already won.
"My unsaintly mind, with deeds malignant,
Demonic frame is made up of ignorance.

"For the cause if He incarnateth,
I'll sure cross bar, falling to the combat.
"And if mere men of mortal straw comes in battle,
I shall win both and carry off bride-belle."

Making up mind, drove he chariot and reached,
Where lived demon-wizard Mareech.
Panchvati's story Lord Shiv further voiced,—
"Uma ! Against the Vice, here Ram framed a device.

Couplet: *While Laxman had gone,*
To gather bulbs, roots, fruits,
The divine couple all alone,
Planned demons to uproot. 1

"O Siye! O Virtue! O true in holy vow!
Mansized Me, will act a human now.
"Thy visaged ownself should abide in holy fire,
Until I get rid the Earth of the fear."

Yogic way possessed Self, leaving cast of Her's,
Niching Ram within, She entered the fire of altar.
Shadow looked real, with same mien, merits, modesty,
Even Lakhan could not know this mystery.

There, Ten skulled Raavan reached to Mareech with no pause,
Bowed head the selfish the Vile, as he was.
Bowing of a mean bringeth torments,
'Ts like bending of goad, bow, cat, serpents.

Flowery words of fraud are as risky,
As the colourful blossom of poisonous tree.

Couplet: *Accepting the homage,*
Mareech asked the mission—
"why are you so perplexed?
What purpose bring you O Raavan?" 2

Of his wretched thirst with vain glory,
He spake of his lust and the whole story

"Assume pseudo form of a heartening hart,
Then to carry off princess will be my part."

Mareech replied–

"Listen! Raavan!! tho' He ist man-sized,
He ist Lord of lords, never He be tried.
"By His sufferance we enjoy our life,
We die when He would have us die.

"Very Princes once guarded hermitage of Kaushik,
I wronged them, dared as antagonist.
"With blunt arrow Ram smote, and in a while,
I was thrown at distance of hundreds of miles.

"Still they scare me, in night mare,
Me a gnat, those Great how can I dare?
"The feud is no good, even if they're humans,
For dear son ! they are real champs.

Couplet: *"But could a man break Shiv's bow,*
And kill Tadaka, Subahu,
Brood ! our troops he laid low,
And Khar Dushan He slew." 3

"Poise O Son! Pause upon the fact,
'Ts for welfare of race if you return back."
The demon dwelt in Raavan, swelt, pelted abuses,
"How dare you preach me as Guru O Wretch!"

"No need you suggest, heed only my behest,
I see no warrior that stands as my match."
Then Mareech thought and mulled over
"Such friend, such foe is disaster ever.

Sufferance=moderation.
Hart=deer.

"The chief, the chef, the chit, the champ,
The cheat, chatty, cheap, the charlatan, the chump,
"None of these nine should be made foe,
Go for their ego and have no row."

He saw death hovering overhead either way,
Hence he saught the refuge in Ram for his last breath.
"The wretch would kill me, if I row,
Why, then should I not be killed by Ram's arrow.

Dipt in Ram, dopped in the thrill,
His joy before Raavan, tho' he did not reveal.

Mareech brooded—

Stanza:

" My insight's in zest, my eyes will feast,
The very sight of Ram's feet,
I feel gay, in His own play,
I 'm His prey so He'll follow me, *A*

"I'll turn and gaze, He 'll run and chase,
In His feat, 'He follows His fleet game,'
He will chase me, and 'll slay me,
And His own abode I will attain. *B*

Couplet:

"That scene I muse,
In His Leela of the game,
Ram chases me confused,
None else's so blest as I am." *4*

Thus tried to brave, the knave Raavan,
With deceit drew to the slumbering Sylvan.
Mareech keeping Ram's visage in heart,
Assumed false appearance of a hart.

Leela=exploit, deed; Chit=younglady; chatty=vain glorious; charlatan=quack; chump=fool

The spell caster feigned in a splendorous built,
With gold strips on glaring skin of gilt.
The body of gold, artistically inlaid,
Such beauty Siya saw with marvelled gaze.

Seeing brilliance Siya got mesmerized,
And asked Shri Ram 'get me that wight.'
There upon Ram arose even tho' He knew,
What glitters was elusive untrue.

The doer of heaven's cause, at deer casting gaze,
For His dear Siya, prepared Self for the chase.
Ram asked Lakhan to stay back,
"Take care of Siya from savages.

"demons roam, danger hovers in the dense,
Make use of your strength and sense."
"if it's infernal I will shot at,
Lest a play thing for Siya, I will bring intact."

Deer took to flight at the sight of the Lord,
Ram ran after it pulling His bow-cord.
All illusion who createth as own toy,
Strange ! He ran in pursuit of spell's ploy.

Wight=rare, divine.

Now nigh at hand, next hied with distance,
At one time came to view, out of sight next, went.
Thus revealing-concealing practising all fraud,
Far and far away, the strange thing took the Lord.

Ram then let fly fatal shaft, while the animal fell,
Hart's screams echoed the woods, when yelled.
"Alas! Laxman!!' calling in loud words,
But in the mind invoking Shri Ram afterwards.

It gave up it's ghost, came in real form,
Reverently gasped in his last 'Shri Ram.'
Tho' demon, His inner love Ram kent,
Conferred on him the state, which was due for saints.

Couplet: *Heaven rained blossoms,*
And sang, Lord's paeans,
He blest even the demon,
The fiend, as a friend. 5

The moment Lord had slain the wretch,
With quiver and bow Ram turned back.
When Sita heard the yell of distress,
She was seized with excessive dismay.

'Quick !' Said Siya 'He is in threat,'
Smiling to this, Laxman said
"Heed ! O revered ! ! the very play of Ram's eye brows,
Masterth, the entire mundane's show.

"No power can lessen Him to cry for help,
And me, no power to save Him, He is saviour Himself.
'Could He be ever in danger?'
But Siya urged him with hard words

"Your brotherhood is on test at this ordeal,
Even newish friends would, at this hour, prove themselves.

"deliberately you stand, O Lakhan ! unmoved,
Your selfish fear prevails, it proves.

"You leave for His help, Lest I leave this frame,
And be ready for loads of all ill fames."
Piercing words for Laxman, piercing to the quick
Fates were at work, his resolution turned weak.

Entrusting Her to all Sylvan deities' grace,
Facing dilemma Laxman left the place.
Availing himself of this lonely cottage,
Raavan emerged disguised as a sage.

Couplet: *In whose terror ever quivered,*
The heavens and the havens,
On mission of thieving, like a cur,
Stands the same Raavan. 6

One who violates virtues, in that villain,
Vision, vim, vigour, wisdom turn Volant.
Came before Siya the satan, disguised as saint,
Alluring anecdotes-quotes he did invent.

Using menace, grace, rage, the knave tried to woo,
Naive Siya saw him with strange look.
"Listen O pious father ! in you speaks a villain,"
Then Raavan revealed self, his name he mentioned.

Scared-stiff She, plucked all Her courage,
Said " stay a while, my Lord cometh O wretch!"
"Even as a hare would dare lioness' wedlock,
So have you wooed your own havoc."

Raavan's eyes of blue thirst, turned red,
On the ruining route of rue Raavan proceeded.

Volant=vapourous ; Cur=worthless dog; Rue=repent, remorse.

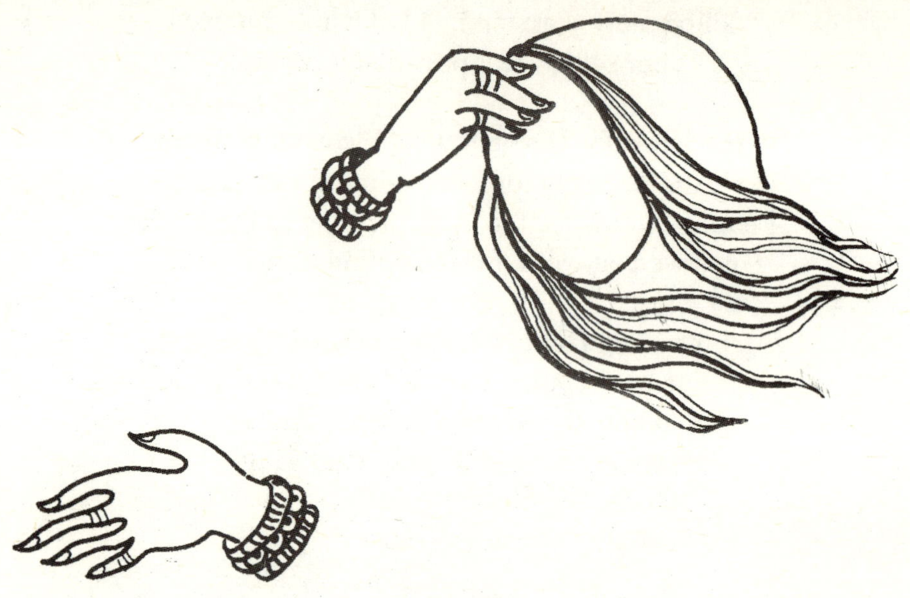

Couplet: *Now, Raavan full of wrath,*
Carried Siya to his rath.
Unnerved drove thro' aery path,
Scarcely could drive scared. 7

CONFRONTS JATAYU

Siya wailed—

"O! peerless champ of the cosmos!
What fault of mine brought this catastrophe?
"O Dear! O Doer!! O Reliever! Saviour!!
Thou hearest every vesper, every whisper.

"The fault is none of yours Lakhan! Alas!!
I have reaped the fruit of My bias.
"Of Me to My Lord who will apprise,"
—Such lamentation pierced the vault of skies.

Meek trees, peaks, laes, bees, 'neath heard Her cries,
Divine eagle Jatayu recognized voice.
Eagle kent Raavan takes Siya thro' sky route,
Like a holy heifer had fallen in catch of a brute.

Winged warrior tho' old but with heart of gold,
"O daughter ! fear not" thus the bird consoled.
Itself hurled bird on Raavan as missile.
"Stop ! O thief !! hold on O vile !!"

Hovering on wounded Raavan's head,
With senile wings, but spiked beak he attacked.
While the death on Raavan's head whirled,
Benumbed his hold of the bridle

"Is it gliding mount or sliding thunderbolt,
Is it winged colt or is it wind's jolt?"
As he thought thus, the bird came nigh,
His panic fled when he recognized

" Ah! came to my pilgrim hands aged Jatayu,
His dying breath to bid adieu."
The Eagle grappled on Raavan as embodied weapon,
Banged, turned, clanged, returned again, clashed upon.

"Listen Raavan ! Leave Siya alone,
Follow my advice, return safely home.

"Lest, in inferno of Shri Ram's wrath,
Your race will be consumed like a moth."

Colt=horse

Kept Raavan silence, tho' was bellicose,
But now was a thief, had no words to cross.
The Bird rushed as Raavan was running riot,
Clutching demon by scalp pulled from chariot.

Placing Seeta safe, Jatayu turned once more,
With the beak, his arms, his armour, the bird tore.
For a while benumbed retched, the wretch,
To ward off he wary, then his sabre stretched.

He severed bird's wings with severe sabre,
Recalling wondrous Ram, fell Ram's warrior.
Invoking Ram the bird fell in own gory pool,
Raavan took again Siya, while bird saw this drooped.

Raavan drove off the chariot, in haste,
Greatly alarmed, over fields and forests.
Was borne thro' air, delicate princess wept,
As if scared doe, in snare was trapped.

Looked She, some monkeys perched on hill top,
Uttering Lord's name some attires she dropped.
Thus taking away Seeta, Raavan drove
The chariot, and placed Her in Ashoka* grove.

Couplet:
Every way of threat, in vain,
Endearment, the wretch assayed,
Kept in grove when hopes waned,
In vigile of demonesses. 8

She niched the impression in heart,
The image which appeared in the last,
The chasing of elusive hart
Muttered She 'Hari-Hari', all lost. 9

Retched=turned sick, heaved; Bellicose=warlike ; Cross=oppose.
**Jonesia asoka.(Bot.)*

THE BEREAVED WANDERER

Here when Ram saw approaching Lakhan,
Outwardly He expressed much concern.
Against my words leaving Siya alone,
—'all abou' the woods Alas ! demons roam.'

"Great misery, now may await,
Siya is not there, I do suspect."
Lakhan clasped Ram's feet, spake grieved heart
"O Lord ! no fault lies on my part."

With brother, Lord Ram swiftly went back,
Bereft of Siya He saw the cottage.
In man-sized frame, the affliction is giant,
Pain turns, malignant, when soul is benign.

Perturbed He was like a man of Straw,
In many way, was consoled by His fra.
He peeped thro' vista asked the leafy boughs
The creaking glades showed no trace of Her go.

From droning bees, drowsy laes, lowing roe,
Asked He "Let me know where did She go?
"O thrilling blooming buds! O trilling birds!!
O rolling floods! O rocking scuds!!

"O Winged! O finned!! O creature limbed!!!
All ye were Hers daily play things.
"O petals! ye graced Her, O pebbles! ye caressed ways,
O pets ye were pals, of Her Sylvan days.

Scuds=clouds; Glade=paths in jungle.

"*O moon, minnow, peahen! O parrot! O pigeon!
O lightening welkin! O blooming Sylvan!!
" ** O lotus ! O jasmine ! O sparkling meteors !!
Whirring bees! warbling birds !! whirling creepers!!!

"Unabashed ye rejoice, now that Seeta is not seen,
Glad today ye gained the reign, of the beauty supreme.

"Siye ! the vista looks hollow, hills, rills sick,
Why do You not reveal Yourself quick.
"Alas ! Feeling of my loss will never fade old,"
—Thus grief puffed a humble human in Supreme soul.

Uxoriously He lamented, sore smitten with blues,
Through the pellucid bosom, welled pellucid dews.
The Immortal cometh shaped as a mortal,
He behaved like a mortal to set a morale.

Further on They saw, the Jatayu was laid,
Dipt in Ram's thoughts, with sinking breath.

Couplet: *Moved Ram, moved to the bird,*
Stroked head with healing touch,
When Ram to the fore appeared
His pain ceased, his sighs hushed— 10

JATAYU'S LIBERATION

For devout's sore no doubt, to the fore cometh Ram,
Ram ist the nostrum, Ram ist the balm.

---

*/**Shri Ram here exhausts the list of animals and inanimate objects looking to which reminds Him of some aspect of mien of His consort Seeta. Of these, moon to Her face, Minnow(fish) to eyes, peahen to delicacy and overall beauty, the Neck, Nose to that of parrots beak, Neck to that of pigeon, complexion to lightening, blooming to freshness and fragrance, Lotus to lips, jasmine to teeth, sparkling meteors to smile,
Bees to curls of tresses, birds to Her voice and creepers to Her waist.
Uxoriously=with extreme fondness for wife.

With labouring of breath, and melting wounds,
Gathering toiled frame he spake recouped

"Hear ! Ram ! for mirky mare, Thou, the barge,
Raavan reduced me to this plight, and is still at large.
"Same wretch carried off Siya, took Her away,
She kept screaming as a humble prey.

"Fought, tho' my pinions were short to strive,
Only to behold Thou, I still survive.
"My sapped wounds waited Thy divine touch,
No wings I need to hop the perch.

Grave-words Ram said "Live more," yet,
With smile the senile tongue thus spake
"muttering whose very Name at the final gasp,
Ways to final beatitude so declare veds,

Pinions=wings ; To hop the perch=to die.

"To the fore, His very presence in palpable form,
Should I retain this frame still long?"
Regarded bird's words Ram thro' His tears
"duty, deeds devotion fulfilled thy quietus.

"Blessed art they for others who sacrifice,
Rest art more dead than alive.
"Nothing is unattainable in this world and the next,
Accomplished thou may proceed leaving smitten cage."

Couplet: *"On reaching the final aim,*
Tell not my father 'bout Siya.
If I am what I am,
Raavan's feat will bring him fatal end." 11

The spirit of divine bird, dropped the frame,
With vitelline glory, the vital of vulture came.
Sublime soul shaped in human, with boundless bliss,
Burst into praises and the Lord's worship

Hymns: *"O Ram! O Might!! Thou art the light,*
In Thy shadow we take delight—
Glory be to Thou! who bringest glory to devout,
My slight death, Thou fillest with life. A

"O All-wise ! came man-sized
For the mirth of heaven and human,
Heeding the Earth, for hearts and hearths,
Came, ridding all of herds of heathen. B

"Thy long arms art the charms of friends
Thy prompt arms are harms of fiends,
Thy strong arms, to right the wrongs,
Will prone demon's throng in one fling. C

Vitteline=golden yellow; fling=shot
prone=lay down flat.

"In all, who pervadeth; now on forest glades
That Ram doth roam to grace sages,
To ravage the reckless, Thou raged on savage
To reck hermitage, hallowed pages, holy pages." *D*

Couplet: *Asking the Bhakti incessant,*
Fulfilled spirit bade adieu,
Ram performed with own hands,
Reverently the obsequies. *12*

In time, Lord's pastime ever viewed,
He bestowth upon devout with determined pursuit.
On vulture, mere bird, flesh eater, smeared,
With slurred mien, sluttish beak, a smudgy bird,

Own highest abode Shri Ram conferred,
Which is solicited ever by seers and friars.
Knowing this they who lift no hands of worship,
Heed Uma! * they are ill-starred, indeed.

The two brothers further proceeded in Siya's quest,
Even as they went, marked thickening of the forest.
Thick groves of trees, with drove of bees,
were inhabitated by wild life livid.

On the way Ram overdrewth Kabandh, the demon,
His malison today turned into benison.

Said dying demon Kabandh–

"The rage of a sage became my plight,
By Thy sight, the sin has now been wiped."

Page=servants (devotees of Lord) ; holy pages=veds.
Obsequies=funeral rites
*Shiv said to Uma(adding his remarks in Ram's narrative.)

Lord replied "O Gandharv! all ye should know,
The hostile to the pious, is My foe."

Couplet: *"The Almighty Master is,*
Mastered by them, who
In thoughts words and deeds
Service to the pious, do." 13

THE BLEST SABARI

"So declare saints and the holy texts,
Even harsh words of the pious are blessed."
The malison on Kabandh brought him benison,
Lord instructed him to His own devotion.

Coming to early-form of celestial songster,
Ascended he upheaven, his curse was over.
Further on, Ram stepped for the senile eyes
Of Sabari who waited since she was a child.

Devotee hath no name, no self of own,
So was she, lost in Lord with name unknown.
The remote 'Sabar-tribe' which she belonged,
She was a name among the pious, tho' low-born.

Her great faith and still greater fortitude,
Her endless penance, since her childhood,
—Brought Lord Ram to her own abode,
In her very hut, commenced and finished her road.

The pilgrim soul was glad at heart,
To find to the fore her Own Lord.
One with swarthy, one with the fair, charming hue,
Sabari fell prostrate before, the two.

Gandharv=celestial songster; Malison=curse.

Matted tresses, hermits dresses with princely face,
Graced ‘wreaths’ on breasts and quiver on waists.
B’cause her clairvoyance, in very visage was dipt,
So recognized she and laved their feet.

Her accomplished penance stood embodied to the fore,
Her lips failed and words were needed no more.

Couplet: *Loving offer of the sloe’,*
Fruits, bulbs and roots
Relishing honey of her love
With her hands Ram partook. 14

Joining palms stood she to the fore,
As she gazed Lord, her love waxed yet more.
“O Unknown! Unknowable!! I know no worship,
I ’m low descent and as well as low wit.

“More over a woman, hath a limit
Still Thou gracedst my long cherished wish.”
Ram called the unnamed “O pious! pilgrim soul!!
I dwell in devouts, no else kinship I know.”

“No castle, no cavelery, no clevery, no crusade,
No cachet, No commerce, clout or coinage.
“No caste, craft, creed nor colour nor customs,
I do care cordial call of the common.”

“I never dost see the sourness of sloe,
Accept ‘Bhog’ looking at the honeyed soul.

“No worth is the man with no reverence,
It’s waterless cloud with no rains.
“A man with no devotion is a fruitless toil
Of shuttling to and fro, a worthless life.

Sloe=wild plum (Ber)
Clout=strength; Cachet=stature; cavelary=troops; Bhog=ritual offering of food.

"Nine paths of devotions now I describe,
Heed ! O good lady! on the qui vive.
"Firstly fellowship with hallowed and next,
Is listening anecdotes of the holy text.

Couplet: *"Service to Guru's feet is*
third form of devotion
and fourth form consists
singing my praises, paeans. 15

"The Jap of Name with unceasing faith,
Constitutes fifth form of the homage.
"Self mastered soul sublimeth to altitudes of rectitude,
Constitutes sixth form of faith with fortitude.

"My existence in every bit who perceives,
He is goer of seventh type of the worship.
"Who wait at Me sated, in whatever they get,
They cultivate devotion's form eight.

"Dependth on Me with no I am ness who,
With nor bloom on cloud nine, nor gloom of the blues,
"Him, the guileless fine, I takest as Mine,
And I do define this path, the nineth."

"Here, goer of even any one of nine ways,
Is dear to Me I do care his tread.
"You, O good lady! simply you trod,
All of these long devotion's road.

"Your walk begun in this hut, and reached the goal,
Your inner journey deified in you, a pilgrim soul.
"The inner expedition in such holy quest,
Tho' Soul remains unstirred, but yet on the pilgrimage.

---

on the qui vive=attentive, alert.
Rectitude=virtues, righteousness.

"Now, if you know anything about
My loss; then tell me of my spouse."
"O All-wise Ram! Thou knowest every thing,
Thou askest, nevertheless, to sublime me.

"Thou wilt meet Sugriv, go to Pampa lake,
O Ram! He will tell Thou, the fact."
Repeatedly at Lord's feet she bowed,
How Presage of the Sage* now was fulfilled, she told,

And in hollow vista, and empty sleuth her eager eyes,
How roamed for Ram, all days and nights.

Stanza: *What the sage* had presaged in her childhood,*
Her eager gaze watched for Ram's Visit,
Her gaze had rummaged for the visage of Ram,
And roamed she, in woods, dipt.
Through filled eyes welled cataracts,
*And fulfilled soul casted off the cage,***
As the sage did forebode, got she high abode,
Now Laureates praise her with great éclat.

Couplet: *In Guru-n-in herself she relied,*
Thus accomplished the watch of a child,
waited for Lord till her unceased sight,
turned creased and senile. 16

WAYS TO SOUTH TO PAMPA LAKE

Folly of my mind's still in mundane's fix,
tho' I see Lord conferth to devout, the bliss.
Further on, further on in deed and deep,
Two princes crossed through untrodden cliffs.

Sleuth=Pedestrian's ways.
*Guru Matang (preceptor of Sabari); **soul left the body; Rummage=carefully searched.

The Lord walked through the sleuth, slopes and steeps,
Matched with ascends and descends of a Bereaved within.
“Lo! Lakhan blossom, brooks, beasts, birds and bees,
All look unstirred of my grief.

“How could I hope that other should,
Seeing me, fade their vernal mood?
“In the row of roes as if this talk goes,
Fear not! He cameth searching deer of gold.

“Beasts roam with mates to teach me how,
Should a man take care of his spouse.
“Touch of silk clad shrubs, and velvet of the glades,
Turns Me more bereft, the breeze’s pat.

“The cupid had charmed the Sylvan, laden it with blossom,
Yet, upon Me further he hath laden My bosom.

Couplet: *“The Cupid found Me alone,*
Made against Me foray,
With verdant paint, bees drone,
And the trilling birds’ lays. 17

“However wind spied found Me with brother,
Cupid held up with troops besieged Me as it were.
“Creepers have entwined its twigs around trees,
Spreaded as the tentered canopies.

“Cupid crayoned the canvas with vernal brush
Over the drowsed drone hills; and to ponds rills rushed.
“Boughs are bowing on creepers with blossoming bouquet,
As if wooing them to adorn and to bonnet.

“Through trilling birds and whispering breeze,
Through appealing parrots, swans, patridge,

To bonnet=to veil with head-dress.

"Beguiler Cupid wooed nature with these troops,
Seemed bugled he the challenge through coos of cuckoos.

"While in man these troops ever combat without and within,
Lakhan ! they are real champs who remain firm.
"Rare are the men who escape this trap,
Which is dissolved in the world as the thirst of no shape.

Couplet: *"What that limits the wit,*
And hit even minds of hermits,
Are the Lust, choler and greed,
With in the man have their seat. 18

"Desire is the face of greed,
Harsh words. the fuel of choler,
Lust thru blue eyes speak,
They ever need be mastered." 19

Ram, is the Master who masterth all puppets,
All acts of animate and inanimates.
Greed, grudge, guile, grafts and lust,
Ram's grace eliminates from these mundane's curse.

'the Divine concern for wife hath increasing reverence',
Lord's pastime conveyed this message to mundane.

(Shiv further added)—

"O Uma ! realized the very Ownself in Me—
To revere Ram is real, rest in world is reverie."

Further Ram wayed southern, reached Pampa Lake,
It's water was as limpid as the heart of a sage.
The aquatic birds, all about it, frolicked,
Like the anchorites wander free and easy.

Reverie=delusion, fantasy; Mastered=controlled; Graft=illegal practice.

Like the hallow touch relieves world; the various beasts
Were lulled there by the lullaby breeze.
The beauty of the lake was the lesson,
How the nature's home was preserved by men.
To reach down to marge, the lake had,
On all its sides, charming flights of steps.

Distich:— *Green disky leaves*
Of lotus was spreaded on surface,
Thro' its carpet, water not perceived,
Like the Maya veils the Truth's face. 20

Couplet: *"In the fathomless lake,*
Their abode, had the fish',
The pious, even as
Dipt in Lord, live in peace. 21

Open lotuses welcomed the arriving Sun,
But at Ram's sight the abashed petals crimsoned.
Swans, waterfowls frolicked made such a noise,
As tho' burst into Lord's praises in own voice.

Little finned jumped above waves in an arch,
Little winged hopped on pinions on the marge.
On the land clad in very green richness,
All resigned sages had thatched their cottages.

Lofty hands of nature overlaid loppy lofts,
And the hush of sky was sages' posh toft.
Steep leap of the Blue on the stretched boughs,
Seemed toiled to embrace hands of trees on toes.

Fruits florets fragrance adorned the face
Of all the canvases of nature's grace.
Murmurs of rills medleyed in melody of trills,
Stirred ever the sages' meditating drills.

Loppy=overhanging ; toft=dwelling place.

Couplet: *Weighed down the laden boughs,*
Kissed ground, the gristle.
Like the blest souls bow,
With riches grow more humble. 22

NAARAD VISITS

Nature conveyed in mind healing thoughts,
Delighted Ram took into Lake, the bath.
Sat Ram and Lakhan under a huge tree,
On crib of the Earth, under green canopy.

Sages rushed recognizing the Lord,
And met the god in Man and man in God.
The Divine Sage Naarad, once accursed
Ram ; he realized-'the Lord sufferth for his words.'

The pangs of bereaved he sufferth for me,
This moment chanced me, the opportunity.
Reflecting thus in mind, with lute in hand,
Where Lord was sitting, there, Naarad went.

The divine lute's thread thus jingled,
And the melodious hymns filled the jungle.
Naarad threw himself at the feet of Ram,
Lord lifted him up and clasped into arms.

Lord seated him nigh, with great love,
While the sage's feet, Laxman reverently laved.

Couplet: *Naarad's worships sublimed,*
And filled milieu of Jungle,
Most humbly, the humble hymned,
Lauded the Lord on lute's jingle. 23

Crib=cradle ; Gristle=flexible.

Then divine sage Naarad spake joining palms
"O Generous! as Thou art; Listen! O Ram,
"Even unattainable may be attained by Thy grace,
Grant me, tho' Thou knowst, still I beg,

"O Ram ! Thou knowst every niche of heart,
That is the hitch, how should I ask?"
"Sage ! my heart and hands are ope to devouts,
None the object I hold, so dear in shroud.

"True heart, true worship is dearest to Me,
None I may withhold from such a votary."
"Never ! never !! give up this faith even by mistake"
At this Naarad delightedly spake—

"O unknowable ! as Thou art, known by many names,
Each is greater than rest for reverence.
"This is the boon I presume to ask,
Let very name, 'RAM' O my Lord! surpass,

"Among all other names in ridding of the sin,
And in the din of riddles of atheism."

Couplet: *"May the very name 'Ram'*
Be the might of all Thy names,
May come nor query nor qualm,
In me and in minds of mundane." 24

With certain smile Ram affirmed
And said—"so be it"
"All names are expression of One,
The difference is, of the wit." 25

Naarad in delight bowed at Lord's feet,
Lord's disposition inspired him further to speak—
"Thou hadst lavished with wisdom my dolish mind,
O Ram ! while dazzled by Maya, I was blind.

Ram replied—

"I extend parent's hands in devouts every dip*,
To whispers of worship I bestow my wardenship.
" 'Ts no fault of infant who runs to catch the fire,
To care is the duty of mother, the very Saviour.

"Likewise, humble devouts are my own infants
And the Wise are like my grown up sons.
"while wisdom works with own genius' wit,
The Bhakti, on Me, depends for every bit.

"Both wisdom and Bhakti have anger, lust, ego,
All go along the pious paths as the foe.
"Pondering thus, Prudents dipt in devotion
Adore Me; even after attaining wisdom-vision.

Couplet: *"Sins have satanic heptad,*
The troops of ignorance,
The wrath, sloth, lust and craft,
Envy, ego, esurience. 26

"from ages, thus alleged, by holy pages and sages,
—The ignorance flourishes in lustful cages.'
"The Clouds of ignorance shroud the piety's sun,
In frost of lust blights the crop of wisdom.

"Nay to parch the brooks of devotion and wisdom,
Lust is the scourge of scorching simmoom.
"Hails of folly that storm the mind's sky,
There emerge out, hibernating frogs of ire, err and envy.

"Weeds of sins among good crop of penance,
Need to be weeded off every now and then.

---

*dip=decline, fall; Bhakti=devotion.
Heptad=group of seven.
Simmoom=dry, hot storm of desert.

Ever Mirky cloud of folly, fill furrows of mind,
Mere one miss, turns, for ever, the vision blind.

"I master the wisdom and Bhakti as well,
So it's folly to think wise of yourself.
"Fog of Maya fadeth the wisdom's path,
But let not delusion ever surpass.

Couplet: *Of all, the lust is root,*
Of all woes and throes,
So I ever prevent the crude
Step of devout, as my vow." 27

'The saviour saveth at every step',
pondered Naarad 'every breath is His very debt.'
Thrill ran in veins and along the heart,
More intense, Naarad felt the grace of the Lord.

If knowing such, who lift no hands of worship,
Dipt in deceit, they are nitwit.
Naarad asked the Lord reverently once more,
'Tell O Lord ! the signs of sacred lore.

'Tell of distinguishing marks of 'a human' in man,
How such a soul sublimeth, deifies to a saint?"
"Who have tamed O Sage ! untamed passions,
In stacks of wisdom who have stoic vision,

"Unattached to the gross, lost in Lord,
Tho' part of the world but still apart,
"who discern, who learn, earn*, one just the Truth,
Who behold Truth, bold for it, hold none but the Truth,

* Earn=attain.

Couplet: *"Mine and the soul of a saint,*
Are made of the same,
Rather He is more Myself,
Than what I am." 28

"In the very micro of every micro
Of macrocosm, they see My glow.
"In Every bit, every beat, every breath they see,
Every sight they delight finding full of Me.

"Their own praises they hear and they blush,
Tho' for praises of others, they never hush.
"They abandon their 'I-am-ness',
Their words, deeds thoughts are ever guileless.

"Their placid even-mind is their might,
Every odds of penance, they perform with delight.
"Pregnant with celestial fervour they,
Are firm, friendly never betray faith.

"No glitter of gold but with splendour of soul,
They, the selfless multitudinists enlighten the whole.
"No err, ire, ego ever touch them,
They would lose ownself to resolve other's pain."

"Their piety, penance hath patience, not passion,
Their non-partisan bosom is ope to pantheon.
"Living for others are, real saints-true devouts,
Rest spin to and fro in vain, no doubt."

Stanza: *Being fortunate, Naarad, the great sage,*
The embodied faith was elated,
Once again bending to the Lord,
His lotus feet he clasped.

Multitudinist=who hold the principle of interest of multitude; Non-partisan=unbiased ; Pantheon=gods of all faiths.

Then glad he, bade he, adieu to the two,
And left the dense.
Steeped in love, stepped Naarad back,
Blest he returned to his plane.

Couplet: *In all odds of mundane,*
Who chant Ram's paeans,
Ram's grace pour upon them,
Even with no piety no penance. 29

Lust is the worst flame,
Be not a moth to it,
Just chant and chant very 'Name'
Let err, ire, envy quit. 30

□

KISHKINDHA KANDAM

Weakness is the one cause of suffering

—Samarth Guru Ramdass

STROPHES

Like the sun Two scions of Raghus,
And the race's very crest,
The wondrous Wonders in woods,
Wander on untrodden glades.
The Divine descent was divined
As His grace on our humble race,
Me request the Two to bless me
Journeying on Siya's quest. 1

With chants of the Holy Name
Whose pious souls are elixired,
They are real blest
Never ever with err stirred.
From old anecdotes, ved's quotes
The Name 'Ram' Who churned
From seekers who learned, what seers discerned;
Are blest; this Name who earned. 2

Me, O moron ! on mundane not fie,
for it hath Holy Ganges
where Shiv's own town Kashi, lies,
for riddance from freight.

How is it for me, the stupid —
-'Lord Shiv who know'
And lift no hands of worship,
I am my own woe. 3

MEETING GRIEVED SUGRIV

On the cool roads at the banks of Pampa lake,
The two walked appreciating the Brahma's make.
Over hung with flowering creepers and fruit trees,
Wanderers touched, drank, the water to drain fatigue.

Ram and Lakhan still further moved,
And approached near range of Rishyamuk.
There dwelt Sugriv with counsellors, in hides,
He saw the two brothers as enemy's spies.

Dismayed Sugriv dazed with splendour,
Seeing them he ran further up from fear.
"Lo ! Here come the two men towards us,
Hanuman ! They look comely and tough."

"Disguise yourself and guess their design,
Inform me fitly by means of signs.
"If they have been despatched by Bali,
At once this hill I should leave."

Taking form of Brahman Hanuman rushed,
Bowing head he accosted them thus-
"O Stranger ! O Wonder!! Thou appearest warrior,
In guise of hermit how roamst in here."

" One with dark hue and other the fair,
Gladly tread on tough glade on feet tender.
"In sun and storm all along the glades,
Thou comest as comely solitary guests.

---

glade = paths of forest

"Dost Thou count in Trinity, I guess,
Or art Thou the twin divine sages?*
"O Tiger amongst men ! youthful and brave ,
So inseparable Thou seemst, so stranger Thou behave,

Couplet: *"Art Thou the Supreme, come disguised?*
The prime cause of all existence.
Descendth man-sized
To relieve Earth of its burdens." 1

"Came from Awadh, we are sons of King Dashrath,
Have come to the forest on father's behest.
"We, the two brothers by the name of Ram and Lakhan,
With us came my comely lass, carried away by some one.

"We are moving about in Her quest,
O Pious ! This is our account's present state."
Agelong waiting ended, Hanuman realized,
His piety was accomplished, while Lord cometh man-sized.

He fell at Lord's feet, lost flesh,
That divine bliss even no divine word can express.
Most blest was he, achieved the Final at his sill,
He clasped Lord's feet, ran through limbs a thrill.

His unstirred gaze, stirred his soul,
In acme of emotions, words remained untold.
Tough as lions, soft as lotuses,
Dashing frames in dash of dresses, Hanuman gazed.

Steeped in love, in stupour of emotions,
He stood stooped in wordless welcome.
Recovering he uttered ' O Master beloved !,
I questioned Thou, it was quite behoved.

"but that Thou asked me, doth it meet?
O All wise ! Is it Thy pastime in it?

---

*Nar and Narayan-the two divine sages.
Behoved=befitting, dashing=elegant, dash=style.

Couplet: *" Blurred by ignorance, I*
Wicked at heart, espied,
Alas ! Could not recognize,
Befo' the divinity I was blind." 2

" More over, Thou had'st forgotten me,
Earthly eyes are now blest with vision, and I see.
" 'm full of faults and folly tho'
But let not the servant be ignored.

"Thro' only Thy grace a man can rid
Of mirky mires, of mundane's dips.
" On the top I know, no piety, no penance,
Have no reverence, no reference, no claim for preference.

" But depend on Master, me Thy page,
As a child on the mother's lap ."
So saying, at Lord's feet, Hanumaan fell,
Manifesting own form, with love overwhelmed.

Lord lifted him and clasped as lost bosom friend,
While Hanumant was lost within the Ancient hands.
"A pal, a page, are pellucid, O Hanuman! Heed!
You are twice as dear to Me as Lakhan indeed.

" 'Ts said that with same eyes I do see,
But devout is distinct, as he looks, at none, but Me.

Couplet: *"He, alone is exclusive devotee,*
Who is truthful and oblate,
Whose sight ever perceives Me,
In whole animate-inanimate." 3

The gracious hand of Master that crowned his head,
Proved to be panacea of his long distress.
" My Lord on this hill dwells Sugriv,
Tho' he is Thy devout but is grieved.

"O compassionate ! Grace ! Make him co-mate,
In his very interest, be his intimate.
" Rid the afflicted of all fears,
Thy endearment will clear his weights of years."

" He is chief of Monkeys' sylvan troops,
In quest of Mother Siya they 'll search every route."
Thus he shouldered the odds of both (sides') grief,
And took Ram Lakhan on his shoulders to Sugriv.

The keen Sugriv kent over yonder,
Two divine visage on Hanumant's shoulder.
Enamoured he saw now Them to the fore,
He reverently rushed to Ram with raves in core.

In a mo veiled His revenge and pangs,
Within him prevailed only reverence.
He fell at Lord's feet, Ram embraced in return,
Sugriv thought 'May the Two be ever my friend'.

Couplet: *Hanuman then said entire*
The narratives and all odds
Making witness the sacred fire,
He resolved the two friend's knot. 4

Unreservedly Lakshman exchanged mutual pangs
Thus was concluded the firm alliance.
Said, Sugriv with eyes brimmed with tears,
'Mother Siya, O Lord !, Will be surely recovered."

" Once deliberating here, on one noon,
While the Sylvan was in careless swoon.
" When She saw us down, she dropt Her scarf,
Fallen in foe's hands She cried 'Ram ! Ram ! -Alas !!"

Raves=rapturous welcome; To shoulder=to bear, to take up.

" being borne through the air the loud wail..."
Ram interrupted, asked, Sugriv gave apparels.
Ram caressed apparels with soul's touch,
Pressed to His heart and grieved much.

Soon, He soothed His soul to courage,
Then steeped in love, stooped Sugriv said-
" Me, a pal, a page' will render service to Thou,
Soon Ma Seeta cometh, 'ts my aim now."

Hanuman had already lighted a fire close by,
as witness of purity of new ally.

Couplet: *With warmth of firm friend,*
And fire of the mettle,
Ram asked in strange-
"How you live in jungle?" 5

Sugriv poured melancholy and not just words,
Dew blurred his eyes, emotive speech slurred-
"Thou Lord hath fraternized man with man,
Mundane's evils break this divine chain."

Thus His own story Sugriv began,
" Me and brother Bali were fraternity's name.
"Faith and fidelity faded in my fra,
When a fiend Mayavi came in town Kishkindha.

"To meet the challenge Bali Sallied forth to fiend,
I too had accompanied him behind.
"During endless duel they entered a cave,
Some hurried instruction to me Bali then gave.

" Await my return till a fortnight,
Take me as slain if I return not in time.
A month time passed, echoed in cave roars,
Then on floor I saw streaming gore.

"Bali was slain this inference I drew,
O Ram ! I thought, the fiend would kill me too.
"So, I filled the cave with rock and fled,
Brooding 'the race of monkeys is now Masterless.'

"When the counsellors learnt that town had no upper hand,
Then they forced me to accept the reign.
"Meanwhile, Brave Bali had killed the knave,
Returned ired he most severely behaved.

" He robed me of all and my wife too,
Since then I rove in fear in wood.
"Of foolish understanding, he deprived
Me of every living of the life."

Ram thought and said,-"foe of friend is my foe,
My vow is to row to relieve devout's woe,"

Couplet:

"Be relieved ! O friend heed !!
'ts my single arrow,
Is for all ill deeds,
And fit to lay him low." 6

" A true friend ever is other Own,
Friendship is worship' this is world known.
"The cordial soul, every kinship hath,
And the intimate hands are at its helm.

"In need, extended the sharing hand,
Of friend, for friend is largess from heaven.
"The divinity in a man that dwells,
In shape of a pal, the very Same helps.

"No limits meet in friendship, i.e. just to play,
As Guru he guideth, when from right you stray.

"Dwelling in soul deeps, a friend on the truth keeps,
Oneness in joy joys, oneness in sorrow weeps.

"Living long for years Bali never did meet,
As we, the two are old friends at first speech."
"So grieve no more, I am here to rescue,
Rely on Me and on your own Truth."

" O Ram ! Bali is a name, a prow in rows,
Counted are the days for his foes."
At this, Ram showed a glimpse of His Might,
Then Sugriv's reverence and love touched new height.

Till he knew not abou' Ram's shaft, Sugriv grieved,
With just one shaft Ram turned tree rows to rampike.
With the dawn of wisdom fled mirk of qualm,
He bowed again and again at feet of Shri Ram.

His folly faded on his mind's horizon,
He was enlightened by Ram, the very Sun.
" I, Sugriv, 'll render my services to Ram,
Renouncing home, fame, name and pomp."

" In endless show, the mundane is employed,
In the fane of melancholy deludes niched joy."
"My fraternity is fulfilled now,
Bali is the cause that I have met Thou.

"Had thought of him a foe, I feel abashed,
Now waking from dream, I know he hath blessed.
"If mind abides in Thee, even for a mo,
it wipes all nescience, the root of sorrow.

"had I known O best of Raghus!, I am Thy portion,
I would not have mourned for worldly concerns,
"Now my heart cherishes after meeting Thou,
Like oblate I may worship, all may I renounce.

To row=to fight.

"Your mind is true" Ram said and smilt—
"But my words can never be otherwise".
The Lord maketh us all dance; even as a juggler
Would make his monkey dance; Veds so declare.

Taking Sugriv with him, Ram, the single handed Army,
Said "Go! Up!! May good betide thee"
Hearing Sugriv's roar Bali sallied forth,
But his wife clasped feet and saw, "its not worth."

"The Sugriv's alliance with two brothers, is his prowess,
Ram Lakhan, princes of Awadh canst conquer the Death."
"Ram of auspicious fortune is now his intimate
Sugriv's challenge is call of thy death"

Couplet: *"Dear wife! Ram ist unbiased,*
Even if He killth, will be no a waste
In here, what Sugriv had, had,
I'll have same nexus in the next." 7

THE BELLICOSE BALI

So saying he sallied forth in great wrath,
Thinking no more of Sugriv, then blade of grass.
The two closed head on with each other,
Bali brow beat Sugriv, roared thunder.

His fist on Sugriv as thunderbolt fell,
Distressed dismayed then Sugriv fled.
"O gracious Lord! He is grievous I said,
This is not my brother but the death himself."

"The two of you are so identical,
I didn't lay him down, I wast puzzled."

Nexus=alliance, relation; The next =After death

With healing touch of Ram, the confused frame
Was relieved of pain, he gained new strength.

Ram garlanded Sugriv then with bays,
As the sure victory was backing him at the back.
Hanging wreath bays became cuirass,
To protect him from Bali's wrath.

With great speed like an elephant in rut
Sugriv with new force to Bali rushed
Again the two fought in many ways,
They battled, struggled in cudget-play.

Iron-fisted they fought in tyranny,
While the Lord watched them from behind a tree.

Couplet: *But then drained Sugriv's Sinew,*
Muscles slipped, his heart he lost,
An arrow then Ram drew,
Thro' sternum of Bali He shot. 8

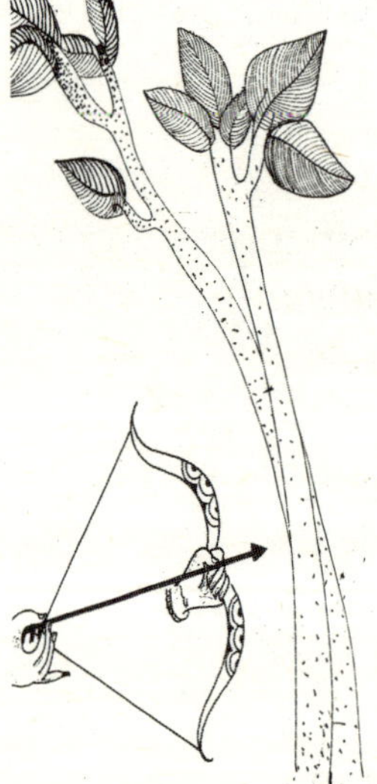

Thro' pierce of shaft fountained the gore,
Fell, sprang up, sat finding Ram to the fore.
Seeing Matted tresses and drest as hermit,
He forgot all pain, in visage he was dipt.

Tho' sinking was the gaze, yet his eyes he fixed,
Fixed his pain-free soul, on Lord's lotus feet.
Recognizing the Lord his glow revived—
'The death hath given me more than life.'

Lord's shaft exorcised all hardness of his heart,
But his lambasting tongue was still harsh-
"tho' Thou havest come, the wrongs to right,
Thou laidst me down like a game in wild."

Bays=wreath of victory, Cuirass=breast plate (armour); Cudget-play=fight with clubs.

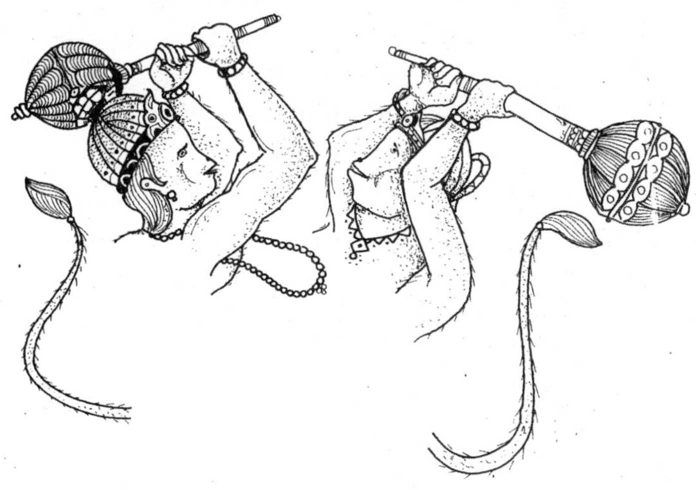

" You transgressed all limits O Bali ! O wretch!!
Lust for other's woman is great fall from grace.
"I view all diabolic heart in lewd,
Your blue eyed thirst hath caused this feud.

" Laden with ire, ego, err and lust,
To zap such a wretch is lightening the earth.
"If someone relieveth the mankind from terror,
No sin anyone would incur.

"The traitors, the perpetrators of Adharma
never can stand before my vow firm.
"Moreover, You knew 'Sugriv is in my refuge'
Yet your ego was engaged in the mortal fued.

Couplet: *"O Ram ! My crafts conclude,*
Before Thy mighty shaft,
At death I found Thy refuge,
Am I a sinner yet?" 9

Lambasting=scolding (crude), Exorcised=driven out (for evils), Lewd=sensual, lustful.

In most tender voice Bali confessed,
With a touch Ram, balmed his pangs and spake—
"You may keep your vital, I'll say 'no' to death,
With immortality I bless your breath.

" O Lord ! For chains of births, the sages strain,
But forget Thy very Name while soul is drained.
"The Very Name 'Ram' is the last missive,
For riddance it is imparted by Shiv.

"While He hath appeared as feellable Himself,
Shall ever I get such a blest death?

Stanza: *"Saints dost penance, for births' chain,*
Yet not certain, Thou wouldst come to core,
I'm no devout, yet appeared Thou,
No doubt now to the fore.
"My deep sins, thro' my deeds brimmed,
Still Thou longed to prolong my life,
Me, a victim, my death is esteemed
Is it still prim, for life I thrieve? *A*

"Now as O great ! My death is blest,
Let me have one boon, in me I cherish,
The fate after death, whatever comes next,
May I be ever annexed to Thy feet.
"Now, the son of mine, O Divine! is Thine
Angad by name, O Ram ! have,
Refined by me, designed for army
Will be defined now as Thy slave. *B*

Couplet: *Bali casted off the mould,*
Death brought the reward of life.
Fixed was, on Ram his soul
Lord sent him to Own paradise. 10

Riddance=get rid of births and birth's chain.
Annexed=affiliated (attached); Prim=Proper, fit.

News of Bali in the town spreaded,
People hied in distress and sighed in dismay.
There came she in tottered gait and tousted tress,
Wife of Bali, Tara keened in many ways.

Beholding her distress Ram consoled,
With words of wisdom he soothed her soul-
"O Queen ! This quince frame is a quinary coil,
Death sublimeth the soul above mortal frame of soil.

"Undying soul sets loose, but what you see before eyes,
Drowned in endless sleep, only mortal noose lies.
"Frame is alien, Soul is ancient,
For whom then, you now lament?"

Thus Lord many ways consoled the grieved,
Then gave Ram command to Sugriv.
Who performed with regard due, the obsequies,
"Go ! And enthrone Sugriv" then Ram viewed.

With Sugriv Ram sent Lakhan as well,
Bowing head to Ram all they left.

Couplet: *Plebs and priests were called*
By Lakhan forth with,
Sugriv as King was installed
And Angad as crown prince. 11

RAM IN RETREAT, IN RAINS

"O Uma* ! Ram is the friend, the only friend,
All kinship is new He, the most ancient."
Nor parent nor pal nor preceptor nor priest,
Is so benefactor as the Lord is."

Keen=wailing at the dead; Tousted=Uncombed (scattered)
Quince=peer shaped fruit (shrifal-coconut) quinary = made up of five elements.
*Shiv in His narrative of Ramayan said to Uma, His consort.

"All kinships other than the Lord's love,
Have their selfish motive all above.
Same timid Sugriv who was so afraid of Bali,
Who had many a sores in soul and body,

The Lord befriended and ceased his ill at ease,
And the same was made, the King of monkeys.
Who lift no hands of worship, knowing such grace,
No wonder should be caught he, in the mundane's mesh.

Lord then sent for Sugriv and instructed the art
Of path of duty and principles of state craft-
"I may not enter town for years forteen,
Listen ! Summer is over and fall is setting in.

"So I shall encamp no far from you,
On some hillock in purlieu.
"You and Angad go and rule over Kingdom,
And ever cherish Ram's mission in bosom."

Thus Sugriv and Angad returned,
Ram took up abode on hillock 'Pravarsan'.

Couplet:

The nature had shaped,
In welcome of the Lord,
Already made ready the cave,
In the heart of the hillock. 12

The sylvan deity with rapturous welcome,
Sent troops of bees with songs of hum.
Bees were busy in greed of honey,
And trees danced in the breeze running.

The untouched treasure of the Nature's charm,
Was further raised by sojourn of Ram.

In the form of birds-beasts, the gods in zest,
Rendered their services to the Divine Guests.

All riches of heaven descended and adorned,
The woods during the Lord's sojourn.
Even inanimate antique soul of crystal rock,
Waited since aeons and aeons for the Lord.

Lord sat on that rock discoursed with Lakhan,
The roads, quotes, anecdotes of the devotion.
Seeing swarthy hue of Lord leaned the swarthy welkin,
dews wetted dense canvas 'rains were set in.'

Couplet: *"Lo ! Here O brother Lakhan!!*
Peacocks parade the beauty,
And dance on rich pinions
Like a recluse tho' housed devotee. 13

Swarms and swarms of the clouds vied,
To share with the land the bliss of sky.
"Lo ! Pencilled peaks faded on the horizon,
Cotton's drifts erased them into cloudy vision.

There, in ope mouth of clefts poured, was the elixired drinks,
here, keeping not a drop the blossoms did shrink.
The clefts are like greedy ever ope mouth,
Saints, the blossom live in rich rain, yet without.

Fits of flashes of lightening came and died,
Like the befriending a knave, never abide.
Richly laden clouds stooped to the land,
As with love the reverence of man further bends.

Rave rivulets roared, revived by rain,
Like a braggart brags with a bit of gain.
The moment water touched earth, it turned turbid,
As the soul is pellucid, Maya is the only culprit.

Rave=enthusiastic; Abide=stand/continue.

Water in to the pools gathered from many routes,
Even as goodness finds ways to hearts of virtues.

Couplet:

Weeds chocked the glades,
Over the green carpets,
As go obscured, the veds
In the heretic tenets. 14

The delightful croaking of frog do befog,
As if in abbeys, the pupils are on chanting jobs.
New twigs on trees look fresh with winsome glow,
As the seers glow by achieving light in marrow.

The Varsha rid the environ off the dust,
Just as piety rids the man off the lust.
Shows, the delicate grass withstanding the hail,
High head may be uprooted but the humble prevails.

The mild dawn that brings a diffused sun,
Says 'even the Brightest have some cloudy season'.
The stars, as if descending taking form of glow worm,
Looked bereaved of the moon with burn in bosom.

In good rain some odds to green; creepers' are rot,
Even as in the good reign, the crooked plans are sought.
In the torrential rains, all embankments are breached,
Its like the ungoverned emotions of bereaved.

"The nature hath Lakhan ! Many things to show,
To sooth us in our possessed sorrow.
"I blame no work of nature but Me, a bereft.
Have feeling of loss, that'll ever be fresh."

Heretic tenets=atheist belief (godlessness.)
Glades = pedestrian path in forest.
Befog=confuse; Varsha=rain.

Couplet: *Capered the roe, hares would borrow,*
None dared the wind's blow.
Bowers would stand stretched bough,
As firm as friars' vow. 15

Every eve the solitary two brothers,
In the intimate company lovingly conversed.
One such rainy eve Lakhan wished
to know the path of faith and worship-

"O Raghav! O Brother-Lord!! declare unto me,
the path for the world and for Thy devotee.
"With faith in Me, serving My Creation",
Ram said "it's the foremost devotion.

"The faith imparted through texts or Gurus,
Should not fragment My world unto feuds.
"All faiths all worships lead to Me,
All truths are one, so are all worships.

"Clincher of this and this and that faith,
Is sin no worships, I do laugh at.
"The boast of the worship is like the worship by the beast,
To the Human, whom I created; it never befits.

Couplet: *"I appreciate the love,*
for Me, that brims,
For devotee but it not behoves,
Others worships who envies. 16

"Unbiased who serve the Human and cow,
As first worshipper I accept them, its my vow.
"Up with flag of truth, who on fields, have deceased,
Those warry martyrs, are My Pujari of peace.

"One who follow the Guru and Holy text,
Duty and piety who perform as per Veds,

“and the ways of worships as I told to Sabari,
any one of that path leadth to Me.

“Recalling Me within, in pompless caves,
or with the pealing anthem in festive raves,
“Every worship, every vesper reach to Me,
every offer to the altar reach to Me.

“No prayer is primitive, no prayer is mature,
‘None else but mine is pure’- this verdict is impure.
“Some through beads and some through deeds,
Some through service to my idol, but all, at par, to Me reach.”

Couplet: *Thus time engulfed eventides,*
The sky, the forests, the twilight.
Poured the rain, out side,
And poured in the cave, Ram's eyes. *17*

Ram grieved over loss of Devi Seeta,
As, an ordinary man is grieving over ordinary woman –
“O morn! Bring fast the hope to My grief,
To the ghastly forest, colours of some relief.

“My grief opens, at the dawn, its bud,
The opening flower is full blown when night thuds.”
Each Night would scorch Ram as ordinary bereft,
Till the East would torch into cave’s depth.

Then, the nature would paint the vista with coloured streaks,
And silent cotton would linger on the far peaks.
“with wiped out clouds the sky weeps no more,
Lakhan ! Rains are fed up with its chore.

Couplet: *“Before raging ego of wind blow,*
Vied and flied sparrow,
But cloud dispersed, high trees bowed,
Lo! Sun painted the rainbow.” *18*

Wiped out=tired; Chore=routine work.

" The nature wipes the wides off the humid,
Autumn reflected thro' water-currents limpid.
"On bare welkin, the cotton silhouettes,
Drift not, waiting for the wind they meditate.

Kas-grass have gained height, crowned with white floret,
As if rainy season hath exposed its preying old age.
"Had I been the painter of this pellucid canvas,
I would have put in Siya, My lass, Alas!

"From the moorage and glades the muddy dust sloughed,
Tho' sun of kwanra* scorched, but soothing breeze puffed.

Only here and there it drizzled discrete,
The onus of canopus from canopy to meet.
"Heed! Birds warble lays of lucky lovers,
Those scorch My soul, My sore uncovers.

Couplet:

Pilgrims now step out,
From their rainy sojourn,
Islets in rivers jut out,
The routine world hath begun. 19

"With a straw in the beak toiling for nest,
Birds begun the job, as well the man thatched.
"Finned have their own world in the fathoms,
Like a refined soul finds own world in bosom.

"In the clear welkin fly in gyres the falcon,
Like the clear thoughts sublime a soul, on wings of freedom.
"Like the Absolute takes a form, the lotuses bloom,
On the pellucid waters of the lagoons.

"From the matins to the descending noon,
From vespers to lifted moon, nature seemth a boon.

---

*month of September; Silhouettes=outline shapes; Canopus=constellation of Agasthya.

" Lo ! Wrinkling moon lingers on silvery gush,
Rippling is heard nigher in the slumberous hush.

" In this rippling, warns the rustling crawls—
Caution the men of steps of faults.
"Till the crimsoned knock awakes, sleepth mother-nature,
On the silver carpet adorned by moon's silver.

Couplet: *"Gnats, insects have perished,*
With advent of the autumn.
Just as ills of men vanish,
When Guru in life doth come. 20

"Tho' nature spreadth its glorious work,
But the melancholy in my bosom do lurk.
"Rains are over, barbs me the bare sky,
Yet no news of Siya hath arrived.

"Her where abouts, had I come to know,
Even of the Death, I would recover Her in a mo-
"where ever She may be, its My vow,
Lakhan! I would rescue Her, no doubt anyhow.

"Sugriv too hath ignored Me now,
Getting sovereign, squads, slaves, sparkles, spouse.
"What I used in favour, with the very same arrow,
I'll shoot the fool, the very dawn of morrow.

'The One, who bestowth grace, holdth arrow in rage',—
Such pastime ist mystery even for the Veds.
The anger of Ram, had knitted Lakhan's brows,
He strung His bow, took, in hands, arrows.

Lurk=lie in wait, hide.

Couplet: *Ram, the Lord of compassion*
Guided Lakhan then-
"Only frightening Sugriv's passion,
Give him right guidance." 21

"The crown, shrouds often
The bosom of crony.
On fire of entente
Sets ashes of luxury. 22

THE SEARCH OF SITA

"Just a frightening puff will get rid,
Sugriv of folly, his reverence to lit.
'With more riches, more love should dwell in us,'
-To see this, is a friend's onus.

There, Hanuman within himself asked,
Hath Sugriv 'forgotten his task.'
Hanuman rushed to Sugriv, panic of his torpor,
He convinced in words of lore, adore*, force, and terror.

Sugriv from craddle of lavish luxuries,
Woke up stirred from his sensual sleep-
"My mind was robbed by luxuries and lust,
Now I shall not fail before Lord's trust.

"Let's call envoy to go all sides taking huge strides,
For monkeys troops from all heights, hides, all wides.
"Let my behest be widely conveyed,
Who ignoreth will sure invite his death."

There upon, Hanuman, sent for envoy,
Most politely their duty, he employed.

Entente=friendly feeling, Crony=bosom friend.
Torpor=passivity, *adoration.

Devoted envoys proceeded in hurry,
And the very moment Lakhan, entered in fury.

Couplet: *Monkeys ran helter-skelter*
Seeing Lakhan's brows on the tenters,
And the town tottered
Most humbly Angad entered. 23

He cringed at feet and made humble petitions,
Lakhan took him in protecting arms there upon.
When report of Lakhan's wrath reached Sugiv,
Pangs of his conscience remorsed and grieved.

He was panic-struck to assuage Lakhan's rage
He asked Hanuman to find some ways.
Hanuman then with the queen Tara went at ingress,
With grace they escorted Lakhan to palace.

After laving Lakhan's feet, offered him a seat,
Then Sugriv most reverently bowed at feet.
Lakhan picked him up and embraced,
And embarrassed Sugriv then spake-

"The Senses O Lord ! Oft cross wisdom's fence,
Even sages could not keep themselves sane."
Lakhan was gratified with his humble excuse.
Then Lakhan reassured with healing views-

"Repent not Sugriv ! Maya dopeth maketh slave,
Who hath won Cupid, is the real brave."
Hanuman told him what happened in meantime—
Batches of spies had been sent primed.

"Ten thousand monkeys are already sent,
To bring bears and monkeys from all continents.

Ingress =entrance (of palace); Cringed= to bow servilely.

Couplet:

Full to the banks glad,
With Angad and many more,
Placing Lakhan at the head,
To Ram, Sugriv went forth. 24

Sugriv rushed cringed at feet of Ram,
He oped his heart joining palms—
"For what I have done, may I not be abandoned,
O Gracious Ram ! Save me from abaddon.

" It's pomp of Maya that spread so wild,
Sans Thy saving hands, senses are survile.
"A man is a mould of malign senses,
More, I'm brute monkey, a born unchaste.

"The one, wakeful in the night of crude choler,
Who is watchful of the lewd glamour.
Nay, the one who mastered the greed's hunger,
Ist as good as Thyself! O Master of masters!

"Such a virtue, can't be attained by our endeavour,
'Ts by Thy grace, tho' man aquireth it rare."
Thereupon Ram smiled and answered,
"With Bharat you share my affection dear!"

"Now I find you on zenith of zest,
So Make some planned effort in Siya's quest."

Couplet:

While thus they discoursed,
Multitudes of monkeys coursed,
Legions from all wides poured,
And gathered the huge force. 25

" O Uma* ! That time I peered through perch,
Full to horizon from all sides they emerged.

Survile = slavish; Abaddon=Hell; Sans=without; *Shiv addressed to Uma.

For the cause of Ram, for the cause of Truth,
Poured and poured the endless troops.

Reared in kulachal hill, in battle all skilled,
Monkeys came capable of assuming any form at will.
"They are here O Lord! with strength of elephant,
Some are like mountains, all are belligerents.

"Chief of bears Jambvaan of great intelligence,
Leads bears, who join us in millions.
"Gavya, Gavaksha, Gaja, Mandav are chiefs of monkeys,
Panas, Balimukh, Dadhimukh, Susena and Kesari.

"And this is Hanuman with great wit and valour,
Great prow as he is, the chief among ministers,
"Some principal leaders are named by me.
But yet millions of such are all devoted to Thee",

Sugriv further to the Lord spake-
"All have given up their lives for Thy sake."

In varied colours, clans and creed,
They crowded and bowed at Shri Ram's feet.
No one remained in the legion entire,
Whose welfare Ram didst not Himself inquire.

This is no a miraculous miracle of Holy Miracle,
Who, in every individual doth dwell.
All troops stood in the martial array,
Sugriv ordered for "Ram's mission I exhort ye."

" I commission ye O monkeys hosts!
In quest of Siya, in every direction go forth,"
" but in a month ye should return brethren!
Failing shall bring your death at my hand.

Couplet: *The troops proceeded on behest,*
In haste at once,
In zest for Siya's quest;
And then Sugriv called Angad, Hanumant. 26

A TROOP TO THE SOUTH

"Listen ! Nil, Angad, Hanuman, Jambavaan,
Ye all art full of valour-wisdom.
" Proceed ! All ye warriors to the south,
Inquire into Siya's whereabouts.

" Your eager efforts 'll bring success,
If this true mission lingers in your breast.
"The Master must be served servilely,
Presenting the whole of your being.

"Discard to and fro business of mortal clay,
To be blessed in the next* the chance cometh to ye.
"The perfection of Human birth is achieved
In worship of the Lord Ram, the Infinite.

"That man of fire, that man of flair is favoured,
Who looks for Ram, finds Him everywhere.
"To transform into smile, the mankind's woe,
Is mission of Ram; on this revered road ye go."

Instant they started, bowed to Sugriv,
Glad they bade to Sugriv adieu.
They bowed to Ram; the last to make obeisance,
Was the son of wind-god, warrior Hanumant.

Lord knew him as epitome of valour, wisdom,
This, a genuine warrior will accomplish the mission.

---

*next=lasting happiness of next world; Epitome=embodiment.

Kennnig Hanuman a perfect, the Lord called him,
He stroked his head, gave him signet ring.

"Finding Seeta, Her mind you console,
Tell Her of grit of My shafts and of grief of My soul."
Very reward of his being, Hanuman felt,
Tho' Ram knew everything, yet He honoured devotee.

Should the mission of Master be passion of devotee,
And they proceeded on path of worship, the duty.

Couplet: *From near to remotes they ransacked,*
Rivers, ravines, ranges,
Scoured they every place,
Lost flesh in Ram's business. 27

Where they met demon they would zap,
Effortless, enthusiast in one slap.
On and on they moved, looked each recess of forest,
They would surround the hermit where ever they met.

While sinew felt done, but unfatigued was heart,
That put to the weary fatigue, depart.
Tho' torched with the thrust, parched with the thirst,
They found no water and felt nonplussed.

When the sap drained, and drained the hope,
Hanuman loped, climbed on a hill top.
He looked all around and found a strange cavern,
Hovered at it wren, bittern, herons, terns and ernes.

Winged were making way into cavern in cheer,
Wise Hanuman concluded water body was there.
Coming down the hill Hanuman showed the way,
Heading the troops Hanuman entered the cave.

Bittern=crane; Thrust=drive; Tern=bird of sea; Erne=Eagle.

Couplet: *Going further, was further strange,*
The cave had a comely garden,
A blossomed lake, a winsome fane,
The milieu, relieved their pain. 28

Their nervousness drained, new verve they gained,
Rejuvenated, as they were, once again.
The breathing statue near the fane,
They saw, austerity incarnate, a woman.

From a distance they bowed in reverence,
When asked they told of themselves.
She then blessed them all and said with love—
'Drink the water and partake fruits of the grove.

Quenching the thirst, partaking the fruits,
Before anchoress once more they stood.
"You're on true mission hence heaven helpth ye,
Lord helps such people with His wondrous way.

"May help ye! the marvel of my yogic strength,
Now, shut your eyes, me help the errand."
Champs closed eyes and ope again,
And they found themselves at the marge of ocean.

Couplet: *There the helping anchoress,*
To Ram on her part went.
Lord granted Bhakti endless,
Then to Badrivan she was sent. 29

MONKEYS AT SEA

Here monkeys brooded we sit like a drone,
The time has elapsed yet the job is not done.
"The Blue sets at nought, our blues do wave,
At the end of journey a nought we have.

The blue=sea; To set at nought=to consider worthless; Nought=Nothing; do nothing.
Drone=idler

Nothing about Siya, we did obtain,
Returning back either will be in vain.
With an ocean in eyes Angad said,—
"failing the duty ist worse than death."

"The tidings of Siya, we have failed to derive,
We have tided yet tides of the shore do deride.
"The Deep defies us being unfathomable,
The death is inevitable to our denial.

"Death is no death if its warmth lifts the head,
But failed life is a chill as good as dead."
There, vapours aired lingered on horizon,
Here, clouds of despair shrouded wisdom.

When the troops heard the Angad's woe,
They remained plunged in sorrow for a mo.
On the sandy shore their thoughts were drowned,
Their sand-castle of hope tumbled down.

But then on quick-sand, they with firm footings,
Decided not to return without Siya's tidings.
In firm core their resolve uproared,
Spread Kusa there, they squatted on shore.

Angad still had ill at ease,
Jambavan spirited him and preached—
"Dear child ! Percieve Ram as above earthlings,
Unborn, Almighty, All-wise, Supreme.

"He hath accepted us as His help,
Such a blessed we art, its Lord's grace.

Couplet: *"The Absolute cometh man-sized,*
Descendth for the innocents,
Performth many exploits,
For the content of heaven and men. 30

Tided=worked hard; The Deep=ocean.

"And survilely Devouts no doubt full of eclat,
Worship the Wight Absolute, when incarnateth."
This discourse reached to nearby cavern,
Were lived Sampati, an aged erne.

He peeped out and saw swarms of monkeys,
Was happy that God hath provided him feast.
Tho' declining were wings but had strong beak,
As old heart hath oft young greed.

He wished to zap monkeys in a slap,
To accomplish beak's greed and belly to sate,
Tho' nature fulfils needs of life,
But to greed's drive, it can't survive.

When the monkeys learnt the Erne's intent,
All alert, alarmed looked frightened.
But then Angad extolled Jatayu's devotion,
Who sacrificed self for Ram's mission.

When the news of Jatayu to this vulture reached,
Filled He was with joy as well as grief.
Sampati drew near the monkey's swarms,
And they told how Jatayu sacrificed life for Ram.

Couplet: *Stirred of brother's death,*
Sampati offered exequies,
The Erne wept "his brother's death,
Hath earned life to species,"* 31

"My proud brother hath sacrified his life,
Tho' declined age, yet I should help with my Eagle's eye.
"With my tubular long sight I peep,
And make ye succeed whom ye seek".

Erne=Eagle, Survilely=Completely dependant.
*species of birds specially Vultures; Exequies=rites after death.

Then, Sampati performed brother's obsequies,
Which reminded him of fraternal love between the two—
"Once we vied up and up near the sun,
I continued to fly up while Jatayu returned.

"In the childish quest I scorched my wings,
Withered I dropped down with pinions singed.
Crippled I crawled to this cave,
Then a kind sage encouraged me and presaged—

"In Treta age the Supreme 'll come man-shaped,
To His Legion of religion, You be a help.
"Take your pains as part of penance,
Pass days on account of the Ultimate gains.

"You 'll be instrumental in the divine errand,
Worry not ! Your wings 'll sprout again."
" The divination by divine soul, in me still echo,
With such a boon, now I am bestowed."

"With it's pomp falling on the ocean all around,
Lanka, city of Raavan stand on Trikut mount.
"This fanatic fiend lives with all fanfaronade,
I see, grieved Siya, in Ashok Grove is lodged."

Couplet: *"For the endless vulture's sight*
I see Her and ye not,
I would have helped ye but plight
Of the age makes me tight." 32

"At banks of brine ye may be at sea,
But the steadiest could leap over this sea.
"Ye look at me and take courage,
See ! How I feel enlivened winning the age.

Presage=foretell.
Divination=foretelling.
Plight of age=sorry condition of age.

"Bravo ! Ye have been chanced to serve Lord,
Even His very Name makes you able, cross.
"So as His very spies, never be strained,
To cross 'ts a lesser ocean than the mundane.

Then, in a wingy move, on enlivened flying thing,
The divine erne left them, in a wink.
Amazed they now talked of their strength,
But doubted the ability to leap over the Main.

Said Jambvan my courage was a name, full of sports,
Age, now hath tamed my sinews short.
"Under my bare skin flabby fishes crawl,
The Age at sea, this bare truth, bawls.

"Youth have little hours and it drains,
While age lingers with its long span.

Couplet: *In my youth, the Lord descended,*
In colossus form of Vaaman,
Yet i circumabulated,
Devoutly to the count of seven. 33

"I would leap across" then Angad said,
"but I doubt about my getting back."
The big bear interposed tho' you are competent,
But the leader of us all, how can be sent?

Towards' Hanuman then Jambavaan turned-
"Listen ! Hanuman, How's that you keep mum?
" O Son of wind ! You possess same spirit,
To beat the hassle, your grit, wit, befit.

"None the task is so snag, that thou canst not venture,
O Hanuman ! thou canst accomplish any tough juncture.

Wingy=fast, Tame=suppress; Bawl= Scream, Cry.
Big bear= Jambavan, Grit=Strength, Wit=Intelligence.

"For the service of Ram, thou hast come on earth,"
Hearing words Hanumaan grew colossus.

His splendorous hue fell on the monkey's troops,
As if before them hath mount of gold stood.
Jamwant reminded him of his inner treasure,
Of his hidden power which could do wonders.

Now again and again he roared like lion-
"Its easy to spring across the ocean."
"My earnest, enlivened, elated mind
Due to Ram's grace shall leave rival waves behind.

"Along with his army the devil Raavan I'll kill,
Even I can uproot the Trikut hill.
"But I ask thou, now tender me advice."
Jamwant said, 'that would be wise.'

"Go ! be for others, the giver of life,
Come back with tidings that will suffice.

Stanza: *"The only behest was Siya's quest,*
Lies the rest with Lord Ram,
With His fierce arms, in his long arms,
He wilt knock off the demon's Swarm.

Couplet: *Dwelth He within sages,*
Becometh He the guest of abbeys,
To accomplish their faith,
Lord treadth thro' untrodden ways. 34

Khar Dushan He slayth,
He blesseth Jatayu's death,
Let His pastime prime the astrayed,
On the mundane's narrow ways. 35

☐

|| SUNDER KANDAM ||

None but the bravest deserves the salvation.

—Swami Vivekanand

STROPHES

1

I pray Ram, who blesseth balm of beatitude,
The Lord of fate, Shiv revere whom as 'The Ancient'
From eon to neo, who ist Constant,
The Ram, the Calm Himself, Thro' Veds who ist kent.

Who, In the Epic descendth, thro' own magic drive,
The Sins of mundane to shrive,
O Absolute Ram ! Thou comest man-sized
Whom, the Shiv within own bosom ever derive.

2

O Raghupati ! soul of all souls and of mine,
Thou art the Truth, in whatever ist divine.
I do crave none of cravings, but faith in Thine,
Ever, for ever in me, be enshrined.

Shrive=purge, eliminate.

3

Bold spirited as thunderbolt,
Colossus as mount of gold,
A torching fire within the Wise,
And Scorching inferno for infernal souls.
*O Adored Bhakt Hanuman! The very son of the Wind**
I worship the Virtue Incarnate, O Ruin of the fiends!!

THE LEADER LEAPS

The drive of Jamwant was a sapient's voice
Inner size of own grit-n-wit Hanuman realized,
Now enlightened Hanuman with new fight within,
Highly heartened was ready on his mission,

Said he-"Brethren ! at marge wait and live,
On feast or fast what ever this shore gives.
"Even whose very Name maketh us to cross mundane
With Ram's signet ring where stands this Main.

"Vast content in me, ope horizons of scope,
Inner happiness bringeth message of new hope."
Bent he to all, and bade them adieu,
Enshrining in heart 'Ram', with new shine he moved.

With the truth of the Troth, with tour de force
He sported and mounted on top of a tor.
He gave out a roar and the tor he shoved
Wow ! the Monkey-hero!! here drove his go.

Then, the Kapi** rocketed himself with vital force,
Trees, boughs as well were sucked and rose.
Those bergs immersed into nether in speed,
On which Hanuman hopped and leaped.

Infernal souls=diabolic souls, demons; *Wind-god(Pawan)
tour de force=skillful performance;Tor=hill;Troth=belief, faith;
Shoved=expelled, pushed off; Main=sea.
**Kapi, Monkey Hero, synonyms of Hanuman; nether=Paataal

His arms spreaded, tail erect, head straight,
Eyes looking up and legs contracted.
Even as, Ram's own unfailing shaft
Hanuman coursed thro' sky ahead.

In His speeded flight leaves, boles were sucked
Behind him; and followed waves, weeds, scuds.
Like a mount he rocketed far and far,
Soon at the shore, looked like aureate meteor.

The Ocean, as the natural help in Ram's errand,
Asked gold mount-Mainaak, be helping hand.
'O Gold! thou canst go down and up
to comfort Hanuman I prompt thou to rise up."

Couplet: *Stood Mainaak befo' Hanumant,*
He just touched in reverence,
"for me who, goes on Ram's errand,
Where is the need for rest." 1

For the noble cause ever cometh hindrance,
Oft by the heaven to test strength.
Seeing speedy traveller and his zeal
Gods, godules sent Surasa to test his skills—

"Go ! create to great monkey some snag,
Assay him whether he lasts or lags"
Surasa, the mother of snake's race,
Assumed a monstrous and ugly face.

"My lot hath brought me what an aliment,
So I am eating you up instant"
"In informing 'bout Siya to Ram, should I not fail,
This mission is my life, then I 'll be thy morsel".

---

boles=stems; scuds=clouds

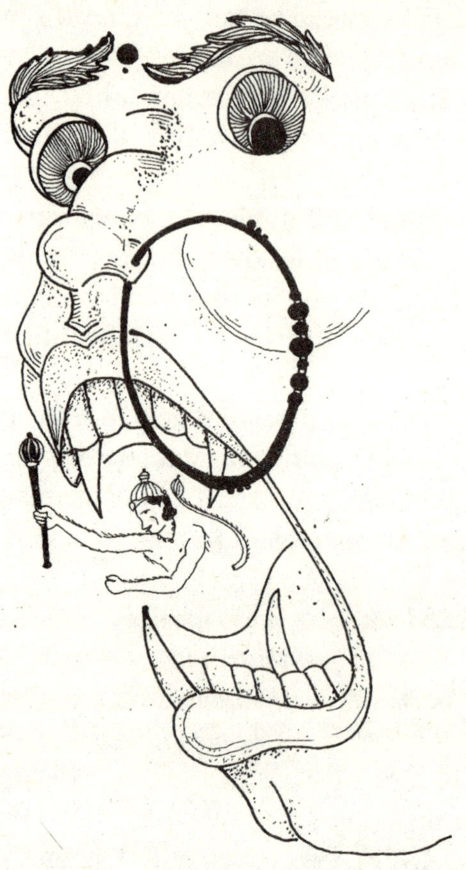

"I 'll return once Ram's mission is fulfilled,
I shalt return as thy food, at thy sill."
By no means when she let him not go,
Then, said noble monkey "why not me swallow?"

She opened her mouth to a yojan size,
Kapi extended the frame doubly-wide.
Her sky scraping jaws she opened,
On the double Kapi doubled to cross the welkin.

Her body even as Surasa grown,
Twice to it Kapi his form shown.
Mouth she oped to centuple size,
The Wise, assumed size of a thumb, in a trice.

On the double =rapidly; Welkin= sky

Nimble he entered mouth and came out at once,
And begged adieu bowing head in reverence.
"Celestials sent me to test competence,
I have weighed your skill, spirit, strength.

Couplet: *"With such a grit, wit, spirit,*
The success ist at hand,"
Wishing this she took leave,
"Go! and fulfil Ram's errand." 2

Into scudding drifts Hanuman further leaped,
Across the ocean as the phenomenal feat.
This part of ocean was an ogress's toft
Any winged shadow she would possess by dodge.

She would seize shadows of the feathered sky,
Thus she would wolf ever their lives.
In turn, on Kapi she turned her trick,
Quick witted Hanumaan discovered her deceit.

Thus provoked on his way this noble prow,
Slayed this prowler 'Sinhika' in one blow.
Thus on his firmness and faith's wings,
Hanumaan traversed across the ocean.

High soul Hanumaan from on high,
gazed Lanka through amazed sight.
Woodland full of rocks and flocks of trees,
With buzzing bees and blowing gentle breeze,

Ope hands of nature filled the purlieu,
as blossoming garland around the Trikut .
Vast mountain range he saw ahead,
He ranged and mounted up with no dread.

Prowler=one who roves for prey.

*Uma! Its none of the Kapi's eminence,
Who devours death, it's that Lord's excellence.
He peeped into Lanka from the holt,
Its splendour was lightening as thunderbolt

Forts, sky-scraping with moats around walls,
Its golden splendour in its water did fall.

Stanza: *Ramparts worked with gem's art,*
Rammed abodes with lavish pomp.
Cross roads, haats, alleys, ways,
Were decked to sway through spell of charm.

Far and near, tier above tier,
Sky-scraper towers had Lustre n look.
Mounts, mules, elephants, plentiful,
Countless were militants' troops. *A*

The mazes, alleys, meadows, groves
Lae, lands, lagoons looked a magic.
Damsels danced worth, gibed nymphs of their dearth,
Dames did exhibit their glitz.

Treasured mammon of no account,
Warriors mammoth like mounts.
Restless champs, wrestled and chased,
In melee challenged like blood hounds. *B*

Canny champs, in many camps,
On agile vigil guarded with zeal,
Low demons swallowed cows buffaloes,
Cannibals feasted on Lavish heaps.

Holt=a hill near forest.
Ramparts=Walls of fort; Glitz=Glamour; mammon=wealth, riches; Canny=careful
*Shiv continues to narrate Ram's story to His consort Uma.

Tulsi did deliberate, as Ram's laureate,
And did narrate in short demon's state,
For sure, even impure souls,
liberate,dying at Ram's shafts. C

Couplet: *For Lanka, Kapi then mused*
'Its impermeable, war-like,
Assuming the form minute,
I'll enter city at night.' 3

KAPI AS A SPY

Kapi assumed a gnat like form,
Then made way to Lanka recalling Ram.
There, deity of Lanka, the heedful Lanka-Shri,
Asked "where you go ignoring me? '

"You Know Fool ! none can Penetrate through
He ist my Food, one who intrudes".
With thump of a blow the Great Kapi dealt,
It was as warm as the chill of the death.

Tumbled on ground, she belched gore,
In fright, upright she then implored–
'In, times gone by, Brahma divined O monkey!
With such a blow when you feel queasy,

"When a monkey subdues you by his prowess, then
Know the plight of demonry, for certain,
"I must have earned some merits dear !
My blest eyes feast upon Ram's messenger.

Queasy=Nauseating

Couplet: *"Nor Nirvana nor the Heaven,*
Canst bring that delight
What with communion of saints,
Is gained in a trice. 4

ROAMING ON RAM'S MISSION

"Keeping Ram enshrined in thy heart
Make for the town O Brave! now free thou art"
Foes turn to friends, the mission cometh to reach,
Once for Ram's errand, one hath reached fever-pitch.

Before the Determined, the Mount amounts to sand,
On him mercy of Ram ever commendth.
Thus, absorbed in 'Ram' Kapi assumed form wee,
And with hushed steps Hanuman moved in.

The tofts, forts, courts, Kapi espied,
Champs, dames, vamps, vampires crossed thro' his sight.

The boast of the town stood with its splendorous pomp,
In the Raavan's palace Kapi moved unalarmed.

Rammed with rummaged riches he saw the mansion,
Raavan's greed reflected in his pomp of mammon.
Sunken in the silken pool, of cot of the gold,
Deep slumbering Raavan, Hanumaan did behold.

Continued his quest of the Revered visage,
He searched niche, pitch, perch, porch every place.
Among odds of Lanka, Kapi did find,
An elegant edifice with Shri Hari's shrine.

Arrect he was arrested, amazed,
Finding predella with 'weapons of Ram', sketched.

Couplet: *A predella on walls showed,*
The revered 'weapons of Ram',
Viewing sapling Tulsi-rows
Charmed Kapi was filled with warmth. 5

"Among oddity is it true
That a pious liveth here but how could?"
Kapi's midnight toil in this wee hour,
Gave him glimpse of the hope so near.

Many thoughts but crossed Hanuman's mind,
And Vibhishan* woke up at the same time.
He poured his heart in the milieu as he rose,
And honeyed air with 'Ram-Ram' echoes.

Words as Nostrum elixired monkey's vitals,
To make compeer of stranger his core compelled.
Twin vital word 'Ram' maketh soul to soul chain,
How such a kinship ever remain strange.

Wee=tiny; Arrect=alert (heedful)
Predella = wall painting (behind altar); *Brother of Raavan, yet virtuous soul.

'For certain ! With this Pure I'll make acquaintance,
As no detriment is ever done by saints.'
Assuming holy form of Brahmin, kapi went nigh,
At the call Vibhishan hurriedly arrived.

More than formal reverence the two aliens,
Met each other clung to the unknown chains.
"O guest! In me the brimming reverence,
Its flood hints to my clairvoyance.'

"either thou art a pious votary
Or the Lord Himself hath come for me."

Couplet: *Kapi, then revealed his truth,*
And told about Shri Hari,
Thrilled was Vibhishan all through,
Meeting His Lord's emissary. 6

Vibhishan said—

"My breath here is a puff of plight,
Amidst teeth poor tongue liveth, its alike.
"Me think, the ocean all around is captive's tears
O Kapi ! Which is filled in thousand years.

"In the dearth of pure souls, I was deprived,
Thou Kapi ! Havest come as finding of my life.
"My filthy flesh in the diabolic frame,
Knows no piety, no penance, no anthem.

"But me the forlorn, thro' petrified gaze
The call of gratifying visage ever waited.
"In my hopeless mirk, thy little touch,
Hath enlightened me with new flamed torch.

Clairvoyance=intuition.

"Lord's grace reflects if one meets a saint,
His favour bestowth here, I'm confident.
"No just a chance that thou chancedst to meet me,
'Ts only Lord's grace that I do see.

Hanuman replied—

"Listen! O Vibhishan!! the Lord's own ways,
He careth his devotees, always.
"Look at me! What worth I do possess,
A lissome, low bosom yet He lifted.

"Tell! What superior clan can I claim,
Monkey is low so much so; for our name,
"If one mentions at peep of eastern hail,
His full day will sure go without morsel.

Couplet: *"O pal ! I am so wretched,*
More so in virtueless mould,"-
Remembering how Ram blessed,
Shine in his eyes brimmed and rolled. 7

"If knows, yet lift no hands of worship
Over slips of mundane how could he skip?
"No wonder, the one wanders ever strayed,
Who stays not on Hari, walks heretic ways."

—Thus hearkening to each other's speech,
The two devouts turned soother to each.
Vibhishan told then how did Janaki pass Her days,
Confined in Ashok-vana, all apart yet.

"Ashoka Vana is Raavan's favourite retreat,
With parks, grottoes, meadows and trees.
"Among lofty greens, withered She alone,
Could be seen dipt in Ram, uttering moan.

"The guarding hands are too crude to console,
Those brinish tears of the Bereaved, that roll.
Kenning Kapi much keen, Vibhishan revealed ways,
To reach to Siya, the entire finesse.

Anew taking up tiny form, Hanumant went fast,
To the Ashoka grove, very abode of the pining lass.
Kapi saw under tree, was sitting the Mother,
Like the scorched heap of holy thing in altar.

Sleepless stars wandered about wilting morn,
Her morn came-n–went-n-came but for moan and moan.
Search was over, he perched on Sinsupa foliage,
Mentally he saluted the Embodied pilgrimage.

Couplet: *Dipt in perpetual moan,*
Lean She to the bones,
Seeing Her With Her sorrow's alone,
Kapi then much mourned. 8

SEETA IN ASHOKA GROVE

With unbraided locks, the Auspicious mien,
Sat on bare ground, body weak and lean.
Hidden while he was, brooding further plan,
At the same came there, demon's King Raavan.

Shrunk to unnoticable form, Kapi shinned up,
Within thick foliage kept himself enveloped.
Pranked Raavan, keeping with him troops of damsels,
Came and revealed many tricks, Siya to prevail.

Siya shivered finding Raavan to the fore,
Even as a plaintain in the cloud's pour.
even as a doe from its herd was abandoned,
Looked like drooped lotus in scorching sun.

By hook and crook the Crooked tried to sway,
"O pretty !, I make you here my prime mistress."
"Mandodari and other my queen mistresses"
The knave declared- "are now your maids."

"Entertain true look at me as your beau,
Accept my suit it befits you.
"I have sent spies to search that Ram,
And found the two brothers are least alarmed.

" Here melancholy is your abigail alone,
All the bliss waits you, so be my own.
"I offer everything, abandon Your gloom,
Take all my splendour dear! now You bloom."

Feared, shivered but with confident face,
Thro' veil of grass blade, Siya thus spake—
"O Night ranger! with gloom of glowworm,
Could ever the bloom of water-lily blossom.

"O Knave! Raavan ! you dared enough,
Are you heedless of Ram's arms tough?
"I was by Myself you carried Me off O Base!
O Imposter! unblushing!! Are you shameless?"

Couplet: *Pierced by stinging words,*
Those trembled his ego,
To batter drew he his sword
In wrath began to crow— 9

"Seete ! You are not versed of my worst rage,
And know not the thirst of my sword's edge.
"Bow Your Will, be it for me,
Lest a pretty life's loss that would be"

Seeta replied-

"lei of long arms of Lord around My neck,
Or your brand should abate unrest of this Bereft."
"Me accept either of the two,
O low ! listen My firm words are true.

"O Chandrahass* ! relieve Me of My agony,
The fire of anguish is scorching Me.
"Mastered by hilt can't you brandish yourself,
And put to the sword My overlived neck."

"O Crescent* ! piercing art thy rays
But may acme of sorrow be edged."
"O Rakshas ! you deserve be ashes through my chaste hands,
But for permission of Ram, I do restrain.

Enraged Raavan stepped forward to behead,
His queens asked their master to master his, self.
"Seete ! Your life is going to be cut short
Else in a month bow Your words to this sword.

Asked he, his guards of distorted faces
To make Her convince through tempts or threats.
" Ogresses ! Surround Her tremble Her with dismay,
So much so that for life She begs".

"If She agrees to be mine in a month**, lest
Kill Her and for my meal cook Her flesh.

Couplet:

His words alternated between,
Tempts and the threats
Raavan used all means to win,
Then he returned back. *10*

Brand = sword, *Chandrahaas name of sword of Raavan.Literary meaning of chanrahaas is the moon. Seeta asked either of the two(punning word) **Two months mentioned in Valmiki Ramayan.

Like the nightmare , hovered all around Siya,
The ugly ogresses, the Embodied awe.
Their very weird forms displayed the ogresses
And dismayed as if they would eat up Her flesh.

Named Trijata was the ogress one
She had Ram as Lord in her perfect vision .
She had an insight into Sita's mind
Said –'ye! Eat up me, I keep Her behind'

"In my inner truth, I have experienced, just now,
A dream, all terrible even to think about .
"Great conflagration is towering the towers,
Ram's messenger turns Lanka to flaming altar.

"I saw, on donkey Raavan goes nude,
Shorn head , torn arms and subdued.
"The demonry is won over by divinity.
Perversions are won by penance, piety.

"All fiends and friends of Raavan, failed in the field,
The womb of the future, thus my dream hath revealed.
"Among, dins of keens of queens at the king,
In town trumpeted Lord Ram's triumph."

"This dream for sure I do state,
In a few days will be a fact."
Would it be real or a reverie,
All fell at Siya's feet reverently.

Couplet: *All Demonesses dispersed,*
Siya felt approaching ill,
While a long month lingers,
Only afterwards the sword will relieve. 11

Keen=weeping at the dead.
Reverie=dreaming

She beseeched Trijata with folded hands
"Ma ! thou being My pal in pains,
"Devise quick means may I cast off this mould
Shafts of bereaving pierce, I can't now hold.

"Bringing chunks, trunks, bark, bring about a pyre,
Then My frozen soul and Me be set on fire.
"May the bark be the bark on ocean of all ills,
May warmth of pyre, melt away My life's chill.

"Raavan, the loud mouthed lout, is a loose lore,
Hath lopped My life, loaded My lofty core.
"Let this Mould, in to the embers con,
To uphold My love in My immortal form.

Trijata solaced counting Ram's praises,
"Mourn not O Child! Courage! Courage!!"
"Glory of Ram for demons is huge inferno,
Let that fire relieve chill of your woe."

"Your truth is the sacrificial fire,
And chastity will be demon's pyre.
"You ask me for fire in vain,
Fire in You 'll enlighten the chaste women.

"I know not a little of fire can harm
You; being beloved devotee of Ram."
Saying so Trijata then went back
Keeping Her on the course of providence to reck.

Siya averred "providence is adverse,
A little of fire may relieve me of curse.
"This bare sky shares not my woe,
Earths not a single ember from starry show.

Con=assume
To reck=to take care

"And tho' moon is fiery sends no fire,
Of My ill-stars, as if he is aware.
"justify thy name O Ashoka grove!
Thou art named that ends all sorrow.

"Like flames, Neo twigs dance on thy perch,
But help me not to hop the perch.
"Ere My ache reach its acme,
O Ashoka! Send little of fire to Me."

Monkey was moved by mourning voice,
For him seemed, lingered as kalp, that trice.

Couplet: *Up there Kapi pondered,*
And dropped the ring signet.
Siya picked as if ember,
Had come God sent. 12

KAPI RELIEVES THE BEREAVED

She picked it up but to Her surprise,
Engraved 'Ram' on it with a thrill She eyed.
Recognized signet ring, amazed She gazed,
In the tides of thought She felt perplexed—

'Ram' and His signet could ever be won,
By any illusion this can't be done.'
Within Her eddied some grief, some relief,
Hanuman then poured reverent words, honeyed.

Hanuman began paeans of Ram,
To calm Her core, Her sores to balm.
From thick foliage Ram's praises echoed,
And filled the milieu of the Ashoka grove.

To hop the perch=to die.

Ram's narratives to the pensive Siya,
Worked as to the moribund, the Ambrosia.
Enlivened She with the pouring in nectar,
Siya asked, " who ar' you, why not appear?"

Monkey of the size of Kalavinga bird,
Prostrated before Seeta, now, came forward.
Hanumant there upon drew nigh,
Frightened she turned back and saw with wondered eyes.

"By merciful Ram, My words are solemn,
O Mother! As messenger of Ram I came.
"Any doubt may not linger in Thy mind.
Ram conferred me signet ring as the messenger's sign.

Moribund=dying

Kapi told 'how it chanced that monkey and men,
Came to each other and allied as friend.'

Couplet: *Listening to messenger of Ram,*
Her grief, she felt assuaged,
Vanished all Her qualms
In him, Siya eyed, Ram's true page. 13

Siya saw the Kapi as the Embodied hope,
Before Her She felt now paths to life ope.
When the emissary of Ram before Her stood,
Her eyes brimmed and thrill ran thro'

"O great Monkey! you are wise indeed,
You have shrunk ocean with your heroic leap.
"Immersed in the ocean of pangs deep,
To me, a ship, you happened to be.

"O messenger, I wish Ram's tidings,
To elixir Me, the Sinking; the vital thing.
"He is soul of My soul, He is My Lord,
You tell how He hath turned hard.

"The soul of devotee is ever resigned,
To the Lord's image in the mind.
"My sight is blind to every gaze,
Of each panorama lacking Rama's visage.

"Could ever the eyes of this deprived Bereaved,
Perceive sight of Ram and be relieved.
"Does He ope My remembrance from His limpid marrow,
But afraid I am to be cause of His sorrow.

"Olden delights of the golden moments,
Delight not but are cause of more pangs."

True page=honest servant.

Her voice choked, eyes filled with tears
"O Naath! Thou havest turned utter oblivious."

Siya's sorrow pierced thro' marrow of Kapi,
Keeping up, politely the Kapi did speak—
"Ram out of sorrow for You, I tell,
Hath no enthusiasm for anything else.

"In Ram's worldly deeds of the earthly freight,
The ancient love of divine couple, can't be weighed.
"That mutual fire, here, fills eyes with tears,
There, in Ram it fills eyes with raging embers.

Couplet: *"O Holy mother ! Hark !!"*
The Ram's very message now,
Kapi said with filled heart
"And be assuaged Thou." 14

"Maa ! the message of Ram is full of pangs,
His melancholy, in words can't be condensed."
"Words are too shallow to say of the deep grief,
Tho' the Lord keepth silence yet we can read.

"In Thy parting, Ram sent few words,
Listen! O Holy one! what hath turned untoward.
"Siya! not seeing Thou since long odds
I pass helpless days counting drifts of orbs.

"Every night turned upon Me a dire night,
Scorched My bosom, even the moonlight.
"The canvas of lotuses paints in Me the blues,
Cataracts look tears of gloomy milieu.

"Winds scorch, cloud pour boiling oil,
Cushioned meadows seem groves of cactii.
"Who were to ease, are now tease,
Like snake's hiss blows the soft cool breeze.

"With the shared pains, little of woe wanes,
Whom should I dole out;the dole none kens
"The kindred element that binds Thou-n-Me,
O beloved ! My crony soul alone can see.

Ever to Thee, current of My soul abides,
"Its essence of My love; know this in brief."
Touch of Lord's words was so intense,
Vaidehi immersed, went in to trance.

"Gather Thyself O mother!" Kapi said-
"On Lord Ram, fix Thy all consciousness."
"Take in these words, shake off all dismay,
Keep at heart the ways of Ram and His sway.

Couplet: *"Monsters are swarms of moth*
Ram's arrows are inferno
O Mother ! keep the heart,
All them as ashes; Thou know." *15*

"Had shri Ram ever any of Thy news,
Would not have delayed the Lord of Raghus.
"As the mirk vanishes at the pop of the Sun,
Before Ram can't stay the pomp of demons.

"Even now I would take Thou back,
But this page is bound to His Master's behest
"Be patient ! it will not be very long,
Raghuvar 'll come with monkeys' and bears' throng.

"He will uproot demonry for the men and Heaven,
And this pastime will be stake for mankind to come."
"But O son! Tiny monkeys are demon's morsel,
Over mammoth monster how'll monkeys prevail?"

Vaidehi= one name of Seeta which means whose thoughts are above body.

"Over ocean of my faith, come vapours of doubt,"
Enlarging his form, Kapi fanned apart those clouds.
He swelt like gold mount so great a miracle,
Mettled and mighty, terrible in battle.

Siya was convinced by Kapi's mettle
Son of wind, then assumed the form, subtle.

Couplet: *"O mother ! monkeys possess none,*
Of own fight or insight,
Even asp eats up an erne,
By Almighty's might. 16

Amazed, assuaged by courage of the page,
Knowing him Lord's loved, Siya thus blessed—
"O Son ! be full of valour and virtues,
Be retort of my rueful days, to those rudes*.

"Be ageless, ceaseless, full of goodness,
May Lord bless you with His endless grace."
Hearing such blessing words-'May Lord bless'
Deep absorbed Kapi, lost his flesh.

He bowed, cringed, bowed, cringed fell at feet,
Getting largest largess and greatest gift.
"O Mother ! now that I am so content,
For Thy Ashish; is renowned as certain.

"Maa ! now my fulfilled soul, hath something more,
Needth be done, as extension of my chore.
"To my soul, mother's blessings are most worthwhile
Now I see fruity grove for my belly and bite.

"Attractive fruits make me more hungry,
May I go if Thou dost agree.

Asp=small snake; Erne=Large eagle; *demons; Ashish=blessing; Retort=hard reply

"But the grove is guarded O my child!
By valiant varderers and vedettes wild.

"Mother! I am not afraid of fiends,
Only if Thou art really convinced.

Couplet: *"Kapi's verve and nerve she viewed,*
And let him go
Then adopting a fierce mood,
Kapi moved like a tornado. 17

LANKINESS OF LANKA

He entered Raavan's grove and savoured fruits,
And began to tear trees and sever roots.
There were champ-varderers not a few,
Some he slew, rest rushed for rescue.

"There turned up O Master! One monkey robust,
Who hath overturned Ashoka grove to the dust.
"Among creaking falling trees, screeching of birds,
He hath crushed in dust our varderers.

Enraged Raavan sent champs and champs more,
In thick of the fray* Hanumaan uproared.
With playful slaps troops he zapped,
Yet, yelling a few half dead escaped.

Raavan then sent the chief, Jambumali,
Hanuman overlooked his valour, his volley.

King's stranged anger, heard of latest defeat,
Whose lust ever heard of triumph and triumph.

Varderer=guard of groves
*At war

He sent Satjivha, Rudhiraksh, Raktrom, Shurdrust.
Satanic Vyaagrh with chivalry and chariots.

All were minister's sons, all firing bellicose,
Soon in own gore, splashed their carcass.
Then Raavan sent prince Akshay,
He moved with countless convoy.

New rows of foes Kapi did behold,
Like a thunderbolt he hurled a bole.
In speed like the wind itself,
Some quitter escaped but Prince Akshay was zapped.

Couplet:

Some he slew, a few smashed,
Some he mashed in dust.
Dismayed a few escaped
'Lord ! He is too robust.' 18

Warriors with war-lust were smashed to dust,
Stationed Kapi there, awaiting for more Rakshas'.
In sorry chill of son's death but still sultry,
Raavan dispatched Indrajeet, the boast of soldiery.

"Son! sever not, him you tether,
Whence Monkey came, let me be clear.
"He seems to be like wind, he is like fire,
Yet victory is sure for you, O great archer!"

The seasoned warrior went in great speed,
Kapi gnashed teeth, roared as he saw Indrajeet.
One huge bole he uprooted, and running riot
Hurled over demon crushing his chariot.

On Hanuman rows of arrows he did pelt,
But to swifts of Kapi all his skill failed.

Zapped=killed; Bole=huge stem of tree; carcass=dead remains.
Sultry=in hots (rage), tether=bind, tie

Kapi clutched, clenched and crushed the troops
To attack over Indrajeet again he moved.

Kapi shinned up a tree and gave him a bash,
At this sudden clash, demon was stunned for a flash.
Gathering self the demon, worked mystic delusions
But wind-god's son was not to be won.

Son of Raavan, the clever was ever winning,
Resolved in his mind 'how to catch hold of him'.

Couplet: *The Brahma-missile he aimed,*
At Kapi; who deemed,
'ts unending esteem ends,
If divine weapon is not esteemed.' 19

Hanuman pondered within himself,
'Thro' missile, The blessings to me Brahma hath vouchsafed.
I have to respect the missile of the Selfborn one,
And submit to it and let its purpose won.'

Kapi bowed to missile and even as he dropt,
He crushed the warry crew of fops.
'Monkey had swooned', when Indrajeet viewed,
Tethered with serpent-noose he swooped up n moved.

Even whose very Name ever frees
For cause of same Lord, Kapi kept unreleased.
Knowing 'monkey is bound', demons with haste,
Gathered in assembly all in jest.

Captors dragged him to Raavan's presence,
Court's ample grandeur had great appearance.
What a form, what valour, what a pomp and power,
The court seemed as the custody of all Wonders.

Celestials, deos, gods and godlets,
All alarmed stood before Raavan as slave.

Couplet:

Breaking up at Kapi,
He, with a bitter grin,
But mourned of Son's death,
He spake grim- 20

"Where have you come from O Ape !
Your appearance seems to be mere camouflage.

"How are you so fearless of my reign and race,
O wretch ! did you not know my prowess.
"You encroached and killed champs in their house,
You have crossed the limits, the life, to hold out.

Hanuman replied-

"Be attentive Raavan! and hark!
Who ist the microcosm of the macrocosm.
"Who is splendour in Trinity's errand,
To create, to destroy as well to maintain.

"in whose hand, work, as puppets,
The galaxies and galaxies, planets to comets.
"Who cameth mansized, the mankind to rescue,
And to teach the lesson to wretches like you.

"who had severed Shankar's severe bow,
And shattered at the same all king's ego.
"The valiant awe of world, unmatched,
Khar, Dushan, Trisir, Baali who had dispatched.

Fop=hypocrites.
Camouflage=Disguise; Prowess = power

Couplet: *It's your might and main,*
Stand little before whose strength,
With whose power you reign,
His envoy I'm. 21

"Boast of your glory, I know very well,
With Sahastrabahu you had a duel.
"Vying with Baali you won the mark,"
-deliberately Raavan ignored Kapi's remark.

"Me, was hungry so fruits I savoured,
Broke boughs as is, a Monkey's nature.
"Of the precious body, the creature is slave,
O Lord! I was but then battered by the knaves.

"They attacked to kill me, in great rage,
So I had to kill them in defence of self.
"I battered those who battered me,
Thine injust son then tethered me.

"Being bound I'm not a little ashamed,
I long to do my Lord's errand.
"Hark! Raavan! The ego which in thou dwells,
With it, as ever, the sin, as well swells.

"Look at thy lineage with lore,
Surrender thy go and ego before the Lord.
"Who is fire for the life and a chill for the Death,
Who unburdenth the Earth from unchartered weight.

"Never make Him a foe, at any turn,
Mine asking, Holy Jaanaki thou return.

Couplet: *" O Raavan! dare not*
Ram, the Super personage.
He, with care wilt adopt
And forgive thy deadly lapse." 22

"Let within you Ram's lotus feet be niched,
Hope! Thy kingdom only then may not cease.
"Thy lineage ist like moon unstained,
In that should thou not put taint.

"Consider my words; forgoing ego, ignorance,
Without His name, life goes in vain.
"Its like a pretty damsel but for apparels,
Doth not appeal, tho' all jewelled.

"Opposed to Ram, all riches and fame,
Will vanish soon as if never obtained.
"Rivulets that have no water source,
Just dry up when rainfalls are no more.

"To the changes, the real-Self, is unaffected witness,
Concern to changes, belongs to Body- mind complex.
"On whom, Ram is bent on destroying rage,
For sure! None comes for his salvage.

"Before His Supremacy leave thy contumacy,
Lest, to protect thou, none I do see.

Couplet: *"Thy folly bringeth ego,*
That ends ever in woe,
Pray! On right path thou go,
And sinful deeds forgo." 23

Tho' Kapi's voice was worth,
Contained faith, wisdom, in every word.
To the words of virtue, his mind was locked,
Calling Kapi his 'Guru', Raavan mocked.

"O Monkey! the death stands by you,
So you try to tutor me, the virtue."

Contumacy=perverseness.

Kapi returned words, "deluded are thy views,
Surely just the vice versa is true."

" O degenerate! Crores of Raavan can't be my peer,
As I am the very Truth's messenger."
On words of Kapi, turned he raving mad,
"Blockhead monkey at once be executed".

Demons as rushed to follow behest,
Vibhishan entered there, the very next.
Reverently Vibhishan, most humbly did submit,
"Capital sentence to envoy doth not befit.

"O King! Be pacified, master thy anger,
Award punishment which behoves a messenger.
"He may be disciplined thro' very many means,
Flogging, whipping, slapping, branding the limbs.

"Let on messenger's body the marks of bruise,
To thy foe, take the script of abuse."
All favoured, Raavan too agreed, the same,
"Dispatch the monkey with limbs maimed.

Couplet: *"The tail is monkey's asset,*
It's a fact I do tell,
To the fire, the tail be set,
Swathing it with oiled apperels." 24

THE CONFLAGRATION

"How'll be the look of this macrurous,
Monkey's asset will, then be his curse.
" He will, then, with his Master 'll return for battle,
Let me as well witness his Master's mettle.

Macrurous=one, having a long tail; mettle=bravery, boldness.

"Monkey hast praised those beggarly fellows,
I will see yes! They are pseudo-prows."
Who are averse to Ram, their wisdom turns adverse,
On the rest, it bestows endless favours.

Here, wisdom deity helped Lord's man to prevail.
There, demons crowded around the Kapi's tail.
On Raavan's command, the demons, stupid,
Began to do as was bid.

The heroic monkey turned to real macrurous,
Stretched his tail to the size enormous.
Wrapped tail they with rags, robs, soaked it in oil,
Robs and oil exhausted for the tail size.

Playfully he let the town to make his fun,
For he knew it was all part of his mission.
They kicked, mocked, ragged, dragged Kapi,
Drumming clapping they took him around the city.

Then they ignited the tail to the flames,
In a trice, triced Kapi, assumed small frame.
Thus his bond loosened, now ready to raid,
Climbed to one of high rival garrets.

The vaulter by nature, monkey vaulted over vaults,
To subdue the demons' boasts and vaunts.

Couplet: *In his boisterous dare,*
Made he boisterous blare,
The fire in tail flared,
Forty nine winds, the heaven aired. 25

Body colossal but with nimble leap,
From towers to towers the fire he lit.
Crores of frightful flames are crowning inferno,
Terrorized citizens are on the run, lo!

"Alas! Splendorous Lanka now sinks,
This heroic monkey hath come as jinx.
"Save me! Save me! Through the blazes echoed dins,
"He is none but the Embodiment of our sins.

"He is no monkey but the messenger of Ram,
He'll turn into ashes our diabolic pomp."
"Such is the reward of saint's disregard,
The state is so burning as has no lord.

" Lankiness of Lanka came evident in a mo,
Woe is me!! see!! ashes of el-dorado."

Garret=Atari, triced=tied up with ropes, in a trice=in a moment.
Vaulter=jumber; to vault=to leap; Blare = roar, vaults=arched roofs; Jinx=bad luck; Lankiness=weakness, El-dorado'=the state made of gold;

Melting gold spangles rolled on charred bricks,
Nude towers stood as glory's relics,

Flames engulfed all, from towers to the tuft,
Excepting the one, Vibhishan's toft.
Thus to Uma! the sacred narrative,
Was detailed pouring soul by the Lord Shiv–

"Uma! Kapi himself was spared,
Being messenger of Him, who is the Sire of fire.
"Seeing Cimmerian fumes from cinders of shines,
Content Kapi leapt in to the brine.

Couplet: *The tail quenched he, toil relieved,*
The small form regained,
Before daughter of Janak, he
Joining palms did stand- 26

VICTORIOUS RETURN

"Just as the Lord conferred to me, signet ring,
Pray! Thou mayest as well grant me something."
Taking She from Her locks, the crest-jewel,
And gave it to Hanuman enthralled.

"Son! convey My regards to the Lord,
Even in stretch of distance, whom, I canst not part.
"Token of my reverence in this crest jewel shine,
O Lord! it reminds Me of Thine pastime.

"The reverence, that dwell in Me, is My jewel,
Its fountain from My bosom ever well.
"O Tender to tender! Recall Thy splendour,
And cease My severe sufferings, O Saviour!"

Brine=sea, Cimmerian=extreme dark, Cinders=ashes; relics=remains, ruins.

"O Thy grace cared for my trivial graze,
The crooked crow's* gaze was prey of Thy rage.
"its truth I tell, when I do mention,
I shall keep my breath not beyond a month.

"I have overlived in this prison,
Glimpse of hope came with Kapi! my son!
"Thy visit now you bid to curtail,
My sorrow, with your farewell will prevail.

Couplet:

Hanuman then convinced,
With words and deeds,
Bowing head to Her Lotus feet,
The farewell he did bid. 27

Hanuman next rose, with great uproar,
Struck with awe the demoness's core.
He leaped over clouds that seemed great bark,
And headed to the northern marge.

Again he rose high up the sky,
From clouds to clouds across like missile.
Reverberating sound the Kapi made,
Eager eyes shone, delighted the comrades.

Greeted them he with shrill echo of joy,
They could envisage the fulfilled envoy.
From beaming face and blooming visage,
'The mission was achieved'- all comrades guessed .

They felt as if they had been born a new ,
With blithe energized, the crew then moved .
Some embraced Hanumaan, some kissed own tail,
For they had won the unfaught battle.

---

*Jayant's story; graze=wound, sore.
Bark=ship, envisage=visualize.

Querying and quoting the events recent,
To Lord of Raghus they moved content.
Zip is verve of the steps on path,
It had shortened the journey of monkeys to Raghunath.

Cared not varderers, they entered royal parterre,
Went to rave there under Angad's care.
Dadhimukh, the keeper saw the forbidden entries,
To protect parterre he sent santries.

Santries when appealed, interferred and pealed,
They replied with the fists, till they took to their heals.

Couplet: *Santries rushed and messaged*
"Crown prince is messing the garden'
Sugriv felt elated-
'they must have accomplished the mission.' 28

'Had they not achieved the mission,
Could ever comrades rade the royal garden.
Sugriv mused they merry on a destructive spree,
It indicateth the very task is achieved.

While he was musing, the very same mo,
The troops of monkeys reached and bowed.
King Sugriv met them all with warmth,
Before his asking eyes, they merrily informed—

"By the grace of Lord, Hanumaan had attained
The mission; and lives of legion he maintained.
Hearing this Sugriv, embraced him a new,
They all then went to the Lord of Raghu.

Zip=enthusiasm, Parterre=garden(madhuvan)
Took to heels=ran away
Spree=lively frolic.

Ram saw them coming in merry mood,
Cringed before Him everyone of the troops.
Making full prostration, the noble monkey,
Hanumaan worded 'Discovered is Devi.'

Couplet:

Sitting on crystal rock,
Heard words as pouring nectar,
Hailed-hugged each of the flock,
Felt much delighted the two brothers. 29

Jamwant said "O revered Ram ! hark !!
In the darks of folly Thy grace is the torch.
"Thy gracious look ist the unceasing nerve,
That doth fill the sinew and soul with verve.

'Ts all Thy splendour that glorifieth us,
Thy grace ever deifieth our opus.
"He becometh a name, he is victorious,
Lest a man with no grace ist nonplussed.

"Thy compassion, is just enough,
To accomplish mission whether easy or tough.
"even myriad tongues, would be short.
For Hanumaan, who hath achieved the task".

High-deeds of the heroic Kapi,
Were highlighted to Lord by Jamwant.
The Merciful Lord, full to the banks,
Embraced tight, Hanumaan once again.

"Dear! Now you say, Siya in what way,
Doth keep Her life, and pass Her days."

Couplet:

"Her withered frame is fane,
*With doors of muttering lips**
Her gaze is tightly fixed
Her soul finds no way to slip. 30

---

*muttering name of Ram.

"She hath sent as token this crest-jewel,
And sent word to Thou as well."
Crest jewel He took, touched it to the core,
His pangs, flooded His eyes further more.

"Her dress, Her tress and Her face,
Not a little, than Her words, spake–
"Thou Lord! Hast forgotten Me
By words, mind, deeds, I'm Thine devotee.

"My breath, I confess, is blame worthy,
At separation why did it not cease?
"Me Lord! That vice lies with My eyes,
The soul to depart, My eyes deny.

"To the scorching pangs My breath puffs
the fire to consume Me; now I have lived enough.
"It's own interest of eyes that pour and pour,
And body ist not burnt in parting-fire in core."

"Seeta's utterly consumed by distress,
O Lord ! the better, if said of that less."

Couplet:

"Every moment O clement!
Passes like an age,
O Ram! Ravage the Savage,
Be quick to salvage." 31

"Who ist Embodied bliss in Himself,
Ran along His veins the pain, 'knowing of Siya's wails.'
His cloudy heart poured through eyes,
'Should ever My devout be in such way, tried.'

How could She be subjected to such mayhem,
While, She ist more Myself than I am.
"By words, minds, deeds who is My devotee,
Should never face such luck O Kapi!"

Kapi said, "I value the life, out of luck,
Whose godless mind, the worship chucks.
"What worth of demons stands before Thou,
Thy pastime hath ever succoured the devouts."

"Obliging, as you are, O Hanumant!
None I find on earth nay in heaven.
"My words, my blessings or any largess,
For you, stay short, my ope hand grace.

"Listen ! I'm unable to repay, but for my embrace,
I now offer you all that I have."

Couplet:

Lords' bosom reflected in eyes,
Grace poured through the gaze,
Ram felt great delight,
Kapi sunk in His tight embrace. 32

Lost in Lord's embrace, the highest largess,
Half slipt he stayed, genu-flexed.
To pick him up, lo! Prabhu trieth and trieth.
But being Love immersed, Kapi loves not to rise.

Lotus hand of Lord on Kapi's head,
Lord Shiv was lost, immersed in that state*.
Regaining Himself once again Lord Shiv,
Began to narrate the winsome narrative.

Picking up Hanumant, Prabhu embraced,
Holding by hand, seated him very next.

Couplet:

"What an ease Thy grace bringeth,
in the puzzle of maze.
A zing in the world's labyrinth,
Thou art, the courage. 33

Chuck=Abandon.
*Shiv while telling Ram's story was lost.

"Lord! Thy Bhakti is the Final bliss,
Grant me that, and may it not cease."
On straight words of simple spirit
Prabhu granted him 'so be it'

Thus Shiv continued to tell Ram's deeds—
"One who, discovered Ram, what else he needs.

"Uma ! in whose core this discourse has coursed ,
Bhakti to the Supreme, Sure he procures."

Here Lord poured more blessings on troops blest,
Echoed- Jai Ram ! jai Ram !! eclat.

Thoughtfully then Ram summoned Sugriv,
"The victory has already begun, so be quick.
'Ts no matter to linger any longer,
Sugriv! To comrades send orders.

"O Gay! Gavay! Dwivid! Sushen! Jamwant!
O leaders! Take position all around and infront!"
Whether Prabhu needth troops or troops need Prabhu,
Heaven rained flowers, for they knew what was true.

Couplet: *Sugriv summoned quick,*
Champs, commanders, comrades.
In swift move of fleet,
Stood before Ram, the Array. 34

THE MARCH

Unmatched valour in many hues,
Stood before Ram, the militia troops.
At Lord's lotus feet all bent and bowed,
And filled the milieu with zealous bellows.

With gracious look Ram eyed the arrays,
With long sublimed arms He hailed and blest.
The blessings of Ram was the chiefest found,
Energized as if they were winged mounts.

And with zest, shri Ram then sallied forth,
Hosts of good omens made its show.
For who is in Himself the Auspicious incarnate,
—Good omens appeared before Him to prove themselves.

Intuited the beats of Siya's bosom,
Throbbing Her left arm told of good omens.
Within Her weary breaths, the cheery soul,
Told, Her Lord had sallied forth,

Omens to Siya were gracious,
Same presages to Raavan were ominous.
Countless monkeys, regardless of life,
To sacrifice Self, moved for heroic strife.

Well equipped with rocks, trees and well-drilled,
Soldiery in offence and defence was skilled.
Some succeed because they are destined to,
But ever, the determined get through.

Trampetted elephants, monkeys bears uproared,
Trembled all quarters as they sallied forth.

Stanza: *Trampetted elephants, shaken mounts,*
The Earth trembled, Ocean bubbled,
All Gods, demi-gods, Sages and Naags,
Kinnars pleased at ceasing trouble.
*Resolved braves of Ram*did go,,*
Scudded and scrambled,
Some hustled, Some trailed, All hailed Ram,
His paeans they warbled. *A*

---

*Brave Warriors of Ram.

The soldiery and bravery of monkeys,
Was the delight of Ram
The Delight was not just might of arms,
But Ram was charmed by the fight within swarms.
*As they moved, the Shesha's hood**
Hardly could hold this drift,
The Shesha took pains, the Earth to balance
With bliss he could poise the axis. B

Couplet: *In hurried move Ram coursed,*
And reached the Sea-coast;
Spreaded all along the shore,
Mighty monkeys' bears' hosts. 35

THE RAVENOUS RAAVAN

Welcoming forest of Sahya and Malay,
Brought, among troops a very new joy.
Scion of Agasthya, kaatav, Malayaran,
Aalar, Irulav, Urali, Arwalan**, Welcomed.

There, humiliated Lanka lived in odd silence,
Fright and panic had its governance.
Every anxious mind of denizens,
Thought-'should we, the notorious now learn'.

" The tiny macrurous monkey burnt
And demonry to save, we found none.
"The Might of whose envoy is so ineffable,
What doom should we get on His arrival.

To Mandodari permeated people's message,
And wise queen felt utterly perplexed.

---

* the base of the earth was supposed to be supported by Shesha(the poetic imaginary support of the Earth.)

** All ancient tribes still live in east and west part of Sahya, Malay jungles.

At feet of her consort, Raavan, she fell,
Humbly she spake of morals-

"O lord ! discard with Hari, the discord,
May my fair words in bosom you record.
"Every heart every hearth is filled with panic,
Looking at the ashes of His envoy's deeds.

"O lord ! brood over, call your court,
Return His wife, your fault you cure.
"Your blooming lotus-race will wither,
For Seeta is here like a frosty winter.

"You return Devi Siya, listen to me!!
Lest, sins summed up are your enemy.

Couplet: *"Your fiends are frogs,*
Ram's arrows, the serpents,
Will devour the fiend-flocks,
Divine is Ram, not a mere man. 36

Inflated Raavan airly was not keen,
High headed jeered at words of queen—
"Fright is females' a factual feature,
You, faint hearted in our revel, fear.

"When monkeys, our food, do arrive,
Hungry demons 'll devour them and survive.
"My might sways over with spreaded panic,
Its not fair, if my queen is timid."

With tittering utterance he reassured,
Then the careless Giant moved to his court.
Mute appeal of The Doom, queen could read,
'Adverse fate to her consort hath reached.'

Airly=heedlessly.

Lanka meanwhile, is rebuilt by Maya, the architect,
Raavan now forgot the moments of setback.
There, Raavan was informed in the court,
Big legion had camped on the northern coast.

"He called counsellors behind closed doors,
'We are challenged by mere Ape not a warrior.'
He saught opinion of his mentors,
They laughed it off, for not a moot matter.

"While you have won, the earth hades and Heaven,
Of what account be Monkeys and humans.

Couplet: *When medics, mentors, ministers kneel*
To flatter out of fear,
The mammon, mettle, morals, the three
Forth with shall shatter. 37

It so happened in Raavan's case,
All acclaimed only at his face.
Rightly came Vibhishan at that mo,
Laden with all reverence he bowed.

Most humbly he bowed and bowed again,
With sanction, Vibhishan prayed then-
"If thou askest me, I say to my mind,
Sure thy lofty dignity to find.

"The welfare cometh not thro' wanton-mood,
deeds need be undone that yield no good.
"On strange chaste Devi*, thy lust,
Will bring to us none but the erebus.

Erebus=hell; *Seeta.

"On demonry, the face of that Revered woman
Is severe as forthmoon*, the ill omen.
"One who is hostile to Prakriti, the law of Nature,
Such adverse fault is, of all, worst.

"Cerebrity, celebrity, all gains are in vain,
If greed of soul is unrestrained.

Couplet: *"The haptad sins** are troops,*
The loops of hellish ignorance.
From them keep aloof,
Revere Ram whom revere saints. 38

"As dwells the world, so in world to dwell,
The Supreme Ram behaveth as mortals.
"Tho' wise do discern, foolish fail to see,
Might of unborn Almighty, and His Infinity.

"All humane Lord, assumed human form,
Determined came to right all worlds' wrongs.
"He'st kind to mankind, deadly to even the Death,
The protector of virtues, the saviour of holy texts.

"Discard the discord, before Him thou bow,
To Him if one goes, He relieveth his woe.
"O Naath ! Cure fault, return Janaki,
For, this fault will lead to fatal enmity.

"Pray to Ram, He will forgo your sin,
One, who faces world rancour, He saves even him.
"Whose very name overthrows three throes,***
Hath descended as Ram O brother! You know.

---

* forth day moon after the full moon is said to be ill-omen.

** seven sins-anger, lust, pride, sloth, lovetousness, envy, gluttony.

*** Physical, mental, super natural.

"My advice is pure, as a fra, as a pal,
To perish present-ills, to save from future faults.

Couplet:

"I bow at feet as fra,
O Elder ! to implore,
Forgo ego and euphoria
The Lord of lords Ram, you adore." 39

"This is Pulastya's attitude
And is mine too,
With all my promptitude,
I have conveyed to you. 40

Words of Vibhishan delighted Malyavaan, the mentor,
Further added the learned teachings, in that court, the rare-
"Hear! Dear! Rare words of morals
Keep to your bosom Vibhishan's principles.

"Morals may not come in modest words,
But should the discourse of lore be heard."
Wrath and ego doubled Raavan's tyranny,
Cried-"Both ye! fools!! praise my enemy."

Then veteran counsellor retired back,
But Vibhishan, a new joining hands pleaded-
"O lord! holy texts havest ever warned,
In every heart dwell the right and the wrong,

"Wealth of wealth is wealth, when mind is set on right,
Evils and wrongs ever end in wails otherwise.
"wrongly in wrongs your mind finds joy,
In bad your sceptred hand is employed.

Fra- brother

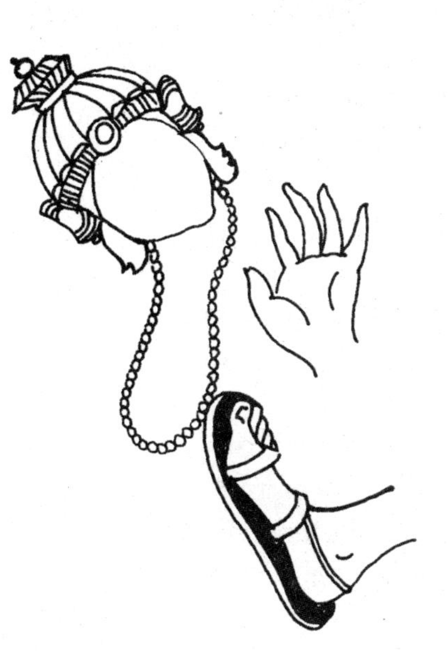

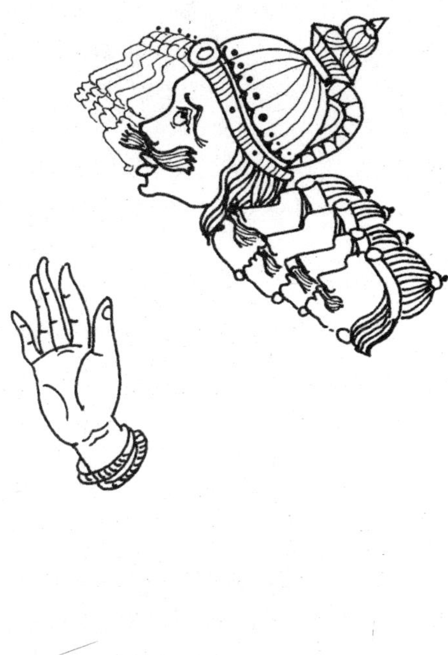

Couplet: *"Should demonry not decline,*
I pray to you and cringe,
Heed prayers of mine,
Lest, the ruins that Devi brings. 41

"O Aine! O mine !! return Siya otherwise,
I have no doubt, of rising sorrow's tide."
Words of wisdom from veds and olds
Morals, ethics Vibhishan did quote.

True duty of brother, is be aloud to say
The very truth; tho' the unwise may cast words away.
Raging Raavan rose and roared- "O wretch!
Its not you speak but speaks your death.

"Ever you survived, of my mercy-revival,
But O wretch ! you revel in , with rivals.

Aine=elder brother.

"You doubt my valour O silly!
Tell me! who can, in world, dare me?

"Living with me, you love two ascetics"
He screamed-"Scram! Silly!! Teach them ethics.

Infuriated Raavan then kicked his brother,
He clutched his feet over and over.
"Uma ! its kind nature of saintly kinsmen know,
Even to evil doer, their goodness they bestow.

"You may pummel me or pamper, its right of parents,
But only worship of Ram 'll exempt."
Renouncing cloudy riches of guilt laden souls,
Announcing their fates, Vibhishan thus told-

Couplet: *"Ram ist embodied Truth,*
This fake court is death damned,
To Ram's refuge I route,
Now may I not be blamed." 41

VIBHISHAN IN RAM'S REFUGE

Might of truth hath fearless speech
The hostile court listened to him; palsied.
Saying so, the moment , Vibhishan left,
All the assize of Raavan seemed consigned to death.

Ignoring enlightened words is a deed berserk,
It's bound to bring in life, the mirk.
Since Raavan lost kindred claim,
Luck, lustre, lack fame instantly he became.

From clouds to cloud **Vibhishan scudded to Ram**,
With the flesh thrilled, mind with flashes of warmth.

Scram=go away quickly, pummel=beat; Assize=court.

"From ages and ages this very day I yearned,
My fortune I earned while to Lord I turn.

"I'll see His feet, the source of all glee,
I'll see Him who trod all the way, for me.
"Very feet salvaged Ahalya petrified,
Very feet bestowed into Dandak*, the life.

"Very feet those lie in Siya's heart,
Those chased delusive deer and lost.
"Those feet rushed after ruse deer,
That parting-visage, Janaki ever doth bear.

"Its glimpse brings to Shiv bliss of trance,
A glance of those feet, is now my glad-chance.

Couplet: *"On whose sacred sabots*
Mind of Bharat is fixed,
With these fleshy orbs
I'll see those holy feet." 42

Pondering so, with all his devotion,
Swift he came to this side of ocean.
When monkeys eyed Vibhishan nigh,
In him the enemy's spy they espied.

Detaining him they approached Sugriv,
'Is he a friend or came to deceive?
Sugriv said, "O Ram! be heedful!!
How come he comes? Is he foe's tool?

Lord asked them to make a guess at,
Sugriv said, "In every bosom Thou dwellest.
"Yet Heed! Be heedful of disguise,
Far to discern are demon's designs.

---

*Dandak=the forest(in the southern part.)
Sabots=wooden sandals.

"To spy secrets with hidden hatred,
If he comes; I apply tit for tat"
" O Sugriv!" Said Lord "due check you make
But My vow makes My refugee unafraid;"

"Saying I am Thine"- whoever comes to Me,
My refuge is ope wide for him, O Sugriv!"
Hanuman amused for he knew 'Lord rescueth,
And careth the one who comes in His refuge.'

Couplet: *A refugee is God sent,*
And so is the duty,
Weigh no loss or gain,
The Conscience hath it's own security. 43

"Even gross sinners, who all evils endure,
If come to Me, I embrace them as Pure.
"With Me every soul hath silent pact,
I reveal it the moment he lookth at (Me) .

"Every soul and Mine are made of the very Same thing.
Innate attraction sublimeth the soul to the Supreme.
"Man is freed from billions of his sins,
If confesses, regrets and looks at Me .

"If know this they, who lift not hands of prayers,
They are inborn Stubborn, evil creatures.
"Had this new comer, been, at heart, a savage,
To face Me could ever he hath courage?

In limpid soul, with liquid eyes,
My Soul, in his, his in Mine soul resides.
"But false, falls, fibs, fake fie! fie!!,
Are lapses of life, I do never like.

"Even if, Raavan had sent him with some evil ,
Truth is truth, in truth nothing is concealed.

"O friend ! All fiends in world who dwell,
Lakhan could finish, in a flash spell.

"But if in My refuge, feared he came
He is to Me more Myself than I am .

Couplet: *"Both ways greet with Ope arms",*
—Thus said Lord with beam,
Champs with éclat of Ram,
Moved to receive him. 44

With all heart and no hurt keeping him ahead,
To the Merciful Ram all they proceeded.
The wight visage of the two*, with wide eyes,
From a distance his thirsty sight imbibed.

He fixed on Ram, his winkless gaze
Benumbed steps stopped he stood amazed.
Long arm as they are, eyes ruddy lotus,
Body swarthy tender, at the same robust.

This handsome frame and winsome visage;
He did drink it with dazed gaze.
Thro' his body thrill ran and gathered in eyes
Plucking up himself, he spake polite-

"In demonry, I was born and bred,
Being brother of Raavan, I am thing of hatred.
"My wile frame is shaped on demonic anvil,
As the owl likes dark, I like the evils.

Couplet: *"Worthless I am, still*
Have come to Thou O saviour!
Relieve me of my ills,
Save me! In Thy shelter." 45

---

*Ram and Lakhan
Anvil=Smith's working tool.

His sighs melted the sandy shore,
His long sufferings, now his life adorned.
As he cringed before Lord's feet,
Long arms of Lord picked him up, to meet.

Humble warm words first touched Ram's breast,
Instantly Ram took him in arms very next.
In embrace he felt a welcoming wreath,
What his soul deserved truly found that bliss.

Two brothers hugged him and seated him very next,
As pal took the devotee to dispel his dread.
Ram asked-"Lankesh*! Tell 'bout yourself,
And your kindred, do they keep well?

"Where soul turns to slave of pomp, its worth not to dwell,
Lest, from heaps of false amples, soul falls to the hell.
"O friend! Among fiends how do you reside?
Keeping virtues among odds is noble pride.

"in troublous days, your virtues you maintained,
Hardship, for you, was worship, and pain, the penance.
"The hell is no hell, its far better,
May nemesis place with knaves never."

Said Vibhishan-

"Lord Ram! Thine grace is the divine balm,
My bruises turned to bliss by touch of Thy warmth.

Couplet: *"I roamed; the peace I searched,*
But found thro' hands sublimed,
Unless washing hands off lust,
No Calm Cometh even in dream. 46

"Satanic sins in my mind prevailed,
Virtues failed and vices swelt.

---

*King of Lanka.

"So long till I declared myself Thine,
Only then Thy shining visage within me enshrined.

"Lust's tender arms with wealth of passion jewelled,
Delight us, as in dark-night, the owl revels.
"The night of lust, should go must,
At horizon of mind, with the rise of orb of trust.

"Sight of Thy feet bringeth me now ease,
Thy blessings bringeth my fortunes increase.
"I 'm well, my folly-fears are now fled,
At the very sight of, O Ram! Thy feet.

"Thy ope hands bestow a lavish spread,
With our little hand we could pickup very less.
"Inborn debase as I am,
No virtues no good, I can claim.

"Even from sage's contemplation Thou dost escape,
My fortune brings me to Thy embrace.

Couplet: *"O Lord! The Heaven! Thy grace*
And my astral influence,
Chanced me 'Darshan' of Visage,
The rarest of rare gain." 47

Ram replied-

"Easy to access, I am ope to all,
O pal ! but for the want of true call."
"Even if a man earns world's enmity,
But with humble heart, looks at Me;

"freeing him from ego, esurience and wrongs,
Into a Virtuous, I soon him transform.
"The tender threads of kins and kindred,
Let all these emotions be put together,

Esurience=Greed.

"Gathering all these make a rope ladder,
Meet Me sure, with trusty steps clambered.
"Who hath no bias and no passion,
Unstirred by pain, pleasure or affliction,

"I keep in My soul, that soul of pious man,
Just as a greedy man keeps in heart, the mammon.
"For the longing hopes cherished by people like you,
For those hopes I descend, and the saints to rescue.

Couplet: *"In every bit, breath, every beat,*
Who perceive Me,
My Evident form they meet,
Ever path of Dharma who see." 48

"Touchstone of troth gets, to the worthy soul,
With shine of trust, the Truth as gold.
"Whose self is diffused to all, with no 'I'- Sense.
My binding to him is more intense.

"You're just right with sure merits Lankesh!
And it's meet to keep you, in My embrace".
Grace, Courtsey and Lord's path of dignity,
Elated monkeys raised words of Ram's glory.

With wreath of blooming words, Vibhishan was bound,
In the ocean of bliss, lost flesh he was drowned.
He adored lotus feet over and over,
Heart brimming thro' eyes, he was much enamoured-

"O warmth of every flame! O glow of every lamp!
O End of every aim! O Name of every fame!
"O goal of every soul ! The whole who creates!
O Saviour hand! O Player of puppets!

Clambered=climbed up.
Troth=faith.

"I had cheap obstacles of desires a few,
In love flood of Thine feet, those flew.
"The Wealth of wealth is faith in Thee,
'let this pellucid stream flow in'; Grant me".

"So be it"The divine Divinity divined,
Same moment asked He for water from the brine*.
"O pal! You have never craved tho' for worldly pleasures,
More so right path in itself is a treasure,

"And as My 'Darshan' is fruit of fruits,
So it behoveth Me to anoint you."
So saying Lord of lords performed coronation,
Welcomed by the presence around, and the Heaven.

Couplet: *Words of Vibhishan fanned,*
The fire of Raavan's rage,
Lord rescued scorching Vibhishan,
And granted him Lanka's reign. 49

Where Raavan offered heads ten,
To get from Shiv, the affluence,
To Vibhishan the same reign,
Ram granted with diffidence. 50

If knows Ram, they lift no hands of worship,
In the jungle of mundane they roam like beasts.
Came in refuge Vibhishan, left with Lord the rest,
Bonds of soul and the Supreme, everyone greeted.

Lord meetth in all souls, and all souls, meet in the Lord,
Diffused in all forms, tho' from all, all-apart.
For cause against demonry, Who came as the Evident,
The Protector of Dharm spake then-

---

*sea water required for coronation of a king.

"O Vibhishan! Prow Sugriv!! Lo!!! This matter is grave.
How the legion will brave, the raves of waves?
" 'Ts full of snakes, crocs and sharks,
Thro' the Deeps, how the troops 'll cross?

Vibhishan said, "Listen! To my petition,
'Tho' Thine arrow canst swallow the ocean,
"But let our anxiety may cherish courtesy.
Thou may reach to beseech the deity of the Sea.

Couplet:

"Tho' Thy shaft may sear sea,
But in sea Thy sires we see,
May he extend some courtesy,
Seeing Thy army at sea. 51

" O friend! Cherished-friendship is ever boon,
To pray to Ocean let Me go soon.
"Friendship from ruin saves, in hour of strife,
Let's do with the hope, that the Deo will oblige.

Perplexed Lakhan liked not this modest part,
"Way-laid bars need be razed in war.
"Only Thy mettle in any battle works,
Lord! Sink this ocean itself, into low world."

" In strife, the heroic greatness of Heroes,
Is in fury and not in kindness to foes.
"Only fainéants have the faith in fate,
The troth of Truth lies in Champ's biceps."

On words of worried Lakhan Ram Smiled,
In mild words solaced He with stable mind.
'To do the same' but little later; Ram assured,
In sweet simplicity then He went to the shore.

Legion=Army; Fainéants=lazy.
Sear=dry up; Sires=forefathers, paters, At sea=perplexed.

Bowing His head, He first saluted,
With grace He sat on the Kush- mat.
Stubborn mind but may melt before patient heart,
And hurdles may depart, even with no use of dart.

Lo! Spies, after Vibhishan sent by Lanka,
Beheld Ram's pastime in great awe.

Couplet: *They kept perched in disguise,*
And could not be caught,
Ram's love for refugee they eyed,
And praised Ram in manners, odd. 52

The worshiper of cruelty adored Ram's love,
Whose noble Excellence is all above.
Monkeys discovered them as spies,
To Sugriv they brought them in ties.

"Hear! O champs" Sugriv exclaimed-
"These diabolic spies should be maimed."
Monkey rushed as a child rushes to toys,
Tied paraded in joy gushed cries 'hoys'.

Monkeys began beating them right and left,
They yelled for help, but not left.
"who seize, tease us we adjure him by Ram,
We'r ashamed, don't maim, do us no harm"

One who is abashed of base deeds, thus is claimed.
'His burdened soul is lightened by the cure of shame.'
This pulling and hauling Lakhan did heed,
Felt pity abou' them, with jeer he freed–

"Take this epistle for Raavan, the gross.
This war will be his life's last.

Epistle=a letter with message.

Couplet: *"My words tell to him straight,*
Firing at him this message,
Return Devi Seeta, Lest
Numbered are your days". 53

Demons as they were, with touch of truth,
Transformed, bowed to Lakhan departed the two.
With éclat of Ram, they scudded thro' clouds,
About doom of Raavan they had no doubt.

Entered into Lanka talking of Ram's feat,
Bowed they their heads at Raavan's feet.
Carelessly Raavan from them asked-
"Shuk! What to ask of assigned easy task?"

"yet ye tell of Vibhishan, a pseudo-kindred,
Silent steps of own death who hath not heard.
"Who forsook Lordship of Lanka, the silly!
Evil-starred will be now weevil of barley.

"Lavish monkeys bears how do ye estimate,
Who are our food, our palates can't wait.
"for the ocean is saviour of their lives,
Fast! finish them, they have over-survived.

"Forget not to tell drama of two ascetics
Who must be getting pale of panic.

Couplet: *"Hearing my thew and sway*
Are they not still dismayed?
Do there they stay or flew away?
....But how ye look so dazed?" 54

Slurred words Shuk* Pushed thro' choked throat,
But in eager silence of court his words echoed-
"Lord! We two went their as reign's spies,
You may confide in us as your own eyes.

Shuk=chief of spies.

"Lord! thou havest cherished a confidence and relied,
Shouldst thou now admit our view likewise.
"with his virtue Vibhishan was weighed as a Saint,
Ram anointed him at once granting thy reign.

"Monkeys discovered us in disguise,
They seized us, teased us and tied.
"They made fun of us and tied to harm,
But released, when we adjured them by Ram.

"Where ever sight reached on northern shore,
More and more were adding to the endless horde.
"Flooded up the troops in many hues,
With visage warlike, horrific and huge.

"One who killed thy son and keeled capital
Among mammoth champs, is just a little.
"The marshalled champs colossal and tough,
To say of their power is never enough.

Couplet: *"Dwivid, Mayand, Nil, Nal,*
Angad, Gad, Viktaas,
Jaamwan, Nisath, Collosal
Their vigour doth surpass. 55

"Keen to keel Lanka, and victory to achieve,
Spirited all they, are like Sugriv.
"Before ocean their thirst of triumphant mind,
Would leave depth of the Brine, behind.

"From the marge of sea to the marge of sky,
We espied millions of them, far and nigh.
"They treasure grace of the Almighty, to add to their might,
Now the legion's exploit, may prove Lanka's plight.

Horde=army, legion.

"It's no hearsay, I have confirmed
The legion have millions of chieftains.
"Lord! That horde hath not a Vaanar single,
Who could not brave you in the battle.

"All are wringing hand in the rabid hate,
Could act but for Raghuveer's behest.
"The flaming rage would dry the sea, it seems,
Or would they fill with mounts and rocks, the Deep.

"Dragon breathes in their flaring wrath to their lips,
They could zap you and all demonry as if.
"Their soldiery fears no weapons, no wounds,
They are sure 'Lanka is now doomed'.

Couplet: *"Treasured with vim profound,*
All the army's limbs
With Ram their chiefest found,
Even the Death they could win. *56*

"The truth of the leader and troth of the soldier,
Put together, what not can conquer.
"sizeable fire is ever monkey's flair,
With added Ram's care, the Death they could dare.

"My emptiness keeps mum to say of the Almighty,
Words are palsied, demonry is too pigmy.
"With a knit of His bow, He couldst split the sea,
Yet He askth Vibhishan out of courtesy.

"On advice of Vibhishan He worshipped the brine,
'mid hurdling waves some ways to find."
Jeered Raavan in a boisterous hoot,
Felt relieved thinking, matter was not moot-

The Deep=Ocean
Flair=aptitude, nature.

"The wisdom of ascetics** seems offspring of their mind,
'ts out come of foolish counsel we find.
"His power reflects in His allies with monkeys,
As He offerth His foes, plentiful for the feast.

"In the shades of words of the coward-inborn*,
He standth before ocean, as a child stubborn.
"O fool! In your praise I see hidden lies,
I see shallow brags in rival allies.

"With Craven counsellor like Vibhishan who ties,
Their crowing will prove, a knife to their lives.
"The defeat of their master is gift of the craven counsels,
With such counsellor only infamy prevails,"

Big mouth Demon-King bragged all odds,
Uneased spies then gave, the letter, they had brought-
"O King! may this epistle bring peace,
Regard it's words, Lest the grief, we meet.

"The race secure, on your lore depends,
Thy dexterity will change the foes to friends."
Over the left mind he took in the left hand,
To read it out he summoned his man—

Couplet: *"Forgo ego O knave!*
And do not wreck your race!
The hostile to Ram, none is saved
Even in refuge of Mahesh. 57

"Follow Vibhishan's Steps of love
Lest your days are done,
Leave your folly's fort,
Which keeps pervert mind hidden. 58

**Ram and Lakhan
*Vibhishan
Over the left=negatively.

"Be the bee of Lord's lotus feet,
Lest you, in fire of Ram's arms as moth be extinguished."
Tho' feared as he was, but in mask of cheer
Raavan bragged once again for all to hear-

"Sick He!! Lies on dust, heaven he seeks,
'ts a mock mention of younger ascetic."
Shuk, the spy appealed lordliness to eschew,-
" the view in the letter are all true.

"Discard the discord, the ruins it brings,
The truth wins ever, this truth you should ween.
"Ram masterth all thro' unseen threads,
And this right sceptre ever protects.

"what are they, the name, riches and the crown,
All in vain, if the Almighty frowns.
"From the enmity grows abundant woes,
When sins remorse, wealth of grace bestows.

"If you forgo ego, He wilt forgive you,
Lest on ruins if you live, you'll live to rue.
"You return Siya, the dignity of womanhood,
Or shame will fall upon this unmanly mood.

Siya to waive, as they prayed,
In return to advice, were kicked by the Knave.
Company of evil should better be left,
Bowing head, the farewell spies bade.

Self guided they rushed to the north,
Their worthy steps reached where camped the Lord.
Saluting Ram, they did state,
Their story, and achieved erst fate.

Eschew=avoid/shun.
Rue=regret, remorse; Ween=think over.
Waive=Renounce, Surrender; Erst=previous.

"Uma !" Said Shiv "it was Augasthya's malison,
He the saint, had turned to maligned demon.
Malison of saint proved to be benison,
They attained endless bliss, returned to their havens.

Couplet: *Here, three days had elapsed,*
Heedless ocean remained crass.
Ram then showed His rage,
For, the gross ever heeds harsh— 59

SUBDUAL OF THE OCEAN

"With no heed to worship; sleeps The Deep in sloth,
Now My wrath will dry it, into froth—
"who is dull, in the noble attempt,
Should get the reward of contempt.

"The ocean, fostered indolence within breast,
Will get the sentence through my firing shafts.
"The modesty have brave but folded hands,
Before knave but should it brandish hidden brand.

" O fra! Bring my bow-arrow, the awe,
On the path of Truth, any hurdle is straw.
"To pray to dull, to love deceiver,
Teaching of charity to the born-miser,

"Words of wisdom before the wanton,
Sermons of dispassion to greedy one,
"Gains none, virtuous words to vicious bosom,
Are like the seeds wither on the earth-barren.

Malison=curse.
Crass=thick, stupid.
The Deep=Ocean; Brand=sword.

" Face! May it be ocean against My determined cause,"
-Saying so, Ram aimed at the Ocean His shaft.
In the firm steps, reside noble pride,
Any depth of hurdle to set right.

Awesome shaft awed waves far and wide,
In the core of ocean raised inflamed tides.
Crocs, snakes, sharks, fish flocks were at sea,
Scorched the biota, when the Sea did see,

At sea, then the Sea, the sea-diety appeared,
With jewelled salver before the Saviour.

Couplet: *Take pains and water the plaintains,*
Won't fructify unless pruned,
Prayers for the Base are in vain
While reproach makes him prone. 60

At the Lord's feet fell deity of the Sea,
"Me Lord! Forgive me! Save me!!
"Earth, ether, air, water and fire,
These are thick by nature O Master!

"Thou Thyself havest characterized these five elements,
None can transgress, Thy ordinance.
"Thou begotest micro and macrocosm,
And havest inspired the limits to their form.

"Under Thine behest we survive in limits,
For every element it ever befits.
"Pampering a base like me, is of no use,
But sugarcane profits even the men who bruise.

"Drums be battered on beats, dames be ushered on beats
Ah me! Oaf, a beast need a different beat.

At sea=perplexed; Ushered on beats=escorted on the path.

"Through Thy perfect might and perfect will,
Thou mayst dry my pit in a handful spill,

"and the force will cross through empty pit, free,
But what honour, what glory it brings to me.
"Veds admit Thine behest hath no limit,
Making course for the Force, I will split.

"Me, the Thine element will do to my best,
Any wonder, O Wonder! On Thy wondrous behest.

Couplet: *All pouring of the nectar Lord listened,*
And deity's malisons turned.
"O Ocean ! O Elderun !
Find some ways for legion." 61

Sea-deity replied humbly–

"This situation to win befits, Nal, Nil the twins
The sage's curse*, this day the boon, brings.
"O Wonder! Their wondrous touch to big rocks,
Will make them float, on waves as logs.

"Over through the brine, Thine splendour thus, wilt bridge,
For the legion to go across with ease.
"Conches, pearls, cones, oysters-shells,
Molluscs, crocs, fishes also will help.

"Lord! Bless them make a bridge on the brine,
Should it be ever inspiring force to the mankind.
"Thy shaft may be dispatched on sinner hosts,
The wretches who live on the Drumakulya coast.

---

*The sage accursed once Nal and Nil, that any stone thrown by them will float in water.
Drumakulya=Land of sinful creatures(abhira tribes);

Lord glimpsed deity of the Blue, looked blue,
Then the Almighty Ram, quickly rescued,

The Sea worshipped Him, and bade farewell,
Thus embodied Sea, evanesced in waves.

Stanza: *Ram blessed the Ocean,*
then evanesced the ocean,
Went back and bade adieu,
Thus descends the Ancient,
For relieve of pangs,
The earth to rescue,
for the worth of virtues. *A*

The muses of bard,
before grace of Lord,
Standshort, ever for His paeans,
He is bliss of friends,
and blitz for fiends,
None can pen His paeans
With the Mortal acumen. *B*

Couplet: *The one who is ever dipt,*
In Bhakti-waves of Ram's paeans,
They, the blessed one without ship,
Will cross the mundane ocean. 62

□

Looked blue=looked perplexed.
Acumen=Keenness, intelligence

YUDDH KANDAM

24

The truth is the highest motive power.

—Brahmrishi Vishwatma Bawra

STROPHES

1

O Bliss of devouts ! O blitz for demons!!
Thou, the All wise comest mansized O Non menon !
O doer of everything ! O Dear of Earthlings !!
For my poorest soul Thou art the mammon.

Fervour of friar, fire of warrior,
Could both be seen in One,
Me, the man of straw, whose vision ever saw,
Adore that, Ram at the shore of bliss-ocean.

2

Shiv, beyond all ages, Shiv, fond of the Ganges
For sages who defined the narrative of Ram,
Who, adore ever Ram, Ram ever adore whom,
I do worship that divine Shiv of Ram.

Who is soul of Ram's soul, whose Mould Ram mouldth,
With own hands at sandy threshold,*
I revere that Shankar, who dwellth at Rameshwar,
*Thus poesy of old bards** on the old palms echoed.*

* At sea shore of Rameshwaram.
** Tulsi, Valmiki, Ezhuthachan etc.

Couplet: *That warrior Ram why,*
Should I not worship?
Whose bows pelt at sin and vie,
The Sun beam's swift fleet. 1

RAM-SETU AND RAMESHWARAM

Most humbly what the Sea-deity told,
Filled all the troops with a new soul.
'Why delay?' asked Ram 'none could withhold.'
'raise a bridge across, make chains of shoals.'

"Ram ! Thy name !" some said " itself is bark,
To cross over the mundane's ocean bar.
"This a few yojan's sea is a little span,
'Ts too little a hurdle for Thy name's strength."

Hanuman added "Lord's fury had already sucked,
The sea; but filled again with foe-women's eyes flood.
"We find anew the waves of brine,
But it's eyes of foe's wives pouring saline.

All amused the Hanuman's hyperbole,
More bold, then, Nal and Nil told—
"It's no our tact but the Supreme architect,
That Very Ram will join two coasts thro' His own act."

"Lo! Troops ye ! hear little request of mine,
Engage self in His sport, He in heart be enshrined.
"Go forth ! bring heaps of trees, rocks, mounts,
For the divine bridge of Ram across the brine.

Hyperbole=exaggeration.

Hurrahing, in hurry, the troops set forth,
With ballad's roar and belauding Ram in core.

Couplet: *Making ballad's uproar;*
In mere sports
Lifting up mounts and boles
They would bring them to the shores. 2

Nal-Nil would fathom the depth of shoals,
As well as the enthusiasm of monkey's souls.
The height of their souls and the depth of shoals,
Both would help twin architects to achieve the goal.

Toilless Brigade brought mounts and boles,
Were received by Nal-Nil like play-balls.
Perfected their part they, to make peerless pier,
And their unslothful hands got prevailing power.

The mounts, boles, rocks splashed on the brink,
But troops toils went in vain, disappeared every thing.
Brooding Ratnakar approached Lord Ram,
"everything is being eaten up by monsterous fish swarms."

Then, from pier in tiers Nal-Nil made, mesh,
While monsterous fishes fled, habitant aquatics helped.
On pillars of self trust, belayed arches of troth,
Engineered by the thrust, maketh bridge of the Truth.

Thus, trust, troth, thrust, truth are supports,
In hardships and hurdles, to manly efforts.

Tides of trouble like those waves tumble on,
With welcome of toiling hands, those are gone.
From the brink with every little of blink,
The bridge began to shape link by link.

Tumble on=drop head on; Ratnakar=Sea diety; Pier=base of bridge.

On the boles and stems floated rocks, by Ram's grace,
At the end of day, upto ten yojan, they could make.
Next morn determined Hanuman, the zealous monkey,
Reached to the coastal range of Suvẹladri.

He uprooted mounts Hemkoot, Naag, Simhachal,
Like a ball brought these mounts to Nil-Nal.
All to just finish the gap of ninety yojan,
And in few hours, thus, bridging work was done.

Where the might is, with wisdom, enriched,
Rowing billows of troubles can be easily bridged.
The mortal hands, Built in the immortal style
The bridge; Lord observed and smiled—

"Manly efforts ever gets support of nature,
The determination hath built ageless architecture."
"This glorious spot to coming men will guide,
Firm hands could achieve any paradise.

"Excellence of the Spot inspires Me,
To install here Lingam of Lord Shiv.
"Lord Shiv, is reverence in every prayer,
Lord Shiv is confidence in every warrior.

"Shiv is the element in every mould,
Which awakes vitality in the soul.
Ram sent for sages from hermitage and holts,
And welcomed them all and extolled.

Reverence that was enshrined within Ram,
As Lingam, the emblem of Shiv, took form.
With due solemnity He installedst the Shiv's emblem,
And imparted the divine Element into the same.

Said-"Shiv ist the very Self of Mine,
Thro' benign worships of Shiv, one can achieve the Divine.

"Hostile to the faith's of different hue,
His devotion to Me, never could achieve his due.
"Any faith, any path sure to Me, lead,
Hostile to other's worship, is ego of nitwit."

Couplet: *"Calling him a votary of Mine,*
And keep enmity with Sivaites,
His worships I decline
How doth hostile to Shiv, be right." 3

"Shiv, my pal, My Lord as He is,
As Rameshwaram will accept every worship.
"To lave Lingam, holy Ganges who ever brings,
Will be worth to achieve the final bliss.

"Worship by any Name, Shiv and Ram art the Same,
Rather He is more Myself than I am.
"Who so ever visits the bridge of Ram,
Will be able to cross the ocean of mundane.

"Who belauds Me as warrior or warbles ballads,
At war or worship, I cherish him in Heart."
All rituals were performed, the sages witnessed,
Gladdened heart they, then returned back.

Swift, skilled Nal and Nil were through,
Wide spread was the bridge and their names too.
Thus, hundred yojan long and ten yojan wide,
Holy Bridge became the whole mankind's pride.

Corals supported, and rocks floated as rafts,
As the moral sinks not in presence of Lord's grace.

Is't skill of a Vaanar, is it will of the Deep?
Is't virtues of rocks, or trees those bridged?
Nor the monkeys, mounts, Main, nor man's mortal hands,
Indeed its deed of the Lord, Himself.

Couplet: *It's gravity of the Supreme,*
Which helped the rocks to float,
'Ts His will and His vim,
Which bridged the parted coasts. 4

Know Him, who raise no hands of worship,
Know Him, who keep mum, praying lips,
They are dead only their machined carcass' live,
Their ope orbs see, but minds' eyes sleep.

Gigantic opus by the mortal hands,
Is achieved not just thro' excellence but with inner reverence.
Bridge-job was worked from shore to shore,
With weeds, trailers ties, they made it secured.

Ullulations, yodelling, ballowing uproars,
With more rave and more rage troops moved to the shore.
Unrocky steps moved on bridge's rocks,
Beyond all tellings was the march of the flocks.

From a height Ram blessed them with grace of His sight,
And gazed the raves of Braves, with waves of might.
Surfaced themselves, eager inhabitants of the sea,
To imbibe the visage of the Fountain of mercy.

Aquatic lives, gathered nigh marge with zeal,
Crocs, alligators, corals, fishes, sharks, snakes, eels.
Their innate enmity they all forgot,
They vied to have just a look of the Lord.

Perched on billows from heights saw some,
Some dared to come on diluvium.
The wrinkled Blue looked hued carpet,
While aquatic lives filled it's surface.

Billows=huge waves ; Diluvium=sand and gravel left behind the flood of waves.

Army proceeded on Lord's behest,
The Bridge looked as if sucking host's vastness.

Couplet: *Bridge being jammed with crowd,*
Some hopped over monsters on wave,
Some crammed the clouds,
And all along scudded.

Their every step, with fire of eager soul,
Before tides of sea-waves, heightened many fold.
Rocky bridge turned smooth, with million's move,
For the lotus feet of two brothers to soothe.

With the stride of zeal, on wings of Lord's grace,
Flood of troops marched with marshalled pace.
At the amusing spectacle Lord Ram laughed,
Along with troops, two brothers too marched.

Ram walked over bridge reached the southern coast,
Words had limit for infinite of the hosts.
Then Lord encamped; asked the troops,
To go and regale themselves on fruits roots.

On behest, glad mood, Monkeys-bears force,
Ran off all about for the lavish source.
Nature had already laden trees for legion,
Keeping away the regard of the season.

They would eat the picks to their fill,
And would hurl fruit stones towards Lanka from hills.
If they ever found a straggling demon,
They all hemmed him, nay, they would maim.

Those who had thus lost ears and nose,
Rushed crying to the Raavan's court.

Straggling=wandering.

The mo, Raavan heard sea had been bridged,
Awe creased on foreheads he exclaimed in unease—

Couplet: *"What ? Has He ? is it true ?*
Bridged the Deep, the Main, the Brine,
The Billow, the Waves, Sea, the Blue,
The Tides, Ocean, the Hyaline * 6

THE BRAGGART KING OF LANKA

To mask his nerves he stretched his lips
To smile; but in distress he was dipt.
For his palace he hopped and left the court,
Welcomed by pensive Mandodari, his consort.

She had already known, the foray across the waves
In mere sport; of troops of braves.
She was caught in the puzzle of dilemma,
Between duty for consort and the truth of Dharma.

She bowed her head as humble supplicant,
And spake to him in honeyed accent
"Get rid O Lord ! of these stormy Clouds,
On Lanka lo! A disaster crowns.

"Bow thy will before the Lord of lords,
Be heedful ! discard the discord.
"forgo ego, listen to my love,
We 'll be woes' target, if Ram is thy foe.

"I see blood sheds on thy sable dress,
I see the disaster on thy able race.
"Keeping hostility, with Him is not worth,
Who hath come to relieve the burdened Earth.

---

*Raavan the ten headed monster, worded the ocean in different ten names.

"Master as He is masterth time and fate,
Revere Him, Lest its call of sure death.

Couplet: *"Thy craze at this age,*
Will raze thy savage race,
From desires thou must retire,
My privilege may not be reveged. 7

"Bow thy will, bow thy head,
Keep my affection, keep what i said,
Restore Siya to Him, It's only worth,
Pass reign to thy son, retire to Vanprasth.*

"Renouncing to worthless charms, glittering pomp,
Retire to forest and worship Lord Ram.
"Ram ist a warrior and a saviour too,
If thou go submissive, He wilt rescue.

"Thy lust and desire should have sated by now,
None is left in world to be won by thou.
"Thou art a triumphant from end to end,
It's a trend, the reign should go now to next hands.

"This maxim is declared by ancient wise—
'A monarch should retire in fourth stage of life.'
"The man, might, mammon, military go down,
If Master of all the Creation frawns.

"He who creates, develops, destroys,
Worship the self same Ram, forgo earthly ties.
"Thy reign is so trivial to renounce,
On thou,if in barter, His blessings crown.

"For lives and lives sages thrive to realize,
'ts His grace that His grace, at thy door hath arrived.

---

* a retired life in woods for spiritual gain.

"My advice will surely bring,
Not the infamy but the great esteem.

Couplet: *"I clasp thou by feet,*
Worship Ram and His feats,
For thou it doth meet,
Thy 'I-am'ness' is thy defeat." 8

Unstirred ego of the wretch, rocked not,
His own glory he himself harped—
" O Honey ! be no prey of idle fear,
What a warrior am I, who is my peer?

"Behave thyself like my bold queen,
Feared are numbered with dead, O craven thing!
"Earthlings nay gods godlings, goddesses,
At my service, all are my puppets.

"The clock, Age, Death I have conquered,
Then why thy liquid eyes are dimmed with fear?"
Ego deafened the King and the Queen turned dumb,
Helpless she conceived, the ill-doom hath come.

'Ego's his folly maketh him blind-deaf,
He seeth nor listenth the hovering death.'
Left palace reached court inflated he,
Asked the counsellors of war strategy.

"Why ask this Lord? 'ts no matter moot,
Men, monkeys and bears are our food."

PRAHASTHA'S ADVICE

Couplet: *Prahastha* thus reacted*
"claques in counsel are foes
Should flattery have no place
Their words are, thanatos." 9

Thanatos=instinct for self destruction/death; Claques=flatterers; *Son of Raavan.

"Its brand's deeds not blarney of stupids,
With which thy Kingdom wilt succeed.
"Recall ! strange monkey sprang across the brine,
Took away town's sleep and the shine.

"They crow here, who dared not that Prow,
Their bragging could not quench inferno.

"When that Vaanar keeled town; knelt champs of this court,
Arson of Lanka was his mere sport.
"What ! where was your diabolic fight then?
What ! did none of ye have appetite then?

"Heed me ! O Sire ! be heedful to His deeds,
Could He be a Mortal who had bridged the sea?
"Pleasant are ever the flannel words,
But then in crude hours are not worth.

"In mannerism of court, the courtiers boast,
But belied bragging in the Bella bringeth remorse.
"This might, magnificience, mammon is waste all,
If true words keep a hide in the court hall.

"Most salutary I say, yet jarring may be,
Turn Ram and his army from enmity.
"Let the malice die off, on my request,
The Ruin will reign thy realm, lest.

Couplet: *"Return his consort back,*
Lanka, from war 'll be free.
Giving up enmity itself,
Ist a joy of the victory." 10

"My salutary advice tho' may jar,
But saves from havoc of impending war.

Belied=false ; Bella=war; Arson=firing the house as an assault; Blarney=flatter talk.

"send envoy the nobbled Siya may be returned,
And nobleness of thy race may be retained.

"Shun passion, smiling face thou mayst wear,
Return Her ; foe may, as friend appear.
"Shift thy Noble mind, for mea culpa,
Shrift by the Absolute wilt absolve thou from awe.

"War ist internecine, my words are all-love,
My hilt is strong, yet in heart lives a dove.
Raavan erupted at his son,-
"fool ! Who hath taught you such lesson.

"Craven-thing in you speaks, Be bold !
They nothing own, who own no verve of soul.
"Not the size of sword but the size of soul,
On the fate of war, hath true control.

"How will you face fight with a dove within you,
Which flatters here for foe to woo.
"Coward's words in the counsel who share,
Better leave they ! the burthen court'll not bear."

On hearing the harsh words those barbed,
Prahastha left court uttering bitter remarks—
'Where wrong prevails and truth fails flat,
There swift and sure cometh doomed fate.'

Vapouring he left the court in eve,
Gazing own ego, Raavan was easily deceived.
To the towering height among garrets and turrets,
Went he for dance and music to divert and relax.

He sat to hang loose in the hour tough,
Songsters, nymphs danced, lauded; he was further puffed.

Nobbled=kidnapped; Internecine=murderous; Mea culpa=confession; Shrift= free from sin.
Garret=Atari ; Turrets=Small towers.

Couplet: *Dipt he in lavishes of lust,*
Blinded by the luxuries
Sick of puppet's lustre,
With temper of temerity. 11

All-cheek, all-sick and weak at lust,
Had not tic on face, for the risks' outburst.
And here, Ram encamped on ranges of Suvel,
With his vast army of bellicose, all marshalled.

THE CAMP OF RAM

Spotting very lofty lovely shining peak,
Laxman spreaded blossoms and tender leaves,
Which he covered with furred mat,
On this seat Himself the Merciful rested.

Lord Kipt, kept bow, quivers on His left and right,
Under Canopy of starry vault of the night.
Lord placed His head on lap of Sugriv,
With Ram, the war was won, all believed.

Eager Champs gathered all about,
To prolong waking hours of His drowse.
Angad, Hanumaan kneaded His lotus feet,
How blest were they indeed.

And then Laxman sat on waking vigile,
Lo ! how doth he, his devotion fulfils.

Couplet: *On Earth no couch, on grass, no silk,*
Thus rested Shri Ram,
Blest are those, who are dipt,
In this 'calmed image' befo' storm. 12

Temerity=risk taking of fool hardiness.
Kip=to lie, to sleep.

In the Lord's lulling eyes,
Came in tranquilized moon,
'just look!' Ram voiced,
" King of night with starry cordon." 13

"Lo! Nectariferous moon rainth its ambrosia,
May it's elixir fill our militia.
"Bowers seem host of imposters in sable dress,
Exposed by the flambeau of moon rays.

The Night has curfewed life, nay, air dare not,
Only milky orb marches on stellar path.
Lord continued, " now brethren ! I ask ye!
Say ! what's that dark spot on moon's face, Phoebe?

The chief of army, Sugriv thus said
'it's only shadow of Earth that reflects
Said some, "The Rahu gnaws and the moon wanes,
Its scar thus left on moon in crescent."

"No ! when the Creator fashioned the design of beauty,
From the frame of phoebe it scooped some honey.
"The selene is serene shows stoical attitude,
Even with gloom in heart, it's face blooms.

Lord said, "Bane is moon's brother, most beloved
That is why in his heart he kept,
"His poison, through his envenomed rays,
Abseils to torment the souls of berefts."

Couplet: *"Being worthy votary of Thine,"*
Hanuman thus spake—
"Thy swarthy visage he enshrines
That appears, like a dark patch." 14

Flambeau=flaming torch(mashaal)
Selene=Moon; Bane=deadly poison; Abseil=to descend by means of rope.

Ram heard Hanuman
'the depth of words has love b'neath,'
Ram smilt and reckoned
'Eyes perceive what the heart seeth. 15

" O Vibhishan !" Ram said, " Lo ! gathering fast scuds
And heed ! near and far the thundering thuds."
"See ! the lowering of the misty helm,
I fear, may ensue the severe hail."

"O Lord" ! from Vibhishan came reply,
"Nor the hail nor the helm but the hell that Thou dost espy."

"It's no thunderous hail, no cirrus no nimbus
It's a Brute's presence that accursed us.
Ravenous Raavan witnessing music and dance,
On a boasting tower luxuriating in lust.

Spreading over his head a regal tabernacle,
That appears as thick clouds sable.
Jewels of queen Mandodari and other damsels,
Like flash of the lightening, those resemble.

Sound like thunder which is incomparable,
Is the sweet rumbling of tabors and cymbals.
With smile, single shaft was aimed by Ram,
When He perceived Raavan's arrogant pomp.

Couplet: *Swift shaft of Ram struck,*
Queen's jewels Raavan's Chhatra and crown,
Every eye was awe-struck,
None knew, what went wrong? 16

Scud=wind driven clouds ; Cirrus/ Nimbus=Heavy rainy clouds.

THE FIRST WARNING

Couplet: *A marvel, the shaft performed,*
And returned to quiver of Ram,
Whole assembly was alarmed
At hindrance of their daily charm. 17

Nor the seismal thrust nor blustery gust,
Nor did they see attacking missiles' rush.
Nevertheless, they figured it as ill-omens,
As a forwarning for the Chief of demons.

Raavan laughed off " how can be mere falling of crown,
Be doomed, who's booned with heads dropping down.
"The fright was never lankiness of Lanka,
How ye be awe's target who are the embodied awe?"

All returned, but in queen's heart qualm lodged,
Since she knew not her jewels-how to dust dropt?
Her lachrymose eyes bleached her face's rose,
Funk face she prayed on knees and toes.

"O King ! He is no a mortal thing, indeed,
Do not slight the might of His wight feat.
"No the fiend's, but cherish in, a heart of friend,
To the boon, turns the bane, from ill it defends.

Couplet: *"Believe me ! what I believe,*
Might of man can't cross mighty Main,
Him as Almighty, O King ! perceive,
May He be a boon not bane. 18

"He is endless wide from hyades to Paradise,
With His Own will, He came mansized.

Blustery=wind strong and noisy; Lankiness=weakness.
Lachrymose=tearful; Wight=Suprahuman ; Main=ocean.

"He, the Master who masterth thine and mine soul,
Nay, He disciplineth cosmos and planets' roll.

He, the vital of every beat, integral of every bit,
Life and death depend on His brows' knit.
Through pious verses His speech is holy text,
His silence is lash to fiends, His hush is devout's test.

The greed His lips, Maya* the glittering teeth,
His endless gesture controlth galaxies.
"The fire, His mouth, The Water, His gesture,
Mountains, His crest, veins denoted by rivers.

"Laes, trees, jungles, groves, meadows,
On the Earth spreaded are His pilose.
"Brine's His belly, pearls, jewels His organs,
Thus universe is the sketch of His person.

Couplet: *"Lord Shiv is His ego,*
The Creator is His reason,
Divinity is His mind,
Trinity is His vision. 19

"Same divineness cometh in His person,
Malice with Him is malison,
Not enemy but enmity be won,
Ego is thy foe, needs be shunned." 20

Raavan laughed off hearing his wife,
For her folly that was blind at her husband's might.
"Wifely love leads to craven path,
Scared who are lost, those champs won't last.

"All skinny, no heart, no mind, no soul,
Ill, unskilled, chilled is the woman's mould.

Pilose=soft hair over body; *cosmic illusion.
Malison=curse.

"Folly, timidity are woman's name,
Such backings to warriors are, loss to claim.

"Armed Kings, who in fields, armlets of queens hear,
Revels of laurels they never share.
"O Dear ! what ever illusive tricks my foe knows,
Are finally all under my control.

"Worthless panic in you, O beloved ! stay
So you ask me at this moment to parley.
"Knowing my splendour, hope !, you are not alarmed,
May Your genuine heart, not fear rampant Ram."

Couplet: *'Befo' vain glory words go in vain,'*
The queen was thus convinced,
'Death had deluded husband',
My lord is ' slave of sins.' 21
The intripid, as he was,
At every advice he joked
Thus Stupid's night passed,
With more proud his dawn broke. 22

Reeds heed no vernal note,
Have no blossom, no fruits but mere nodes.
Just the same, fools heed no thought,
Even tho' the Lord Himself hath taught.

Half wit, Highheaded blinded by proud,
Entered the court, sat on boastful couch.
Here, Shri Ram woke, at the eastern break,
And asked counsellors "what to do next?"

"Bellicose troops are not just to sing ballads,
Neither they are here, my paeans to belaud.

Parley=to talk for peace with enemy.

"A quick course now we must adopt,
From the sick Earth demonry must be knocked.

Chief of bear's race Jamwant spake
"to my own light, wisdom I do suggest,
"Ram ! Thy eyes bringest calm, while brows are alarm,
Thy arms embrace the blest, while armed hands art storm.

"May be sent an envoy, Angad is exact,
With courtesy, Counsel, counters and courage."
Taking counsel Ram turned to Angad,
"Go to Lanka dear son ! for my purport.

"Go with stud of Truth, and steady troth,
Talk to serve my cause, and to interest foes.
"Mighty lore of the clever envoy should,
Bring winning joy with no gore imbrued."

Couplet: *Blest with Ram's behest,*
Bowing head Angad arose—
"Thy command is Thy grace,
Thine cause, my life's purpose." 23

□

Gore=blood; Imbrued=Stained.

This rascal ego must be obliterated.

—Ram Krishna Paramhans

ENVOY ANGAD IN RAAVAN'S COURT

Angad said—

Couplet: *"Once comes in Lord's thought, the object*
Is ever self- accomplished,
Lord asked me the task, yet,
To honour, what I wished." 1

With steady eyes and fearless steps,
Bowing head to all, Angad departed.
A gallant, as he was adept in warfare,
So moved he, his Lord's splendour to declare.

He escaladed swift over the carbels,
Playfully from bailey jumped in ballium of castle.
Soon, Raavan's son Prahastha came across,
Both were unrivelled bellicose.

As they met they had debates, backchats,
Soon they both tilted at skirmish combat.
The stiff Angad seized that demonic stuff,
And scoffed and with tough hands dashed him to turf.

Bailey=outerwall; Ballium=courtyard of castle; Tilt at=fight; Carbels=brick projections on wall(of city).

Whoever witnessed this event,
Ran away and screamed-"O that same! not again!!"
Demons scattered helter-skelter,
Scared realizing their days are numbered.

Cries and screams filled milieu with awe
'Same monkey had come who had burnt Lanka.
'What reward he brings now'-every mind was dismayed,
Unasked, but the citizens showed him the way.

The brave went and rent thro' the crowds,
If he but looked at anyone he would dry out.

Couplet: *Witty Angad, knitting brows,*
Fixing mind on Shri Ram
Entered Raavan's court,
With gestures all unalarmed. 2

Lionized Raavan with lion's countenence,
Sable dressed he saw Angad with eager glance.
A hush stretched as if the Death was passing by,
Raavan laughed at this and cried

"Go ! and drag him before my presence,
Does his death wait for my hands."
With the boast of bravery he kept sitting alone,
Marshals brought him before Raavan's throne.

With the weight of ego, Raavan was sunk in throne,
'As a sign of sinking of his reign' Kapi reckoned.
The Envoy of Ram enjoyed being caught,
Eagerly inclined to perform his Lord's cause.

Sable dress, dark face Raavan looked as heap
Of collyrium, breathing deadly hiss.

Rent=splitted into two(the crowd).

Like crawling snakes moved his limbs, arms,
Like palm-leaves appeared his palms.

His mouth, lips, ears looked as caves and chasms,
So pranked he was, as flaunter of mammon.
With inflincing mind as the monkey entered,
Abruptly assembly rose at the sight of Angad.

Even before his presence, Raavan saw the court awed,
Filled with great fury he looked further odd.

Couplet: *Braved he, being Envoy-O-Ram,*
Bowed he, employed courtesy,
And stood there unalarmed
As a boastful lion among beasts. 3

Raavan roared "O monkey ! dared you how?
" Me, the messenger of Ram, came to advise thou."
" I owe to thy intimacy with my father,
Entirely thy interest hath brought me here."

The sweatless face, with sweet of his voice,
Such envoy of choice, his Lord employed
" O High-born ! High brow !! O Worshipper of Shiv !!,
Since my childhood, I have heard thy narratives.

"Being Shiv's favoured, crowned with His blessings,
Thou havest won gods, godlings, earthlings.
"But the Kingly pride had blinded thou, the worst,
Thy folly, carried off, Siya, the Maa of Universe.

"O crony of my father ! listen my friendly advice,
Lord Ram may absolve thy every vice.
"With eyes low, head bowed, O man of straw !
Go to Lord Ram for mea culpa.

Flaunter=who exhibits (as show off.); Mea culpa=confession of guilt.

"Go with queens, kins, kids, keeping ahead Siya,
Thus, repair to Him, shedding all awe.

Couplet:

"And the saviour Ram may be prayed,
"Save me! Absolve me!!
I am transgressor, a sinner yet,
I am at thy mercy." 4

"Such petitions full of all contritions,
Will absolve sinning soul of all malisons."
These words of Monkey put Raavan's monkey up,
" O lemur ! O langur !! mind your lapsus.

" O fool ! it's your folly that dogmatise,
I'm avowed foe of men and gods all wides.
"Yet tell ! O Chap !! the kinship you made,
And said of your father, claimed 'was my comrade."

"I'm Angad, Baali's son, didst thou ever meet him?"
Hearing Baali's name, Raavan seemed trimmed.
Gathering self, coming out of unease he spake
"There was a Vaanar Baali, I do remember, yes !

"But then being Baali's son, your race how you ruin,
Your pomp, prowess, pranks need be pruned.
"In case, Ram's envoy you call yourself,
In vain, where you are born, goes that race.

"Now tell me of Baali, how is he?
Angad laughed at this and reparteed
"Ask me not, wait just ten days,
Thou wilt be sent soon, your friend to embrace.

"The fate of hostility to Ram; your friend
Will tell thou, 'bringeth none but the bane.

Absolve=forgive a sin.
Trimmed=conquered; Contrition=remorse for sin; Dogmatise=speak in overconfidence.

"A bosom with no blessings is a barren land,
But then rain of prudence may seed in foe, a friend.

Couplet: *'Me' the ruiner, thou the saviour of race,'*
Thy sins in thou thus brewed,
Even the blind and the deaf,
Know everything what's the truth. 5

"How hard is thy heart, how strange is thy thought,
That burst not cherishing such odd."
Raavan blasted, "O Wretch ! I put up with you,
As I am bound to decorum and my virtues."

Angad replied–

"I have heard O Raavan! of thy true decorum,
From the fact that other's wife thou havest stolen.
"Too pity ! thou didst uphold piety,
Even when thy sister was maimed, thou possessedst modesty.

"So benign thou art, that thy malignant ire,
Fled while lanky Lanka was set to fire.
"Thou didst free that monkey forgiving his wrongs,
I am chanced to see in you, O King ! a monk.

Couplet: *"Prate no more now shut !*
O monkey ! enough is enough
Lest the death can, but, make you butt
My choler is tough. 6

"My palms could lift the mount Kailash,
How did you keep from my vast glorious past?
"Listen ! Angad ! war is no perching up tree,
It's nor hop-jump; nor for plum, a melee.

"Ye 'll be snatched out of your life,
O Fool ! O food ! on ye demonry survives.

Butt=victim

"Your bereaved Master is already weak,
Similarly grieved seems the younger ascetic.

"Who else can encounter me in war,
Try not ye to catch a tartar.
"Sugriv and Jamwant wait for last pyre,
Lesser use of them in battle, the better.

"While Nal-Nil play their tricks on brick,
As warrior, these architects will not click.
"But then there is one, whose might I approve,
A macrurous, tailed with some explosive.

"With arsons who spreaded ado, the same envoy,
In battle with that toy, I'll enjoy.
"Don't tell !" funny!" cut in Angad "that puny monkey
Could burn down thy boastful city."

"How a petty runner of Sugriv, here became a champ
'Ts beyond belief, thou must havest dreamt.
"He is very little thing, for thou, to impress,
Among millions of warriors, he is puniest.

Couplet: *"Yes ! seems he must have burnt,*
Without behest of Lord
That's why he hath not returned,
And remained in hiding, awed. 7

"What thou dost declare
I hear with no rage,
For the courage of our warriors
Fighting thou, bringeth no grace. 8

Catch a tartar=fight with very strong enemy.
Puny=weak

"With equals, make friend
And peers should be foes,
It 'll be aberrant,
If lion kills the frog." 9

"It 'll on Ram's part, tho'
Belittling to make thou a foe,
Killing thou, wilt be greater blame,
Like punier is punished by a prow." 10

—Pert expert monkey pelted
The Sarcastic pelters
Raavan showed no hatred
Tho' simmered yet he simpered— 11

Raavan laughed at—

"The virtue of mockery, monkeys ever possess,
And dance for their Master any where unbashed.
"Bravado for a monkey to hop in some hope,
But for his Master, traps of woes, it may ope.

"Your race serveth Ram, so Ram you worship,
For the same Ram you dance and skip.
"So your race, how could you deceive,
I respect your mind full of glib speech."

Quick wit Angad provoked Raavan
"Thou art really kind to killer of thy son.
"Thy glory is told extolled by Hanumant,
Who killed demons, and The Lanka who burnt.

"Who killed thy sons, keeled town by arson,
Thy amiablility saved him from thy action.

Simmered=in state of suppressed anger ; simpered=to smile in affected manner.
Pert=smart/over smart.

"What Hanumaan witnessed I find in thou, the same,
O Kind ! thou havest no anger, no remorse, no shame."

Tho' simmered but simpered, then burst in guffaw,
The Kapi enjoyed, the courtiers were filled with awe.
"Baali's name, O monkey ! is your shield,
I desist, lest I would have killed(you).

"You talk what you have been taught,
Be not victim of folly, for no fault on your part."

"O Vile ! be not boaster of those ascetics' exile,
While Baali was my pal, why you go hostile.

"Hostility with Raavan, is to claim the death,
Be not my game, lemming's life will be waste.
"If a prince careth not his race at war,
Revenue and reverence from state depart.

"For your folly knows not Raavan's great name,
Unshamed you stand, own loss you claim."
"I know many faces of Raavan", monkey said,
"One was tied by children when he went to Hades."

"King Sahastrabahu captured another Raavan again,
Kept with him for fun as a thing strange."

Couplet:
"Yet for one Raavan I tell,
With much of diffidence,
Under Baali's arm who was held,
I ask 'was he different?" 12

"Heed ! O Vaanar, Valour of these very arms,
Which lifted mount Kailash, the same I am.

Lemming=self destructive person ; Game=prey.

"In worship of Shiv I offered as blossom,
Own heads, but I never plumed."

"My lofty-line keeps me from saying my greatness,
With your littleness you boast your prowess.
"Winds know my pace, thunders know my voice,
The sun knows my rage, heaven knows my choice.

"I master the seasons, I control cloud's pinions,
Orbs of welkin are puppets nay I control moon and Sun.
"When I step mounts move; oceans lull in awe,
My face scares lions, what of men of straw.

"Do you know me not? Are you lying prattler?
World knows me as prow, of peerless power,"
" O puny wretch! I have fathomed you well,
Belittling Raavan you extol mortals."

Couplet: *The boastful Raavan bragged,*
Thro' his long winded spiel,
His lust consumed his shame,
A ghost in him unveiled. 13

Raavan's own fanfaronade and Ram's disregard,
Raised Angad's rage and raised discord—
"O mindless wretch ! mind !! what you say
Revere Ram; Severe cometh your way, lest.

"How He be simply a flesh and breath,
He ist Creator of life, He ist above death.
"Who puffth soul into every mould,
Who ist Ancient of the oldest of the old.

"The Lord, who broke the bow of Shiv,
And thus pensive Janak who had relieved.

Plumed=boasted.

"In Swayamvar, herds of, kinglets gathered with ego,
He broke the Shiv's bow, their ego also.

For the bays in the same arena you failed,
Once again a belial in you prevails.
"Is paragon just a stone, is the Sun just planet,
Is the Ganges just the stream, are Veds just a text.

Couplet: *"He's Supreme, O dullard !*
He cometh here man-sized,
How "Pranav" be plain word,
Can paradise be called satellite?" 14

"Further how you call Hanumaan, mere Monkey,
Your son who killed, Great Lanka who keeled.
"Unhurted, Whole Lanka, who destroyed,
Not the mere Monkey, Hanumant is Ram's envoy.

"Still you have chance, discard ! the discord,
Give up hypocrisy, Surrender to the Lord.
"O King but of fools ! brag not in vain,
None can save if, you go against.

"Still now if you don't listen to me,
Your heads for monkeys 'll be plaything.
"All-wrongs, what your heads ghostly brewed,
Will be daubed with your own ghastly dews.

"Such bouncing verve of your nerves 'll melt,
In battle when Ram his enraged darts 'll pelt."
The Devotional flambeau with which Angad was torched,
With its heat Raavan's heart got scorched.

Unflattering lips and fearless eyes,
Firm, faithful voice, should be face of envoy.

Belial=devil; 'Pranav'= OM (sonic manifestation of the Supreme.)
Ghastly dews=blood.

"The immodest words may bring death of envoy,"
Ravenous Raavan thus began his reply.

Couplet: *"Kumbhkaran my beloved fra,*
Is a giant goliath,
My son Meghnaad, foe's awe,
Are my right and left. 15

"Their valour had made them greatest victor,
Together our might multiplies further.
"In a mo could I go seven billows, across,
These biceps have observed me lifting the Kailash.

"Fire in me ashenth the envied heaven,
Poor gods, godules hanker after my mammon.
"If your Master hath bridged the brine,
Even then I call him not the Divine.

"O fool ! puny birds with puniest pinions,
May fly across the tides of ocean.
"My eyes are oceans, my rage it's billows,
The heavens, the Earth in it I would swallow.

"If some trick ; some magic your Master knows,
Yet I keep Him not in the count of heroes.
"My arms are oceans with flooding strength,
And tides of awe, 'll drown your legion.

"An earthly prince you do glorify,
Should He be Lord, why He sends envoy.
"See my gigantic arms, then see ascetic Ram,
Then you extoll Him, even then if He charms.

Hanker after=long for/crave for.

Couplet: *With lot of go and ego*
Own prowess he crowed—
"The one and only Hero,
That's me, only me, I know." 16

"I offered my heads as flowers to Shiv,
Narrative of lifting Kailash every one knew."
"The divined prophecy I know to be false,
How me, the immortal, be killed by mortals?

"My beheaded heads, I do not vaunt,
Havest divine power to replant.
"The Ancient Brahma was too senile,
For prophecy of my death to divine.

"Yet on my face, you exalt some else as champ,
All-mouth you have crossed all decorum and shame.
Angad replied, "As you are shame faced,
It seems, abashed you are, hearing own brags."

" 'Ts only Mount Kailash, is in reverence of your mind,
Hence you have just told me that twenty times.
"Not the brags of words but the edge of the swords,
Ever rage of the truth, that hath conquered."

Couplet: *"Boast not self as behemoth,*
Ponder your existence in cosmos,
Before Almighty's firing shafts
You are a little moth." 17

"Moths immolate in flame, donkeys lift loads,
But they are never considered heroes.
"It's folly in you, only that dares,
Voice of lore should, learned advice share.

Vaunt=boast.
Behemoth=monsterous giant; Immolate=sacrifice.

"If folly is deaf, keeps self untaught,
Himself, the man plays doom's part.
"My task of envoy hath bound me in chains,
Lest I would have be lesson to your ignorance.

"In limits of envoy I smashed not your jaw,
And not have recovered back Maa Siya.
"In you braggart ever reflects a coward,
I would have taught you lesson, but for my Lord's words.

"Your deeds proved you a coward, that you have stolen,
Another's wife, O thief ! while She was alone.
"If I were not afraid of Ram's insult,
I would have wrought a wonder before your court."

Couplet: *"Dashing you to the ground,*
Smashing your all army,
Mashing the messed town,
I would take your wives with me." 18

"It would not bring me any grace even then,
How it brings a kudos to slay a slain.
"Who are strayed off the path of virtue,
The holy text, whose ego, disapprove,

"Who are hostile to benigns, bovines and the Blue*,
O Raavan ! Whose ravening thirst is ever new,
"Who are hostile to innate worshippers of Vishnu,
Who tempt other's faith to impose own view,

"Who try to whitewash** their black hand's hue,
Who polish their wrongs by hook or by crook,
"Whose malignant mind ever spoils benign milieu,
Who terrorize the Earth with ghastly dew,

---

* blue (used for nature, the sky and ocean.)
** justify; ghastly dew=blood shed; Ravening=greedy.

"Vile, senile, fragile, anile, are the few,
They are more dead than alive, just like you.

"O Ravenous Raavan ! I see you as a corpse,
From killing you, So, my hand stops."
Thus the monkey put Raavan's monkey up,
His volcano burst out with furious puff—

"Your Lord can't save your breath, O Ape !
Tho' pigmy but big mouth, from my extreme step.

Couplet: *"Me, Raavan, a Throned king,*
Raven heaven and mortal coils
While Ram is a Thrown thing,
By His own king into exile. 19

"Man is demon's palate,
Your Lord is one such,
Should He realize His fate,
Learn! this fact, cease! to be perverse." 20

While the Vile demon, against Ram reviled,
Enraged Angad turned further wild.
for, who is not sick, hearing polemics of Hari-Har,
A greater sin he ever incurs.

Struck he mighty arms against ground in ire,
In furious protest then he clamoured.
Earth trembled, courtiers tumbled in awe,
Some slipped, some slipped away in phobophobia.

Ten headed Raavan, too, was about to topple down,
Recovered he, stood holding his crowns.
Yet fell on the ground some of his diadems,
Angad hurled them to his Lord's camps.

Phobophobia=being alarmed of approaching fear; Revile=aroused; Polemic=abusive criticism.

Monkeys fled seeing speedy diadems as meteors,
'is it volley of weapons by Raavan in ire.
'Ram smilt "nor meteors nor weapons, nor planets,
They are diadems of Raavan which Angad despatched."

Couplet:

Playfully Hanumaan sprang,
Caught in hands the diadems,
Monkeys, bears gazed, stranged,
The dazzling like huge diamond. 21

Here, diadems were placed,
Near Ram by Hanumant,
There, Raavan cried enraged
"Catch and zap him at once." 22

"After killing him sally forth at once,
Devour all monkeys, bears leaving not the one.
"Nay, let the Earth be cleaned of all the beasts,
Then go and capture alive the two ascetics.

Angad yelled as he got engraged
"You wag your tongue like a shameless.
"O imposter ! do ever your dull mind espy
'Such is my sin'- ever you realize.

"Wine of mineness and meanness hath sloshed you,
Your delirious abuse will, your ruin, prove.
"O Perverse ! sure the death hath taken over you,
You will reap doom soon, when our troops belabour you.

"What the consequences are knocking your door,
Lesser said of that, the better.
"Why's your tongue, that abused Ram, fell not,
No wonder ! on battlefield with your heads will drop.

Wag=rock/move.

Couplet: *"Your eyes have no light, and mind no lore,*
That The supreme cometh mansized,
Ram's shafts are thirsting for your gore,
O dull of unworthy womb! fie!!" 23

"I spare you b'cause He mayst be annoyed,
I limit my task, I am here as envoy.
"But for behest of my Master that restrains,
Lest I would have smashed you with these hands.

"My rage hath no permission of Lord, to reveal,
Lest you and your Lanka I would have keeled.

"Lanka is my fruit but I will not eat,
B'cause insect like you reside here to rot it.
Raavan smilt, " Who hath made you such vaunting liar,
Must be those Two, never boasted your father."

"O Raavan ! till I tear your arms,
Till I shatter your head, blustering liar, I am.
"My fixed mind, firm step is a fancy, sure,
Till from your cut throat sprout fountains of gore."

Saying so, recalling Lordship of his Lord,
Angad planted his foot in midst of the court's quad.
"If you can but stir my foot a little bit,
I shall accept defeat, Ram 'll return forth with."

"My foot is firm, as the footings of my faith,
Potentiated by my Lord, you yourself assess."
Yelled Raavan "champs ! seize the Monkey by the leg,
To the ground dash him enough he hath bragged."

With delight rushed many warriors stout,
Employed their vices, devices and clout.

Keel=overturn; Court's quad=open square space (in assembly.)

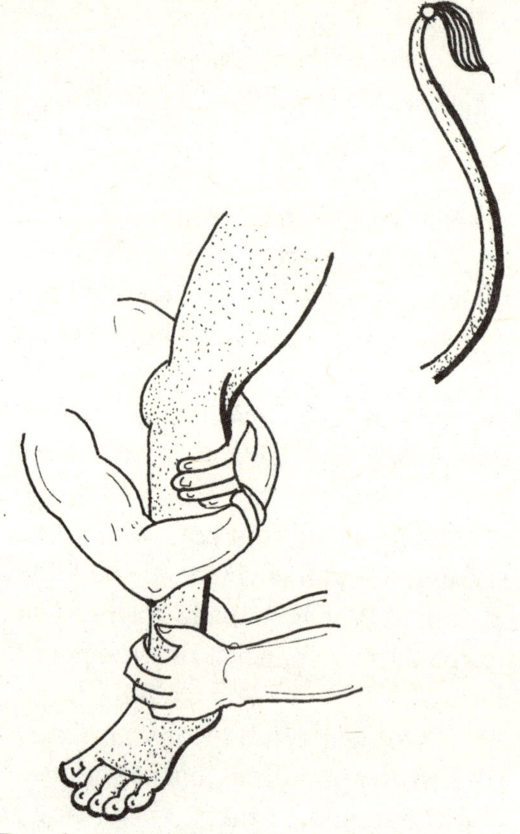

But the foot of Angad refused to stir,
Thus the diabolic power before Truth was jeered.

Then the tired champs retired back,
Toiled face, soiled lustre, coiled head they sat.
Gathering anew, their thew in sinew,
They dashed forward, foot remained unmoved.

Foot remained unstirred like a devout's trust,
It moved not a bit like sensual's lust.

Couplet: *Myriads raided to thrust,*
Swooned down clung again,
But the foot did not budge,
All vices' devices went in vain. 24

Budge=to move slightest.

The Faith of envoy and the Truth of a prow,
Was elixired with a go to defeat pride of foe.
With own shrewd deeds who never shrunk abashed,
Seeing Angad's strength, all they were embarrassed.

While the court is defeated, shrunken King must be,
But Raavan himself rose on the challenge of monkey.
Even as Raavan moved, his foot to grasp,
Monkey said, " bowing to my feet you can't be saved.

"Stupid ! go and cling to Shri Ram's feet"
Words bruised, he blushed, he turned to his seat.
All faces looked bleached, faded pomp and mammon,
Even as glory of moon fadeth before the infant sun.

As if despoiled of all riches, into throne he coiled,
Tho' he foisted smile, but his face looked foiled.
Gold, glory, grandeur, are all soil,
for, whose deed, and mind, to Ram, are hostile.

"It's brows' play for Ram to dissolve and create
The souls; nay earths, nay galaxies and planets."
With these comments further proceeded Lord shiv,
And continued relating the pleasing narrative.

'He hath vitalized each gravel with power great,
Each of bits in it's core, thunderbolt's power, has.
So how His envoy's vow should stand not,
But the shameless Raavan sat with no guilt for own faults.

Court witnessed unstirred challenge of Angad's foot,
And witnessed unstirred revenge of the his mood.
"O Raavan! Here, I have sported with you,
I will daub warfield to last of your dews."

Angad departed from the court saying so,
Glorifying His Lord's splendour all above.

Foist=impose upon; foiled=frustrated.

Chill of hush filled the court, and rushed along their veins,
Courtier's heart froze on Angad's challenge.

Couplet: *Winning even before, 'the war is faught',*
Keeping Shri Ram in thought
Setting Raavan's might at naught
Angad returned to his Lord. 25

WIFELY ADVICE TO THE VICE

Raavan seeing chilli's red on the horizon west,
In chill of chagrin he returned to palace.
To the vice, queen Mandodari advised,
'O Wise! feud with Ram is claiming the high-price.

"Abandon perversity, ponder in thy mind,
Thou couldst not cross even Lakhan's thin line.
"Whose messengers do such strange feat,
How dost thou expect Him to defeat.

"Who bridged across waves with troops of monkeys,
To me looks our Lanka, mere Lanky.
"None can forget, the one, who laid waste Ashoka grove,
Nay, he killed thy beloved son under thy nose,

"Do not be indulged in empty pride,
Thy ego betrayth thou and misguideth.
"He ist Lord, Himself and no mere earthling,
He ist Ruler of Creation, King of the kings.

"In arena of Janak He only could tore bow,
Marich, Khar, Dushan had suffered fire of His arrows.
"thou, if are blind with twenty eyes to perceive
The might of Ram ; then ownself, thou dost deceive.

Couplet: *"Mind maketh thou a fop,*
Recognize His Perfect acts,
Who zapped Baali, Cyclops
His feats revealth the facts. 26

"How a mere man, could cross the Main,
'ts His divine feat that hadst made it certain.
"On mount Suvela, He hath encamped,
In thy interest, the envoy He hath sent.

"The size of fight, which the puny envoy has,
In ope court, thy might, that has embarrassed.
"Thy courtiers, too crow, the empty brags,
They are lesser counsellors, more claques.

"Call Him not a mortal, He hath wight's might,
Whom, thy wit, vim, whim, weapons canst not vie.
"Piled up charms, barm, arms and pomps,
The ruins, they claim, if are hostile to Ram.

"Our mortal clay hath numbered breaths,
In vain thou burdenst the pride on thy crest.
"The death, doth not smite with uplifted rods,
He strays victim's mind, his reason he robs.

Couplet: *"I saw ashes of my sons,*
And saw the capital burnt,
Turn to Ram, and not to bellum,
The good name, shouldst thou won. 27

"Sin ist name of defeat, maketh a man wallower,
Adore Him and win Him as His follower."
Words of consort pierced him like shafts,
Crawled his sleepless night, left palace at day break.

Fop=arrogant, boastful; Cyclops=one eyed demon (Kabandh)
Claque = flatterer
Bellum = war

Now he was unconcerned of words of his consort,
In his excess pride, all his fears blurred.
With which Raavan swelt, was empty pride,
The real pride of Suvela*, jewelled with Ram's camp this side.

Angad bowed at Ram's feet, as he arrived,
Lord lovingly seated him very nigh.
"Well done ! Angad I'm eager to know,
How did you fulfil task, I ask, Bravo!"

"Demon-king is cheered for his peerless might,
How your strange hand, reached his crest's height?
"How that wonder you little ! made possible,
And tossed his four crowns to this mount Suvela.

Angad mildly said, "O Lord Omniscient !
None of the crown of Lankesh, I have sent.
Those were four virtues those left, the king of cruel reign,
Like husk is weeded out by tender grains.

"Virtues that abide within king of right sceptre,
Are the genility, grace, goodness, grandeur.
"These are four footings of nobility,
So they themselves had stepped to Thee.

Couplet: *"With no pity, no piety,*
Dipt in ill-deeds, the heedless,
Lack-lore, on throne lordly,
Sure he waits for reaching death." 28

THE IMPENDING WAR BEGINS

At Angad's ingineous reply,
Noble minded Lord Shri Ram smiled
'Pacific words are not for that perverse'
Ram realized and swiftly summoned counsellors.

---

* the mount.

"Barbarian's town have massive four barbicans,
Take counsel as to how we should beset them."
Sugriv, Jambvaan, Vibhishan then recalling Ram,
Putting heads together reached to definite plan.

They divided monkey-host into four brigades,
To each appointed a General for each of the gate.
Then, the champ commanders they summoned,
Getting higher orders they rushed roaring like lions.

Mount peaks in hand, keeping Ram in core,
With din of roars, looking grim they sallied forth.
"glory be to Ram! glory be to the Lord!!
Ram's army moved, to the high-rampart.

Along sky they scudded, on ground they flooded,
Their furious faces, with ire, were studded.

Couplet: *The Ovations filled milieu,*
'Glory be to the Best of Raghus,
With eclats of Lakhan, Sugriv,
Troops drew with great thew. 29

The rumpus filled Lanka with scenes of bedlam
'The town is besieged by the rampant Ram.'
Raavan heard it and smilt with ego,
"the cheekiness of the monkeys, lo!"

"Monkeys seemed winged to die like moths,
Fate brought them nigh the hungry mouths."
The belial king was blind at thronged bellicose,
Belittled he, the matter, bursting in to belly laughs

Barbican=fortified gate

Raavan ordered-

"Sally forth all champs, seize those worms,
Catch and dispatch them in ditches, devour them on berms."
Sable vanguard and terrible infantry,
With maces, lances, machetes, axes, they sallied.

The foes to dismay, they displayed thirsty edges,
And lobber-heads lobbed in marshalling arrays.
Cannibals in ghastly lust to leech,
Rushed lechers in wish to relish on monkeys' lich.

Couplet: *With throws, bilbos, arrows-bows,*
Climbed up they rampart turrets.
On the barbican belial bellicose
waited to rebuff attack. *30*

The sable, vigil-rush on the auric rampart,
Looked like, on Mount Meru hang clouds dark.
Tocsins of impending blitz was heard,
Sparked off more chaos on rampart.

A chill ran along the demon's veins,
When they witnessed monkeys-bears from end to end.
Hiding on battlement they peeped thro' holes,
And saw closing in monkeys like boles.

Clefts, valleys, moats, would be none to their on-rush,
Robusts were closing like swarms of locust.
Then, bulky roars bullied from both sides,
Calling here on Ram, their on Raavan from height.

War- like warriors from the outer bailey,
Jumped on berms like worms for the array.
The heroes both sides fearless did stand,
To wound the foes and glorious wounds to sustain.

Ditch=moat around fort; Berm=A passage between fort–wall and moat; Bellicose = fighter
To leech=suck blood ; Lich=dead body.
Rebuff=repel
Blitz=attack (war); Tocsin=Alarm bell.

Stanza: *Barbarians jumped from barbicans*
And ran to clash with attackers,
And here, fierce monkeys, bears
Hurled rocks as spears over ogres.
They Smashed some, they dashed some
To the ground seizing by the legs;
The Ram's pages, in the rampage
With raised rage, began carnage.

Couplet: *Undoubted redoubtable champs,*
On escalade, the most agile,
Echoed glory of Lord's names,
Thus begun bellum-lethale. 31

Attacking demons, on them, Monkeys hopped,
With demons beneath, then they jumped from top.
Agile monkeys climbed up turrets, pierced thro' the fort,
And milieu filled with 'Jai Ram' echoes.

Sable host was smashed, mashed, crushed,
And was incapable to rebuff wild gush.
Then the rampant invaders havoced rampart,
Made a chaos among opposing vanguards.

As the clouds are scattered by strong blast,
Fled away sable infantry and vanguards.
Lamented peopled air in awe,
Once more they realized the lankiness of Lanka.

They rebuked 'Raavan's deeds as devil's greed
'now we'll be weevil of barley.'
When Raavan heard that demons had beaten a retreat,
Further more champions he rallied

"Not stand fierces but in fears who fled,
For them, thirsty edge of my brand waits.

Redoubtable=terrible; Bellum lethale=deadly war; Rebuff=drive back.

"You consumed on all lavishes in your life,
In battle now be ready for sacrifice."

Couplet: *The stern words put them to shame,*
Gathering innerself to die,
Shedded fears, realized champs
'fie ! turning back in strife." 32

Now, to sable storm, monkeys turned tails,
Tho' in the end the Truth 'll prevail.
It's size of fight in the hour of strife,
Not the might of weapon, that strikes.

Blazing Sun there seemed backing the defence,
Some puzzle monkeys faced in dazzlement.
While the troops were breaking on the western gate,
Hanumaan took the charge, the array to reshape.

This gate, where himself Meghnaad Led,
Baffling was rebuff of western barricade.
Plucky Kapi Hanumaan as the Death incarnate,
Sprang with roar and reached the turret.

He rushed at Meghnaad, seizing a rock,
Overthrowing charioteer, shattered his chariot.
Next, he kicked Meghnaad at his chest,
Funk defence picked the distressed prince and escaped.

Couplet: *Vigilant Angad heard,*
'Hanuman fights alone',
A single bound, he hopped
Reached top breaking merlons. 33

The go of the two prow monkeys,
In battle, rattled fort's every gold brick.

Merlon=Solid sections of parapet.

Leaving deads, half deeds in din of their groans,
Fighting like lightning, the two reached donjon.

Raavan's raven flags they unfurled,
Hurled those to ground, overthrew with pinnacles.
Demon King was dismayed when he saw this,
Such ire of invaders, was his irony.

Bluebeard demon's damsels blubbered
"Now two monkeys have come to double the trouble."

With monkey's pranks they made monkey of queens,
Frightened they with tricks and mischieves.
Auric oriels then the two reached,
And exclaimed "let us do little more mischief."

Then the two bellowed, jumped below on ballium,
Bashed demons with fist, with foot mashed some.
Monkeys cried "for anarchy, face our wrath",
The two slapped whoever, they gasped their last.

Couplet: *On the ballium, in bellum-lethale,*
Victim's heads, monkeys pulled apart,
To the Raavan's presence they hurled
Like clay- pots they dropt. 34

Where ever they found foe's chieftains,
They would seize by leg, to Ram sent them.
In taco of flight, the whole demon corps,
In fright of death, reached to Ram as corpse.

"Makraksha, this Surripu, Virupaksh, and that
is Prajangh, Eupaksh, Kumbh all killed in combat."
Vibhishan would mention the names of deceased,
The merciful Lord assigned their souls, the peace.

Donjon=topdome of fort; Raven=jet black
Bluebeard= man of many wives; Blubber= to weep noisily; Pinnacles = kalash
Made monkey of=made fool of; Auric oriels = window of gold
Ballium = inner court-yard of fort.

Cads, carls, carnals, cannibals and cheats,
Like candid and chaste to Ram's abode they reached.

Long arms of Lord art ever stretched,
Keepth every child like an infant in lap.
He ist the light in His shadow every one,
Biota, iota, heaven, men and demons.

Even if know this, no hand of prayer who rai se,
Ill-luck makes him the target.
Then, Angad and Hanumaan, On the rampage,
Have intruded into fort propelling hurdles on their ways.

Couplet: *Mighty slaps like thunder bolt,*
Zapped the chatelains,
Closing of day when the west told,
Toilless they returned to camps.. 35

Quietly returned they, bowed heads at Master,
Whose eyeful look appreciated warriors.
Lord's fatherly look ran along their veins,
Thrilled they, all their fatigue drained.

When the troops learnt that the two champs had left,
Monkeys bears too retired back.
But then the night- wanderers were night mare,
For in murk of night, their might would recover.

Night had multiplied vim of sable defense,
Attackers turned knowing of retaliating demons.
Demons' count multiplied, demons' clout multiplied,
They did take-up the battle in back up of the night.

Two formidable armies stood to forage,
The sable's might was intensified by night's face.

Chatelain= castle keeping guard; Clout = influence.

The creeping armies were now nighing in,
Came to a fierce fight without giving in.

The dim, turned more grim, the demonocracy,
But then keen legion here, was not lesser a crazy.
Like the eclipse moved in the sombre crew,
But great thew of monkeys bears was not Sober too.

Akampan, Atikaya* were two commandants,
When they perceived losing ground of their sable legion,
They employed instant their illusive spell,
They poured the gore with rocky hail.

Couplet:

The obi of ogres,
Obscated whole milieu,
Chaos filled the monkeys bears,
With hue and cry in their troops. 36

The Arcane trick Shri Ram Kent,
He then summoned Angad and Hanumant.
Shri Ram briefed them of illusive mischief,
And then sent the two chiefs into the field.

He then drew His bow, let fly a fiery dart,
And benighted field lighted and none was dark.
The night of ignorance even as,
Is wiped by the dawn of knowledge.

Relieved the legion once again enlivened,
And put their souls into deadly bellum.
Hanumaan Angad thundered at the battle-field,
Fled at their roars the battered fiends.

But the monkey bears seized the demon crews,
And crushed them, dashed them like a cruse.

Somber crew = Demon's army; *Sons of Raavan.
Obi = magic illusion; obscated = darkened; Cruse = Earthen pot.

Some tried their flight in great speed,
But in gory mud slipped, caught in stampede.

Field looked, filled with deads and half-deads,
Like carpet of chintz in blacks and reds.
Over grounded corpses of sable corps,
Thro' clear spaces monkeys hopped to cross.

Couplet: *Demons thus were slain,*
Yet a few clambered the fort,
Having hostile forces drained,
Ram's legion gave a loud roar. 37

□

Chintz = glazed print

26

Let us perfect the means, the end will take care of itself.

—Samarth Guru Ramdass

COURT OF CLAQUES AND EUPHORIC KING

All monkeys returned, it was now night,
The gory day brought glory to their might.
Ram casted a benign look on them,
The same mo all fatigue of monkeys drained.

Raavan there, summoned minister's assemblage,
Told them killing of champs in the carnage.
The counsel of cannibals gathered to cabal,
"Should what make us able to save force of Sables?

Ghatkarn in pride informed to the counsel,
"tho' his son Kumbh died, but chief Dwivid, he killed.

"On the rampage, monkeys have ravaged,
Laid waste, half the legion of savage in carnage.
"And who survived are no better than the dead,
Have no hopes for their spirit to be fed."

Grey and hollow voice of aged Malyavan floated.
He spake all wisdom, with soul devoted –
"Listen to my voice what Veds quoted,
Who is hostile to Ram, his mind is doted.

To Cabal = to make plot (secret), doted = to be silly minded

"Son! you carried off Siya ever since that date,
Lanka has become ill-omen's target.

Couplet: *"The same, Ancient of the days,*
Who rights ever every wrong,
Who shuns devil and his dam,
Hath now descended as Ram." 1

"It is quite out of question,
One who dwellth in thou and me,
Who is person in each person,
Can He be enemy?" 2

"Shouldst thou please ! Discard the discord,
And adore Him, the Lord of lords.
"He descendth for His own cause ,
Thy mind's eye ist blind at His deeds, Alas!"

Words of Hoar, poured lava on Raavan's core,
He roared "kick this thick from the court
"O Vile! O senile!! Away O wretch !!!
Such accursed face, I leave, for your age."

Left the courtier Malyavan, the doyenne of court—
"The Death hath ravaged ravenous Raavan's lore."
"Morrow wilt be mine" Meghnaad uproared,
"The spirit of my marrow, is now zeroed on foes."

"In the battle I'll accomplish too much,
Why should I talk and belittle its worth".

Meghnaad roared in the court-

Couplet: *"In own house a bluff huffs,*
A Tough never puffs up
In the house a tough keeps hush,
Tho' his valour in fields speaks tough." 3

Hoar=old, grey haired ; Doyenne=Eldest member; Huff = offend, (brag)

THE DIABOLIC MEGHNAAD

At the crimsoned east, gold fort looked blushed,
Once again to assail here monkeys rushed.
Dismayed Lanka while was filled with hay and cry,
Demons darted, hurled rocks from rampart's height.

Both sides hurled weapons, were in myriads,
To hurt, blitz had from both sides cannonades.
Murky defence was attacked by plucky warriors,
They battered demons, maimed and severed.

Fearless fierce Meghnaad with fiery efforts,
To defeat foe, with feat of fight , he sallied forth—
"O men ! O manikins !! Come on ! fight !!
Keep not ye into the mazy hides.

"Where is Vibhishan, the traitor of the king?
At the cost of kins, with aliens who did cling.
"Where are Nal, Nil, Sugriv, Hanumaan,
Seeing my challenge are ye all gone?

—Thus the embodied venom saying so,
Discharged a volley of arrows on the foe.

Couplet: *In fight he was a staunch*
Rained shafts like serpent's pelter
The Death over monkeys danced,
and laid low monkeys, bears. 4

The ghastly warmth of gore of brothren,
Chilled the bosom of monkey's, bear's legion.
The chiefs Panas, Pavan, Govay, Gavaaksh,
Sharabh, Gaj, Kumud, Mayand, all felt harassed.

He disbanded the marshalled troops,
Seeing this, Hanumaan, in rage swooped.

Kapi tore up and hurled a huge rock,
Gliding up into air Meghnaad left chariot.
Perished charioteers, horses and the wheels,
He dared not for duel nor he kneeled.

Hurled weapon, dared not he to vie with Hanumaan,
For he knew him, came not nigh to Hanumaan.
He rushed thro' the clouds like storm,
And tried maces, missiles against Shri Ram.

Massive maces, missiles he aimed at Lord,
Tho' with utmost ease He cut them off.
All illusive devices, the vice then tried,
Ram enjoyed as if eagle with snakelings toys.

Couplet: *The gross, tries on Him in vain,*
Who, on the canvas of the cosmos,
Every iota biota who paints
With His delusive brush who draws. *5*

In his delusive trick he mounted up clouds,
He rained fire, issued on earth water-spouts,
Fiends danced freak on the fallen and deads,
'Miam and kill' in the fields they yelled.

Rained odds, slod, smut, mud and blood,
Spurted dirt, crud, curd, clod flood.
Now Meghnaad hurlt a volley of stones,
Pelted bombs and discharged smokes.

Heated coal here, there snowy hail,
All engulfed was the field, with murky veil.

Disband = breakup/scatter (army)

All odd cloudy canopy choked,
And further tortured the monkey's flock.

Ram smilt at petty ploy of the perverse,
At the same saw monkeys at their worst.
With a single arrow He broke illusive web,
And nipped instantly, the nuisance of the knave.

Ram then graced monkeys with His healing glance,
To be restrained from fight lo! they grew strong,

Couplet: *Taking umbrage Lakhan was scorched,*
Accompanied by many chieftains,
Asking leave of Ram he marched,
With bow and arrows in hands. 6

Red threads in eyes knitted his brows,
Face shone as eoan rays on peaks of snow.
Ebon brigade of brute and bogies,
Bellowing rushed like billow on monkeys.

Seeing daggers, sabers, swords, rapiers,
Rampant fighters of Ram turned more rampageous.
There, Bilbo, bills, and brandishing wrists,
Here, rocks, boles, mounts, claws, jaws and fists.

The eager edge of array of monkeys hastened,
In heroic rush to meet the demons.
Boisterous bellicose brigade in broil,
Agog to win clashed both the sides.

'Lay!' 'Slay!' 'Slap'! 'Zap'! 'Kill!' 'Punch'! 'Lynch!'
'Seize!' 'Maim!' 'Aim! 'Sever'!—Made severe din.

Ploy = (trick) job; Nip = check / cut
Taking umbrage = being angry
Bills=Axes; Eoan=dawn; Ebon=black(like ebony)

Smiling splits of the wounds, spewed gore,
The scene, heaven saw, now assured, now soured.

Couplet: *Long wounded was Earth's core,*
Now reddened with ghastly dew,
To heal needed demon's gore,
But few sacrifices were due. 7

Warriors were fearless of weapons and the wound,
Doomed demons' souls were granted blest boon.
Cries, sighs echoed up and up high,
They vied till the profuse wounds denied.

All kerns, knights may be too keen at war,
But the army kneels, where no fit chieftains are.
Lakhan and Meghnaad in mounting up anger,
Grappled each other but none was the lesser.

Resorted to unfair means, was, the Meghnaad,
Running riot, rampant Ram's brother tore his chariot.
Smitten by Lakhan, demon was all but dead,
To escape he turned finding him in straits.

Before he fled, a javelline he threw,
Lo! He succeeded in swift of his move.
Now, in hands of Meghnaad, now on breast of Lakhan,
So smart, like the lightning was the throw of weapon.

Venomed by the prick, swooned the prince,
Meghnaad went near, fearless, convinced.

Couplet: *As ever the proud Earth,*
Took the son on her lap;
For swooned son's comfort,
Fondled the air, a freshet. 8

Kern = foot soldiers ; straits=difficult conditions.

LAKHAN'S SWOON/HANUMAN'S RESCUE

In the battle field was laying the swooned champ,
Striving to lift him, came the devils and his dam.
But how could Lakhan be lifted thus,
Hence demon-champs returned smarting with blush.

Warrior like Lakhan who dared jaws of death,
Is firm support to the truth of the Earth.
When into the sea damped the western lamp,
With cramp in hams, champs returned to camps.

Different troops began taking the count,
But Ram's fond Lakhan, the chiefest-found was not found.
Meanwhile Hanumaan brought him in soft embrace,
The distress of all, came on Lord's face.

Jambvaan said, "Susen, Lanka's royal medic,
Someone should bring him here quick."
Hanuman moved swift in panic,
Brought with house and his all, the medic.

Couplet: *The duty of a medic,*
Is blind at bounds of hatred,
Transparent eyes with no malice
See, that weeping wound is ever red. 9

Susen, the medic bowed at Ram's feet,
Mentioned the name of herb needed to treat.
Told of the mount from where it could be had,
"Quick go! Mac-wind, Hanuman!!"- He added.

Assuring the Lord of task, Hanuman departed,
From clouds to clouds he rocketed.
There, spy disclosed secret to Raavan,
Who asked 'Kalnemi' to be snag in mission.

Snag = hurdle

"A hurdle to him? Who burnt your capital,
O King ! desist from vain prattles, lord! Cease the battle.
"Adore Raghuveer in thy own interest,
In interest of demonry's whole race.

"Should die thy folly or thy family,
Shed off idea of 'Mine' and 'Me'.
"Arise ! Awake ! From deep slumber,
Lest thine and mine days are numbered,

Couplet: *Ravenous Raavan raved,*
Tho words were rational.
Kalnemi reasoned to himself,
'The death is inevitable'. 10

"for this sinner revels in his load of wrongs,
Should I rather die at hands of man of Ram.
So thinking of warlock, Kalnemi departed,
War-like, to his black art, he resorted.

Thro' clouds to the north as Hanumaan went,
The demon created a lake, a grove, a fane.
The demon sat there disguised as hermit,
The courtesy forced Hanumaan, him to visit.

With reverence Hanumaan bowed the head,
In return he recited Ram's praises.
He posed-'he knows the visitor's crunch,
And knows of everything of war thro' his intuitive hunch.

'It's now, nay the days to come, I have beheld,
Victory will bow to Ram, Ram's sena 'll prevail.
"So relax O brave! And quench your thirst,
And with fresh thrust you go forward.

Warlock = black magic; Crunch = crisis; hunch=feeling.

For pearls of fatigue that I see on your face,
Take a plunge in the lake and swift come back.
"Then, I 'll initiate you with spiritual insight,
that will add up further to your fighting size".

Couplet: *As he stepped into the lake,*
A crock seized him by ankle,
Hanumaan zapped it by a thwack,
Crock's frail form turned celestial. 11

Absolved of curse shedding form of a crock,
Grateful in new form he then spoke—
'O monkey! Your very sight hath absolved me
Of curse of great sage and of all sins.

"This is no hermit but a demon hurdling triumph"
So saying left to heaven the celestial nymph.
Returned monkey "Guru! take first the fee,
Then sacred insight impart into me."

Kapi knocked down the knave, by his tail's clasp,
Demon muttered 'Ram', at his last gasp.
Even demon's muttering 'Ram' poured in Kapi, honey,
With new verve, he proceeded on journey.

Tracker of truth are ever trapped by traitors,
But before commitment they are ever battered.
Found the mount but, to single out the herb; he failed,
So, lost no time, in uprooting, the mount itself.

Holding the mount over palm, he rocketed back,
Happened to cross Ayodhya while night it was yet.

Couplet: *Vigil Bharat espied-*
Some odd collosus goes,
With headless shaft's strike,
Hit the one, who encroached? 12

Thwack = big blow

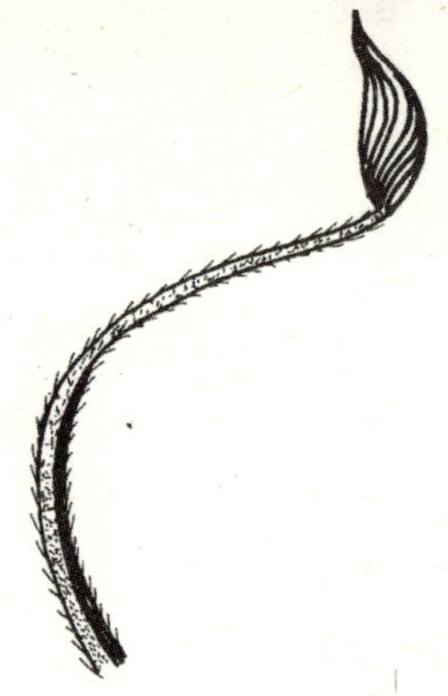

Struck, stunned, swooned dropped from sky,
Drawled "Ram! O Ram! "O Raghuveer!!" he sighed.
Hearing sighs post-haste Bharat rushed to his side,
To bring his consciousness, every mean he tried.

Creases of melancholy drew on his face,
Shone by brimming eyes of dews of sadness —
"The fate hath alternated me from Ram's love,
Anew, maketh sinner; Doth it behove?

"If my heart and soul are true to my Lord,
If I cherish truth in my deeds, words, thought,
"Then O Ram! O my Lord!! relieve him of his pangs,
Lest, my too and fro puffs toil in vain.

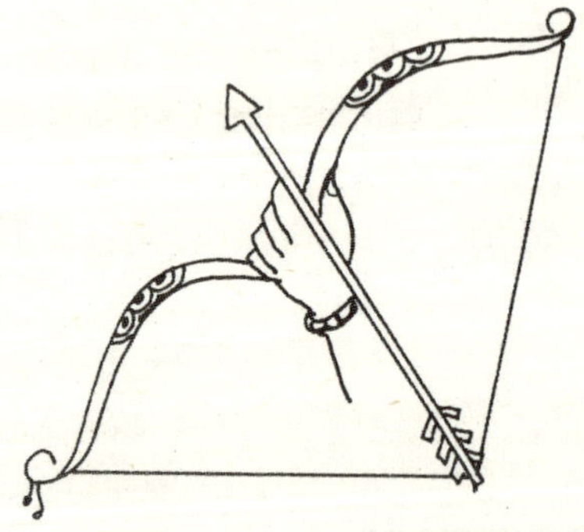

Drawl = to speak in low tone.

Words like elixir poured into his ears,
The monkey, chief arose, sat up with 'Jai Raghuvar.'

Couplet: *Finding the devout of Ram,*
Thrill ran thro' Bharat's veins,
Bharat shackled him in arms,
Like a kin; that very alien. 13

In Bharat, Kapi saw his Lord's visage,
Delight in surprise revived him awake.
Bharat asked "You seem to be companion
Of Ram in woods Alas! to me an alien."

"Let me know abou' Ram, maa Siya, Lakhan."
Hanumaan briefed him all that happened.
"Woe is me! Why should I have been born,
In the blossomed family, as futile thorn."

"What's worth that I come to this world,
If I could not be of any service to my Lord."
But then collecting himself gallant prince added,
"The prime mission is timed, you should not delay,"

"So ascend on my arrow that'll missile you to shore ,
Timely herbs make sure, the cure ,"
"I'll send you straight into presence of Lord."
But then pride of Kapi doubted hearing Bharat's words.

"How this tiny arrow'll bear my weight?
But then recalled Ram's glory which operates.
Abashed of his doubt, he bowed his head
To Bharat, Lord's Brother, and humbly spake—

Couplet: *"Your sight is a gift,*
Touch of this land is reward,
Now I speed swift
With might of the Lord" 14

As he journeyed forth,
Hanuman extolled,
Bharat's thoughts, virtues, worth
Which Ram ever recalled.

There on Suvel* befitting as mortals
With a soft gaze at Lakhan, He, the Lord wailed.
Sad Ram could not restrain His pain,
Eyed and sighed He, eyed and sighed, again.

"Lo! the glittering rush of the hostile sky,
Seems faster, as Hanumaan yet hath not arrived."
Every elapsed mo put Ram, on test of His patience,
Ram clasped Lakhan and sunk in him.

"O brother! You could never bear, see Me pained,
My ache never crossed acme's such extent.
"You chose untrodden woods for My love,
Shredded princely colours, O floret of royal grove!

"Is that same love lost in deadly silence,
For benumbed response on My comments.
"Had I known, its at cost of My brother,
I would never have obeyed My sire.

"Kins, mammons, sons and tenements,
Are the lost and found chains of mundane,
"But the real brother once lost is lost,
Alas! Can not be had again.

"If the death deceiveth Me compelth Me to live,
I'm wingless bird, a fish without dew."
"Warmth of fraternity should melt your swoon,
Lest Ram's life 'll be a rampike pruned.

"Love is the elixir, a panacea
Should it make you arise O beloved fra !

"Recall your old love, and arise! Awake!
Lest my living, O tenderling! is at stake.

"No land, legion, law, Lineage is worth,
Its love of Lakhan that lays Awadh.
"I would have rather suffered world's obloquy,
Then, losing you, and go to Awadh empty.

You are soul of the soul of mother, Sumitra,
Who entrusted her son to Me.
"My incapable lips babble, yet fathom not,
Like a pebble of the sea of melancholy in heart."

With the honey that Ram had, for his brother.
Thus, for ages to come, fraternity was elixired,
Thus, Lamented the One, who dispels sorrows,
To purge devout's heart His tears flowed.

Tenderling=beloved, Elixired = vitalized.

Couplet: *In the hush, the host stood statuesque,*
Only wails of Ram echoed
And Arrived Hanumaan in his rush,
Like a heroic lay in midst of pathos. 16

All swooned and the Lost, found themselves enlivened—
"Bravo! The brave have achieved the mission."
Content Ram embraced Hanumaan to bosom,
Quick Medic, mean while, picked the Nostrum.

At the same Susen applied the herb,
Soon Lakshman rose from swoon; and got up.
Gush of rejoice wiped out the gloomy hush,
All saw embracing brothers and the divine nexus.

Hanumaan took the medic, back, before the east break,
Like had brought him he, the same way.
In utter despair the king-monster heard this
And remembered KumbhaKaran* at this fix.

For this colossus monster from his hibernating sleep,
In waking, they used drums" din to succeed.
He sat up; from his eyes the death peeped,
First he poured in his belly wines and heaps.

Then he asked! "O elder! now you tell,
What had caused you that you look so pale?"
Own timid vain-glory as great bravery,
How he carried off Siya he bragged all story.

"But then unwonted chaos killed some champs,
And keeled Lanka to unwanted extent.
"If I'm not wrong, they were no little
warriors; who have fallen in field of battle.

Statuesque = like statue
*younger brother of Raavan (A Giant); Unwonted = abnormal (unusual)

"Like a tempest on us foe is rolling on,
But when I see you, I find all they gone."

Couplet: *KumbhKaran felt guilty,*
Laden with wrongs of King—
"teasing 'Maa of totality',
Fool! Still you hope the win." 17

KUMBHAKARAN, THE GIANT

"Thou havest acted O King! All unwise,
Now how thou askest me 'Arise'.
"Ego had ever faded glory of the crown,
Who giveth no thought to deeds sheds off his renown.

"Yet! Forgo ego and go to Ram,
Thou wilt be blest, with no harm.
"Alas! I was asleep, and thou wert blind,
A mere man, in the King of kings, thou didst find.

"Thou havest courted war with the Divine itself,
I see on race, darkening eve's shades.
"Alas! Being born in race of demonry,
Who dwellth in my bosom, in bellum is my enemy.

"Should a devoted soul fullfil devoir to the soil,
And should moil for his onus, in hour of turmoil.
"Embrace me! I fare thee well now,
Even my last breath will fight 'its my vow'."

Couplet: *He imagined swarthy visage,*
Lost in the Man-sized form,
Now pondered of His grace,
Now planned to fight shri Ram. 18

Devoir = respect (due to the soil) (mother land); Moil = work / toil.

The barbarian troops, through the barbican passaged,
With no trace of scar, with no scare's trace.
With heaps and wines he inflated his fill,
Then he roared a thunder crossing the sill.

Intoxicating-juice hath the spelling charisma,
It squeezes all the chill of the awe—
A lush full of passion for the war
The Giant crossed over in a step the rampart.

Seeing his brother, Vibhishan came to the fore,
And fell at his feet with reverence in core.
Revenge faded witnessing brother's reverence,
A blest devout, in Vibhishan he Kent.

Vibhishan informed—

"O brother! Raavan spurned me and exiled,
When I gave him most salutary advice.
"Disgusted I came in my Lord's refuge,
I stay with Truth, in this feud.

"Hark! Vibhishan!! The Death maketh blind and deaf,
He nor seeth nor heedth to the best,
"O blest! Devout of Ram, O blest ! Ram's beloved,
You as the jewel of the race, your deeds proved.

"On the path of the Truth among all odds,
Unstrayed you trod, towards the Lord,

Couplet: *"Brother! Be benign to the Divine,*
Now my fiend's frame I leave to fate
The Right-wrong, I can't define,
For doomed as I am to death." 19

Vibhishan turned back in Shri Ram's presence,
"A mountainous monster moves to us, the moribund".

Moribund=on the brink of death.

'He puffth in clouds to quench his thirst,
The typhoon cometh as the tempest's out burst.

"The bold robust, with some resolve, cometh fast,
Lord ! do the feat that yields the bliss, at last."
Meanwhile monkey troops rushed in frolic,
They plucked up trees and mountain peaks.

Hurled them on the Giant gnashing their teeth,
In vain, hardly to the thighs reach.
He ignored attack of pigmies in the field,
Stood with undaunted zeal and unstirred steel.

Hanumaan then struck his full fist,
He fell on the field in confused fit.
Recouping himself he hit in riposte,
Sans weapons he became the warfield's boast.

Hanumaan was stunned and fell to the ground,
He overthrew Nal-Nil, many champs he knocked down.
Here, there, everywhere he spreaded,
The dead and dying, where ever he raided.

Panting with pangs monkey host stampeded,
The confused troops, vamoosed and fled.

Couplet: *"Angad, Sugriv, Many chiefs,*
Swooned many bellicose;
Pressing Sugriv in armpit,
Soon the Giant went off." 20

"Uma ! ebbs and rise in war were feats of the Lord,
As vulture would play with snakes, before it devours.
"Where mere knitting of brows could turn Trikut*,
How could He be engaged, with grace, in such feud.

Vamoosed=ran hastily; Riposte=quick retaliatory action.
*Trikut=Mount on which Lanka existed.

But Ram with own will, with own cause descendeth,
For, His paeans to take, men across mundane.
Now, Hanumaan woke began to look for Sugriv,
Meanwhile Sugriv recovered, slipped out of Giant's grip.

His escape KumbhKaran could discover,
When Sugriv bit off his nose and ears.
Demon caught Sugriv against ground him he dashed,
With great agility Sugriv hit him back.

The warrior then returned into Lord's presence,
With some bruisy wound, that knew no pains.
Maimed of nose ears the Giant demon,
In fury looked more and more awesome.

Couplet: *The monkeys presently foreyed,*
With heroic howls,
With a new fire, anew they fired,
Volley of boulders and boles. 21

With lust of battle, maddened with rage,
The robust demon rushed against foe like Death.
Many monkeys he seized and sucked into mouth,
As the swarms of locusts enter a cave of the mount.

Some, he seized, squeezed and thus slew,
He crushed, smashed and mashed a few.
Some he levigated between palms and laps,
Many puffed out of nostrils and mouth, and escaped.

Frenzied of the battle like a nasty sport,
The bellicose, rolled on field as Catastrophe.
Now, what ever comes in way he devours,
Seems, he'll finish monkeys bears, nay the universe.

Quite ahead of him vamoosing monkeys create a vaccum,
Faster he chases, frets and fumes.
Lo ! sable army behind with Giant also sallies forth,
Learning Kumbhakaran is dispensing the foe's host.

Ram beheld 'to the bitter end the belial comes',
To buoy up the battered He joinedst the bellum.

Couplet: *"Listen ! Sugriv! Vibhishan ! Lakhan !*
Care ! lesions of the legion,
Now ! I go to fathom,
the real size of demon in Demon." 22

Taking in His hand bow, named Sarang,
His waist was with a quiver, fastened.
Raghunath moved forth to crush foe's ranks,
His bow, playfully the Lord first twanged.

The sound pierced through the bone marrows,
The twang twinged the troops-n-troops of the foes.
The Din deafened them, field turned to bedlam,
Awe struck they screamed 'Here ! Here ! cometh Ram.'

Myriads of arrows Shri Ram discharged,
With hiss those sped like winged cobras.

Odd mesh of arrows, awed army of foes,
All milieu showed the demons-mowed.
Demons champs wert chopped into chunks and pieces,
Field was carpeted with miamed limbs and liches.

Jetting torsos whirled and fell,
In the gory pools with ghastly splash.
Some of the heathen herd, rushed with lust of fight,
But Ram's newer pelter they didn't survive.

---

bellum=war; Vamoosing = flee hastily.
Pelter=rain (of arrows); Lich=dead body; Twinged=pained.

Couplet: *In a trice, Ram's arrows,*
Mowed down hosts of foes,
Finishing the punishing show,
Into quiver returned His arrows. 23

Battle field resembled shamble of sabled array,
Perceiving this Kumbhkaran ran in fury.
A mount he tore to Ram he hurlt,
With a shaft Ram turned it into dust.

Even as eclipsed orb cometh out of clouds
From the dusty mount Kumbhkaran came out.
Ram saw 'the black mount as if cometh close',
He pulled bow-string to his knitted brows.

On the rampage, Shri Ram pelted new strike
Of volley of shafts that filled the sky.
Thro' the body of the Giants, arrows so pierced,
As the flashes of lightening into clouds disappear.

Gush of gore spurled from the limbs and torso,
Looked, erupting lava from the black volcano.
The Giant was in flurry, from hides monkeys saw,
In hurry they dashed shedding off their awe.

Couplet: *Wary Giant fearless of*
The wounds, weapons and war,
In own and other's gore daubed,
Rushed to catch a tartar. 24

His thirst of the gore and lust of war,
Even with fatal wounds faded not.
His diabolic roar vibrated welkin,
Monkeys bears fell in thrust of the din.

Shamble=place of slaughter.
Flurry=panic

Once again he began the monkeys to sieze,
Flesh pulped through webs, as with palms he squeezed.
Monkeys bears turned tail in feared chill,
Their palsied limbs forgot marshal skill.

"The Giant is an embodied famine, who wrought,
In the field of war for primates*, a draught.
Laden heart, but on pinioned limbs,
Filled they, the field with their screams—

"Hurry! O Lord Hari ! for this Hurricane,
He is hell in battle, our army's bane."
As the Lord heard the pathetic words,
With his bow and arrow He cameth forward.

Placing army in rear, Raghunath marched,
Discharged hundreds of shafts, flushed with wrath.
Winged serpents flew and pierced through,
The body of demon, but to hurt not a few.

Demon ran, he tore up a rock,
But the arm that bore it, Ram cut off.
Hawkish he hurried with hillock in left hand,
Instant even that arm Shri Ram maimed.

Couplet: *With shorn off arms,*
In fury, he hurried to Ram,
Witnessing this, the celestial swarms,
"Oh no !" yelled in alarm. 25

Sanguinary scene was too foul to perceive,
The heaven was perplexed seeing the war grim.
Hearing demon's uproaring shouts,
With the flight of His arrows Ram blocked his mouth.

---

*Monkeys; Sanguinary=bloody, (bloodshed)

He looked living quiver of Death himself,
On the rampage, rampant Ram beheaded
Off his body with a sharp shaft,
And his head dropt in front of Raavan, the wretch.

With the burden of the trunk, the earth sunk beneath,
And as well the earth sunk under Raavan's feet.
Ruddy fountain, out of trunk did sprint,
And sprayed to the wides of the fields, gory chintz.

There upon, Ram severed his trunk in two,
Like meteors the parts fell on his own troops.
Demon's spirited-halo sublimed and diffused within Ram,
From heaven to the Earth all felt relieved.

Heaven expressed delight thro' lightening and rains,
Naarad came that mo, and extolled paeans.
Hovering over billet Naarad prayed,—
'Now despatch the wretch quick, it's belated'.

Stanza: *The lord Shri Ram, up in arms,*
in divine form to combat,
The Matchless in strength, Ram the rampant,
marched forth with Army of primates. *A*

With dew of toil, on His face, graced,
In hue of red eyes, the rage imaged,
The Supreme, as He is, in the age of crisis,
He cometh to ravage the savage. *B*

Couplet: *Ram took him as crony soul,*
And blest him final bliss,
Dolt, are they, who don't extol,
His such mercy. *26*

Billet=camp of army.

THE DEADLY WAR

Sanguinary battle-field looked as if,
The west sky, spreads the orb's dip.
Most strenuous was the day even for the bravest,
With drooped weapons, dropping wounds, retuned dragging gait.

From the battle to billets the sighs and yells,
On both the sides, the pain prevailed.
Ram's grace blest warmth to the sinew's chill,
Ram's grace was balm for wounds to heal.

Their parched lips, sick faces turned vivid,
Again now were ready, bellum-lethale to meet.
Named, unnamed Monkeys struggled for the cause,
Reverse, the demons faught for own applause.

The sanguine flood in battle hath no name,
But the genuineness churned in fight, they claim.
Raavan, lamented clasping head of his fra,
Paying tributes to his extraordinary awe.

At this loss, Meghnaad came and solaced,
"The primates are pea-nuts before our penates.
"The better ; battle be called a frolic,
I have for my toys, the two ascetics."

While son-father were engaged all night in reverie,
Monkey's army woke up with reveille.
Swarms of Monkey besieged all the four gates,
There, demon army stood with their champs as death.

Couplet: *Meghnaad on his charmed chariot,*
The sky, to ascend up, he tricked,
He chortled but was running riot,
And began on primates, the blitz. 27

Blitz=attack; Chortle=laugh in loud manner; Primates=monkeys, bears.

He discharged shafts, swords, spikes and pikes,
Mounts, mortars, maces, machetes and missiles.
Rained He, the outpours of mystic weapons,
Like an outburst of hell on monkey's legion.

'Seize ! kill ! Sieze ! Kill ! ' echoed all about,
None knew 'who sends the pelting bout.
Among the primates there was all chaos,
Yet the boles, and boulders they tossed.

Tossed trees, rocks fell back on them again,
Now the palsied legion could hardly stand.
Thro' Maya, Meghnaad made moats, mines, mounts,
In its labyrinth, the monkeys, to confound.

Prime champs of primates too, were perplexed,
Imprisoned legion cried now for help.
On Lakhan and Vibhishan he assailed anew,
And pierced their limbs through and through.

Then he let fly arrows those turned into
Serpents, even as they struck Lord of Raghus.
In a trice, the trick of the vice, wrought,
Surrounded by the serpents in its noose, Lord let Himself caught.

'Lo ! who is free of feud, fight and fate,
He let Himself tied as mortal puppet.
Thus, the Supreme in various ways doth act,
This time, the glory, to the battle, to invest.

Couplet: *"Uma* ! He, Himself nay whose*
Very name cuts bondages,
Shouldth He fall in noose,
And be victim of coils of snakes? 28

Bout= encounter;
Confound=confuse, put to perplexity.
*Lord Shankar narrates the story to Uma, His consort.

When the Supreme compactth into man-size,
For His deeds, none the reason, need be applied.

Bhakti is the torch of mind's eye to deem,
To enlighten the soul from enthymeme.

The troth is the true path of the Truth,
And the faith should prevail in the inner feud.
Now, bewildered monkey's turned more wild,
Revealing himself, then the Vile* reviled.

Abuses, He poured from up sky,
Old bear** challenged "wretch remain there a while."
He, the spit- fire further fretted,
Liking a fuming hot- coal he, the fated, said

"O fool ! for your age I spared,
O weak ! still cheek, how you dare?"
So saying he hurled a huge trident,
How ever the old champ caught it in his hand.

And darted it back in swift response,
Struck in chest, Meghnaad, dropt head on.
The bear conculcated and knocked him with knees,
Half dead was seized, dashed, and again seized.

His pluck was now plucked by his sorry plight,
But by virtue of boon he did not die.
Jamvaan hurled, seizing him by the ankle,
Tossed he, dangled over castle's crenelle.

Here, the divine erne, Garuda*** was despatched,
By sage Naarad for coils of the snakes.

Reviled=abused; Enthymeme=suppressed reasoning (logic); Bewildered=confused.

* Meghnaad.

** Jaamwant; Conculcate=trample under feet.

*** Garuda-the divine erne is devotee of Vishnu.

Couplet: *The erne devoured and dispelled,*
The spell of snaky swarm,
The noose of snakes failed,
Failed it's elusive charm. 29

The snakiness of the sneak
Worked snare of snake's spell,
Was snipped by the erne's beak
Thus the devout won laurels. 30

Rejoiced host of monkeys uproared ballads,
Rushed, army armed with rocks, boles, claws.
Recovered Meghnaad dragged back to the fort,
Felt much ashamed finding his father before.

With no other thought he betook himself to oubliette,
To perform Tantrik worships for maligned object.
Which would render him invincible,
for pelf, power, profit and would win him laurels.

Here Vibhishan went to Lord Shri Ram,
"Listen ! O Generous ! Meghnaad performs,
A malign latry for more sortilege,
Cryptic diabolism, who already has."

"Doing dirty incantation for unholy cause,
The heaven to scourge, the human to scorch.
"O Nonmenon ! the splendour of Thy bow,
Nor I could fathom, nor I know,

"Yet with holy power, he goes beyond reach,
That is my frenzied anguish.
"If his odd sacrifice is allowed to complete,
He 'll prove to be tough-nut to defeat."

Snakiness=guile.
Win laurels=acquire glory ; Oubliette=secret cave.

Gratified Ram to warriors sent call,
"Go with Lakhan Ye ! brethren all."
"Ye ! all wreck the tricky sacrifice of the wretch,
Hear Lakhan ! Here the demon should be dispatched.

"Earthlings and godlings have suffered enough,
Tough lesson is now due for satanic stuff.
"Meet the enemy with all grit and wit,
Should his deeds meet now nemesis.

"Go with covering troops O Vibhishan! O Sugriv !!
For easy victory and not the one, expensive."
In a voice as thunder Lakhan then spake,
With all courage and the rage medleyed

"No wight- might can now fight me,
Could a foe ever stay befo' Ram's devotee?
"If I daub not this eve's west, with his gore,
Ram's man, should I be called no more!!"

Couplet: *So saying Lakhan bade adieu,*
And set out at once,
All sinew fevered with thews,
And accompanied by champions. 31

Angad, Hanumant, Mayand, Nal and Nil*,
Moved with crude weapons but with fire of zeal.
All they reached oubliette with silent foot,
Bivouaced demons failed to see sniper troops.

They saw Meghnaad and environ unsecred,
He was offering other's blood for sacrilege.
Monkeys attacked and wrecked the altar,
They spurned him yet he did not stir.

Sacrilege=godlessness; Biavouaced=watched at night ; Sniper=attacker from dark dusk.

Then they caught him by hair and dragged,
Now, he turned to monkeys on the rampage.
Monkeys fled behind Lakhan, but then Hanumant, Angad,
In between the two, came forward.

Before they could plump, they managed got up,
And got even with him, with great pluck.
In great wrath, the two sabaoth,
Like one other's death stood in fighting lust.

Lakhan attacked with volley of arrows on the wretch,
In his elusive trick the wretch evanesced.
He revealed and fought in Various guise,
With his limited weapons, yet unlimited inner fight.

Primates were dismayed for the demon proved be tough,
Here Lakhan decided 'now this play is enough.'
Deft Lakhan then defiantly zeroed his aim,
And arrow sunk in breast, Meghnaad's death claimed.

Couplet: *"Come on ! Ram !! Lakhan !!"- he bellowed*
-n-croaked frame gave up his ghost,
Lo ! demon's life was low,
Yet his death was thus hallowed. 32

Angad Hanumant on his lips whispered,
'O blessed ! indeed blessed is your mother.'
—An unblessed life of an unblessed womb,
Calling 'Name' in the Last, frees absolved from doom.

Hanumaan lifted him, at maingate placed him,
And the troops returned with glorious triumph.

The Heavens, up there, drummed in delight,
In the havens, down here, returned paradise.

Evanesced=disappeared ; Plump=fall ; Sabaoth=armies.

In the hope of returning of the repose,
Spreaded relief in, long suffered cosmos.

The Lanka in it's lankiness made Lamenting din,
Then, hush of melancholy filled every scene.
Fort looked robbed, among sobs of queen,
By the sleeping prince, whole gynaeceum keened.

People accursed Raavan, the anarchy incarnate,
'should he be now beggar at fate's gate.'
The stone within Raavan melted in his eyes,
In chill of sad news he stood petrified.

Couplet: *Then, Raavan solaced women folk,*
"No tears ! till war is won,
The Death, when meets, I'll ask,
To return back, my son." 33

Whole gynaeceum was then more upset,
For Raavan did not know what he said.
Raavan's solace was so wholesome,
Tho', Euphoria overpowered his own wisdom.

So frequent are the feign preachers,
But who implement on ownself are rare.
There, Lanka's night was a nightmare,
Here, before revellie got up monkeys bears.

Recalling Hari, all hurried as hurricane,
And stormed over the four barbicans.
Raavan summoned champs, cannibals,
For tactics in battle they caballed.

Demon King said, "war is passion—
Let it be voice of the nation.

Cabal=to make secret plot(action)

"Any one could even now quit battle,
But before foe no heart should quail.

"My ego hath never seen defeat,
I shall meet enemy with reply that befits.
"Heaven and Humans have learnt to adore me,
I'll see today who dares before me."

Swift he moved on his chariot,
Ill omens occurred which, he heeded not.

Couplet:

On Chariot of ego,
With ire unbridled
In careless confidence he goes,
Into bellum-lethale. 34

□

27

Within or without, fight bravely!

—Samarth Guru Ramdass

RAAVAN IN THE BATTLE

Stanza: *The fop's weapons dropt, as he hopped up the cart,*
Fell his crown, champs fell down,
Yet in lack of reason, heedless of omens,
In fighting passion his mind was drowned.

Dogs whined, eagles, jackals wailed,
Sabled cats yelled shrill cry.
On the wings of ego, demon King goes,
Lord Ram to try but just to die.

Couplet: *Who needs the innocent's gore,*
Own thirsty deeds to sate,
Whose core is never pure,
He is now own ill's prey. 1

Can ever anyone think of mind's calm,
Sans moral ever dipt in sensual pomp.
Thus, in anxiety, Raavan with demon swarms,
Assailed forward, the hostile to Ram.

Demon's host defied calculations and marched,
All four, the chariots, elephants, foot and horse.

On foot the brutes, recruits rushed,
Even as the endless swarms of the locust.

Marched like windy clouds the elephant's stroops,
Marched like flood of soot, the rampant troops.
Resolved to fight the bellum Lethale,
Were pouring in the field of the battle.

Dragons, dragoons were coming nigh in speed,
Heard shrill din of neighing steeds.
Ghostly troops for the ghastly shows,
Moved in revenge of lost day's woes.

The savage army for carnage, onward goes,
All lessoned to lesson the legion of foes.
Fronting infantry was topped with casques,
Looking like closing in the poppy-crops.

Unnamed waves stirred the sea-benthos,
Mounts rocked, as the army trod.
With Firing lust, they gushed in battle field,
Shroud of dust made to the firing sun a shield.

Stanza: *The demonry's boast, behested his host—*
"Go ! forage the courage of monkeys,
All you ! pierce through, with fierce crews,
And here I slay the two pigmies."
When monkeys troops received the news,
They jumped in bellum, rammed with tantrum,
They assailed, in foray, they held
Boles, boulders in arms, Lord Ram in bosom.

Couplet: *With shouts of martial strains,*
Both sides came to clash,
All breaths puffed the revenge
In and in now closed the phalanx. 2

Benthos=sea-bed ; Casque=soldiers' helmet.
Tantrum=great fury.

Vibhishan saw Raavan on the chariot,
And Ram without; put him in puzzling crux.
Fondness for Ram made him sickly obscessive,
For His protection he turned pensive—

'Enemy cometh swift on the wheel,
Lord, here, hath nor armour nor shield.'
"Thou havest Lord! came in field bare-foot?"
"Listen! Vibhishan, I have with Me, the Truth.

"Nor the chariot, clarionet, nor weapons nor din,
'ts Truth that fights from within to win.
"The chariot that triumphs is quite unique,
It hath wheels of valour on dogged axis.

"With truth, troth, thoughts, the triumphant flag is designed,
Hath conduct, courage, curb, celibacy as powered equines.
"Fastened to the Rath with steady-steadfast cord,
devotion is it's driver, dispassion is sword.

"The reason its weapon, judgement, the javelin,
Mores the mace, bliss, the blitz winning.

"The Honour, to the pious and to the own preceptor,
Is the impenetrable shield of armour.
"Who owns such chariot of piety in battle,
O Pal ! he is ever and ever be invincible.

Couplet: *"With tides of flow and ebbs,*
The mundane is mighty foe,
Such tough chariot who possess
O pal ! can only overthrow." 3

Dogged=determined; Mores=morality.

Contented Vibhishan said,—
"Making most of the opportunity,
While the phalanx stand at bay,
Its Great; Thou exhortedst me. 4

Demons' chariot sped through in revenge,
Here Angad, Hanumaan threw their challenge.
There, sable monsters, here able bellicose,
Clashed, crossed and varied weapons they tossed.

Demons, dragons, dragoons, flung like tornado,
Lo ! Monkeys, bears rushed on toes to the foe.
In hush the Heaven, up witnessed the hell,
What went on Earth, the bellum-lethale.

'Alas ! It needth the benign sacrifice,
To bring on the mundane's get up, the paradise.
The Creator, gods, godules lowered themselves,
And watched the combat from the cloudy veils.

Passion of war on both sides was wide spread,
Wary heads played game of blood sheds.
Both sides champs gazed Ram's martial zeal,
With Lord's might, monkeys led the field.

Ducking dragons of demons, monkeys closed in duels,
Dashed, smashed, mashed, zapped then hurled the cruels.
Tearing heads off, they, pelted them as cannonade,
Plucked up arms with jaws, ripped up bellies with claws.

Stanza: *Here, bears in wrath, Buried demons like moth*
And piled over them Heaps of sand—
Champs slapped, trapped, Trampled and snapped,
zapped then, the opponents *A*

Stand at bay=ready to combat.
Dragoon=cavalary troop ; Cannonade=bombard.

Monkeys seized, the warry sneaks
Tore ope the cheeks, ripped up bellies—
They spared none, they sparred demons,
They marred, maimed them Like prey easy— B

Couplet: *Seeing own troops in disarray,*
Raavan puffed in huff—
"Fools ! turn back ! be tough !!
Finish it all, 'ts enough." 5

On the Rampage, the Ravaging Raavan ranged,
He knew no bounds as he rolled in revenge.
But the Hari's warriors hurried as well,
To confront him with glee, they yelled.

Taking in their hands mounts, trees, stones,
They hurled on him all at once.
But the mounts as they struck the adamantine frame,
Those broke into dust, the very moment.

He planted chariot in midst of battle-field,
Remained firm as a mount, and not flinched.
Scorched by the rage, he darted hither-thither,
And his pelter began crushing monkeys bears.

Screaming for help they took to their heels,
In deadly pour of the Death, faded their zeal.
His blitz laid monkeys some dead and half dead,
Rest took a dip, hopped, ran and fled.

Stanza: *None dared, the rare slayer, in warfare*
Field turned bare, monkeys bears fled—
In fits of ego, he fitted arrows,
In huge bows, those pelted as death. A

Spar=hit with fist ; Huff=anger.

The pelters of shaft, like fierce snakes,
Filled environs, the Earth even, the ether,
All in sore, monkeys corps roared
'Pray ! O Hari ! Hurry !! O Saviour !! B

Couplet: *Every even turned odd, in awe,*
Then, to master the mystic mess,
Lakhan bowed head to his Fra,
And sallied forth in rage. 6

" O wretch! make not the primates, the target,
Here I come Raavan ! as your death.
"O Knave! you braved and accursed the Earth,
Now face anathema, that you deserve."

"Are you same Lakhan, my son, who slew?
Since then I was looking for you, two.
"My scorches will only be then soothed,
When your chilly corpse I get stewed."

So saying he discharged many arrows swift,
But Lakhan shivered them each, into hundred pieces.
Again the demon hurled myriads of missiles,
Lakhan reduced all into smoke, in a while.

Lakhan got even with him, now with shafts,
Killing charioteer, the chariot he smashed.
Again one volley of shaft transfixed then,
The heads of that monster who felt, sick.

Lakhan pelted shafts now on his breast,
He fell from his chariot, perplexed.
Regaining his nerve he hurled Divine Lance,
Through ordinance which he gained from Brahma's ordnance.

Annathema=curse.
Ordinance=rituals, penance; Ordnance=store of weapons.

Stanza: *Through the ordinance, the thew he gained,*
Brahma from his ordnance gifted that lance,
That struck Lakhan, on the bosom,
In field of bellum, he fell in pain. *A*

While Lakhan swooned, Raavan tried to swoop,
But Lankiness of Lanka's King it proved,
He little knew, of Lakhan's sinew,
And feud with Lakhan he undervalued. *B*

Couplet: *Perceiving the threat brews*
To Lakhan, rushed Hanumaan swift
Seeing monkey, the monster blew,
With his terrible fist. *7*

Hanumaan sank on his knees and swiftly regained,
Rose in wrath, and struck Raavan returning the same.
Even as thunderbolt falls on huge styrax,
Hit Kapi's fist, and the Demon fell genu flexed.

From spell of his swoon, soon he recovered,
Abashed he admired the monkey's power.
"O Raavan ! shame on myself, fie !!
None is my valour, if you'r still alive."

—Now Hanumaan carried off like a child, Lakhan,
The bewildered Vile at this sight was stunned.
In presence of Ram, brought, was Ram's brother,
Ram elixired his swoon with nectarian words.

Words of loved brother, worked the nectar,
In a trice rose Lakhan from stupor.
Lakhan came post-haste to the field determined,
Again he darted through thick and thin.

Styrax=A thorny tree(like babool)
Through thick and thin=at any risk, resolutely determined; Stupor=unconsciouness.

Stanza: *In wrath, on the wretch, Lakhan despatched*
Myriads of the shafts,
Running riot, he smashed chariot,
In vortex of shafts, charioteer retched. A
With the dizzy blitz, Raavan was hit
In fit of unease, he fell to ground,
One able charioteer, seeing King in trouble,
On the double, took him away to town. B

Couplet: *The valiant Lakhan returned,*
From the front in utter ease,
While demons were stunned,
The field hushed in seeming peace. 8

Belittled Raavan for his brittle might,
To get new mystic height, he sat to perform sacrifice.
Here, Vibhishan got news from spies,
Hastening to the Lord everything he apprised–

"Now, he has realized' he catches a tartar,
For unholy gain he is on mystic altar.
"Once he completes this unholy sacrifice,
In its divine shield, he will never die.

"So, my Lord ! send some warriors at once,
So that the wretch may be compelled to return."
Lord sent Hanumaan, Angad, as the day broke,
Fearlessly they escaladed over the fort.

Through ballium and bailey crossed to belial's palace,
In a sacrifice, they saw him engaged.
'O goose !' Said Kapi 'You vamoosed from bellum,
In business of pomp, you lost aplomb."

Vortex=Dizziness ; Retched=fell sick, (vomited)
Vamoosed=fled hastily.

"You doubt yourself and your own might,
So you sit here idle, and escaped the fight.
"Your malign-latry for more sortilege,
Here I ravage, O wretched savage !"

So saying Angad struck him with foot,
But the fool overlooked absorbed in own pursuit.

Stanza:

Struck by foot, yet he overlooked
And kept absorbed in his persuit,
When he refused to look, monkeys abused
Bit him, hit him yet he kept mute. *A*

Enraged they then, grabbed him by locks
And dragged away the wretch,
Finally, in choler, he rose from altar,
By then, the sacrifice was wrecked. *B*

Couplet:

His diabolic soul abetted,
For malign-latry,
Raavan felt discomfitted
For the hope was vanished by monkeys. *9*

Having done the job monkeys returned safe,
While chagrin set him out ablaze.
Evil omens occurred as he proceeded,
Vultures, crows flew and perched on his head.

Being in jaws of death, he heeded none,
And exclaimed "call to arms, beat war-drum."
Endless champs from camps, caves hides and flanks,
Marched on foot, wings, horses, chariots, elephants.

All marshal demons embittered the phalanx,
Arrayed to face Lord, as the moths dart to the flame.

Malign-latry=unholy worships; Sortilege=magic power.
Abetted=supported to commit sin

Celestials approached Ram to His billet,
'Demon's end is belated, no more the war be played.'

With mettle, up in arms, on head matted locks,
To heal the Human, Heaven, He turnedst to havoc.
The ghastly dews, which had daubed the world,
All appeared in His ruddy eyes, in thready curls.

He fastened His quiver with xanthic cloth,
Took in His hand formidable Saranga, the bow.

Stanza: *Took in hands the bow, in quest of foe*
To His waist fastened winsome quiver—
Post haste, to ravage the savage
In great rage, raided the Supreme soldier. A

The ancient bard, Tulsidas
Belauds his Lord, the bellicose,
Up in arms Ram, charmth the swarms of
Friend and fans and alarmth foes. B

Couplet: *Mark! Ram taketh by the storm*
Himself fronted in field,
To right the world's wrongs
For glory to friends, gory end to fiends. 10

THE BELLUM LETHALE

Lo ! there ! arriveth demon host with crowded ranks,
And vastly arrayed in wide phalanx.
Here primates are rushing to meet their foes,
Like the clashing clouds, are making chaos.

Like the gleam of thunder look swords, bilbos,
And many hues of monkeys are making rainbows.

Take by storm=attack.

Trumpeting of elephants and rattling of chariots,
With added shrilling cries, making din of thunderbolt.

Both armies here stand at bays,
Like rain, here begins the pelting of shafts.
This day, see! on the top, leads the Best of Raghus,
And ist continually wounding the demon crew.

As the shafts of Ram, are piercing through,
In dizzy gyri they are falling in gory stew.
Some unsoldierly demons are now on back foot,
Yet most of hosts are trying to prove.

Stanza: *The Ghastly dews of ghost's crew*
Overflew as ruddy flood
On corpse of champs, fell limbs maimed
Yet some aimed forward daubed in blood. *A*

Over field in clash, shafts made a mesh,
And smashed fiends in great carnage
And some belials, in bellum finale,
Assailed again, regaining courage. *B*

Couplet: *Over the carpeted deads, half deads,*
Hopped and crossed the monkeys through;
And pierced through the fields spread,
The demons looked subdued. *11*

Now new set of giants, ghosts, genii, goblins,
In spleen attacked on monkeys in full swing.
For vultures, crows, field served lavish treat,
On grim wings they flew with flesh in beaks.

Crows, kites flew off with arms and flesh,
Which they snatched from one another and ate.
Through adulterous bellies of belials they probed,
And flew with hanging guts, from beaks blood daubed.

Bleached faces rounded and rounded in blank,
Till in own pool of gore their bodies sank.
As the injured ones, on the half deads, collapsed,
Helpless moved they not, and finally gasped.

Diabolic souls to leave frame, strained,
Till wounds had squizzed their last drain.
Spirits-specks, on the corpes dandled,
Took to storing the blood in skulls.

Vampires chuckled seeing field, the shambles,
Thrilled they sang shrill clashing skulls as cymbals.

Stanza: *'T was feat of Death, feasted wraith,*
Ravaged in battle, relished on the dead,
Ghosts in gustos, frolicked on torsos,
While 'Jai ho' shouted the beheaded's heads. *A*

Spirits-witches, danced on liches
On ditches of gore they quenched the thirst,
Fox' Jackals, dogs mongrels
Gulped, when surfeited, they snarled worst. *B*

Couplet: *Raavan brooded in panic—*
I am left all alone,
Yet I have with me tricks
Let me spell illusions. *12*

Many headless trunks trotted along the field,
While heads shouted shrill "Kill! Kill!!",
Struck by blitz of Ram's shafts,
On the lap of death demons were laid.

All souls sacrificed their mortal frame,
Whether friend or foe, reached Ram's own promised land.

Lich=dead body ; Wraith=phantoms, ghosts ; Gusto=entertainment.

Seeing Lord bare foot, the heaven was abashed,
Forth with, his own chariot Indra despatched.

Delighted Matali* alighted it on the field,
Gladly Lord Ram, mounted it.
Driven by four horses, as swift as the thought,
On war path the horses knew no sloth.

With renewed vigour monkeys rushed forward,
When they saw Lord Ram, mounted a chariot.
To Lord Ram, the spell of Raavan, stood feeble,
While monkeys nay Lakhan took it for real.

Monkeys witnessed among the demons swarms,
A number of forms of Laxman and Ram.

Stanza: *Monkeys' swarm, was alarmed,*
Had qualms, finding numerous Lakhan-Ram,
All stood in awe, like in predella
Gazed, were dismayed, bellum turned bedlam. *A*

Ram smilt, at the exploit of the vice
And his spell that widely swelt,
For Ram's mettle, it was too little,
In short spell He dispelt the spell. *B*

Couplet: *Lord Himself now assailed*
Seeing own champs toil-worn,—
"Stay ! ye now watch my duel
With stubborn Raavan, the hell-born." *13*

He recalled Lord Shiv even as He moved,
Who is warrior in 'every warrior of Truth'.
Poisonous Raavan with toxic heart,
Sick in rage, now darted to meet Lord.

Sloth=laziness; *Indra's charioteer.

The King of Savage, gaged in rage—
'Heed ! this is war path, not a hermitage!"
"I am Raavan, a name of steel,
Many braggart are beggared in my bastille.

"Even Heaven dareth not my glory to challenge,
How You dare ! hermit ! to take revenge.
"Killing a hermit 'll bring me penitence,
Go for penance, now Your mind, You change.

"I knew, Khar, Dushan, Baali you slew,
They had the thew of feud in them a few.
"Even as a hunter would shoot his game,
But then in warfare he hath no name.

"Tho it brings me no grace to combat,
With You a midget and army of primates.
"Yet for Kumbhkaran and Meghnaad, I'm vengeful,
I'll fight till from battle You vamoose.

"Me, Raavan, relentless, is no less than Death,
Here, I writ Law of tit for tat.

Stanza: *Ram spake, standing at bay—*
"Your thew was true but now it's trite
"now crow no more, show your valour
At your door hath come now the fight." *A*

"Human was pale, heaven was a hell,
Demonry prevailed, it was tough,
No toft for the troth was left
Tophet tortured the Earth enough." *B*

Gaged=challenged ; Bastille=fort prison.
Toft=home ; Troth=faith (virtues) ; Tophet=hell ; Stand at bay=at war ; Trite=old/stale, weak.

Couplet: *Raavan laughed off Ram's words—*
"O feared ! it's mere spiel
Not the words but the sword,
That works in the battle." 14

Then, In reply to torching* words of Lord,
Raavan uttered bitter all scorching to heart.
In fury then the demon King hurried forth,
And despatched arrows like thunderbolt.

Various designs of his shafts were tough,
Filled dense, every flank like catastrophe.
Speedily dispatched arrows namely Bhak, Kiti
Sharabh, Ushtha, Phani, Shuk, Vakra, Keet, all horrid.

Gandak, Balaak, Sharp like missiled pelted on Ram
Looked like swift invading locusts' swarms.
Same mo, Raghu's Hero, fretted and fumed,
Let fly dart, and demon's bolts were consumed.

Raavan ground his teeth out of chagrin,
Making din he then hurled a fierce javelin.
But Ram sent it back with own guided dart,
Thro' demon's body pierced its smarting part.

Came demon with new volley of discs and tridents,
With no toil in a trice Ram frustrated them.
The unending attacks of Raavan, He rebuffed,
He then was stirred up with terrible huff.

Stanza: *Bearing the brunt of raiding front*
Every gush of thrust Ram rebuffed,
Now, in war to end war
Ram marred and warred, full of huff. *A*

Spiel=long winded talk.
*Enlightening; Smarting=pain giving.
Rebuff=repel an attack.

The field rocked, fiends shocked
Hearing havoc of twang of His bow,
Arrows in quiver, vied one other
In endeavour to shoot forth. B

Couplet: *Ram drew bow-string,*
And let fly volley of darts
There quaked heart of queen,
Here, keen heaven frisked at heart. 15

Hissing arrows flew like firing squad,
Laying low charioteers horses in first spell.
Next shafts tore off banners and flags,
Now, demon's inner core had within him failed.

Yet, he roared and rolled on to other chariot,
In wrath from new Rath the missile he hurlt.
Even as goes in vain the crafty man's ruse,
All incursion of missile's volley was diffused.

Then Raavan hurled ten pikes anew,
Thus four divine horses of divine chariot were overthrew.
Ram raised horses and in new coarse raid,
With volley of arrows to the foe He sped.

Like the sting of wasps enter lotus-bed,
Waspish shafts conveyed and pierced Raavan's head.
Fresh pelter of shafts now, pierced thro' his brows,
From the mountainous demon, gory cataracts coursed.

What his demonry did, over Earth's face, before,
Same way the sinner's face was daubed with own gore.
Like a moving mount with ghastly founts,
Tho' afraid but headed forward on the front.

Ghastly founts=fountains of blood; Ruse=trick

One by one Ram then, with shafts shot down,
Monster's head and limbs, to the ground.
Time after time Ram smote heads and limbs, but
They were renewed as soon as, were cut.

His heads-arms, over and over Ram maimed,
Seemed Ram took delight in playing such game.
Several heads limbs were replaced by the new,
Infinite of such hovered all over milieu.

Stanza: *The heads beheaded as soon as shed*
Were superseded by the new,
The milieu was filled with heads and limbs
Like the meteoric Rahu-Ketu. *A*

Ram's arrows fierce, through the heads pierced,
Severed shattered them into bits,
Arrows flew, transfixing through,
Making lour view most horrid. *B*

Couplet: *Nor the demon's heads, nor arrows,*
Exhausted in this battle,
Nor Ram's go, Nor Raavan's ego
Was spent in the duel. *16*

War-field depicts mundane and arrows, the trust,
While renewing heads depict the man's growing lust.
Raavan now perceived 'I am deathless,'
'and savage in me withstands the damage.'

With renewed heads, limbs and renewed ego,
Raavan despatched rows of arrows and arrows.
In this thick pelter the chariot of Ram went unseen,
Monkeys in chagrin, in chaos made screams.

Lour=threatening.

In the lust of war, Raavan threw tridents and discs,
Ram was lost to sight like the Sun in the mist.
The Earth sighed, cries came from on high,
Lord intercepted demon's arrow with new strike.

Ram struck off anew his renewed heads,
Bewildering thro' air those, flew and bled.
Gory heads shouted "Glory! my glory!! Jai ho!!,
Come on Ram! Lakhan! Sugriv" they echoed.

Stanza: *Myriads of heads, as they sped*
They shouted 'Where is Ram?'
Fiend's heads as they fleyed
From the field, fled monkey's swarms. *A*

Heads hovered fleyed, on field stacked
All were awed in odd lour
Now at war, to end the war,
Rampant Ram marred with new pour. *B*

Couplet: *Raavan, but, getting brief chance,*
At war, to get even,
Hurled forth his terrible lance,
Like the Death towards Vibhishan. *17*

The saviour, as He is of the supplicants
Became shield for Vibhishan, instant.
Himself to the force of lance, He exposed,
Lord showed unease tho' a mere sport.

Seeing Ram hurt; burst in reprisal rage,
Vibhishan rushed to the vile seizing his mace—
"O Knave ! you braved humans, havens, heavens,
Now this battle will bring to you a bitter end.

Fley=terrify(cause fear)

"O Ten headed monster ! better be said 'fat head',
You offered one head to Shiv, got in return myriads.
"You have terrorized heaven above and havens beneath,
Yet have been spared till now from death.

"O fool ! how you seek in life smiles,
To no avail is glory to Ram's hostile."
So saying Vibhishan struck him right on chest,
Raavan tumbled to the ground at sudden impact.

Stanza: *At potent impact of cogent mace*
On Robust chest, Raavan came to dust,
Rival Raavan rivelled, yet picking self
He the hurt, hurlt shafts in outburst. *A*

Now two champs, for the duel came,
They wrestled, tumbled in terrible row
Size of fight inside Vibhishan
Was a prized might that Ram bestowed. *B*

Couplet: *Befo' Raavan who remained on knees,*
With the size of Truth within
Remained not meek weak,
Belittled him in battle field. *18*

Raavan was stunned at stern attack
Of Vibhishan; who made him sweat.
On Vibhishan's face too, appeared weary pearls,
Hanumaan took up battle a rock he hurled.

The horses he hurled, charioteer he harled,
At the same gave Raavan a kick on vault.
In the dizzy whirls, Raavan kept standing tho'
There upon he challenged the Monkey Hero.

Mace=club with spikes; Harl=drag along ground.

The tail is certain weapon of a Monkey
Hanumaan spreaded his tail quick.
Raavan held tail but Hanumaan flew up,
Now turning again, closed with him in high huff.

Hovering like prey in paws of eagle,
Raavan was caught in big ordeal.
From field it seemed a black gem,
Was a locket hung through a gold chain.

When burden couldn't be over thrown by trick of thrust,
Hanumaan invoked his Lord and trust.

Stanza: *Niching in heart Ram, perching on head of demon,*
Hanumaan crowned him with a kick,
With full blown hit, the demon's grip,
Slipt from tail, he fell on the field. *A*

Hanumaan in delight, did alight
To resume fight fell on foes
From sides both, the brute force
Sallied forth and champs closed. *B*

Couplet: *Here Battle-mad Raavan, crushed,*
Primates' army with arms.
Then Ram in ire rushed
For now Raavan unfurled his charm. *19*

Now Raavan evanesced, now revealed in multiples,
Some forms were battle-mad, some waited as murals.
His forms multiplied into one for one,
Feared monkeys, bears vamoosed passim.

Thundering darted forth in every scene, the Knave,
Dismayed primates fled crying "O Ram ! Save."

Ordeal=difficult situation; Passim=here and there.

With the pithing roar of demon, the army got palsied—
'Among fragile chances, confide no victory.'

"While the heavens, havens are subdued by the Knave,
Now that he is multiplied let's hide in caves.
"Now that hopes are at the other end of the rope
Help Ram ! Help Lakhan ! thou art our prop."

It's no better to say of army of primates
Nay, the gods godules in panic fled.
Only soldierly soldiers and the seekers seers knew,
The fate of fight, their insight hath deja vu.

Stanza: *Army of primates, in the fright of fate*
Fled finding multiples as real.
Monkeys, bears hosts, here valour lost
Cried 'O Saviour ! save from ordeal. A

Raavan spreaded sleight, to slight
the might of Lord in field,
Yet, Hanuman raided, Raavans myriads
Many killed by Angad, Nal, Nil. B

Couplet: *Lord Kent heaven's pangs*
The mortals' fright
*Fitted shaft in His Sarang**
Thus, all sleight of Raavan was wiped. 20

In a trice Lord dispersed the whole show of phantom,
Even as mirky canopy is torn by the Sun.
Heaven, then rained abundant blossoms,
For the vernal relief in their bosom.

With the chagrin within, Raavan now kent,
His cunning treasure was being spent.

Deja vu (*F*)=already seen.
*Name of bow of Ram; Sleight=Indrajaal

Fearless monkeys rushed, the Lord they extolled,
And raided there, where tides of battle rolled.

Seeing marshalled monkeys Raavan thought,
"they think I am now reduced to a naught.
"I 'll be the cause for their final hush"
—so saying he sprang into air with great thrust.

Struck with awe, sky turned unmanned,
But to catch hold of him Angad sprang.
Seizing Raavan by ankle he threw him down,
In his way gave him a kick and shown him ground.

Stanza: *Having seized the Knave, a kick he gave,*
In din of pibroch, him he reproached.
Angad bellicose, breaking his cuirass,
His weapons he tossed, then to Ram he approached.

Raavan then rose, with shrill roar,
In vain-ego he rained arrows,
From front to flanks, wounding foe's ranks
he rated his pranks as prow's show.

Couplet: *Once again Ram with new blitz*
Tore off Raavan arms heads,
He regained through his weirds,
Like in the woods grow weeds. 21

Monkey chagrined by renewal of his heads—
'would he ever to accursed nature pay the debts.'
All the chiefs were chafed by clumpy craft,
All together they darted for joint on- slaught.'

Hanumaan, Angad, Sumukh, Nal-Nil,
Sugriv and others all marshalled martials,

Cuirass=breast plate ; Pibroch=battle cry ; Weirds=magic.

With rocks and trees they besieged,
And hurled upon Raavan making a heap.

Bursting the heap the Giant came up with outburst,
Rushed to prove himself, the monkey's accurse.
All champs unstirred kept standing at bay,
Closed in with Raavan to prove themselves.

Some perched over nape and tore his scapulae,
And slided in play along vertebrae.
Others escaladed over knees, waist, chest,
And braved to attack him face to face.

They tore mesomorphic flesh with claws,
Seeing wounds he felt troubled at heart.
The Giant could not catch nimble monkeys,
they hovered around him like bees.

He could succeed to catch some in grip,
But through webs of the Giants the pigmies slipped.
He gnashed, smashed and mashed some champs,
Hanumaan and other chiefs turned senseless.

Having rendered, in swoon, Hanumaan and all chiefs,
He further rejoiced to see "night has reached."
Now the second-line headed by Jamvant,
Rushed forward with bears carrying hills trees.

In ire irksome Raavan dashed bear flocks,
Teased, seized, squeezed creating a havoc.

Stanza: In puff of ire, demon cuffed bears,
Clutching them with fluff, them he flung
They flumped like a lump,
to get even the sum, Jamwant jumped on his bosom. *A*

Mesomorphic=strong built.
Fluff=hair of bear; Flung=threw on ground; Flump=fall with sound.

The bear-chief in ire chafed,
He, the great champ, stamped on his breast,
Struck on heart, swooned the demon fell on cart,
Flurried carter hurried him back. B

Couplet: *Here, Masters of eve's fight*
Recovering; in delight returned,
There, Raavan was circled by fright
For the swooning night they earned. 22

SIYA, WITH HER INNER BATTLE

Reached to Ashok grove some battle-drums' hums,
For Siya those buzzes were puzzling, dolsome.
Demoness Trijata reached to Siya that very eve,
And told Her the whole very narrative.

When She heard demon's heads got renewed,
She turned further more and more pensive.
'O elder ! what is going to happen?
How the world 'll be relieved of pain?

"The overlived demon outlives Lord's shaft,
Is he blest by the perverse fate.
"Nay, it's My ill fate that he overlasts,
Same ill luck keepth Me away from My Lord.

"I have paid dearly for gold dear,
That phantom still frawns at Me, I fear.
"Same providence prompted Me to be harsh,
To Lakhan, in the moment of trial, Alas!

"Same words revert to Me as tempered shafts,
And wound through My tender heart, bereft.

Dearly=with great loss.

"I survive it is He who keepth Me alive,
He alone as well is conserving Raavan's life.

"A war in Me goeth day and night,
Nor My breath ends nor my inner fight."
Invoking Her Master, thus Siya cried,
With healing touch then Trijata replied—

"With an arrow in heart Raavan will sure die,
He striketh not, He knowth in his heart 'Siya abides'

Stanza: *"Ram striketh not, with this thought*
That in demon's heart, he hides Siya.
And Ram dwellth in Siya, further in Ram,
Dwellth all iota, all biota." *A*

Thus Trijata briefed, Siya was filled
With mixed thought of bliss and grief,
"the Qualm, you shake off, Ram 'll knock off
Raavan; certain! for world's relief. *B*

Couplet: *"With repeated cropping of heads,*
Disconcerned when he feels perplexed
When Thy thought from his heart escapes,
By Ram then he'll be zapped." *23*

With such soft reasonings Trijata solaced,
Leaving Her alone, then returned back.
War was prolonged with ghastly shed,
This added the pangs in Siya, already bereft.

Around Her the murky night was enveloped,
The sickle-orb was chiselling Her hope.
In the ocean of melancholy Her bereft core,
Had its sinking bark with no prop, no oar.

The twin lonesome eyes eyed starry road,
In the stretched night, the stars trod with sloth.
Clouds drifted in sky, veiled Her heart too,
On Her alone, the Grove's breeze blew.

Overhung trees with the breeze moved,
Even as a prey was besieged by phantom's crew.
As the night had stretched to the length of an age,
Her soul too wrenched within Her cage.

As Her eyes poured from Her cloudy heart,
To wipe Her doubts some good-omens occurred.
She felt she was no lonesome in that grove,
She had truth, had troth, and true love.

She felt good omen's affirmative nod,
As a blessing touch among all the odds.
There; from swoon Raavan recouped,
His carter who saved him, he reproved—

"Shame ! on you that incurs disgrace,
You brought me alive, me, the deadly to the Death."
His lust of war could hardly wait dawn,
He sallied forth ignoring shady horizon.

News of Raavan in the monkey's camp reached,
With boles, boulders they rushed gnashing teeth.

Stanza: In wee hours, hurried the monster,
Raided bears, forayed monkeys
They hurled forth, with full of force
Mounts and boles on sable army. A

The fiends, afraid from fields fled
Monkeys further assailed in the next spells.
They sieged, teased Raavan,
And seized and bruised him with jaws, claws and nails. B

Couplet: *The levied foe he could not face,*
To prevail this battle spell,
In forlorn hope he evanesced,
And reft the illusive juggles. 24

RAAVAN'S LAST WAR

Ballads

1

In that bellum-lethale ;
The wretch stretched spells,
Against teamed monkey's host;
He teemed goblins, ghosts,

2

And phantoms with bow, arrows ;
Yoginis with bilbos
Some huffed and some laughed ;
Half deads' blood, they quaffed.

3

They lauded their lord ;
In loud loury ballads.
With shrill yells, the belials,
Assailed the monkey's marshals.

4

Ope mouth ogres oped upon,
And now alarmed the monkey's swarm.

Reft=took by violence

Aghast by the ghastly ghosts,
Took to heel the monkey's host.

5

Where ever monkeys bears,
Veered, were deterred,
By the pyres mire or fire
Scared they all quivered.

6

Raavan uproared and now poured
Showers of gore to the fore.
In the mayhem of haemal hail,
Fagged monkey's wer' appalled and failed.

7

The flair of fronting flanks
In a flash, turned fagged and flail.
Champs, in chaos fell lost flesh,
And Sugriv Lakhan fainted as well.

8

He teemed now many form,
Of Hanuman those sieged Ram
They gnashed their teeth,
In rash act rushed to meet.

9

Screamed the teemed forms,
"grasp Ram! and zap Ram!!"

Fagged=tired; haemal=bloody, gory.

Stanza: *The Lord Ram, in midst, the form mystic,*
Charmed in arms, in thick of fray,
On the rampage, he darted shafts,
That erased all savage's mirage. A

Illusions dispersed, monkeys-bears cheered,
Again they arrayed and forayed.
Sans peur, monkey force
To make sure the win, they attacked. B

With knitted brows, Ram fitted arrows,
To right all the world's wrong,
Ram's assail, in the bellum lethale,
Can't be scaled in any bard's songs. C

Couplet: *For the size of fight, faith, fret*
For the mettle in the battle,
For wit, spirit of the primates
'words' are not created yet. 25

In the hour of great strife,
Fearless of wounds, arrows,
Not they, but fought their sacrifice,
In the great show of prows. 26

Gore, wounds and pain know no words,
Yet the sacrifices, in stoned eyes glitter.
The sacrificing dews from wounds are sacred,
From soldierly soldiers live or dead.

Lord struck off heads and arms many times,
For Ram it was simply a pastime.
Fresh crop of heads Raavan regained,
Like the covetousness grows with every gain.

In thick of fray=at war; Sans peur (fr)=fearless.

War stretched, the wretch could not be zapped
By the Lord then Vibhishan was looked at.
'Uma ! whose Will cause even death to the Death,
There by He tested his devout's faith.'

Vibhishan said "Lord! he is playful prey,
Of Thine who survives this thick of fray."
"Thy game dies not in bellum lethale,
For the ambrosial sac in his navel."

"Thou art All-wise, yet I do my part,
World's dark Thou mayst wipe with one dart."
Thus rejoiced Ram took terrible shafts in hands,
Decided to war, for the war to end.

Lankiness of Lanka became obvious,
Many ills presaged, presently themselves.
Echoed donkeys', dogs', jackals' howls,
Crows perched on demon's head and eagles whirled.

Comets appeared all over the sky,
The warbling birds made shrill cries.
Many solar orbs appeared but nipped,
By untimely occurrence of eclipse.

Idols shed tears in gynaeceum's niche,
Shed ruddy tears the pillars' caryatids.

Stanza: *Mandodari was perplexed, as the idols wept,*
Lightening torched, trees got scorched.
Quacked Lanka, queen recked in awe,
For lanky Lanka prayed her parched gorge. *A*

Cried the winged, for bones and minced
In sky they miffed, for gore and flesh,
As final bugle, in lethal battle,
Against baleful belial, Ram drew shafts. *B*

Gorge=throat ; miffed=petty quarrel.

Couplet: *The teeming Belial's heads,*
Were earth's bale and heaven's hell,
Ram attacked those with ballistic shafts,
Like the Death itself. 27

THE WAR IS WON

The bitter battle was a fun for the Lord,
Yet in the combat He played man-sized part.
With the Sarang he let flow shafts thirtyone,
In a wink they flew and the war was won.

Twenty armed monster, the Ten headed,
Was struck by thirty thirsty shafts.
One guided arrow which was left,
Struck and sucked up navel's depth.

Deuced torso headless and armless,
Danced on the battle field most devious.
Whirled deviously his diabolic trunk,
And already burdened Earth further sunk.

Ram drew and darted a shaft on torso,
That split it in two in a mo.
His heads roared, shouted, murmured and gasped—
"Where is Ram! Ram!!, let him not escape."

His torn wrists brandished weapons that held,
The earth reeled as the monster fell.
In sluggish widening, knees of the two halves,
Kneeled and on the field he, thus dropt.

His knocked off heads, arms declared itself,
The end of demonry and bellum lethale.

---

bale=load.

Guided darts took heads from field-O-bellum,
And reposited heads before queen at the bellium.

Thus the guided darts accomplishing job,
Into the quiver of Lord Ram galloped.
The immortal part of demon's mortal frame,
Dissolved within Lord as effulgence.

In the heavens and havens returned paradise,
'Victory! Jai Ho!! Glory to Ram!!!' filled the skies.
"O Saviour! O Liberator!! O Bliss!! O Truth!!
Glory! Glory be to Thy peerless virtues."

Stanza: *Gods, godules trumpeted*
Chanted lays of the Almighty's might,
Paradise wayed to Earth, heaven rejoiced in mirth,
Breeze breathed relief, through all wides. A
Elated gods, indebted to the Lord
Contented decanted floral rains,
For fulfilling the Cause ; in thrilling applause
Gods belauded loud, the Lord's paeans— B

"O Lenient!, Thy advent,
As Ram is balm to wounded earth,
Thou havest pleased heavens, relieved havens
n-blest calm to hearts and warmth to hearths. C

Couplet: *Thus, ended the endless frays,*
Were freight on Earth's face.
Lord dispelled the dismays
With a glance frought of grace. 28

Effulgence=flooded light(of spirit).
Decant=pour off.
Frought of=full of.

WAILS OF MANDODARI

Heads of Raavan laid in the bellium,
Spake of itself the end of the bellum.
Chiselled by the hammering melancholy,
Turned to idol of grief, Queen Mandodari.

Other queens too rushed to the spots,
Mandodari in grief fainted and dropped.
To the Raavan's remains came all queens,
Surrounding the debris all they keened—

Their hair flew loose, sat they lost flesh,
They set up shrieks, out of breath.
Caressing his carcass, they took heads on lap,
"Alas the day!" many ways they wept—

"My beloved! my lord! here lie low,
Sun-moon's haloes looked to whose glow.
"Who turned into heifer, the Earth's ego,
That beloved lord, here lie low.

"who was terror from Hades to the High above,
That beloved Lord here lie low.
"who dipt the heaven in flood of hellish flow,
That very beloved lord, here lie low.

"who robbed nature's robes of vernal show,
That beloved lord here lie low.
"Who conquered even the Death in row,
That beloved lord here lie low.

"O prow! O high brow!! didn't you know,
That Master masterth all above.
"nor sons, demons nor weapons, mammon,
Are of avail while you lie forlorn.

"What forced you O Raavan! to be ravener,
Being rival of Ram everything turned worst.
"The height you gained, now reduced to plight,
You vied the Might of Ram, the Wight.

"Alas ! Now jackals feast on your heads and arms,
But such sorry fate is due for the foe of Ram.

Stanza: *"Vied you, with the Wight thew,*
And tried you to slight His might.
It's Lord's way, the Ancient of days
As mere clay, He cometh man-sized. *A*

"You ever charmed, to harm others,
Wronged ever O Embodied Sin!
O Robust King ! your unjust sting,
The ruin, to your reign now brings. *B*

"Your lecherous core, your treacherous lore,
Secured valuables not the values
Your hatred, the Lord accepted
Yet in Own-self He absorbedst you. *C*

Couplet: *"We the queens bow to the Supreme,*
For He uplifted the evil-spirit,
And bestowed upon him,
Final bliss, the rarest gift." *29*

RELIEVED HEAVENS AND REVIVED HAVENS

The Queen Mandodari keened but her wise utterance,
Gratified the sages, seers, yogis, saints.
The Heavens, havens, human and hermits,
Looked at Supreme-wonder's wondrous deed.

Since ages the Earth had no free breath,
And suffered sacrilege by savage's saboath.
Seekers, seers, sacred souls now overwhelmed,
Feasted on Ram's visage with eyes brimmed.

Winning joy but in Vibhishan, scarce seemed to be,
Lamentation of women filled him with grief.
Seeing scattered, shattered his brother's thew, sinew.
Something within him seemed shattered too.

Seeing fate of strong brother, his heart burnt,
Eased by recalling, what he in the last earned.
As he approached into the bellium,
Shrieks and cries embraced him in welcome.

Heavily he walked, with heavy of heart,
There upon, Laxman was sent by the Lord.
Laxman solaced him and brought him to the Lord,
Through His eyes Lord pouredst compassion on sick-heart—

"The Life is a melee in life unto death,
Between mellow shines and melancholic shades."
"So win over sorrow and perform obsequies
The funeral rites, which are now due."

Vibhishan then performed with due reverence,
All obsequecies following ordinance.

Couplet: *Whose life was death of life,*
Of innocent biota,
Lord lavishly granted him
State of 'Ne plus ultra'. 30

Solaced and convinced with the Destined,
Praising Lord Ram, returned from the ballium, the queens.

Saboath=Armies; Sacrilege=profanation of sacred things; Melee=confused fight.
Ne plus utra=ultimate perfection

Gathering himself getting over the fix,
To his Lord then Vibhishan reached.

Lost flesh he stood bowed head,
To the need of time Lord Ram said—
"Lakhan ! hear me and ye champs,
Go Ye all !! and arrange crowning of Vibhishan."

"Your tender heart now aches for the loss,
But Vibhishan ! it's for betterment of the Mass.
"For my words not I go, but send monkeys,
And Lakhan who are as good as Me.

On behest of the Lord all proceeded in haste,
And enthroned Vibhishan with due reverence.
Thus demonry ended and taking place of the awe,
With hopeful shine began new era.

Who struggle with woes those silent hearts,
From them the faith put to the woes, depart.
With Vibhishan they all returned back,
Gratified Lord Ram then addressed—

Stanza: *To hear Lord, cheered all*
In honeyed words Lord gave hail—
"O Warriors! your valour
Hath won over, O dear!, Laurels; A

Monkeys race, now won the bays
And blaze of glory as well they won.
Vibhishan won his realm, And won his Ram as well,
Warbling this paeans, man will crosss mundane.

Couplet: *Blessing words of Lord Ram,*
In sweet honey imbued,
Sated not the monkeys' swarms
With words like nectar dew. 31

"Go now Hanumaan! to Siya with sure words,
The talk of town She may be taking as canard."
"Unstirred devotion and love have streak of qualm,
She may not trust, trustworthy news of Ram.

"Tell Her battle is now won, but not with arms,
But O Siye! it's all Thy faith in Ram."
Swift Hanumaan entered the peopled town,
Citizens ran in homage and bowed down.

Gratified they conducted Him to Ashok grove,
As he saw the Devi, Hanumaan bowed.
Him, recognised She as Ram's envoy,
Eager eyes looked at him with dews of joy.

"Dear Son! your presence tho' itself speaks,
Yet tell Me, of Lord, His fra, and monkeys."
"O Mother! Thy faith hath won the laurels,
Raavan hath been conquered in the battle.

"Vibhishan ist now the sceptred King,
It's all Merciful Lord's blessings."
She heard the nectarian words of envoy,
Thrill ran along Her veins with flood of joy.

Stanza: *Thrill ran, along Her veins,*
Her pain, drained in flooding tears
"Son ! none values, that equals the news,
What should I give you? What should I confer? A

"O Maa ! Heed !! What else I need,
Lord Ram hath won the field,
Raavan's razed, Savage is ravaged
Mankind is safe Lord's will is now fulfilled." B

Canard=fabricated story.

Couplet: *"O great warrior! little son!!*
May in you all virtues abide,
May Lord Ram and Lakhan
Ever within you reside." 32

THE EMBODIED BHAKTI, SEETA

"Now Son ! devise means, where by,
I may behold My Lord with Own eyes."
Treasuring Her words between folded palms,
Tarried not Kapi, hurried to Ram.

While the palms of Kapi touched Ram's feet,
those spake and apprised Ram, tho' remained meek.
Apprised of the prize of Siya's tidings,
Ram gladly called Vaanar prince and the sceptred King.

"Accompany Hanumaan both of you,
And escort Siya here, with regards due."
Where Siya was, gladly they stepped,
Found demonesses waiting on Her, over-modest.

They jewelled Her with ornaments and worshipped,
Then brought divine palanquin duly equipped.
With the flood of rapture, She entered palanquin,
With Her thoughts fixed on Ram, the Supreme.

The ravelling monkeys, rival on toes stretch,
And followed palanquin with eager gaze.
Ram said " let Monkeys see Her as they would
See their own mother, so bring Siya on foot."

Monkeys bears rejoiced to hear Lord,
And for echos of éclat the sky seemed short.
Oniy Ram was witness of Her pining image,
That was shadow element of Her divine visage.

For Mansized feats Ram had secured Her
Divine visage, into sacred fire.

Couplet: *Only the Divine-couple knew,*
What went in actual
But then Lord asked Her to prove,
In the fire, ordeal. 33

It was Ram's feat to bring Her back
From yogic fire; seemed a severe test.
The epitome of Bhakti, Her Lord to obey,
Filled with celestial fire, Siya then said—

"My Wed-Lord ist world-Lord as well,
So the truth should come to world through ordeal.
"In this sacred rite, Laxman ! be a priest,
Kindle me a fire and be swift."

Felt Lakhan, pining fire in words of Siya,
Scorching Lakhan was caught in dilemma.

With wet eyes he joined his palms,
But could not wait against behest of Ram.
Reading Ram's tacit go-ahead in His looks,
Laxman ran and brought some fire woods.

With bliss in Her heart, Siya flinched not,
For Her staunch faith and true stance—
"If I'm true in thought, words, deeds,
May this fire become like sandal to Me.

Stanza: *Fixing her thought on Her Wed-Lord,*
Performed Her part, for the World- Lord Ram,
Princess of Mithila, Goddess Siya,
With no trace of awe entered into flame.

Ordeal=trial by fire.

She whispered as She entered
Into fire 'Glory to Ram, Jai Jai Raghuvar.'
The Earth's awe worldly stigma,
With shadow of Siya, burnt in blazing fire.

It was Lord's feat, that was mystic
Quizzed by civic, but was right,
Gaining own real, through fire-ordeal,
She Shone on Ram's side, a Couple-Wight.

Couplet: *Real paradise descended,*
With the union of Siya-Ram,
Charm reappeared in Heavens,
In havens returned calm. *34*

Gods painted cosmos red,
And songsters revelled,
Peopled air was so glad
At the sight of the Divine-Couple. *35*

Monkeys, bears, here shouted and revelled,
"Glory to the Lord! Jai divine-couple!!"
Charioteer did his job to the best,
On Ram's behest Mataali returned back.

Now, came gods-godules fearless,
Ever who lived to selfish interest—
"O friend of meek ! O pal of the weak !!
Thy mercy hath lavished, the grieved.

"Through his own sins, Raavan hath been perished,
Thou havest accomplished everyone's wish.
"Thou art real ethereal, shapeless tho' shaped,
Thou are nascent as well the Ancient of days.

"Thou art power within every minim,
Thou art thunderbolt within every atom.

"O Nameless tho' named, O frameless tho' framed,
In every Divine shine, Thou art Latent.

"Unborn Thou art, beyond almanac's dates,
From gnats to planets all art Thy puppets.
"for heavens and havens Thou assumest form,
To right every bit of earthly wrongs.

Couplet: *"Accept our worship*
Of our shallow souls,"
—Now the Creator with own lips,*
Prayed with flooded love— 36

BRAHMA'S WORSHIP

Hymns: *"O Abode of bliss, Lord ! Jai !!*
Thou the Lord of lords ! Aye
"Glory be to Thou, Thy Jai !
O dispeller of sins of mortal clay. 1

"Thy worships, nay, mere Name,
Makest cross the mundane.
"The compressed thew in each atom,
Is thy wonder O Non menon! 2

" O Master thou masterest,
Galaxies, planets and planets.
"Blue of welkin and Ocean's blue,
Ist gleam of Thy swarthy hue. 3

"The micro in every micro
Of macrocosm is Thy glow
"The mettle, metal and mammon,
Is all Thy Maaya in mundane. 4

Almanac=calendar (Panchang)
*Creator(Brahma), one of the Trinity; Non-menon=Unknowable.

"Sans Thouself, the Sansaar is what?
'ts corpse when soul sheds off.
"to rid burdened earth off its weight
Thy 'Sacred-coming' Thyself made. 5

"Thou, the Shapeless takes up the shape
To shape up the distorted snags.
"With our words, our heart do voice,
The lips are short to show the rejoice." 6

"Thou camest to the Earth for mankind,
For empty eyes, for laden whines.
"Blessed are the monkeys and the primates,
No ifs and buts are known to whose faith. 7

"While accursed is our immortal existence,
Knowth no reverence, our deifed frame.
"Our ethereal bodies lackst in devotion,
Ever dipt in merriment and passion. 8

O Compassionate ! it's Thy mercy,
Ist the perennial source of the blessings. 9

Couplet: *Thus the Creator Brahma,*
Prayed in His own ways
As relieved his creation's awe
Of inevitable damage. 37

There descended from high planes,
Paters of Raghukul and it's manes.
Celestial souls of paters and manes,
Back in every loss, bless in every gain.

Dashrath's soul beheld Son's deed,
Appeared on scene, could not restrict.

Whines=sign of pain.

Ram and Lakhan made obeisance,
And received blessings of father and manes.

"O revered father ! it's due to thy virtues,
The invincible ravenous Raavan I slew.
"In making of This Ram, I do see,
O father ! It's foresight of Maa Kaikeyi."

Father, Dashrath in his celestial forms,
Was overwhelmed hearing Lord Ram.
Ram perceived same warmth of old affection,
Lord, then, bestowed on him the firm wisdom.

Detailing narrative Shiv explained—
"Uma ! Moksha beatitude Dashrath didn't attain,
For the reason, his soul was set on 'Bhakti'.
Like devotees, he maintained separate identity."

The final beatitude, Moksha some devouts spurn,
In the depth of devotion, the height they earn.
Bestowed with more and more devotion,
Rapt in Bhakti, Dashrath then returned.

Couplet: *Perceiving Almighty's might,*
Came King of the heaven, Indra.
Relieved and filled with delight
Most humbly he worshipped— 38

INDRA'S WORSHIP

Hymns: *"O Lord ! man sized Thou comest,*
God, saints, innocents to bless
"Glory to Ram Gloria ! Gloria !!
For sick earth who is panacea.

"Glory to the slayer of demonry,
Through Thou, virtues getst glory.

"Glory to the reliever of Earth's burden,
Glory to the reliever of hearths and heavens.

"O Unborn! O Ancient of days!!
Thou camest for truth in various ways.
"Thy shapeless formless unpalpable form,
Havest shaped into Lord Ram.

"Thou art the troth within the truth,
For the seekers Thou art the sleuth.
"Thou art the breath and death in one,
Thou art the innocence of wisdom.

"Through Veds we read, O non menon!
Thy mystic feat and wondrous lesson.
"for some minds Thou art Absolute,
For some hearts Thou dost attribute.

"Veds declare Thou as unmanifest,
Seekers discovered Thou by inner quest.
"For truthful core and truthful lore,
For devotee Thou descendst to the fore.

"My words are words of every bosom,
Accept my prayers, the Te Deum."

Couplet: *"Thronged up gods, godlets,*
Polite, in delight prayed,
Then the Lord, the Compassionate,
To the celestial crowd spake— 39

"My Martial monkeys-bears never tired,
And faught for cause till martyred.
"In deep silence they now lie on field,
Their wreaked havoc is now, veiled by dumb chill.

Sleuth=path trodden on foot; Te Deum=hymns sungs as thanks giving.

"Sacrificed their lives, for my cause ; they
O Indra* ! puff their souls in their clay."
How mysterious were these words,
For the Lord who canst create and raze.

He wished only to give Indra respect,
Lest, Death and life art His puppets.
With ambrosial showers blessings rained,
Martyrs, warriors rose from the Dead, again.

Tho' showers could not distinguish between two,
But its effect as mastered by backing of Truth,
Here, souls of bears monkeys alone that revived
There, demon ghosts refused to regain such a life.

More so demon thought of Ram, only Ram at the end,
So, were rid of the bonds of mundane.
As for monkeys, bears they were celestials,
All manifested in mortal-size themselves.

Above all, it was Will of Shri Ram,
And His love and blessings over monkeys', bears' swarms.
And Liberated demons, attained exalted state,
The Lord is ever so kind even to afflicted.

Couplet: *Thus gods returned to their planes,*
Here, Shiv with rejoice and reverence,
Arrived in Ram's presence,
In moment expedience. 40

Lord Shiv, in form of 'bum'.
In emotion, was benumbed,
Thrilled all over with goose bumps,
Whispered thro' voice almost dumb— 41

---

*King of heaven; Bum=menidicant, beggar.

WORSHIP BY SHIV

Hymns: *"With bow and arrow in Thy hands,*
Save men ! the very mammon of mundane.
"For clouds of folly be the windy gale,
Be the fire for dense doubts' jungle.

"In the wave of mundane's mayhem,
O Lord ! for the innocents be the helmsman.
"Thou art shaped pearl, shapeless water too,
Thou takest attributes tho' boundless of attribute.

"In the delusive sky of cloudy mind,
In the frost of folly, thou art the Sun-shine.
"For the beastly thoughts of pride and passion,
To kill such prey, Thou art the lion.

"For the lotus bed of lust to blast,
Thou are the chill of severest frost.
"For the depressed pits of melancholic thoughts,
Thou art the rain that falls on such draught.

"Thou art spectrum of every complexion,
On vernal canvas Thou art vivid paint.
"Thou art the devotion in my bosom,
Thou art the emotion in my paeans.

"Which fills wordless galaxies, that is 'Om'
O Ram ! Thou art its condensed epitome.
"O Raja Ram ! with Lakhan and Siye,
Make My heart Thy dwelling place, aye.
O Pal of supplicants ! count Me as devotee,
*O Saviour of VedVyas, take care of Tulsi.**

Couplet: *Now, I take leave, O All-Lord !*
When as Awadh's king
In Thy feat, be crowned
I'll come to catch glimpse. 42

---

*Tulsi (prays for every devotee.); Aye=ever ; Epitome=Embodiment

VIBHISHAN'S WORDS

All witnessed this modest talk fest,
Shiv bade adieu ; rest kept stood lost flesh.
The Sceptred King Vibhishan, was so obliged,
Bowed to the Lord approaching nigh—

"My words of prayers and my tongue of flesh,
Lacks to express Thy divine grace.
"I am meek, nay a mean and low born too,
I know nor morals nor virtues.

"A worm embedded in mundane's moss,
A gross creature of the cosmos,
"is bestowed with real ethereal mercy,
Me, deserve not those, for my ill-deeds.

"Enriched with Thy grace as I am,
I see no shine in Lanka's pomp, gold, gems.
"the sheen, silk, riches of Lanka are not mine,
All art owned by Thy divine shine.

"Now consecrate Lanka with Thy sacred presence,
And monkeys may be bestowed with opulence.
"I'm, I was and will be Thy own,
With men, mammon, manors of this throne.

"Now Thy toiled frame of battle field,
Should give chance to Lanka's luxuries.
"Before journey to Awadh, take little rest O Lord!
Then take me up along, as escort.

Stanza: *"O Vibhishan ! it's your devotion,*
What you told, ts soul you poured,
Your faith is sure, your heart is pure,
Your view is true in your core.

You yourself, your pearls and pelf,
Are all Mine-you do say
But any how, for Bharat's vow
Must I go now, with no delay. B

Couplet: *"He waits for Me, and scores,*
The course of each Sun,
His petrified eyes are sure,
That with in term I'll return." 43

"If passeth the term of my exile,
I shouldst not expect my Bharat's life.
"to him, I may soon be able to reach,
Therefore, arrange O friend! I beseech."

Ram's love for brother was full to the banks,
And the Ocean of love hath the pearls of Pain.
A panic appeared on His brow,
As He recalled again and again Bharat's love.

Overcoming emotions Lord asked Vibhishan—
" O friend ! now enjoy your sovereign,
"For as long as you wish and you can
Then like a saint to my abode ascend."

The blessings that stand all above,
Is the crown of the bliss, Ram bestowed.
Delighted bears and monkeys too,
Clasped they Ram's feet recounting His virtues.

Vibhishan then withdrew to the palace,
And the divine aerial car he, himself decked.
With jewels, laurels and florals,
And pearls, apparels and rare articles,

Pelf=riches.

'Pushpak-Vimaan', as it was called,
Was brought and set before the Lord.
Ram asked looking large troops nigh and far—
"Vibhishan ! drop largess' rising up in aerial car."

Rising up in 'Vimaan', over the benign belligerent,
He dropt from aerial car jewels, pearls, gems.
Picking up the stones each took a fancy to,
Took in mouth, the uneatables, and would throw the unvalued.

Not in benign primates, but with civic sense,
The dispute evolves for the pomp of gems.
Siya-Ram-Lakhan felt amused at primate's innocence,
For they valued gems, as would value, the saints.

Couplet: *To say about whom,*
Even sages, veds are confused,
With monkeys, that very Ram,
In diverse ways thus amused. 44

Piety, prayers and penance,
May fail to evoke
Lord's grace ; to the extent
As does the pure love. 45

Having secured thus ornaments, raiments,
Bears monkeys adorned their person with the same.
All appeared then before Lord of Raghus'
He once again felt amused—

"O Warriors ! it's all through your thews,
I succeeded in defeating Raavan and his troops.
"Fear none ! to your home-forests ye return,
Ages and ages will sing your paeans."

Monkeys' bears' troops of various hues,
Replied "it's none of our might and thews,

"Our martial spirit only this much knows,
Perching up the trees we caper on boughs."

"its well becometh of Thou, what Thou sayst,
It's none our share, lest, in conquest.
"Mankind and monkeys are Thy manikins,
Thy shelter maketh, anyone's win.

"While Thou mentionst of our prowess,
We shrink within self and feel abashed.
"Could ever the Swarms of the gnats,
Help the Divine Erne to aviate?"

They had no inclination to return home,
Their words choked in deep emotion.

Stanza: *With fixed devotion, with mixed emotions,*
They sticked to command of their Lord,
They all dispersed; on trees they perched
Niching Ram's visage in their heart. *A*

Mixed with joy and blues, they bade adieu
Bowing anew, they departed
Angad, Nal, Nil and Hanu thrilled
And looked at Ram, intently rapt. *B*

Couplet: *With empty face, filled eyes,*
All martials and chieftains,
Stood joined palm, hushed voice,
With silence of prepense. 46

BACK TO AYODHYA ON PUSHPAK

Before Ram, the troth of devotee's bow,
But Ram dost bow before truth of love.

Erne=golden Eagle (divine vulture, Garud.)
prepense=predecided intention.

Mounting up on the vimaan Ram with Lakhan and Siya,
Took chiefs and Vibhishan, up with love.

Reverently Ram bade adieu to penates of the land,
'Vimaan' now moved to north on Ram's command.
The Vimaan took off with intense din,
And shouts of 'Jai Ram!' filled the welkin.

On a lofty throne of Pushpak Shri Ram sat,
And Lordess Siya, accompanied on His left.
From clouds to clouds it scudded in speed,
From on high stranged mirthful eyes peeped.

Broad canvas of the land looked splendid,—
One, very Earth, with no men's boundaries.
"Lo Siye !" Said Ram "see the field's spread,
With demon's gore Lakhan have daubed it red.

"Now Mark Siye ! Here Laxman slew
Meghnaad; Here Hanuman laid the demon's crew.
"Here fell Raavan the Brave, but the Knave,
Thus ended demonry, the Earth to save.

"Here see across ocean the bridge,
I installed here 'Rameshwaram', the symbol of bliss."
So saying Ram and Siya both made obeisance,
And thus aerial car crossed the northern banks.

The earth was apparelled by Sylvan greens,
With lappet of silky frills of wrinkled ocean.

Couplet: *Every spot in the dense,*
In the path of the quest,
Where ever Lord Ram encamped,
To Siya He mentionedst. 47

Lappet=loose part of garment.

The ascending smokes spotted the hamlets,
With rare-spread along the forest-bed.
Birds, on high, those stood on gyrating wings,
Looked at the passing Vimaan, as strange thing.

Forthwith 'Vimaan' reached the Dandak forest,
Where delighted Ram reverently alighted.
Here Ram visited havens and ashrams,
Then flied to Chitrakoot, the sanctum-santorum.

Gratifying huts, havens, Kaamad hill of Chirtakoot,
Aerial car speeded further on the northern route.
Swarthy stream of Yamuna passed next,
There-after they espied the holy Ganges.

The Divine couple then made obeisance,
At the crest of holy places, the Prayag confluence.
The native breeze filled the bosom and eyes too,
Dipt they, in essence of homely milieu.

Couplet: *Here landed Ram with bliss,*
And bathed in holy confluence,
At peopled shore granted gifts,
To the hearths, hermitages, havens. 48

The Lord then instructed Hanumaan—
'Go ahead of Us to Awadh O Hanumaan !'
Takeup guise of a pupil, tell Bharat of our coming,
And come back swift with his tidings.

Hanumaan left, for what was asked,
Lord then called on the sage Bharadwaj.
The sage offered Him worships with Prayag's folks,
All blessed, Shri Ram for the coming epochs.

Santum Sanctorum (L)=holiest of holies.

Lord in turn, praised the sage, hermitage, its aim,
Mounting car, flied across the Ganges' banks.
Nishaad rushed hearing that the Lord had come,
Summoned his men, and came to this bank.

Siya offered here all kinds of worships,
In gladness of soul, Ganges bestowed blessings.
Nishaad ran to his Master, in bliss rapt,
And fell flat on sand, all lost flesh.

With all warmth Lord clasped Nishaad,
His ownself Lord Himself too lost.

Stanza: *Shri Ram clasped, the two lost flesh,*
Regaining Self, Lord seated him next,
Ram inquired, his welfare
"Ram ! Thou art near, so all is blest." A

"With my faulty core, and crafty lore,
I do adore, a Laud of a lout.'
O Benign ! ignore me a maligned,
I adore O Divine! Take me as Thy devout." B

Lord rapt, like Bharat himself,
In arms clasped him again and again,
One, who warbles lays, of this warry frays,
Crosses the waves of warring mundane. C

Couplet: *With warmth of war, who listens,*
The warrior Ram's paeans.
Unending victory, wisdom,
Saves him from warring mundane. 49

Warring Devil ever tortures,
The divinity within self,
Inner Ram who discovers,
Wins in Kaliage the laurels. 50

□

‖ UTTAR KANDAM ‖

28

Each nation has a mission for the world.

—Brahmrishi Vishwatma Bawra

STROPHES

1

The praise worthy Absolute,
in His Swarthy form I recall,
and Whose hue reflects in the Blue,
very same Ram I extol.

2

Armed with bow and arrow, Charmed in yellow
Mounting on Pushpak, pointing to Ayodhya,
The Lord of lords, Shri Ram I belaud,
Glory be to thou, O Ram! Gloria!!

3

Let me be, the thirsty bee
Of Thy lotus feet, O Prince of Ayodhya,
Whose, narrative blossom, in Shiv's bosom
plucked by Tulsi, as panacea.

(Gloria = Glory be to)

4

I adore, the statue of Truth,
Truer than the Truth, The comely Lord Shiv,
Slaying Kaam, praying Raam Detailed who,
To the world, Ram's narrative.

THE RETURN

Couplet: *Pencilled towers Ram viewed,*
From, on high, the aerial car,
Pushpak alighted in purlieu
When the town came steps far. 1

Awadh was not an Awadh,
While Ram was in exile,
People counted crawling period
Every mo lingered too wild. 2

Petrified eyes watched the path,
Panic was at its climax,
Every mo like an age passed
Long bereaved no more could wait. 3

Now, the peopled air was lavished,
With good omens all about,
All ills now vanished,
Festive mood permeated into crowd. 4

Spread of mellow milieu,
People felt in their marrow,
Clairvoyance clearly viewed,
Life 'll come to Awadh, morrow. 5

Queen-mothers were all inwardly glad,
As if someone was about, good news to tell.
Overjoyed Bharat counted the end of the term,
But with anxious heart, felt panic again.

Bharat goeth in grotto and cometh out again,
No where he stayed for a moment.
But for just one day, term of exile ends,
Bharat's heart was filled now with pangs—

"How is it that my Lord didth not turn up?
Must He be thinking of me, a corrupt.
"Woe is me! Abandoned by Lord, Alas!
Ram knew me to be perverse and false.

"Along with Him, He tookth Lakhan, the blest,
He is the real fortunate, the Embodiment of faith.
"For my life to stay, just a day is left,
Shouldst He forsake my faults, for my sake.

"Lord overlookth faults and lookth at devotee,
So earnest ist my intent, that should earn Him for me.
"But if I out live and Exile term dies,
No one would be so wretched as I.

Couplet: *At sea in will-o' the wisp,*
Of scuppering marshy views,
Came Hanumaan, the son of Wind,
Like a ship to his rescue. 1

Through Bharat's grim eyes brimmed love,
Found seated on Kus-grass,
For brother, like Bharat, it behoves
To be so anxious, as he was. 2

Grim=determined; Scupper=to sink (a ship); At sea=Confused.

Recognizing Hanuman as Ram's envoy,
His arrival filled Bharat with joy.
The great envoy of Ram, to balm his sore,
Spake all honey from nectarian core-

"You are framed melancholy, in whose absence,
Your every breath for whom is aimed
"You sorrowed day and night in your mould,
Yet your soul followed and was one with Whose soul,

"The battle He hath won to rescue every one,
That Ram, very Ram hath safely come.
"The comely couple along with Lakhan,
Wilt come soon at the end of the term."

Word poured as on thirsty draught nectar- rains,
He forgot years and years of his pains.
"This news in itself that you have brought,
Is no lesser than very sight of my Lord.

"What you told proves to be soul to my soul,
This joy, this bliss how can I hold?"
And his bliss streamed through his eyes,
But were different tears, than that rained days and nights.

"What you brought that content, to contain O pal!
My heart nay whole Awadh is too small.
"At your very sight, Kapi ! my woes have fled,
Himself, my very Ram, in you I have embraced.

Bharat, reverently saying so,
Took Kapi to the bosom with flooded love.
"Nothing can match this peerless news,
I am, thus unable to repay my debts to you."

Then Hanumaan bowed head with folded palms,
And narrated meritorious deeds of Ram.

"Tell me Hanuman ! my Lord with His grace,
Ever remembered me as one of His page."

Stanza: *"Did Ram's grace, ever recall this page?"*
-His words filled with thrill Kapi,
Joy ran, along Kapi's veins,
Reading Bharat's modesty. *A*
At feet Kapi fell, spake to self,
Whose praises even Ram reciteth,
It behoves, for such beloved
Of Ram, to be such a polite.' *B*

Couplet: *To Bharat, Hanuman told*
"What in Lord I have viewed,
You are soul of His soul,
My words are truer than truth. *3*

Bharat embraced again and again,
With joy which couldn't be contained,
Kapi forthwith returned then,
To Shri Ram where He encamped. *4*

Bharat too returned with joy profound,
Informed Guru, then palace, then the town.
On wings of joy he himself informed all,
'Ram is coming soon safe and sound.'

Life returned in the gynaeceum,
Glow in mother's empty eyes returned.
Bharat personally eased mothers,
Informing to them Lord's welfare.

Crowded roads flew out of southern gate,
While damsels filled path's flanks with stately gait.
They all went as if river goes to meet ocean,
With revealing joy making rippling din.

All sallied forth making a great gush,
Wishing to quench own eyes thirst, first.
They ran as they were, leaving children, old folks,
'Brothren ! where is Ram ?' one and other they asked.

Nature too did ope it's treasures,
Thro' breeze, blossoms adding to pleasures.
Rippling waves of Sarayu welcomed,
With its clear stream, full to the banks.

Couplet: *With Guru, Shatrughan, Kins men,*
And host of the priests,
Bharat flooded with affection,
Set forth to receive. 5

Some women climbed up attics,
Looked up for aerial car,
The moment, they espied it,
They began melodious choir. 6

Just as in full moon ocean swellth
Same way citizens behaved,
While men swelt full to banks,
Women moved to and fro like waves. 7

Here Shri Ram showed from height,
The charming city to the monkeys, with delight.
"Sugriv! Angad!! Vibhishan!! listen!!
Holy is this city, homy is this land."

"Tho' Veds extolled paradise as divine,
Yet it's not so dear to Me as this city of Mine.
"To its north flows the holy Sarayu,
Sacred is its air, and whole milieu.

"Contented to breath in native air,
This is My dwelling place, so I declare.

"He, whoever dwells in this land,
I consider him more Myself than I am.

"Towers, doors seem to be, of boles, bricks,
But see ! City hath a spirit, full of bliss.
"Mortal coil may be decked with glittering spoils,
But the man's soul is made of native soil.

"Thus mother-land is the first diety,
Her first worship ist Mine and your duty."

Delighted Monkeys said within self-
'Ram dost worship Ayodhya, its indeed blest.'

Through the dense peeps of purlieu,
Crowded up people, Ram viewed.
Some keen perched on the trees,
To welcome some kneeled on knees.

Some kept on their stunned view,
Some danced, some kept stood as statue.

Couplet:

Ram too was eager,
To meet Bharat and subjects,
He urged the aerial car,
To halt on lae very next. 8

Pushpak landed, Lord alighted from it,
And returned it back to its owner Kuber.
Emaciated in body with just bone and skin,
Even in this joy, subjects' lean years could be seen.

When Lord saw the great sages Vamdev and Vashishtha,
He ran with Lakhan to clasp their feet.
Vashishtha embraced and asked if all was well,
Ram said 'in thy grace alone, Our welfare dwells.'

Virtuous Ram now turned to the priests,
And bowed His head to the pious gathering.
Meanwhile Bharat clasped Lord's lotus feet,
The love, none the verses can word, can meet.

He laid prostrate on the earth,
Lord took him to bosom, both lost in each other.
In the coupled statue of the fraternity,
Bharat rapt in affection lost identity.

Lean years=barren years of separation from Ram.

Stanza: *In love's depth, Brother Ram clasped*
Beloved Bharat again and again,
Then rapt Ram, left not arms
Of Bharat as if regained the lost reign. *A*

In hush of voice, in gush of eyes
The brother's fervour needed no word,
Laureates confused, with defeated muse,
Can not bring the scene to the words. *B*

Citizens all wides, by these love-tides
Were dipt and floated all around,
Bliss was deep, beyond reach
Of worldly speech to recount. *C*

Couplet: *Lord gladly met Shatrughan,*
Pressed him to His bosom,
Laxman next in his turn,
Embraced two brothers with affection. *9*

The three devoted brothers of Ram,
Met each other with same old warmth.
Bharat shatrughan went ahead gladly,
And bowed their heads at Seeta's feet.

Citizens were transported at sight of Ram,
To years long sore, it worked a balm.
All mirks of melancholy eloped,
With coming up rising sun of hope.

All the life in peopled air began taking shape,
In wake of bliss, woes, worries escaped.
Every citizen wished Ram's same grace,
Like Bharat, as was taken into His embrace.

In countless forms, Ram appeared forth with,
And embraced everyone, as they wished.

Lord greeted them all in a moment,
Uma !* this mystery none could comprehend.

From the palaces ran queen mothers,
Even as cow would run at little heifer.

Stanza:

Rushed mother too, towards purlieu,
Like a calved cow rushes to heifer.
Sons and mothers, met each other,
Ram revered them with honeyed words. *A*

Thus Ram arrived, people derived
Beyond measure, endless rapture.
This sacred eve, became festive,
For long bereaved, brought elixir. *B*

Couplet:

Proud-son was embraced
By queen mother Sumitra,
But Kaikeyi felt embarrassed
While meeting Ram and His fra. *10*

With blessing warmth kaikeyi embraced,
Flood in her eyes washed Lakhan's bitterness.
Even as the lost infant finds mother's lap,
Siya rushed and mother's feet She clasped.

She kept Herself in the lap flesh lost,
Mothers crowned Her with blessings, fondling Her lot.
Eyes do read heart and speak in tears,
Of somber soul as well of heart in cheers.

Remembering it was occasion of rejoice,
Mothers checked tears that rose in their eyes.
Lighting festal lamps in gold salvers,
They waved lamps with flooding heart of a mother.

(*As narrate by Lord Shiva to deity Uma.)

Gazing upon soft tender sons; Kaushalya,
Recalling war, was amazed, yet today was awed—
"Too delicate are my two boys,
How havest they have killed the lord of Lanka.

Couplet: *She realized "a son is real son*
If He fulfils common cause,
Not for luxuries He was born
But to fight as great bellicose. 11

"for a son's born not to stay back,
Once he dents in warfields, the debt of womb he repays."
Between pride of lauerels and panic of battle,
Soft as well strong heart of Kaushalya wobbled.

Then she, with blessing gaze and grand merci,
Looked at the strange host of kapis.
Stood Sugriv, Nal, Nil, Angad and Vibhishan,
Jambavan, other chieftains, in the last Hanumaan.

Citizens welcomed and cheered up them all,
And greeted them as Ram's beloved pals.
Strange was Bharat's love, that strangers revered
His piety, psyche, purity, penance, prayers.

They extolled citizens seeing their life style,
Their lifeless life, while Lord was in exile.
Then He called comrades and warrior chiefs,
To clasp feet of Guru, the sage Vashishtha;

Saying "O pious! they are as so many barks,
Who took Me across the waves of war.
"Dearer to Me even than Bharat, them I take,
They put their lives, in My cause, at stake.

Psyche=soul; Grand merci (*F*) =many thanks.

Rapt they all heard the Lord's words,
Every moment brought neo joyous spurt.
Lord then summoned crony, play-mates nigh,
And met them all, as another, I.

Couplet: *Kapis reaching to Kaushalya,*
Touched feet, poured heart before,
In her they all saw,
Blessing soul of own mother. 12

Kaushalya blest them all with warmth,
"Ye art all as dear to me as my Ram."
People thronged up on barbican and rampart,
Through petals, florals all poured their hearts.

Peopled attics envied for Lord's view,
Paradise permeated through out the milieu.
Wishing Ram wilt soon come to the fore,
With welcome-gold-urns people decked their doors.

They set festoons, flags, and lamps with glow,
This welcome proved to be, a glad show.
From hither to horizon the spread of heaven,
Was filled with essence, fountains, plantains.

From haats to hearths every citizen poured,
His heart into town to deck every door.
Amusing music and muses filled the environs,
With the din of lute, flutes, kettle drums and gongs.

Stanza: *Damsels warbled, ballads festal,*
Belauded Lord in chorus psalms.
Graced ladies, gathered in bevies,
Scattered offerings all about Ram. A

Waved the lamps they, warbled lays,
Their crazed ways were enfete.
The city, sacred, extolled by Veds,
In glad-show was painted red. B

Couplet: *Nature spreaded all vernal,*
In the gardens and groves,
Lord of lords to welcome,
Such gala of nature, behoves. 13

While on the lanes of Awadh, Ram passed through,
Good omens occurred themselves to prove.
Thus the sun crossed half arch in pace,
While Ram came back, the day itself turned blest.

Greens, teens, to veterans all followed behind-
His home coming, with homage in mind.
Lord came to know that Kaikeyi was abashed,
To reassure her, first He went to her palace.

Gratifying her much in various ways,
Reassured Ram then came to His palace.
Sage Vashishta, summoned priests and spake thus-
"The day, hour nay everything is today auspicious.

"May to every concerned it be known,
Ram getth on this very day, long waiting throne."
The resolved plan of the sage Vashishtha ,
In the joyous hour, added further bliss.

For, Ram's Rajya was dream of world itself,
It would be not just regal, but for plebs.
Virtuous deed is said best performed,
To right all wrongs, if men it prompts.

Enfete(*F*) = in festivity.

Couplet: *"At the very first chanced luck,*
O Sage ! linger no more,
Apply to His head 'Tilak'
To make Ram Rajya sure." 14

THE CORONATION

People of Awadh thus requested,
For Ram's reign enough they had waited.
The sage summoned Sumantra and instructed,
Gladly he got ready the force's parade.

For the ceremonial occasion of Ram's sovereign,
In houses, huts, haats, havens, preparation began.
The festivity painted the town red,
Here, priests chanted loudly the Ved.

Ram, then, called His staff, serfs and chefs,
To attend hosts of comrades and chiefs.
Prince Ram called beloved Bharat, then,
Unknotted his matted locks with Own hands.

Ram, who is so fond of His devotees,
Now bathed and dressed His closed three.*
Old fraternal togetherness to find,
Their faces shone flood of rapture so divine.

Then Ram disentangled His own matted tress,
Bathed and Appareled regal on Guru's behest.
Decked Self with trappings, edgings, hangings,
Nay, the ornaments looked decked on Him.

There, Siya in the gynaeceum was,
Most lovingly was graced with rich robes.

---

*Lakshman, Bharat, Shatrughan.

From the tresses to the toes was adorned worth
To the daughter of Janak and the queen of Awadh.

Couplet: *Heavenly thus adorned;*
To the left of Lord Ram,
Siya, Herself now shone,
With glow-in mellower tone. 15

The queen mothers on the acme of delight,
Felt fully rewarded by their lives.
The Paradise descended on the Earth,
Celestial beings came to witness the mirth.

With the charmed gaze rapt Vashishtha looked at,
Sent for regal throne, for coupled visage.
Regal retinue brought divine throne at once,
Its splendour put to shame hundreds of suns.

Bowing His head to the Pious presence,
Ram along with Siya took the seat then.
"Brahmans then recited Vedic hymns,
Pious crowd shouted 'Victory! Victory!"

Vashishtha first of all applied Tilak mark then,
As a mark of beginning of Ram's reign.
To do likewise, he directed blest Brahmans,
Thus began the Vedic usage of coronation.

The joy that had densely filled the milieu,
Was seen condensed on Mother's faces too.
Waves of bliss filled them, full to the banks,
They waved Aarti lamps about Ram again and again.

Surprises and prizes, on every one they bestowed,
Gave the beggars so much that they begged no more.

Stanza: *The Heaven descended on the Earth,*
And immersed in the mirth on Earth-,
For Ram's reign, itself the Heaven,
Left heaven and it was worth, A

To have a glimpse, of gala of triumph,
hovered nymphs over Awadh,
Alighted from above, delighted drove
Of deities deos to join this mirth. B

Siya Ram shone, on regal throne,
Every one within own, Kept this panorama,
They all enshrined, in soul and mind,
The couple-divine, Ram and Ramaa. C

Further in sight, came on left and right,
Bharat, Laxman, Shatrughan,
Then rest shone, by the side of throne,
Vibhishan, Angad and Hanumaan. D

Couplet: *The dazzling diadem shone,*
Became shine of every eye,
Ram's reign became everyone's own,
B'coz His voice was every one's voice. 16

The delight and its height,
For the limit of mortal words,
Every description, 'll defy
Only Shanker knowth its sapor. 17

Personified as Laureates,
Then came the holy texts,
Only Siya Ram kent them as Veds,
Mystic they, then recited- 18

---

*Ramaa name of Laxmi, (Siya)
Sapor=taste

Stanza:

We art in fact, embodied veds
And as Lauretes praise Thou as Attribute,
O Master! Thou masterth,
As pupetts, the galaxies, planet; O Absolute! A
Thou art Helmsmen, in wavy mundane,
To save from waves, Thou art at helm,
Thy paeans, we Veds do hymn
O Supreme! hail! O Lord!! hail!! B

Each beat of biota, each bit of iota,
In Thy Maya, hath Thy nuclei,
Mellow of Veds, hallow of texts
O All wise ! its all Thine. C

*The Sacred sages, devoted pages**
With no I am ness who look at Thou,
Sure their troth meetth Thy Truth
Which is route of bliss without doubt. D

O! Thou can't, be thus kent,
In Thy unborn absolute form,
We now so, before Thou bow
And chant the glories of Attribute form. E

Couplet:

Veds worded grand worships,
Then returned to their abodes.
Soon, their came Lord Shiv
His voice in prayers choked- 19

Stanza:

*"Hail to Thou O Raam ! O Ramaa** !!*
O Reliever of afflictions of all awe !
Hail to Thou ! O king of Ayodhya !
World is obsessed with the phobias. A

* devoted servants (Daas)
** Ramaa name of Laxmi (Siya)

Pray! exend thy shelter to all,
From to and fro journey's call.
Folly chilled the soul hiemal,
Thy touch wouldst make it vernal. B

"May texts monitor the minds,
Of the overtaxed mankind.
May the strayed ways, none find,
At the call of monsterous giants. C

"May the world bear soul of a child,
Which looks up mild with smiles.
May battle fields turn to meadows,
May world's hollows be filled with mellows. D

"Not on spikes but on Thy lap,
May man's dream take supreme shape.
Not the auric hue but ethic's virtue,
The value of man should approve. E

"Hungry steps are strayed on greed,
Binded by folly they gather weeds.
The untrodden path of Thy moral deeds,
May fulfil their life, after-life's needs. F

"As the mind grows, may the reverence grow,
May ego not make heart bare of Love.
While the lust and the Just conflict
Must, the Just prevail all-above. G

"Deep and deep in the benthos,
Of the ocean of devotion, who goes
The pearls of bliss he acquires
Lest rest get froth and mire. H

Hiemal=wintry.
Benthos=bottom of sea.

"Bhakti, Thine Bhakti is panacea,
To cure all afflictions and all-awe.
Should the Ram's reign with ageless glory come,
To void wrong, add the virtuous sums. I

"O Light of virtues! O Delight of Raghu!!,
Cast a glance on Thy humble devouts. J

Couplet: *"Again and again I ask*
Grant me devotion and reverence,
Should, Bhakti, ever-last,
And the company of the saints." 20

Lord Shiv thus having hymned,
To Ram bade adieu
Now, monkeys were assigned homes
With comfort of habitué. 21

This winsome panaroma of Ram's narrative,
Through out was witnessed by Lord Shiv.
Who narrated to Uma, from saints came to men,
Then hymns by men winged to reach avians.

And Crow-saint, by name Kakabhusundi,
Narrated among birds this story-
"O Garud ! it purifies heart, the heart of ego,
And rids the fears of swinging to and fro*

" The Narrative of Ram's blest coronation,
Brings festive suns and moons of dispassion.
Who sing His paeans, with same holy motive,
Attain happiness and the aim they achieve.

Habitué=family guest(frequent guest)
*affliction between birth and death

The pilgrimage, every verse; as it is,
At the end of earthly career, brings final bliss.
In gloom of life it's panacea,
In bloom of life it's ambrosia.

Every sun beheld a new joyous glow,
Ram's reign performed everyday a new glad-show.
Largesses so Lavished, left no lazarus,
Haats gained new heights in commerce.

Couplet: *Here, monkeys were dipt,*
In joy of love and faith.
All were devoted to Lord's feet,
Thus six months had elapsed. 22

FAREWELL TO COMRADES

Kapi's rapt in service to their Lord,
Their own home all they forgot.
Ram, then called all His comarades,
All came and reverently bowed heads.

Most lovingly the loving Ram seated them very next,
Then, in tender words Lord Ram addressed-
"Ye have rendered service to My cause, My aim,
I feel 'ye are more Myself than I am.'

"Your glad-home, your glades, ye left gladly,
Hence ye have endeared yourselves most to Me.
"My fra, frau, family, my fort, my fate,
All art dear to Me, but ye are dearest.

"For all my devouts its not untrue,
Simply My nature I reveal to you.

Lazarus=poormen, beggar.
Fra=brother, Frau (Germ) =Wife.

"As a rule, the Master controls his cortege,
But I, for one, am mastered by my page."

Couplet: *Tho' ye are inexpensive*
I ask ye with diffidence,
Return home to the land native,
Knowing Me as omnipresent. 23

Benumbed all, perplexed they,
Heard Ram's voice, all lost flesh.
They knew no words in reply,
Only bleached face spake, spake unwinking eyes.

Perceiving fondness thus in winsome words,
Ram recommended the duty over piety.
Lord said "Hark ! heart and hands work must
Together, for the home and native land first.

In presence of Lord they had no words,
And to word the tumult that within them occurred.
Ram then called for the jewels, costumes of various hues,
With which first Bharat invested Sugriv.

Bharat invested Kapis, then one by one,
With a different set Lakhan invested Vibhishan.
Seeing all friends invested, Ram was gladdened,
But Angad kept sitting even as unconcerned.

Couplet: *Jaamwant, Nal, Nil and others,*
Enshrining Lord's visage.
With in core of their core;
They trailed in snail's pace. 24

Angad kept stuck in court,
And refused to move.
Thus was not called by Lord,
Perceiving his love. 25

Cortege=servants.

In the court spreaded a chill of hush,
Angad's blank gaze was on Lord, continuous.
But then gathering himself in honeyed voice,
His laden heart melted thro' his eyes—

"I am dimwit to perceive Thy omnipresent form,
While I see the feelable warrior king Ram.
"It was in Thy charge I was left,
Without Ram, I am bereft rampike, lest.

"Thou art Master, parent, preacher, pal, all in one,
So, recall Thy vow that protects a forlorn.
"Severed from Thou, of what use is my home sill,
Of its bricks, stones, sabres, sapors, scents, silk.

"Cozy shelter of Thy feet is my asylum,
Keep me as pilgrim soul in this sanctum sanctorum.
"Let Thy home be my home for this menial page,
Tho' this haughty, naughty knows no homage.

"Save me ! keep me not away from eyes"
These beseeching words choked his voice.

Couplet: *Words went home to Lord's heart*
Within Him, He embraced.
"Angad! duty is piety's part,
For Mine and for duty's sake." 26

"The duty is deity of first worship,
Every duty is holy tho' seldom sweet.
"Duty is sweet only through the love,
To mother and Motherland, keep duty, all above.

"In essence of your soil, find My soul,
Serve Me; Comforting all My carved moulds.

Sanctum sanctorum (*L*)= holy of the holies.

"More bread, more bloom among all his subjects,
Is the worship of Divine; be it regents' object."

Then the All-wise advised and consoled him,
When Angad left the scene, every eye brimmed.
Being conscious of devout's faith, every bosom throbbed,
Bharat, Lakhan and younger went to see them off.

Angad again would turn to Ram's face,
To have one more look at Ram, eyes to sate.
He would repeatedly cringed himself on floor,
In hope that Ram might ask him to stay more.

His Lord's mind, and His expression, he kent,
Enshrining Ram's visage then, Angad went.
To depart from part of heart is hard,
Harder, for Angad's soul who was all soul for Lord.

Having seen all Kapis off with utmost respects,
Bharat and his brothers returned back.
Reading Hanumaan's mind, Sugriv asked—
"Hanuman ! your life is, for Shri Ram, tasked."

Thus all monkey departed forth with,
But Angad tarried, here to say this—

Couplet: *"Convey my worships to Him,*
Joined palms I beseech you.
At times, remember me to Supreme,
As the part of His retinue." 27

Saying so, Angad bade adieu,
Hanumaan kept standing till he disappeared from view.
Hanumaan returned and told to Lord his feelings,
Those were supremely ecstatic for the Supreme.

Harder than adamant as the Ram's heart is,
Softer than inflorescence as the Ram's heart is.
It was daily joy for Guh, the Ram's intimate,
"Back home Go O pal! to banks of Ganges."

For a friend or friendship, needs whatelse,
Enriched with Ram's amity, the richest jewel.
"Following dictate of abnegations, devotion,
O Bosom friend Guh ! now return back home.

"For you, my fraternal love is as deep
As it's for Bharat my beloved indeed.
"For My sake, every now and then,
You visit Awadh and Me, O bosom friend !"

In his bosom's fane*, thus Guh did find,
Bosom friend's image was already enshrined.
Guh returned back keeping this image,
Banks of Sacred Ganges applauded, ' Here cometh the blest.'

Couplet: *All with natural hearts had,*
Innate love with natural chain.
'One home the Awadh, one family the subjects,
In Ram's reign became. *28*

THE RAM – RAJYA

None of Somatic, Cosmic, no extrinsic torments,
In the whole Ram's reign, none such remained.
Knitted by love all the hearts, all hearths,
Lived as family unit in dominion of Awadh.

Truth, purity, compassion and charity,
Became integral part of the society.
No one even dreamt of the sin,
Ram's reign brought calm to subjects within.

---

* Temple

The honest lead of Ram made everyone a leal,
In the natural bosom of people, vernal heart revealed.
Lofty living had no lack of life or loaf,*
Yet in lavishes of luxuries none was found lost.

Duty, piety, chastity, charity,
Such findings were mankind's identity.
'Ts said ' being humane- the species of men,
Since then, is named 'the species Human'.

---

leal=honest; *Loaf=food (Roti)

Devoted to Lord Ram and to Ram's reign,
All had right privilege for the beatific gain.
Peopled air had no complaints, no cries, no sighs,
Had no sick, weak, twit, no unriped demise.

Couplet: *In the sovereign of Ram,*
Men, nay, animate had no menace.
No ban, no bane, no bam,
No lacks, no tax, no perplex. 29

Across seven oceans and seven lands,
Awadh's reign was the one undisputed sovereign.
Laes, clouds, seeds, soil, mounts and woods,
Performed own jobs to the best, they could.

Nature was not exploited by the men,
And thus the preserved nature bestowed with ope hands.
Moon blushed to see the splendour of Awadh,
Most heavenly the heaven enveloped the Earth.

Souls of stars, planets and comets descended,
In globalized Awadh, to be glorified subjects.
The pious souls from different planes,
Crowded up the land with their descent.

But restless orbs, in their disciplined
Orbits; could witness very little.
Such marvellous Lordship was nothing great,
For Him, who, in a mo, createth worlds in myriads.

Couplet: *Here dwelt pilgrim souls,*
In this place of pilgrimage.
The bliss they could not hold,
And shared, squandered among them. 30

Twit=Fool.
Bam=falsehood, Ban=curse, Bane=poison.
Perplex=perplexity, confusion; Menace=danger, evil.

Splendour and shine had it's own grace,
Every home, every sill looked a palace.
No clangs of cross swords but with chyming peals,
No wars but, the people wished to win mind's field.

People's mind had placid stream
Of pellucid flow of calm in Ram's realm.
Duty to soil every soul knew,
They preserved the infant-world's milieu.

All lavish trees with laden boughs,
And the floral carpets, decked the groves.
Beasts, birds forgot animosity,
Their habitat jungle left autarchy.

Robed in verdurous apparels, rocks, peaks,
Were decked with silky frills of cataract streaks.
Herbages, hermitages, as the real asset,
Bestows mankind, tho' stand meak.

Couplet: *The grandeur of holy text,*
Got printed in subject's bosom.
They trod and path they lead,
For the time and men to come. 31

All hearths had warmth, all hearts had Ram,
Mines yielded jewels and the mind, jovial charm.
Hymns of Veds were revealed in men's thoughts deeds,
Their sated needs, never set them to greed.

No chaos of arguments, over words of text,
To confuse varitable path, they had.
Before first Master, first Mirth, first marvel,
All the subjects strieved to excel.

Awadh, itself dwelt in their heart,
In which they enshrined Awadh's Lord.

Rivers, rills rippled kissing the pebbles,
Their drops quenched souls, every crop they jewelled.

On the land, the elixir, from paradise dropped,
Making ramal lavishes and golden crops.
Ponds and meres were flooded with merry making finned,
Aquatic birds all about made the warbling din.

Couplet: *The moon enveloped earth in silver,*
The Sun gilded it in aurum.
Clouds showered when asked for,
Nature helped the natural bosoms. 32

Even plebs, peasants had say in governance,
Their toil dews yielded gratifying gains.
Eager seeds ever waited for the soil,
The first touch, seeds greeted with sprouting smile.

Where, inert seeds, thus, sincerely served,
There, no words could say of service of the Nerved.
Moon dissolved its silver in streams, sands, torrents,
Beamed brush of Sun painted in gold, the grains.

Lo ! pearls gathered on lap of lotuses,
Nature greeted with salvers of pearly largess',
Nature's kingdom and Lord Ram's Lordship,
Bestowed all wides, bliss-n-bliss.

And the Lord Himself, the champion of Virtues,
Ever went with the sacred vedic views.
And as meek statue of virtues on the throne,
As queen of Awadh, Seeta, on Ram's left shone.

Couplet: *Siya, the queen, the parent,*
Of creation as She ist,
Took care of the subjects,
Every beat, and every bit. 33

Forgetting Her own natural kudos,
She served ever with no pride no ego.
Beatific beauty and Her modest majesty,
Was revered thro' out the worlds' society.

Epitome of fraternity compressed in brothers
Of Ram; revealed in the way they served.
With love their keen gaze ever looked at,
To serve and follow their beloved Eldest.

The mutual love which bound them among,
In four frames, was the Soul one.
Under every roof, in Ram's realm, it does behove,
Dwelt a bound family with boundless love.

Vedic, mystic, cryptic, heroic, yogic, medic,
Teachings had no bias of race or creed.
Innovations, researches, discoveries in that age,
Added further a mark in the knowledge, ahead.

Couplet: *The divine seekers toiled,*
To find truth behind truth,
Scholars burnt midnight oil,
To explore the Absolute. 34

They trod and explored the untrodden paths,
Of artistic science and scientific art.
Pundits took knowledge to every door,
Oblates perfused morals in every core.

Truth was natural finding in the deeds,
Pledge, mortgage, swearing, were no tongue's need.
Lightened by literacy and liturgy,
Ram's grace put society under the lee.

Under the lee=defended, protected

Whether plebs, pupils, peasants or pundits,
Ever spake true words with truer deeds.
There was no sin, no blemish, no weakness,
But the purity, patience and perseverance.

People's deeds and thought had no 'me and mine'.
Their thoughts, words, deeds were perfectly aligned.
Needed no menacles, no bars, prisons, fetters,
In the discipline of Ram, the very law of nature.

Couplet: *The ethics was Oneness,*
Manifested by the love.
The faith in every breath,
Looked for His behest all above. 35

Ram's Name filled matins of people,
Very Name they repeated in vespers and vigils.
Siya gave birth to two pretty sons,
Lava and Kush by name, whom Veds have sung.

Other brothers too had two sons each,
Thus the regal groves, corridors were accomplished.
Innocent shouts of innocent cheer,
Added more bliss every where.

In models of their father's very image,
Past time's pastimes were recalled by the palace.
Throughout the day the little steps,
Played unweary in laes, groves on nature's lap.

In fun and frolic their bruised knees sobbed,
With mother's touch, very next mo, they laughed.
The innocent wanderers of palace and town,
With weary return into mother's lap, would drown.

Perseverance = steady work.

Couplet: *The same shapeless Absolute,*
Thus didth come man-sized,
Who ist Unborn, the final Truth,
Performth an ideal life. 36

After taking morning bath at Sarayu's banks,
Lord Ram joined the holy séance.
Sage Vashishtha expounded the holy Veds,
Ram listened, tho' He ist Creator of all the texts.

He wouldth then perform Yog and matins,
Then reverently wouldth visit mother-queens.
Here, brothers and Hanumaan would go to some grove,
And Hanumaan would detail Ram's virtues with love.

Hanumaan's intellect would plunge into,
The ocean of His Lord's virtue.
The cause, the remedy who possessth within His own,
He carried out state-causes from Awadh's throne.

Nature of mild Ram, His discourse as child,
As warrior in wilds, and as Lanka's turmoil,
Such diverse virtues and this holy exploits,
Everywhere, everybody, everytime did recite.

Couplet: *Prospered by daily bliss,*
Treasured with blessings,
That Awadh, none could depict,
Where Ram reigned as king. 37

Where for mankind Lord cameth mansized,
That Awadh's spread was wide globalized.
Beyond seven seas, seven lands, seven heavens,
Ram-Rajya cared from end to end.

Passionless life was the only passion,
Subjects thrieved for lustless ambitions.

Pompless life was painless too,
All did do what Ram would approve.

Where king sitth on throne with pensive mind,
Indeed, His virtues in deeds of subjects, find.
For times to come, to guide, Lord came,
As a guide to the coming mortal realms.

Ram reigned the Reign that brought paradise,
On the land of man, as mankind's pride.
Lord came Man-sized; the man to deify,
His surprised coming, became man's priced prize.

Couplet: *Where king regardth virtues,*
Where right sceptre wields,
Subjects yield splendorous hue,
In every and every field. 38

Where Truth lives in soul of King, enshrined,
And He Himself, lives in soul of the mankind,
Where sentinels repel not, but help subject,
They bring praises to the king, for easy access.

Where above swords, spike, spears, sabres,
Holiness is the greatest power,
Where holy texts command the throne,
Where every sigh, to the king, is known,

Where selfless building of national pride,
Is the goal of every bosom all wides.
Where commerce grows for the man's common need,
Where hearts are innate, ignorant of greed,

Where king dwelth in subject's heart and subject in His,
Where ope hands, ope minds, ope hearts exist,
There, reign right sceptre, the Ram's realm,
Should it be people's and regal aim.

Couplet: *Heavenly souls and sages*
Keen on sight of the Lord.
Saw the Earth with dazzled gaze,
There 'Viraag' they forgot. 39

THE AYODHYA OF RAM

Awadh's rampart hath great work of bricks,
Fine hands carved superb arches, attics.
Meditated work synchronized with lumbricals,
Enlivened on woods and stones, a marvel.

Carved stones, painted murals, they embossed chalks,
And chiselled xylographs on wainscots.
On lattice', attics and arched bricks,
Made they Lord's pastime depicts.

Fine hand miniatures, free hand collages,
Dazzled passer by all along their ways.
Artistic artisans poured soul in predella',
In lively depicts of Ram and Siya.

On barbicans barbarian havoc was so shown,
Would melt the petrified soul of same stone.
Here artisan made artless Earth, grieved,
As a heifer, on relievo, prays for relief.

Couplet: *Inner bailey and balustrades,*
Showed welcoming caryatids,
Diorama of Rama were so made,
Seeming palpable, the depicts. 40

Viraag=self abnegation to the worldly life.
Lumbricals=fine muscles of hand responsible for art.
Relievo=Sculptures where figures half project from flat background.

Lo! the Vulcan hoverth here on altar with an urn,
In the same nativity, Kaushalya's Ram cometh.
In the same row, carved, an intaglio,
Having the pranks and freaks of divine child's show.

Here child Ram from Dashrath's lap,
Endeavourth in innocent wish to escape.
In a still, the luck of crow, here prevailed,
The divine Infant feedth him with own morsels.

Reverence of pupil Ram, love of Vashishtha, the priest,
Tutelage that binds, stones do speak.
Here Ram roams with brothers in a grove,
Silent lips, stilt eyes but tell of citizens' love.

The divine weapons here, Vishwamitra bestows,
Here Taarakaa the demoness lays low.
Here with abigails Siya walks thro' alleys,
Here happen to meet, the Couple Ancient of days.

Roar of breaking Shiv's bow is heard in silent clay,
Here Siya garlandeth Ram with the wedding bays.
But then blank faces depicted the black night,
In the festivity fallth, on Awadh, the plight.

Couplet: *Only sculpture half done,*
Which had chiselled Awadh.
Scene of Ram's exile to sylvan,
Hands on chisel denied work. 41

Helmsman's luck surpasses, takes them across Ganges,
Ram Siya Lakhan here treadst in glades.
Gaze of eager plebs of passing hamlets,
Here surrounded holy strangers, under some tree shades.

Vulcan=firegod; Nativity=painting representing Lord's birth.
Bays=wreath of victory.

On square they erected Dashrath's shrine,
Whose life was worth and death was divine.
Here rippling waves through pebbles, just now would
Speak of panorama of Ram's Chitrakoot.

Bharat taketh here, Ram's sabots for the throne,
Here, fraternal love almost hath melted the stone.
The diorama of Rama's Grotto next see !
At the holy banks of holy Godawari.

Lo ! on long canvas a composed montage,
See ! bliss among sages, see ! blitz on savages.
Here awesome minx by Lakhan is maimed,
In full tilt here Ram at gold hart aimth.

Couplet: *All mastered maestros failed,*
To depict its ever hard.
To draw theft of Siya and Her wails,
They left empty canvas, odd. 42

On an cenotaph see! old eagle's statue,
'Ts to honour the sacrifice of Jatayu.
See ! the depict, which is most favourite,
Is the Ram's embrace when Hanumaan meets.

Lanka with lankiness in havoc of inferno,
Is sketched and above flames Bravo! Hanumaan, the hero.
Xylographs on the doors, they engraved,
See ! the foray of Vaanars and bears brave.

An artisan sees through the avian eyes,
The bridge he makes across the Brine.
A pagoda over crosslanes stands,
With episodes of war and echoes of Ram's paeans.

In full tilt= In full speed.

Severed shatterd corpe of Raavan sunk in own gore,
This sketch sayth demonry stays no more.
In a sketch, the delight cometh with same good luck ,
Awadh returns in Awadh with alight of Pushpak.

Couplet: *Thro' chisels and brushing hands*
In Awadh alights heaven.
Here, Gnostic minds ordain,
Martials, merchants, men, mammon. 43

Lo !Roads squares are paved with various colours,
The celestials nay sages to enrapture.
Shining pinnacles over towering fanes,
Put to shame the sun and moon's effluence.

Inverts, arches are illuminated by jewels,
Attics, lattices are made of corals crystals.
Every house hath doors that never close,
Rooms adorned with frescos of Ram's court.

Dance through oriels, lancets, the tapestries,
Topiary seemed even as house is wreathed.
Parterre is made from door to the gate,
Every sight looks as if landscaped.

As a boast of house the trellis is grown,
On its floral bed bees make sweet drone.
Reared by children in playful delight,
Birds are warbling melody in their flight.

Repeated the words, Mainas and parrots,
'Ram! Ram!!' as is learnt by rote.
Splendour of commerce falls on bazaar,
Where need and supply ever is at par.

Oriels, lancets=windows, effulgence=lustre, Topiary=designed gardens.
Trellis=canopy of climbers.

Couplet: *Commerce has honest trade*
Sans bluff or blurb,
Ope vendee and shops flooded,
Makes it perfect marketing hub. 44

Lo! Nigh blooming flowers with burst of buds,
Lo ! High boasting towers on Rajpath.
Crowning on heavenly laes, the elysian palm trees,
Bow and rock in tickling by the breeze.

Disciplined display of fountains is teased,
By whispering thrust of notorious breeze.

And for subject where reignth as king, the Lord Himself,
His Lordship expends weal as lavish wealth.
The Rajpath here ends to the north,
From the top of slope, see! the rows of ghats.

To the stretch of Sarayu, the very life of town,
Look! clear wide steps neatly laid down.
Ghats, aquatics, quick sands, rippling rapids,
Are cared together by men on helms and hands on beads.*

Couplet: *Frolicking waves plop,*
Against charming ghat's steps.
Is enlivened by little hops,
Further by youth and greyed. 45

Filled with melody of chimes, hymns, chants,
Ghats have no mire, mud or drains.
They care the stream, the stream, the men,
Men preservest nature and the nature, the men.

Blurb=Propaganda.
Men on helm=helm'sman; * hermits and sages.
To plop=to splash; little hops=child's play.

The boast of rows of ghats is the 'Ramghat',
Sans caste creed, race, ope to all for bathe.
High fanes with vying towers and pinnacles on it,
Look ! some neo designs and some antiques.

Dwells, on banks, Sages, recluses, friars, ascetics,
Ever taking dips in devotions and gnosis.
All along the banks stood parterres,
Reared by sages, of charming Tulsi herbs.

Gaze far! Tortuous Sarayu into green carpets' view,
Disappears into the thicket of purlieu.
Back to town see ! coliseum, colosseum* , meadows,
Tanks, ponds, green lees, orchards and groves.

Couplet: *Kissed by humming bees,*
Lotuses blush in lakes,
Cooing birds on trees,
Are wooing Nature's riches. 46

Natural hearts thus preserved Nature's face,
As should Awadh have, that very Awadh's grace.
Pencilled horizon on far southern back drop,
Hath bleak rocks, meak hillocks and green hassocks.

Thro' the duct of vista the filtering sun,
All along the concourse seemed as beacon.
Thus every landscape had vernal hue,
Heaven painted the canvas of every milieu.

Among pals, in stalls, in halls and chaupals,
Ram is ever talk of town, people did exalt.
Anima, Garima and other super powers,
Ever in Ayodhya, were ready to serve.

Gnosis=spiritual wisdom.
* Arena(stadium.)
Concourse=wide road; Bleak rocks=bare, treeless hills; Hassocks=grassy peaks.
Anima=Superhuman power to assume atomic size.

Where joy, riches, peace forever stayed,
No words can portray, but can only be felt.
Like Roses' essence, honey's elixir, viol's euphony,
The feel, is the feeling, hath no glossary.

Couplet: *In eight classical circles,*
With huge gates nine,
The Ayodhya, land of celestials,
*As if human body, it defines.** 47

THE DAWN OF RAM'S GLORY

And Whose delight reflectth in the Sun,
Night orb reflectth Whose cool,
Millions of galaxies Who governth,
Man sized, the Awadh, He ruleth. 48

The Immortal cometh in Awadh man-sized,
To bring to the mortals, the immortal's paradise.
In azure above reflects whose swarthy hue,
Whose mystery is deep as depth of the Blue,

Who is life in the Life, who is death of the Death,
Who is truth of the Truth, and fact of the faith,
To the frost of folly, who is sunlight,
Who ist frost too, to destroy lust-gnits.

Who is Unborn, yet breaths in every born,
For the mirk of thanatos, who is instinct of morn.
In the draught of passion, who is fount of wisdom,
To soothe the agony of scorching bosom.

---

* Yogic metaphysics defines human body with eight Chakras (eight vital centres of energy in the body) and nine portals.

As nectar in vernal blossom dwellth He,
As throb in every bosom dwellth He.
Nay, in every inert as well
As, alert nucleus He dwellth.

Couplet: *Thus all goodly heart they exchanged,*
With brimming praises of Ram.
In return they all gained,
Benignant grace of Ram. 49

Ram's splendour lightened like dazzling sun,
Delighted hearths to hearts, from hurst to the horizon.

White lily in the shape of anger and lust,
Closed, as if, in this dazzling sun was accursed.
Thieves like worthless-charms and wanton warmth,
Had no occasion to trick in sunny glory of Ram.

In rays of bliss, vanished the mist of the blues,
Lotuses of wisdom opened in ponds of virtues.
In clear sky of mind, birds in shape of dispassion,
Flied to sublimed Sun of His glory on wing of realization.

In the upright wind, clouds in shape of doubt
Scudded; and in view, staunch mount, came about.
His solar glory fell on mortal soil grange
Of mortal souls; that gained immortal grain.

Couplet: *When Ram's glory illumines,*
A saintly wisdom dawns,
Scampers, the scamp from within,
Vanishes dimness of sins. 50

Hurst=shore (near edge)
Grange=form
Scamper=run away; Scamp=knave, mean fellow.

Such dawn brings for new heifer of the soul,
Freedom to caper, ope meadows to roll.
Sun of Ram's glory, on nite at sixes and sevens,
Dawns for this benign heifer to bring heavens.

Lord's glory with its confident rays,
Thro' the eclipse of doubts and dismays; penetrates.
This dawn, frees from the nest, the nestling,
Thus, lofty spirit sublimeth on dauntless wings.

Bringeth waking call, the Ram's glory,
To the antic slumber of idle psyche.

Sun of His glory in miniated envelop,
Bringth light of East, with its first pop up.
Its nimbus fills every nidus, nest, niche,
With epistle of love, fraternity and peace.

Bird of wisdom is drawn, to this glorious morn,
On free wings towards virtuous horizon.

Couplet: *All the pompous twinkles of nite,*
Mayst dazzle due to illusion,
But then wisdom shineth bright,
When His glory riseth as the Sun. 51

□

At sixes and sevens=in great perplexities.
Miniated=painted with vermillion (vermillionated)depicting the sunrise.

The fear of God is the beginning of religion but the love of God is the end-goal of religion.

—Swami Vivekanand

A MELIC AGAINST MELEE

Thus Glorious Sun of culture from the East,
Shouldst illumine ages and ages with peace.
Should this Sun enlighten benighted road,
Its peaceable tread with no wound no sword.

With this Sun, 'true decorum' of Earth be preserved,
B'cause, its glorious light* every soul doth deserve.
Who follows not the dignified path of peace
In spite of all learnings, earth's decorum doth breach.

Should this eastern Sun not pervade with sword,
Should this, conquer the man thro' true words.
To find man in man should this holy text,
Among offspring texts**, should have unbiased taste.

Should the world of the Supreme Creator, Brahma,
Come under one faith of Human's umbrella.
Should Lord's paeans and His pastime,
Paint forth the colours of rapture so divine.

Benighted=ignorant; *light of the East; **all texts of world are derived from Veds.

Couplet: *Over chilly veils of mounts*,*
Should this luminous orb of the East,
With warmth of sacred sounds,
Reach like a Priest. 1

Should golden rays of love with its solemn sound,
Murmur epistles in every mellow founts and hallowed mounts.
In icy white outs, or sandy havocs,
Should this Luminous orb clear confused fog.

Should the liberal text be the path of mankind,
Should steps find oneness in holy lines.
Should holy pages meet, should meet carols, prayers,
Not with numbers, not with letters but with hearts' share.

Should sacred words bring faultless gains,
Should in learned scholar dwell more reverence.
Zeroing on holy text, should make wide
The spectrum of vision, not the tubular sight.

Should not the ego in folly of the mind,
Split the very spirit of mankind.
Should all good thoughts and good pages unite,
Should view thru' it, one Truth, one Light.

Couplet: *The land of peace and no war,*
Which is named 'Awadh',
Should very same, spread far,
Beyond seven seas, on the Earth. 2

AN AYODHYA WITH IN

Ayodhya is a never-never land,
Find it very nigh in fraternal essence.

---

*High-headed ego with narrow peaks of vision.

The soil where blossom, bosom friends,
There Ayodhya lies in crony hands.

In the breasts where truth is enshrined,
There divinity of very Ayodhya, find.
Where vernal smile welcomes at door,
There in homes, hearts, Awadh dwells sure.

Where unbias justice heals a humble sigh,
Find Awadh, where the king satisfies.
Where abundant share is due in smiles and assets,
There Heaven as Awadh, descends for subjects.

Where annals and archives have waving white flag,
In nonviolent ordnance, the Ayodhya stays.
Fanatic ordinance and fierce ordnance,
It hath anguish of abyss, not the bliss of Awadh's land.

Couplet: *Where abundance crowns the field,*
'ts Awadh, the greater heaven.
Where right sceptre wields,
'ts true reign, very Ram's reign. 3

With no farce, folly, foul, flaw and fallacy,
With force, fisc, friend, fra and fidelity,
With treasured five these and truncated five those,
Into any kingdom, Ram-Rajya grows.

Heads with nerve, hearts with verve and hands that serve,
It be named 'Ram Rajya', that kingdom deserves.
Any kingdom mayst make dream of Ram Rajya true,
Through valour, verdict, vigils, values, virtues.

Where liberal hands with zeal, care of people's weal,
There Ram's reign by itself reveals.

Annals and archives=historical records; Fanatic ordinance=Pretensions, Heresy
Fisc=state treasury; Farce=worthless deeds.

The fortified, yet where King hath, easy access,
There sure Ram's reign rules thro' palace.

None the brick, that upholds the fort,
Should in such reign be slopped by the gore.
Glee, gleam, glory of Genius and Gallants,
Should be treated in the council like gems.

Couplet: *Where stay no breaches,*
Between people and the palace.
There Ram's reign itself reaches,
With its true decorum and grace. 4

The ambrosia of mutual reverence,
Is the thing that binds prince and peasants.
Where patriotic pride fills peopled air,
There subject get shelter of solemn care.

No coins of treason but treasure of devotion,
Upholdth the subjects and commerce of nation.
With zeal of civism and civic discipline,
Subject people are guarded by a soldier within,

And mutual reverence in a kingdom,
Bringeth reign of Ram and it's true decorum.
Divine decorum and modesty of Ram's reign,
Canst not be portrayed by mortal's pen.

Where the Supreme descendth that very Awadh,
None can portray, the Awadhian's worth.
Where Ram, Modest Ram, very Ram dwelt,
There glory of very blest people swelt.

People's sincere duty and riper wisdom do share,
King's liberal hands of fatherly care.

Civism=patriotism.

Dutiful wisdom is the national pride,
Joy is its charioteer for people's ride.

Flag wavers with people's strong grip,
Before lust and lure, which never slips.
Very spirit of Ayodhya from fraud preserved
Pure; by Lord's nerve and people's verve.

Couplet: *Awadhians and the Lord of Awadh,*
For coming ages and ages.
Hath made perfect Rajpath,
For populace and the palace. 5

THE DAILY JOY OF AYODHYA

Lord and Awadhians were thus a perfect match,
Where men, mansion, milieu are marked blest.
Eternal blessedness descended in Awadh for aye,
And increasing Bhakti for Ram, became daily joy.

In one such leisure stretch of the day,
Ram with brothers and Kapi went into some thicket.
Welcomed blossoming trees, the inclining boughs,
And the humming bees and warbling echoes.

Finding the chance and hour just right,
Sage Sanaka with his brother arrived.
Sage brothers are first progeny of Creator,
They are still living, the Ancients beyond clock.

Couplet: *They are the ageless divine,*
Figures of Spiritual glow.
With lost flesh, mind,
For the Supreme, are filled with love. 6

With infant's face, with love aeons old,
How deep (in them) Ram dwelth, their calm eyes told.
Melody of some canticle ever kissed their lips,
Their sight looked, beyond the present, ever dipt.

To spread spirituality, their hobby was,
They ever roamed all about for Ram's cause.
They ever backed steps, those aimed to spiritual height,
In light of clairvoyance, the insight.

In hallowed company, in mellow mood,
To uplift mankind, they ever moved.
Since world was infant, with own flambeau,
They torched every soul with spiritual glow.

They, the wight being, to right the wrong,
Ever appeared to make humanity strong.
Leisurely they stepped, bare foot,
Before Ram's company, serenely they moved.

Couplet: *The ancient sages tho' were infants,*
When appeared to the fore,
With esteem Ram welcomed,
With flood of bliss in the core. 7

Lord spreaded yellow scarf for them to squat very next,
Princes and Kapi then, prostrated themselves.
In infants, the divinity, as it happens,
Seemed more intense and more ripened.

Beholding Ram the sage brothers, the blest,
Were beside themselves with bliss, lost flesh.
The ambrosial visage they did drink,
With no wink gazed, gazed and remained gazing.

Canticle=short hymn

The Lord in His turn bowed His head with reverence,
Seated them very next, taking by hand.
"O Sages ! the hour, the place and I am,
All blessed today, in Ayodhya ye came.

"Ye havest witnessed the infant world,
Thro' Creator's hands 'how the life got unfurled.'
"Ye art progenitor of line of saints,
O most pious creation of the Divine hands!"

Couplet: *Lord's words filled their souls,*
With nectar to the brim,
All they begun to extol
Lord's praises they thus hymned— 8

"O Infinite ! O Unborn Lord !!
Immutable, All-wise as Thou art,
"Thy very touch makest any one, a pious,
O begetter parent ! Veds reveal thus.

"Who revereth Thou, ist revered too
Thy glory maintain in him the 'Truth'.
"Thou havest consecrated itself the Holiness,
Thou havest graced the divinity's grace.

"Thou art nameless yet every name ist Thine,
O Formless ! Thou makest every form divine.
" O Unborn ! dateless beyond almanac,
Thou art Ancient, beyond clock of days.

" O Unknown, Unknowable !! as Thou art,
Yet omnipresent in every heart.

Couplet: *" O Saviour ! Save us from,*
Senses and from the self**.*
O Formless ! Thy human form,
May in our conscious dwell. 9

---

*sensuality; **Egoism(vanity)

"The Mind, that perceiveth, not, Thy existence,
Any wisdom is no wisdom, it's folly in vain.
"Any glory, if not surrendered to Thou,
Is vain glory remained short lived, no doubt.

"Any sheen is the shining dazzle of pomp,
If thro' it reflects not the splendour of Ram.
"Any hymn is a versified limerick,
Till, flood of devotion, thro' it not brims.

"Pray ! grant us the unceasing Bhakti,
That destroys all Mundane's agony.
"Thy Bhakti ist wish yielding tree,
That rids soul of to and fro journey.

"Thy Bhakti ist the bark of hope,
To cross the bar of worldly woes.
"Thou art the flambeau to enlighten, the astrayed,
On the mirky paths of mundane ways.

Couplet: *"Thou art firm bosom of friend*
Thou art tender heart of mother,
Thou art the father's hand
To wipe forlorn tears. 10

"Thou art custodian of vedic laws,
For flaws and sins Thou art catastrophe.
"In ocean of mercy, Thou art pearl of boon,
For the tides within saints, Thou art Bhakti's full moon.

"In metempsychosis, soul swirls in eddies,
Thou are deep wave of devotion, that frees.
In the gloomy chill of frosty night,
Thou art East with breaking light of delight."

–The hymns they chanted and thus they extolled,
That further hallowed their own holy souls.

Again and again then the sage-brothers bowed,
And returned back to their sacred abodes.

Here, Bharat and youngers were too modest,
Looked at Hanumaan to continue the chat.
All wished to hear from Lord's lips,
Something that would eradicate earthly slips.

Couplet: *Any wish, that sprouts*
In the heart of the devout,
Or cometh to the mouth,
Foreruns before the Lord, no doubt. 11

With favoured gesture Lord looked at,
Diffident but with fervour Hanumant spake-
"O Compassionate ! as Thou art for the meek,
Yet Bharat, is too diffident to speak."

"Kapi ! Me and Bharat art two names,
But One soul breathing in twin frames.
"My deals, thoughts words are just the same,
Rather, He ist more Myself than I am."

"Bharat's transparent mind and ope heart
And wordless lips know no art.
"Bharat ist the fraternity's towering fane,
Over world of kinship, should his glory reign.

"The unseen bond that bindth the two,
Ist the vital binding of transparent glue."
Loaded with love Bharat bowed at Lord's feet,
Flooded bosom forced his choked throat to speak-

Couplet: *"Deep soul or shallow face,*
O Lord! Lord's eye canst read
What ever cometh is Thy grace
None ist mortal clay's deed. 12

"Here I make bold to make one request,
O Supreme soul ! O Goal of every soul's quest.
"O Hymns of Himalaya ! O Chimes of holy bells !!
Thou art psalms of Ved and rhymes of Craddle.

"Thou art prayer, prayee and the wish, all in one,
Thou art wishes accomplished and the sublimed orisons.
"O Strength of Truth ! O Depth of the Troth !!,
Behind bone, flesh, gore, Thou art something dwellth in us.

"O Divinity of Paradise ! O Chastity of Ganges !
O Depth of knowledge ! O Mystery of Veds !
"O Truth of the Troth ! O firmness of the faith,
O Master of fate ! O Ancient and Ultimate!!

"I would fain hear, I do supplicate,
Draw distinct traits of good and wicked."

Ram replied—

"Like an axe are the wicked; and the good,
Bharat ! are like the sandal wood.
"Be cut, should, the sandal tree by the axe,
Yet in it's turn, it perfumes the edge.

Couplet: *" 'Ts why Saintly Sandal is*
Placed on the forehead
While axe is punished in heat
And beaten by mallet. 13

"Saints as rule are devoid of the lust,
Their thought, words deeds are ever Just.
"Not by own grief, but other's joyous drive
The envied wicked can not survive.

"O Bharat ! brave, naïve, grave* and sincere,
Chaste, honest, modest, to Me are dear.
"Who work with no motive of their own claim,
With my earnest feelings I own them.

"Patriots who worship the Nation first,
Whose gore is prompted for battle-field's thirst,
"The nation's whose parent, it's soul whose soul,
People's smile who treasure as gold,

"Whose noblest life impregnates hearts,
With humanity, hope and no hates no hoax,
"Who serve my cause, and never swerve,
Service and duty as 'Dharma' who observe,

Couplet: *"Unpossessed by Maya,*
Bhakti is whose possession,
They are Saints, art bound to Master's law
Mastered by the true reason. 14

"Who barter not principles for pottage,
For mankind to follow, who make foot tracks,
"With realistic eyes new ways who invent,
Against slave-bangles of corrupt trends.

"Slogans-sermons become when blunt,
The Saints on helm make society on the abrupt turn,
And guide the untrodden path of wisdom,
And rid the men of old corrupt customs.

"Meaning of the words and that of lines of text,
Should evolve 'to suit' need of time and age.
"True secret of devotion is evolution,
To discover the goal of the very perfection.

---

*Sober, thoughtful.

"And the perfection is a relative term,
Differs for Gods, godules, saints, man and little worm.
"Iota-biota may evolve to the God of tomorrow,
But evolution cometh not out of the zero.

Couplet: *"The evolution is the change*
By which the little soul,
Transcending the sense,
and reach, nay, become the Supreme soul." 15

"One particle of matter has whole energy within,
Same way, every soul hath same divinity of Supreme.
"Sublimed souls that descend on earth,
For My love and grace, those saints, are worth."

"Saints, devoted to Me, them I ever like,
They regard both obloquy, and praises alike.
Saints do have a Selfless self,
Research, reverence, reason in them dwell.

"The truth of the theism is their thews,
Their vim and views are guided by virtues.
"Saints, like flint, even if dipt in worldly ocean,
They possess ever fire of faith, within.

"Distinguishes the touch stone, between gold and brass,
Ascetics-heretics can be tested on tough task.
"Among rights and wrongs in the mundane; the Saints,
Pick sugar from the sand, like an ant.

Couplet: *" Hear ! of wicked and impious-*
Wearing deceiving masks
They are vampires dubious
And wild canine or fox." 16

Flint=match-stone; Theism=believing; Thews=power, strength.

"Seeing whom, the innocent faces turn pale,
With in him, sure, a vampire dwells.
The men's environ whose sins suffocate,
They are wild with strayed thoughts, steps."

"Whose smile is hiss, with touch of scorpion,
Ever refrain from them and let them alone.
"They get filled with scorches of agony,
And are burnt by others' prospering glory.

"Wicked are like sieve that throws away the worth,
And keeps the junk within it's girth.
Wicked are like the hollow shell's ewer,
Even filled with Ganges it remains bitter.

"In heart's quicksand of Saints, Veds get imprints,
But are unworkable on wicked concrete.
Holy words are like sprinkled dew,
Go in vain on hot iron of wicked's view.

Couplet: *"They, the personified toxins,*
With bosom of poisonous urn,
Ever, are, prompted at sin
The Delight, in other's woe they earn. 17

"Like a peacock they speak so sweet,
Flint hearted they, on snakes tho' feast.
"False is meal, zeal, false is their deal,
False is their feel, they are never leal.

"With askance, look at other's woman, other's mammon,
In human skin they are real demon.
"Greed is their wear, lust is their quilt,
Their pocket hath thirst for gold and gild.

Ewer=cucumber shell pot.
Flint hearted=hard hearted; Leal=faithful.

"Viewing Others' thews, views and virtue,
Their sinews droop as tho' suffer ague.
"On others' throes, woes, torts and sorrows,
With rejoice they tread on their toes.

"Self centred devoted to own interests,
For towering pomps they ever are dipt in debts.
"The cheat, as they are all cheek, and cheap,
They bargain, for gain, the values, for greed.

"Absorbed in lust, usurp wealth of others,
In robes of ascetics, they are heretic robbers.

Couplet: *"In the age of the truth,*
In epoch of the infant world,
The Era is vestal Satyug
Have no place for vile, vandals." 18

"In Tretayug as well dwells no traitor
In Dwapar their strange presence appears.
"While the viles in Kaliyug will crop forth,
Against truth and troth making traitor's force.

"But hark ! 'ts today or any era to come,
The Truth is the power above any weapon.
"O Brother ! meaning of life is benevolence,
And meanness of life is the very violence.

"Highest virtue is in service and grace,
While biggest vice is the deed that oppress.
"Who are root cause of men and mankind's woe,
Their hellish trafficking suffer traps of to and fro.

Ague=shivering fever; To tread on their toes=to wound their feelings.
Usurp=seize against
Vestal=chaste(pure) ; Vandal=ruiner.

"Should my these words echo for ages to come,
are all texts' epitome and pearls of wisdom.
"For shortlived bones, skin and mortal flesh,
Men toil hard for the selfish interests.

"Thus, they ruin own today and the next world,
Trapped in gyres of the mundane whirls.

Couplet: *"Every dazzling pomp hath,*
The mirky shades behind
For glitter of sinful acts,
The wise are never blind. 19

"Short gains may lead to the long loss,
Such greed, the surpassing souls ever bypass.
"Utterly consumed and loaded with greed,
From mesh of pangs, such soul is never freed.

"Robed in daubed seven tinge* cloth,
Bare soul gets astrayed from heaven's path.
"I ever back soul against sins' sabaoth,
Of pride, envy, gluttony, lust, greed, wrath, sloth.

"Saints are riant blossom in my grove of bliss,
While viles are thorns thrown into abyss.
"Thus in same tree both sages, savages are born,
But the fate is diverse for flowers and thorns.

"Sublimed souls take refuge in Me,
While the rest odds whirl in eddy of destiny.
"Maya creates shadow-glow, gloom-bloom, wrong-right,
My refuge is ever ope for the Bona-fide.

Couplet: *"In Maya's mayhem,*
Merits-demerits confuse,
When wit is driven by ignorance,
'Bhakti' is only refuge." 20

Sabaoth=Armies, *Seven sins.

All brothers rejoiced full to the banks,
Again and again they bowed in reverence.
Lord's words were all showers of blessing,
For Hanumaan in particular immensely heartening.

Then Lord of Awadh retired to own abode,
Thus with daily joy he enacted a new sport.
Celestial Sage Naarad made frequent visits,
And sang the paeans of Ram's sacred deeds.

He witnessed a greater heaven in Awadh,
Naarad recited Lord's leela* and blest Awadh's worth.
"Dear son !" said to Naarad overwhelmed Brahma**
"Ram is intense form of His own immense Maya."

"His paeans, even with no music, no muses,
May it be slight work of slight poets,
"Even in unlettered compositions of crude consonents,
May it be babble of the verses plain,—

Couplet: *"Yet Every hymn of His praises*
Hath words impregnated with love,
'ts troth maketh no trophy raises,
But the soul sublimeth all above." 21

THE EPIC BLESSED BY BRAHMA

"'Ts every word in worldly whirls is bark,
For men, in mundane to cross the bar.
"Should this little world with His vast paeans,
Be filled with His deeds full to the banks.

"Should His feats command little hand's deeds,
And envelop gentlier around every spirit.

---

* Exploits of Ram
** The Creator.

"Should the hymns of praises, be the light,
To free the shadowed life piled on life.

"Should these pealing strophes echo beyond icy range,
And fill with kindred fire the envied men.
"Should these rhymes bring, into calculative brains,
Among nonplused Sums, the logarithum of innocence.

"Should these sweet words be sweetest to His ear,
As to father, soft touch of his child is dear.
"Should those songs paint forth flood of bliss so divine,
And the kindred spirits fill canvas of mankind.

Couplet: *"Should the ballads in the Epic,*
Right all worlds' wrongs
And the touch of it's lyrics
Make life simple as folk songs." 22

"Should the epicure be cured by this sacred Epic,
And heal cramped thoughts of the sick.
"Should caring Ramlala*, the infant,
Bring riant face to world and to saints.

"Should hymns of Advent and the Berceus,
To the anxious world bring lulling comfort.
"Should pupil Ram bring wisdom and valour,
Should Nuptial songs be festivity's source.

"The Melancholy, is to breath, stitched,
Between desire and destiny, there is breach."
—Should this message fill The World of many desires,
And the duty be revered above the Empires.

"Should psalms convey that on throne or thorns,
May life be tuned to stoical songs.

---

*Child Ram; Epicure=lewd, Sensuous; Berceus=Craddle songs.

"Should the latent chain between Ram and Bharat,
Fill with fraternity, the kindred spirits on the Earth.

Couplet: *"The Human race is honoured*
When the Supreme cometh man-sized,
Epic inspirits god in Vaanar,
See ! How the Bhakti is prized?" 23

"God in man, man in God this epic brings,
Should with pealing anthems, swell blessings.

"Should determinations of little hearts be accomplished,
Through epic the Will and the Goal be bridged.

"Shouldst the Warrior Ram, whom (even) battle-field belauds,
Inspirit soldier's sinew with echoes of ballads.
"Should essence of Awadh and the RamRajya,
Swell beyond the oceans to serve man's cause."

Further Creator Brahma said to Naarad "Dear Son !
Again and again recite to Me Ram's paeans.
"Me, the Creator, lack skill to create such Awadh,
The holy place of His feats, holy place of noble birth."

Naarad visited Ayodhya again and again,
To elixir the souls with essence of Ram's reign.
Ever dipt in reciting paeans and praises,
Naarad became name of the delight of sages.

Truly, there must be a heart of granite,
In hymns of Lord, who takes no delight.
The heavenly hymns raised to the Heaven,
Heaven turned to Awadh, Awadh, into heaven turned.

Couplet: *Ever pious spirits were absorbed,*
In the conscious-free planes,
Descended to the blest orb,*
To witness Ram's paeans. 24

---

* The Earth.

RAM'S SERMON TO AWADHIANS

The daily Sun thus saw the increasing bliss,
Every moment, every event, was every soul's gift.
One such morn Ram called every one,
Came priests, pious-class, people, peasant, plebians.

Then the Master of devouts, who is mastered by devouts,
Spake in arena before the blest crowd-
" 'Ts not my request nor my behest,
Ye may or not follow, ye are not put to test.

"'Ts a divine favour that your very soul gets,
Into Human frame; its rare largess.
"For, 'Human' is only form suits for spiritual attempts,
Lest the soul toils to and fro, in vain.

Couplet: *" Who miss the sacred aim,*
And earn none but the sacrilege,
Should time, fate, God not be blamed
Deeds seeded, same is the harvest. 25

"The world, is not be-all and end-all of human,
Ends in sorrow ever, short lived fun.
"A corrupt is sorrow's easy target
With ambrosial hands, toxic-bane who selects.

"Elixir stone is My pen, by which
I make, on human palms, the crease'.
"Should Human hands with excelled deeds,
Gather for here and for the next, gold yields.

"Short-lived glittering harvest is not the gold,
Something that is carried, to next world, is the shine of soul.

Elixir stone=philosopher's stone (paras), which converts base metal to gold.

"Astrayed souls as wandering accursed spirits,
Go around in eighty four lacs of species.
"The spirit is immortal, but is Maya's toy,
In wandering drifts it's ever employed.

Rarely Lord favourth 'Jiva', and bestows
The human form; Lest in low forms it roves.

Couplet: *"This good form; with good gumptions,*
And to Guru great devotions,
Above all My compassion,
Taketh him across the ocean. 26

"In fortunate wind of My grace,
With Guru at the helm,
Alas ! some luckless yet
Miss the final aim. 27

"If Ye seek the bliss here and here after,
Should My words guide the lost wanderers.
"The smooth, to soothe Brethren ! a pleasant road,
Is 'Bhakti' told by saints and Veds extolled.

"Many tortuous, steep, craggy paths do perplex
With Bhakti and surrender find Me, very next.
"If Ye look to Me, I look to ye,
Making glades, roads, bridges and cause-ways.

"Bhakti' need no trodden path, no foot prints,
'Bhakti' is independent, it surrenderth and wins.
"Surrenderer is winner, in the path of Bhakti,
That's easiest road for a natural devotee.

Jiva=a soul
Gumption=sagacity, cleverness.
Bhakti=devotion.

"Fellowship of saints maketh path smooth,
Holy text maketh path pleasant to soothe.
"Your Merits are your virtuous steps,
That help to access saints and holy texts.

Couplet: *"The man is the best mirror,*
In substance; the soul purer
In him reflects deified figure
Of the Divine more clear. 28

"Real man, so is one and infinite
With potential of perfection, in him exists,
"Man is thinking being, innately deemed,
The infinite dreamer Alas ! dreaming finite dreams.

"The man is degeneration of what 'He' was
From the Best unto the beast debauched.
"A 'Man' within man is first to be saved,
Its only then way to perfection can be paved.

"Man's will, ready for mankind, to sacrifice
Contains infinite message of the Most High.
"Man's progress to Truth is not from the error,
But from truth to the Truth, from lesser truth to the Higher.

"And body of man can be a 'Teerth' in itself,
Search the Divinity which within ye dwells.
Immortal is the soul, goal is not life in the cage,
Far-beyond what goes with, is that earning, always.

Couplet: *"In Chains of journey man learns*
The evils to spurn,
What ever the mind, discerns,
those virtues, the immortal soul earns. 29

Teerth=spot of pilgrimage.
Spurn=repel.

“Earned by short-lived minds and frames,
all virtues add to immortal soul’s balance.
“Human body is greatest body in universe,
Human being, greatest being, make this not worse.

“The essence in deserts, unknown to the world,
In the floor of benthos, the unnoticed pearls,
“Hands that toiled for mankind, those incognito,
Those unnamed as best names, I know.

“With a wish to be perfect, even gods and angels,
All need to descend as men, to excel.
“On dial of eternity, the time makes no mark,
Ever born, never dies, soul is endless spark.

“Tho’ nothing is created absolutely evil,
And none is nihil of evils, none has merits nil.
“Shedding evils for betterment may the souls strieve,
The evil means less good, darkness is less light.

Couplet: *“Night-day, the bad and the good*
Are depiction of relative virtues,
I am the only Absolute,
The Truth with all Attributes. 30

“The Good-bad virtues and their attributes,
With its burden, the little souls get confused.
“What should be-all, end-all of the human,
Is the whole creation’s and My concern.

“I love my Bhakta, because he is lovable,
To his love I am ever available.
“The desire is sire of the disaster
Love of Bhakta masters the love of the Master.

Incognito=unknown.

"Perfectly resigned from Maya's gloves,
Bhakta is intensely assigned to My love.
"His I-am-ness evaporates in warmth of his love,
With him I am ever, he needs not rove.

"Among ways to Me, Bhakti, is Smoothest all above,
This love is only form in which the Love is loved.
"Bhakti is self-surrender to ope impossible gates,
It opes as well universe's secrets.

Couplet: *"For any good-things done,*
'ts love that propels,
And hatred is just none,
But killing the self by the self. 31

"Bhakti is manifestation of love and reverence,
Most visible thing of natural hearts, it represents.
"Man is the quinary elements' matter* but
Till in his bosom, the Bhakti spurts.

"While motif of Bhakti in the bosom lies,
No motive stands, and the method dies.
"The True Bhakti has one request to ask,
That merely Bhakti is the sole task.

"Bhakti inspirits, the mere matter
By force of love, with its elixir.
"In Bhakti love dwells; all fear it repels,
Bhakti is recompense of Bhakti itself.

" 'Ts basic instinct to express infinite unity,
Of infinite bond between Ye and Me.
"Bhakti is the perfect way of worship,
Above mages' magic, above sages' logic.

Motif=Predominant feature (idea); * five elements-Fire, Earth, Sky, Water, Ether.

Couplet: *"The nature hath drenched;*
With Bhakti all equal,
The nerves of the men,
Nay, matter's nucleus as well." 32

"Little separate-self must be sacrificed
Bhakti is beyond I, this fact to realize.
"Big phenomenon 'me' maketh a puny self,
Thus punary of mind, deprives man from the real pelf.

'Bhakti' drives in man 'a second-less One',
Can be attained thro' saints-union.
"A thin glade, in the jungle of weltshmerz,
In life through devotion it, emerge.

"This path, this glade, is lighted by saint's-union,
To guide astrayed souls for perfect communion.
"but then saints are accessible to stocks of merits,
These come through truth in thought, words deeds.

"Only seed of Bhakti is the need, to succeed,
no beating of beads nay even vedic deeds.
"For mortal coils it's a toilless path,
Needs no yog, penance, piety nor fasts.

Couplet: *"The artless art of living*
Is the science of every-living soul,
Reward of Bhakti, the 'Bhakti' brings
Should it be every mould's goal. 33

"Bhakti brings bliss, the form of real Self,
While miseries in this pseudo mind dwells.
"On wings of bliss in Bhakti's welkin,
Real self sublimeth to the heaven within.

Pelf = real wealth (the Bhakti)
weltshmerz (Ger) = world-sorrow.

"To the higher conciousness, more free and free,
Beyond infinite planes he cometh to Me.
"It is all He and it is all I,
At the same time within, doth realize.

"With natural instinct of Bhakti, you are pure,
That sure is within ye, by itself explores.
"All holy texts, teerths, temples are one projection of the Self,
Find its voice, its truth in every cell.

"Nothing that is worth knowing, can be taught,
All ope up of itself in realized heart.
" In mines of knowledge, gems of Bhakti shrine,
That deifies man into the High Divine.

Couplet: *"Human race in haphazard pace*
In good or evil move,
Is motivated on path sacred,
Ever his divinity to prove." 34

Further blessing, thus, the blest citizens,
Ram fulfilled every soul with nectarian sermon.
In arena Master's voice so echoed,
That it filled texts, hearts, even for ages to come.

All, accomplished full to the banks, then extolled-
" O Ram ! Thou art soul of our souls.
" O Saviour! O Supreme ! O Most high!
We art so blest to find Thou nigh.

"May the theme of our lives be to gather,
The spiritual forces and not the matter.
" A parent's soft touch, a preceptor's great precept,
A pal's warm bosom, in Thy words we did get.

" Let this be our greatest haves,
Accept us as slave of Thy slaves.

"Thou art parent, preceptor, a pal in one,
Thou art our mind, marrow, motive and mammon."

Couplet: *Steeped as they were*
In love and devotion,
Flooded with rapture,
Back home citizens returned. 35

Spirituality filled the peopled air,
Blessedness filled citizens with colours of rapture.
Its spirituality, and not the rocks and bricks,
That makes the towers of national edifice.

Truth was pecularity of Awadh's growth,
Citizens were very picture of dedicated troth.
In this blessed land, the foundation and the backbone,
And life centre was the Truth and Truth alone.

Apparently Awadh was mastered by Ram on throne,
But the mass was ideal, ruled by very Ram within own.
Where ruled Lord Ram, the King of the kings,
People were destined to do great to greater things.

Ope hands of men made no line of fragments,
All Oceans, all lands, Lord of Awadh reigned.
There was only one sect that prevailt,
And Dharma of peace and harmony dwelt.

Couplet: *Words issued from holy lips,*
Electrified the mankind,
Tempered with Gyan, the worships,
Purified them unto 'Divine'. 36

□

30

God is a circle whose circumference is no where and whose centre is everywhere.

—Swami Vivekanand

VASHISHTHA'S SUBMISSION

Couplet: *One such joyous day, Sage Vashishta,*
Called at Palace of Ram
Lord Ram laved his feet
With great reverence and warmth. 1

Sage Vashishtha said—

" I know not, earning of what virtues,
That maketh me the Omniscient's Guru.
"O Begetter of Veds! and Creator of all texts,
Being Thy preceptor, I am so blest.

"A pigmy soul of the feeble race,
In gaining such height, I see Thy grace.
"Utterly consumed with diffidence,
As Guru I, accepted Thy reverence.

"More I tought Thou, more I learnt fact,
Mystery of Thy deeds to detect I lack.
" I know not, how many birth's cycles,
I wished for 'Thou as my pupil'.

"My virtues, with all piety or penance,
And my real worth such reverence can't claim.
" O Obedient pupil ! of my hermitage,
Fulfil my wish taking it a behest or request—

Couplet:

" O Ram ! the Preacher of preachers,
I would ask for the one wish,
May love for Thou in future,
Ever be lavished, never be languished. 2

"The spotless devotion, as is virtue's name,
What greater than 'Bhakti' can feeble race obtain.
"If by love and virtues, mind and soul is reigned,
Of the beings, it's the perfect gain.

"Life dedicated to Thy True name,
If blameless; then Thy grace, may claim.
"In course of my coming future births,
The guileless path of Bhakti may make it worth."

VASHISHTHA'S MISSION

Fulfilled thus Vashishtha, the Sage priest returned,
His eyes brimmed, for the countless blessings he earned.
Lost flesh he sat under Banyan tree,
The 'Guru' evanesced, appeared in him a devotee.

A devotee, no praises, no glory, who claims,
Who hears 'Name' in silence or pealing anthems.
Vashishtha then summoned his pupils,
And revealed before them his Will—

Couplet:

"In the proses and verses,
In His strophes, narratives, metres,
Nay even in unlettered praises,
Ram Himself appearth. 3

"The ambrosial muses of Ram's narrative,
Very first appeared in conscious of Lord Shiv.
"He, then, revealed it to the blest sages,
Thus this nectar was availed to the human races.

"With muses, the Narrative, turned to strophes,
And descended through pencil of Valmiki,
"And inked as scripture the palms,
To reveal the Unseen in palpable form.

"And elixired the vitality of hearts of the plebs,
And poured life into hushes of caves.
"Muses carved a bard out of barbaric rock*,
Muses inspired unlettered words of folks.

"His strophes puffed life in idle thoughts,
Its words poured nectar over seekers' hearts.
"Halos of hallowed verses lighted road
With spirituality; that plebs and pious together trod.

Sage Vashishtha told to his pupils—

Couplet:

"May world be more glorious,
O pupils! O my sons !!
So serve ye my purpose
That I see in my vision. 4

"Restricted was it not, just in men's race,
Under the Mains, over the Mounts sung with great éclat.
"Among winged, finned this epic equally traversed,
'The winged warbled the verse', the finned deep in it immersed.

"Bees hummed, truly hymned into florescence,
And filled vernal canvas with it's life and essence.
"Perching din of primates, mooing meeks on meadows,
Heigh ho** ! its all expressioin of the Most Hallowed.

---

*Referred to Valmiki's previous life; ** Heigh ho!(sign of surprise).

"Thro' bells, bangs, beads, the every breath prays,
But the belief on The Believable ever wins the bays.
"Infinite ist Ram, Infinite ist His Name,
Birth by birth every soul hath a closer claim.

"This sacred epic is in every soul niched,
Reveal it within, for nearing His reach.
"As was obvious in birds' séance,
Recited the holy crow* perched on the Banyan.

Couplet: *In the far-north, in the vales,*
Of the peaks of Himalaya,
The crow-sage to the birds tells
This epic, the Ambrosia. 5

"There stood bo-tree, mango, a banyan and a fig,
The feathered with faith listen to this epic.
"Holy place is untouched to worldly dins,
Birds' souls are ignorant to worldly sins.

"It's the perfect place for Ram's narrative,
As a swan, there sojourned ever Lord Shiv.
"The intense-bliss ever welled over the peaks,
Thus Avian world is filled with this epic.

"Thus in mains, mounts, men and men's primates,
The bliss, this faith of Truth, impregnates.
" Further, be, the hymns of Himalaya melt as Ganges,
Or come as muses of bards on holy pages.

"Be it a dent on the heart's quick-sand,
But hath indeleble impression in the end.
"They, who feel sated holy words to hear,
Have little known their own peculiar sapor.

Séance=spiritual meeting; *Kaagbhushundi
Bo-tree=Peepal

Couplet: *"For the sake of His devotees*
The Divinity came man-sized,
And performed sacred deeds
The Bliss is personified. 6

"Now listen to my teachings absolutely true,
Echoed by oldest texts yet ever new.
"Ages of feeble men creeped on the research,
Imprint of conclusion thus emerged.

"Men's vision rocketed thro' the universes,
Within the self found conclusion of all researches.
"Worship is the ship in ocean of delusion,
Through gyre of brains, keeps heart at the helm.

"Lord loveth every micro of His macro,
But to Human being imparts, His maximum love.
"Further He loveth pundits well-versed in the Veds,
Loveth more, who, vedic path, tread.

"Among well-versed in Veds, Vedic path who traverse,
Dearer are, to pomp and pleasure who are averse.
"Yet dearer the truthful wise, full of lore,
Then the Man of realization He loveth further more.

Couplet: *"Yet, who servilely depend,*
On Him with no other hope,
To those devout, His own servant
His warm arms are ever ope. 7

"And the humblest soul, of a truthful devout,
Is the dearest, that is His solemn vow.
"And truthfulness is earned thro' moral virtues,
Such is declared by the texts old or new.

" Impurity of mind can never sustain long,
Soul is naturally right ever prevails over wrongs.

"Guided by pure soul on the glade of Veds,
Its innate love, the Bhakti for the Supreme that treads.

"Bhakti is the mute instinct that maketh distinct,
Among dins of envying siblings.
"See ! a father has a number of sons,
Each differ in temper, conduct and vision.

"One is wise, other is given to austerities,
One other is enlightened, fourth one is rich.
One is generous, a genius, a genial all are gems,
But a father loveth all equally the same.

Couplet: *"The one, dedicated to his father,*
Be he ignorous tho'
Own breath father shares
He is soul of father's love. 8

"Thus among human, sub-human, super human species,
It's love and devotion that the Lord seeth.
"Luck, lore, light is the Lord's benison,
But then devotion is the man's option.

"Thus, the Lord, and His benisons are at man's reach,
This now sums up my sermon, my speech.

Now, Vashishtha initiated pupils—

" O proud pupils ! of this pious abbey,
Ye are blest to follow the great way.

"Be the wandering monk, on the path of Dharma,
And fill with spiritual fire every bosom.
"Be the conquering soldier in the field of Dharma,
To implant theTruth, wide and firm.

"Spread! And run like a fire to all places,
With warmth of love against chill of hatred.
"Be the missionary for the cause of Ashram-
For soil, soul, nay for, Supreme, be a factotum.

"Go ! in every run, make the fields pious,
My morale is, O pupils ! Your moral onus.

Couplet: *"Intensify the morals in world,*
As the cherished heritage,
Aquaint to the world, the internal world,
And let with God be the rest. 9

"O Children of this land ! the Punya-Bhumi !!
Deluge the world with tides of spirituality.
"From this ancient land, where wisdom made its home,
Take light of divinity to the world of dazing pomp.

"I clearly see my vision come true,
Rejuvenated on my mission when I see you.
"May the message of the land of eight rivers* go wide,
And illumine the world with spiritual light.

"O Arya ! Son of soil of Aryavart,
May through missionary peace and harmoy spurt.
"Some of ye should, to the north step,
Beyond Himawant range of tiers of snowcaps.

"All along the quick sand of Sarayu,
Up go passing through Shravasti's purlieus.
The withered sinew and your aching calves,
By sweet breeze of Himalaya, will be halved.

Factotum=dedicated devotee.

*Ganga, Yamuna, Godawari, Saraswati, Narmada, Sindhu, Kaveri, Krishna rivers.

Couplet: *Impending smile of buds,*
But shivering lives in huts,
And the lightening scuds
'll sure assay you first." 10

"Tho' Himalaya welcometh with pearls of dew,
Along untrodden vista of cedar's avenue,
"Further up on chilly crags, as you'll step,
Hopping rivulets roll to heal your blebs.

"Saved from rage of storms, worse than death,
Eventides will nurse you in the caves.
"Then, the murmur of a dream 'll fill you with
Determined nerves and verve of bliss.

"Mind ! you be the glowing flambeau,
To enlighten world with Ram's virtues.
"Your determined warmth will sure melt a pass,
Through the icy peaks of sacred Kailash.

"Shining sores, shining soul 'll prove,
Your mission for men, Lord hath approved.
"Spreading 'Lord's message' in the sacred sojourn,
that strange land 'll be your bourn.

Couplet: *"Be ready the very next,*
Some of my blest youths,
Crossing Kanyakubj state,
Swift reach to Chitrakoot. 11

"Tho' for my own pupil I have no doubt,
Yet, in holy Ganges forget not, to take a vow.
"Mind again ! you be a glowing flambeau,
To enlighten the world with truth of the Truth.

Bourn=journey's destination.

The land of peace in the heart of Aryavart,
Will welcome with hills hamlets, huts, hearths.
You will cross Vindhya range with same zeal, same awe,
Till you reach land's coronary flow, the Narmada.

Stream's every pebble is Shiv in itself,
And tells of the very benign heritage.
Along peals of waves, the skilled oar,
Will take you to Malav state's door.

"O travellers ! ye 'll rush to the fascinating call
of chants and clangs in the fane of Mahakal.
"Studded Avantika town with pearls, gems, brings the thought—
That ocean must be left with salt and froth.

Couplet: *"My missionary travellers*
Are not made to be dazed by pomp,
Shall soon proceed further
On the errand of Ram. 12

"Now thro' opaque greens of Dandkaranya,
Piercing you will err and err and learn.
"Jaws, claws and caves and unknown traps,
Strange threats will welcome your every step.

"But then determination is the boldest weapon,
Holding its' hilt, any threat is won.
"In the way, awake Kishkindha, awake Malay,
Should the sway of Ram, stay aye.

"Should elixir, the Rameshwaram's dust,
The life of world with more trust.
"And the shoals of shore and that of the bridge,
Be the mean to cross the bar, to release.

"With you I send my soul, only to return,
When, O Sons ! accomplishes my mission.

"Next, to farther east I send you, oblates !
To carry the echo of east into every breast.

Couplet: *"Sarayu meets holy trunks in Magadh,*
Next, sail to land of many rills.
Flood ! the peopled and palmed banks, with troth,
Reach to land's eastern doorsill. 13

"Oceans are no limit to oblates,
When folly on the different land, waits,
"Sailing thro' high waves of ordeal,
It reveals, sure ! the voyage is ideal.

"A saint, in determined sailor, nagivates,
And even wakes of the boat ever make awake.

"Mind ! sailor monks !! be the glowing flambeau,
Save the men drowning in misery's crew.

"From Mahendra, to Malay along the east coast,
Imbibe the Darshan, then turn to east, the boat.
"My behest, your zest will be the oar,
To take you to Java, Sumatra's shore.

"Not the brandishing arms but the cherishing arms,
Will lavishly fill world with charms of Ram.
"My conscious is ever with my pupil at task,
Thus, in the frost of folly may world bask.

Couplet: *"Now some missionaries I expect,*
To cross the land of Koshal,
Beyond the Kurukshetra,
In scorching days, and chilly Lulls. 14

Wakes=waves left by moving ship.
Bask=delight in warmth of knowledge.

"Go ! and untie man's meshy labyrinths,
In the sand, in the planes beyond Sapt-Sindh.
"Mind ! warrior monks ! be the glowing flambeau,
Win ! not with swords but with words of Guru.

"To Kaikey, Gandhar, and beyond further to unlettered sands,
Take to the nascent world, hand of earliest friend.
"The message of Awadh is message of mirth,
For real ethereal souls to save the earth.

"The pomp hath seen the shortlived triumphs,
In fleshy frames go! And puff ! soul of pilgrims.
"The very cause of the Supreme's advent,
Is destined now, be done thro' your hands.

"The Bhakti moves on wings of dove,
Cuts trawls of hates, where moves the love.
"Flood ! the world with life-blood of Bhakti
Lest the Maker is making frames of travesty.

Couplet: *"Take the ages of the learnings*
Make it guiding motto,
Be it mankind's earning
That every coming man 'll owe." 15

Seamed face of Guru with sheen so divine,
With grit and spirit filled pupil's mind.
" O revered one ! thou havest revealed the Truth,
Now purpose of our life, is to distribute."

Dedicated pupils thus transformed to determined monks,
Their short stride became East's leap long.
through the untrodden paths, the perpetual wanderers,
Since then, are whispering essence in stagnant air.

Trawls=Net; Travesty=misrepresent, perversion.

Their flesh tho’ hath turned to fossils and rocks,
Yet spirit warbles in folks of the flocks.
Lost flesh they in marines with no obsequies,
But still they thrieve for mortal’s release.

Their lonely feet fell tho’ in icy caves,
Yet the footings for mankind their foot-prints paved.
In thirsty parched sands, their poor graves,
With thrust of trust, rich heritage, engraved.

Couplet: *Their grit and their Spirit,*
Ever perpetually exist,
Meet them in Valmiki’s lyrics,
And in Tulsi’s distitch. 16

Beyond clock of time, the very soul of true mission,
Hath impregnated souls with fire of devotion.
As scions of natural soil, the natural sons,
Held upright the torch, for illumination.

Their bones, flesh died at clay, hay or at bay,
Old bequests and new quest stay, yet, aye.
Thus, Narrative of Ram is the heritage gift,
It impregnates with divine fire; the spirit.

To the odd eddies of fragmented world,
It elixirs lull of peace, in envied rivals.
Along its verses, traverses the gnosis,
The Visage, Men’s vision visits thro’ visive vis.

Incomparable as Ram is, has no compeer,
He alone is His peer, so Veds declare.
Mortal minds of the feeble race,
Picked some pearls from ocean of His depth.

Bequest=heritage.
Visive vis=power of realization.

Couplet: *Little lives for ages rolled,*
For a glimpse of the Ancient of days
Once, realized, the bindings old
Found Him in own image. 17

THE EASY KALIAGE

Soul realizeth in the very mortal frame
'Lord is more myself than I am'.
The Kaliage hath many draw backs,
But for little life of man it hath advantage.

In the pious-Ages, Satyug, Treta, Dwapar,
Then the Truth and Troth were truer,
In that age, even Venial faults negated the Gains,
Then, needed perfect penance and repentance.

While in Kaliage the Sins to remit,
Soul just need, His very Name to repeat.
With the faith and the fortitude,
Bhakti redeems from sins and rescues.

Kaliage keeps so low the threshold,
Little efforts for release, the high hopes, hold.
Simple man's simple steps are leaps,
To cross the very bar steep.

Couplet: *Simple whispering chants in this Kaliage,*
Sound, resound and are heard,
Remitting sins, the virtuous acts,
Get the high and highest reward. 18

This age, in mundane is right sojourn,
Where soul simply canst reach its bourn.

Venial=minor, excusable; Bourn=final Destination.

The piety as is, to take pity on the Jeev,
And the service to the Jeev, perceiving in him Shiv.

Whole struggle, from ages of men, is about,
To reveal Satyug within and without.
Matter and marrow are linked with a knot,
To untie that verses of Veds taught.

The devices are little in this world,
To untie the knot of meshy curls.
Gyan, the Gnosis is deep and steep,
Difficult to practise, difficult to achieve.

Path of wisdom is foot print of stalwart,
A sleuth made on the edge of sword.
It's folly to be wise on this track,
Rarest could attain the final state.

Couplet: *It's loving faith, fortitude,*
The path ever which welcomes,
For the final beatitude,
Through practising devotions. 19

LYRICS OF THE METAPHYSICS

Inevitable is the cycle of births,
But then, the devotion is the apt option on the Earth.
Veds and old text in holy lyrics,
Have made the path of metaphysics.

Bhakti as established doctrine emerged,
After ages and ages of Seeker's research.
The gem of Bhakti sheds its radiance,
Such enlightenment needs no 'Gyan-lamp'.

Sleuth=foot-lane.

No blast of argument can extinguish it,
Being light of gem and not the weak wick.
Radiance of this gem hath no 'neath shadows,
Its glow illuminates where ever it goes.

'Bhakti' is chaste and crest of piety,
It guides man to work to his duty.
For the Lord approves His own vow,
He loveth equally praying hands and hands at plough.

Couplet: *Hold the Lord with hand one,*
To the work, other hand be engaged,
Once the work is done,
With both, the Lord be grasped. 20

The duty is piety for body and mind,
Piety as duty, to the very soul binds.
All our duties are truely His,
Let the paths and goal take care of fruits of bliss.

The sapling souls need disciplined duties,
Tho' hedge will be hindrance for a grown tree.
And then, gigantic wisdom need no hedge of duty,
With height of the conquered Will, such souls are free.

One for duty, for piety one, two hands, the Maker made,
Lest the vegetative frame is named, a quadruplet.
The Ancient bards poured their souls,
The brutes unto men unto gods, to evolve.

A verse, nay a word of hymn may enlighten,
Lest in vain, words may crowd the cramped brain.
In conduct, if reflects prayers of holy text,
Then only, the scripture is, well-read.

THE TRIBUTE TO RAM'S LAUREATES

Couplet: *The Ram's saga of Valmiki,*
Casted a great spell,
And in Tulsi's epic
Lord Ram Himself dwellth. 21

What appeared on leaves of Kamban,
Is versified saga of his own vision.
He echoed banks of Godavari and Kishkindha,
And flooded the lives with Rama's saga.

And the rejuvenated Malay have Sung,
Chants of Ramayan by Ezhuthachan.
Thus ancient bards elixired world of myth,
With truth of the Truth, the spiritual pith.

Ved vyas had lit the Ancient flambeau.
Came to Ramanand, Ramteerth, Nanak, the Guru.
Many unclaimed limericks of the unknown,
Inspirited mankind with devotional tone.

The muses, those murmur and penetrate through,
Its solemn sound, the souls approve.
'Very souls of words' never wish to be liberated,
Those graced Holy text, Holy text, them, graced.

Couplet: *'Syllables' were sound hollow,*
Till those appeared in Ram's paeans.
Their meanings have hallowed
And proved the pilgrim presence. 22

Words of the paeans and Ram's narrative,
Keep secure of Maya, the soul-n-mind, attentive.
Blest dialogues between Uma and Lord Shiv,
From, mirks and mire of mundane, relieve.

These primeval poems of pious primitives,
From ages to the men are persuasive.
Words appeared in world of sword, with motive,
In the self, the True Self to perceive.

Verses make traverse the finite thoughts on the road infinitive,
Up high and high nearer to Shiv.
In selfless self, make these hymns, believe,
That 'I' never lived, only 'He' in me lived.

The hymns for spiritual needs are inexpensive,
It directs, heart to forgive and the hands to give.
Ram is the Ancient, so is His narrative,
And 'Name' is earliest with vivid viv.

Couplet: *Acts of Ram who, listens n narrate*
Here and here after, are blest,
Ram's glory rewarded laureates,
They became part of the holy text. 23

Stanza: *Ram's narrative, for the pensive,*
told by Shiv, is panacea,
Immortal comes, for mortals to learn
the lesson of Ambrosia. A

The Lord cometh mansized, for the man to realize,
—'For souls, human frame is a prize.'
A devout in man, no doubt in man,
Sprouts in man, a paradise. B

Very self's intimate, the Ancient laureates,
Sung the Great acts, with great éclat.
The bards are bark, with lore as oar,
Make us cross with freights the mundane's spate. C

Persuasive=fascinating.
vivid viv=Intense vitality.
Spate=flood.

O'er limits of languages, inspirited sages,
Sung infinite praises of the Infinite,
May my hollow soul, now extol,
And with hallowed light may be lit. D

Couplet: *I'm man of straw,*
A bubble of feeble race,
With body, the target of awe,
And frame the soil and ash, 24

—For this miserable as I am,
The shield is lustless Bhakti,
O Ram ! Thou art path, Thou the Aim,
Only Thou mayst to Thou take me. 25

O Tulsi ! O divine lauraete !!,
For my dunce attitude, excuse !
For it hath fortitude and faith,
Though may lack in Valmiki's muse. 26

□□□